Our Sexuality

Second Edition

ROBERT CROOKS

Portland Community College

KARLA BAUR

The Oregon Health Sciences University

THE BENJAMIN/CUMMINGS PUBLISHING COMPANY, INC.

Menlo Park, California · Reading, Massachusetts · London
Amsterdam · Don Mills, Ontario · Sydney

Sponsoring Editor: Jane R. Gillen
Production Editor: Patricia S. Burner
Developmental Editors: Beverly Azarin and Jean Stein
Art Director: Bonnie Garmus
Photo Researchers: Lindsay Kefauver and Barbara Hodder
Book and Cover Designer: Christy Butterfield
Cover Artist: Heather Preston
Drawings on pages 1, 85, 193, 262, 263, 273, 277, 279, 280, 281, 323, 491, 530, 532, 536, 537, 543, 544, and 587 by Heather Preston
Other Illustrations by Barbara Hack and Connie Warton
Cartoons on pages 62, 226, 237, and 497 by Martha Weston

Credits may be found beginning on page C-1.

Library of Congress Cataloging in Publication Data

Crooks, Robert
 Our sexuality.

 Bibliography: p.
 Includes index.
 1. Sex   2. Sex customs—United States.
I. Baur, Karla.   II. Title.
HQ21.C698   1983   612.6   82-17836
ISBN 0-8053-1914-X

cdefghij-HA-8987654

The Benjamin/Cummings Publishing Company, Inc.
2727 Sand Hill Road
Menlo Park, California 94025

About the Authors

The integration of psychological, social, and biological components of human sexuality in this text is facilitated by the blending of the authors' academic and professional backgrounds. Robert Crooks has a Ph.D. in psychology. His graduate training stressed clinical and physiological psychology. In addition, he has considerable background in sociology, which served as his minor throughout his graduate training. He is currently involved in a number of research and writing projects, and teaches psychology and sexuality classes at Portland Community College. Karla Baur has a master's degree in social work; her advanced academic work stressed clinical training. She is currently in private practice as a psychotherapist, and is a clinician at the Elahan Center for Mental Health and Family Living. She is also a Clinical Associate Professor of Obstetrics and Gynecology at the School of Medicine, Oregon Health Sciences University.

The authors have a combined total of 21 years of teaching, counseling, and research in the field of human sexuality. Together they team taught sexuality courses at Portland Community College for a number of years. They present workshops and guest lectures to a wide variety of professional and community groups, and they counsel individuals, couples, and families on sexual concerns. The authors are also involved in ongoing research pertaining to sexual attitudes and behaviors of college students. Their combined teaching, clinical, and research experiences, together with their graduate training, have provided them with an appreciation and sensitive understanding of the highly complex and personal nature of human sexuality.

It is the authors' belief that a truly sensitive understanding of our sexuality must be grounded in *both* the female and male perspectives and experiences. In this sense, their courses, their students, and this text have benefited from a well-balanced perception and a deep appreciation of human sexual behavior.

Foreword

*I*n 1970, while an Assistant Professor of Psychology at the University of Oregon, I developed, as a new offering in the undergraduate curriculum, a course on human sexual behavior. When developing the curriculum for this course, I found myself considerably frustrated by the available textbooks. At that time, and to a lesser degree today, most of the books available were basically sex education texts. Rather than focusing on human sexuality—attitudes, emotions, behavior patterns, and so forth—these books dealt mainly with the "plumbing" aspects of sex—anatomy and physiology of the reproductive system. Furthermore, many of these books were really very value laden, often with basically conservative and sexist values.

In using this type of sex education oriented text over a few semesters, the feedback from the students confirmed my initial misgivings. The students didn't find the anatomy and physiology very interesting—they wanted to know about *sexuality*, not about reproduction. The conservative values struck many of the students as hopelessly out of touch with current reality, and many students were offended by the implicitly sexist views in these books.

Not being too obtuse or a terribly slow learner, I eventually stopped using this sort of text, and instead began to use collections of articles from professional journals. However, this alternative turned out to have two problems: First, the articles were often over-detailed and uninteresting to students. Second, without using a text which covered anatomy and physiology, many of the students lacked the basic knowledge required to understand the lecture material. This sort of material is a very necessary, if not sufficient, part of a course on human sexuality.

I eventually arrived at a combination of a basic physiology text, a collection of readings, and some mimeographed material gathered from a variety of sources. What these readings didn't cover was the *human* or personal side of human sexuality. Obviously, a course in sexuality has enormous personal relevance to the students, and their reactions to both readings and lecture material is often more personal than intellectual. My office hours began to assume certain aspects of a sex counseling service. I reached the point where I was actually *glad* when a student would come in merely to complain about a grade. Reflecting on the students' reactions to the course and readings, it became clear that the students needed and wanted something that would help them to integrate their own life experiences—exciting, confusing, gratifying, or frustrating—with the academic material.

During this period, I often found myself wishing that my life could be much less complicated. If there were a single really good sexuality text available, it would be much easier to teach human sexuality. In thinking about what would constitute an ideal text, I came up with a shopping list:

1. The basic biology of sexuality must be thoroughly covered.
2. The psychology and sociology of human sexuality must be emphasized, covering behavior patterns, emotions, sociocultural factors, and so forth.

3. There should be some integration of both sorts of academic material with personal experiences of real people.
4. Self-help problem-solving advice in the text would be useful.
5. The text should not be overly political or stridently polemical about sexual and sex-role values, in either conservative or liberal directions. Instead, the text should be value free as much as is possible. Given that some values obviously must appear when presenting life histories and self-help material (points 3 and 4 on this list), my preference would be for a book committed to equality in male and female roles and relationships, and to acceptance of a wide range of sexual life styles as normal and healthy.

Over the next few years, I evaluated each new textbook that appeared against this five-item shopping list. Some excellent texts appeared, including ones that met almost all of my criteria. What never did appear was a solid academic text with a personal focus, that is, one which included life history and personal problem-solving material. Thus, when I first saw a new text by Robert Crooks and Karla Baur, I was immediately intrigued. Here, at last, seemed to be two people who obviously had taught human sexuality for some time and had been willing to listen to their students and respond to *their* needs in writing a text.

The first edition of this text was an excellent book, and was very well received. Indeed, this book has become one of the most widely used (if not *the* most widely used) texts in college level courses in human sexuality. This success has been well deserved. Among the book's virtues, the academic material is presented clearly, yet is not oversimplified. The personal material is fascinating, and makes the text one that students read out of interest rather than to study for the exams. The self-help material is very straightforward and is useful and relevant to students. The values of the authors are not presented in a strident way, and are indeed equalitarian and nonjudgmental. Finally, the technical aspects of the book are outstanding—good graphics, a highly readable writing style, excellent accompanying Instructor's Guide and student Study Guide, and a good slide set for lecture use.

Not content to rest on their laurels, Crooks and Baur have now produced a second edition, updating, revising, and adding to an already outstanding book. The latest advances in sex research have been integrated into the existing chapters, and new chapters added. The new chapters focus and expand on the issues of historical perspectives, gender roles, love and the development of sexual relationships, and sexual victimization (including incest and rape). These are all topics of great interest, and about which much current sex research and public policy debate centers. These new chapters will certainly be of great interest and relevance to the students.

In closing my Foreward to the first edition, I concluded that at last an academically sound, personally relevant text teaching package was available for courses in human sexuality. This second edition only improves on an already excellent text. The current generation of students taking a course in human sexuality—and their instructors teaching the course—are indeed fortunate to have this book available.

Joseph LoPiccolo
State University of New York at Stony Brook

Preface

*O*ur major goal for the second edition of *Our Sexuality* is essentially the same as for the first edition: To provide a comprehensive and academically sound introduction to the biological, psychosocial, behavioral, and cultural aspects of sexuality, in a way that is personally meaningful to students. The enthusiastic response to the first edition of our text has been gratifying, and has encouraged us to revise the book with the dual aim of updating it and making it even more effective as a learning tool.

Like the first edition, the second edition covers a broad array of subjects in considerable detail. We have included some topics that are frequently either omitted or discussed superficially in other texts—for example, gender identity and gender roles, methods of sex research, love and the development of relationships, communicating about sex, improving sexual satisfaction, sexuality throughout the life-cycle, and cross-cultural variations in sexual expression. While we have avoided being overly technical in our presentation of data, we have been scholarly and thorough in our review of the human sexuality research. The second edition has been updated in every area and includes many new citations from the recent literature.

NEW IN THIS EDITION

This new edition has benefited greatly from the comments and suggestions of the many instructors and students who have used the book. Several modifications and additions are worthy of special mention.

- ☐ MORE ON THE HISTORY OF SEXUALITY An expanded first chapter puts present-day views of sexuality into historical and cultural context.
- ☐ NEW CHAPTER ON GENDER ISSUES The new Chapter 2 provides solid treatment of the fundamental issues of gender identity and gender roles.
- ☐ NEW CHAPTER ON LOVE AND THE DEVELOPMENT OF SEXUAL RE-LATIONSHIPS A full chapter (Chapter 7) is devoted to these complex and important topics.
- ☐ MORE ON COMMUNICATION We have expanded the highly praised chapter on communication (Chapter 8). The roles of both sexual partners have been given more attention throughout this edition.
- ☐ SEPARATE CHAPTER ON SEXUAL VICTIMIZATION Now in a chapter separate from other atypical sexual behavior, the discussion of sexual victimization includes expanded discussions of rape, the sexual abuse of children, and sexual harassment (Chapter 20).
- ☐ SPECIAL TOPIC BOXES This edition includes many new boxes, on such topics as the effects of alcohol on sexual arousal (two examples of experimental research), sexual fantasies, a letter from a gay man to his parents, and how to tell a partner about a sexually transmitted disease.

A PERSONAL APPROACH

Users of the text have responded very favorably to our attempts to humanize and personalize the subject matter, and in the second edition we have retained and strengthened the main elements that contribute to our approach.

□ READABLE, PERSONAL STYLE   The book is written in a clear and interesting style that facilitates understanding. We have maintained a personal focus throughout its pages. For example, when we present the anatomy and physiology of sexual functions, we frequently provide perspectives of people's feelings about their bodies.

□ AUTHORS' FILES   Excerpts from our files relating experiences and observations by students, clients, and colleagues are interspersed throughout the text. In some instances, they were provided to us in the form of written personal reflections. Here, only minor changes have been made to preserve anonymity (any names which appear are fictitious). In other cases, where they were related verbally, we have recorded the accounts as accurately as our memories allow. These quotations, printed in color, help dramatize important concepts and the many dimensions of human sexuality. The second edition includes many new quotations of this type.

□ NONJUDGMENTAL PERSPECTIVE   Consistent with our personal focus, we have avoided a prescriptive stance on the issues introduced in the text. We have attempted to provide information in a sensitive, nonsexist, nonjudgmental manner that assumes the reader is best qualified to determine what is most valid and applicable to his or her life.

□ PSYCHOSOCIAL ORIENTATION   We focus on the roles of psychological and social factors in human sexual expression, reflecting our belief that human sexuality is governed more by psychosocial factors than by biological factors. At the same time, we provide the reader with a solid basis in the anatomy and physiology of human sexuality.

□ PRACTICAL INFORMATION   Many chapters offer practical information and suggestions for readers to use, if they wish. Some examples include: how to enhance sexual communication, options for contraception and childbirth, how to improve sexual satisfaction, how to avoid contracting sexually transmitted diseases, when and where to seek professional counseling, and how to deal with sexual harassment on the job.

□ SUPERB ILLUSTRATIONS   The biological and diagrammatic art is clear and instructive. Many sensitive drawings and photographs enhance the text. Widely praised in the first edition, these illustrations are not limited to portrayals of young and attractive couples but include a wide variety of individuals.

ORGANIZATION

The organization of the book has been modified from the first edition to reflect a more logical progression of topics. We begin, in Part One, with the social and cultural legacy of sexuality in our society, and this discussion flows logically into a detailed exploration of a variety of gender issues. We then describe how major research studies have increased our knowledge in recent years, and discuss the difficulties of gathering information in this sensitive area of human behavior. The three chapters of Part Two present the biological foundations of sexuality, with sexual arousal and sexual response patterns integrated into one chapter, Chapter 6. A variety of sexual behaviors are discussed in Part Three. In Part Four, we discuss contraception, pregnancy, and issues pertaining to sexuality throughout the life cycle. The sources and nature of sexual problems and their treatments constitute the three chapters of Part Five. In the final section, Part Six, discussions of atypical sexuality, sexual victimization, legal aspects of sexuality, and cultural differences in sexuality complete the circle, arriving back at the cultural basis of sexuality that was introduced in Chapter 1.

LEARNING AIDS WITHIN THE TEXT

Individuals learn in different ways. We therefore provide a variety of pedagogical aids to be used as the student chooses. Each chapter opens with an **outline** of topic headings. **Key words** are italicized within the text. **Color** is used to highlight major topic headings and in many of the drawings. Each chapter is followed by a **summary** in outline form for student reference. Annotated **suggested readings** are included with each chapter, and a complete **bibliography** is provided at the end of the book. A comprehensive **glossary** facilitates quick reference to terminology.

A COMPLETE PACKAGE OF SUPPLEMENTS

Lecture preparation and student understanding are enhanced when the complete teaching package is employed.

- ☐ The student STUDY GUIDE, newly revised by Professor Gary R. Lesniak of Portland Community College, contains many devices that a student can use to check comprehension of the text material. It includes lists of key terms from each chapter, together with multiple choice, matching, and short-answer essay questions. Answers to the multiple choice and matching questions are provided. Questions for "personal reflection" and discussion are also included.
- ☐ The INSTRUCTOR'S GUIDE contains a large number of test items, as well as audiovisual suggestions, recommendations for classroom activities, and a questionnaire for measuring student knowledge, attitudes, and behavior before and after the course.
- ☐ The SLIDE PACKAGE consists of a set of 60 color slides. Approximately half of the slides are reproductions of art from the text; the other half are photographs from the text and other sources. These slides are designed to enhance classroom understanding and appreciation of a variety of topics.

ACKNOWLEDGMENTS

This book represents a combination of talents and insights that extend beyond those of the authors. We are particularly indebted to the reviewers of our manuscript, the staff of Benjamin/Cummings, and our students, whose combined contributions have added much to the quality of the text.

As we worked on this project, we came to appreciate the indispensable value of the review process. Individuals representing a variety of disciplines and perspectives read and evaluated our first edition manuscript at various stages of completion. For help with the first edition we owe special gratitude to Carol Ellison, author, clinical psychologist, and instructor of human sexuality. Our work on the second edition was facilitated by the invaluable suggestions of Valerie Pinhas, John Petras, and Joseph LoPiccolo, who reviewed the manuscript throughout its development. Other reviewers who made important contributions to the first and second editions are included in the lists that follow the Preface.

Additional individuals contributed their talents to the second edition. Sally Adelman's skill and resourcefulness as a research assistant was highly valued. Susan Birkemeier, a practicing gynecologist, contributed her medical expertise to several chapters in the text. Joni Marie U. Johnson was a major contributor to the historical aspects of Chapter 1, and Jean Stein did a special developmental edit of the same chapter.

The staff of the Benjamin/Cummings Publishing Company has consistently performed beyond our highest expectations. Our sponsoring editor on the first edition, Larry Wilson, maintained a sense of perspective, direction, and infectious enthusiasm and humor that saw us through many difficult times. Jane Gillen, who assumed the role of sponsoring editor on the second edition, provided invaluable direction and support. Margaret Moore and Pat Burner, production editors on the first and second editions, respectively, deserve a special thanks for providing the kind of efficient organization essential to the success of a project of this nature. The developmental editing by Jean Stein and Beverly Azarin was extremely valuable and contributes much to the book's quality. The artists, Heather Preston, Barbara Hack, and Connie Warton, together with cartoonist Martha Weston and photo researchers Barbara Hodder and Lindsay Kefauver, have contributed an attractive and informative visual component. We are also indebted to Peter Martin and Bonnie Garmus for their coordination of these graphics and their sensitivity to our purpose.

We are deeply grateful for the loving support and encouragement our families and friends have so generously and patiently provided throughout the writing of this book.

Finally, we owe our greatest gratitude to the thousands of students who have attended our classes. In many ways, *Our Sexuality* reflects the thoughts and experiences of this diverse group. Their contributions have enriched the text. We hope that readers of our book will derive at least a portion of the benefits that we have gathered from our opportunity to share in this collective fund of human experience.

Robert Crooks/Karla Baur

REVIEWERS

First Edition

Marvin J. Branstrom, Cañada College

David R. Cleveland, Honolulu Community
College

Alan G. Glaros, Wayne State University

Eric Golanty, University of California, Davis

Miriam LeGare, California State University,
Sacramento

Joseph LoPiccolo, State University of New York
at Stony Brook

Thomas Tutko, San Jose State University

John P. Vincent, University of Houston

Elaine Walster, University of Wisconsin

Dan Schrinsky, Obstetrician/Gynecologist

Denis Moore, Honolulu Metropolitan
Community Church

Marga Sarriugarte, Portland Rape Victim
Advocate Project

Barbara Safriet, Lewis and Clark Law School

Peter Vennewitz, Portland Planned Parenthood

Second Edition

Jane Blackwell, Washington State University

John Blakemore, Monterey Peninsula
College

Bruce Clear, The First Unitarian Church,
Portland

Brenda M. DeVellis, University of North Carolina

Judy Drolet, Southern Illinois University

Andrea Parrot Eggleston, Cornell University

Catherine Fichten, Dawson College

Glen G. Gilbert, Portland State University

Claudette Hastie-Beahrs, Clinical Social Worker

David Johnson, Portland State University

Teri Nicoll-Johnson, Modesto Junior College

Richard A. Kaye, Kingsborough Community
College

Roger W. Little, University of Illinois, Chicago
Circle

Joseph LoPiccolo, State University of New York
at Stony Brook

Leslie McBride, Portland State University

John Money, Johns Hopkins University

Bruce Palmer, Washington State University

Monroe Pasternak, Diablo Valley College

John W. Petras, Central Michigan University

Valerie Pinhas, Nassau Community College

Deborah Richardson, University of Georgia

Cynthia Schuetz, San Francisco State University

James E. Urban, Kansas State University

Michael G. Walraven, Jackson Community
College

Marianne K. Zalar, University of California, San
Francisco

Brief Contents

PART ONE: INTRODUCTION 1

  1 Perspectives on Sexuality 2
  2 Gender Issues 19
  3 Sex Research: Methods and Problems 58

PART TWO: BIOLOGICAL BASIS 84

  4 Female Sexual Anatomy and Physiology 86
  5 Male Sexual Anatomy and Physiology 125
  6 Sexual Arousal and Response 151

PART THREE: SEXUAL BEHAVIOR 192

  7 Love and the Development of Sexual Relationships 194
  8 Communication in Sexual Behavior 222
  9 Sexual Behavior Patterns 252
  10 Homosexuality 290

PART FOUR: SEXUALITY AND THE LIFE CYCLE 322

  11 Contraception 324
  12 Conceiving Children: Process and Choice 373
  13 Sexuality During Childhood and Adolescence 409
  14 Sexuality and the Adult Years 448
  15 Sexuality and Aging 473

PART FIVE: SEXUAL PROBLEMS 490

  16 The Nature and Origins of Sexual Difficulties 492
  17 Increasing Sexual Satisfaction 524
  18 Sexually Transmitted Diseases 556

PART SIX: SOCIAL ISSUES 586

  19 Atypical Sexual Behavior 588
  20 Sexual Victimization 601
  21 Sex and the Law 626
  22 Cross-Cultural Variations in Sexual Expression 646

Glossary G-1
Bibliography B-1
Credits C-1
Index I-1

Detailed Contents

PART ONE: INTRODUCTION   1

1   Perspectives on Sexuality   2

THE AUTHORS' PERSPECTIVES   3
A Psychosocial Orientation   3
Our Cultural Legacy: Questioning Two
        Themes   5
A CROSS-CULTURAL PERSPECTIVE:
        SOCIAL NORMS AND
        SEXUALITY   6
Mangaia   6
Inis Beag   7
The Dani of New Guinea   8
The People's Republic of China   8
THE SEX-FOR-REPRODUCTION
        LEGACY   10
THE GENDER ROLE LEGACY   12
SEXUALITY: PERSONAL OR PUBLIC
        DOMAIN?   16
SUMMARY   17
SUGGESTED READINGS   18

2   Gender Issues   19

MALE AND FEMALE, MASCULINE AND
        FEMININE   20
Sex and Gender   20
Gender Identity and Gender Role   21
GENDER IDENTITY FORMATION   23
Gender Identity as a Biological Process   23
Social Learning Factors in Gender
        Identity   33
The Interactional Model   35
A Special Case of Gender Identity Difficulty:
        Transsexualism   36

GENDER ROLES   41
The Socialization of Gender Roles   43
The Impact of Gender Roles on Our
        Sexuality   47
Transcending Gender Roles: Androgyny   52
SUMMARY   55
SUGGESTED READINGS   57
BOX 2.1 Maleness as Better   42

3   Sex Research: Methods and Problems   58

RESEARCH METHODS   59
Surveys via Questionnaires or Interviews   59
Case Studies   63
Direct Observation   64
Experimental Research   64
SOME WELL-KNOWN STUDIES   66
The Kinsey Group   66
Masters and Johnson   72
Hunt   75
The Redbook *Report*   76
The Hite Report on Female Sexuality   77
The Hite Report on Male Sexuality   78
Sorenson   78
Zelnick and Kantner   79
Bell and Weinberg   80
WHAT TO BELIEVE? A STATEMENT OF
        PERSPECTIVE   81
SUMMARY   82
SUGGESTED READINGS   83
BOX 3.1 The Elegant Prostitute: An Example
        of Case Study Research   65
BOX 3.2 The Effects of Alcohol on Sexual
        Arousal: Two Examples of Experimental
        Research   67
BOX 3.3 Sex Research and Technology   68

PART TWO: BIOLOGICAL
BASIS 84

**4   Female Sexual Anatomy and
Physiology** 86

GENITAL SELF-EXAM 87
THE VULVA 89
The Mons Veneris 89
The Labia Majora 91
The Labia Minora 91
The Clitoris 91
The Vestibule 92
The Urethral Opening 92
The Introitus and the Hymen 93
The Perineum 94
UNDERLYING STRUCTURES 94
INTERNAL STRUCTURES 97
The Vagina 97
The Cervix 103
The Uterus 104
The Fallopian Tubes 104
The Ovaries 105
*Surgical Removal of the Uterus and
    Ovaries* 106
THE BREASTS 106
Breast Self-Exam 108
Breast Lumps 110
MENSTRUATION 111
Menstrual Physiology 113
Sexual Activity and the Menstrual Cycle 118
Menstruation: Mood and Performance 119
Menstrual Cycle Problems 121
Toxic Shock Syndrome 122
SUMMARY 123
SUGGESTED READINGS 124
BOX 4.1 *How to Examine Your
    Breasts* 109
BOX 4.2 *Men, Lovemaking, and
    Menstruation* 120

**5   Male Sexual Anatomy and
Physiology** 125

SEXUAL ANATOMY 126
The Scrotum 126

The Testes 127
The Vas Deferens 131
The Seminal Vesicles 132
The Prostate Gland 132
The Cowper's Glands 133
Semen 133
The Penis 134
MALE SEXUAL FUNCTIONS 137
Erection 138
Ejaculation 139
SOME CONCERNS ABOUT SEXUAL
    FUNCTIONING 142
Penis Size 142
Circumcision 146
SUMMARY 149
SUGGESTED READINGS 150

**6   Sexual Arousal and
Response** 151

SEXUAL AROUSAL 152
The Role of Hormones 152
The Brain 156
The Senses and Sexual Arousal 158
Foods, Chemicals, and Sexual Behavior 162
SEXUAL RESPONSE 167
Kaplan's Three-Stage Model 167
*Masters and Johnson's Four-Phase
    Model* 168
Some Differences Between the Sexes 185
SUMMARY 189
SUGGESTED READINGS 191
BOX 6.1 *Subjective Descriptions of
    Orgasm* 180

PART THREE: SEXUAL
BEHAVIOR 192

**7   Love and the Development
of Sexual Relationships** 194

WHAT IS LOVE? 195
Measuring Love 196
Jealousy and Love 197

FALLING IN LOVE: WHY AND WITH
    WHOM? 199
LOVE AND SEX 201
SEX AND RELATIONSHIPS ON YOUR
    TERMS 202
Know What You Want 203
Friendships Without Sex 204
*Saying "Not Yet" to a Sexual
    Relationship 205*
Guidelines for "Casual Sex" 206
Caring Endings 207
Managing Rejection 207
TYPES OF LOVE 208
Passionate Love 208
Companionate Love 210
THE DEVELOPMENT OF INTIMACY 211
Self-Love 211
The Phases of Relationship 211
MAINTAINING RELATIONSHIP
    SATISFACTION 214
The Inclusion-Response Foundation 216
Individual and Relationship Growth 217
Sexual Variety, An Important Ingredient 218
SUMMARY 220
SUGGESTED READINGS 221
*BOX 7.1 Two Contrasting Definitions of
    Love 196*

**8 Communication in Sexual
    Behavior** 222

THE IMPORTANCE OF
    COMMUNICATION 223
SOME REASONS WHY SEX TALK IS
    DIFFICULT 224
TALKING: GETTING STARTED 227
Talking about Talking 227
Reading and Discussing 228
The Media As a Stimulant 228
Sharing Sexual Histories 229
LISTENING AND FEEDBACK 229
Be an Active Listener 229
Maintain Eye Contact 230
Provide Feedback 230
*Support Your Partner's Communication
    Efforts 230*

*Express "Unconditional Positive
    Regard" 231*
Use Paraphrasing 231
DISCOVERING YOUR PARTNER'S
    NEEDS 232
Asking Questions 232
Self-Disclosure 234
Comparing Notes 235
Giving Permission 235
LEARNING TO MAKE REQUESTS 236
*Taking Responsibility for Our Own
    Pleasure 236*
Making Requests Specific 238
Using "I" Language 239
DELIVERING CRITICISM 239
Be Aware of Your Motivation 240
Choose the Right Time and Place 240
Temper Criticism with Praise 242
Nurture Small Steps Toward Change 243
Avoid "Why" Questions 244
Express Anger Appropriately 244
NONVERBAL SEXUAL
    COMMUNICATION 245
Facial Expression 246
Interpersonal Distance 246
Touching 247
Sounds 248
IMPASSES 248
SUMMARY 249
SUGGESTED READINGS 251

**9 Sexual Behavior
    Patterns** 252

CELIBACY 253
MASTURBATION 254
Perspectives on Masturbation 254
Purposes of Masturbation 256
Masturbation through the Life Cycle 258
Self-Pleasuring Techniques 261
EROTIC FANTASY AND DREAMS 265
SHARED TOUCHING 270
*Manual Stimulation of the Female
    Genitals 272*
*Manual Stimulation of the Male
    Genitals 272*

ORAL-GENITAL STIMULATION 273
ANAL STIMULATION 275
COITUS AND COITAL POSITIONS 275
Man Above, Face-to-Face 277
Woman Above, Face-to-Face 278
Side Position, Face-to-Face 280
Rear-Entry Position 281
SEXUAL ADJUSTMENT AND
    DISABILITY 281
*Stereotypes about Sexuality and
    Disability 282*
Body Image 283
*Sexuality and Medical and Institutional
    Care 285*
Spinal Cord Injury 285
Cerebral Palsy 286
Blindness and Deafness 287
Developmental Disabilities 287
SUMMARY 288
SUGGESTED READINGS 289
*BOX 9.1 Masturbation: An Historical
    Opinion 255*
*BOX 9.2 Masturbation: A Contemporary
    Account 259*
BOX 9.3 Sexual Fantasies 267

10 **Homosexuality** 290

A CONTINUUM OF SEXUAL
    ORIENTATIONS 291
Defining Bisexuality 293
SOCIETAL ATTITUDES 293
Homophobia 295
"CAUSES" OF HOMOSEXUALITY 297
Psychosocial Theories 298
Biological Theories 300
LIFE STYLES 303
Homosexual Relationships 304
Sexual Expression 307
"Coming Out" 310
GAY RIGHTS AND ANTIGAY
    RIGHTS 314
SUMMARY 319
SUGGESTED READINGS 320
BOX 10.1 The Homophobic Scale 296

*BOX 10.2 Examples of Childhood Gender
    Nonconformity Reported by
    Homosexual Adults 302*
BOX 10.3 "Dear Abby" 313
*BOX 10.4 A Letter from a Gay Man to His
    Parents Who Were Recently Told of His
    Sexual Orientation by His Angry
    Ex-Wife 315*

PART FOUR: SEXUALITY AND
THE LIFE CYCLE 322

11 **Contraception** 324

HISTORICAL AND SOCIAL
    PERSPECTIVES 325
Birth Control in the United States 325
Birth Control As a Contemporary Issue 326
SHARED RESPONSIBILITY 327
CURRENTLY AVAILABLE METHODS 329
*A Comparison of the Most Commonly Used
    Methods 329*
Oral Contraceptives 330
Intrauterine Devices 337
Diaphragms 342
Cervical Caps 346
Vaginal Spermicides 348
Condoms 350
Methods Based on the Menstrual Cycle 354
Other Methods 357
Postcoital Contraception 358
INDUCED ABORTION 359
Right-to-Life Versus Prochoice 360
Medical Procedures for Abortion 360
Pregnancy Risk-Taking and Abortion 363
STERILIZATION 364
Female Sterilization 365
Male Sterilization 366
NEW DIRECTIONS IN CONTRACEPTION 368
New Directions for Men 368
New Directions for Women 369
SUMMARY 370
SUGGESTED READINGS 371
*BOX 11.1 Using Backup Methods to Increase
    Contraceptive Effectiveness 332*

12 Conceiving Children: Process and Choice 373

PARENTHOOD AS AN OPTION 374
BECOMING PREGNANT 377
Infertility 377
Enhancing the Possibility of Conception 379
Alternatives to Couple-Intercourse for Conception 380
Preconceptual Sex Determination 381
Pregnancy Detection 382
Spontaneous Abortion 382
A HEALTHY PREGNANCY 383
Fetal Development 383
Prenatal Care 385
Amniocentesis 388
Pregnancy after 35 388
THE EXPERIENCE OF PREGNANCY 389
The Woman's Experience 389
The Man's Experience 391
Sexual Interaction During Pregnancy 393
CHILDBIRTH 394
Stages of Childbirth 395
Childbirth Practices: Past and Present 396
Birthplace Alternatives 398
Medical Interventions: Pros and Cons 400
POSTPARTUM 402
Parent-Child Contact 402
Breast Feeding 404
Sexual Interaction after Childbirth 406
SUMMARY 406
SUGGESTED READINGS 407
BOX 12.1 Are We Parent Material? (or, Am I? in the Case of Single Parenthood) 376

13 Sexuality During Childhood and Adolescence 409

SEXUAL BEHAVIOR IN CHILDHOOD 411
THE PHYSICAL CHANGES OF ADOLESCENCE 417
SEXUAL BEHAVIOR DURING ADOLESCENCE 419
The Double Standard 419

Virginity or "Sexual Liberation"? 420
Masturbation 421
Petting 422
Ongoing Sexual Relationships 422
Sexual Intercourse 424
Homosexuality 428
SOME KEY INFLUENCES ON PSYCHOSEXUAL DEVELOPMENT 429
Dirty Diapers, Going Potty, and Related Issues 429
Reactions to Masturbation 430
Positive Models 431
The Question of Nudity 435
Independency Issues 437
Privacy Concerns 438
SEX EDUCATION 439
ANDROGYNOUS CHILD-REARING AND SEXUALITY 443
SUMMARY 445
SUGGESTED READINGS 447

14 Sexuality and the Adult Years 448

SINGLE LIVING 449
COHABITATION 451
Personal Reasons for Living Together 451
The Social Impact of Living Together 453
MARRIAGE 454
Changing Expectations and Marital Patterns 455
Why Do People Marry? 457
Sexual Behavior within Marriage 458
RELATIONSHIP CONTRACTS 460
EXTRAMARITAL RELATIONSHIPS 461
Nonconsensual Extramarital Relationships 461
Consensual Extramarital Relationships 463
DIVORCE 467
Interpreting Divorce Statistics 467
Adjusting to Divorce 468
WIDOWHOOD 470
SUMMARY 471
SUGGESTED READINGS 472

15 Sexuality and Aging 473

SEXUALITY IN THE LATER YEARS: EXAMINING THE MYTHS 474
The Double Standard of Aging 475
Sexuality and Aging in Nursing Homes 477
PHYSIOSEXUAL CHANGES AND SEXUAL RESPONSE: THE OLDER FEMALE 478
Estrogen Replacement Therapy 479
The Sexual Response Cycle of the Older Female 480
PHYSIOSEXUAL CHANGES AND SEXUAL RESPONSE: THE OLDER MALE 481
The Prostate Gland 482
The Sexual Response Cycle of the Older Male 482
MAXIMIZING SEXUAL FUNCTIONING IN THE LATER YEARS 484
Potential Problems and What to Do About Them 484
Sexual Expression in the Later Years 485
SUMMARY 488
SUGGESTED READINGS 489

PART FIVE: SEXUAL PROBLEMS 490

16 The Nature and Origins of Sexual Difficulties 492

ORIGINS OF SEXUAL DIFFICULTIES 493
Cultural Influences 493
Personal Factors 499
Interpersonal Factors 501
Organic Factors 504
DESIRE PHASE DIFFICULTIES 506
Inhibited Sexual Desire 507
Sexual Aversion 509
AROUSAL DIFFICULTIES 509
Inhibition of Vaginal Lubrication 509
Erectile Inhibition 510
ORGASM DIFFICULTIES 511
Anorgasmia 511

Rapid Ejaculation 515
Ejaculatory Inhibition 517
Faking Orgasms 519
VAGINISMUS 520
SUMMARY 521
SUGGESTED READINGS 523
BOX 16.1 A Case Study in Psychologically Based Erectile Inhibition 512

17 Increasing Sexual Satisfaction 524

THE PLISSIT MODEL OF SEX THERAPY 525
Permission 525
Limited Information 525
Specific Suggestions 526
Intensive Therapy 526
SELF-KNOWLEDGE 526
Self-Awareness 526
Self-Stimulation 528
SHARING WITH A PARTNER 528
Communicating Feelings and Problems 529
Sensate Focus 530
Active-Receptive Communication Exercise 531
Self-Stimulation with a Partner Present 532
SPECIFIC SUGGESTIONS FOR WOMEN 533
Becoming Orgasmic: Strategies for Women 533
Experiencing Orgasm with a Partner 535
Dealing with Vaginismus 538
SPECIFIC SUGGESTIONS FOR MEN 539
Lasting Longer 539
Dealing with Erectile Difficulties 545
Reducing Ejaculatory Inhibition 549
TREATMENT FOR INHIBITED SEXUAL DESIRE 550
GUIDELINES FOR SEEKING PROFESSIONAL ASSISTANCE 551
Selecting a Therapist 551
Fees and Ethics 553
SUMMARY 553
SUGGESTED READINGS 555

18   Sexually Transmitted Diseases   556

TWO COMMON VAGINAL
        INFECTIONS   558
Trichomoniasis   558
Moniliasis   561
GONORRHEA   562
SYPHILIS   567
NONGONOCOCCAL URETHRITIS   570
HERPES   571
PUBIC LICE   577
GENITAL WARTS   578
PREVENTION OF SEXUALLY
        TRANSMITTED DISEASES   578
Some Steps for Prevention   580
SUMMARY   583
SUGGESTED READINGS   585
BOX 18.1 Telling a Partner   564

PART SIX: SOCIAL ISSUES   586

19   Atypical Sexual Behavior   588

EXHIBITIONISM   590
OBSCENE PHONE CALLS   593
VOYEURISM   594
SADOMASOCHISM   595
FETISHISM   596
TRANSVESTISM   597
SUMMARY   599
SUGGESTED READINGS   600

20   Sexual Victimization   601

PEDOPHILIA   602
INCEST   603
SEXUAL HARASSMENT ON THE
        JOB   606
Varieties of Sexual Harassment   608
*Effects of Sexual Harassment on
        Victims   609*

How to Deal with Sexual Harassment   610
RAPE   610
Contemporary Issues   611
False Beliefs about Rape   613
Rape Victims   616
A Partner's Response to Rape   617
Men Who Rape   621
Treatment of Rapists   623
Rape of Males   623
SUMMARY   624
SUGGESTED READINGS   625
BOX 20.1 Dealing with Rape   618

21   Sex and the Law   626

ADULT CONSENSUAL SEXUAL
        BEHAVIORS   627
Nonmarital Intercourse   627
Specific Sexual Behaviors   628
Homosexual Behaviors   629
PORNOGRAPHY   630
Three Legal Issues   632
Effects of Pornography   634
PROSTITUTION   637
Female Prostitutes   638
Male Prostitutes   640
Economics and Profit from Prostitution   641
Issues of Legal Status   641
SEX LAW REFORM   643
SUMMARY   644
SUGGESTED READINGS   645
*BOX 21.1 States with Consenting Adult Laws
        as of 1982   630*
BOX 21.2 Books Banned in Schools   635
*BOX 21.3 Sexual Exploitation of Children in
        Prostitution and Pornography   638*

22   Cross-Cultural Variations in Sexual Expression   646

SOCIETY AND CULTURE: DEFINITIONS
        AND OBSERVATIONS   647
DATA SOURCES: METHODS AND
        LIMITATIONS   649

COMPARATIVE ANALYSIS OF SOME
    SELECTED SEXUAL
    BEHAVIORS 650
Sexuality During Childhood 651
Coitus Before Marriage 654
Marital Coitus 657
Extramarital Coitus 658
Female Orgasm 659
Noncoital Sex Play 661
Sexuality and Aging 662

Homosexuality 662
SUMMARY 663
SUGGESTED READINGS 664
BOX 22.1 Female Genital Mutilation 660

Glossary G-1
Bibliography B-1
Credits C-1
Index I-1

PART ONE

Introduction

1

Perspectives on Sexuality

THE AUTHORS' PERSPECTIVES
    A Psychosocial Orientation
    Our Cultural Legacy: Questioning Two Themes
A CROSS-CULTURAL PERSPECTIVE: SOCIAL NORMS AND SEXUALITY
    Mangaia
    Inis Beag
    The Dani of New Guinea
    The People's Republic of China
THE SEX-FOR-REPRODUCTION LEGACY
THE GENDER ROLE LEGACY
SEXUALITY: PERSONAL OR PUBLIC DOMAIN?
SUMMARY
SUGGESTED READINGS

*P*erhaps all of us have had the experience of walking into a class for the first time, wondering what the course and the teacher will be like. On that first day, the instructor's candor in freely expressing the philosophies and focus of the course is a great help in setting the stage for all that is to follow. Our primary purpose for including this opening chapter is the same as that of an instructor's opening remarks—to acquaint you, the reader, with the focus, philosophy, and perspectives we bring to this text.

We offer you this book as a step in the development of your own personal perspectives on human sexuality. While we will present a wide array of information about attitudes, ideas, and behaviors, we wish to emphasize that the final expert on your sexuality is *you*. Thus, we encourage you to evaluate all the information we present within the framework of your own experiences and convictions.

THE AUTHORS' PERSPECTIVES

It is safe to assume that any controversial topic (and what sexual topic is not controversial?) will elicit a wide range of responses. In any beginning sexuality class—or in almost any other group, for that matter—attitudes toward sexuality will likely range from very liberal to highly conservative. It is also reasonable to assume that students in sexuality classes represent a wide range of sexual experience and preferences. Some have shared sexual encounters with one or more partners; some have had long-term partnerships in marital or other ongoing frameworks; others have not been sexually intimate with another individual. Many people prefer to relate exclusively to members of the opposite sex; others prefer sexual relations with the same sex; still others may feel comfortable relating to either sex. There are virtually no universals in sexual attitudes, experiences, or preferences.

With this broad spectrum in mind, we have attempted to bring a pluralistic, nonlimiting philosophy to this text. We think a human sexuality text should be written for all prospective readers, not just for one or two groups that may happen to be statistically more common than others. We hope there will be something of value in the following pages for all our readers. At the same time, we do speak from a distinct point of view. It is appropriate to tell you about our perspectives here, so you can recognize and evaluate them for yourself as you read the text.

A Psychosocial Orientation

This book has a *psychosocial* orientation, reflecting our view that human sexuality is governed more by psychological factors (motivational, emotional, attitudinal) and by social *conditioning* (the process by which we learn our society's expectations and norms) than by the effects of biological factors such as hormones or instincts. The psychological and social factors are so intertwined that it is often difficult to distinguish clearly between the two.

We may not always be aware of it, but our sexual attitudes and behaviors are strongly shaped by our society. The subtle ways in which we learn society's expec-

Sexual attitudes and experiences vary from person to person.

tations regarding sexuality often lead us to assume that our behaviors or feelings are biologically innate, or "natural." However, an examination of sexuality in other societies (even in different cultural groups within our own society) and in other time periods of history reveals a diverse range of acceptable behavior. For example, lovers rubbing noses, brides experiencing coitus with many men on their wedding day, and children being masturbated by parents are all legitimate forms of sexual expression in certain other cultures, though certainly not in North American society. What we regard as "natural" is clearly relative.

Many contemporary sex researchers think that there has been an overemphasis on the biological determination of sexual behavior. Evidence from studies of human sexual response patterns, together with investigations of sexual behavior in different societies and in different species, shows that there is much more to human sexuality than biology. However, it is clear that the physiology of sex plays an important role, and we will be looking in some detail at the biological foundations of sexual behavior. But understanding the impact of culture and individual experience can make it easier to make decisions about our own sexuality. Thus, our major emphasis in this book will be on the psychosocial aspects of human sexuality.

Within this psychosocial perspective, we admit to a few biases. These have to do with our opposition to two sexual themes that are long-standing in our culture and in most other Western cultures.

One of these legacies is the idea that the only legitimate purpose of sexual activity is reproduction. This theme is rooted deeply in our heritage. In our culture one of the most prominent ways that the reproductive theme is expressed is in the notion that sex is synonymous with penile-vaginal intercourse (or *coitus*). Certainly coitus can be a very fulfilling part of sexual expression. However, we believe that excessive emphasis on intercourse often has negative consequences. For one, it perpetuates the notion that sexual response and orgasm are supposed to occur during penetration. Such a narrow focus places tremendous performance pressure and expectations on coitus itself, for both women and men.

The sex-for-reproduction view also may result in devaluating other forms of sexual behavior. Some activities—for instance, affectionate kisses, body caresses, and manual or oral stimulation—are often relegated to the secondary status of *foreplay* (usually considered to be any activity before intercourse), to be followed by the "real sex" of coitus. Many people have learned to view these and other practices, such as masturbation, sexual fantasy, and anal intercourse, with suspicion. The same is true of sexual relations between members of the same sex, for these certainly do not fit into the standard model of intercourse for reproduction. All of these noncoital sexual behaviors have been defined at some time, past or present, as immoral, sinful, perverted, or illegal. We will present them in this text as viable sexual options for those people who do, or who would like to, engage in these behaviors.

A second cultural legacy is the distinction between male and female roles. This distinction reflects far more than the physiological differences between the sexes. Research does indicate the presence of certain minimal sex differences in behavioral predispositions. However, it is the impact of the socialization process that shapes and exaggerates our biological proclivities. Human beings begin learning in early infancy to be "opposites." For example, one of our students describes seeing this behavior at a baby shower for fraternal twins:

Except for the color of their clothes, the twins sure looked the same to me. But the women handled each of them differently: they gave soft, cooing sounds and delicate touches to the girl and energetic words and bouncing to the boy. (Authors' files)

It is our belief that rigid gender role conditioning acts to limit each person's full range of human potential, producing a negative impact on our sexuality. For example, "appropriate" personality characteristics delegated to men and women may contribute to the notion that the man must always be the initiator and the woman must be the receiver. When this arrangement is the status quo, we believe it places tremendous responsibility on the male and severely limits the woman's likelihood of discovering and meeting her own needs. It discourages the man from expressing his receptivity and the woman from experiencing her assertiveness.

These three author biases—our psychosocial orientation, our opposition to the sex-for-reproduction theme, and our belief that gender roles are limiting—will appear again and again throughout this text. In this chapter, however, we want to take the opportunity to explore these ideas more thoroughly, first through a cross-cultural and then an historical perspective.

It is difficult to understand how deeply culture shapes our attitudes and feelings without some grounds for comparison. In the next section we will look at four twentieth-century societies to see how their sexual norms vary from one another and from those of our own culture. After that, we will take a brief, selective look back through our Western cultural heritage in a search for the "roots" of the two legacies of sex-for-reproduction and rigid gender roles. Hopefully, appreciating these two themes as they are reflected in their cross-cultural and historical contexts will help us to more fully understand conflicts they may present in our own lives.

A CROSS-CULTURAL PERSPECTIVE: SOCIAL NORMS AND SEXUALITY

What constitutes "normal" sexual behavior? Many of us have our own ideas about what is normal and what is not, but often, people do not stop to realize how fundamentally these ideas are affected by our own social context. For instance, in the ancient Greek city-states of Athens and Sparta, it was normal for men to engage in *pederasty,* a practice in which an older man would take a young man as a lover, providing not only affection but also intellectual and moral guidance. (The Spartans encouraged pederasty for military purposes, for they believed that a man in love with a fellow soldier would fight all the more fiercely in battle to protect his lover.)

Today, as in Western culture for centuries, we define pederasty more narrowly as the sexual attraction of an adult for a child, and as such it has not only been condemned but also made a crime. This is but one example of how "normal" varies from one era to another; and it also varies broadly in modern cultures. We will look briefly at four societies—those of the Polynesian island of Mangaia, the Irish island known as Inis Beag, the Dani people of New Guinea, and the People's Republic of China—that illustrate four very different views toward sexuality. (More will be said about the first three of these societies later in the text, in Chapter 22.)

Mangaia

Mangaia is the southernmost of the Polynesian Cook Island chain. The island was studied in the 1950s by anthropologist Donald Marshall, whose accounts of Mangaian sexual practices have been widely quoted.*

*In Mangaia, as in all human societies, behavior patterns change with the passage of time. In the years since Marshall's visit, Mangaian life style has undergone many changes, as were noted during a visit in 1982 by one of the authors, Bob Crooks. Some of these more recent observations will be discussed in Chapter 22.

When Marshall visited Mangaia, he observed a society in which sexual pleasure and activity is a principal concern, starting in childhood (Marshall, 1971). Children have extensive exposure to sexuality: they hear folk tales that contain detailed descriptions of sex acts and sexual anatomy, and they observe provocative ritual dances. With puberty, both sexes receive active and detailed sex instruction. Males undergo an operation called "superincision" that consists of cutting the tissue on top of the penis and folding it back, exposing the glans. During this period the boy is provided detailed information about various sexual techniques. He is taught how to stimulate a woman's genitals and breasts with his mouth, to bring a partner to orgasm, and to control his urge to ejaculate. A Mangaian girl is also instructed in sexual activity. She is taught the importance of being responsive and active during sexual encounters.

Once their instruction is completed, boys begin to seek girls. Sex occurs in "public privacy" as young males engage in a practice called *sleepcrawling*. At night, the boy creeps quietly into the family home of a young woman with whom he wants to have sexual intercourse. If awakened, the other five to 15 family members in the home politely pretend to sleep. (In the 1950s, when Marshall conducted his research, most Mangaian houses had only a single sleeping area.) Parents approve of this practice and listen for sounds of laughter as a sign that their daughter is pleased with her partner: they encourage the young woman to have several encounters so that she may find a sexually compatible marriage partner. The young men gain social prestige through their ability to please their partners. These patterns persist on a daily basis throughout the adolescent years for unmarried males and females.

Sexual relations continue to occur frequently after marriage. An 18-year-old male is estimated to experience three orgasms per night *every* day of the week—and if he is skilled, his partner experiences three orgasms for each one of his. A wide range of sexual activity is approved, including oral-genital sex and a considerable amount of touching before and during intercourse. Among the Mangaians, then, a high degree of sexual activity is not only condoned but is actively encouraged as the norm. A sharp contrast is provided by the community of the Irish island known as Inis Beag.

Inis Beag

The inhabitants of Inis Beag (a pseudonym given to protect the privacy of this Irish island) have a very different attitude from that of the Mangaians (Messenger, 1971). Sexual expression is discouraged from infancy: mothers avoid breast feeding their children, and after infancy parents seldom kiss or fondle them. Children learn to abhor nudity. They learn that elimination is "dirty" and that bathing must be done only in absolute privacy. Any kind of childhood sexual expression is punished.

As they grow older, children usually receive no information about sex from their parents. Young girls are often shocked by their first menstruation, and they are never given an adequate explanation of what has happened. Priests and other religious authorities teach that it is sinful to discuss premarital sexual activity, masturbation, or sex play. Religious leaders on the island have denounced even *Time* and *Life* magazines as pornographic.

The average age for marriage is older than in many societies (36 for men and 26 for women), and marriages are often arranged. One of the reasons for late marriage may be the limited land resources: a man must usually wait to own land through inheritance. Marriage partners generally know little or nothing about precoital sex play, like oral or manual stimulation of the breasts and genitals. Beyond intercourse, sexual activity is usually limited to mouth kissing and rough fondling of the woman's lower body by the man. Males invariably initiate sex, using the man-on-top intercourse position. Sex usually occurs while both partners are wearing night clothes. After ejaculation, men tend to fall asleep. Female orgasm is unknown or considered a deviant response.

Sexual misconceptions continue through adulthood. For example, many women believe that menopause causes insanity, and some women confine themselves to bed from menopause to their death. During menstruation and also during the months following childbirth, men consider intercourse to be harmful to them. Many men also believe intercourse to be debilitating, and they avoid sex the night before a strenuous job. In general, anxiety-laden attitudes and rigid social restrictions are the normal elements of sexuality in Inis Beag.

The Dani of New Guinea

In both Mangaia and Inis Beag, sexuality receives a great amount of attention, if in different ways. Is this characteristic of all societies? A look at the Dani culture of the mountains of West New Guinea indicates not.

The Dani people seem to be largely indifferent to sexuality (Heider, 1976). Children are raised gently, with little stress: their toilet training and education are relaxed. Sexual activity is infrequent among adults. There is almost no premarital sex, even when courtship covers an extended period. (Marriages are held only during a certain feast that occurs every four to six years.) After marriage, a couple abstains from sex for at least two years and then has infrequent intercourse. Following the birth of a child, the couple abstains from sex for four to six years. During this time there is no reported masturbation and extramarital sex is rare.

According to Karl Heider, who studied this society in the 1960s, the Dani culture does not attempt to overtly enforce these behavior patterns. Heider also saw no indications of hormonal or physiological deficiencies that could result in low sexual interest. In general, the Dani are relaxed, physically healthy people who live in a moderate climate and have an adequate food supply. They appear to be very calm, only rarely expressing anger. Heider believes that the apparent infrequency of sexual activity reflects the Dani's relaxed life style and their low level of emotional intensity.

The People's Republic of China

There is still a fourth variation on the theme that sexuality reflects society. More so than in the three previous examples, sexuality in the People's Republic of China reflects official policies and attitudes of government. The policies seem to have been effective: the sexual mores of the one billion Chinese (one out of every four people in

A family planning worker in China provides contraceptive information.

the world) who live in the People's Republic of China appear to be quite homogeneous (Hamburg, 1981). Prostitution and sexually transmitted diseases such as gonorrhea and syphilis are reported to have been eliminated from mainland China. Also, the media does not commercialize sex as is typical in the United States.

As one method of controlling the growth of the country's enormous population, the government has an incentive program for married couples to have only one child. Couples who limit their families to one child receive a monthly subsidy, free education for the child, and priority for housing. Penalties are assessed to families who have more than one child—for instance, parents have to pay for the second child's schooling. Also, a comprehensive network of family-planning workers teaches couples about birth control to help them limit their family size.

In general, sex seems to be a low priority in the lives of most Chinese. There is little or no talk about sex between parents and children; likewise, there is little or no formal sex education in the schools. (Sex education is reported to be important only for adults about to be married.) Sex is uncommon prior to marriage. Abortions are available, but few unmarried women request them.

The broad range of sexual attitudes and behaviors among the Mangaians, the people of Inis Beag, the Dani, and the mainland Chinese helps to show how society shapes sexuality. Though we may not always look at it in the same light, our own customs, practices, and attitudes reflect a parallel process of social shaping. This becomes clearer if we explore the origins of our sexual mores in Western history.

THE SEX-FOR-REPRODUCTION LEGACY

We have noted that a strong theme in our culture is that the purpose of sexual activity should be procreation. Where did this theme come from, and how relevant is it to us today?

The idea of sex for reproduction is associated with Judeo-Christian tradition. Childbearing was tremendously important to the ancient Hebrews. Their history of slavery and persecution made them determined to preserve their people—to "be fruitful, and multiply, and replenish the earth . . ." (*Genesis* 1:28). Yet to "know" a partner sexually, within marriage, was also recognized as a profound physical and emotional experience (Carswell, 1969), and the Song of Solomon in the Old Testament contains some of the most sensuous love poetry in Western literature:

The bridegroom speaks:

> How fair is thy love, . . . my spouse!
> how much better is thy love than wine!
> and the smell of thine ointments than all spices!
> Thy lips, oh my spouse, drop as the honeycomb:
> honey and milk are under thy tongue. (Solomon 4:10-11)

And the bride:

> I am my beloved's and his desire is toward me.
> Come, my husband, let us go forth into the field;
> Let us lodge in the villages . . .
> There will I give thee my loves. (7:10-13)

This kind of appreciation of sexuality was a part of Judaic tradition, just as was the notion of sex for procreation. It would later be eclipsed, however, under the teachings of the medieval church. To understand why this happened, it is necessary to look at the social context in which Christianity arose. By the first century B.C., after the Roman Empire had reached its height, social instability and sexual decadence were pervasive. Many exotic cults were imported from places like Greece, Persia, and Palestine to provide sexual entertainment and amusement. The cult of Bacchus (god of wine) became one of the most notorious. In the "Bacchanalia" ceremony (which ultimately became so offensive that the Roman Senate banned it), young male initiates raced to the banks of the Tiber River, where they were forced to have intercourse with members of the cult or be killed.

We know very little about Jesus' views on sexuality. But in the years after his death, his followers were to show their reaction against activities such as the Bacchanalia by their association of sex with sin. Paul of Tarsus, whose influence upon the early Church was crucial (he died in 66 A.D. and many of his writings were incorporated into the New Testament), described the importance of overcoming "desires of the flesh" (including anger, selfishness, hatred, and nonmarital sex) in order to "inherit the Kingdom of God." He equated spirituality with sexual abstinence, and he saw *celibacy*, the state of being unmarried, as superior to marriage. Other church fathers expanded on this theme in the following centuries. Augustine (353–430) declared that lust was the original sin of Adam and Eve, and he formalized the notion that intercourse could only take place within marriage for the purpose of procreation.

The belief that sex is sinful persisted throughout the Middle Ages (the period dating from the fall of the Western Roman Empire in 476 A.D. to the beginning of the Renaissance (about 1400); and Thomas Aquinas (1225–1274) further refined it in a small section of his *Summa Theologica*. In a detailed list of rules about sexual behavior, Aquinas maintained that man's sexual organs were designed for procreation and that any other use (homosexual acts, oral-genital sex, anal intercourse, or sex with animals) was against God's will and therefore heretical. Aquinas' teachings were so pervasive that from then on homosexuals were to find neither refuge nor tolerance throughout the Western world (Boswell, 1980).

The ideas of Augustine and Aquinas dominated Western thought until the Reformation in the sixteenth century. One of Martin Luther's (1483–1546) disagreements with official church doctrine centered around chastity and celibacy. Sex, he believed, was as necessary to humans as eating and drinking. He believed the clergy should be permitted to marry, and after he left the priesthood he married, and fathered several children. Another reformer, John Calvin (1509–1564) recognized that sex could have other purposes besides procreation. Sex was permissible if it stemmed "from a desire for children, or to avoid fornication, or to lighten and ease the cares and sadnesses of household affairs, or to endear each other" (Taylor, 1971, p. 62). The Puritans, a group who are often maligned for having rigid views about sex, also shared an appreciation of sexual expression within marriage as a part of their emphasis on the importance of the family unit. One man was expelled from Boston when, among other offenses, "he denied . . . conjugal . . . fellowship unto his wife for the space of 2 years . . . ." (Morgan, 1978, p. 364). While necessary for procreation, Reformation groups also saw intercourse as a human necessity, with marriage providing the proper outlet for it.

One other influence should be mentioned in any discussion of the sex-for-procreation legacy: the availability of modern contraception, which more reliably permits intercourse without procreation. Contraceptive devices have been used for centuries (Pomeroy, 1975). Condoms made from goat bladders were used by men since ancient times. In Rome during the first century B.C., women used amulets, magic, and the rhythm method (which was ineffective because the Romans believed the most fertile period was at the end of menstruation). They also inserted soft wool pads to block the cervix. The modern diaphragm, which was developed in Europe in the 1870s, was not introduced to the United States until the 1920s.

With the possible exception of the diaphragm, none of these methods were as reliable as the Pill, introduced in the late 50s and early 60s, soon to be followed by the intrauterine device (IUD), "morning after pills," and spermicides. These contraceptives have given women increased independent control over their reproductive capacities, and their widespread acceptance has permitted sexuality to be separated from procreation in a way that it had never been before. The world has changed, too, so that today many people are concerned with the costs of bearing children (both ecological and economic), costs that were not as relevant in the preindustrial world. Despite these changes, however, the legacy of the Old and New Testaments, of St. Augustine and Thomas Aquinas, and of the Reformation is still very much with us. Thus, the twentieth-century Western perspective of the sex-for-reproduction issue represents a complex conflict between personal pleasure, practicality, and tradition.

THE GENDER ROLE LEGACY

A second issue about which we admit to a bias is the impact of gender roles. Roles of women and men are changing in modern Western society, but each change, going as it does against tradition, has been difficult to achieve.

How far back do we have to look to find the roots of these traditions? Certainly by the time Hebraic culture was established, gender roles were highly specialized. The Book of Proverbs lists the duties of a good wife: she must instruct servants, care for her family, and keep household accounts. In addition, she must look on the future with optimism, be kind, and never be idle. Charm and beauty were not required, but bearing children (especially sons) was essential; so was obedience to her husband. In return for all this, the wife was granted the right to her husband's sexual favors—although she might share this right with one or more secondary wives or concubines!

If the Old Testament seems to embody a double standard, it is egalitarian compared with the gender roles that evolved in ancient Athens, where women had no more political or legal rights than slaves. In the sixth century B.C., the lawgiver Solon institutionalized these distinctions. He regulated women's dress, food, and drink and their right to appear in public. Women were subject to the absolute authority of the male next-of-kin. They received no formal education and spent their lives in women's quarters within their homes.

Not all ancient societies had the same inflexible double standard. In fact, the cultural climate was very different in the sixth-century Greek societies of Sparta and Lesbos. The city-state of Sparta was determined to produce the most feared and dedicated army in Greece. Women were valued. Both sexes trained from birth under severe discipline, both sexes were educated, and both were encouraged in athletics (on the theory that strong women produced healthy babies). Sexual relationships between women, as well as between men, were accepted. Women were also valued in the island culture of Lesbos, from whose name *lesbianism* (female homosexuality) has been derived.* What explains the difference between these two societies and Athens?

---

*In Greek classical literature, however, Lesbos is actually linked with both heterosexual and homosexual eroticism; even the famous poet Sappho, who lived on Lesbos at this time, seems to have been bisexual (she had a husband and a child).

Sparta and Lesbos seem to have accepted erotic attachments between women because women themselves were considered important (Boswell, 1980; Dover, 1978; Pomeroy, 1975).

Christianity reaffirmed Judaism's traditional sex roles. One of the major themes of the writings of Paul of Tarsus was the status of women. Paul looked to man's creation before woman's and Eve's disobedience to God to explain why women should be submissive:

I permit no woman to teach or to have authority over men. . . . For Adam was
formed first, then Eve; and Adam was not deceived, but the woman was deceived
and became a transgressor . . . (*I Timothy* 2:11–15)

This was the status quo throughout the Middle Ages. During this period, however, two contradictory images of women were to evolve, gaining strength so that each had its own impact on women's place in society. The first of these was the cult of the Virgin; the second, the image of Eve as an evil temptress.

The cult of the Virgin was imported by crusaders returning from Constantinople, and it transformed and exalted Mary's image from a vague figure of secondary importance to a gracious, compassionate mother to the poor and wretched who became a focus of religious devotion. The practice of *courtly love*, which evolved at about the same time, reflected a compatible image of woman as pure and unreproachable. Ideally, a young knight would fall in love with a married woman of higher rank. After a lengthy pursuit, he would find favor; but his love would remain unrequited because her marriage vows ultimately proved stronger. Just how many such affairs actually took this course is a rather fascinating question. However, the idea caught the medieval imagination, and ballads of courtly love were performed by troubadors throughout the courts of Europe.

Another medieval image provides a counterpoint to the unattainable, compassionate "madonna"—the image of Eve as the evil temptress of the Garden of Eden. This view, promoted by the church, reflected an increasing emphasis on Eve's sin and an antagonism toward women. It reached its climax in the witch hunts that began in the late fifteenth century—after the Renaissance, which also elevated women's status, was well under way—and lasted for close to 200 years. Queen Elizabeth I (1533–1603) was a true "Renaissance woman" who brought England to new heights of power; yet at the same time, thousands of women were being tortured and executed as witches in both Europe and America.

Witch hunting had ended by the time of the eighteenth-century Enlightenment, which was partly a product of the new scientific rationalism, and women were to enjoy a new equality, at least for a short time. Women like Mary Wollstonecraft of England were famous for their intelligence, wit, and vivacity. Wollstonecraft's book, *The Vindication of the Rights of Women* (1792), attacked the practice whereby young girls were given dolls rather than schoolbooks. She also asserted that sexual satisfaction was as important to women as to men, and that premarital and extramarital sex were not sinful.

In the Middle Ages, two contradictory images of women prevailed
—women as pure and unreproachable, exemplified by
courtly love, and women as evil, which reached a climax in the
witch hunts.

These views did not prevail. The Victorian era, which took its name from the woman who ascended the British throne in 1837, brought a sharp turnaround. Both genders had highly defined roles. Victorian women were valued for their spirituality and delicacy—an image that was reinforced by clothing like corsets, hoops, and bustles, which all but prevented a woman from freely moving her body. Popular opinion of female sexuality was reflected by the widely quoted physician, William Acton, who wrote, "The majority of women are not very much troubled with sexual feelings of any kind" (Degler, 1980, p. 250). Women's duties centered around fulfilling their families' spiritual needs and providing a comfortable home for their husbands to "retreat to" after working all day. Ladylike manners and domestic skills were considered very important, and magazines such as *Godey's Lady's Book* instructed women on the proper form for such virtues. The world of women was clearly separated from that of men, and intensely passionate friendships developed between women, providing the support and comfort often absent in marriage.

Victorian men were expected to conform to the strict propriety of the age, but (alas!) they were often forced to lay aside morality in the pursuit of business and political interests. They sometimes laid aside morality in the pursuit of sexual companionship, also, for the clear separation of the worlds of husbands and wives imposed an emotional distance on many Victorian marriages. Ironically, prostitution flourished at the same time as propriety and sexual repression. Victorian men could smoke, drink, and joke with the women who had turned to prostitution out of economic necessity. Added to this was the social pressure that encouraged men to marry only after they had accumulated money and established a comfortable home. Confronted with many years without a wife, followed by marriage to a sheltered bride many years younger than himself, a man paid prostitutes for companionship as well as sexual release.

Perhaps more than any age, the nineteenth century was full of contradictions. Some women were put on a pedestal of asexuality and piety at the same time that others were exploited as sexual objects. Men were trapped between the ideal of purity and the frank pleasures of physical expression. The nineteenth century French writer Gustave Flaubert captured this feeling:

A man has missed something if he has never woken up in an anonymous bed beside a face he will never see again, and if he has never left a brothel at dawn feeling like jumping off a bridge out of sheer physical disgust with life. (Baldwick, 1973, p. 106)

The twentieth century, however, changed this precarious status quo. The suffrage movement, which began in the late nineteenth century with the goal of giving women the right to vote, grew out of several related developments such as the temperance movement, the abolition of slavery, and the demand that women be

In the Victorian era, the marriageable woman possessed morals that were as tightly laced as her corset. Ironically, prostitution flourished at this time. Clearly, a double standard existed.

permitted to attend universities and hold property. Equality was not ushered in, however, with the passage of the Eighteenth Amendment in 1920 enfranchising women, but an environment for its growth was encouraged during World War II when thousands of women left the traditional homemaker role as they took paying jobs. Not until the 1960s, after the flurry of postwar marriages, the baby boom, and a broad-scale disappointment in the resulting domesticity, did a new movement for gender role equality begin. This movement, still under way, has had its victories. Yet we still carry the legacy of Victorianism and earlier traditions in the gender roles we all learn as children in our society, and this legacy acts to limit both men and women. Chapter 2 will discuss the impact of gender roles on contemporary men and women.

SEXUALITY: PERSONAL OR PUBLIC DOMAIN?

The historical perspective we have used in this chapter may help us appreciate the unique position in which we currently find ourselves. Men and women today have new freedoms and responsibilities. To a far greater degree than was possible for the ancient Hebrews or Athenians, the early Christians, the Europeans of the Middle Ages, or the Victorians of a century ago, we may define our own sexuality on the basis of personal morality.

This responsibility has been hard won, and it is largely a result of the combination of psychological, scientific, and social advances that have taken place primarily in the twentieth century. Psychological advances came with the work of people like Sigmund Freud (1856–1939) and Havelock Ellis (1859–1939), who recognized sexuality in both women and men as natural and also recognized that different individuals had differing sexual needs, and Theodore Van de Velde (1873–1937), who emphasized the importance of sexual pleasure and satisfaction. As these ideas became accepted by more people, the result was a growing tolerance for a wider variety of behaviors.

Findings of sex researchers like Alfred Kinsey added scientific data that brought further acceptance of masturbation, homosexuality, and nonmarital intercourse as normal expressions of sexuality, and research such as that of William Masters and Virginia Johnson brought a greater public understanding of the sexual response cycle. (We will look at the work of these and other scientific researchers in Chapter 3.) This new awareness of sexual interests and individual variations also contributed to a greater tolerance and respect for the individual's right to make sexual decisions.

In the early 1960s, the invention of the Pill and the increased availability of other reliable contraceptive devices helped to bring sexual decisions even more firmly into the private domain. By the end of that decade, contraception had become accepted as a matter of personal decision. Moreover, in 1973 the U. S. Supreme Court ruled in a landmark decision that abortion was a woman's personal decision, one that the government could not prohibit. In the increasingly tolerant atmosphere of the 1960s and 1970s, attitudes began to change about another traditional taboo, homosexuality. Homosexual men and women began to openly declare that their sexual orientation was a personal matter and should not affect their rights and responsibilities as citizens. However, the popular stigma surrounding this practice has only recently begun to lessen.

These many changes have come rapidly, and society is still in a state of flux. One result has been a sense of displacement and uncertainty. At the same time that young men and women have had access to information, contraception, and medical care, there has been an epidemic of sexually transmitted diseases, a rise in illegitimate births, and widespread confusion about personal values. Still another result has been the growing interest of some groups in limiting personal control and bringing many decisions about sexuality back into the public domain. For example, antiabortion or "right-to-life" groups are attempting to make abortion illegal. Others want to require federally funded clinics to notify parents of adolescents who obtain contraceptives. The "moral majority" opposes homosexuality, pornography, sex outside of marriage, and easy divorce; and their intent is to enact social policy to support their views. The conflicts between personal choice and social control in issues pertaining to sexuality is likely to be a recurring theme throughout the 1980s.

SUMMARY

THE AUTHORS' PERSPECTIVES

1. The psychosocial orientation of this book stresses the role of social conditioning in shaping human sexuality.

2. The book will critically explore the impact of two pervasive themes related to sexuality: sex-for-reproduction and inflexible gender roles.

A CROSS-CULTURAL PERSPECTIVE: SOCIAL NORMS AND SEXUALITY

3. A high degree of sexual activity and extensive sexual instruction of youths is the norm on the Polynesian island of Mangaia.

4. On the Irish island of Inis Beag, sexual expression is discouraged from infancy through old age. Sexual misinformation is common, and female orgasm is practically unknown.

5. The Dani people of West New Guinea demonstrate little interest in sexual activity and abstain from sex for years at a time.

6. The government of the People's Republic of China as a matter of social policy limits sexual expression and reproductive choice.

THE SEX-FOR-REPRODUCTION LEGACY

7. The ancient Hebrews stressed the importance of childbearing and had an appreciation of sexuality within marriage.

8. Christian writers such as Paul of Tarsus, Augustine, and Thomas Aquinas contributed to the view of sex as sinful and justifiable only in marriage for procreation.

9. Leaders of the Reformation of the sixteenth century challenged the necessity of celibacy for clergy and recognized sexual expression as an important aspect of marriage.

10. Technical advances in contraception in the twentieth century permitted people to separate sexuality from procreation to a degree not previously possible.

THE GENDER ROLE LEGACY

11. The gender role differentiations between men and women were well established in ancient Hebraic culture. Women's most important roles were to manage the household and bear children, especially sons.

12. Women in ancient Athens had no legal rights and spent their lives within women's quarters within their homes. In contrast, women in Sparta were educated and trained in athletics.

13. The New Testament writings of Paul emphasized the importance of submissiveness for women.

14. Two contradictory images of women developed in the Middle Ages, the pure and unattainable woman as manifested by the Virgin Mary and courtly love and the evil temptress represented by Eve and the persecution of women accused of witchcraft.

15. The view of women as asexual was emphasized in the Victorian era, and "proper" Victorian men and women's lives were separate. Men often employed prostitutes for companionship and sexual relations.

SEXUALITY: PERSONAL OR PUBLIC DOMAIN?

16. Greater knowledge, more reliable contraceptives, and legal decisions have increased the contemporary individual's ability to make personal decisions regarding sexuality. Social policies and laws can either restrict or expand personal choice.

SUGGESTED READINGS

Boswell, John. *Christianity, Social Tolerance, and Homosexuality.* Chicago: University of Chicago Press, 1980. This book is a comprehensive study of Western beliefs concerning homosexuality from ancient Greece to the fourteenth century.

Calderone, Mary (Ed.). *Sexuality and Human Values.* New York: Association Press, 1974. Presents values and perspectives from many writers in the area of sexuality.

Degler, Carl. *At Odds, Women and the Family in America from the Revolution to the Present.* Oxford: Oxford University Press, 1980. A survey of American women and family history.

Gordon, Michael (Ed.). *The American Family in Social-Historical Perspective.* New York: St. Martin's, 1978. A collection of writings about sexuality and the family in America.

Pomeroy, Susan. *Goddesses, Whores, Wives, and Slaves: Women in Classical Antiquity.* New York: Schocken, 1975. A scholarly and readable work on women in ancient Greece and Rome.

2

Gender Issues

MALE AND FEMALE, MASCULINE AND FEMININE
   Sex and Gender
   Gender Identity and Gender Role
GENDER IDENTITY FORMATION
   Gender Identity as a Biological Process
   Social Learning Factors in Gender Identity
   The Interactional Model
   A Special Case of Gender Identity Difficulty: Transsexualism
GENDER ROLES
   The Socialization of Gender Roles
   The Impact of Gender Roles on Our Sexuality
   Transcending Gender Roles: Androgyny
SUMMARY
SUGGESTED READINGS

*E*xamine the following sentence and fill in the blanks: In this particular society "the _____ [is] the dominant, impersonal, managing partner, the _____ the less responsible and the emotionally dependent person." Did you assume that *man* goes in the first blank space and *woman* in the second? In fact, the reverse is true. But how can this be? Is it not human nature for men the world over to take charge in their relationships with more dependent women? Things may be getting a bit more equal between the sexes (at least in some societies), but a complete reversal of these traditional roles? How can this happen?

This is the first, incredulous comment people typically voice after being told about the Tchambuli Indian society of New Guinea, where traditional masculine and feminine behavior patterns are complete opposites of those typical of American society (Mead, 1963). This cultural difference raises certain fundamental questions:

1. What constitutes maleness and femaleness?
2. What is the relationship between male and female and masculine and feminine?
3. Which of the behavioral differences between women and men have a biological basis? A psychosocial basis? Both?

MALE AND FEMALE, MASCULINE AND FEMININE

Through the ages people have held to the belief that individuals are born males or females and just naturally grow up doing what men or women do. The only explanation required was a simple allusion to "nature taking its course." There was a simplicity about such a viewpoint that helped to make the world appear to be an orderly place. However, closer examination has revealed that there is a much greater complexity in the process whereby our maleness and femaleness is determined and the manner in which it influences our behavior, sexual and otherwise. This fascinating complexity will be our focus in the pages that follow. But first, it will be helpful to clarify a few important terms.

Sex and Gender

Many writers use the terms gender and sex interchangeably. However, each of these words has specific meanings. *Sex* refers to our biological maleness or femaleness. There are two aspects of biological sex: *genetic sex*, which is determined by our sex chromosomes, and *anatomical sex*, the obvious physical differences between males and females. *Gender* is a concept that encompasses the special psychosocial meanings added to biological maleness or femaleness. Thus, while one's sex is linked to various physical attributes (chromosomes, penis, vulva, and so forth), gender refers to the social concomitants of sex, or in other words, our masculinity or femininity. In this chapter we will be using the terms masculine and feminine to characterize the behaviors that are typically attributed to males and females. One undesirable aspect of these labels is that they may limit the range of behaviors that people are comfortable expressing. For example, a man might hesitate to be nurturing out of a concern that he would be labeled feminine and, conversely, a woman might be reticent to act assertively for fear she would be considered masculine. It is not our intention to perpetuate the stereotypes often associated with these labels. However, we do find it necessary to use these terms when discussing gender issues.

When we encounter people for the first time we probably quickly note their sex and make certain assumptions about how they are likely to behave based on their maleness or femaleness; these are gender assumptions. For most people gender assumptions are an important part of routine social interaction. For example, think back on the last time you were unable to determine someone's sex. Perhaps you were as flustered and perplexed as the man in the following account:

One day I stopped in the park to watch a pick-up soccer game involving several men and women. One player, who immediately caught my attention, seemed to flow across the field with graceful, almost sensuous movements. From a distance this person's face was striking and incredibly androgynous. The bulky clothes being worn (cold day) didn't give me any clues as to the sex of the wearer. With all the noise and hollering going on, I couldn't distinguish this person's sex by voice. The hair was cut short in a masculine style, but the movements reminded me of a woman. When the game disbanded, she or he walked alone to the parking lot. I was torn by indecision. I wanted to go up and strike up a conversation. But what if she had been a he? What would I have said?—"Say, I followed you over here to the parking lot to tell you I liked the way you play soccer." To this day I regret my inaction and still wonder who this person was— woman or man? (Authors' files)

Many of us may find it hard to interact with a person whose gender is ambiguous. People are either the same sex or the other sex. (We have avoided using the term opposite sex because we believe this term overstates the differences between males and females.) When we cannot be sure in our identification of another's gender, we may become confused and uncomfortable.

Gender Identity and Gender Role

Gender identity refers to our own personal, subjective sense that "I am a male" or "I am a female." Most of us realize that we are either male or female, masculine or feminine, in the first few years of life. However, there is no guarantee that a person's gender identity will be consistent with his or her biological sex, and some people experience considerable confusion in their efforts to identify their own maleness or femaleness. We will look into this area in more detail later in this chapter.

Gender role (sometimes called sex role) refers to a collection of attitudes and behaviors that are considered normal and appropriate in a specific culture for people of a particular sex. Gender roles establish sex-related behavioral expectations that people are expected to fulfill. Behavior thought to be socially appropriate for a male is called masculine, for a female, feminine. When we use the terms masculine and feminine in subsequent discussions, we are referring to these socialized notions.

© Jerry Marcus. Reprinted by permission of Jerry Marcus and *The Ladies Home Journal.*

"Well, for heaven's sakes, which one is the opposite sex, you or me?"

Gender role expectations are culturally defined and vary from society to society. For example, the Tchambuli Indian society considers emotionally expressive behavior to be appropriate for males. Obviously, American society takes a somewhat different view. A kiss on the cheek from one man to another is considered a feminine act, and therefore inappropriate in American society. In contrast, such behavior is consistent with masculine role expectations in many European and Middle Eastern societies.

In addition to being culturally based, our notions of masculinity and femininity are also era-dependent. For example, if an American male went to a hairdresser for a permanent in the 1960s, he would probably have been ridiculed for his "effeminate" behavior. In the early 1980s, an abundance of curly-headed men indicates that gender role expectations for hair style have changed significantly. Such changes are becoming increasingly common; more than at any other time in our history, the present era is marked by great upheaval and redefinition of male and female roles. Many people are no longer content to live with traditional gender roles. Many of us, who have grown up subjected to strong gender role conditioning, are now exploring how these roles have shaped our lives and are seeking to break away from their limiting influences. Being part of this change can be both exciting and confusing. We will consider the impact of traditional and changing gender roles later in this chapter (and also throughout our text). But first, let us turn our attention to the processes whereby we acquire our gender identity.

How do we acquire a realization that we are either a boy or girl, masculine or feminine? Is this a "natural" process or does our gender identity emerge from an array of social learning experiences? In this section we will attempt to unravel some of the mysteries surrounding these questions. The mechanisms through which people attain their gender identity have been the subject of much research and theoretical discussion. Some theorists have emphasized the role of biological conditions; others have argued that social learning factors are most crucial in the formation of gender identity. Today, however, most theorists recognize the importance of both of these forces. We will begin by outlining the biological factors that play a part in the development of our sense of maleness or femaleness.

Gender Identity as a Biological Process

Gender identity is unquestionably influenced by our biological sex, which is determined by a complex set of variables. Our physical maleness or femaleness is not simply a function of the makeup of our sex chromosomes or the type of gonads we possess. Rather, there are at least five separate biological categories or levels of sex determination: chromosomal sex, gonadal sex, hormonal sex, sex of the internal accessory sex structures, and sex as determined by the external genitalia. Under normal conditions these five biological variables interact harmoniously to determine our biological sex. However, as we shall see, errors may occur at each of these levels. The resulting abnormalities in the development of a person's biological sex may seriously complicate acquisition of a gender identity.

Chromosomal Sex   At the first level our biological sex is determined by the chromosomes present in the reproductive cells (sperm and ova) at the moment of conception. With the exception of the reproductive cells, the body cells of humans contain a total of 46 chromosomes, arranged as 23 pairs (See Figure 2.1). Twenty-two of these pairs are the same in both male and female. These matched sets, called *autosomes*, do not significantly influence sex differentiation. One chromosome pair, however—the *sex chromosomes*—differs in females and males. For females the combination is XX. For males the pair is XY.

As noted above, the reproductive cells are an exception to the 23 pairs rule. As a result of a biological process known as *meiosis*, mature reproductive cells contain only half of the usual complement of 46 chromosomes. (This process is necessary to avoid a doubling of the chromosome total when sex cells merge at conception.) A normal male *sperm* cell contains 22 autosomes plus either an X or Y chromosome. A normal female *ovum* (or egg) contains 22 autosomes plus an X chromosome. Thus, the ovum bears only an X chromosome, but the sperm may carry either an X or Y chromosome. Fertilization of the ovum by a Y-bearing sperm produces an XY combination, resulting in a male child. Conversely, if the ovum is fertilized by an X-bearing sperm, an XX combination is produced, resulting in a female child.

FIGURE 2.1 MALE HUMAN CHROMOSOMES

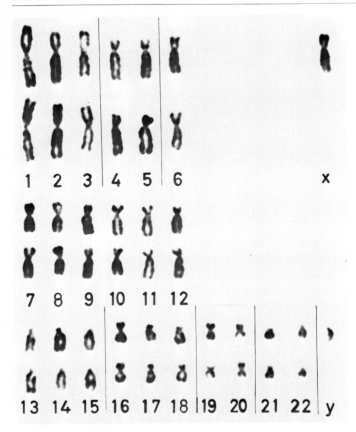

Science is far from a complete understanding of the role of sex chromosomes in the determination of biological sex. However, certain facts do seem well established. The Y chromosome must be present to ensure the complete development of internal and external male sex organs. The presence of at least one Y chromosome—regardless of the number of X's present—allows the development of these male structures. In the absence of a Y chromosome, the individual will develop female external genitals. However, two X chromosomes are needed for the complete development of both internal and external female structures.

Some writers have argued that the only function of the sex chromosomes is to determine the characteristics of the sex organs. However, it now appears that this is an overly simplistic view. Both X and Y chromosomes contain *genes* (the basic units of heredity) that influence many other structures and functions. Some researchers contend that the Y chromosome adds a "male" quality to development that may help account for certain physical and behavioral differences between the sexes (Hutt, 1973). Studies of sex chromosomal abnormalities—variations on the normal XX or XY combinations—provide important evidence on this issue. In the following para-

Turner's syndrome is a rare condition characterized by the presence of only one unmatched X chromosome. It results when an atypical ovum, containing only 22 autosomes, is fertilized by an X-bearing sperm. (The same atypical ovum fertilized by a Y-bearing sperm does not survive.) The resulting chromosome number in the fertilized egg is 45 rather than the normal 46. Such individuals, generally designated as XO, develop normal external female genitals. Consequently, they are classified as female. However, their internal reproductive structures do not develop fully (ovaries are absent or represented only by fibrous streaks of tissue). Turner's syndrome females do not develop breasts at puberty (unless given hormone treatment), do not menstruate, and, of course, they are sterile.

Since the gonads are absent or poorly developed and hormones are consequently deficient, Turner's syndrome permits gender identity to be formed in the absence of gonadal and hormonal influences (the next two levels of biological sex determination). Turner's syndrome individuals are likely to identify themselves as female and, as a group, they are not distinguishable from biologically normal females in their interests and behavior (Money and Ehrhardt, 1972). This strongly suggests that a feminine gender identity can be established in the absence of ovaries and their hormone products.

A much more common sex chromosome error found in humans is *Klinefelter's syndrome*. This condition results when an atypical ovum, containing 22 autosomes and two X chromosomes, is fertilized by a Y-bearing sperm, creating an XXY individual. In spite of the presence of both the XY combination characteristic of normal males and the XX pattern of normal females, people affected by Klinefelter's syndrome are anatomically male. This lends support to the view that the presence of a Y chromosome triggers the development of male structures. However, the presence of an extra female sex chromosome impedes the development of male structures, and these individuals typically have undersized penises and testicles and are sterile. Their interest in sexual activity is often weak or absent (Money, 1968; Raboch et al., 1979). (Presumably, this low sex drive is related, at least in part, to deficient production of hormones from the testes.)

A third type of sex chromosome error is the *XYY male*. This chromosomal anomaly results when a normal ovum is fertilized by an atypical sperm bearing two Y chromosomes. XYY individuals develop the normal sex organs and characteristics of males and are thoroughly masculine in appearance. They are unusual in that most tend to be quite tall, over six feet on the average.

Some years ago the XYY condition received a great deal of publicity. Some investigators suggested a link between the so-called "supermale syndrome" and violent, aggressive, criminal behavior (Jacobs et al., 1965). This conclusion was reached largely because studies of this anomaly revealed a significantly higher proportion of XYY males in prison populations than in the general population (Gardner and Neu, 1972).

Some writers have proposed that the extra Y chromosome somehow adds an aggressive component to the individual's character. Others have suggested that XYY males tend to be overly impulsive, a trait that can result in trouble with authority. More recently, a number of investigators have questioned this last interpretation and some have noted that prison samples may be highly biased (Unger, 1979). Prisoners are obviously a unique study population in that only the more severe behavioral manifestations of the XYY condition may come to the attention of investigators. What about all the other males with the same chromosomal variation who are never identified and studied because they do not end up in prison? Perhaps further research will clarify the causal relationship, if any, between this chromosomal abnormality and behavior. Meanwhile, current thinking generally holds that the case for the alleged link between the "supermale syndrome" and violent behavior has been overstated.

These varied examples of sex chromosome errors provide evidence that adds to our understanding of the role of chromosomes in establishing patterns of maleness or femaleness. It is now well established that at this first level of biological sex determination, maleness depends on the presence of a Y chromosome. Femaleness develops in its absence. We will now consider the way in which chromosomal sex influences the second level of biological sex determination, gonadal sex.

Gonadal Sex   During the first few weeks of prenatal development it is impossible to distinguish the sex of a human embryo. The *gonads*—ovaries in females and testes in males—look alike. Without a chromosome analysis, it is impossible to tell whether the gonads will develop into ovaries or testes.

Beginning about six weeks after conception, however, the gonads begin to differentiate. If a Y chromosome is present, the inner portion, or *medulla*, of the gonad undergoes a rapid phase of development that ultimately results in the formation of a mature testis. In the absence of a Y chromosome, the outer portion, or *cortex*, of the gonad develops into a mature ovary.

A great deal of research has been conducted in an effort to understand the process whereby gonadal tissue differentiates into either testes or ovaries. It is now apparent that without specific masculinizing signals, the primitive gonads will undergo ovarian differentiation (Haseltine and Ohno, 1981). Recent evidence has implicated a substance called *H-Y antigen* that appears to be under the control of male-determining genes on the Y chromosome and is present on the surface of cells in all normal male tissue. In some complex way, as yet not fully understood, this substance triggers the transformation of the embryonic gonads into testes (Bernstein, 1981; Haseltine and Ohno, 1981). In the absence of H-Y antigen, the undifferentiated gonadal tissue develops into ovaries.

Errors may occur at the gonadal level of biological sex determination just as they do at the chromosomal level. Perhaps the most unusual gonadal error is a rare condition known as *true hermaphroditism*. True hermaphrodites (after the mythical Greek deity Hermaphroditus, who was thought to possess attributes of both sexes) are individuals who have both ovarian and testicular tissue in their bodies. They may have one ovary and one testis or two ovaries and two testes. Some possess sex glands that contain mixtures of ovarian and testicular tissue (called *ovotestes*). The external genitals are often a mixture of male and female structures. A vaginal opening is frequently present beneath the penis and many true hermaphrodites menstruate. Occasionally, the uterus is developed to the point of being fully functional.

Investigations of true hermaphroditism have stimulated speculation about whether such individuals might both impregnate as a male and conceive as a female. Some years ago this speculation took a bizarre twist when Brazilian physicians reported the case of a pregnant true hermaphrodite who claimed to be both mother and father of the child. The uterus and ovaries of this person were fully functional and the testicles were sperm-producing. While this is certainly a fascinating case, the claim of dual parenthood was not clearly substantiated and remains highly doubtful (Money, 1966).

As we have seen, genes on the sex chromosomes trigger differentiation of the gonads into ovaries or testicles after six weeks of prenatal development. At this point the fetus's own gonadal sex hormones (the third level of biological sex determination) begin to direct the differentiation of the internal and external sex structures (the fourth and fifth levels). In the next section we will consider these final three levels.

Sex Hormones and Differentiation of Sex Structures   As soon as the gonads differentiate into testes or ovaries, the control of biological sex determination is passed to the sex hormones and genetic influence is relinquished. It will be easier to understand these complex hormonal processes if we first briefly examine the endocrine system and its function in human sexual development and behavior.

The *endocrine system* consists of several ductless glands located throughout the body. The major endocrine glands include the pituitary, the gonads, the thyroid, the parathyroids, the adrenals, and the pancreas. Each of these glands produces hormones and secretes them directly into the bloodstream. Our interest here is with the gonads and the sex hormones they secrete that influence biological sexual differentiation and development. All the sex hormones belong to the general family known as *steroids*. The ovaries produce two classes of hormones: the *estrogens* (the most important of which is estradiol), which influence development of female physical sex characteristics and regulation of the menstrual cycle, and the *progestational compounds*. Of these, progesterone is the only one known to be physiologically important. Its function is to help regulate the menstrual cycle and stimulate development of the uterine lining in preparation for pregnancy. The primary hormone outputs of the testes are the *androgens*. The most important androgen is testosterone, which influences both the development of male physical sex characteristics and sexual motivation. In both sexes, the adrenal glands also secrete sex hormones, including small amounts of estrogen and greater quantities of androgen.

A considerable amount of research has revealed the manner in which gonadal sex hormones contribute to differentiation of the internal and external sex structures. If fetal gonads differentiate into testes, the testes soon begin to secrete androgens. These androgens stimulate the development of male structures. If for some reason a male fetus does not produce enough androgen secretions, its sex organs will develop to be morphologically female (that is, female in form and appearance) despite the presence of the male chromosome (Money, 1968). Thus, in the absence of male hormones, the developmental pattern is female. A specific female hormone is not necessary to instigate development of female structures in a fetus. Maleness, however, depends on the secretion of the right amount of male hormone at the crucial time.

FIGURE 2.2 PRENATAL DIFFERENTIATION OF INTERNAL SEX STRUCTURES

Prenatal development of male and female internal duct systems from undifferentiated (before the sixth week) to differentiated (by twelve weeks).

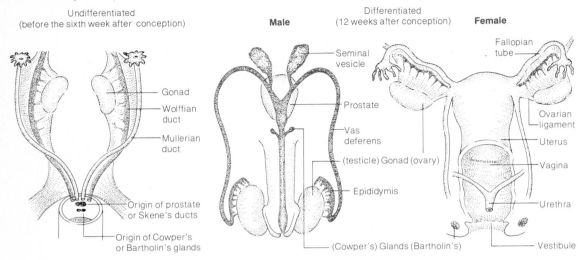

Sometime after six weeks of prenatal development, internal sex structures begin to differentiate. Each embryo contains two internal duct systems, as shown in Figure 2.2. Depending upon the gonadal sex of the embryo, one of these duct systems evolves while the other degenerates. In males, fetal androgens cause the *Wolffian ducts* to grow into male structures: the testes, epididymis, vas deferens, seminal vesicles, and prostate gland. The testes of the male fetus also secrete a substance known as *Müllerian inhibitor* that suppresses growth of the female structures. In the absence of these testicular secretions, the *Müllerian ducts* develop into the female internal organs: the fallopian tubes, uterus, and ovaries.

External genitals develop according to a similar pattern. Prior to the completion of the sixth week of prenatal development, all human fetuses possess undifferentiated external genital tissue, located below the umbilical cord and known as the *genital tubercle*. This tissue, depending on the presence or absence of androgens, develops into either male or female external genitals. When androgens begin circulating in the bloodstream of males, the genital tissue begins to differentiate into male external sex structures. By the twelfth week, this differentiation process is complete: the penis, scrotum, and other external sex structures are recognizable in males; the clitoris, labia majora, and other genital tissue can be identified in females (see Figure 2.3).

Because they originate from the same tissues in the earliest weeks of life, the sex organs in each sex have corresponding (or homologous) parts in the other sex. Table 2.1 summarizes these male and female counterparts. We will look at the form and function of all of these organs in more detail in Chapters 4 and 5.

FIGURE 2.3 PRENATAL DIFFERENTIATION OF EXTERNAL GENITALIA

29

Prenatal development of external male and female genitalia from undifferentiated (before six weeks) to fully differentiated stage.

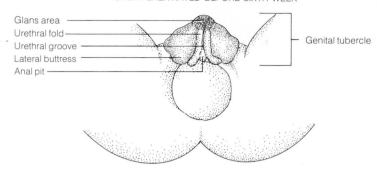

UNDIFFERENTIATED BEFORE SIXTH WEEK

Glans area
Urethral fold
Urethral groove
Lateral buttress
Anal pit
Genital tubercle

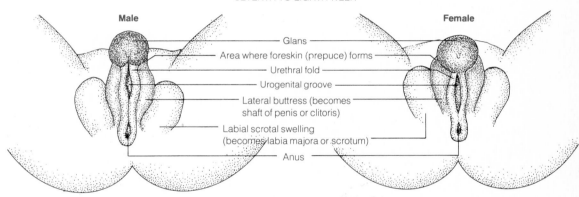

SEVENTH TO EIGHTH WEEK

Male **Female**

Glans
Area where foreskin (prepuce) forms
Urethral fold
Urogenital groove
Lateral buttress (becomes shaft of penis or clitoris)
Labial scrotal swelling (becomes labia majora or scrotum)
Anus

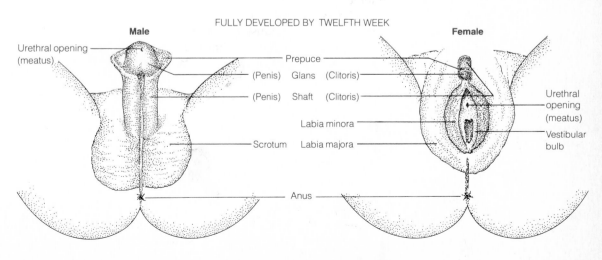

FULLY DEVELOPED BY TWELFTH WEEK

Male **Female**

Urethral opening (meatus)

Prepuce
(Penis) Glans (Clitoris)
(Penis) Shaft (Clitoris)
Labia minora
Scrotum Labia majora
Anus

Urethral opening (meatus)
Vestibular bulb

TABLE 2.1 HOMOLOGOUS SEX ORGANS

Female	Male
glans of clitoris	glans of penis
shaft of clitoris	shaft of penis
hood of clitoris	foreskin of penis
labia majora	scrotal sac
labia minora	underside of penile shaft
ovaries	testes
Skene's ducts	prostate
Bartholin's glands	Cowper's glands

As we have seen, formation of the gonads, duct development, and differentiation of the internal and external sex structures occur under the influence of different time and cue factors. When these factors deviate from normal patterns, the end result can provide contradictory information in terms of sex. Individuals who possess contradictory sex characteristics are sometimes called *hermaphrodites*.

In the previous section we noted that a true hermaphrodite possesses functioning gonads of both sexes. This condition is exceedingly rare. More commonly, the term hermaphrodite is applied to any person in whom there is an inconsistency between the various levels of biological sex—that is, between chromosomes, gonads, hormones, and internal and external sex structures.

For most people, there is consistency across the various levels of biological sex determination. Most males have XY chromosomes, prostate glands, testes, and penises, are reared as male, and think of themselves as male. Conversely, for females, a parallel and consistent set of female characteristics exists. However, the sex of a hermaphrodite is biologically ambiguous. The internal and external reproductive anatomy may demonstrate a combination or mixture of male and female structures or the structures may be incompletely male or incompletely female. Furthermore, they may not be consistent with the person's chromosomal sex. Such cases are particularly interesting in that they provide data that helps to clarify the relative roles of biological and social learning factors in the formation of our gender identity. Let us consider some of the evidence.

A number of biological accidents may result in hermaphroditism. One is the situation in which a chromosomally normal female (XX) is exposed to an excessive amount of androgens or androgen-like substances during the critical period of prenatal sex differentiation. There are two possible sources of these androgens: they may be produced by the fetus's own body or be introduced as drugs her mother takes during pregnancy. In the 1950s, some pregnant women took a synthetic hormone drug to prevent miscarriage. The physicians who prescribed the drug (progestin) were unaware that it would have the same effect on the fetus as a dose of male hormones. (Progestin and androgen have similar chemical structures, and as the drug circulated in the mother's bloodstream the developing fetus was essentially exposed to a high dose of male hormones.) Sometimes a female fetus's own adrenal glands malfunction and produce abnormally high amounts of androgen.

Regardless of the source of these prenatal androgens, the effect at birth is similar. The internal structures of these chromosomal females do not appear to be affected. However, the external genitals are masculinized and resemble those of male infants to varying degrees (see Figure 2.4). The clitoris is often enlarged and may be mistaken for a penis. The labia are frequently fused so they look like a scrotum.

In the not too distant past the assignment of biological sex at birth was based solely on the appearance of a newborn's external genitals. Thus, in some cases of babies born with genital ambiguities, sex assignment was a toss-up and the assigned sex might not have been consistent with the chromosomal sex. Today, however, physicians faced with such ambiguities obtain additional information about the composition of the chromosomes and the nature of the gonads. Thus, most masculinized female infants are correctly identified and reared as females. Usually only a relatively small amount of surgery and hormone therapy is necessary to make the appearance

FIGURE 2.4 MASCULINIZED EXTERNAL GENITALS OF A
FETALLY ANDROGENIZED FEMALE

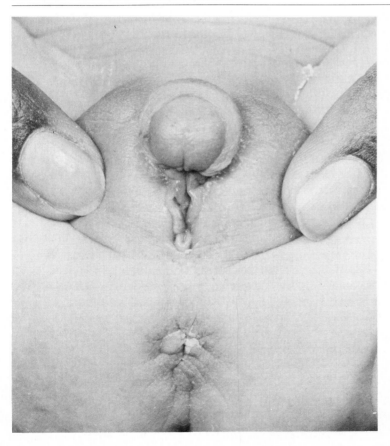

32

of their external genitals consistent with their chromosomes and internal sex structures.

Some years ago John Money and Anke Ehrhardt (1972) provided some fascinating evidence from their extensive study of 25 fetally androgenized females. These 25, all of whom had received appropriate medical treatment and had been reared as girls from infancy, were matched by age, intelligence, race, and socioeconomic status with a normal group of nonandrogenized girls. There were marked differences in the behaviors of these two groups. Twenty of the 25 fetally androgenized girls identified themselves as "tomboys." Their parents and friends agreed with this label. They tended to be active and aggressive and preferred to engage in traditionally male activities (such as rough and tumble athletics and pushing trucks in dirt piles). They demonstrated little interest in bride and mother roles, disliked handling infants, and were uninterested in makeup, hair-styling, and jewelry. In contrast, only a small number of the girls in the matched normative sample claimed to be tomboys and then only to a limited extent. The fetally masculinized girls demonstrated a significantly greater amount of dissatisfaction with their gender identity than the normal sample, although none expressed a desire to actually change her sex.

Money and Ehrhardt's research sheds considerable light on the ongoing debate between theorists who view gender identity formation as a biological process versus those who maintain that social learning factors are more important. Proponents of this latter viewpoint argue that fetally androgenized girls will manifest gender role behavior consistent with their upbringing despite being subjected to prenatal hormone errors. However, the actual results of this research suggest that the prenatal hormones masculinized not only the girls' genitals but also their nervous systems and behavior as well. While this inference is somewhat controversial, this research demonstrates that biological factors may reach far beyond birth to influence the ways in which our gender identity is formed and expressed.

Male children are occasionally affected by a similar abnormality known as the *testicular feminizing syndrome.* Individuals with this rare condition are chromosomally normal males (XY) whose gonads differentiate into testes that produce normal levels of prenatal androgens. However, as a result of a genetic defect, their body tissues are insensitive to the action of male hormones and consequently their prenatal development is feminized. These infants have internal sexual structures similar to those of a normal male, but their external sexual structures fail to differentiate into a penis and scrotum, and the testes do not descend. Instead homologous female genitalia are formed: clitoris, labia, and so forth. At birth their external genitals appear to be completely female. Nothing unusual is suspected and consequently such babies are classified as girls and reared accordingly. The error may not be discovered until adolescence or later, usually when efforts are made to see why they have not menstruated.

Money and his colleagues reported an in-depth study of 10 individuals with testicular feminizing syndrome (Money et al., 1968). All ten had been reared as girls. Only one, a young girl with a very disturbed family background, showed any gender identity confusion. The other nine were strongly identified as female by themselves and others. As a group they demonstrated strong preferences for the role of homemaker over an outside job, fantasies of becoming pregnant and raising a family, and inclinations to engage in typically female play with traditional girls' toys (dolls and the like). In a word, there was nothing that could be viewed as traditionally masculine in the way the girls behaved despite their XY chromosomes and male gonads.

These studies of hormonally based differentiation errors have some important implications. We have seen that chromosomal females, masculinized before birth from exposure to excessive androgens, tend to manifest typically masculine behaviors after birth in spite of being reared as girls. In contrast, chromosomal males insensitive to androgens behave in a typically feminine manner consistent with the way they are reared. Within a theory that considers social learning factors to be the sole determinants of gender identity formation and gender role behavior, these two observations seem to be at odds. Proponents of this view argue that if an individual is reared as a girl, the person should behave in a feminine manner regardless of whatever biological anomalies may have occurred during prenatal development. Yet, while this prediction holds true for those individuals with testicular feminizing syndrome, it is not confirmed by studies of prenatally masculinized girls.

This apparent inconsistency may not be contradictory at all when evaluated from a biological perspective. There is evidence that prenatal androgens may masculinize the human brain as well as the sex structures (Dorner, 1976; Ehrhardt, 1977; Money and Ehrhardt, 1972; Phoenix et al., 1959). (Animal research suggests that differences between male and female brains, in an area called the *hypothalamus*, may have behavioral consequences; however, the degree to which this occurs in humans is subject to considerable debate.) This could account for the masculine behavior of fetally androgenized females. The same genetic defect that prevents masculinization of the genitals of individuals with testicular feminizing syndrome may also prevent the masculinization of their brains. Thus, prenatal androgens may be important not only for the proper differentiation of biological sex but also for the development of gender role behaviors consistent with a person's gender identification.

The results of experimental investigations of these varied biological accidents raise some fundamental questions. Just what makes us male or female? Our chromosomes? Our hormones? The characteristics of our sexual structures? The sex we are assigned at birth? Clearly, a person's biological sex is determined by a complex process involving several interacting levels. Many steps, each susceptible to errors, are involved in sex differentiation prior to birth. We will now turn our attention to the various social learning factors that influence gender identity formation after birth. Perhaps this information will help to clarify some of the unanswered questions emerging from the biological data.

Social Learning Factors in Gender Identity

Thus far we have only considered biological factors involved in the determination of gender. Our sense of maleness or femaleness is not based exclusively on biological conditions, however, and in recent years an alternative explanation of the shaping of gender identity has emerged. This social learning interpretation suggests that our identification with either masculine or feminine roles or a combination thereof (*an-*

drogyny) results primarily from the social and cultural models and influences we are exposed to during our early development.

For example, at birth parents label their children as being male or female with the announcement "It's a boy!" or "It's a girl!" From this point on children are exposed to people who tend to react to them in a manner dictated by their culture's gender role expectations. Parents typically dress boys and girls differently, decorate their rooms differently, provide different toys, and even respond to them differently.

Parents and others actively teach little boys and girls what gender they are by the manner in which they describe them. Certainly, expressions such as "You are a sweet little girl" or "You are a bright little boy" are commonly heard. While small children may not comprehend what makes them biologically a male or a female, they definitely are not confused about whether they are a boy or a girl (just try calling a two-year-old boy a girl, or vice versa, and observe the indignant manner in which they set you straight).

Understandably, parents and others have certain preconceived ideas about how boys and girls differ, and they communicate these views to their children from the very beginning. For example, in one study (Rubin et al., 1974) parents were asked to describe their infants within 24 hours of birth. All babies included in this sample were of the same approximate height, weight, and muscle tone. Parents of girls tended to describe their daughters as soft, sweet, fine-featured, and delicate. On the other hand, parents of boys were inclined to use words like strong, well-coordinated, active, and robust to describe their sons. These perceptions remain after the child is brought home from the hospital, and they may influence the nature of parent-child interaction.

A child's own actions probably strongly influence the process whereby his or her gender identity is established. Most children have developed a firm sense of being a boy or girl by the age of 18 months. Once this takes place, they typically acquire a strong desire to adopt behaviors appropriate for their sex (Kohlberg, 1966); that is, they try to find out how boys or girls are supposed to behave and then act accordingly.

Anthropological studies of other cultures also lend support to the social learning interpretation of gender identity formation. In several societies, the differences between males and females that we often assume to be innate are simply not evident. In fact, Margaret Mead's classic book, *Sex and Temperament in Three Primitive Societies* (1963), reveals that other societies may have very different views about what is considered feminine or masculine. In this widely quoted report of her fieldwork in New Guinea, Mead discusses two societies that minimize differences between the sexes. She noted that among the Mundugumor of New Guinea both sexes exhibit aggressive, non-nurturing behaviors that would be considered masculine by our society's norms. In contrast, among the Arapesh of New Guinea both males and females exhibit gentleness, nurturing, and nonaggressive behaviors that would be judged feminine by our societal norms. In a third society studied, the Tchambuli of New Guinea, Mead observed an actual reversal of the typical masculine and feminine gender roles. You will recall from the opening page of this chapter that the Tchambuli females tend to be dominant, assertive, and very much in charge, while their male counterparts are quiet, undemanding, and emotionally dependent. Since there is no evidence that people in these societies are biologically different from Americans, it seems that their often diametrically different interpretations of what is masculine and what is feminine must result from different processes of social learning.

Some of the most impressive evidence in support of the social learning viewpoint has emerged from the research of John Money and his colleagues. Perhaps the most persuasive of these studies have concerned children whose external genitals represent such a mixture of male and female characteristics that biological sex identification is difficult. Money and his co-workers found that in most of the cases they evaluated, incorrectly identified children, whose assigned sex did not match their chromosomal sex, developed a gender identity consistent with the manner in which they were reared (Hampson and Hampson, 1961; Money, 1965; Money et al., 1955; Money and Ehrhardt, 1972).

One particularly unusual study of two identical twin boys (Money, 1975; Money and Ehrhardt, 1972) has frequently been cited in support of the social learning interpretation. At the age of seven months, a circumcision accident destroyed most of the penile tissue of one of the boys. Since no amount of plastic surgery could adequately reconstruct the severely damaged penis, it was recommended that the child be raised as a female and receive appropriate sex change surgery. At 17 months, the parents decided to begin raising their child as a girl. Shortly thereafter, initial genital surgery was performed. Follow-up studies of these unusual twins revealed that, in spite of possessing identical genetic materials, the twins responded to their separate social learning experiences by developing opposite gender identities. Furthermore, the child reassigned to the female gender appeared to demonstrate no confusion about her identity during her early developmental years.

If the story of these twins ended here, we would have strong evidence of the dominant role of social learning in gender identity formation. However, in 1979, the psychiatrist following this case revealed that the assigned female member of the pair is having considerable difficulty making her adjustment as a woman (Williams and Smith, 1979). Thus, it appears that efforts to alter her biological potential as a male have not been completely successful. The reasons for this are not entirely clear; maybe her parents waited too long to make their decision (the probability of successful reassignment of sex diminishes with increasing age). Perhaps prenatal masculinization of the brain, via androgens, may be a factor in this case. To the extent that we believe biological and social learning factors interact in the formation of gender identity after birth, the unfolding results of this twin study may be understandable and perhaps even predictable. In the next section we will briefly explore this interactional interpretation of the formation of gender identity.

The Interactional Model

We have seen that even though learning plays a crucial role, biology is also important in gender identity formation. Some people have concerns about the implications of the biological evidence. They may fear that acknowledging the role of physiology in gender development somehow implies that gender roles are unchangeable and denies the importance of life experiences in establishing our own subjective sense of masculinity or femininity. However, few researchers today believe in a simple, inflexible biological basis for maleness or femaleness. The evidence supporting the role of social learning is simply too pervasive.

In the interactional model, gender identity is seen as a result of a complex interplay of biology and social learning factors. The question of which plays the greater role in shaping gender identity will probably continue to be debated as additional evidence is gathered. Perhaps the best clarification of the interactionist position is presented in the book *Man and Woman/Boy and Girl* by John Money and Anke Ehrhardt (1972). The approach of these writers is an integrative one that attempts to avoid some of the extreme dichotomies (such as genetic versus environment, instinctive versus learned) that have characterized thinking in this area.

In our view, the Money–Ehrhardt position represents an enlightened interpretation of present data. Our own perspective tends to place a somewhat greater emphasis on the role of social learning in shaping gender identity and gender roles. From birth to death, our social environment continues to demonstrate that the sexes act differently. This is not to say that biological factors are unimportant. But it does seem that the gender role differences between males and females (and the sexual behaviors based on them) are influenced to a greater extent by our respective environments.

A Special Case of Gender Identity Difficulty: Transsexualism

The *transsexual* is a person whose personal gender identity is opposite to his or her biological sex. Thus a male transsexual, before surgical alteration, feels like he is a woman betrayed by some quirk of fate that provided him with male genitals. He is a woman-identified-man, and this is the source of his acute discomfort. He wishes to be identified as a woman, who he sincerely believes himself to be. Rather than experiencing sexual excitement when cross-dressing, as is the case with *transvestism*, such activity might give him his few moments of comfort with self. (We will discuss transvestism in more detail in Chapter 19.)

Studies have revealed an apparently higher incidence of males wishing to be women than the converse (Block and Tessler, 1973). However, this statistic may be compromised somewhat by the fact that identified transsexuals are generally those who come forth for surgical treatment. Male-to-female alteration is considerably more successful than the results of female-to-male surgery.

Most transsexuals are biologically normal individuals with healthy sex organs, intact internal reproductive structures, and the proper complement of XX or XY chromosomes. Nevertheless, the transsexual rejects his or her anatomy. In some cases, in fact, the external sex organs have become such hated objects that attempts at self-mutilation have occurred.

What causes transsexualism? There are many theories. Some writers maintain that biological factors may play a decisive role. Research with animals has revealed that masculine behavior can be increased in females by artificially inducing high levels of male hormones in the prenatal environment. Conversely, prenatal males who are deprived of sufficient levels of male hormones often later exhibit female behavior (Goy, 1970). Studies of prenatally masculinized human females (discussed earlier) provide additional evidence that biological errors may result in gender identity confusion during the developmental years.

In spite of this biological evidence, most theorists hold to the view that social learning experiences contribute to the development of transsexualism. A child may be exposed to a variety of conditioning experiences that support behaving in a manner traditionally attributed to the other sex (Green, 1974; Money and Primrose, 1968). The child may develop a close, identifying relationship with the parent of the other sex that may be strongly reinforced by the adult's reaction. The little boy may play at being a girl and, conversely, the girl may be "Daddy's little man." Such cross-gender behaviors may be so exclusively rewarded that it may be difficult or impossible for the individual to develop the appropriate gender identity. To the extent that this interpretation is accurate, we might expect to see less clear-cut transsexualism in the future if society moves in the direction of androgynous childrearing (see Chapter 13).

As difficult as it is to determine what factors might contribute to transsexualism, it is often even harder to find a way to resolve these instances of reversed gender identity. Most transsexuals follow a heterosexual script and prefer to have sexual relations with a member of the other sex. However, for them the other sex happens to have the same genitals. Whom then do they relate to sexually? Most want to interact with heterosexual individuals: a male transsexual wants to be desired as a woman, by a heterosexual man, and most transsexual women would not be satisfied with a lesbian relationship.

These sexual needs are often hard to meet. Unlike heterosexuals and homosexuals, who can generally find willing sex partners who match their orientations, most transsexuals are trapped in the frustrating, painful world of someone whose most desired sexual partners would reject them offhand for making "unnatural" advances. Occasionally, they may try homosexual encounters, but most find them unrewarding, as revealed by the following interview.

TRANSSEXUAL: For a while I thought the homosexual life would be the answer, and it wasn't.

DOCTOR: Why wasn't it?

TRANSSEXUAL: I found it revolting. To me the idea of two men in bed with each other is sickening, while a man and a woman together is perfectly natural. I am a woman. I have a problem, a growth, but I'm a woman. I am in no way like a male.

DOCTOR: Except that you have a penis and testes, and you don't have a uterus, and you don't have ovaries.

TRANSSEXUAL: Yes.

DOCTOR: So, anatomically—

TRANSSEXUAL: Anatomically, I am female, with those things stuck on. (Green, 1974, p. 47)

Psychotherapy, without accompanying biological transformation, has generally been reported to be unsuccessful in helping the transsexual make a personally satisfying adjustment to life (Benjamin, 1967). Therefore, it would seem that a potentially beneficial course of action is to change the body to match the mind, through surgical and hormonal alteration of the genital anatomy and body physiology.

Beneficial as it may be, however, the process of medical alteration is not a simple solution, for it is both time-consuming and costly. The initial step involves extensive screening interviews during which an individual's motivations to undergo the change are thoroughly evaluated. Those with real conflicts about their gender identity (who are not really sure which sex identity they prefer) or those seeking the operation on a whim are typically removed from consideration as a candidate for surgical alteration. After the initial screening, the next step is to provide hormone therapy, a process designed to accentuate some of the latent other-sex traits residing within their bodies. Most professionals providing the sex-change procedures require that an individual live for some time (a year or more) as a member of the other sex, while undergoing hormone therapy, before moving to the final, more drastic surgical stage. At any time during this phase the process can be successfully reversed, although few transsexuals choose to do so.

The final step of a sex change involves surgical procedures that are far more effective when applied to men wishing to be women. As Figure 2.5(a) shows, the scrotum and penis are removed, and a vagina is created through reconstruction of pelvic tissue. Some of the genital tissue is maintained so that the individual, now a woman, may be able to achieve orgasm. Intercourse is possible although use of a lubricant may be necessary. Hormone treatments may produce sufficient breast development, but some individuals also receive implants. Biological females who desire to be male generally have their breasts, vagina, uterus, and ovaries surgically removed. An artificial penis may be fashioned from synthetic or available tissue as shown in Figure 2.5(b). Technology has not advanced to the point where it can fashion an organ capable of erection, but significant advances have been made in recent years in this aspect of surgical reconstruction. The failure to develop a functional penis may account in part for the drastically lower incidence of female-to-male transformations.

Postoperative follow-up of transsexuals' lives reveals contradictory findings. For example, several major studies indicate that when a candidate for sex change surgery is carefully selected, there is a strong likelihood of a satisfactory outcome (Baker, 1969; Pauly, 1968; Randell, 1969; Walinder and Thuwe, 1974). However, several writers have considered these early reports to be overly optimistic and have objected to them either on methodological grounds (Lothstein, 1978) or by making reference to the increasing number of reported failures of sex reassignment surgery (Childs, 1977; Eber, 1980; Van Putten and Fawzy, 1976). Research at a major center for sex change surgery, Johns Hopkins Hospital, failed to demonstrate any differences in long term adjustment between transsexuals who undergo surgical alteration and those who do not (Meyer and Reter, 1979). However, these findings have been called into question and may have been biased by some serious methodological problems (Fleming et al., 1980).

FIGURE 2.5 THE GENITALS FOLLOWING SEX CHANGE
SURGERY

39

Surgical procedures are generally more effective when applied to
genitally altering a male to female **(a)** rather than the reverse of a
female to male **(b)**. (Courtesy of Dr. D. Laub, Gender Dysphoria
Program, Department of Plastic and Reconstructive Surgery,
Stanford University.)

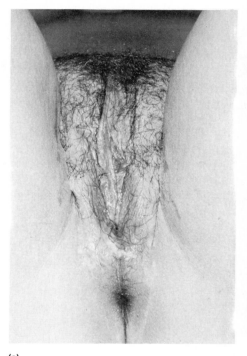

(a)

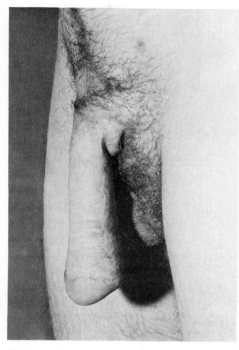

(b)

Two recent research endeavors have provided some optimistic results. One
study used the Minnesota Multiphasic Personality Inventory (MMPI) to assess psychological adjustment levels of pre- and postsurgical transsexuals. Both before and after
surgery groups contained an equal number of male-to-female and female-to-male
individuals, all of whom were matched within sex by age and education. MMPI scores
revealed that postsurgical subjects had a higher level of psychological adjustment than
their presurgical counterparts (Fleming et al., 1981). Another report provided data
from a two-year follow-up of 21 postsurgical transsexuals (Lothstein, 1980). While not
as optimistic as some of the earlier reports, this study did reveal moderate improvements in the social and sexual adjustment of postsurgical patients.

At the time of this writing there is considerable confusion in the scientific
community over just how beneficial sex change surgery is. Some writers are even
suggesting that psychotherapy by itself, contrary to earlier assumptions, may be a
sufficient treatment for many transsexuals (Lothstein, 1977; Lothstein, 1979; Morgan,

1978). Clearly, we do not have the complete picture at the present time, and there is a vital need for continued research in this area.

Many people react very strongly to the phenomenon of transsexualism, perhaps viewing it as an attack upon traditional gender assumptions. We are concerned that a "backlash" against sex change surgery may reduce the availability of an important option for transsexual individuals. Clearly, such an attitude is not what is needed now. Rather, we need continued careful, well-designed investigations of both the appropriateness and effectiveness of surgical sex reassignment.

Finally, we must not overlook what transsexuals themselves have to say about this controversial process. Many finally feel "out of prison," and their accounts are often poignant. One of the most widely read personal accounts of the transsexual experience was recorded in a book titled *Conundrum*, written by Jan Morris (1974) after she had undergone the transsexual change. The photographs in Figure 2.6 show her both before and after the sex change. She summarizes her motivation for undergoing the change as ". . . mending a discrepancy. . . . I found that when people took me to be unquestionably a woman, a sense of rightness calmed and satisfied me. . . . I felt myself to be passing through an anteroom of fulfillment" (pp. 130–131).

FIGURE 2.6 SEX CHANGE: MALE TO FEMALE

(a) James Morris prior to sex change surgery.
(b) Jan Morris after sex change surgery.

(a)   (b)

The issue of gender goes beyond the processes whereby we acquire our own subjective sense of maleness or femaleness. Society is not content to merely allow us to identify our gender. Rather, it ascribes to us a set of behaviors that are considered normal and appropriate for our particular sex. These normative standards are typically labeled gender roles (or sex roles).

The ascribing of gender roles leads naturally to certain assumptions about how people will behave. For example, men are expected to act independently and aggressively, while women should be dependent and submissive. Once these expectations are widely accepted, they may begin to function as *stereotypes.* A stereotype is a generalized notion of what a person is like that is based only on that person's sex, race, religion, ethnic background, or a similar criterion. Stereotypes do not take individuality into account.

There are many common gender-based stereotypes that are widely accepted in our society. Some of the prevailing notions about men maintain that they are aggressive (or at least assertive), logical, unemotional, independent, dominant, competitive, objective, athletic, active, and above all, competent. Conversely, women are frequently viewed as passive, nonassertive, illogical, emotional, dependent, subordinate, warm, and nurturing. While these gender role stereotypes are not held by all people, there is strong evidence of their pervasiveness within our society (Broverman, 1972; Siiter and Unger, 1978; Unger, 1979).

Stereotyping people based on biological sex can help to make the world appear to be more orderly, but it may also produce a number of undesirable outcomes. Certainly it encourages us to prejudge individuals and to expect them to act in certain ways just because they happen to be female or male. Often these stereotypic assumptions act to limit the nature of human relationships and sexual interaction. For example, consider the following two observations expressed by former students during small-group discussions:

If a woman makes the first move and says she would like to sleep with me, I'll probably take advantage of the opportunity. But you can bet I won't see her again. Any woman who is that easy isn't the kind of person I would really like to get to know. (Authors' files)

Sometimes when I am making love, I would like to tell my partner how I like being touched. But I am afraid he would think I was too pushy or aggressive. Men like to run the show and they get threatened if you give them any instructions. (Authors' files)

It appears that both of these individuals may be victims of societal notions about how men and women are supposed to behave. Neither seems to be looking beyond these confining assumptions, and consequently their relationship options are unnecessarily limited. The man expressing the initial observation is unwilling or unable to acknowledge that "good women" can take the lead in initiating sexual contact. Consequently, he shuts himself off from sexually assertive women who step out of

BOX 2.1 MALENESS AS BETTER

As a result of gender role stereotyping, males and females are frequently perceived as possessing different characteristics. However, these characteristics are not necessarily viewed as being of equal value in our society. A number of research studies, outlined in the following paragraphs, suggest that men and masculine traits are more highly valued than women and feminine traits. Furthermore, both sexes tend to view male qualities as being more desirable.

In one widely quoted study, psychologist Philip Goldberg (1968) asked female college students to read excerpts from actual journal articles in the fields of law and city planning (professions strongly associated with males), dietetics and elementary school teaching (strongly associated with women), and linguistics and art history (not strongly associated with either sex). The articles were assembled into two equal sets of booklets; however, the same article was attributed to a male author in one set and to a female author in the other. The women were asked to rate each article for value, competence, persuasiveness, and writing style. The results revealed that articles associated with a male author's name, regardless of occupational field, were consistently given higher ratings than those supposedly written by a woman. Even in fields strongly associated with women, men were per-

ceived as more effective. In a similar study, it was found that women tended to place higher value on abstract paintings attributed to male artists than the same paintings credited to female artists (Pheterson et al., 1971). Both the Goldberg and Pheterson research indicates that women may actually be prejudiced against other members of their sex.

Even studies that employ the concept of androgyny—having both feminine and masculine traits simultaneously (discussed later in this chapter)—reveal that male traits are more highly valued by both sexes. For example, when people were asked to indicate personality characteristics that they considered to be most desirable for an adult, sex unspecified, they were much more likely to choose traits typically considered masculine rather than feminine traits (Rosenkrantz et al., 1968). In another study, both men and women who rated themselves high in the possession of male-valued traits had higher self-esteem than subjects who rated themselves low in male-valued traits (Spence et al., 1975).

These findings suggest that gender role stereotyping does more than limit our options. It may also lead people of both sexes to arbitrarily discount women and elevate men simply on the basis of physical sex, rather than because of personal qualities.

---

their traditional gender role. Conversely, the woman voicing her concerns in the second example suppresses her inclinations to be assertive during lovemaking because she assumes males see this as their role and would be threatened by any woman who crosses these gender-imposed boundaries.

Gender role stereotypes also tend to restrict our opportunities. For example, a woman might not enroll in a mountaineering class because she considers such an activity to be within the male domain. She may be concerned that others would view her expressed interest as a sign of inappropriate masculinity. Similarly, a man might hesitate to stay at home and provide childcare and domestic services while his female partner pursues her career in the working world. Even though he may find such activities to be quite rewarding at a certain point in his life, he nevertheless might be concerned that others would think he was unmasculine.

In a subsequent section of this chapter we will consider in detail some of the possible negative effects of gender role assumptions on sexual sharing. But first, let us examine the socialization processes that introduce these limiting roles into our lives.

The Socialization of Gender Roles

In spite of the potentially limiting impact of rigid and stereotypic gender roles on our lives, many men and women behave in a manner remarkably consistent with the norms these roles establish. Certainly many individuals are comfortable fulfilling a traditional masculine or feminine role, and we do not wish to demean or question the validity of their life style. Rather, we are concerned with why these gender roles are so prevalent in our society. Are they biologically mandated or are they learned? It seems reasonable to suspect that at least some of the behavioral differences between males and females may be related to biological factors such as differences in muscle mass, hormonal variations, and brain differences (Diamond, 1977 and 1979; Diamond and Karlen, 1980; Reinisch and Karow, 1977). Nevertheless, most theorists, including the authors, believe that gender roles result largely from the manner in which we are socialized as males and females. *Socialization* refers to the process whereby our society conveys to the individual behavioral expectations for his or her gender. In the following sections we will examine the role of parents, peers, schools, textbooks, and television as agents in the socialization of gender roles.

Parents as Shapers of Gender Roles   Parents play a powerful role in the socialization of gender roles in their children. The manner in which they interact with their children, the behaviors they encourage or discourage, and the roles they model all help to shape traditional gender behaviors. Their influence probably begins right after birth. As we have seen, most parents tend to have different perceptions and expectations of a newborn depending on his or her sex. These sex-based assumptions are likely to result in at least some differences in how parents treat boys and girls from birth on. For example, girls are often treated as if they were more fragile than boys. Instead of being subjected to the rough and tumble play that often characterizes parents' play with boy children, little girls are frequently handled very delicately in the course of quiet play (Lewis, 1972; Moss, 1967). There is also evidence that girl babies are more likely than boy babies to be talked to and smiled at by their mothers (Thoman et al., 1972).

Research indicates that parents become increasingly likely to treat their girl and boy children differently as they grow older (Block, 1976). "As the child moves from

The establishment of stereotypic masculine or feminine roles may
be greatly influenced by traditional child-rearing practices.

the infant to the toddler stage, somewhere around age two, gender-typing increases. Boys are told that 'Boys don't cling to their mothers,' and 'Big boys don't cry.' Boys' independence, aggression, and suppression of emotion are rewarded, and failure to comply brings increasing disapproval. Girls are encouraged to display opposite characteristics" (Gagnon, 1977, p. 70).

Although increasing numbers of parents are becoming sensitive to the gender role implications of a child's playthings, many others encourage their children to play with toys that help prepare them for specific adult gender roles. Girls are often given tea sets, miniature ovens, dolls, and dollhouses. Boys frequently receive things like trucks, guns, and footballs. Children who play with toys thought appropriate only for the other sex are often rebuked by their parents ("Boys who play with dolls are sissies" or "Nice little girls don't play with guns"). Since children are sensitive to these expressions of displeasure on the part of parents, they usually develop toy preferences consistent with the gender role expectations of their parents. In fact, there is evidence that this process takes place in children as young as 20 months (Fein et al., 1975). Play activities are similarly gender stereotyped by many parents. Girls are typically encouraged to play house, change the diapers of dolls who wet, jump rope, play hopscotch, and color. Boys are more likely to receive support for building erector set bridges, exploring, playing cops and robbers, or pushing trucks around dirt piles.

These differentially rewarded toy and play preferences undoubtedly influence men and women to adopt different roles as adults. Is it really surprising that boys who have been encouraged to be active and adventurous in their play activities often grow up to be men who are comfortable with being in charge, assertive, and competitive? On the other hand, the typical play of girls certainly inclines them toward being nonassertive, compliant, and nurturing as adults.

Parents can also influence the emotional development of their children along gender lines. Boys sometimes learn that they should limit their emotional expressions ("Be strong like a man"). Girls are frequently encouraged to be nurturant ("Nice girls help others") and are allowed to express their feelings more openly. There is also evidence that from around age nine to late adolescence, girls are more likely than boys to experience being nurtured by parental displays of affection, support, and acceptance (Armentrout and Burger, 1972; Hoffman and Saltzstein, 1967). This early socialization undoubtedly accounts, at least in part, for the fact that many adult females are more inclined toward emotional expression and nurturing behavior than their male counterparts.

The Peer Group   Parents are not the only people who play an important role in the socializing of gender roles. The peer group may exert a strong influence, particularly during the adolescent years. Most teenagers have fairly rigid views of what constitutes gender appropriate behavior (Adams, 1973). For girls, being popular and attractive to boys may be very important. In contrast, boys may try to prove their worth on the athletic field. Teenagers who do not conform to these traditional roles may be subjected to a great deal of peer pressure. Boys who seem sensitive or nonaggressive may be ridiculed. Girls who behave in an independent and assertive manner may be ostracized or criticized.

One particularly negative aspect of adolescent gender-typing is the notion that one cannot be both feminine and an achiever. The potential impact of this limiting assumption is revealed in the following account:

I like high school and I am a good student. In fact, I could be an outstanding student. But I am afraid what others might think of me if I do too well. My boyfriend is into sports and not schoolwork. We take some classes together. Many times I purposefully score below my ability on tests so as not to show him up. What would he think about his girlfriend being a brain? (Authors' files)

Schools, Textbooks, and Gender Roles   Schools may exert a particularly strong influence on a child's development. They can also be quite influential in the development and perpetuation of gender roles (Dweck, 1975). Teachers' responses to their students are often guided by their own stereotypes about males and females. It is common for them to expect girls to excel in subjects like English and literature, while boys are often believed to be naturally more proficient in math and science. Guided by such assumptions, teachers may differentially encourage and reward boy and girl student performances in these particular subjects.

Schoolchildren are also frequently encouraged to engage in different activities on the basis of sex. For example, boys may help move desks and tables around while girls are encouraged to perform secretarial tasks such as making lists on blackboards. This segregation of activities on the basis of gender reinforces the notion that important differences between boys and girls do exist.

Until recently, textbooks created for children have also tended to perpetuate gender role stereotypes. In the early seventies, a task force of the National Organization for Women (NOW) conducted an extensive analysis of 134 children's readers published by 12 different companies. The results of this investigation, published in a monograph entitled *Dick and Jane as Victims* (Women on Words and Images, 1972), were quite dramatic. Extreme gender role stereotypes were pervasive in these books, with girls portrayed as domestic, fearful, dependent, unambitious, and not very clever. In contrast, boys were brave, strong, independent, ambitious, clever, and successful. In addition to gender stereotypes, these books tended to perpetuate the notion that boys are more important than girls, as evidenced by a 5 to 2 ratio of boy-centered to girl-centered stories. The findings of the NOW task force were confirmed by another analysis of grade school textbooks (Saario et al., 1973). These investigators reported that boys in these books were portrayed as good at problem solving, very active (even aggressive), and in charge of their fates. Girls were depicted as followers, likely to engage in fantasy, not very successful, and less in control of their destinies.

There are indications that many elementary and high school textbooks now in use do seek to avoid gender role stereotyping. A number of states have recently adopted criteria pertaining to the portrayal of gender roles that govern the adoption of textbooks. For example, California guidelines require that males and females be portrayed "in a wide variety of occupational, emotional, and behavioral situations, presenting both sexes in the full range of their human potential" (California State Department of Education, 1979, p. 3). Textbook publishers obviously want their books to be adopted. Consequently, many now put considerable effort into avoiding gender role stereotypes.

Gender Role Stereotypes Via Television   Television is another pervasive part of our lives that may have a significant impact on the establishment of gender roles. Many children regularly spend long hours in front of a TV set, and it would hardly be surprising to discover that television portrayals of men and women influence their learning of gender role behaviors.

Television is often quite blatant in depicting stereotyped gender roles. For example, two separate analyses of television commercials found that men were featured far more than women (particularly if any type of authoritative pronouncement was called for) and that both sexes were usually cast in roles that supported gender stereotypes (McArthur and Resko, 1975). Men are depicted as authoritative figures while women are usually portrayed as experts only about domestic functions and feminine hygiene needs. What is the potential impact of this imbalanced treatment on the viewer? It seems probable that many watchers internalize a sense of the greater importance of males versus females.

The impact of television on gender stereotyping is not confined to commercials. The same NOW task force that examined children's readers performed a similar analysis of prime time television story lines (Women on Words and Images, 1975). They found that females were commonly portrayed as seductive sex objects, incompetent, domestically inclined, supportive, passive, and even unintelligent. Males were typically shown as being in charge, competent, brave, active, and intelligent.

There have been few notable changes in the last few years in television's gender role stereotyping (Atkin, 1982). Men, who continue to outnumber women by a wide margin, remain typecast as strong, intelligent decisionmakers. Women, who often occupy secondary roles, continue to be depicted as passive, supportive, and dependent. However, the recent advent of several television series that portray women in active, assertive roles (programs such as "Maude," "Alice," "Nurse," and "Hill Street Blues") may signal a slight shift in traditional gender role typecasting. Nevertheless, such positive characterizations constitute only a small percentage of television's total offerings. There has also been a slight reduction in stereotyping via commercials, but men continue to sell computers and women remain entrenched in the kitchen. "One distinct sex disparity remains unchanged: more than nine of ten off-camera voices that provide the authoritative information about the product are male" (Atkin, 1982, p. 67).

We see, then, that family and friends, schools, and television frequently help develop traditional gender role assumptions and behaviors within our lives. To some degree, we are all affected by gender role conditioning, and we might discuss at great length how this process discourages development of the full range of human potential in each of us. However, this is a text dealing with our sexuality, and so it is the impact of gender role conditioning on this aspect of our lives that we will examine in greater detail in the following section.

The Impact of Gender Roles on Our Sexuality

Gender role expectations exert a profound impact upon our sexuality. Our beliefs about males and females, together with certain assumptions about what constitutes appropriate behaviors for each, may have an effect on many aspects of sexual sharing. Our assessment of ourselves as sexual beings, the expectations we have for intimate relationships, our perception of the quality of such experiences, and the responses of others to our sexuality, may all be significantly influenced by our identification as male or female.

In the following pages we will examine some of the potential effects of these gender role assumptions on relations between the sexes. However, we do not mean to imply that only heterosexual couples experience these potentially limiting influences. Gender role stereotypes may affect people regardless of their sexual orientation. However, individuals with a homosexual orientation may experience them somewhat differently than those with a heterosexual orientation. For example, problems of initiating may be particularly pronounced for a lesbian couple, both of whom have been socialized not to initiate, whereas a male homosexual couple may have difficulty establishing an emotional bond in their relationship, since both were probably socialized to hide their feelings.

Women as Undersexed, Men as Oversexed A long-standing, slow-to-die assumption in many societies is the mistaken belief that women are inherently less sexually inclined than men. Such gender stereotypes may result in women being subjected to years of negative socialization during which they are taught to suppress or

48

deny their natural sexual feelings. Legions of women have been told by parents, peers, and books that sex is something a woman engages in to please a man, preferably her husband. A related gender assumption pervasive in society is the onerous view that "normal women" do not actually enjoy sex as much as men.

Although these stereotypes are beginning to fade as people strive to throw off some of the behavior constraints of generations of socialization, many women are still burdened by such views. How can a woman express interest in being sexual or actively seek her own pleasure if she is laboring under the mistaken assumption that women are not supposed to have sexual needs? Some women, believing that it is not appropriate to be easily aroused sexually, may direct their energies to blocking or hiding these normal responses. Some people adhere to these stereotypes so rigidly that they believe any woman who openly expresses sexual interest or responds sexually is "easy," "sleazy," or a "slut." However, men who manifest similar behavior may be characterized as "studs," "casanovas," or "playboys," terms that are often ego-enhancing rather than demeaning.

Males too may be harmed by being stereotyped as super-sexual. A man who is not instantly aroused by a person he perceives as being attractive and/or available may feel somehow inadequate in his male role. After all, are not all men supposed to be instantly eager when confronted with a sexual opportunity? We believe that such an assumption is demeaning and reduces men to insensitive machines that respond instantly when the correct button is pushed. Male students in our classes frequently express their frustration and ambivalence over this issue. The following account is typical of these observations:

When I take a woman out for the first time, I often am confused over how the sex issue should be handled. I feel pressured to make a move, even when I am not all that inclined to hop into the sack. Isn't this what women expect? If I don't even try, they may think there is something wrong with me. I almost feel like I would have to explain myself if I act uninterested in having sex. Usually it is just easier to make the move and let them decide what they want to do with it. (Authors' files)

Clearly, this man believes he is expected to pursue sex, even when disinclined, as part of his masculine role. This stereotypical view of men as the initiators of sex in developing relationships can be distressing for both sexes, as we shall see in the next section.

Men as Initiators, Women as Recipients   In our society, men traditionally initiate intimate relationships, from the opening invitation for an evening out to the first request for sexual sharing. As the following comments expressed by men during small-group discussions reveal, this can make males feel burdened and pressured:

Women should experience how anxiety-provoking it can be to provide an invitation with the ever-present potential of being turned down. (Authors' files)

I feel that every woman I date expects me to put the move on her. (Authors' files)

I am never sure when I should ask a woman to sleep with me. If I am in too much of a hurry, she may say no and I'll probably feel rejected. If I wait too long, she might get the wrong idea about me. Either way, you run the risk of coming up short. What a hassle. (Authors' files)

During lovemaking women usually expect me to make all the initial moves. Sometimes I wish I could just lie back and be taken over sexually instead of being the one who must orchestrate the whole thing. (Authors' files)

This last comment reflects a concern voiced by many of our male students and clients. Men who grow up being socialized to be active, assertive, and even aggressive are usually accustomed to being in control in most situations. It may be very difficult to relinquish this role in the bedroom. Thus, even though a man may fantasize about being taken over sexually, actually having such an experience can be stressful, as the following account reveals:

I consider myself to be somewhat avant-garde when it comes to changing roles of men and women. I like it when a woman is assertive in her relationship with me. For quite some time I fantasized about meeting someone who would assume the role of sexual aggressor with me. Well, it finally happened with unexpected results. I was asked out by an extremely attractive, charming woman. After dinner she invited me to her place. We talked, listened to music, and drank some wine. As the evening progressed I noticed her looking kind of strangely at me. Finally, I asked her what she was thinking. Her response knocked me over. She said "I was thinking that I would like to take you into my bedroom and ball your brains out." Unreal! My fantasy translated into reality. But, alas, when we ended up in bed, my body wouldn't respond. I guess the traditional tapes are stronger than I thought. (Authors' files)

This man's candid revelation details an event that, while unexpected by him, seems quite predictable in view of the strong impact gender roles have on our lives. We grow accustomed to behaving in certain ways that are consistent with our biological sex. Therefore, being asked to act in an alternative manner, while a potentially enjoyable and emancipating experience, can lead to considerable confusion and anxiety.

Even in established relationships, men are frequently expected to initiate each sexual encounter. This may result in sex becoming more of a duty than a pleasure.

My wife never initiates sex. It is always up to me. It's almost like making decisions about sex has become my job in the relationship. I wish she would hustle my body for a change. Maybe then sex would be a little more unpredictable and exciting for me. (Authors' files)

On the other hand, it is not necessarily satisfying to be cast into the stereotypical mold of the recipient in matters of intimacy. A woman who feels compelled to accept

50

the female role of passivity may have a very difficult time initiating sex. It could be even harder for her to assume an active role during sexual sharing. Many women are frustrated, regretful, and understandably angry that such cultural expectations are so deeply ingrained within our society. The following comments, expressed by women talking together, reflect some of these thoughts:

I would like to ask men out, but it is real hard to take this step. Women are simply not brought up to see this as an action consistent with the female role. (Authors' files)

It has been my experience that men may say they want women to be more assertive, but when we take the initiative they frequently act shocked, put off, or threatened. (Authors' files)

When I feel like getting down with a man, I'd like to just let him know up front what I'm thinking. But I usually keep my mouth shut and wait for him to make the first move. What a drag, particularly if he doesn't get the message. (Authors' files)

It is hard for me to let my man know what I like during lovemaking. After all, he is supposed to know, isn't he? If I tell him, it's like I am usurping his role as the all-knowing one. (Authors' files)

The last comment relates to another common gender myth about sexual functioning—the notion that men are more knowledgeable and better able than women to direct a "successful" sexual encounter.

Men as "Sexperts" Considering that gender role socialization conditions males to be competent leaders, and females to be not-so-competent followers, is it any wonder that men are typically expected to carry on this role as experts in sexual matters? Men are not the only ones who see themselves as the experts; women too may coerce men into the expert role by subscribing to this mistaken notion. In one study, roughly one-half of the women questioned indicated they believed that a "real man" should be skilled in bed (Tavris, 1977).

Some men enjoy being cast as "teacher" or "mentor." However, others may feel quite burdened by the need to play the expert, and thus, by implication, to be responsible for the outcome of sexual sharing. As one man states:

Sometimes sex is more like work than fun. I have to make all the decisions—when and where we are going to have sex and what we are going to do together. It's my responsibility to make sure it works out good for both of us. This can put a lot of pressure on me and it gets real tiring always having to run the show. It would be nice to have someone else call the shots for a change. Only it has been my experience that women are real reluctant to take the lead. (Authors' files)

Women may be reluctant to take the lead for good reason. They learn their roles just as well as men, and they may be just as burdened by them, perhaps more so. Some women may actually believe that men understand women's sexual needs better than women themselves. If things do not work out, they may even blame themselves

Part One: Introduction

for being "frigid" or unresponsive, never realizing that the real problem stems from gender role assumptions that inhibit them from communicating their needs.

Certainly there are many women who realize that they are much more aware of their sexual needs than any partner they may encounter. Nevertheless, they also may succumb with their silence to the "men as sexperts" myth, but for a different reason. As one woman noted:

I know what I need sexually to experience real pleasure. I have been masturbating for years and believe me, I know what feels best. The frustrating thing is that I can't bring myself to tell my boyfriend how I like to be touched. If I could just show him, our lovemaking would probably be much better. There he is, laboring away, doing all the wrong things, and me laying there with my mouth glued shut. The thing is, I'm concerned he would get real threatened or angry if I started telling and showing him what I like. It would be like I was saying he didn't know what he was doing and I'm afraid his male ego just couldn't handle it. (Authors' files)

This is not an uncommon concern of women. Many of our women students express reluctance to take responsibility for their own satisfaction during sex play because they are concerned that their partners will misinterpret active involvement as an attack on their personal prowess as lovers. Fortunately, some of these destructive patterns are showing signs of eroding. Many of our men students speak with a sense of delight and relief about their sexual encounters with women who initiate sex, play an active role during lovemaking, and assume responsibility for their own pleasure. In recent years, women, too, seem more inclined to view men as sexual equals rather than all-knowing experts.

Women as "Controllers," Men as "Movers" Many women grow up believing men always have sex on their minds. For such women it may be a logical next step to become the "controllers" of what takes place during sexual interaction. By this we do not mean actively initiating certain activities. Rather, a woman may see her role as controlling her male partner's rampant lust by making certain he does not coerce her into unacceptable activities. Thus, instead of enjoying how good it feels to have her breasts caressed, she may concentrate her attention on how to keep his hand off her genitals. This process may be particularly pronounced during the adolescent dating years. It is not surprising that a woman who spends a great deal of time and energy regulating sexual intimacy to preserve her "honor" (something else she learns from gender role conditioning) may have difficulty experiencing sexual feelings when she finally allows herself to relinquish her controlling role.

Conversely, men are often conditioned to see women as sexual challenges and to go as far as they can during sexual encounters. They, too, may have difficulty appreciating the good feelings of being close to and touching someone when they are thinking about what they will do next. Men who routinely experience this pattern may also have a hard time being receptive rather than active during sexual sharing. They may be confused or even threatened by a woman who switches roles from "controller" to active initiator.

Men as Unemotional and Strong, Women as Nurturing and Supportive

Perhaps one of the most undesirable of all gender role stereotypes is the notion that being emotionally expressive, tender, and nurturing is appropriate only for women. We have already seen that men are often socialized to be unemotional. This conditioning can make it exceedingly difficult for a man to develop emotionally satisfying relationships. A man who is trying to appear "strong" will find it difficult to express vulnerability, deep feelings, and doubts. In such a situation it can be very hard to share intimately with another person.

For example, a man who accepts the assumption of nonemotionality may approach sex as a purely physical act during which expressions of feelings have no place. This may result in a limited kind of sharing that can leave both parties with feelings of dissatisfaction. Women often have a negative reaction when they encounter this characteristic in men, and it is understandable that such traits may not be welcome in a relationship where openness and willingness to express feelings may be important to the female partner. However, we need to remember that many men must struggle against a lifetime of "Marlboro Man" conditioning when they try to express long-suppressed emotions. For some, even an expression of tenderness may be an exceedingly difficult break from the tough guy image.

Women in turn may become tired of their role as nurturer, particularly when their efforts are greeted with little or no reciprocity. For each of us, tenderness and emotional supportiveness can dwindle rapidly unless fueled by similar acts directed toward us by others whom we care for.

We have discussed how strict adherence to traditional gender roles may act to limit and restrict the manner in which we express our sexuality. While these cultural legacies may often be expressed more subtly today than they were in the past, rigid gender role expectations linger on, inhibiting our growth as multidimensional persons and our capacity to share intimacy with others. Also, while many people are breaking away from stereotyped gender roles and learning to accept and express themselves more fully, we cannot underestimate the extent of gender role learning that occurs in our society. Pictures like the photographs on the next two pages underscore this point; they will probably cause most readers to do at least a slight double-take.

In recent years there is increasing evidence that many people are striving to integrate both masculine and feminine behaviors into their life styles. This new trend, often referred to as *androgyny,* will be the focus of the final section in this chapter.

Transcending Gender Roles: Androgyny

The word *androgyny* means "man-woman," and it is derived from the Greek roots *andr* = man and *gynē* = woman. Sometimes androgyny is confused with hermaphroditism, implying a kind of mixed biological gender. More appropriately, androgyny is used to describe flexibility in gender role. Androgynous individuals are those who have moved beyond traditional gender roles. They are people who have integrated aspects of masculinity and femininity into their life styles in their pursuit of an individual sense of well-being. Androgyny offers the option of expressing whatever behavior seems appropriate in a given situation instead of limiting responses to those

Many individuals are now expressing aspects of themselves previously discouraged by stereotypic gender roles.

considered gender appropriate. Thus, androgynous men and women might be assertive on the job and tender and nurturing with lovers.

Many people hold the mistaken notion that one is either masculine or feminine and that it is not possible to be both. From this perspective, a man who chooses to do domestic chores and provide childcare is somehow less masculine and more feminine. Conversely, a woman who enrolls in auto mechanics at the local community college

might be viewed as rejecting her femininity in favor of a masculine pursuit. However, many men and women possess characteristics consistent with traditional gender assumptions but also have interests and behavioral tendencies typically ascribed to the other sex. Actually, people may range from being very masculine or feminine to being both masculine and feminine (that is, androgynous).

A well-known social psychologist, Sandra Bem, has developed a paper-and-pencil inventory for measuring a person's degree of androgyny (Bem, 1974). Armed with an empirical device for measuring androgyny, a number of researchers have investigated how androgynous individuals compare with strongly gender-typed people. The results of some of this research will be briefly outlined in the following paragraphs.

As we might expect, androgynous people are more likely to engage in behavior typically ascribed to the other sex than are gender-typed individuals (Bem, 1975). Gender-typed individuals may adhere so rigidly to role expectations that they will avoid cross-gender behavior even when such choices are not in their best financial interests (Bem and Lenney, 1976). Bem suggests that these studies demonstrate that androgynous people are more flexible and less stifled by gender role assumptions. Research has also demonstrated that masculine individuals and androgynous people of both sexes are more independent and show less of a tendency to have their opinions swayed than individuals who are strongly identified with the feminine role (Bem, 1975). In addition, feminine individuals and androgynous subjects of both sexes appear to be significantly more nurturing than people who adhere to the masculine role (Bem et al., 1976). Finally, there is evidence that androgynous individuals of both sexes have higher levels of self-esteem than gender-typed people (Orlofsky, 1977; Spence et al., 1975).

These studies suggest that androgynous people are able to approach life with more flexibility than strongly gender-typed individuals. They also indicate that people who are able to transcend traditional gender ideas may be able to function with greater comfort and effectiveness in a wider range of situations. Androgynous individuals are able to select, from a broad repertoire of feminine and masculine behaviors, whatever actions seem most appropriate in a given situation. Thus, they may elect to be independent, assertive, nurturing, or tender, based not on gender role norms, but rather on what provides them the greatest personal comfort and satisfaction.

What about androgyny and sexual behavior? There is evidence that androgynous individuals, both male and female, have more positive attitudes toward sexuality than individuals who are traditionally gender-typed (Walfish and Myerson, 1980). Furthermore, we believe that transcending rigid gender role expectations may encourage the development of more egalitarian, fulfilling relationships and sexual encounters between individuals. We have already outlined, in some detail, the potentially adverse influences of gender role conditioning on our sexuality. Perhaps many of these old, negative patterns will fall by the wayside as increasing numbers of people begin to embrace androgynous styles of living and loving.

SUMMARY

1. The process whereby our maleness and femaleness is determined and the manner in which it influences our behavior, sexual and otherwise, is highly complex.

SEX AND GENDER

2. Sex refers to our biological maleness or femaleness as reflected in various physical attributes (chromosomes, genitals, and so forth).

3. Gender refers to the social concomitants of sex, or, in other words, our masculinity or femininity.

GENDER IDENTITY AND GENDER ROLE

4. Gender identity is a term used to describe our personal, subjective sense that we are either male or female, masculine or feminine.

5. Gender role refers to a collection of attitudes and behaviors that are considered normal and appropriate in a specific culture for people of a particular sex.

6. Gender roles establish sex-related behavioral expectations that people are expected to fulfill. These expectations are culturally defined and vary from society to society and era to era.

GENDER IDENTITY FORMATION

7. Gender identity formation is influenced by both biological conditions and social learning factors.

8. Research efforts to isolate the many biological factors that influence an individual's gender identity have resulted in the identification of at least five separate biological categories or levels:

chromosomal sex, gonadal sex, hormonal sex, sex of the internal accessory sex structures, and sex as determined by the external genitalia.

9. Under normal conditions these five biological variables interact harmoniously to determine our biological sex. However, errors may occur at each of these levels. The resulting abnormalities in the development of a person's biological sex may seriously complicate acquisition of a gender identity.

10. The social learning interpretation of gender identity formation suggests that our identification with either masculine or feminine roles results primarily from the social and cultural models and influences we are exposed to.

11. Most contemporary theorists embrace an interactional model, where gender identity is seen as a result of a complex interplay of biology and social learning factors.

12. Transsexualism is a special case of gender identity difficulty in which a person's gender identity is opposite to his or her biological sex. The scientific community has not reached a general consensus as to the causes and best treatment of this condition.

GENDER ROLES

13. Society ascribes to us a set of behaviors that are considered normal and appropriate for our particular sex. These normative standards are called gender roles.

14. Widely accepted gender role assumptions may begin to function as stereotypes, which are notions about what people are like based not on their own individuality but rather on their inclusion in a more general category such as age or sex.

15. There are many common gender-based stereotypes in our society that may encourage us to prejudge individuals as well as act to restrict our opportunities.

16. Socialization refers to the process whereby our society conveys to the individual behavioral expectations for his or her gender.

17. Parents, peers, schools, textbooks, and television all act as agents in the socialization of gender roles.

18. Gender role expectations exert a profound impact on our sexuality. Our assessment of ourselves as sexual beings, the expectations we have for intimate relationships, our perception of the quality of such experiences, and the responses of others to our sexuality may all be significantly influenced by our identification as male or female.

19. Androgynous individuals are those people who have moved beyond traditional gender roles by integrating aspects of masculinity and femininity into their life styles in their pursuit of an individual sense of well-being.

Allgeier, Elizabeth, and McCormick, Naomi (Eds.). *Invisible Boundaries.* Palo Alto, Calif.: Mayfield, 1982. An interesting and diverse collection of articles dealing with the impact of sex roles on our sexuality.

Bem, Sandra. "Androgyny vs. the Tight Little Lives of Fluffy Women and Chesty Men." *Psychology Today*, September 1975, 58–62. A renowned experimenter in sex roles reports her intriguing research on androgyny. Must reading for anyone interested in learning more about an androgynous life style.

Bermant, Gordon, and Davidson, Julian. *Biological Bases of Sexual Behavior.* New York: Harper & Row, 1974. A rigorous text with a wealth of information about the physiological correlates of sexual behavior. Of particular interest are several chapters dealing with hormonal and neural determinants of sexual activity. Also contains an excellent chapter on sexual differentiation.

Diamond, Milton. "Human Sexual Development: Biological Foundations for Social Development." In F. Beach (Ed.), *Human Sexuality in Four Perspectives.* Baltimore: Johns Hopkins Press, 1977 (also available in paperback from Johns Hopkins Press, 1978). A discussion of early sexual differentiation and later sexual behavior from a biological perspective. Presents the provocative thesis that genetic and hormonal factors establish sex differences in the brain that determine gender differences in behavior throughout life.

Mead, Margaret. *Sex and Temperament in Three Primitive Societies.* New York: Morrow, 1963. An eminent anthropologist's analysis of three societies in which male and female gender roles differ from those of North American society.

Money, John. *Love and Love Sickness: The Science of Sex, Gender Difference, and Pair-Bonding.* Baltimore: Johns Hopkins Press, 1980. A complex and scholarly text that covers a broad range of topics in human sexuality, including some provocative new concepts related to gender identity and gender role.

Money, John, and Ehrhardt, Anke. *Man and Woman, Boy and Girl.* Baltimore: Johns Hopkins Press, 1972. An in-depth analysis of the psychosocial and biological factors that influence the development of gender identity. Must reading for anyone desiring a more thorough understanding of the processes of gender identity and gender role.

3

Sex Research: Methods and Problems

RESEARCH METHODS
  Surveys via Questionnaires or Interviews
  Case Studies
  Direct Observation
  Experimental Research
SOME WELL-KNOWN STUDIES
  The Kinsey Group
  Masters and Johnson
  Hunt
  The *Redbook* Report
  The Hite Report on Female Sexuality
  The Hite Report on Male Sexuality
  Sorenson
  Zelnick and Kantner
  Bell and Weinberg
WHAT TO BELIEVE? A STATEMENT OF PERSPECTIVE
SUMMARY
SUGGESTED READINGS

Articles and books that claim to contain the latest research on human sexual behavior are plentiful, and they are readily available to anyone who is interested. "Scientific polls" urge readers to accept their findings as Truth—despite the fact that these may contradict another survey published just a month earlier. At present, there is an extensive body of scientific sex research, and it is rapidly growing. Some of this research is excellent and rather remarkable; other findings have proven to be less than noteworthy. How can a reader learn to distinguish the wheat from the chaff?

You may find it helpful to keep in mind that sex research, despite its rapid growth, is still in its infancy. The pioneering work done by Kinsey, who was the first to conduct an extensive general survey of American sexual behaviors, took place only in the late 1940s and early 1950s. Sex is as old as humankind, but it is a newcomer as a subject for serious research.

It is also important to realize that the study of sexuality shares the same problems that handicap all research into human social behavior. Human subjects cannot be placed in the same kind of experimental situations as other animals: ethical considerations limit the researcher's range of options. Human thought and behavior are extremely complex, and this fact poses even more serious research problems. For instance, subjects second-guess the researcher, altering their responses to coincide with their expectations of what the researcher (or society) wants to hear. The very private and sensitive nature of human sexuality further complicates the process of data collecting: many people simply do not want to be "researched."

Despite these problems, research provides a growing body of knowledge about human sexuality. In this chapter we will acquaint you with how we have come to know certain things about sexual behavior. As we discuss particular methods, problems, and examples of sex research, you may begin to appreciate what we know and do not know, and how confident we can be in the available knowledge. You may also begin to sense the directions we can take to further expand our scientific knowledge of sexual behavior. Perhaps at some future time you will contribute to our knowledge of this important area of human experience. We invite you to do so.

RESEARCH METHODS

There are a number of methods for studying sexual behavior. They range from detailed case studies of specific individuals, often in a clinical setting where the subject is being treated for a specific behavioral or medical problem, to questionnaire or interview surveys that typically produce less depth of coverage about a much larger group of people. Two less frequently used research methods are direct observation and experimental laboratory research. Each of these strategies has advantages and disadvantages for researching various kinds of questions.

Surveys via Questionnaires or Interviews

Most of our information about human sexuality has been obtained by *surveys* that ask people about their sexual experiences or attitudes. This information may be obtained in two ways: either orally through a face-to-face interview or in written form on a paper-and-pencil questionnaire. There is no single way of administering questionnaires: questions may range in number from a few to over a thousand; they may be multiple-choice, true-and-false, or discussion questions; they may be done at home alone or in the presence of a researcher.

Each of these survey methods has its advantages and shortcomings. Questionnaires are more anonymous, and for some people, this may reduce pressures to distort information about their sex lives by boasting, omitting facts, and so on. (The presence of an interviewer may encourage such false responses.) Questionnaires have another advantage in that they are usually cheaper and quicker than interview surveys. However, interviews have the distinct advantage of flexibility. The interviewer may clarify confusing questions, and vary their order if necessary, to meet the needs of the participant. A competent interviewer can establish a sense of rapport that may encourage more candor than that produced by an impersonal questionnaire. On the other hand, data obtained through oral interviews may be subject to bias as a result of inaccurate interpretations by the researcher.

While the methods are somewhat different, the intention of both written and oral surveys is the same: to use a relatively small, representative population (the *survey sample*) to draw inferences or conclusions about a much larger population group—for instance, married adults or high school adolescents.

The ideal sample is called a *probability sample*. Here, every individual in the total population of interest has an equal chance, or probability, of being included in the limited sample actually studied. We can use an example to show how the probability sample works.

Let us assume that you wished to survey the attitudes and behavior of American, high school-aged males regarding birth control. In order to draw broad conclusions about the general population (all American male adolescents), your sample would need to be representative of it. How could you ensure this? You could begin by obtaining the rosters of all male high school students in a variety of geographic areas throughout the United States. These regions would be chosen very carefully to reflect the manner in which the American population is distributed. If 20% of American male adolescents live in the South, for instance, 20% of your lists would be drawn from the South. Likewise, if 30% of southern male high school students live in rural environments, 30% of your southern sample must be country dwellers. Once your rosters were compiled, the next step would be to select the actual participants by some method that would ensure equal probability of inclusion, such as a table of random numbers. Provided your final sample was sufficiently large, you could be relatively confident in generalizing your findings to the entire population of American high school-aged males.

Actually, obtaining a probability sample for this hypothetical survey would be a difficult, if not impossible, task in real sex research. This is because it is often quite difficult to get people to participate in studies of this nature. Assuming you had used proper sampling procedures to choose your target sample of male high school-aged students, how many do you think would actually be willing to answer your questions about their sexual attitudes and practices? (Even if the individuals were willing, how many school officials and parents would object to such participation?) *Nonresponse,* the refusal to participate in a research study, is a common problem that consistently plagues sex survey research. This difficulty, together with issues related to data inaccuracy, will be explored in the following section.

Problems of Sex Survey Research: Nonresponse and Inaccuracy   No one has ever conducted a major sex survey where 100% of the randomly selected subjects voluntarily participated. In fact, some studies include results obtained from samples where only a small minority of those asked to respond actually did.

Nonresponse presents a major complication in human sexual research. No matter how careful the researcher has been in selecting the sample population, that sample may be distorted by the subjects' *self-selection*. Are the individuals who agree to participate in sex research surveys any different from those who choose not to respond? Perhaps they are a representative cross-section of the population—but we have no theoretical or statistical basis for that conclusion. As a matter of fact, the opposite might well be true. People who volunteer to participate may be the ones who are the most eager to share their experiences, who have explored a wide range of activities, or who feel most comfortable with their sexuality. (Or it might be that the most experienced people are the ones who are least willing to respond, because they feel their behaviors represent atypical or extreme levels of activity.) A preponderance of experienced, inexperienced, liberal, or conservative individuals might bias any sample.

A limited amount of research on "volunteer bias" has provided contradictory results. For example, one study compared individuals who had volunteered for Alfred Kinsey's research with those who did not volunteer (Maslow and Sakoda, 1952). These investigators found significant differences between the two groups; the volunteers demonstrated higher levels of self-esteem and more sexual activity than those who did not volunteer. In contrast, a more recent study found no important differences in sexual attitudes and experience between men and women who volunteered to fill out a sex survey questionnaire and those who had to be persuaded to participate (Bauman, 1973). It is apparent that additional research is necessary to clarify whether people who willingly participate in sex research differ from those who do not.

Other kinds of problems might result from subject selection. For instance, demographic bias has been a problem in many studies. Most of the actual data available from sex research have come from samples weighted heavily with Caucasian, middle-class volunteers in the United States. This was certainly true of the monumental studies of the Kinsey group in the forties and fifties and of Masters and Johnson in the sixties. Typically, college students and educated white-collar workers are disproportionately represented in these samples.

How much effect do nonresponse and demographic bias have on sex research findings? We cannot say for sure. But as long as elements of American society, including the less educated and ethnic and racial minorities, are underrepresented, we must remain cautious in generalizing any findings to the population at large.

A second problem that hinders sex survey research has to do with the accuracy of information provided by subjects. Most of our data about human sexual behavior are obtained from respondents' self-reports of their experiences. How closely does actual behavior correspond to these subjective, after-the-fact reports?

A variety of factors may reduce the accuracy of individual reports of sexual behavior.

For many reasons, there may be considerable discrepancy between actual behavior and the way people report it. One potential complication involves the known limitations of the human memory system. For instance, how many people remember accurately when they first masturbated and with what frequency? Ask yourself (if applicable) at what age you first experienced an orgasm. It may be quite difficult to accurately recall some information.

Some people may consciously or unconsciously conceal certain facts about their sexual histories because they view them as abnormal, silly, or perhaps too painful to remember. In areas of sexual behavior where there are strong social taboos (such as those regarding incest, homosexuality, and masturbation), people may feel pressure to deny or minimize such experiences in their own lives. Others may purposely falsify their responses to inflate their own sexual experience, perhaps out of a desire to appear to be sexually liberal.

Occasionally, false reports may result simply from misunderstandings. For example, a person with little education might answer no to the question "Have you experienced penile-vaginal intercourse prior to marriage?" simply because he or she was not familiar with the terminology. That same person might respond affirmatively to the question "Did you go all the way before getting hitched?" Language is a problem in many types of social research; this is especially true in sex research where there is a virtual absence of any sexual language common to all groups in our society. That is why the wording of questions becomes such a critical issue.

Sample surveys via questionnaires and interviews are the most commonly used methods for studying sexual behavior and attitudes. They provide a relatively inexpensive way to obtain information about a broad range of topics from many individuals. But we cannot expect to learn all there is to know about sexuality from sample surveys. Other important sources of information include case studies, direct observation, and laboratory research.

Case Studies

There are numerous references in the existing literature to *case studies*. These are in-depth explorations of single cases or of small groups of persons who were examined individually. Unlike surveys, case studies obtain a great deal of information from one or a very few individuals.

Often people become subjects for case histories because they have some physical or emotional disorder or because they have manifested a specific atypical behavior. Thus, much of our current information about sex offenders, transsexuals, incest victims, and the like has been obtained through this approach. Also, a large portion of our information about sexual response difficulties (for instance, male erectile inhibition and lack of orgasmic response in women) has been obtained from studies of individuals seeking treatment for these problems.

The case-study approach allows for flexible data-gathering procedures. These range from well-structured questions that offer specific response alternatives to open-ended queries that provide considerable flexibility to respondents. Some researchers deplore the fact that this approach offers little opportunity for investigative control. Unlike survey methods, case studies often provide opportunities to acquire insight into specific behaviors. The highly personal, subjective information about how individuals actually feel about their behavior represents an important step beyond simply recording activities. So, while this method sacrifices some control, it adds considerable dimension to our information. Case studies have another advantage. Because of their clinical nature and the fact that they may continue for long periods of time (months or even years), the researcher is able to explore cause-and-effect relationships in detail.

There are some important limitations to the clinical case study, however. Since proper sampling techniques are rarely observed (how could they be?) it is hard to draw generalizations to the rest of the population. This potential source of error is illustrated in many writings that have presented a pathological model of homosexuality based on case studies of homosexuals who had sought treatment. As in the self-selection that can take place in survey sampling, there may be pronounced differences between homosexuals who are not trying to change their sexual orientation as contrasted with those who seek therapy. In other situations, where individuals with known mental or physical disorders have been studied in depth, applying the resultant information to healthy people is questionable. For that matter, how do we know that individuals under treatment or observation are representative of the subpopulation to which they belong? For example, incest-committing fathers who have been identified by the court may not be representative of all fathers who engage in incestuous relationships with their offspring. All of these general cautions can be applied to the cases we cite in our authors' files sections throughout this book. We think these cases represent especially relevant experiences and feelings, but our purpose is for readers to draw perspective from them, not conclusions. An example of case study research is provided in Box 3.1.

Direct Observation

A third method for studying human sexual behavior is *direct observation*. This type of research may vary greatly in form and setting, ranging from laboratory studies that observe and record sexual responses to participant observation where the researchers join their subjects in sexual activity.

Observational research is quite common in a variety of disciplines, particularly the social sciences of anthropology, sociology, and psychology. However, very little research of this nature occurs in the area of sexuality. Sexual expression, being a highly personal and private experience, does not readily lend itself to direct observation.

When it has been well-conducted, thorough direct observation produces valuable information. There are some clear advantages to seeing and measuring sexual behavior firsthand, instead of relying on subjective reports of past experiences. Firsthand direct observation virtually eliminates the possibility of data falsification through memory deficits, boastful inflation, or guilt-induced repression. Second, records of such behaviors may be retained indefinitely via videotapes or films.

But there are also some disadvantages associated with this approach. A major problem lies in the often unanswerable question of just how much a subject's behavior is influenced by the presence of even the most discrete observer. This question has been asked often since the publication of the Masters and Johnson studies (1966), which used the direct observation method to document male and female sexual response patterns. Researchers employing direct observation often attempt to minimize this potential complication by being as unobtrusive as possible (for example, observing from a peripheral location or behind one-way glass, using videotapes to be viewed later, and so forth). But the subject still is aware that she or he is being observed. The reliability of recorded observations may also be compromised by preexisting biases in the researchers. For example, if the observer believes "swingers" experience only nonemotional sexual involvements, she or he may be less likely to interpret their interactions as manifestations of affectionate intimacy.

Experimental Research

A fourth method, *experimental research,* is being utilized with increasing frequency in the investigation of human sexual behavior. In experimental research, subjects must be confronted with certain specific stimuli under controlled conditions where their reactions can be reliably measured. For example, if you designed an experiment to

BOX 3.1 THE ELEGANT PROSTITUTE: AN EXAMPLE OF CASE STUDY RESEARCH

In 1958 Harold Greenwald, a psychologist, published an in-depth social-psychological study of "call girls" appropriately titled *The Call Girl*. An updated edition of his study, *The Elegant Prostitute* (1970), describes how call girls are the elite of the world of prostitution: they make appointments by phone, dress elegantly, and live in expensive apartments. Before Greenwald's study, little was known about the factors that contribute to call girls' choice of occupation. Greenwald became interested in the subject as a result of conducting therapy with six call girl clients. These six shared certain experiences and attitudes, and Greenwald began to wonder if these similarities extended to other call girls. He explored this question by conducting in-depth interviews with 20 additional women who practiced the profession.

All 20 were working as call girls at the time of the interviews. They ranged in age from 19 to 43 years. Most had a high school education or better. A substantial majority had been reared in middle and upper-income families. Most of the information about these women was obtained by interviews that employed open-ended questions such as "Tell me about yourself" or "What has your life been like up to now?"

After sifting through large quantities of interview data, Greenwald made some observations about the family backgrounds, life styles, feelings, and attitudes of the women in his research population. There was a marked similarity among the family atmospheres in which they were reared. "I found not one example of a permanent, well-adjusted marital relationship between the parents" (p.165). Affection between parents was rarely or never displayed, and 19 of the subjects reported feeling rejected by both parents. Fifteen found themselves in broken homes before they reached adolescence, and as a result, many were passed from family to family or lived in a succession of boarding schools.

Ten of the subjects reported that at an early age they had engaged in sexual activity with an adult that resulted in some kind of reward such as affection or privileges. Greenwald suggests that these early experiences may have established a pattern of giving sexual gratification as a way of temporarily overcoming feelings of loneliness and unworthiness. Furthermore, such experiences led the women to recognize early in life that sex was a commodity they could barter with.

Greenwald found that virtually all of his study population expressed anger and even rage over being deprived of affection and stability during their formative years. Their anger was often turned inward, resulting in very negative self-images and varying degrees of anxiety and depression. Most of them found it extremely difficult to maintain satisfactory relationships with other people.

In light of their family backgrounds and resulting negative self images, Greenwald theorized that "becoming a call girl appeared to offer a desperate hope of halting the deterioration of self, but . . . their choice of profession made these conflicts more intense and more self-destructive" (p. 187).

compare the sexual responses of males and females to visual erotica, you would subject both sexes to the same stimuli under controlled conditions and then use a reliable method for measuring the results (such as physiological measures of penile erection, vaginal engorgement, and so forth). An experiment of this nature was conducted a few years ago in Germany with rather interesting results (see the discussion of the Schmidt and Sigusch experiment in Chapter 6).

A laboratory experiment offers the major advantage of control over variables that are thought to influence the sexual behavior being studied. Often such an approach allows for direct statements about cause and effect that would be more speculative with other methods of data collection. However, the somewhat artificial nature of the experimental laboratory setting may influence subjects' behavior. As in direct observation research, the very fact that people know they are in an experiment can alter their responses from those that might occur outside the laboratory. An example of experimental research is provided in Box 3.2. Box 3.3 describes some applications of technology to sex research.

SOME WELL-KNOWN STUDIES

Studies conducted by sex researchers over the years have covered the range of methods just described. A few of these studies are repeatedly cited by writers in the field; some are even household names. In the following pages, we will look at nine of them. The main features of the studies are summarized in Table 3.1. As the table shows, all but one belong in the survey category of research methods. Findings from these studies will be cited throughout the book; outlining their scope, strengths, and weaknesses here can provide you with a solid frame of reference for making subsequent interpretations.

The Kinsey Group

Alfred Kinsey, with his associates Wardell Pomeroy, Clyde Martin, and Paul Gebhard, published two large volumes in the decade following World War II. One, on male sexuality, was published in 1948; the follow-up report on female sexuality was published in 1953. These volumes contain the results of extensive survey interviews whose aim was to determine patterns of sexual behavior in American males and females. These remarkably ambitious investigations still remain unique in the annals of sex research as the most comprehensive of all *taxonomic* surveys (that is, investigations aimed at classifying people into behavioral categories for statistical comparisons).

Kinsey and his associates believed that attempts to secure sex histories from individuals selected by random sampling methods would result in so many refusals to participate that randomness would be destroyed. To minimize this problem of nonresponse they elected to seek subjects in the memberships of a variety of social groups or organizations (such as college classes, professional organizations, residents of rooming houses, and so forth). Initial contacts who willingly participated were then urged to convince their friends to get involved. In some cases, this use of peer-group

BOX 3.2 THE EFFECTS OF ALCOHOL ON SEXUAL AROUSAL: TWO EXAMPLES OF EXPERIMENTAL RESEARCH

People often report that alcohol increases their level of sexual arousal. In one major survey of 20,000 middle-class and upper middle-class Americans, 60% of the respondents reported that drinking increased their sexual pleasure (Athanasiou et al., 1970). However, most surveys have been limited to asking people what they *think* happens when they drink, and these subjective assessments may not match up with objective reality, as was found in two experiments on the actual effects of alcohol on human sexual arousal.

Both investigations were conducted at Rutgers University's Alcohol Behavior Research Laboratory. The first experiment involved 48 male college students between the ages of 18 and 22 (Briddell and Wilson, 1976). During an initial session the researchers obtained baseline data on flaccid penis diameter for all subjects. The participants were then shown a 10-minute erotic film of explicit sexual interaction between male and female partners. Penile tumescence (engorgement) was measured continuously during the film by penile strain gauges (see Box 3.3). In a second session, held one week later, all subjects drank measured amounts of alcohol prior to viewing a somewhat longer version of the erotic film. Subjects were assigned to four experimental groups, with 12 subjects in each group. Each subject, depending on his group assignment, consumed 0.6, 3, 6, or 9 ounces of alcohol. After a 40-minute "rest period" the subjects viewed the film, during which each person's sexual arousal was assessed by his score on three measures of penile tumescence: increase in diameter, time required to obtain an erection, and duration of the erection. The results indicated that alcohol significantly reduced sexual arousal, especially at higher intake levels. Even at low dosage levels, alcohol did not enhance penile tumescence.

The second investigation was conducted with 16 college women between the ages of 18 and 22 (Wilson and Lawson, 1976). The research design was somewhat different from that employed in the Briddell and Wilson study of men: "During weekly experimental sessions, each of 16 university women received, in counterbalanced order, four doses of beverage alcohol prior to viewing a control film and an erotic film" (p. 489). Alcohol dosage levels were approximately 0.3, 1.4, 2.9, and 4.3 ounces. The control film was a boring 12-minute review of the computer facilities at Rutgers University. The erotic film portrayed explicit heterosexual interaction. Vaginal changes reflecting sexual arousal were measured continuously during film viewing by use of a vaginal photoplethysmograph (see Box 3.3). As expected, "subjects showed significantly more arousal in response to the erotic than the control film" (p. 493). More importantly, there was clear evidence that alcohol significantly reduced the sexual arousal of these women. The inhibitory effects were greater at higher dosages.

These two experiments suggest that "increasing intoxication in both men and women results in progressively reduced sexual arousal in response to visual erotic stimulation" (Wilson and Lawson, 1976, p. 495).

BOX 3.3 SEX RESEARCH AND TECHNOLOGY

Experimental research and direct observation studies of human sexual responses often employ measures of sexual arousal. Until recently, researchers had to rely largely on subjective reports of these responses. However, recent advances in technology have produced two devices for measuring sexual arousal: the *penile strain gauge* and the *vaginal photoplethysmograph*.

The penile strain gauge (sometimes called a penile plethysmograph) is a flexible loop that looks something like a rubber band with a wire attached. It is actually a thin rubber tube that is filled with a fine strand of mercury. A tiny amount of electrical current from the attached wire flows continuously through the mercury. The gauge is placed around the base of the penis. As an erection occurs, the rubber tube stretches and, in turn, the strand of mercury becomes thinner and changes the flow of electrical current. These changes are registered by a recording device (a polygraph). This apparatus can measure even the slightest changes in penis size, and in fact is so sensitive that every pulse of blood into the penis can be recorded. In the interests of privacy, brief instructions from the experimenter will permit a subject to attach the strain gauge to his own penis.

When a woman is sexually aroused, her vaginal walls fill with blood in a manner comparable to the engorgement of a man's penis. The vaginal photoplethysmograph is a device designed to measure this increased vaginal blood volume in a sexually aroused female. It consists of an acrylic cylinder, about the size and shape of a tampon, that is inserted into the vagina. It contains a light that is reflected off the vaginal walls and a photocell that is sensitive to this reflected light. When the vaginal walls fill with blood during sexual arousal, less light is reflected to the photocell. These changes in light intensity, continuously recorded by a polygraph, provide a measure of sexual arousal that is comparable to the penile strain gauge. And, like the male device, it can be inserted in privacy by the female research subject.

---

assurances or pressure produced virtually 100% participation by members in the target group.

The final Kinsey subject populations consisted of 5300 white males and 5940 white females. They included people from both rural and urban areas in each state—people who represented a range of ages, marital status, occupations, educational levels, and religions.

Despite the wide subject variability in the two research samples, the failure to use random sampling procedures resulted in the underrepresentation or overrepresentation of certain population subgroups. Specifically, the sample contained a disproportionately greater number of better-educated, city-dwelling Protestants, while older people, rural dwellers, and those with less education were underrepresented. Blacks were omitted from the sample. And finally, all the subjects were volunteers. As we saw

Alfred Kinsey, pioneer sex researcher.

earlier, self-selected subjects can never be viewed as a random sample. Thus, in no way can Kinsey's study population be viewed as a probability sample of the American population. But Kinsey and his associates were well aware of this shortcoming. As the following quotation shows, it is clear that his group made no claim to the contrary:

This is a study of sexual behavior in (within) certain groups of the human species, *Homo sapiens*. It is obviously not a study of the sexual behavior of all cultures and all races of man. At its best, the present volume can pretend to report behavior which may be typical of no more than a portion, although probably not an inconsiderable portion, of the white females living within the boundaries of the United States. Neither the title of our first volume on the male, nor the title of this volume on the female, should be taken to imply that the authors are unaware of the diversity which exists in patterns of sexual behavior in other parts of the world. (Kinsey et al., 1953, p. 4)

Publication of the Kinsey findings generated strong reactions, both positive and negative. The most thorough review of the work was published by the American Statistical Association (Cochran et al., 1954). Despite the acknowledged problems with the sampling methods employed, this review praised Kinsey's group for their excellent use of well-planned interview techniques. While there is always the possi-

TABLE 3.1 A SUMMARY OF KEY SEX RESEARCH STUDIES

Names of Researchers and the Study	Year	Type of Study	Focus and Scope	Strengths and Weaknesses
Kinsey; *Sexual Behavior in the Human Male* *Sexual Behavior in the Human Female*	1948 1953	interview survey	patterns of sexual behavior, the American population	most comprehensive taxonomic sex survey yet conducted; but the large sample overrepresented certain groups (educated, urban dwellers, young) and underrepresented others: (undereducated, older, nonprotestant, rural, and nonwhite)
Masters and Johnson, *Human Sexual Response*	1966	direct observation	female and male physiological responses to sexual stimulation	the only major piece of research to observe and record sexual response (over 10,000 completed response cycles); has been criticized because sample was drawn from narrow-based academic community
Sorenson, *Adolescent Sexuality in Contemporary America*	1973	questionnaire survey	male and female adolescent sexual behavior (ages 13–19)	surveys a broad range of sexual behaviors; has been criticized because of nonresponse bias and length of questionnaire
Hunt, *Sexual Behavior in the 1970s*	1974	questionnaire survey	patterns of sexual behavior, the American population	much information about a broad range of adult sexual behaviors; has been criticized because of high nonresponse, sampling bias from telephone recruitment, and length of questionnaire
The Redbook Report on Female Sexuality	1974	questionnaire survey	female sexuality (behavior and attitudes)	very large sample size (100,000 women); but sample bias due to fact that respondents were *Redbook* readers, not a true cross section of American women
The Hite Report on female sexuality	1976	questionnaire survey	female sexuality (behavior and attitudes)	large number of respondents (3019) provided extensive narrative answers to questions; has been criticized because sample volunteers probably overrepresented young "liberal" women

TABLE 3.1 CONTINUED

Names of Researchers and the Study	Year	Type of Study	Focus and Scope	Strengths and Weaknesses
The Hite Report on Male Sexuality	1980	questionnaire survey	male sexuality (behavior and attitudes)	7239 respondents out of 119,000 questionnaires distributed; strong possibility of volunteer bias; educational levels of volunteers much higher than national average
Zelnick and Kantner, "Sexual and Contraceptive Experiences of Young Unmarried Women in the United States, 1979, 1976, and 1971"	1971, 1976, and 1979	questionnaire survey	pregnancy, use of contraceptives, and premarital sex among unmarried teenage women, ages 15–19 (1979 survey included men, ages 17–21)	good sampling techniques; but a narrow population of interest
Bell and Weinberg, *Homosexualities: A Study of Diversities Among Men and Women*	1978	interview survey	homosexual life styles and sexual practices	most comprehensive study of homosexuality to date; criticisms have centered on sampling biases from recruitment methods
Bell, Weinberg, and Hammersmith, *Sexual Preference: Its Development in Men and Women*	1981	interview survey	causes of sexual orientation	utilization of sophisticated statistical techniques to produce findings remarkable in what they disprove; sampling biases from recruitment methods

bility of distortion whenever interviews or questionnaires are used, the Kinsey interviewers were particularly adept at establishing rapport with their subjects. They accomplished this by asking questions in a way that conveyed acceptance of any kind of response, by modifying language to fit the understanding of respondents, and by spontaneously altering the interview sequence so that particularly sensitive questions could be asked at the best time.

Kinsey's findings covered a wide range of topics, including such things as frequency and kind of sexual outlet (that is, the sources of orgasm and how often experienced), nonmarital coitus, sexual orientation, and sexual techniques. Many of his conclusions produced a great deal of public furor. For example, his finding that approximately one-half of the women in his sample reported experiencing coitus before marriage contradicted the dominant cultural ideal of virgin brides. His observation that many people have varying degrees of homosexual and heterosexual tendencies within them also produced considerable controversy. In later portions of this book, we will discuss several other major findings of the Kinsey research.

Kinsey's studies were published three decades ago, and today many people question whether their findings are applicable to contemporary society. In response to this, it may be noted that information becomes obsolete at differing rates, and certainly many of the Kinsey data are still relevant. It is quite unlikely that the passage of time has altered the applicability of certain findings—for example, that sexual behavior is influenced by educational level and that the heterosexuality or homosexuality of a person is often not an all-or-none proposition. However, certain other areas—such as coital rates among unmarried people—are more influenced by changing societal norms. Thus, one might expect the Kinsey data to be less predictive of contemporary practices in these areas. Nevertheless, even here his data are relevant in that they provide one possible basis for estimating the degree of behavioral change over the years.

In summary, despite the problems inherent in the Kinsey research, it still remains one of the very best sources of information about patterns of human sexual behavior. If the data contained in these two volumes are interpreted cautiously, we are able to secure some important clues about the sexual behavior of Caucasian Americans, if not now, at least several decades ago.

Masters and Johnson

Along with the Kinsey research, Masters and Johnson's study of human sexual response is probably the most often mentioned sex research. The two studies represent distinctly different kinds of research, though, with quite different goals. Kinsey used survey interviews to trace broad patterns of sexual behavior; Masters and Johnson used direct observation in a laboratory setting to learn about physiological changes during sexual arousal. (Their study remains the only major piece of research to do this.) The product was their widely acclaimed volume *Human Sexual Response* (1966), which was based on laboratory observations of 10,000 completed sexual response cycles (see Chapter 6).

Masters and Johnson began their research by studying a group of prostitutes (118 female and 27 male). It was assumed that "...study subjects from more conservative segments of the general population would not be available (a presumption which later proved to be entirely false)" (1966, p.10). Accordingly, they turned to the one obviously available group—professional prostitutes. However, they quickly decided prostitutes were not suitable subjects, for two reasons. First, the prostitutes tended to move from one city to another frequently, a fact that discouraged study over extended periods of time. Second, female prostitutes often develop a state of chronic pelvic congestion due to repeated sexual arousal without orgasm. As a result, their physiosexual responses were somewhat different from those of other women.

Their final research population was obtained by spreading the word in the academic community of Washington University in St. Louis that they were interested in studying normal volunteers. The response was quite enthusiastic. From 1273 who applied, Masters and Johnson selected 382 women and 312 men. They excluded those unable to respond sexually and anyone who showed signs of emotional instability or exhibitionistic tendencies. Their final sample was thus composed of sexually responsive volunteers, drawn largely from an academic community, with above average intelligence and socioeconomic background—obviously not a proba-

Virginia Johnson and William Masters.

bility sample. However, the physical signs of sexual arousal, the subject of their study, appear to be rather stable across a wide range of people with diverse backgrounds.

Masters and Johnson used a number of techniques to record physiological sexual responses. These included the use of photographic equipment and instruments to measure and record muscular and vascular changes throughout the body. Direct observation was also employed to record changes in the primary and secondary sex organs. An ingenious artificial coition machine was designed to record changes that had never before been observed in the internal female sex structures. It was equipped with an artificial penis that could be controlled voluntarily for size and for depth and rapidity of thrust. It was constructed from clear plastic and contained photographic equipment capable of recording changes in the vagina and lower portion of the uterus during sexual arousal. Masters and Johnson recorded responses in a variety of stimulus situations in their laboratory—masturbation, coitus with a partner, artificial coition, and stimulation of the breasts alone. As a follow-up to all recorded observations, each individual participant was extensively interviewed.

Employing this observational approach, Masters and Johnson obtained a wealth of information about the manner in which women and men respond physiologically to sexual stimulation (which is outlined in detail in Chapter 6). Some have suggested that their conclusions are limited because of the artificial nature of laboratory observations. While there may be some merit to this conclusion, time has nevertheless demonstrated that their research findings can be beneficially applied to such areas as sex therapy, infertility counseling, conception control, and general sex education.

While Masters and Johnson are perhaps most acclaimed for their study of human sexual response, they have also contributed information in two additional areas of human sexual behavior: sexual problems and homosexuality. In 1970 they published *Human Sexual Inadequacy*, an outline of the rationale, methods, and successes of a variety of strategies for treating sexual difficulties. In this book, Masters and Johnson reported that only 20% of their patients failed to improve after two weeks of therapy. This was generally interpreted to mean they were curing 80% of their cases in a very short time span, a truly impressive success story.

Their claims went virtually unchallenged for the next decade until two psychologists, Bernie Zilbergeld and Michael Evans (1980) published an incisive critique of their work. This critical review was stimulated, at least in part, by Evans' discovery that he could not find out enough about Masters and Johnson's research methodology to replicate their study with a different population. *Replicability* is an important feature of research. That is, original research must be described in a clear fashion to allow for repeat experiments. Then, other researchers can replicate the study, using the same methodology, to see if similar results can be obtained. Without any hope of conducting valid replication studies, Zilbergeld and Evans chose to make a close examination of the methodology of Masters and Johnson's second major research endeavor. It will be instructive for us to look at a brief synopsis of their criticisms.

It was impossible to determine how Masters and Johnson assessed the outcome of their therapeutic treatments. They did not try to measure success, only failure, and their definition of failure was vague and inexact: "Initial failure is defined as indication that the two-week rapid-treatment phase has failed to initiate reversal of the basic symptomatology of sexual dysfunction. . . ." (p. 352). What exactly did they mean by "initiate reversal"? Apparently, no one has been able to determine this. Without clearly defined criteria of success or failure, replication is impossible and the reliability of their outcome statistics must be questioned. In addition, since we do not know how Masters and Johnson screened applicants and how many were rejected, it is difficult to compare their results to those obtained by other investigators with different treatment populations.

Masters and Johnson report a very low relapse rate of 7%, based on a five-year follow-up of nonfailure patients. However, this figure is also difficult to interpret since they do not specify what criteria constitute a relapse. Furthermore, follow-up data were obtained on only a limited number of cases (35% of the nonfailure group).

In 1979 Masters and Johnson published *Homosexuality in Perspective*, a book that reports their investigation of homosexual behavior over a 15-year period. In the first half of this volume they compare the sexual functioning of homosexual and heterosexual individuals as assessed by observational techniques comparable to those outlined in *Human Sexual Response* (1966). They reported observing no significant differences between homosexuals and heterosexuals in their capacity to respond to effective sexual stimulation. (For example, participants in each group seemed comparable in their ability to reach orgasm.) They did find that members of the homosexual study group seemed to exhibit better sexual communication than their heterosexual counterparts during shared sexual activity. Furthermore, the homosexual couples generally exhibited a greater range of sexual activities with their partners than did the heterosexual couples. These findings, while certainly interesting and provocative, should be interpreted with caution since Masters and Johnson do not provide any relevant information about the subjects' sexual histories or the manner in which their sexual behaviors were rated.

The second half of *Homosexuality in Perspective* reports Masters and Johnson's treatment of troubled homosexuals, both those who wished to function better in homosexual relations and those who reportedly wished to change their sexual orientation to heterosexual. This portion of Masters and Johnson's research program with homosexuals contained many of the same methodological problems outlined earlier in our discussion of *Human Sexual Inadequacy*, including unclear criteria for subject selection and treatment assessment, plus no information about treatment strategies. This aspect of Masters and Johnson's research will be discussed further in Chapter 10.

Hunt

One of the most widely quoted contemporary studies of human sexual behavior is reported in a book written by Morton Hunt, *Sexual Behavior in the 1970s* (1974). It contains the results of a survey commissioned by the Playboy Foundation and conducted by the Research Guild, an independent market survey and behavioral research organization. The goal of the Hunt study, like that of Kinsey's research two decades earlier, was to obtain contemporary information about a broad range of adult human sexual behaviors. But this study failed to match the comprehensiveness and thoroughness of the Kinsey research in several important areas.

Hunt's sample was obtained by randomly selecting names from phone directories in twenty-four cities that supposedly represented the diversity of American urban centers. Although Hunt claimed that his final study group (1044 females and 982 males) closely represented the national population, the sample has been criticized. Serious questions have been raised, for instance, about self-selection biases. Of the original group of people who were telephoned and asked to participate in anonymous small-group discussions of sexual behavior, only 20% agreed to take part.

In addition, the methodology itself created problems. Selecting names from city phone books can easily lead to the underrepresentation of certain categories of people, including isolated rural dwellers and people who have no phones (for instance, the poor and illiterate, people living in institutions, and young dependents). The Research Guild made efforts to rectify part of this omission by interviewing an additional sample of young adults. However, the final survey group can hardly be viewed as representing a true probability sample.

Beyond the sampling methods and the problem of nonresponse, Hunt's survey has been criticized on other grounds. These have to do with the questionnaire and the way it was administered. At the conclusion of the small-group discussion, each individual was given a questionnaire to fill out anonymously. The number of questions on this form ranged from 1000 to 1200, depending on the number of items applicable to a given individual (four separate questionnaire forms were used: for unmarried women, married women, unmarried men, and married men). This is an incredible number of items for one person to answer, and it is questionable whether subjects could have really considered each point thoughtfully. Furthermore, the situation created by Hunt's research setting may itself have created some subject bias. To what degree did the preliminary group discussion affect the participants' responses? Certain group definitions of normality, acceptable sexual behavior, and so forth might have created considerable influence on the subjects' responses.

Despite its shortcomings, though, Hunt's analysis of the survey findings does contain some important information about the current sexual practices of adult Americans. Furthermore, by contrasting Hunt's findings with Kinsey's, we may get some idea of the degree of change over the last three decades in such areas as variety of coital positions used, incidence of extramarital involvements, number of premarital sex partners, and many other areas of sexual conduct.

The *Redbook* Report

The October 1974 issue of *Redbook* included a sixty-item multiple-choice questionnaire on female sexual attitudes and behavior. Over 100,000 women returned the questionnaire, and analysis of the results provided the basis for two subsequent articles in the September and October 1975 issues of the magazine. The complete results of this survey were eventually published in a book titled *The Redbook Report on Female Sexuality* (Tavris and Sadd, 1977).

The certainty of anonymity was well established because responses were mailed, without names or addresses, back to *Redbook*. In spite of its prodigious size, however, the study group cannot be viewed as a random sample of all American women. Groups who were underrepresented included all those who were not likely to read the magazine—namely, women with low family incomes, women who had not finished high school, women over fifty years of age, nonwhite women, and unmarried women. Beyond the bias created by the magazine's limited audience, the ever-present problem of volunteer self-selection bias probably had some effect, too. Did the women who voluntarily filled out and returned the questionnaire differ greatly from those who chose not to do so?

Despite sample problems and possible volunteer bias, the *Redbook* survey is noteworthy because of its sample size. Some of its findings include the following. The majority of married women reported that they were active sex partners (initiating sexual encounters and being active during relations); oral-genital sex was almost universally experienced; 7 out of 10 respondents reported sex with their husbands to be "good" or "very good"; the more religious a woman was, the more satisfied she seemed to be with her marital sexual relations; 3 out of 10 had had intercourse after smoking marijuana; one-third had experienced extramarital intercourse; and finally, 4% had had a sexual experience with another woman by the age of forty.

Data about women who had not been married revealed that 90% had experienced intercourse. In addition, strongly religious women were less likely than others to have experienced intercourse or to have cohabited with a man; and the younger a woman was when she had premarital intercourse, the more likely she was to have extramarital intercourse.

Shortly after *Redbook* published the results of its survey, Shere Hite published her bestseller *The Hite Report* (1976), which records the detailed responses of 3019 women to an approximately sixty-item, essay-type questionnaire. Hite's topic was the same as that of the *Redbook* survey—female sexuality.

The *Hite Report* on female sexuality has been described as a nationwide study. In the sense that responses to her questionnaire came from all over America, this is an accurate statement. However, it would be inappropriate to conclude that her subjects are a representative sample of American women. In fact, they represent a very limited and perhaps quite biased sample. Her sources for respondents were several magazines and organizations. Some people responded to notices in *The Village Voice, Mademoiselle, Brides,* and *Ms.* magazines and wrote for the questionnaire. *Oui* magazine published the entire questionnaire. Mailings to women's organizations and church organizations were also utilized. *The Hite Report* is similar to the *Redbook* survey in terms of the possibility of volunteer bias and in protection of anonymity because, again, responses were mailed. The obvious sampling limitations and possible subject bias present in Hite's research strongly suggest that her findings should be interpreted with considerable caution. Nevertheless, her report has provided valuable information about how some women view sex and consequently offers important insights into female sexuality.

One major finding of Hite's report was that clitoral stimulation (whether direct, through self-stimulation, partner's manual stimulation, oral-genital stimulation, or more indirect, through pressure against the public bone during intercourse) is very important to sexual arousal and orgasm for the vast majority of the women in the survey. Second, many women reported having faked orgasm. A third important finding was that there is great diversity in female sexuality.

Comparing *The Hite Report* and the *Redbook* Report   There are several important differences between the *Redbook* report and *The Hite Report*. The objective of *Redbook* was to examine to what extent sexual practices of women have changed since Kinsey's research. *The Hite Report's* objective was to find out about specific sexual behaviors and to explore women's in-depth feelings about sexuality. These different intentions are reflected by the format of the questionnaires: *Redbook*'s had multiple-choice questions, and Hite's had essay-type questions. Sample questions about orgasm reflect the differences. *Redbook* asked "Do you achieve orgasm . . . A. All the time? B. Most of the time? C. Sometimes? D. Once in a while? E. Never? F. Don't know?" (1975, p. 51). Hite asked "In most of your sexual encounters, does your orgasm(s) usually occur during cunnilingus, manual clitoral stimulation, intercourse, or other activity? Which of these activities usually lead to orgasm? How often?" (1976, p. 585). As a result of these differences, *Redbook* responses can be more definitively analyzed statistically, and the Hite results provide a rich narrative about many aspects of women's sexuality. A substantial portion of Hite's book is composed of personal accounts. Since Hite and *Redbook* asked questions in very different ways, much of the data are impossible to compare directly.

Although the format and perspective of the questions were different, many similar topic areas were covered in the two reports: attitudes and behaviors concerning masturbation, intercourse, oral sex, and sexual relations with women. Each report also emphasized certain areas not dealt with by the other. *Redbook* examined premarital and extramarital intercourse, marijuana use during sexual relations, marital happiness, and the effect of the strength of religious convictions. Hite explored attitudes towards the "sexual revolution," examined techniques of masturbation, and sought information about arousal and orgasm during intercourse and nonintercourse activities.

Given the difference in sources for volunteer subjects, it is likely that *Redbook* respondents would be more "conservative" and Hite respondents more "liberal." A reflection of this difference is that 90% of *Redbook* respondents and about 35% of Hite respondents were married. *Redbook*'s ratio of married to unmarried women is higher than the 70% national average and Hite's is lower. Kinsey (1953) found that marital status was related to orgasmic response, and this factor may contribute to differences. Additionally, a higher percentage of Hite's respondents had had sexual experiences with other women or were currently in same-sex sexual relationships.

Both of these studies give us some valuable information. The fact that they surveyed somewhat different populations using different types of questions provides us with what may be a more composite picture of female sexuality—as well as making an important commentary that research technique and subject selection influence research findings.

The Hite Report on Male Sexuality

In 1981 Shere Hite published *The Hite Report on Male Sexuality*, which records the responses of 7239 men to an essay-type questionnaire. Like the participants in Hite's study of female sexuality, the respondents in this investigation were far from representing a true probability sample of American men. The group consisted largely of men who answered versions of the questionnaire reprinted in magazines like *Penthouse* or who wrote for the questionnaire because they were aware of Hite's work through previous publications or her frequent appearances on television and radio. Of the 119,000 questionnaires distributed, only 7239 were returned, a fact that strongly suggests the possibility of volunteer bias. The educational levels of her respondents were much higher than the national average. One critic of her research sample suggested that "Her respondents seem to be mainly a sexual avant-garde" (Robinson, 1981, p. 81).

The text of her report is so devoid of consistently reported statistical data that it is almost impossible to make meaningful quantitative differentiations among the responses. More than 90% of the book consists of quotations from her male respondents. However, in spite of the probable sample bias and statistical limitations of this report, it does provide some insights into how men experience their sexuality.

Sorenson

An important study of adolescent sexual behavior was conducted in the early seventies by Robert Sorenson, a social psychologist. The results were published in

1973 in a volume titled *Adolescent Sexuality in Contemporary America.* The scope of this study was not as ambitious as that of the Kinsey surveys, but within the narrower target population, relatively good sampling procedures were employed. Initially, 2042 households were randomly selected from 200 urban, suburban, and rural areas throughout the continental United States. This sample yielded a potential group of 839 adolescents within the designated age range of 13 to 19. If all had agreed to fill out Sorenson's questionnaire, the final study group would have been a true probability sample.

However, the design of the study required obtaining written permission first from the parents and then from the respondents. Forty percent of the parents refused to provide their consent. Of the remaining adolescents, roughly one quarter decided not to participate. Thus the final sample contained 411 of the originally selected 839 adolescents. Here again, the problem of self-selection is apparent. Did the nonparticipants—roughly 50%—differ in important ways from those who filled out the questionnaire? And what kind of relationship existed between parental restrictiveness (as might be suggested by refusals) and children's sex attitudes? As always, we can only speculate.

Another problem with Sorenson's research lies in the excessive length of the questionnaire, which was thirty-eight pages long. How many questions can a subject answer alertly? It is possible that some of the subjects may not have carefully considered all the items, particularly those contained in the later pages. Nevertheless, the Sorenson research has some strengths, including the application of basically sound methodology and a commitment to survey a broad range of adolescent sexual behaviors (including activities like petting, masturbation, coitus, and homosexual contact). His finding that 45% of his female participants and about 60% of the males reported having premarital coitus by age 19 is particularly noteworthy (see Chapter 13).

Zelnick and Kantner

In 1971, 1976, and 1979, the U.S. government sponsored national sex surveys aimed at evaluating pregnancy, the use of contraceptives, and premarital sexual activity among young, unmarried American females. The research was directed and reported by two Johns Hopkins researchers, Melvin Zelnick and John Kantner (1977, 1980). Probability sampling techniques were employed to select a subject population of several hundred women in the United States between the ages of 15 and 19. (The 1979 survey included young men, ages 17–21.) The use of a well-constructed questionnaire to assess sexual behaviors and attitudes among a relatively representative sample of American adolescent women makes this research particularly valuable. However, its results are limited by the narrow study population (teenage women) and the restricted range of behaviors evaluated.

Perhaps most noteworthy of Zelnick and Kantner's findings is the fact that by 1976, three years after the publication of Sorenson's findings, the number of 19-year-old females reporting premarital coitus had risen to 55% (an increase of 10% over Sorenson's reported figure). By 1979 this figure had risen to 69%. Zelnick and Kantner also reported a rise in the proportion of all teenage women who have become pregnant before marriage—9% in 1971 compared with 13% in 1976 and 16% in 1979.

Bell and Weinberg

Alan Bell and Martin Weinberg's *Homosexualities: A Study of Diversities Among Men and Women* (1978) was the product of a study originally commissioned a decade earlier by the National Institute of Mental Health. It was an ambitious project, the most comprehensive study of homosexuality to date.

The research team, headed by Bell and Weinberg, used extensive face-to-face, four-hour interviews to survey the sexual practices of homosexual men and women. The study group was recruited in the San Francisco area from a variety of sources, including public advertising, gay bars, personal contacts, gay baths, homophile organizations, and public places (theaters, restaurants, and so forth). The final sample of homosexual individuals contained a large number (979) of men and women, blacks and whites, from a wide range of age, educational, and occupational levels. For comparative purposes, random probability sampling was employed to select a group of 477 heterosexuals who matched the homosexual respondents in terms of race, sex, age, occupation, and education. Most of the interviews for both groups were conducted by well-trained graduate students from universities in the San Francisco area.

The sample of homosexual individuals, although quite large, has been criticized as systematically biased by its manner of selection. Individuals who frequent gay bars, join homophile organizations, or openly acknowledge their homosexuality may not be entirely representative of the general homosexual population. Bell and Weinberg freely acknowledged that the study group was not a random sample.

The nonrepresentative nature of other investigators' samples as well as of our own precludes any generalization about the incidence of a particular phenomenon even to persons living in the locale where the interviews were conducted, much less to homosexuals in general. Nowhere has a random sample of American homosexual men and women ever been obtained, and given the variety of circumstances which discourage homosexuals from participating in research studies, it is unlikely that any investigator will ever be in a position to say that this or that is true of a given percentage of all homosexuals. (p. 22)

In spite of the sample's limitations, though, the Bell and Weinberg report is the most comprehensive examination of homosexual life styles to date. It is an important contribution to the literature, in an often sensationalized and misunderstood area of human experience.

To gain additional insight into the mechanisms by which people form their sexual orientation, Bell and Weinberg, in collaboration with researcher Sue Kiefer Hammersmith, employed sophisticated statistical techniques to analyze the data collected from their sample of 979 homosexuals and 477 heterosexuals. The results of this effort, which put to the test popular theories about the development of sexual orientation, were published in 1981 in a book titled *Sexual Preference: Its Develop-*

ment in Men and Women. In this excellent volume, the authors report that sexual orientation appears to be little influenced by parenting practices or other psychosocial factors. Rather, they suggest the possibility of a biological basis for sexual orientation, although they are unable to pinpoint causal factors. We will examine the various aspects of this important research on homosexuality and the development of sexual orientation in more detail in Chapter 10.

WHAT TO BELIEVE?
A STATEMENT OF PERSPECTIVE

The preceding discussion of the methods and problems of sex research may have left you with some unanswered questions. To what degree can we rely upon the wide array of data introduced in the chapters that follow? We have learned that sex research is often hindered by difficulties in obtaining representative samples and accurate information. We have also seen that sex researchers have shown remarkable versatility in their efforts, using many different approaches to data collection. Thus, a major strength of sex research is its reliance on a wide assortment of methodological techniques.

We believe that any serious student of sex behavior would do well to differentiate between nonscientific polls and opinions and the results of scientific research conducted by serious-minded investigators. However, even in the case of carefully planned investigations, it is desirable to maintain a critical eye and to avoid the tendency many of us have to believe something just because it is "scientific." You may find the following checklist of questions useful in evaluating any particular piece of research:

1. Who conducted the research? Are they considered to be reputable professionals?
2. What type of methodology was employed? Were scientific principles adhered to?
3. How large was the sample group, and is there any reason to suspect bias in the selection of subjects?
4. Can the results be applied to individuals other than those in the sample group? How broad can these generalizations be and still remain legitimate?
5. Is it possible that the method used to obtain information may have biased the findings? (Did the questionnaire promote false replies? Did the cameras place limitations on the response potentials? And so forth.)
6. Have there been any other published reports that confirm or contradict the particular study in question?

Keeping questions like these in mind is valuable in finding a middle ground between absolute trust and offhand dismissal of a given research study.

SUMMARY

RESEARCH METHODS

1. Most information about human sexual behavior has been obtained through questionnaire or interview surveys of relatively large populations of respondents. Questionnaires have the advantage of being anonymous, inexpensive, and quickly administered. Interviews are more flexible and allow for more rapport between the researcher and the subject.

2. Sex researchers who use surveys share certain common problems. These include:
   - The virtual impossibility of getting 100% participation of randomly selected subjects. (There has not yet been a true probability sample survey.)
   - Biases created by nonresponse: Do volunteer participants have significantly different attitudes and behaviors from nonparticipants?
   - Demographic biases: Most samples are heavily weighted toward white, middle-class, better-educated Americans.
   - The problem of accuracy: Respondents' self-reports may be less than accurate due to limitations of memory, boastfulness, guilt, or simple misunderstandings.

3. Another way of studying sexuality is the case study. Case studies typically produce a great deal of information about one or a few individuals. They have two great advantages: flexibility, and the opportunity to explore specific behaviors and feelings in depth. Poor sampling techniques often limit the possibility of making generalizations to broad populations.

4. There is very little direct-observation sex research, due to the highly personal nature of the topic. When it can be done, observation significantly reduces the possibility of data falsification. However, subjects' behavior may be altered by the presence of an observer. Furthermore, the reliability of recorded observations may sometimes be compromised by preexisting researcher biases.

5. Experimental research, while infrequently employed in investigations of human sexual behavior, offers two advantages: control over the relevant variables, and direct analysis of potentially causal factors. However, the artificial nature of the experimental laboratory setting may alter subject responses from those that might occur out of the experimental setting.

SPECIFIC STUDIES

6. The Kinsey surveys remain the most ambitious, broad-scale, taxonomic studies of human sexual behavior. They were somewhat limited by sampling techniques that resulted in overrepresentation of young, educated, city-dwelling individuals.

7. The laboratory observation research of Masters and Johnson provided excellent information about the physiosexual responses of women and men. In spite of the fact that their study population was biased toward high education and socioeconomic levels, their findings have broad application to the general population. Their subsequently reported studies of sexual problems and homosexuality are difficult to interpret because of methodological errors and imprecise reporting.

8. Morton Hunt's survey of sexual behavior in the 1970s was compromised by several limitations, including poor sampling techniques, strong self-selection bias, and excessive questionnaire length. The major strength of the Hunt research lies in the comprehensiveness with which it explored a broad range of human sexual behaviors.

9. The *Redbook* survey utilized a huge sample of women who answered questions about female sexuality. But since the sample consisted of volunteers drawn mostly from the magazine's readership, it cannot be considered a probability sample.

10. Shere Hite's observations of female and male sexual behavior, while obtained from biased samples, provide several valuable insights into human sexuality.

11. Robert Sorenson provided an important study of adolescent sexual behavior, broader in scope than the Zelnick and Kantner surveys but more limited by sampling bias and excessive questionnaire length.

12. Zelnick and Kantner provided survey data pertaining to the sexual activity of American teenage women in 1971, 1976, and 1979. Good sampling techniques and research methodology make this investigation particularly valuable.

13. The most ambitious study to date of homosexual people was conducted by a research team headed by Alan Bell and Martin Weinberg. Their research population was biased by sampling difficulties.

SUGGESTED READINGS

Brecher, Edward. *The Sex Researchers*. New York: Signet, 1969. An easy-to-read account of sex researchers and their findings. Provides a behind-the-scenes perspective and some interesting historical anecdotes.

Brecher, Ruth, and Brecher, Edward. *An Analysis of Human Sexual Response*. New York: New American Library, 1966. In addition to detailing the work of Masters and Johnson, this highly readable book deals with sex research in general, particularly emphasizing its practical applications and its impact on society.

Bullough, V. *The Frontiers of Sex Research*. Buffalo, N.Y.: Prometheus, 1979. An overview of research into various fields of sexuality. Contains several excellent articles dealing with the issues and implications of sex research.

Elias, Veronica. "A Cautionary Note on Sex Studies." *The Humanist*, March/April 1978, 23–25. A thoughtful discussion of the tendencies of some sex researchers to make unwarranted interpretations of their findings. The author urges readers to use caution in interpreting sex research findings.

Pomeroy, Wardell. *Dr. Kinsey and the Institute for Sex Research*. New York: Harper & Row, 1972. An informed and entertaining look at Kinsey and his research as seen through the "insider" eyes of one of his original research colleagues.

PART TWO

Biological Basis

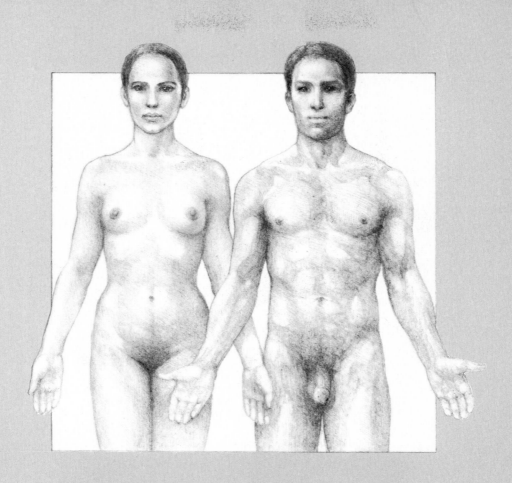

4

Female Sexual Anatomy and Physiology

GENITAL SELF-EXAM
THE VULVA
    The Mons Veneris
    The Labia Majora
    The Labia Minora
    The Clitoris
    The Vestibule
    The Urethral Opening
    The Introitus and the Hymen
    The Perineum
UNDERLYING STRUCTURES
INTERNAL STRUCTURES
    The Vagina
    The Cervix
    The Uterus
    The Fallopian Tubes
    The Ovaries
    Surgical Removal of the Uterus and Ovaries
THE BREASTS
    Breast Self-Exam
    Breast Lumps
MENSTRUATION
    Menstrual Physiology
    Sexual Activity and the Menstrual Cycle
    Menstruation: Mood and Performance
    Menstrual Cycle Problems
    Toxic Shock Syndrome
SUMMARY
SUGGESTED READINGS

I had three children and was 45 years old before I ever really looked at my genitals. I was amazed at the delicate shapes and subtle colors. I'm sorry it took me so long to do this because I now feel more sure of myself sexually after becoming more acquainted with *me*. (Authors' files)

*M*any women are as unacquainted with their genitals as this woman was. However, gaining knowledge and understanding of her body can be an important aspect of a woman's sexual well-being. This chapter presents a detailed description of all the female genital structures, external and internal. It is intended to be easy to use for reference, and we encourage women readers to do a self-exam as part of reading this chapter. We begin with a discussion of the genital self-exam and the external structures, followed by the underlying structures and the internal organs. The chapter closes with information about the breasts and menstruation.

GENITAL SELF-EXAM

We are born with curiosity about our bodies. In fact, physical self-awareness and exploration are important steps in a child's development. Unfortunately, many of us receive negative conditioning about the sexual parts of our bodies even from earliest childhood. We learn to think of our genitals as something "down there" that are not to be looked at, touched, or enjoyed. It is common for people to react with discomfort to the suggestion of a self-exam. A physician's experience, summarized in the following quotation, exemplifies the extent to which we sometimes learn to be alienated from our bodies:

Not infrequently when I ask a patient if she does her own breast exam, she replies "Oh, no! I would never touch myself there!" (Authors' files)

Betty Dodson, an erotic artist and the author of *Liberating Masturbation* (1974), stresses the importance of women *un*learning negative attitudes. Although she is speaking specifically of women, this can also apply to men:

Many women feel that their genitals are ugly, funny looking, disgusting, smelly and not at all desirable—certainly not a beautiful part of their bodies. A woman who feels this way is certainly going to have reservations about sharing her genitals intimately with anyone. We therefore need to become very aware of our genitals. (p. 18)

The following paragraphs describe a self-exploration exercise designed to help you become more aware of your genitals. Some readers may choose to read about the exercises but not do them. Others may wish to try some or all of the steps. If you choose to do the exploration you may experience a variety of feelings. Some people feel selfish for spending time on themselves. You may find it difficult to remain focused on the experience instead of thinking about daily concerns. The exercises may be enjoyable for some people and not for others. Primarily, they provide an opportunity to learn about yourself—your body and your feelings.

FIGURE 4.1 FEMALE GENITAL SELF-EXAMINATION

Routine self-examination is an aspect of preventive health care.

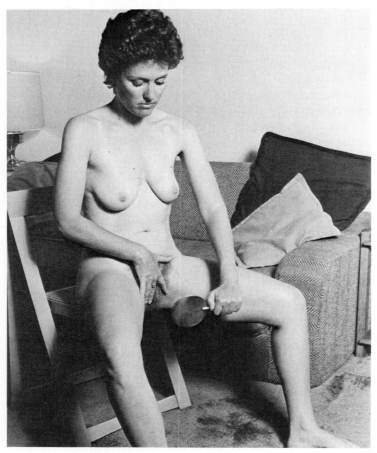

The exercises serve another purpose as well. Besides helping us feel more comfortable with our anatomy and sexuality, periodic self-examinations, particularly of the genitals, can augment routine medical care. (For this reason, we have included other specific suggestions for self-exams throughout the text.) For self-examinations to be most effective, it is best to do them regularly, at least once a month: people who know what is normal for their own bodies can often detect small changes and pursue medical attention promptly. Problems detected early usually require less extensive treatment. If you discover any changes, consult a competent physician immediately. *Gynecology* is the specialty for female sexual and reproductive anatomy.

To begin, look at your genitals thoroughly. Use a hand mirror, perhaps in combination with a full-length mirror, to look at them from different angles and postures—standing, sitting, lying down (Figure 4.1). Notice colors, shapes, and textures. As you are looking, try to become aware of whatever feelings you have about your genital anatomy. You may find it helpful to draw a picture of them and label the parts (these are identified in Figure 4.2).

In addition to visual examination, use your fingers to explore the various surfaces of your genitals. Focus on the sensations produced by the different kinds of touching. Note which areas are most sensitive and how the nature of stimulation may vary from place to place. The primary purpose of this exercise is to explore, not to become sexually aroused. If, however, during this time of self-exploration you become sexually excited, you may be able to notice changes in sensitivity of skin areas that occur with arousal.

After completing an initial self-exploration, you may want to repeat all or parts of the exercises to become even more familiar and comfortable with your body. Women have different kinds of reactions to looking at their vulvas; these reactions include:

I don't find it to be an attractive part of my body. I wouldn't go as far as to call it ugly. I think it would be easier to accept if it was something you weren't taught to hide and think was dirty, but I've never been able to understand why men find the vulva so intriguing. (Authors' files)

I've only looked once, and it seems almost like a foreign object. (Authors' files)

I think vulvas are pieces of art. (Authors' files)

I think it looks very sensuous; the tissues look soft and tender. I was told by a previous partner that my vulva was very beautiful. His comment made me feel good about my body. (Authors' files)

THE VULVA

The *vulva* refers to all of the external genital structures—the hair, the folds of skin, and the urinary and vaginal openings. Even though *vulva* is a clinical term, it seems to be less impersonal than other technical words, and it lacks the derogatory connotations of street language. Vulva will be the term most frequently used in this text when we refer to the external genitals of the female. We will discuss the several parts and their functions one at a time. For reference and identification, see Figure 4.2.

The appearance of the vulva has been likened to that of certain flowers, seashells, and other forms found in nature. Vulvalike shapes have been used in artwork, including "The Dinner Party" by Judy Chicago. This work consists of thirty-nine ceramic plates and corresponding needlework runners representing significant women in history. Many of the plates resemble vulval shapes.

The Mons Veneris

Translated from Latin, *mons veneris* means "the mound of Venus." Venus was the Roman goddess of love and beauty. The mons is the area covering the pubic bone. It consists of pads of fatty tissue between the bone and the skin. Touch and pressure on the mons can be sexually pleasurable due to the presence of numerous nerve endings.

FIGURE 4.2 STRUCTURES AND VARIATIONS OF THE VULVA

The vulva: (a) external structures and (b)–(d) different shapes. There are many normal variations in shapes of external female genitalia. (b) and (c) The vulvas are unopened; (c) shows gray and black pubic hair of an older woman. (d) The vulva is spread open, giving an unobstructed view of the clitoral glans.

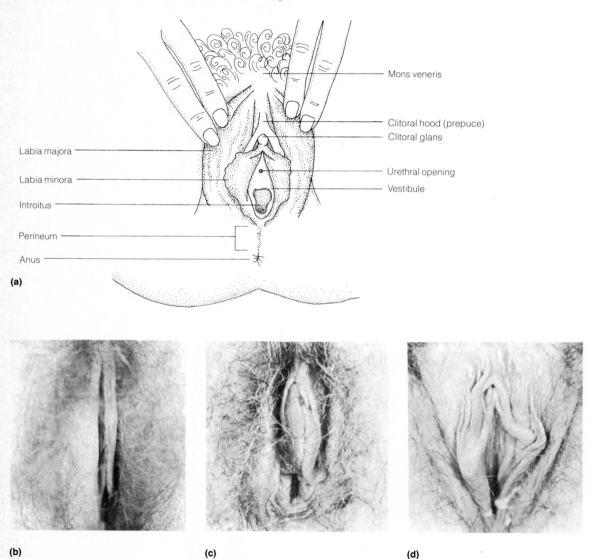

(a)

(b)   (c)   (d)

At puberty, the mons becomes covered with hair that varies in color, texture, and thickness from woman to woman. Sometimes, women are concerned about these differences:

I always felt uncomfortable in college physical education classes because I had very thick, dark, pubic hair, more so than most other women. One day my best friend and I were talking and she mentioned that she felt self-conscious in the showers after physical education class because her pubic hair was light-colored and sparse. I told her my concerns. We laughed and both decided to stop worrying about it. (Authors' files)

During sexual arousal the scent that accompanies vaginal secretions is held by the pubic hair and can add to sensory erotic pleasure.

The Labia Majora

The *labia majora,* or outer lips, extend downward from the mons on each side of the vulva. They begin next to the thigh and extend inward, surrounding the labia minora and the urethral and vaginal openings. Next to the thigh, the outer lips are covered with pubic hair; the inner parts of these lips, next to the labia minora, are hairless. The skin of the labia majora is usually darker than the skin of the thighs. The nerve endings and underlying fatty tissue are similar to those in the mons.

The Labia Minora

The *labia minora,* or inner lips, are located within the outer lips and often protrude between the labia majora. They are hairless folds of skin that join at the *prepuce* (or clitoral hood) over the clitoris and extend downward past the urinary and vaginal openings. They contain sweat and oil glands, extensive blood vessels, and nerve endings. They also vary considerably in size, shape, and color from woman to woman, as Figure 4.2 shows. In the Hottentot culture of Africa, pendulous labia are considered a sign of beauty and women commence pulling on them early in childhood in an effort to increase their size.

The Clitoris

The *clitoris* is comprised of the external *shaft* and *glans* and the internal *crura.* The shaft and glans are located just below the mons area where the inner lips converge. They are covered by the clitoral hood, or *prepuce.* Genital secretions, skin cells, and bacteria combine to form *smegma* that may accumulate under the hood and occasionally form lumps and cause pain during sexual arousal or activity. Smegma can be prevented from collecting in this area by drawing back the hood when washing the vulva. If the smegma is already formed, it can be removed by a health-care practitioner.

The shaft itself can be felt and its shape can be seen under the hood. It contains two small spongy bodies called the cavernous bodies. These become the crura (internal leglike stalks) as they extend into the pelvic cavity.

The glans is also often not visible under the hood, but it can be seen if a woman gently parts the labia minora and retracts the clitoral hood as in Figure 4.2. The glans looks smooth, rounded, and slightly translucent. Initially, it may be easier for a woman to locate her clitoris by touch rather than sight because of its sensitive nerve endings and small size. The external part of the clitoris, although tiny, has about the same number of nerve endings as the penis; the glans in particular is highly sensitive. With other factors conducive to sexual arousal present, some women find that the entire sexual response cycle can be set in motion and maintained to orgasm by light stimulation of the glans alone (Sherfey, 1972). The glans is so sensitive that women usually stimulate this area with the hood covering it, and avoid direct stimulation.

Research into female masturbation patterns has produced findings in keeping with the physiological data about the location and concentrations of nerve endings. As we will see in Chapter 9, clitoral stimulation, and not vaginal insertion, is the most common way women produce arousal and orgasm during self-stimulation.

While other sexual organs have additional functions of reproduction or the elimination of waste material, the only purpose of the clitoris is sexual arousal. The size, shape, and position of the clitoris varies from woman to woman. Although women are sometimes concerned that their clitorises are too small or too large, these normal differences have no known significant correlation to sexual arousal and functioning (Money, 1970). It is possible, though, that these factors may affect the amount of stimulation during coitus and influence arousal levels in this way.

A good deal of controversy has surrounded the role of the clitoris in sexual arousal and orgasm. Despite long-existing scientific knowledge about the highly concentrated nerve endings in the clitoris, the erroneous belief that vaginal rather than clitoral stimulation is—or should be—exclusively responsible for female sexual arousal and orgasm has persisted. However, there are relatively few nerve endings in the vagina as compared with the clitoris. There are some nerve endings that respond to touch in the outer third of the vagina, and almost none are present in the inner two-thirds. (This is why women do not feel tampons or diaphragms when they are in place correctly in the vagina, and some vaginal surgeries are painlessly performed without anesthesia.) However, many women do find the pressure and stretching sensations during intercourse to be highly pleasurable.

The Vestibule

The *vestibule* is the area of the vulva inside the labia minora. It is rich in blood vessels and nerve endings, and the tissues are sensitive to touch. In architectural terminology, the word vestibule refers to the entryway of a house. In the genital area, both the urinary and vaginal openings are located within it.

The Urethral Opening

Urine collected in the bladder passes out of the body through the urethral opening. The *urethra* is the short tube connecting the bladder to the urinary opening that is located between the clitoris and the vaginal opening.

Women sometimes develop bladder infections, or *cystitis*. In fact, some authorities believe that this ailment is the second most frequent illness in women after the common cold (Lapides, 1980). Cystitis is an inflammation of the bladder and can be caused by many things: damage to or irritation of the urethra from coitus, bacteria from one's hands or anus, or infectious agents from a partner's sexual organs (see Chapter 18 for a discussion of sexually transmitted diseases). Bladder infections often occur during periods of frequent intercourse with a new partner and are sometimes referred to as "honeymoon cystitis." The symptoms are usually intensely uncomfortable and include a frequent need to urinate, a severe burning sensation when urinating, blood or pus in the urine, and sometimes internal pain above the pubic bone. Medical treatment may include any of a variety of drugs, including sulfa and antibiotics. Observing a few routine precautions may help prevent cystitis; for example, careful wiping from front to back after both urination and bowel movements helps prevent bacteria from getting close to the urethra. Urinating immediately after intercourse also helps wash out bacteria. Women can use sterile lubricating jelly when vaginal lubrication is not sufficient, since irritated tissue is more susceptible to infection. For those who have frequent problems with cystitis, it can be helpful to drink plenty of liquids, especially cranberry juice, and avoid substances like coffee, tea, and alcohol that have an irritating effect on the bladder.

The Introitus and the Hymen

The opening of the vagina is referred to as the *introitus*. It is located between the urinary opening and the anus. Partially covering the introitus is a fold of tissue called the *hymen*, which is typically present at birth and usually remains intact until initial coitus. Occasionally, the tissue may be too thick to break easily during intercourse; it may then require a minor incision by a medical practitioner. In rare cases the hymen may completely cover the vaginal opening. Once a young woman begins to menstruate, this *imperforate hymen* causes the menstrual flow to collect inside the vagina. When this condition is discovered a medical practitioner can open the hymen with an incision.

Usually the vaginal opening is partially open and flexible enough to insert tampons before the hymen has been broken—contrary to the information provided by a high school physical education teacher in the 1960s:

I'll never forget the day in class when one of the girls asked the teacher if it was OK to use tampons. She replied, "No, it's up to your husband to make you not a virgin." (Authors' files)

Contrary to the preceding quote, a person is considered a virgin until she or he has experienced coitus. (And although cases have been rare, it is possible for a woman to become pregnant even if her hymen is still intact and she has not experienced penile penetration. If semen is placed on the labia minora, the sperm can swim from outside to inside the vagina and fertilize an ovum.)

Although the hymen may serve to protect the vaginal tissues early in life, it has no other known function. Nevertheless, many societies, including our own, have placed great significance on its presence or absence.* The following quote illustrates a

---

*Attitudes and behavior regarding virginity will be discussed further in Chapter 13.

perspective from our own society, from the experience of a woman who was an adolescent in the 1950s:

The hymen obsessed everyone, though it was never called by its proper name. It was referred to as your "innocence," your "purity," your "goodness," your "maiden-head," your "mark," as in "mark of Cain," and your "shield." . . . We were told that "men can tell" and warned not to wipe ourselves too hard, which led to untold confusion about the logistics of sexual congress. We were told everything about the hymen except where it is, what it is, and the whimsical fact that the human female shares this pearl beyond price with no other species of living creature except the elephant, the ass, and the pig. (King, 1976, p. 49)

In our society and many others, people have long believed that a woman's virginity can be proved by the pain and bleeding that may occur with initial coitus. This is not always true. Although pain or bleeding sometimes occur, the hymen can be partial, flexible, or thin enough for there to be no discomfort or bleeding; it may even remain intact after intercourse.

If a woman manually stretches her hymen before initial intercourse, she may be able to minimize the discomfort that sometimes occurs. To do this, she inserts a lubricated finger, using saliva or a sterile lubricant (such as K-Y jelly) into the vaginal opening and presses downward toward the anus until she feels some stretching. After holding this for a few seconds she releases the pressure and relaxes. This is repeated several times. The next step is to insert two fingers into the vagina and stretch the sides of the vagina by opening both fingers. The downward stretching is repeated with both fingers as well.

The Perineum

The *perineum* is the area of smooth skin between the vaginal opening and the anus (the sphincter through which bowel movements pass). The perineal tissue is endowed with nerve endings and is sensitive to the touch.

During childbirth an incision called an episiotomy is sometimes made in the perineum to prevent the ragged tearing of tissues that may happen during delivery. Many medical practitioners believe this incision is essential. Other health-care specialists disagree. We will consider this issue in more detail in Chapter 12.

UNDERLYING STRUCTURES

If the hair, skin, and fatty pads were removed from the vulva, several underlying structures could be seen (see Figure 4.3). The shaft of the clitoris would be visible, no longer concealed by the hood. Also detectable would be the crura, or roots, projecting inward from each side of the clitoral shaft. These bodies extend into the pelvic cavity, and they are part of the vast network of bulbs and vessels that engorge with blood during sexual arousal. The *vestibular bulbs* alongside the vagina also fill with blood

FIGURE 4.3 UNDERLYING STRUCTURES OF THE VULVA 95

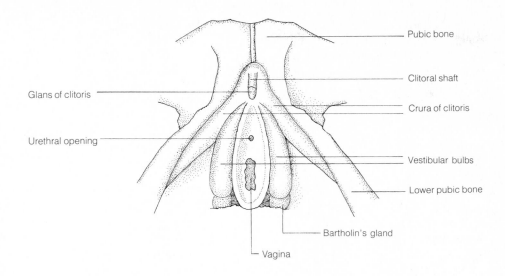

during sexual excitement and cause the vagina to increase in length and the vulvar area to become swollen.

The *Bartholin's glands* on each side of the vaginal opening were once believed to be the source of vaginal lubrication during sexual arousal; however, they typically produce only a drop or two of fluid just prior to orgasm. The glands are usually not noticeable, but sometimes the duct from the Bartholin's gland becomes clogged, and the fluid which is normally secreted remains inside and causes enlargement. If this occurs and the swelling does not go away within a few days, it is best to see a physician.

Besides the glands and network of vessels, a complex musculature underlies the genital area (see Figure 4.4). The pelvic floor muscles, called the *pubococcygeus* or *PC muscles*, have a multidirectional design that allows the vaginal opening to expand greatly during childbirth and to close afterwards.

These muscles contract involuntarily at orgasm; they also can be "trained" to contract voluntarily, through a series of exercises known as *Kegel exercises*. These exercises were developed by Arnold Kegel in 1952, as a way of helping women redevelop control of urination after childbirth. It is common for postpartum women (women who have recently delivered children) to lose urine when they cough or sneeze. This is due to the loss of muscle tone in the perineal area caused by the stress to the muscles during delivery. The exercises are effective in restoring muscle tone, and they have an additional bonus. Many women who practice the Kegel exercises regularly for about six weeks report an increase in sensation during intercourse, as well as in general genital sensitivity. This seems to be the result of the woman's increased awareness and sense of control of her sex organs, as well as her improved muscle tone.

FIGURE 4.4 UNDERLYING MUSCLES OF THE VULVA

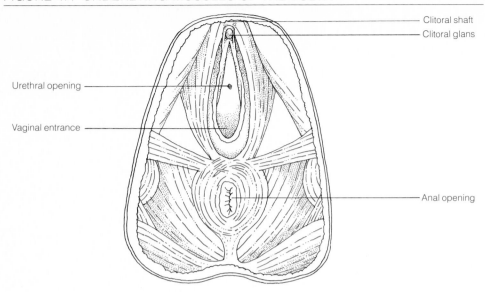

The steps for the Kegel exercises are:

1. Locate the muscles surrounding the vagina. This can be done by stopping the flow of urine to learn which muscles to contract. The muscles that control the flow of urine are the same muscles you contract during Kegel exercises.
2. Insert a finger into the opening of the vagina and contract these muscles. Feel them squeeze your finger.
3. Squeeze the same muscles for three seconds. Relax. Repeat.
4. Squeeze and release as rapidly as possible, 10 to 25 times. Repeat.
5. Imagine trying to suck something into your vagina. Hold for three seconds.
6. Push out as during a bowel movement, only with the vagina. Hold for three seconds.
7. Repeat exercises 3, 5, and 6 ten times each, and exercise 4 once. This series should be done three times a day. (Adapted from *For Yourself*, Barbach, 1975, pp. 54–55).

Unlike most exercises, Kegels can be done almost any time and any place—sitting in a class, at the dinner table, talking on the phone, or during sexual interaction. Some women find the exercises themselves to be pleasurable. As one woman reported:

Kegels are the only exercises I know of that feel good both during and after. (Authors' files)

The exercises have often been reported to have many other beneficial effects. These include increased vaginal lubrication during sexual arousal, relief of constipation, increased flexibility of episiotomy scars, and enhanced pleasure of the male partner during intercourse (Hartman and Fithian, 1974).

Internal female sexual anatomy consists of the vagina, cervix, uterus, and ovaries. These will be discussed in the following sections. Refer to Figure 4.5 for a cross-section of the female pelvis.

The Vagina

The *vagina* opens between the labia minora and extends into the body, angling upward toward the small of the back. Women who are unfamiliar with their anatomy may experience difficulties when they first try inserting tampons:

No matter how hard I tried, I couldn't get a tampon in until I inserted a finger and realized that my vagina slanted backwards. I had been pushing straight up onto the upper wall. (Authors' files)

The nonaroused vagina is approximately three to five inches in length. The walls form a flat tube. The analogy of a glove is often used to illustrate the vagina as a potential rather than actual space, with its walls able to expand enough to serve as a birth passage. In addition, the vagina changes in size and shape during sexual arousal, as outlined in Chapter 6.

FIGURE 4.5 INTERNAL FEMALE SEXUAL ANATOMY

Cross-section side view of female internal structures.

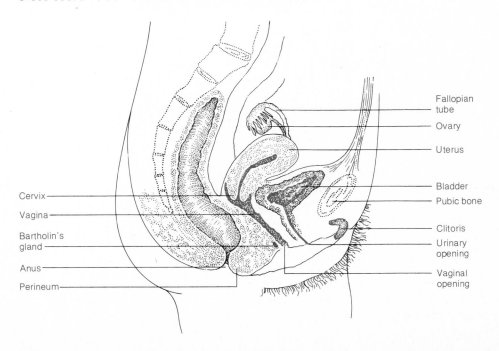

Cervix

Vagina

Bartholin's gland

Anus

Perineum

Fallopian tube

Ovary

Uterus

Bladder

Pubic bone

Clitoris

Urinary opening

Vaginal opening

The vagina contains three layers of tissue: mucous, muscle, and fibrous tissue. All these layers are richly endowed with blood vessels. The *mucosa* is the layer of mucous membrane that a woman feels when she inserts a finger inside her vagina. The folded walls, or *rugae*, feel soft, moist, and warm, resembling the inside of one's mouth. The walls normally produce secretions that help to maintain the chemical balance of the vagina. During sexual arousal a lubricating substance exudes through the mucosa.

Most of the second layer, composed of muscle tissue, is concentrated around the opening region of the vagina. Because of the concentration of musculature in the outer one-third and the expansive ability of the inner two-thirds of the vagina, a situation often develops which can be at best, funny, and at worst, embarrassing. During headstands and certain yoga or coital positions when the pelvis is elevated, gravity causes the inner two-thirds to expand, thereby drawing air into the vagina. The outer muscles tighten, and the air trapped internally is forced back out through the tightened muscles. This creates a sound we usually associate with a different orifice. One student has suggested calling this "varting." The auditory component is identical to the common fart; however, the olfactory element is lacking, thereby distinguishing the two to the casual observer. Varting occurs in gym classes and bedrooms across the nation, and may be cause for great individual consternation:

I stopped taking gymnastics in high school because everytime I did a nice tuck-roll out of a headstand, pppppppppptttt! It was just too embarrassing. (Authors' files)

When I have intercourse on my back with my legs on his shoulders, invariably my vagina fills with air. I just don't know what to do when those sounds start happening except to say, "I promise, it's not the real thing," and laugh. Only laughing just makes them louder. (Authors' files)

When I lived in a sorority in college, one of my sisters had the amazing ability to do voluntary vaginal farts. She would sit upright, crosslegged, lift her abdominal muscles, then push them down and create that all too familiar sound. She could do this repeated times and provided us with great entertainment during finals week. I tried to master this skill myself, but wasn't coordinated enough. (Authors' files)

To our knowledge, this issue has never been included in public discussions of sexuality. However, Richard Pryor, a well-known comedian, is one of the few who have been daring enough to address the subject. He discusses how women are truly amazing in their ability to recover from almost any situation. The example he relates is an experience during intercourse when suddenly, without warning, "Blaaaat." The woman calmly looked at him and said, "She's talkin' to ya, baby!" We hope that this discussion of varting will help people feel more at ease if and when it occurs.

Surrounding the muscular layer is the final vaginal layer. This is composed of fibrous tissue. It aids in vaginal contraction and expansion, and it acts as connective tissue to other structures in the pelvic cavity.

Arousal and Vaginal Lubrication So far in this chapter we have been describing the parts of the female sexual anatomy, but we have said relatively little about how these structures function. Since lubrication is a unique feature of the vagina, it will be presented here. Other physiological aspects of female arousal will be discussed in Chapter 6.

During sexual arousal a clear, slippery fluid begins to appear on the vaginal mucosa within 10 to 30 seconds after effective physical or psychological stimulation begins. Lubrication is the first physiological sign of sexual arousal in women, and it occurs primarily in the early phase of sexual response.

The source of vaginal lubrication was firmly established by Masters and Johnson's laboratory research. A clear, phallus-shaped camera was inserted into the vagina, and filmed the internal changes. From their research, Masters and Johnson describe the process:

As sexual tensions rise, a "sweating" phenomenon may be observed developing on the walls of the vaginal barrel. Individual droplets of the transudation-like, mucoid material appear scattered throughout the rugae folds of the normal vaginal architecture. These individual droplets coalesce to form a smooth, glistening coating for the entire vaginal barrel. (Masters and Johnson, 1966, p. 69)

In the past, both the cervix and Bartholin's glands were believed to be the source of increased vaginal lubrication during sexual arousal. However, Masters and Johnson's research reveals that this lubrication is a result of *vasocongestion*, the pooling of blood in the pelvic area. During vasocongestion, the extensive network of blood vessels in the tissues surrounding the vagina engorge with blood. Clear fluid seeps from the congested tissues to the inside of the vaginal walls to form the characteristic slippery coating of the sexually aroused vagina. (This process is discussed further in Chapter 6.)

Vaginal lubrication is present on the internal walls before it is noticeable at the vaginal entrance. Some women, not understanding the normality of vaginal lubrication, have been concerned that something was wrong with them when it occurred:

When I came into my house after my first date with a lot of kissing and hugging, I noticed the wetness on my underwear. I was shocked and worried. I didn't know what it was and thought maybe I had some kind of disease. After it happened several more times, I realized it was related to being aroused. (Authors' files)

Vaginal lubrication serves two functions. First, it enhances the possibility of conception by helping to alkalinize the normally acidic vaginal chemical balance. Sperm are able to travel faster and survive longer in an alkaline environment than in an acidic environment, and the seminal fluid of the male also helps to alkalinize the vaginal chemical balance.

Second, vaginal lubrication can increase sexual enjoyment. During manual-genital stimulation, the slippery wetness can increase the sensuousness and pleasure of touching. Also, some women's partners experience the scent and taste of the lubrication during oral-genital sex as erotic. During intercourse, vaginal lubrication makes the walls of the vagina slippery, which facilitates entry of the penis into the vagina. Lubrication also helps make intercourse pleasurable. Without adequate lubrication, entry of the penis into the vagina can be very uncomfortable for the woman and often for the man. Irritation and small tears of the vaginal tissue can result.

While lubrication helps prepare the vagina for entry of the penis, the presence of some lubrication does not automatically indicate that a woman is "ready" for intercourse. Some women prefer to wait until they are highly aroused before beginning intercourse. Communication, verbal and nonverbal, is helpful in taking both people's desires into account.

Vaginal lubrication can be inhibited by several factors. Anxiety about one's self, one's partner, or the situation; the use of some drugs; changes in hormone balance—all can influence the vasocongestive response. Some women who take birth control pills find that vaginal lubrication is reduced; others find that for a while after childbirth, lubrication is lessened. Many women experience a decrease in lubrication due to the hormonal changes after menopause. Each of these situations will be discussed in more detail in later sections of the text.

There are several alternatives available to remedy insufficient vaginal lubrication, depending on the source of the difficulty. Changing the anxiety-producing circumstances and engaging in effective stimulation are important. Saliva, K-Y jelly, or a nonirritating, water-soluble lotion can be used to provide additional lubrication. Occasionally, some type of hormone treatment is necessary.

The Grafenberg Spot   The *Grafenberg spot* is located about one centimeter above the surface of the anterior (or top) wall of the vagina between the cervix and the opening to the vagina. This approximately dime-sized area is usually found about one-third to one-half way into the vagina. To locate the Grafenberg spot a woman or her partner needs to insert one or two fingers into the vagina and press from the cervix to the pubic bone along the anterior wall below the urethra. Deep pressure is usually necessary to locate the spot. Initially, stimulation of this area may be somewhat unpleasant, producing a sensation of needing to urinate or of uncomfortable tenderness. However, within a brief period of massaging the area, the sensations usually become pleasant and arousing, although some women report no distinct feeling.

The Grafenberg spot is reported to consist of glands and ducts that surround the urethra. This area is believed to be the female counterpart of the male prostate gland and to have developed from the same embryonic tissue (Belzer, 1981). The Grafenberg spot has generated considerable interest because of reports that some women experience orgasm, and perhaps an ejaculation of fluid, when stimulated there. We will discuss the role of the Grafenberg spot in female sexual response in more detail in Chapter 6.

Chemical Balance of the Vagina   Both the vaginal walls and cervix produce secretions that are white or yellowish in color. These secretions are normal and are a sign of vaginal health. They vary in appearance according to hormone level changes during the menstrual cycle. (Keeping track of these variations is the basis for one method of birth control, discussed in Chapter 11.) The taste and scent of vaginal secretions may also vary with the time of a woman's cycle and her level of arousal. One research study reports that men found the vaginal secretion odors during ovulation more pleasant than during other times in the cycle (Doty et al., 1975).

The vagina's natural chemical and bacterial balance helps promote a healthy mucosa. The chemical balance is normally rather acid (pH 4.0 to 5.0). A variety of factors can alter this balance and result in vaginal problems. Among these are too-frequent *douching* (rinsing out the inside of the vagina) and using feminine hygiene sprays. Cultural negativity about female sexual organs, as well as advertising, have turned misguided attempts to eradicate normal female secretions and scents into an extremely profitable business. Advertisements make statements such as "Unfortunately, the trickiest deodorant problem a girl has isn't under her pretty little arms" and "Our product eliminates the moist, uncomfortable feeling most women normally have just because they're women." However, frequent douching can alter the natural chemical balance of the vagina, thereby increasing susceptibility to infections. "Feminine hygiene" sprays can cause irritation, allergic reactions, burns, infections, dermatitis of the thighs, and numerous other problems. Deodorant tampons are another example of selling women something they do not need: menstrual fluid has virtually no odor until it is outside the body. Regular bathing with a mild soap and washing between the folds of the vulva is all that is necessary for adequate cleanliness.

Vaginal Infections   When the natural balance of the vagina is disturbed or a non-native organism is introduced, a vaginal infection, or *vaginitis*, can result. A number of factors increase susceptibility to vaginitis: the use of antibiotics; heat and moisture retained by nylon underwear; emotional stress; a diet high in carbohydrates; hormonal changes from pregnancy or birth control pills; chemical irritants; and coitus without adequate lubrication.

Usually the woman herself first notices symptoms of vaginitis: irritation or itching of the vagina and vulva, unusual discharge, and sometimes a disagreeable odor. (An unpleasant odor can also be due to a forgotten tampon or diaphragm.) Some of the different types of vaginal infections include yeast, bacterial infections, and trichomoniasis. These are all discussed in detail in Chapter 18.

It is important for vaginitis to be treated and cured. Chronic irritation resulting from long term infections may play a part in predisposing a woman to cervical cell changes that can lead to cancer (Benson, 1971). Some health-care practitioners provide suggestions for nondrug treatment of vaginitis; the following suggestions may help prevent vaginitis from occurring in the first place:

1. Eating a well-balanced diet low in sugar and refined carbohydrates.
2. Maintaining general good health with adequate sleep, exercise, and emotional releases.
3. Using good hygiene, including:
   a. regular bathing with mild soap.
   b. wiping from front to back, vulva to anus.
   c. wearing clean cotton underpants (nylon holds in heat and moisture that encourages bacteria growth).

d. avoiding the use of feminine hygiene sprays, colored toilet paper, bubble bath, other people's washcloths or towels.

e. being sure your sexual partner's hands and genitals are clean.

4. Having adequate natural lubrication before coitus or using a sterile, water-soluble lubricant such as K-Y jelly. Vaseline must not be used because it is not water-soluble and is likely to remain in the vagina and harbor bacteria.

5. Using condoms if either partner is nonmonogamous.

6. Women who are prone to yeast infections after menstruation (menstrual flow increases alkalinity of the vagina and promotes yeast overgrowth) may find it helpful to douch, once the flow ceases, with two tablespoons of white vinegar in a quart of warm water.

Self-Exams and Vaginal Health Care   A self-exam can sometimes help detect vaginal infection. The skin of the genital area may turn red instead of its usual pink, and this along with irritation is a sign that treatment may be necessary.

Many cities have clinics where women can learn to do their own vaginal exams. Some women elect to acquire this knowledge in groups with other women. In self-help learning groups women work together with a trained facilitator to learn about

Women can learn about their bodies in self-health groups.

their bodies and to share information with each other. As a group they may do their own breast, vulva, vaginal, and cervical exams. Proponents of self-health groups believe that women learning about themselves with others sharing the same experience can help demystify health care. The following is a typical reaction to the experience of such a group:

I was very nervous about going to the group I had signed up for. I had a difficult time imagining looking at my vagina in front of other people. But my group leader was so relaxed, that before I knew it I was very comfortable and curious. I was asking questions like everyone else. I had never seen other women's genitals before and was amazed that, even though we're basically the same, everyone was a little unique. (Authors' files)

For women interested in a self-examination group, many cities have clinics or other organizations that provide such experiences.

The Cervix

The *cervix*, located at the back of the vagina, is the small end of the pear-shaped uterus (Figure 4.5). It contains mucous-secreting glands. Sperm passes through the vagina into the uterus through the *os*, the opening in the center of the cervix.

A woman can see her own cervix by learning to insert a speculum into her vagina in a self-health group. She can also ask for a mirror when she has her pelvic exam. A woman can also feel her own cervix by inserting one or two fingers into the vagina and reaching to the end of the canal. (Sometimes squatting and bearing down brings the cervix closer to the vaginal entrance.) The cervix feels somewhat like the end of a nose, firm and round in contrast to the soft vaginal walls.

The *Pap smear*, a screening test for cervical cancer, is taken from the cervix. The vaginal walls are held open by an instrument known as a *speculum*. A few cells are removed with a small wooden spatula; these are then put on a slide and sent to a lab to be examined. A Pap smear is not painful because there are so few nerve endings on the cervix. The test is an essential part of a woman's routine preventive health care. Depending on a woman's individual situation and her health-care provider's recommendation, she may have a Pap smear once every two years, every year, biannually, or even more frequently.

Pap smear results have a diagnostic range of five classes (Benson, 1971). A Class I Pap smear is considered a negative result and indicates normal tissue. A Class II is usually caused by inflammation of the cells from a vaginal infection such as yeast or trichomoniasis. Often, the specific infection is diagnosed, treated, and the Pap smear is repeated to ensure that the infection has cleared up. Other times, a Class II is caused by cells that are just beginning to change to a possibly cancerous state. Class III results usually indicate the presence of some abnormal cells on the surface of the cervix. It is important for a woman with a Class III result to be followed closely by her health-care practitioner and to have more frequent Pap smears while waiting to see if the tissue returns to normal. A Class IV Pap smear indicates severe cell changes and the possibility of superficial cancer cells on the cervix. Class V results indicate the presence of cancer cells.

With Class III, IV, and V results, further tests are necessary for a conclusive diagnosis of cancer cells. A *colposcopy* (an exam using a special microscope) and a tissue *biopsy* (surgical removal of a small piece of cervical tissue which is examined under a microscope) are two of the kinds of further testing that can be done.

There are several simple, highly effective, life-saving treatments for cervical cancer. *Cryosurgery* (freezing of tissues) is one method of removing minimal surface cancerous cells. Elimination of the malignant tissue by a biopsy is also often effective. In more severe cases a woman needs to have a complete *hysterectomy* (surgical removal of the cervix and uterus), a procedure that will be discussed further in the next section.

The Uterus

The *uterus*, or womb, is a hollow, thick, pear-shaped organ, approximately three inches long and two inches wide in a *nulliparous* woman (one who has never had a child). It is somewhat larger after pregnancy. The *fundus* is the top area of the uterus where the uterine walls are especially thick. Longitudinal and circular muscle fibers of the uterus interweave like a basket and enable it to stretch during pregnancy and contract during labor and orgasm.

The uterus is suspended in the pelvic cavity by six ligaments, and it is capable of some movement. It is normal for the uteri of different women to be in various positions, from tipped forward toward the abdomen (anteflexed) to tipped back toward the spine (retroflexed), as shown in Figure 4.6. At one time it was believed that a retroflexed, or tipped, uterus interfered with conception. Women with retroflexed uteri may be more likely to experience menstrual discomfort or have difficulty with diaphragm insertion, due to the angle of the cervix, but their fertility is not negatively affected by the position of the uterus.

Fertilization usually occurs, not in the uterus, but in the fallopian tubes as the egg travels from the ovary. Once fertilization has taken place, the *zygote* (united sperm and egg) travels down the tube and becomes implanted in the uterus, where it develops into the fetus. In preparation for this event, the lining of the uterus (called the *endometrium*) becomes thickened in response to hormone changes during the monthly menstrual cycle, discussed later in this chapter.

The Fallopian Tubes

Each of the two four-inch *fallopian tubes* extends from the uterus out toward the left or the right side of the pelvic cavity. The outside end of each tube is like a funnel, with fringelike projections called *fimbriae* that almost reach the ovary. When the egg leaves the ovary, it is believed to be drawn into the tube by the fimbria. However, the process by which the egg enters the tube remains somewhat a mystery.

Once the egg is inside the tube, the movements of tiny hairlike cilia and contractions of the walls move it along the tube at a rate of approximately one inch per 24 hours. It remains viable for fertilization for about 24–48 hours. Therefore, fertiliza-

FIGURE 4.6 POSITIONS OF THE UTERUS

105

Various positions of the uterus in the pelvic cavity: (a) retroflexed,
(b) midline, and (c) anteflexed.

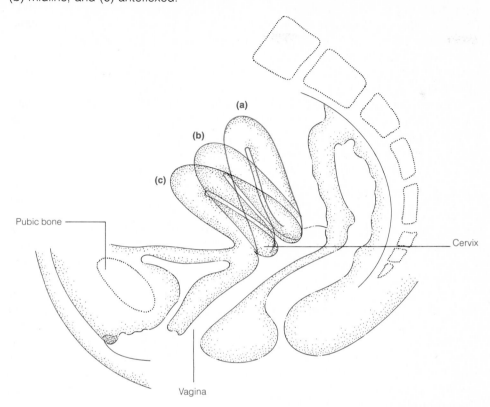

tion occurs while the egg is still close to the ovary. After fertilization, the zygote begins developing as it continues traveling down the tube to the uterus.

In some cases, the zygote becomes implanted in a location outside the uterus. This condition is known as an *ectopic pregnancy*. The most common site of an ectopic pregnancy is the fallopian tube, and so the condition is often called a tubal pregnancy. Research indicates this occurs in one out of 200 pregnancies (Eastman and Hellman, 1961). A tubal pregnancy is often difficult to diagnose because some of the possible symptoms (abdominal pain, a missed menstrual period, a pelvic mass, or irregular bleeding) are similar to other types of problems (Benson, 1974). Without surgical treatment, though, an ectopic pregnancy may ultimately rupture the tube and result in severe bleeding, shock, and possible death.

The Ovaries

The two *ovaries* are located at the ends of the fallopian tubes, one on each side of the uterus. They are connected to the pelvic wall and the uterus by ligaments. The ovaries contain 40,000 to 400,000 immature ova, which are present at birth.

The ovaries are almond-sized and -shaped endocrine glands that produce two classes of sex hormones. The estrogens (the most important of which is estradiol) influence development of female physical sex characteristics and regulation of the menstrual cycle. The progestational compounds (*progesterone* is the most important) help to regulate the menstrual cycle and to stimulate development of the uterine lining in preparation for pregnancy. Around the onset of puberty, the female sex hormones play a critical role in initiating changes in the *primary sexual systems* (such as the growth of the uterus and the vagina) and the *secondary sex characteristics* (such as pubic hair and breast development).

During the years between puberty and menopause, one ovary typically releases an egg each cycle. Egg maturation and release (or *ovulation*) occurs as the result of the complex chain of events we know as the menstrual cycle. We will look at the menstrual cycle more closely at the end of this chapter.

Surgical Removal of the Uterus and Ovaries

Sometimes a woman needs to have a *hysterectomy* (removal of the uterus) and/or an *oophorectomy* (removal of the ovaries). Various medical problems necessitate these procedures including cervical, uterine, or ovarian cancer; the presence of benign (noncancerous) tumors; or severe pelvic infections. The physical side effects of these operations are similar to those of any major surgery. These procedures are performed quite frequently, and it may be especially important for a woman to get a second opinion before agreeing to this type of surgery.

The effects of this type of surgery on a woman's sexuality can vary. Some women may experience alterations in their sexual responses after removal of the uterus. Sensations from uterine vasocongestion and elevation during arousal and contractions during orgasm will be absent and may change the physical experience of sexual response (Zussman et al., 1981). In most cases, how the woman and her partner perceive the surgery is the crucial variable in postsurgery sexual adjustment (Dennerstein et al., 1977). In a few instances, continued general physical or emotional problems may interfere with sexual functioning. These can range from diminished vaginal lubrication (due to the absence of ovarian estrogen) to feelings of depression over the loss of a woman's ability to reproduce or the loss of her symbolic femininity represented by her reproductive organs. On the other hand, some women find that the elimination of medical problems, assured protection from an unwanted pregnancy, and lack of menstruation may enhance their sexual functioning (Woods, 1975). It is important for any woman facing surgical removal of her reproductive organs to obtain, together with her partner, thorough pre- and postoperative information and counseling.

THE BREASTS

Breasts are not a part of the internal or external female genitalia. The *breasts* are secondary sex characteristics (physical characteristics other than genitals that distinguish male from female). In a physically mature woman they are composed internally of fatty tissue and mammary (milk-producing) glands (see Figure 4.7). There is little variation from woman to woman in the amount of glandular tissue present in the breast, despite differences in size. This is why the amount of milk produced after childbirth does not correlate to the size of the breasts. Variation in breast size is due primarily to the amount of fatty tissue distributed around the glands. It is also common for one breast to be slightly larger than the other.

Breast size is the source of considerable preoccupation for many people in our society. Large breasts are often considered to be linked with "sexiness," and cleavage is frequently depicted in advertising to help sell products. Surgeries that are available to enlarge or reduce the size of breasts reflect the dissatisfaction many women feel because their breasts do not fit the ideal "type." (The "type" may be difficult to fit because there are contradictory images of the slender, small-breasted, elegant cover girl and the buxom woman.) Many women believe that their breasts are too small, too big, or not the "right" shape:

In talking with my friends about how we feel about our breasts, I discovered that not one of us feels really comfortable about how they look. I've always been envious of women with large breasts because mine are small. But my friends with large breasts talk about feeling self-conscious about their breasts, too. (Authors' files)

FIGURE 4.7 THE FEMALE BREAST

External and internal structures of the female breast.

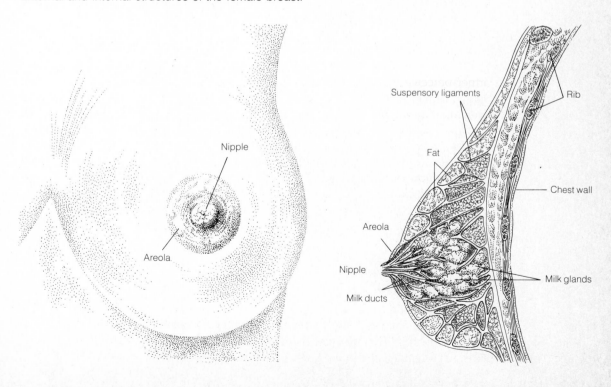

Breast size and shape vary from woman to woman.

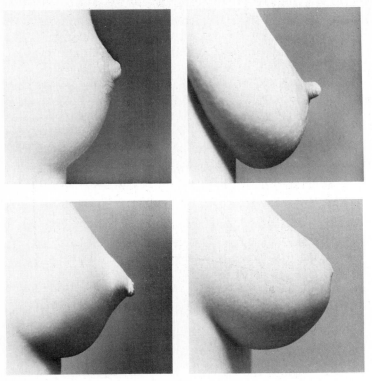

The glandular tissue in the breast responds to sex hormones. During adolescence, both the fatty and glandular tissue develop markedly. Breasts show some size variations at different phases of the menstrual cycle and when influenced by pregnancy, nursing, or birth control pills.

The *nipple* is in the center of the *areola*, the darker area of the external breast. The areola contains sebaceous (oil-producing) glands that help lubricate the nipples during breast feeding. The openings of the mammary (milk-producing) glands are in the nipples. Some nipples point outward from the breast, others are flush with the breast, and still others sink into the breast. When small muscles at the base of the nipple contract in response to sexual arousal, tactile stimulation, or cold, the nipples become erect.

Breast Self-Exam

A monthly breast examination is an important part of self-health care for women. This exam can help a woman know what is normal for her own breasts. A woman can do the breast exam herself and can also teach her partner to do it. The steps of a breast exam are illustrated in Box 4.1. The best time to do the routine exam is following

BOX 4.1 HOW TO EXAMINE YOUR BREASTS

1. In the shower

Examine your breasts during bath or shower; hands glide easier over wet skin. Fingers flat, move gently over every part of each breast. Use right hand to examine left breast, left hand for right breast. Check for any lump, hard knot, or thickening.

2. Before a mirror

Inspect your breasts with arms at your sides. Next, raise your arms high overhead. Look for any changes in contour of each breast, a swelling, dimpling of skin, or changes in the nipple.

Then, rest palms on hips and press down firmly to flex your chest muscles. Left and right breast will not exactly match—few women's breasts do.

3. Lying down

To examine your right breast, put a pillow or folded towel under your right shoulder. Place right hand behind your head—this distributes breast tissue more evenly on the chest. With left hand, fingers flat, press gently in small circular motions around an imaginary clock face. Begin at outermost top of your right breast for 12 o'clock, then move to 1 o'clock, and so on around the circle back to 12. A ridge of firm tissue in the lower curve of each breast is normal. Then move in an inch, toward the nipple, keep circling to examine *every part of your breast*, including nipple. This requires at least three more circles. Now slowly repeat procedure on your left breast.

Finally, squeeze the nipple of each breast gently between thumb and index finger. Any discharge, clear or bloody, should be reported to your doctor immediately.

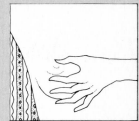

menstruation due to cyclic changes of the breast tissue. For a woman who is not menstruating (either during pregnancy or after menopause or a hysterectomy), doing the exam the same time each month is preferable. Many breasts normally feel lumpy. Once a woman becomes familiar with her own breasts, she can notice changes. If there is a change, she should consult a physician.

Breast Lumps

Three types of lumps can occur in the breasts. The two most common are *cysts* (fluid-filled sacs) and *fibroadenomas** (solid, rounded tumors). Approximately 80% of breast lumps are these kinds of benign (not cancerous or harmful) tissue. The third kind of breast lump is a *malignant tumor* (a tumor that is made up of cancer cells). Approximately 100,000 new cases of breast cancer are detected each year (Cooke and Dworkin, 1979).

Once a lump is found, further diagnostic testing is necessary. *Needle aspiration* involves inserting a fine needle into the lump to determine if there is fluid inside. If so, it is usually a cyst and can be drained. Moisture from the tissue of any lump can be analyzed for cancer cells. Additional tests can be done to distinguish between a fibroadenoma and a malignant tumor.

Once breast cancer has been diagnosed, several forms of treatment may be used. Radiation therapy, chemotherapy, hormone therapy, immunotherapy, surgery, or a combination of these procedures may be performed. How much of the breast and surrounding tissue is removed by surgery varies from *radical mastectomy* (entire breast, underlying muscle, and lymph nodes are removed) to a *lumpectomy* or *partial mastectomy* (the lump and small amounts of surrounding tissue are removed). There is controversy about the effectiveness and survival rate following the more and less extreme surgical procedures. Increasing numbers of physicians believe that many women could have less radical, breast-conserving surgery without compromising their chances of survival. Radical mastectomies are becoming much less common, especially in breast cancer that is detected early. There is, however, a considerable amount of ongoing research on the diagnosis and treatment of breast cancer aimed at determining the most successful and least damaging treatment for the disease.

Breast cancer and its treatments may affect sexual adjustment. Beyond the physical recuperation from surgery and side effects of other treatments, the loss of one or both breasts almost certainly has special meaning to a woman and her present or potential partner. In our culture the female breast is often considered to be a symbol of a woman's femininity and is a vital part of her body image. Breast stimulation—looking, touching, kissing—is often an important component of sexual arousal for a woman and her partner, and consequently surgical removal of one or both breasts may create problems in sexual adjustment (Frank et al., 1978).

A mastectomy presents unique problems to a woman who is not in a long-term relationship. She may have difficulty deciding when to tell someone she is dating

*Minton et al. (1979) believe that caffeine in coffee, tea, cola drinks, and chocolate can contribute to the development of benign breast lumps. They report that breast lumps disappeared in many patients who eliminated caffeine from their diet.

about her surgery. Her own feelings of acceptance and comfort and her judgment about timing are important. Also, she needs to understand that her partner will require some time to adjust to the information about her mastectomy. Still, it may help her to keep in mind that a loving relationship is based on more than physical characteristics.

The American Cancer Society's Reach to Recovery program provides a very important service to these women; volunteers in the program, who have all had one or both breasts removed, meet with a woman who has recently undergone a mastectomy and offer her emotional support and encouragement. They also provide a positive model of a woman who has made a successful adjustment to her surgery.

Fortunately, reconstructive breast surgery or an external prosthesis (an artificial breast) may enhance a woman's general and sexual adjustment following a mastectomy. For example, an exterior silicone prosthesis can be matched to the other breast and worn inside a bra. In some cases a new breast can be made from a pouch containing silicone gel and placed under the woman's own skin. To improve the possibilities for breast reconstruction it can be quite helpful to have presurgical discussions with both the surgeon removing the tissue and the plastic surgeon doing the reconstruction.

It is especially important to remember that early detection leads to less drastic surgery and easier and more successful breast reconstruction.

MENSTRUATION

While menstruation is a sign of normal physical functioning, many societies have seen it as unhealthy or supernatural. Great powers and danger have both been attributed to menstruation. The Roman historian Pliny stated that bees will leave their hive, boiling linen will turn black, and razors will become blunt if touched by a menstruating woman. In other societies, she may be restricted from certain activities or from contact with men. She may also be isolated from the entire community into a menstrual hut, as with the Arapesh in New Guinea. The Bible, Lev. 15:19, states, "And if a woman have an issue, and her issue in her flesh be blood, she shall be put apart seven days: and whosoever toucheth her shall be unclean until the even." Some writers believe that the menstrual myths and taboos serve to control women and maintain their inferior social status (Weidiger, 1976).

Remnants of these attitudes persist in contemporary American society. For example, in the popular television production, "All in the Family," Archie Bunker states:

ARCHIE: Yes, that's right, you don't believe me. Read your Bible. Read the story about Adam and Eve there. Adam and Eve, they had it pretty soft out in Paradise. They had no problems. They didn't even know they was naked. But Eve, she wasn't satisfied with that, see. And one day, against direct orders, she made poor Adam eat that apple. God got sore. He told them to get their clothes on and get the hell outta there. And that's why Eve was cursed. And that's why they call it what he called it, the curse.

MIKE: Well, there you have it, Gloria, straight from the Reverend Archie Bunker. The true story of menstruation.

ARCHIE: SSSHHHHHHH with that kinda word!*

The real "curse" is the continued negative societal attitudes that often affect women. The menstrual taboo may act as a source of embarrassment or a confirmation of a negative self-image. One study found that more than one-third of the people surveyed believed that even at home a woman should conceal the fact she is menstruating (Research Forecasts, 1981).

Common American folklore reveals many interesting ideas about menstruation. It has been thought that a woman should not bathe or wash her hair during her menstrual period because she would become ill or stop menstruation. In the 1920s, women commonly believed that a permanent wave given during menstruation would not curl their hair. Other myths include the belief that it is harmful for a woman to be physically active during menstruation, that domestic animals will not obey a menstruating woman, or that a man can regain his lost ability to have erections if he performs oral sex on a menstruating woman (McCary, 1973).

In spite of these myths and negative societal attitudes toward menstruation, some women and families are redefining it more positively. For example, some may have a celebration or give a gift to a young woman when she starts her first menstrual period. In a few other cultures a woman's first menstruation is described in lyrical words of positive images. The Japanese expression for a girl's first menstruation is "the year of the cleavage of the melon," and one Indian description of menstruation is the "flower growing in the house of the god of love" (Delaney et al., 1976).

One of the aspects of the menstrual cycle that people often see as positive is its cyclic pattern typical of many natural phenomena. The poet May Sarton describes the analogy of the menstrual cycle and nature in this 1937 poem:

There were seeds
within her
that burst at intervals
and for a little while
she would come back
to heaviness,
and then before a surging miracle
of blood,
relax,
and re-identify herself,
each time more closely
with the heart of life.

'I am the beginning,
the never-ending,
the perfect tree.'
And she would lean
again as once
on the great curve of the earth,
part of its turning,
as distinctly part
of the universe as a star—
as unresistant,
as completely rhythmical.

The symbolism of the cyclic nature of menstruation is, among other things, one of the aspects of menstruation about which women report having positive feelings:

*Written by: Michael Ross & Bernie West © Copyright 1973. Tandem Productions, Inc. All Rights Reserved.

Part Two: Biological Basis

I feel menstruation is a part of a woman's beauty. It ties her into the whole rhythm of the tides and the moon. (Authors' files)

Menstruation lets me know that another cycle has passed, and I look back on what I have accomplished. (Authors' files)

It's a nice way to find out I'm not pregnant. (Authors' files)

Some of the things that men report they like about menstruation include:

It's a sign that a woman is healthy. (Authors' files)

Women seem closer to their bodies because of menstruation. (Authors' files)

I like the sexual responsiveness some women have with their periods. (Authors' files)

Knowing your girlfriend is safe after you've been sweating it out. (Authors' files)

Menstrual Physiology

During the menstrual cycle the uterine lining is prepared for the possible implantation of the fertilized ovum. If conception does not occur, the lining sloughs off and is discharged as menstrual flow. The menstrual cycle usually begins in the early teens, between the ages of 11 and 15, although some girls begin earlier or later. Menstrual cycles end at menopause, which in most women occurs between 45 and 50 years. The first menstrual bleeding is called the *menarche*. The timing of the menarche appears to be related to heredity, general health, altitude (the average menarche is earlier in lower altitudes), and body weight (Sullivan, 1971).

The differences in timing of menarche is often a concern for young women, especially those who begin earlier or later than the norm:

I felt very alone when I first started my periods late in the fifth grade because none of my friends had. In our school there were no Kotex machines in the kids' bathroom stalls, so I had to carry them in my purse and was afraid someone would see them. (Authors' files)

Almost everyone had been menstruating for years before I started. I thought something was wrong with me but Mom said she started late, too. (Authors' files)

Many young women are not adequately informed about the developments and changes that attend the onset of menstruation. One study found that 43% of women reported feeling confused, frightened, panicky, or ill when they started their first period (Research Forecasts, 1981). In another study, 20% of mothers had told their seventh-grade daughters nothing about menstruation (Bloch, 1978). The information girls do receive may be scanty, confusing, or frightening:

During the time my breasts started to develop, I came home from school one day to find a pamphlet from Kotex on my bed. Mom never said anything else; I guess she was waiting for me to ask. (Authors' files)

My mother talked to me about menstruation, but my father never did. I felt like it was something I had to hide from him. (Authors' files)

I really avoided boys like the plague after I started because my mom said, "Now you can get pregnant." (Authors' files)

Young men are probably even less likely to receive information about menstruation. One study found that men are most likely to learn about menstruation from friends (31%), school (21%), and mothers (20%). Ninety-one percent of both men and women thought that information about menstruation should be provided in schools (Research Forecasts, 1981).

The menstrual discharge consists of blood, mucus, and endometrial membranes that sometimes form small clots. The length of the menstrual cycle is usually measured from the beginning of the first day of flow to the day before the next flow begins. It is normal for the amount of menstrual flow (six to eight ounces) to vary, and the cycle length also varies from woman to woman (21 to 90 days). These time differences occur in the phase before ovulation. Fourteen days, plus or minus two days, between ovulation and the onset of menstruation is the pattern that prevails even when there is several weeks' difference in the total length of the cycle. If a woman experiences a dramatic change in her usual pattern, she should seek medical attention.

An interesting phenomenon known as *menstrual synchrony* sometimes occurs among women who live together and have considerable contact with each other: they develop similar menstrual cycles. The purpose of the uniform cycles is unknown, but the trigger is believed to be related to the sense of smell (McClintock, 1971).

The menstrual cycle is divided into three stages: the *proliferative phase*, the *secretory phase*, and the *menstrual phase* (see Figure 4.8). The hypothalamus and the pituitary gland (both located within the brain), the ovaries, and the uterus are all interrelated in this cyclic pattern. This is a self-regulating and dynamic process in which the particular level of a hormone retards or increases the production of the same and other hormones.

The hypothalamus interprets the levels of hormones in the bloodstream throughout the cycle, sending chemical messages to the pituitary gland, which in turn sends hormones to stimulate the ovaries. The hypothalamus produces a group of chemicals generally known as *hypothalamic-releasing factors*. These chemicals are produced in response to existing levels of other hormones in the bloodstream. The most important substances related to menstruation are the *gonadotropic-releasing factors*, which stimulate the pituitary to produce hormones that affect the ovaries. Once the pituitary gland receives the appropriate releasing factors from the hypothalamus, it produces *follicle-stimulating hormone* (FSH) or *luteinizing hormone* (LH). These two hormones have the general name of *gonadotropins* because they stimulate the gonads (ovaries and testes). FSH stimulates the ovarian production of estrogen and the maturation of the ova and follicles (small sacs, each of which contains an ovum). LH induces the mature ovum to burst from the ovary, and it stimulates the development of the *corpus luteum* (the portion of the ovarian follicle that remains after the egg has matured). The corpus luteum produces the hormone progesterone.

These glands do not produce a steady stream of hormones; there is a complex interaction between the glands that signals when to increase or decrease secretions. A

FIGURE 4.8 CHANGES DURING THE MENSTRUAL CYCLE

115

The menstrual cycle during (a) the proliferative phase, including ovulation; (b) the secretory phase; and (c) the menstrual phase.

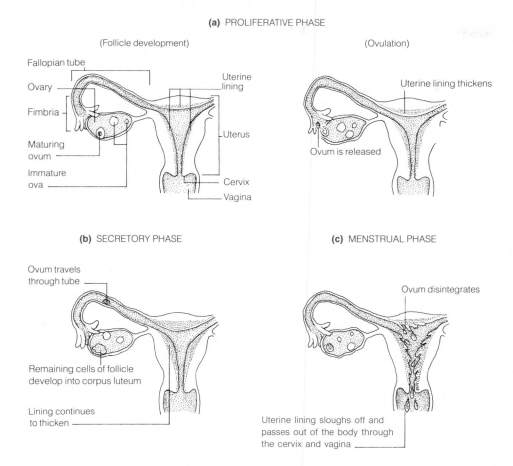

(a) PROLIFERATIVE PHASE

(Follicle development)

(Ovulation)

Fallopian tube

Ovary

Fimbria

Maturing ovum

Immature ova

Uterine lining

Uterus

Cervix

Vagina

Uterine lining thickens

Ovum is released

(b) SECRETORY PHASE

Ovum travels through tube

Remaining cells of follicle develop into corpus luteum

Lining continues to thicken

(c) MENSTRUAL PHASE

Ovum disintegrates

Uterine lining sloughs off and passes out of the body through the cervix and vagina

hormone is secreted until the organ it acts upon is stimulated; at that point, the organ releases a substance that circulates back through the system to regulate hormonal activity in the initiating gland. This *negative feedback mechanism* provides an internal control that regulates fluctuations of hormonal production.

Proliferative Phase During the proliferative phase the pituitary gland increases production of FSH, which stimulates the developing follicles to mature and to produce several types of estrogen, which in turn cause the endometrium to thicken. Although several follicles begin to mature, usually only one, the *graafian follicle*, reaches maturity; the other follicles degenerate. When the level of ovarian estrogen circulating in the bloodstream reaches a peak level, the pituitary gland depresses the release of FSH and stimulates LH production.

At approximately 14 days before the onset of the next menstrual period, *ovulation* occurs. In response to the spurt of LH secreted by the pituitary gland, the mature follicle ruptures and the ovum is released (see Figure 4.9). Some women experience a twinge, cramp, or pressure in their lower abdomen, called *mittelschmerz* (German for "middle pain") at ovulation. Mittelschmerz is caused by the swelling and bursting of the follicle or from the slight release of fluid or blood from the ruptured follicle that can irritate the sensitive abdominal lining. The released ovum then travels to the fimbria of the fallopian tube. Occasionally, more than one ovum is released. If fertilization of both ova occurs, fraternal twins will develop. When one egg is fertilized and then divides into two separate zygotes, identical twins result.

Around the time of ovulation, there is an increase and a change in cervical mucous gland secretions due to increased levels of estrogen. The mucus becomes clear, slippery, and stretchy. The pH (measurement of acidity or alkalinity) of this mucus is more alkaline; as noted earlier, a more alkaline vaginal environment contributes to sperm mobility and longevity. This is the phase in the cycle when a woman can most easily become pregnant.

FIGURE 4.9 OVARIAN FOLLICLE DEVELOPMENT

Cross-section of an ovary showing different stages of follicle development.

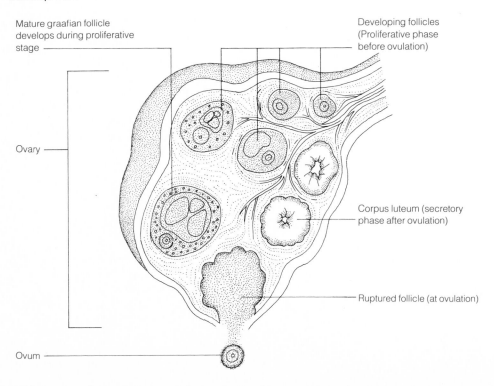

Mature graafian follicle develops during proliferative stage

Developing follicles (Proliferative phase before ovulation)

Ovary

Corpus luteum (secretory phase after ovulation)

Ruptured follicle (at ovulation)

Ovum

Secretory Phase   During the secretory phase, continued pituitary secretions of LH cause the cells of the ruptured follicle to develop into a yellowish bump called the corpus luteum. The corpus luteum secretes progesterone, which inhibits the production of cervical mucus found at ovulation. Progesterone, together with estrogen produced by the ovaries, causes the endometrium to thicken and engorge with blood in preparation for implantation of a fertilized egg. If implantation does not occur, the pituitary gland, in response to high estrogen and progesterone levels in the bloodstream, shuts down production of LH and FSH. This deprives the corpus luteum of the necessary chemical stimulation to produce hormones; the corpus luteum degenerates and estrogen and progesterone production decreases. This triggers the sloughing off of the endometrium during the menstrual phase (Figure 4.10).

Menstrual Phase   During the menstrual phase, the thickened inner layer of the endometrium sheds and is discharged through the cervix and vagina as menstrual flow. Menstrual flow typically consists of blood, mucus, and endometrial tissue. As noted, the shedding of the endometrium happens as a result of reduced amounts of progesterone and estrogen.

FIGURE 4.10 THE MENSTRUAL CYCLE

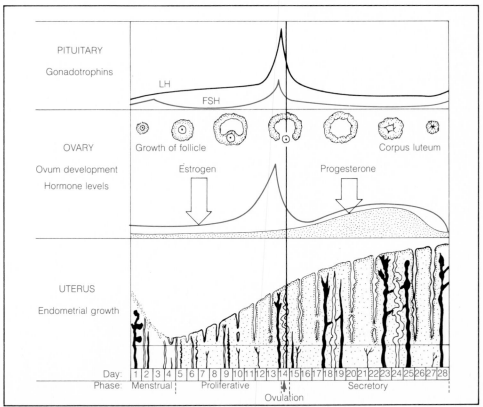

As the hormone level in the bloodstream continues to fall, the hypothalamus responds to the reduction by stimulating the pituitary to release FSH, which initiates the maturing process of several follicles, and the cycle begins again (Figure 4.10).

Sexual Activity and the Menstrual Cycle

While the idea of menstrual huts may seem extreme from our perspective, there are some common menstrual taboos in our own culture. One of these taboos has to do with intercourse during menstruation. One phone interview survey found that 51% of men and 56% of women believed that women should abstain from intercourse during menstruation (Research Forecasts, 1981). However, the women who took part in Masters and Johnson's (1966) menstrual research responded more favorably. Out of 331 women, 33 objected to sexual activity during menstruation for religious or esthetic reasons. Among the others, there were no objections, provided ". . . they (1) were not at a peak of menstrual flow, (2) felt well, and (3) felt no esthetic aversion from the male partner" (p. 125). Well over half of the Masters and Johnson sample said they were interested in sexual activity, especially during the last days of the flow.

Some writers have expressed the view that sexual intercourse during menstruation is immoral or physically dangerous. Although we know today that from a medical point of view there are usually no health reasons to avoid intercourse during menstruation (with the exception of excessive bleeding or other menstrual problems), many couples do so.

Reasons for avoiding sex during a woman's period vary. Some women resist sexual activity because of culturally induced shame about menstruation. Uncomfortable physical symptoms of menstruation often reduce sexual desire or pleasure, and the inconvenience or spillage of flow on sheets can inhibit sexual activity. Personal preference and religious beliefs can also be factors.

If individuals do prefer to abstain from coitus during menstruation, the remaining repertoire of sexual activities is still available:

When I'm on my period, I leave my tampon inside and push the string in, too. My husband and I have manual and oral stimulation, *and* a great time! (Authors' files)

Some women use a diaphragm to hold back the menstrual flow during coitus.

Furthermore, orgasm, by any means of stimulation, can be beneficial to the menstruating woman. The uterine contractions and release of vasocongestion often reduce backache and feelings of pelvic fullness and cramping.

A number of studies have attempted to determine whether a correlation exists between menstrual cycle changes and sexual behavior. Although there is some inconsistency in the findings of various researchers, there is a pattern of increase in sexual feelings and behavior during the ovulatory phase and the *paramenstrual* phase (the time period several days prior to and during menstruation) (Friedman, 1980). There is also great individual variation from woman to woman. We encourage women readers and their partners to notice their own patterns.

Because so many sociocultural, psychological, and biological factors interact, no one research study can completely analyze the complex relationship between behavior and the menstrual cycle (Friedman, 1980). It appears, though, that most women experience mood changes during the paramenstrual period, and there is substantial evidence that women's moods tend to be more positive at other times during their cycles than during the paramenstrual interval. Many women report an increase in feelings of anxiety, irritability, and sadness just before and during their menstrual periods. Some male and female students report these mood changes to be something they dislike about menstruation. Women's comments include:

I dislike the growing sense of concern about my body and sexual attractiveness that I get for two or three days before my period begins. (Authors' files)

I dislike my depressed, teary mood. (Authors' files)

Some men say:

I dislike a woman's irritability and crabby behavior and how that affects our relations. (Authors' files)

Girls are mean because of cramps, but I don't blame them. (Authors' files)

Not all women experience negative mood changes associated with menstruation, and among women who do, individual differences are considerable. Box 4.2 offers some suggestions to men on how to help their partners cope with menstruation.

Some researchers believe that self-report studies of menstrual mood changes may be biased when the subjects know the purpose of the questionnaire is to study menstrual symptoms. Cycle phase differences found in self-reports in which the subjects know menstruation is being studied may reflect stereotypes or social expectations of what is considered to be the typical menstrual experience (Ruble and Brooks-Gunn, 1979). When women are unaware of the nature of the study, they often fail to show cyclic fluctuations of symptoms (Brooks et al., 1977).

Research has also examined the relationship between menstrual changes and the ability of women to perform a variety of tasks. A review of the studies that used objective performance measures like academic examinations, factory production, and reaction time shows no demonstrable changes related to the menstrual cycle. The objective measures of task performance, however, frequently differed from the women's subjective evaluations of their performance. Some women believed that their level of performance decreased during the paramenstrual period (Sommer, 1973). This discrepancy in subjective and objective evaluation of performance may be related to attitudes and expectations. One study indicated that many people believe that menstruation has a significant effect on a woman's ability. For example, 26% of the respondents thought that women could not perform their jobs as well, and 35%

BOX 4.2 MEN, LOVEMAKING, AND MENSTRUATION

Men who make love with women have to deal in some way with menstruation. Caring about a woman's experience of her period may help to avoid misunderstandings and build intimacy.

You might ask a lover if she gets cramps, and if so, how they feel. Pain is not the only consideration. The bloated feeling caused by water retention may not *hurt*, but it can be fairly uncomfortable. In some women with pronounced menstrual water retention, it can feel like the flu.

A man can do several things to help a lover deal with dysmenorrhea. He might make her a cup of soothing herbal tea—chamomile and mint herb teas may be especially effective—or massage her lower back or abdomen.

Try to discuss how a lover feels about making love premenstrually or during her period. Some women prefer not to—discomfort can interfere with the undivided attention lovemaking deserves. On the other hand, some women say lovemaking right before the start of menstruation, or during it, helps alleviate cramps. During orgasm, the uterus contracts and the cervix opens. This helps speed menstrual flow and can reduce the duration of cramps. Men should bear in mind, however, that this is not an experience shared by all women. Also, ask about breast tenderness and keep it in mind during sensual explorations.

Different cultures and religions have different perspectives on lovemaking during a woman's period. As a result, many people—both men and women—have deep feelings about it. It is important to listen carefully to a lover's feelings about making love during menstruation and to try to respect them.

For couples who do make love during a woman's period, there are several things to keep in mind. Menstruation may change a woman's natural vaginal lubrication. Menstrual fluid irritates some penises, and a man can use a condom if this is a problem. Intercourse with a tampon in place is not recommended; a woman might use a diaphragm or cervical cap to catch the flow. Even if a barrier method is not your primary or preferred form of contraception, you may want to use one at this time.

If a couple would rather not have genital intercourse during the woman's period, there are other satisfying ways to make love, though some men prefer not to provide oral-clitoral stimulation during menstruation.

The bottom line is: Try to talk about the issues menstruation raises in your relationship and how you both feel most comfortable dealing with them. (Adapted from Michael Castleman, 1981b)

---

believed that women could not think as well during menstruation (Research Forecasts, 1981). However, further research is required before we can draw conclusions about the cause of this inconsistency in subjective and objective performance.

Most women undergo some physical or mood changes (or both) during their menstrual cycles. In many cases the changes are minor. Sometimes, however, more serious difficulties with the menstrual cycle occur. *Premenstrual tension syndrome* usually begins two to 12 days prior to menstruation and ends with the onset of menses. The symptoms can include a dull pelvic ache, a bloated feeling in the breasts and abdomen, swelling in extremities such as hands and feet, headaches, dizziness, weight gain, and emotional irritability. The physiological causes for premenstrual tension syndrome have not yet been established, but increased progesterone levels are suspected to contribute to these symptoms.

Primary dysmenorrhea occurs during menstruation and is usually caused by the overproduction of *prostaglandins*, a class of chemicals produced by body tissue. Problems with primary dysmenorrhea usually appear with the onset of menses at adolescence. The symptoms are generally most noticeable the first few days of a woman's period and include abdominal aching and/or cramping. Some women may also experience nausea, vomiting, diarrhea, headache, dizziness, fatigue, irritability, or nervousness.

A new treatment for women who experience severe, debilitating primary dysmenorrhea has been recently developed. The development of this treatment was based on more complete knowledge about the role of prostaglandins. Prostaglandins help regulate the contraction and relaxation of smooth muscles in the body, including the uterus, blood vessels, and intestines. In 1957 a researcher noticed that women who experienced severe cramps had larger amounts of prostaglandins in their menstrual fluid than did other women. He suggested that the high level of these substances caused the uterine muscular contractions experienced as cramps. Further research has corroborated this idea and drugs have been developed that inhibit the body's production of prostaglandins. Although these medications have some side effects, they are being successfully used to treat this problem (Heinrichs and Adamson, 1980).

Secondary dysmenorrhea occurs prior to or during menstruation and is characterized by constant and often spasmodic lower abdominal pain that typically extends to the back and thighs. The symptoms are often similar to primary dysmenorrhea and are usually caused by various factors including the intrauterine device (IUD), pelvic inflammatory disease (chronic infection of the reproductive organs), endometriosis (cells from the uterine lining implant in the abdominal cavity), benign uterine tumors, or obstruction of the cervical opening. Following a diagnosis of the causal factor, appropriate treatment can be implemented.

Women may be able to alleviate some of the unpleasant symptoms accompanying menstruation by their own actions (Ritz, 1981). Moderate exercise throughout the month, as well as proper diet, can contribute to improvement of menstrual-related difficulties. For example, an increase in fluids and fiber will help with the constipation that sometimes occurs before and during menstruation. Decreasing salt intake and avoiding food high in salt (salad dressing, gravies, bacon, pickles, to name a few) can help reduce swelling and bloating caused by water retention. Food supplements such as calcium, magnesium, and B vitamins also sometimes help to relieve cramps and bloating. One writer (Burdoff, 1980) recommends small, frequent meals of low-carbohydrate and fat and high-protein foods for women with problems of dizziness. She also suggests cutting down on daily caffeine intake to help reduce breast tenderness during the paramenstrual stage.

When a woman experiences menstrual-related pain, it can be useful for her to keep a "pain diary" to track pain, stresses, and daily habits such as exercise, diet, and sleep. She may be able to note variability that may make a difference. The information may also be helpful for specific diagnosis if she consults a health-care practitioner.

Many people believe that menstrual discomfort is "all in your head." In fact, one study found that about one of every five people believed that menstrual pain had psychological rather than physical causes (Research Forecasts, 1981). While attitudinal and life stress factors may contribute to dysmenorrhea, today a growing number of physicians support the view that anxiety, resentment, and other symptoms are the result of menstrual pain rather than the cause.

Besides discomfort or pain, another relatively common menstrual difficulty is *amenorrhea*, the absence of menstruation. There are two types of amenorrhea, primary and secondary. Primary amenorrhea is the failure to begin to menstruate at puberty. It may be caused by problems with the reproductive organs, hormonal imbalances, poor health, or an imperforate hymen. Secondary amenorrhea involves the disruption of an established menstrual cycle, with the absence of menstruation for three months or more. This is a normal condition during pregnancy and breast feeding. It may also be common for women when they first begin menstruating and women approaching menopause. Sometimes poor health and emotional distress are the causes (Maddux, 1975).

Hormonal problems can also produce amenorrhea. Women with *anorexia nervosa*, an eating disorder that often results in extreme weight loss, frequently stop menstruating due to hormonal changes that accompany emaciation (Clappison, 1981). Women who discontinue the birth control pill occasionally do not resume menstruation for several months, but this situation is usually temporary and resolves spontaneously. It is a good idea for a woman who does not have a period when expected to consult a health-care practitioner.

Occasionally, female athletes experience amenorrhea. For example, approximately 30% of a sample of American female athletes reported missed menstrual periods during training and participation in the Montreal Olympic games (Webb et al., 1979). It is not known whether the lack of menstruation in such women is caused by low body fat, the physical or emotional stress of training and competing, the exercise itself, or a combination of all of these. The amenorrhea may also be due to medical problems unrelated to athletics. Thus, it is important for a female athlete to seek medical evaluation for menstrual irregularities (Shangold, 1980a).

Toxic Shock Syndrome

In May 1980, the Centers for Disease Control published the first report about *toxic shock syndrome* (TSS) in menstruating women. Symptoms of toxic shock syndrome include fever, sore throat, nausea, vomiting, diarrhea, red skin flush, dizziness, and high blood pressure. The exact cause of toxic shock syndrome during menstruation is unknown, but it is believed to be a result of toxins produced by the organism *Staphylococcus aureus*.

Although TSS has received a great deal of publicity, it is important to remember that it is a rare disease, and the chances of contracting it are quite low. When it does occur, it is seen most frequently in women during menstruation. Ninety-six percent of toxic shock cases occur during menstruation and are associated with the use of tampons, especially superabsorbent tampons. The remaining 4% of cases occurred in males (1.5%) and nonmenstrual females (2.5%). Menstrually associated TSS commonly affects young women; 33% of the reported cases were women 15 to 19 years old (Centers for Disease Control, 1981). Because toxic shock syndrome progresses rapidly and can cause death, a menstruating woman with several of these symptoms should immediately consult a physician (Taylor and Lockwood, 1981; Tanner et al., 1981).

Some guidelines have been developed that may help prevent toxic shock from occurring. One suggestion has been to use sanitary napkins instead of tampons. Suggestions for women who want to continue to use tampons include: use regular instead of superabsorbent tampons, change them three to four times during the day, and use napkins sometime during each 24-hour period of menstrual flow. A woman should consult her health-care practitioner for further up-to-date suggestions pertaining to prevention of TSS.

SUMMARY

GENITAL SELF-EXAM

1. Genital self-exploration is a good way for a woman to learn about her own body and to notice any changes that may require medical attention.

THE VULVA

2. The female external genitals, also called the vulva, are composed of the mons veneris, labia majora, labia minora, clitoris, urethral and vaginal openings. Each woman's vulva is unique in shape, color, and texture.

3. The mons veneris and labia majora have underlying pads of fatty tissue and are covered by pubic hair beginning at adolescence.

4. The labia minora are folds of sensitive skin which begin at the hood over the clitoris and extend downward to below the vaginal opening.

5. The clitoris is composed of the external glans and shaft and the internal crura. The glans contains densely concentrated nerve endings. The only purpose of the clitoris is sexual pleasure.

6. The urethral opening is located between the clitoris and vaginal introitus.

UNDERLYING STRUCTURES

7. Below the surface of the vulva are the vestibular bulbs and the multidirectional pelvic floor muscles.

INTERNAL STRUCTURES

8. Most cultures have placed great importance on the hymen as proof of virginity. However, there are various sizes, shapes, and thicknesses of hymens, and many women can have initial intercourse without pain or bleeding. Women who have decided to have coitus can also learn how to stretch their own hymens to help make their first experience comfortable.

9. The vagina, with its three layers of tissue, extends about three to five inches into the pelvic cavity. It is a potential rather than an actual space and increases in size during sexual arousal, coitus,

and childbirth. The other internal reproductive structures are the cervix, uterus, fallopian tubes, and ovaries.

10. Vaginal lubrication, the secretion of alkaline fluid through the vaginal walls during arousal, is important both in enhancing the longevity and motility of sperm cells and in increasing the pleasure and comfort of intercourse.

11. The Grafenberg spot is located about one centimeter above the surface of the top wall of the vagina.

12. The vaginal walls and cervix produce normal secretions. Occasionally, a vaginal infection occurs that results in irritation, unusual discharge, or a disagreeable odor.

13. A hysterectomy or oophorectomy may, in some cases, have an effect—either positive or negative—on a woman's sexuality.

THE BREASTS

14. The breasts are composed of fatty tissue and milk-producing glands. A monthly self-exam of the breasts is an important part of health care.

15. Three types of lumps can appear in the breasts; cysts, fibroadenomas, and malignant tumors. Careful diagnosis of a breast lump is important. Increasing numbers of physicians believe that less radical surgeries for breast cancer are as effective as more severe procedures.

MENSTRUATION

16. The menstrual cycle results from an interplay between the central nervous system and the endocrine system. The cycle is divided into the proliferative, the secretory, and the menstrual phases. While much societal negativity has been historically attached to menstruation, some people are currently redefining it in a more positive fashion.

17. There are usually no medical reasons to abstain from intercourse during menstruation. However, many people do limit their sexual activity during this time.

18. There is conflicting evidence about the effects of the menstrual cycle on mood and performance.

19. Some women have difficulties with premenstrual tension syndrome or primary or secondary dysmenorrhea. Knowledge about the physiological factors that contribute to these problems is increasing.

20. Amenorrhea occurs normally during pregnancy, breast feeding, and after menopause. It can also be due to medical problems or poor health.

21. Toxic shock syndrome symptoms include fever, sore throat, nausea, red skin flush, dizziness, and high blood pressure.

SUGGESTED READINGS

Boston Women's Health Book Collective. *Our Bodies, Ourselves.* 2nd ed. New York: Simon & Schuster, 1976. A thorough exploration of female sexuality, anatomy, and physiology. The book has a strong emphasis on health care and covers such topics as sexual relationships, rape, VD, birth control, parenthood, and menopause.

"Breast Cancer: The Retreat from Radical Surgery." *Consumer Reports*, January 1981. An excellent and informative article detailing the history and current findings of treatment of breast cancer.

Friday, Nancy. *My Mother, Myself.* New York: Delacorte, 1977. A compelling integration of expert testimony and personal insight into many complex aspects of mother-daughter relationships, with an emphasis on the effects of this relationship on female sexuality.

Steinem, Gloria. "If Men Could Menstruate." *Ms.*, October 1978. A humorous, yet provocative, "political fantasy" about how menstruation would be treated in our society if men, instead of women, menstruated.

5

Male Sexual Anatomy and Physiology

SEXUAL ANATOMY
  The Scrotum
  The Testes
  The Vas Deferens
  The Seminal Vesicles
  The Prostate Gland
  The Cowper's Glands
  Semen
  The Penis
MALE SEXUAL FUNCTIONS
  Erection
  Ejaculation
SOME CONCERNS ABOUT SEXUAL FUNCTIONING
  Penis Size
  Circumcision
SUMMARY
SUGGESTED READINGS

Who needs a lecture on male anatomy? Certainly not the men in this class. It's hanging out there all our lives. We handle it and look at it each time we pee or bathe. So what's the mystery? Now the female body—that is a different story. That's why I'm in the class. Let's learn something that isn't so obvious. (Authors' files)

*T*he preceding quote, from a student in a sexuality class, illustrates two common assumptions. The first is that there is a simplicity about male sexual anatomy that requires little elaboration. A second, perhaps more subtle, implication is that female genital structures are, by comparison, considerably more complicated and mysterious. Neither of these assumptions is necessarily true. There is a complexity and beauty in the sexual anatomy of both men and women that transcends description. Although increasing our understanding of often complex biological sexual functions does not necessarily ensure sexual satisfaction, such knowledge may help us develop comfort with our bodies.

In recent years, there has been a strong movement among women to assume responsibility for understanding and influencing their own sexual health. There has not yet been an equivalent movement for men. We are hopeful that this will change; books like Zilbergeld's *Male Sexuality* (1978) may help. This publication provides some excellent guidelines for a self-health program for men.

Perhaps male reluctance to move toward self-health care has been due to the fact that a male's anatomy "hangs right out there." Nevertheless, easy accessibility does not necessarily imply familiarity—and in fact, many men are quite ill-at-ease with the idea of a detailed self-exam. As in the preceding chapter, we encourage readers to use the pages that follow as a reference for their own self-knowledge.

SEXUAL ANATOMY

We will begin with discussions of the various structures of the male sexual anatomy. Descriptive accounts are organized according to parts of the genital system for the reader's easy reference. Later in this chapter (and in Chapter 6), we will look more closely at the way the system functions during sexual arousal.

The Scrotum

The *scrotum*, or scrotal sac, is a loose pouch of skin that is basically an outpocket of the abdominal wall in the groin area (see Figure 5.1). Normally, it hangs loosely from the body wall, although influences such as cold temperatures or sexual stimulation may cause it to move closer to the body.

The scrotal sac consists of two layers. The outermost is a covering of thin skin that is darker in color than other body skin. It typically becomes sparsely covered with hair at adolescence. The second layer, known as the *tunica dartos*, is composed of smooth muscle fibers plus fibrous connective tissue.

Within the scrotal sac are two separate compartments, each of which houses a single testicle. Each testicle is suspended within its respective compartment by the

FIGURE 5.1 THE SCROTUM AND TESTES

(a) The spermatic cord can be located by palpating the scrotal sac, above either testicle, with thumb and forefinger. (b) Sperm is produced within the interior of the testes in the seminiferous tubules and then transported to the epididymis, which serves as a storage chamber.

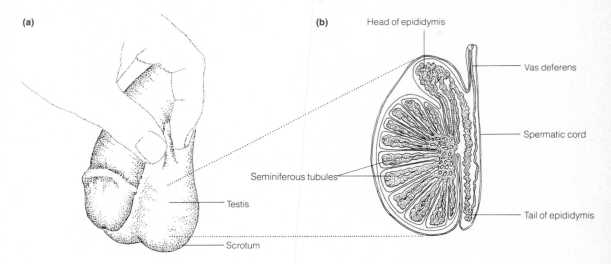

(a)

Testis

Scrotum

(b)

Head of epididymis

Vas deferens

Spermatic cord

Seminiferous tubules

Tail of epididymis

spermatic cord, a structure that contains the sperm-carrying tube, or *vas deferens*, blood vessels, nerves, and *cremasteric* muscle fibers which influence the position of the testicle in the scrotal sac. These muscles may be voluntarily contracted, causing the testicles to move upward. Most males find they can produce this effect with practice; this exercise is one way for a man to become more familiar with his body. As shown in Figure 5.1, the spermatic cord may be located by palpating the scrotal sac, above either testicle, with thumb and forefinger. It is a firm, rubbery tube that is generally quite pronounced.

The Testes

The *testes*, or testicles, have two major functions: the secretion of male sex hormones and the production of sperm. The testes form inside the abdominal cavity during prenatal development. Late in fetal development they migrate from their position inside the abdomen to the scrotum. The route they take is known as the *inguinal canal*.

At birth, the testes are normally in the scrotum. However, in some instances [estimates range from 1% to 7% of males (Campbell, 1970)], either one or both fail to descend. This condition is known as *cryptorchidism* (meaning "hidden testis"). Undescended testicles often move into place spontaneously some time after birth, usually in the first year or two, and no treatment is needed. Occasionally, however, undescended testicles are overlooked into adolescence, primarily because hormone production continues and the changes in body structures at puberty usually occur in routine fashion. The following account of a former student reflects this oversight:

Your discussion of undescended testicles had quite an impact on me. The woman I live with has a 13-year-old son who has this condition. When I asked her about it, she just said, "That's the way it is with him." Obviously, she didn't ask the right questions or got some bad advice along the way. (Authors' files)

It is important to watch out for undescended testicles, especially when both testicles are affected, because the internal body temperature is too high to permit normal sperm production and infertility may result. Surgery or hormonal treatment may be necessary to allow the testicles to descend.

We are not certain of the exact relationship between heat and sperm production, but we do know that the average scrotal temperature is approximately 3.1°C (5.6°F) lower than body temperature (Tessler and Krahn, 1966). In fact, both historical and contemporary writers have suggested that hot baths may be an effective method of male contraception. There is some supporting evidence for this notion; for example, it has been reported that a 30-minute exposure to heat (which is within the tolerable range) can arrest sperm production for as long as several weeks (Dickinson, 1949). Even so, sitting in the health spa steam room or a hot tub is not a recommended method of birth control. Considering the wide range of variables involved (for instance, sufficient temperature, frequency of exposure, or time in the bath), it would be reckless to rely on such a procedure to provide sufficient protection against conception.

In recent years there has been considerable speculation that higher-than-normal scrotal temperature may be related to male infertility. Tight clothing has been implicated by more than one writer. One study demonstrated that men who wore a specially designed jock strap had significant increases in scrotal temperature, with a corresponding lowering of their sperm count (Robinson and Rock, 1967). While it is unlikely that hot baths or tight garments have a significant effect on sperm production in most men, these conditions should not be overlooked as possible contributors in some cases of infertility.

The scrotum is very sensitive to any temperature change, and numerous sensory receptors in the skin provide information that prevents the testicles from becoming either too warm or too cold. When the scrotum is cooled, the tunica dartos contracts, wrinkling the outer skin layer and pulling the testicles up closer to the warmth of the body. This process is essentially involuntary, and the reaction sometimes has amusing ramifications:

When I took swimming classes in high school, the trip back to the locker room was always a bit traumatic. After peeling off my swim togs, it seemed like I had to search around for my balls. The other guys seemed to have the same problem as evidenced by their frantic tugging and pulling as they tried to get everything back in place. (Authors' files)

Another kind of stimulation that causes the scrotum to draw closer to the body is sexual arousal. One of the clearest external indications of impending male orgasm is when the testicles draw up to a position of maximum elevation. The major scrotal muscle involved in this response is the cremasteric muscle, mentioned earlier. Sudden fear may also cause strong contractions of the cremaster. It is also possible to initiate contractions of this muscle by stroking the inner thighs. This response is known as the *cremasteric reflex.*

The movements of the testes and scrotal sac are influenced by factors other than temperature change, sexual arousal, and strong emotion. These structures have the rather amazing property of virtually constant movement, a result of the continuous contraction-relaxation cycles of the cremasteric musculature.

Another testicle characteristic in most men is asymmetry. In Figure 5.1, you will note that the left testicle hangs lower than the right. This is the case for most men, as the left spermatic cord is generally longer than the right. This difference in positioning has often been mistakenly attributed to excessive masturbation. There is no truth to this assertion. The difference is no more unusual than a woman having one breast larger than the other. Our bodies simply are not perfectly symmetrical.

We encourage you to become familiar with the geography of your testicles and to examine them on a regular basis. A variety of diseases attack these organs, including cancer, venereal disease, and an assortment of infections (see Chapter 18). Most of these conditions produce observable symptoms, and early detection allows for rapid treatment and the prevention of more serious complications.

You may examine your testicles in a sitting position (see Figure 5.2), standing, or lying on your back. A good time for this exploration is after a hot shower or bath, since the heat causes the scrotal skin to relax and the testes to descend. In this relaxed, accessible state, it may be easier to detect anything unusual. First, notice the cremasteric cycles of contraction and relaxation, and experiment with initiating the cremasteric reflex. Then explore the testicles one at a time, using your fingertips to gently probe their surface, as if you were examining an egg for imperfections. The surface should be relatively smooth and fairly firm in consistency. There are individual variations in the contour and texture of male testicles. Thus, it is important to get to know your own anatomy so that you can note changes. Having two testicles allows you the opportunity for direct comparison, and this is helpful in spotting abnormalities (although it is common for them to be slightly different in size).

Areas that appear swollen or are painful to the touch may indicate the presence of an infection. Along the back of each testicle lies a structure called the *epididymis*, from which the vas deferens carries sperm upward to the urethra. These structures occasionally become infected, an occurrence that may result in an irregular area that is tender to the touch.

Testicular cancer accounts for approximately 1% of all the cancers that occur in men. Surprisingly, this cancer often has an early onset, typically in the early thirties. That is one reason why it is important to know its symptoms. During the early stages of this type of cancer, there usually are no other symptoms beyond a mass within the testicle. The mass will feel hard or irregular to the fingertips and be distinguishable from surrounding healthy tissue. The surface will often feel bumpy, as though a few

Self-examination can increase a man's familiarity with his genitals.

tiny marbles were imbedded in the testicle. Some men may experience additional symptoms such as tender breasts and nipples and painful accumulation of fluid or swelling in the scrotum. For successful treatment, it is important that this mass be detected as soon as possible.

The Seminiferous Tubules   Within and adjacent to the testes are two separate areas involved in the production and storage of sperm. The first of these, the *seminiferous* (sperm-bearing) *tubules*, are thin, highly coiled structures located in the approximately 250 cone-shaped lobes that make up the interior of each testicle (see Figure 5.1). *Spermatogenesis*, or sperm production, takes place within these tubules. For most males this process begins sometime after the onset of puberty. Men continue to produce viable sperm cells well into their old age, often until death (although the production rate does diminish with aging). The *interstitial* or *Leydig's cells* are located between the seminiferous tubules. These cells are the major source of androgen, and their close proximity to blood vessels allows for direct secretion of their hormone products into the bloodstream. (See Chapter 6 for a discussion of the role of hormones in sexual behavior.)

The Epididymis The second important area for sperm processing is the *epididymis* (literally, "over the testes"). The developed sperm move out of the seminiferous tubules through a maze of tiny ducts into this C-shaped structure that adheres to the back and upper surface of each testis (Figure 5.1). Evidence suggests that the epididymis serves primarily as a storage chamber, where the sperm cells undergo additional maturing, or ripening, for a period of several weeks. During this time they are completely inactive. Based on studies of other animals, researchers theorize that a selection process also occurs in the epididymis, in which abnormal sperm cells are eliminated by the body's waste removal system.

The Vas Deferens

Eventually the sperm move through the epididymis and drain into the *vas deferens* or ductus deferens, a long thin duct which travels up through the scrotum inside the spermatic cord. The vas deferens is close to the surface of the scrotum along this route, and this makes the common male sterilization procedure, *vasectomy* (see Chapter 11), relatively simple.

The spermatic cord exits out of the scrotal sac through the inguinal canal, an opening that leads directly into the abdominal cavity. From this point the vas deferens continues on its journey, looping over the ureter and behind the back of the bladder, as shown in Figure 5.3. (This pathway is essentially the reverse of the route taken by the testis during its prenatal descent.) Turning downward, the vas deferens reaches the base of the bladder, where it is joined by the excretory duct of the *seminal vesicle*, thus forming the *ejaculatory duct*. The two ejaculatory ducts (one from each side) are very

FIGURE 5.3 MALE SEXUAL ANATOMY

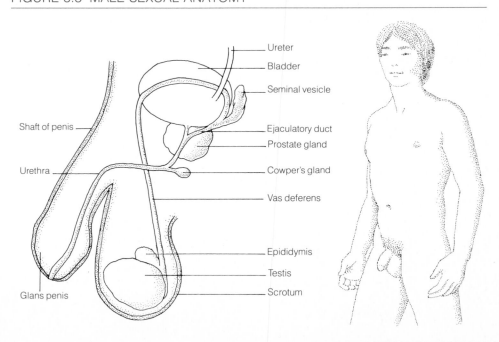

short, running their entire course within the *prostate gland.* At their termination they open into the prostatic portion of the *urethra.*

The Seminal Vesicles

The *seminal vesicles* are two small glands adjacent to the terminals of the vas deferens (Figure 5.3). Their role in sexual physiology is not completely understood at the present time. It was once assumed that they functioned primarily as storage centers for sperm. However, it is now known that they secrete an alkaline fluid that is very rich in fructose sugar. This secretion constitutes a significant portion of the *seminal fluid* (along with secretions of the prostate gland), and its sugar component seems to contribute to both sperm nutrition and motility. Up to this point in its journey from the testicle, a sperm cell is transmitted through the elaborate system of ducts by the continuous movement of *cilia,* tiny hairlike structures that line the inner walls of these tubes. Once stimulated by the energy-giving secretions of the seminal vesicles, sperm are able to propel themselves by the whiplike action of their tails.

The Prostate Gland

The *prostate gland* is a structure about the size and shape of a walnut, located at the base of the bladder (Figure 5.3). As described earlier, both ejaculatory ducts and the urethra pass through this organ. It is made up of smooth muscle fibers and glandular tissue, whose secretions account for the greatest portion of seminal fluid released during ejaculation. When we administer initial questionnaires to our beginning sexuality students, most men and women indicate that they believe the testicles to be the major suppliers of semen. Actually, the contribution of the testes is limited primarily to the millions of sperm cells contained in a typical ejaculate—quantitatively speaking, only a very small portion of the total fluid expelled.

While the prostate is continually active in a mature male, it accelerates its output during sexual arousal. Its secretions flow into the urethra through a system of sievelike ducts, and here they combine with sperm and the seminal vesicle secretions to form the seminal fluid. The prostatic secretions are thin, milky, and alkaline in nature. This alkalinity helps to counteract the unfavorable acidity of the male urethra and the female vaginal tract, making a more hospitable environment for the sperm.

The prostate gland is the focal point of some of the more common physiosexual problems in the human male. Occasionally, it becomes enlarged and inflamed as a result of various infectious agents (such as gonococcus and Trichomonas). This condition, known as *prostatitis,* may occur among men of any age. The symptoms of prostatitis may include any or all of the following: pain in the pelvic area or base of the penis, lower abdominal ache, backache, aching testicles, feelings of urgency (needing to urinate frequently), burning sensation while urinating, a cloudy discharge from the penis, and difficulties with sexual functions, such as painful erections or ejaculations and reduced sexual interest.

Some men also develop cancer of the prostate, and the potential for this becomes greater with increasing age. According to the American Cancer Society, approximately 22,000 men die each year from prostate cancer, the majority of whom would have been saved by early diagnosis and treatment. Consequently, it is very important for men to be aware of the early symptoms of this disease, which may include many of those listed for prostatitis (particularly pain in the pelvis and lower back and urinary complications). However, in its early stages prostate cancer often does not have easily detectable symptoms, and an early diagnosis may be accomplished only by a physical examination.

A physician examines the prostate by inserting a finger into the rectum. Under normal conditions this process is only mildly uncomfortable. During this procedure, the physician may also detect signs of cancer in the colon or rectum. The American Cancer Society recommends an annual digital rectal examination for men and women age 40 and older (women also develop cancers of the rectum and colon—about 53,000 men and women die of these diseases each year).

Many men are reluctant to have this examination. They may be uncomfortable about homosexual associations when the examining physician is male. They may also fear the implications of what the examination may reveal. False information abounds in the area of prostate disease, and many men incorrectly believe that prostate surgery will inevitably block sexual functioning. The reality is that surgery on the prostate only occasionally results in major impairment of the biological aspects of male sexual function. More will be said about this issue in Chapter 15, in which we will discuss sexuality and aging.

The Cowper's Glands

The *Cowper's* or *bulbourethral glands* are two small structures, each about the size of a pea, located on each side of the urethra just below where it emerges from the prostate gland (Figure 5.3). Tiny ducts connect both glands directly to the urethra. When a man is sexually aroused, these organs often secrete a slippery, mucoid substance that appears in droplet form at the tip of the penis. Like the prostatic secretions, this fluid is alkaline in nature, helping to buffer the acidity of the urethra. Furthermore, it is thought to provide lubrication for the flow of seminal fluid through the penis. Contrary to some reports, though, it has virtually no function as a vaginal lubricant during coitus. For many men, these secretions do not appear until well after the beginning of arousal, often just prior to orgasm. Other men report this emission immediately after obtaining an erection, and some individuals rarely or never produce these pre-ejaculatory droplets. All of those experiences are normal variations of male sexual functioning.

While the fluid from the Cowper's glands should not be confused with semen, it does occasionally contain active, healthy sperm. This is one reason among many why the withdrawal method of birth control is not highly effective.

Semen

As we have seen, the *semen* ejaculated through the opening of the penis comes from a variety of sources. Fluids are supplied by the prostate, seminal vesicles, and Cowper's glands, with the prostate providing the greatest portion. The amount of seminal fluid a man ejaculates is influenced by a number of factors, including the length of time since last orgasm; the duration of arousal time before ejaculation; and age (older men tend to produce less fluid). The semen of a single ejaculation typically contains between 200 and 500 million sperm. Chemical analysis shows that semen is also made up of acids (ascorbic and citric), water, enzymes, fructose sugar, bases (phosphate and bicarbonate buffers), and a variety of other substances. None of these materials is harmful if swallowed during oral sex.

The Penis

The *penis* consists of nerves, blood vessels, fibrous tissue, and three parallel cylinders of spongy tissue. It does not contain a bone; neither does it possess an abundance of muscular tissue, contrary to the beliefs of some people. However, there is an extensive network of muscles around the base of the penis, and these help to eject both semen and urine through the urethra.

A portion of the penis extends internally into the pelvic cavity. This part, including its attachment to the pubic bones, is referred to as the *root*. When a man's penis is erect, he can feel this inward projection by pressing a finger up between his anus and scrotum. The external, pendulous portion of the penis, excluding the head, is known as the *shaft*. The smooth, acorn-shaped head is called the *glans*.

Running the entire length of the penis are the three chambers referred to earlier. The two larger ones, the *cavernous bodies* (corpora cavernosa), lie side by side above the smaller third cylinder called the *spongy body* (corpus spongiosum). At the root of the penis the innermost tips of the cavernous bodies (*crura*) are connected to the pubic bones. At the head of the penis the spongy body expands to form the glans. It also enlarges at its base to form the *bulb* of the penis. The relationship between these three structures is shown in Figure 5.4.

All of these chambers are similar in structure. As the terms *cavernous* and *spongy* imply, they are made of a vast array of irregular spaces and cavities, having properties similar to a sponge. Each chamber is also richly supplied with blood vessels. When a male is sexually excited, these structures become engorged with blood, resulting in penile erection. During sexual arousal, the spongy body may stand out as a distinct ridge along the underside of the penis.

The skin covering the penile shaft is usually hairless and quite loose, which allows for some expansion when the penis becomes erect. While it is connected to the shaft at its neck (the portion just behind the glans), some of the skin folds over and forms a cuff or hood over the glans. This loose covering is called the *foreskin* or *prepuce*. In some males it covers the entire head, while in others only a portion is covered. Typically, the foreskin can be retracted (drawn back from the glans) quite easily. *Circumcision*, discussed later, involves the permanent removal of this sleeve of skin.

While the entire penis is sensitive to tactile (touch) stimulation, the greatest concentration of nerve endings is found in the glans. Although the entire glans area is extremely sensitive, there are two specific locations that many men find to be particularly responsive to stimulation. One is the rim or crown that marks the area where the glans rises abruptly from the shaft. This distinct ridge is called the *corona*.

FIGURE 5.4 INTERIOR STRUCTURE OF THE PENIS

135

Three parallel cylinders of erectile tissue (the cavernous bodies and spongy body) run the entire length of the penis.

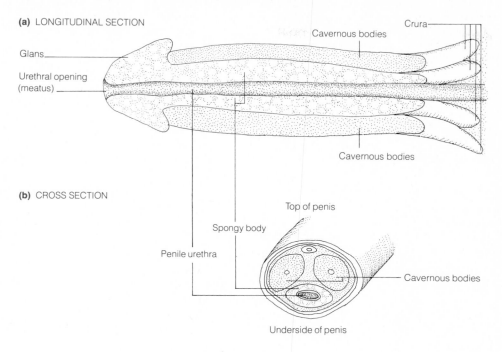

(a) LONGITUDINAL SECTION

Crura

Cavernous bodies

Glans

Urethral opening
(meatus)

Cavernous bodies

(b) CROSS SECTION

Top of penis

Spongy body

Penile urethra

Cavernous bodies

Underside of penis

On its underside, the glans is connected to the foreskin by a thin strip of skin called the *frenum* or *frenulum*. The location of these two areas is shown in Figure 5.5.

While most men enjoy stimulation of the glans, particularly the two areas mentioned above, individuals vary in their preferences. Some may occasionally or routinely prefer stimulation in genital areas other than the glans of the penis. The mode of stimulation, either manual (by self or partner) or oral, may influence the choice of preferred sites. Some of these variations and individual preferences are noted in the following accounts:

When I masturbate I frequently avoid the head of my penis, concentrating instead on stroking the shaft. What happens is that the stimulation is not so intense, and that allows a longer time for build-up to orgasm. The end result is that the climax is generally more intense than if I focus only on the glans. (Authors' files)

Occasionally, when I make love for an extended period of time, my glans gets so sensitive that I can't stand to have it touched or sucked by my partner. In such cases I either have to stop for awhile or start having intercourse so the stimulation is not quite so intense. (Authors' files)

The corona and frenum are two areas on the penis that contain a
great concentration of sensitive nerve endings.

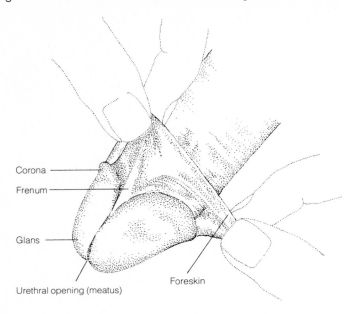

Corona

Frenum

Glans

Urethral opening (meatus)

Foreskin

When I started making love with men rather than women, it was so much easier to
get and give sexual pleasure. We both know where those special pleasure spots
are and how a man likes to have them touched. Before, with women, it was
always a hassle trying to get the message across. (Authors' files)

During oral sex with my girlfriend I sometimes have to put my hand around my
penis, leaving just the head sticking out, so she will get the idea what part feels
best to me. Otherwise, she spends a lot of time running her tongue up and down
the shaft which just doesn't do it for me. (Authors' files)

In addition to demonstrating an array of stimulation preferences in men, these
anecdotes, particularly the last two, reveal a common concern or difficulty that many
of us experience in our sexual lives, namely that it is often awkward to communicate
our sexual needs and preferences. We live in a culture that provides few models of
effective sexual communication. We will address this vital area in Chapter 8.

As previously mentioned, the internal extension of the penis is surrounded by an
elaborate network of muscles. This musculature is comparable to that in the female
body, and strengthening these muscles may produce benefits for men that are similar
to those experienced by women doing Kegel exercises. The following is a brief outline
of these procedures for men, adapted from *Male Sexuality* (Zilbergeld, 1978, p. 109):

1. Locate the muscles by stopping the flow of urine several times while urinating. The muscles you squeeze to accomplish this are the ones you will concentrate on.

2. Begin the exercise program by squeezing and relaxing the muscles in sets of 15 each, twice daily. Do not hold the contraction at this stage (these are called "short Kegels").

3. Gradually increase the number of Kegels until you can comfortably do sets of 60 twice daily.

4. At this point, practice "long Kegels" by holding each contraction for a count of three.

5. Now combine both the short and long Kegels in each daily exercise routine, doing two sets of each per day.

6. Continue with the Kegel exercises for at least several weeks. You may not notice results until a month or more has passed. By this time the exercises will have probably become automatic requiring no particular effort.

Some of the positive changes men have reported after doing the male Kegels include stronger and more pleasurable orgasms, better ejaculatory control, and increased pelvic sensation during sexual arousal.

Caring for the penis is an important aspect of sexual self-health. Be aware of any unusual changes in your penis. A sore or unusual growth anywhere on its surface may be a symptom of a sexually transmitted disease (see Chapter 18). Sometimes the glans and/or shaft of the penis may develop an eczema-like reaction ("weepy" and sore). This may result from an allergic reaction to the vaginal secretions of your partner. Wearing a condom may help to alleviate this condition, but it is important that you consult a physician to clarify its origin and treatment. (*Urology* is the medical specialty that focuses on the male reproductive structures.)

It is wise to avoid abusing your penis by putting it in potentially harmful places such as partners' mouths that have herpes blisters or vaginas that manifest unusual sores, growths, odors, or discharges. There are some sexual gadgets that may also be quite hazardous to penile health. For example, never use a "cock ring" (a tight-fitting ring that encircles the base of the penis). This device, while perhaps successful in accomplishing its intended purpose of sustaining erections, may destroy penile tissue by cutting off the blood supply. Actually, any device that alters natural processes within the penis can be harmful.

Washing the penis regularly with soap and water, at least once a day, is an excellent self-health practice. (There is also evidence that washing the genitals before and after sex may reduce the chances of exchanging infectious organisms with your partner—see Chapter 18 for more details.) If you are uncircumsized, pay particular attention to drawing the foreskin back from the glans and washing all surfaces, especially the underside of the foreskin. After bathing, thoroughly dry all surfaces of your penis.

MALE SEXUAL FUNCTIONS

Up to this point in the chapter, we have been looking at the various parts of the male sexual system, but we have not described their functioning in much detail. In the following pages, we will examine two of these functions, erection and ejaculation.

Erection

An *erection* is essentially an involuntary process coordinated by the autonomic nervous system. When a male becomes sexually excited, the nervous system transmits messages that induce expansion of the arteries leading to the three spongy erectile chambers in the penis. This increases the rate of blood flow into these parallel cylinders. The blood flowing out of the penis, through the veins, cannot keep up with the dramatically increased inflow, and so it accumulates in the spongelike tissues. The penis remains erect until the messages from the nervous system stop and the inflow of blood returns to normal.

The capacity for erection is present at birth. It is very common and quite natural for infant boys to experience erections during sleep or diapering, from stimulation by clothing, and later by touching themselves. Nighttime erections occur during the REM, or dreaming, stage of sleep (Fisher et al., 1965; Karacan, 1970). While erotic dreams may play a role, the primary mechanism seems to be physiological, and erections often occur even when the dream content is clearly not sexual. Often a man awakens in the morning just after completing a REM cycle. This explains the phenomenon of morning erections, which in the past have been erroneously attributed to a full bladder.

While an erection is basically a physiological response, it also involves psychological components. In fact, some writers distinguish between psychogenic (from the mind) and physiogenic (from the body) erections—although in most cases of sexual arousal, there are simultaneous inputs from both thoughts and physical stimulation.

How great an influence does the mind have on erections? We know that it can inhibit the response: when a man becomes troubled by erection difficulties, the problem is usually of psychological origin (see Chapter 16). It is even conceivable, given the developing science of biofeedback, that men might be trained to "think" an erection. Nevertheless, this is an unlikely eventuality, at least for most men. Therefore, a man's penis, unlike other appendages of his body, will continue to act as though it has a will of its own, not always behaving in a way the mind might prefer.

Logically, one might expect erection to occur only in response to obvious sexual stimuli. This is not always the case, however, a fact that can be embarrassing, perplexing, amusing, or anxiety-arousing. Most men can recall episodes of unwanted erections during adolescent school days—the teacher who said "Crooks, come up here and do the math problem on the board," when math was the farthest thing from my mind; the trips down school halls with a notebook held in a strategic location; the delayed exit from the swimming pool after playful frolicking.

Sometimes erections happen in situations that seem entirely nonsexual, such as riding a bike, lifting heavy weights, or straining during defecation (particularly pronounced in little boys). Occasionally, the occurrence of an erection may produce considerable anxiety and cause a person to question his own motivations. This is evident in the following report offered by a father and former student in our sexuality class.

Sometimes when my little girl crawls up on my lap to be cuddled, I find myself getting an erection. This bothers me greatly. Does it mean I have some kind of unconscious, incestuous craving for my daughter? (Authors' files)

This kind of experience, and the anxiety associated with it, is not unusual. It is possible to experience a reflex erection from direct physical stimulation during cuddling with a child. The response may also be psychologically induced, and in this sense it is probably a predictable event in our culture. Consider the following account:

When I was a little boy my father would go away on extended business trips. I missed him terribly and when he returned I wanted to rush across the room and catapult myself into his arms. Instead, like a man, I shook his hand and said "Hi, Dad, good to see you." I guess I started losing little pieces of my humanity even that early. (Authors' files)

Like this person, many men learn very early that it is not "masculine" to cuddle and embrace those near and dear to us. Particularly among adult males in our society, intimate physical contact occurs either primarily or exclusively within a sexual context. With this kind of conditioning, the association of warm embraces and sexual excitation will be quite strong. In this sense, it is not "unnatural" at all for a father to experience an erection when he holds his child closely.

Ejaculation

Besides erection, the second basic male sexual function is *ejaculation*—the process whereby the semen is expelled through the penis to the outside of the body. Many writers equate orgasm and ejaculation in the male. However, these two processes do not always take place simultaneously. Prior to puberty, a boy may experience hundreds of orgasms without any ejaculation of fluid. Occasionally, a man may have more than one orgasm in a given sexual encounter, with the second or third producing little or no expelled semen. Recent research reveals that some men may experience a series of nonejaculatory orgasms culminating in a final orgasm accompanied by expulsion of semen (Robbins and Jensen, 1978). Thus, it is clear that while male orgasm is generally associated with ejaculation, these two processes are not one and the same and they do not necessarily occur together.

From a neurophysiological point of view, ejaculation, like erection, is basically a spinal reflex. Effective sexual stimulation of the penis (manual, oral, or coital) results in the buildup of neural excitation to a critical level. When a threshold is reached, this triggers several internal physical events.

The actual ejaculation occurs in two stages (see Figure 5.6). During the first stage, sometimes called the *emission phase*, the prostate, seminal vesicles, and upper portions of the vas deferens (called the *ampulla*) undergo smooth muscle contractions. This forces their various secretions down into the ejaculatory ducts and prostatic urethra. At the same time, both internal and external *urethral sphincters* (two muscles, one located where the urethra exits from the bladder and the other below the prostate) are closed, trapping seminal fluid in the *urethral bulb* (the prostatic portion of the urethra between these two muscles). The area expands like a balloon. A man typically experiences this first phase as a subjective sense that orgasm is inevitable, the so-called "point of no return."

FIGURE 5.6 EJACULATION

Male sexual anatomy during ejaculation: (a) the emission stage and (b) the expulsion stage.

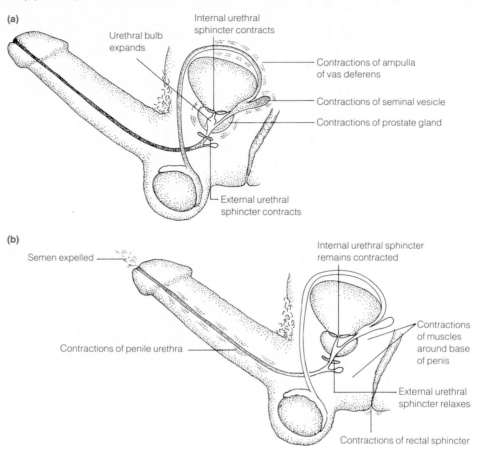

(a)

Urethral bulb expands

Internal urethral sphincter contracts

Contractions of ampulla of vas deferens

Contractions of seminal vesicle

Contractions of prostate gland

External urethral sphincter contracts

(b)

Semen expelled

Internal urethral sphincter remains contracted

Contractions of muscles around base of penis

Contractions of penile urethra

External urethral sphincter relaxes

Contractions of rectal sphincter

In the second stage, sometimes called the *expulsion phase*, the collected semen is expelled out of the penis by strong, rhythmic contractions of muscles that surround the internal bulb and crura of the penis. In addition, there are contractions along the entire urethral route. The external urethral sphincter relaxes, allowing fluid to pass through, while the internal sphincter remains contracted to prevent the escape of urine. The first two or three muscle contractions around the base of the penis are quite strong and occur at close intervals. Most of the seminal fluid is expelled in spurts corresponding to these contractions. Several more muscle responses typically occur, with a gradual diminishing of intensity and lengthening of time intervals between contractions. The entire expulsion stage usually takes place in three to ten seconds.

It is often assumed that once a man enters the emission phase, ejaculation inevitably follows. Well-known research, including the Masters and Johnson study, has supported this view:

In contrast to the fact that orgasmic experience of the human female can be interrupted by extraneous psychosensory stimuli, the male orgasmic experience, once initiated by contractions of the accessory organs of reproduction, cannot be constrained or delayed until the seminal-fluid emission has been completed. Regardless of intensity of extraneous sensory stimuli, the male will carry the two-stage ejaculatory process to completion. (Masters and Johnson, 1966, p. 217)

This observation seems inconsistent with experiences occasionally related to us. The following describes one of these supposed biological impossibilities:

Occasionally, when I feel like I'm going to orgasm, I stop all movement. If my partner cooperates, I have what seems like a little climax, with a contraction or two. Unlike with a normal, complete orgasm, I have no problem maintaining interest and an erection after this "false start." (Authors' files)

We have surveyed large numbers of our male students over the years and have found this experience to be somewhat uncommon but by no means rare. A more detailed discussion of this phenomenon and its implications for sexual sharing is included in Chapter 17.

Some men have an experience known as *retrograde ejaculation* where the semen is expelled into the bladder rather than through the penis (see Figure 5.7). This results from a reversed functioning of the two urethral sphincters. The condition occurs in about 80% of men who have undergone prostate surgery (Hotchkiss, 1971). In addition, illness, congenital anomaly, and certain drugs, most notably tranquilizers, can induce this reaction. Some men have allegedly developed the voluntary ability to

FIGURE 5.7 RETROGRADE EJACULATION

A reversed functioning of the urethral sphincters (internal relaxes, external contracts) results in semen being expelled into the bladder.

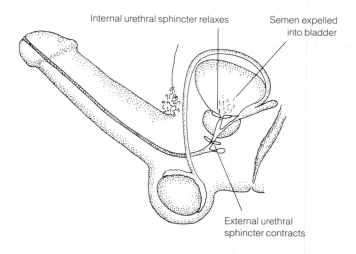

Internal urethral sphincter relaxes

Semen expelled into bladder

External urethral sphincter contracts

produce retrograde ejaculations as a method of birth control. As yet, though, the training techniques for acquiring this capability have not been clearly outlined. While retrograde ejaculation is not harmful itself (the seminal fluid is later eliminated with the urine), a man who consistently experiences this response would be wise to seek medical attention to rule out the possibility of an underlying health problem.

There are instances when a man experiences orgasm without direct genital stimulation. The most familiar of these are *nocturnal emissions* (commonly known as "wet dreams"). The exact mechanism that produces this response is not fully understood. Women also have the capacity for experiencing orgasm during sleep. In a waking state, the possibility of a man using fantasy alone to reach orgasm is exceedingly unlikely, and we have never heard a firsthand account of this phenomenon. Kinsey (1948) stated that only three or four of the males in his sample of over 5000 reported this kind of experience. In contrast, significantly greater numbers of women in his sample (roughly 2%) reported orgasms from fantasy alone (Kinsey et al., 1953). Another kind of nongenitally induced ejaculation that men sometimes report is reaching orgasm during sex play (activities such as mutual kissing or manual or oral stimulation of a man's partner) when there is no penile stimulation.

SOME CONCERNS ABOUT SEXUAL FUNCTIONING

A variety of concerns about male sexual functioning are frequently voiced. Several of these will be addressed throughout our text. At this point we will discuss two areas that receive considerable attention—the significance of penis size and the necessity and impact of circumcision. Claims are frequently made that one or both of these physical characteristics may influence the sexual pleasure of a man or his partner. In the following sections we will examine the available evidence.

Penis Size

When I was a kid my peers were unmerciful in their comments about my small size. They would say things like, "I have a penis, John has a penis, but you have a pee-pee." Needless to say, I grew up with a very poor self-image in this area. Later it was translated into anxiety-ridden sexual encounters where I would insist that the room be completely dark before I would undress. Even now, when I realize that size is an irrelevant factor in giving sexual pleasure, I am still worried that a new partner will comment unfavorably about my less than impressive natural endowment. (Authors' files)

This man is not alone in his discomfort. His feelings are echoed in more accounts than we can remember. Penis size has occupied the attention of most men and many women at one time or another. Generally, it is more than mere idle curiosity that stimulates interest in this topic. For many it is a matter of real concern, perhaps even cause for apprehension or anguish.

A man's self-esteem and sense of identity often are influenced by how he views his penis (Comfort, 1972). We have all heard accounts of the little boy's reaction upon viewing the much bigger penis of his father or older brother. Allegedly, the marked contrast in size may lead to anxiety that affects future well-being. Although this early experience may be important in some cases, in general its effects seem to be a bit overstated. Consider the following account:

One day, while taking a shower with my son, I noticed that he seemed to be overly intrigued by my penis. After his eyes had shifted back and forth between his and mine several times, he expressed the following. "Dad, how come yours is so much bigger than mine?" The unspoken part of this question seemed to be "Will mine ever be as big as yours?" I responded, "Like every other part of the body, it takes time to grow. But yours is a really nice size now, just right for you." He seemed quite content with this simple answer. At least the big smile he flashed did not indicate the presence of any internal conflict, anxiety, envy, or regret. (Authors' files)

It does not take much imagination to understand why penis size often takes on great importance. As a society, we tend to be overly impressed with size and quantity. Bigger cars are better than compacts, the bigger the house the better it is, and, by implication, big penises work better than smaller ones. Certainly the various art forms (literature, painting, sculpture, movies, and so forth) do much to perpetuate this obsession with big penises. Consider the following excerpt from Mario Puzo's novel, *The Godfather* (1969), which describes a sexual encounter between Sonny and Lucy:

. . . She felt something burning pass between her thighs. She let her right hand drop from his neck and reached down to guide him. Her hand closed around an enormous, blood-gorged pole of muscle. It pulsated in her hand like an animal and almost weeping with *grateful ecstasy* she pointed it into her own wet, turgid flesh. The thrust of its entering, the *unbelievable pleasure* made her gasp, brought her legs up around his neck, and then like a quiver, her body received the savage arrows of his lightning-like thrusts; innumerable, torturing; arching her pelvis higher and higher until for the *first time in her life* she reached a shattering climax, felt his hardness break and then the crawly flood of semen over her thighs. (p. 28, italics ours)

The modern Western world is not alone in its preoccupation with penis size, as the photographs on the next page illustrate. Even the fascinating Indian sex manuals, the *Ananga Ranga* and the *Kama Sutra*, classify men according to three categories: the hare-man, whose erect penis measures six finger-widths; the bull-man (nine finger-widths long); and the horse-man (12 or more finger-widths long). In ancient Greek mythology, preoccupation with penis size found a focal point in Priapus, the son of the goddess Aphrodite and the god Dionysus, who was usually portrayed as a lasciviously grinning little man with a greatly oversized penis (see photo on next page).

The result of all this attention to penis size is that men often come to view it as an important attribute in defining their masculinity or worth as a lover. Such a concept of virility can contribute to a poor self-image. Furthermore, if either a man or his partner

Preoccupation with penis size is evident in a variety of art forms. On the left is a pottery lamp in the form of Priapus, the Greek god of fruitfulness.

views his penis as being smaller than desired, this can decrease the sexual satisfaction that one or both may experience. This may occur not because of physical limitations but rather as a self-fulfilling prophecy.

What are the simple physiological facts of sexual interaction and penis size? We will focus on heterosexual penile-vaginal intercourse, since concerns about penis size most often relate to this kind of sexual activity.

As we learned in Chapter 4, the greatest sensitivity in the vaginal canal is concentrated in its outer portion. While some women do find pressure and stretching deep within the vagina to be pleasurable, this is not usually requisite for female sexual gratification. In fact, some women may even find deep penetration to be painful, particularly if it is quite rigorous.

You asked if size was important to my pleasure. Yes, but not in the way you might imagine. If a man is quite large, I worry that he might hurt me. Actually, I prefer that he be average or even to the smaller side. (Authors' files)

There is a physiological explanation for the pain or discomfort some women feel during deep penetration. Since the female ovaries and male testicles originate from the same embryonic tissue source, they share some of the same sensitivity. If the penis bangs into the cervix and causes the uterus to be slightly displaced, this may in turn jar an ovary. The resulting sensation is somewhat like a male's experience of falling off a bike seat onto the cross-bar. Fast stretching of the uterine ligaments has also been implicated in deep penetration pain. However, some women find slow stretching of these same ligaments to be pleasurable.

These observations indicate the importance of being gentle and considerate during intercourse. If deeper or more rigorous thrusting is desired, a couple may experiment by gradually adding these components to their coital movements. It may also be helpful for the woman to be in an intercourse position other than female supine (see Figure 9.6) where she has more control over depth and rigor of penetration.

Occasionally, people are concerned about penis diameter rather than length. There is no physiological reason for this to appreciably affect sensations during coitus. The vagina is amazingly adjustable—it can nicely and firmly accommodate objects ranging in size from one finger to a baby's head.

Most textbooks report average dimensions of penises. We will not do this because such information seems unimportant. As Figure 5.8 indicates, several different flaccid (nonerect) sizes are well within the normal range. It is worth noting that penis size is not related to body shape, height, length of fingers, or anything else. It should also be mentioned that small flaccid penises tend to increase more in size during erection than do penises that are larger in a nonerect state (Masters and Johnson, 1966). These collective facts are reflected in the commentary offered by an extremely tall, husky male:

FIGURE 5.8 VARIATIONS IN MALE GENITALS

There are many normal variations in the shape and size of the male genitals. The penis in the right photo is uncircumcised.

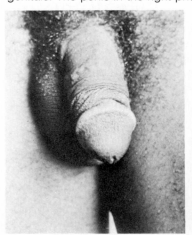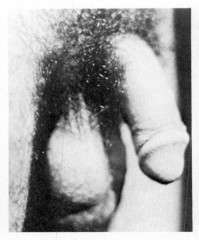

I think most people just naturally assumed, judging from my large stature, that I would have a big penis. Such is not the case. In fact, when I'm flaccid it looks like all I have is testicles and a glans. My shaft is practically invisible. However, when I get hard I know my penis is quite adequate in size. When I was a teenager the problem was how to let my buddies know this when it's not really cool to walk around with a hard-on. What I did was simply avoid taking showers with others if at all possible. Now I feel OK about my body but for awhile there I was really self-conscious. (Authors' files)

One of the most extreme manifestations of preoccupation with penis size is the development of an industry devoted to exploiting this anxiety through advertisements for gadgets and other paraphernalia designed to artificially increase a man's dimensions. For instance, a mail-order catalog originating from Los Angeles listed among its products the "Super Cock," "Big Fat Freddy," the "Super Double Dong," and the "Extensifier." Clearly there is no lack of a market for "easy" ways to enhance one's dimensions.

Circumcision

A characteristic that many people associate with differences in male sensitivity—and also differences in hygiene—is the absence or presence of the foreskin.

Circumcision is the surgical removal of the foreskin shown in Figure 5.9 that is widely practiced throughout the world for religious, ritual, or hygienic reasons. In the United States, this operation is performed on the majority of males (with parental consent) generally on the second day after birth. In certain other cultures the procedure is not accomplished until the onset of male adolescence, when it is a sign of entering manhood, an event which is heralded and celebrated during elaborate rituals. Some religions, including both the Jewish and Moslem faiths, require circumcision.

In this country, the standard medical reasoning behind routine circumcisions has reflected concern about hygiene. These medical arguments have been based on the following. There are a number of small glands located in the foreskin (*preputial glands*) and under the corona, on either side of the frenum (*Tyson's glands*). These glands secrete an oily, lubricating substance. If these secretions are allowed to accumulate under the foreskin, they combine with sloughed off dead skin cells to form a cheesy substance known as *smegma*. When it builds up over a period of time, smegma generally develops a strong, unpleasant odor, becomes grainy and irritating, and can serve as a breeding ground for infection-causing organisms.

There are unsubstantiated claims that penile cancer is more frequent among uncircumcised males (Hand, 1970). There are additional claims that smegma may harbor organisms that can cause a variety of infections in the female vaginal tract. Furthermore, some investigators have suggested that cervical cancer occurs with a higher frequency in women who have sexual relations with uncircumcised partners. However, these assertions have been contradicted by research. For example, one study of Lebanese Moslems and Christians showed that the wives of the rarely circumcised Lebanese Christians had no greater incidence of cervical cancer than their Moslem counterparts whose husbands had been circumcised early in life (Abou-

FIGURE 5.9 CIRCUMCISION

Circumcision, the surgical removal of the foreskin, is practiced throughout the world.

(a)   (b)   (c)   (d)

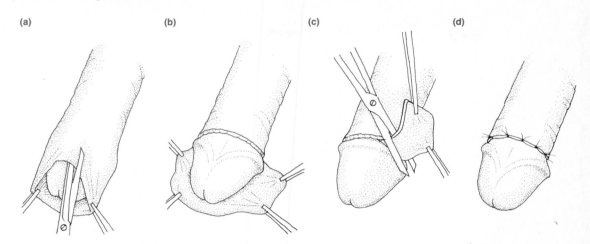

David, 1967). Perhaps the best compilation and interpretation of circumcision research is contained in a recent book by Edward Wallerstein (1980) titled *Circumcision*. After carefully analyzing the available data, Wallerstein concludes that there is absolutely no causal relationship between circumcision and any kind of cancer.

There are several arguments against routine circumcisions, many of which have been raised with greater frequency in recent years. First, it has been suggested that the foreskin may serve some important function as yet to be determined. Second, some have expressed concern that sexual function may be altered by excising the foreskin, as we will see later in this discussion. Finally, such an unpleasant procedure performed on a newborn has been viewed as unnecessary trauma and an invitation to possible surgical complications. Some of the health risks of circumcision include hemorrhage, infections, mutilation, shock, psychological trauma, and even death in rare cases. Certainly the whole question of circumcision as a preventive medical practice is now being seriously questioned. One writer compared the practice of circumcision to pulling out children's teeth when they first appear to avoid possible tooth decay in the future (Street, 1959).

One other critical point should be mentioned. The vast majority of uncircumcised males who practice routine hygienic care are no more likely to encounter health problems than are circumcised males. If this were not so we would expect higher rates of penile infections in Europe, where circumcision is an uncommon practice. This is not the case. It is interesting that even though the medical profession has tended to perpetuate the idea that circumcision equals cleanliness, there is simply no solid evidence to back up this claim. In 1975 the American Academy of Pediatrics asked its Committee on the Fetus and Newborn to review the evidence supporting circumcision as a routine medical practice. After thoroughly examining the available research, the committee concluded that there is no medical indication for circumcision of the newborn, and they recommended that it not be performed routinely (Kirkendall, 1981).

In recent years several American hospitals have established policies whereby circumcisions are performed only at the request of parents or as elective surgery. However, circumcision is still widely practiced. This may be accounted for in part by the fact that established medical procedures are often slow to change. On the other hand, circumcision, a 10-minute operation, may generate fees ranging up to $100 for the surgeon and as much as $300 to the hospital. As one observer wrote, "With more than 1 million babies circumcised in the United States each year, that makes circumcision at least a $55 million business" (Bolch, 1981, p. 4).

It seems that the widely held justification for circumcision creates unnecessary potential for anxiety. In our own classes it is common for most students to assume that circumcision is important for hygiene. How do assumptions like these affect a person's self-image and sexual relations? Consider the following report provided by a surgeon:

When I was serving a stint as ship's surgeon on a large carrier, during the Vietnam conflict, I had a very interesting experience. A young sailor came to me requesting circumcision. When I queried him as to his motivation for undergoing such an operation, he stated that his wife refused to engage in oral sex because she viewed him as unclean. After performing the simple operation, an amazing thing happened. Many more men came with the same request. Apparently the word had circulated rapidly. Their reasons were essentially the same as the first seaman. They either felt unclean themselves or were viewed in this way by partners. (Authors' files)

Accounts like this one are echoed in numerous other reports. With the increasing availability of accurate information, we hope to see a time when the absence of a flap of skin will no longer be considered a sign of personal cleanliness or sexual attractiveness.

Beyond the issue of hygiene, another question has often been raised about circumcision. Do circumcised men enjoy any erotic or functional advantages over uncircumcised men (or vice versa)? Some people assume that the circumcised male responds more quickly during penile-vaginal intercourse because of the fully exposed glans. However, with the exception of a condition known as *phimosis* (an extremely tight prepuce), there is no difference in contact during intercourse. The foreskin of an uncircumcised man is retracted during coitus, so the glans is exposed. It might be assumed, in fact, that the glans of a circumcised man is less sensitive, due to the toughening effect of constant exposure to chafing surfaces. Masters and Johnson investigated both of these questions, and they found no evidence of differences in responsiveness:

The thirty-five uncircumcised males were matched at random with circumcised study subjects of similar ages. Routine neurologic testing for both exteroceptive and light tactile discrimination were conducted on the ventral and dorsal surfaces of the penile body, with particular attention directed toward the glans. No clinically significant difference could be established between the circumcised and the uncircumcised glans during these examinations. (1966, p. 190)

Undoubtedly influenced by the above report, many writers have concluded that the presence or lack of foreskin does not influence sexual function. However, the Masters and Johnson data fail to include the all-important dimension of subjective assessment by men who have experienced both conditions after achieving sexual maturity. Occasionally, we have encountered men in our classroom who have been circumcised during their adult years. Some of these men have reported experiencing physiological differences in sexual arousal—such as a decrease in sensitivity of the glans—as a result of circumcision. But these reactions have not been consistent. Other men afforded this unique comparative opportunity have found no perceivable differences in sexual excitability. It would seem that exploration of the relationship between circumcision and sexual arousability still leaves a number of questions unanswered.

SUMMARY

SEXUAL ANATOMY

1. The scrotum is a loose outpocket of the lower abdominal wall which consists of an outer skin layer and an inner muscular layer. Housed within the scrotum are the testicles, each suspended within its respective compartment by attachment to the spermatic cord.

2. Human testes have two major functions—sperm production and secretion of sex hormones.

3. Sperm development requires a scrotal temperature slightly below that of body temperature.

4. The interior of each testicle is divided into a large number of chambers that contain the thin, highly coiled seminiferous tubules wherein sperm production occurs.

5. Adhering to the back and upper surface of each testicle is a C-shaped structure, the epididymis, within which sperm maturation occurs.

6. Sperm travel from the epididymis of each testicle through a long, thin tube, the vas deferens, which eventually terminates at the base of the bladder where it is joined by the excretory duct of the seminal vesicle.

7. The seminal vesicles are two small glands near the terminals of the vas deferens. They secrete an alkaline fluid (a significant portion of the semen) that appears to nourish and stimulate the sperm cells.

8. The prostate gland, located at the base of the bladder and traversed by the urethra, provides the greatest portion of the seminal fluid released during ejaculation.

9. Two pea-sized structures, the Cowper's glands, are connected by tiny ducts to the urethra just below the prostate gland. During sexual arousal they often produce a few drops of slippery, alkaline fluid which appear at the tip of the penis.

10. Semen consists of sperm cells and secretions from the prostate, seminal vesicles, and Cowper's glands. The sperm component is only a small portion of the total fluid expelled during ejaculation.

11. The penis consists of an internal root within the body cavity; an external, pendulous portion known as its body or shaft; and the smooth, acorn-shaped head called the glans. Running the length of the penis are three internal chambers filled with

spongelike tissue that become engorged with blood during sexual arousal.

MALE SEXUAL FUNCTIONS

12. Penis erection is an involuntary vasocongestive process which results from adequate sexual stimulation—physiological, psychological, or both.

13. Ejaculation is the process where semen is transported out through the penis. It occurs in two stages: the emission phase, when seminal fluid is collected in the urethral bulb; and the expulsive phase, when strong muscle contractions expel the semen. In retrograde ejaculation, semen is expelled into the bladder.

SOME CONCERNS ABOUT SEXUAL FUNCTIONING

14. Penis size does not significantly influence ability to give or receive pleasure during penile-vaginal intercourse. Neither is it correlated with other physical variables such as body shape or height.

15. Circumcision, the surgical removal of the foreskin, is widely practiced in this country. Medical evidence supporting its hygienic benefits is scanty at best, as is data concerning its effect on erotic or functional elements of sexual expression.

SUGGESTED READINGS

Blank, Joani. *The Playbook: For Men/About Sex*. Burlingame, Calif.: Down There Press, 1975. This is an informally written self-awareness workbook for men. It includes topics such as body image, genital awareness, masturbation, sexual response, relationships, and fantasy.

Kinsey, Alfred C.; Pomeroy, Wardell B.; and Martin, Clyde E. *Sexual Behavior in the Human Male*. Philadelphia: W. B. Saunders, 1948. In addition to extensive data on male sexual behaviors, this volume contains an abundance of details about a male's sexual anatomy and the manner in which he responds physiologically to sexual stimulation.

Simon, William. "Male Sexuality: The Secret of Satisfaction." *Today's Health,* April 1975, 32-34,150-152. A noted sex researcher interviews four men of diverse life styles who candidly discuss the meaning of sexual satisfaction in their lives with attention paid to their sexual joys, needs, uncertainties, and fears.

Zilbergeld, Bernie. *Male Sexuality: A Guide to Sexual Fulfillment,* Boston: Little, Brown, 1978. An exceptionally well-written and informative treatment of male sexuality including such topics as sexual functioning, self-awareness, and overcoming difficulties.

6

Sexual Arousal and Response

SEXUAL AROUSAL
  The Role of Hormones
  The Brain
  The Senses and Sexual Arousal
  Foods, Chemicals, and Sexual Behavior
SEXUAL RESPONSE
  Kaplan's Three-Stage Model
  Masters and Johnson's Four-Phase Model
  Some Differences Between the Sexes
SUMMARY
SUGGESTED READINGS

*S*exual arousal and response in humans is influenced by a number of factors: hormones; our brain's capacity to recall experiences and engage in fantasy; our emotions; various sensory processes; the level of intimacy between two people; and a range of other influences. We will begin this chapter by discussing some of the factors that influence sexual arousal. We will then turn our attention to the ways in which our bodies respond to sexual stimulation. We will concentrate primarily on a variety of biological factors and events that are associated with human sexual arousal and response, but this focus on physiology is not meant to minimize the importance of psychological and cultural influences upon these processes. Psychosocial factors play an important and probably greater role in the extremely varied patterns of human sexual response, as we shall discover in later chapters.

SEXUAL AROUSAL

In this section we will single out a number of factors as we explore the complexity of human sexual arousal: the role of hormonal influence; the impact of brain functions; sensory input and the individual ways we interpret it; and, finally, the reputed effects of certain foods and drugs.

The Role of Hormones

Theorists hold differing opinions about the relative importance of hormones on human sexual arousal, for a number of good reasons. For one, it is extremely difficult to distinguish between the effects of strictly physiological processes, especially hormone production, and of psychosocial processes such as early socialization, peer group learning, emotional needs, and the like.

Other reasons for the uncertainty about specific effects of hormones stem from the incomplete data available. Until recently, much of the experimental evidence linking sex hormones to human behavior came from studies of women. This was for two reasons: first, more research funds were available to study female sex hormones (the practical impetus was the development of the birth control pill); and second, we had no reliable method for directly measuring androgen levels in men. However, two recent developments—the introduction of a reliable method for measuring androgen levels and the current search for a male birth control pill—have begun to even out the imbalances in our knowledge.

Another limitation on research into human hormone function as it relates to sexual arousal has been the lack of information about normal males and females. Almost all human data have been obtained from clinical studies of abnormal cases. With the availability of more sophisticated research techniques, however, together with mounting interest in the hormonal bases of sex, we may anticipate that some of the confusion in this area will soon be resolved.

Despite our incomplete understanding of the precise influence of hormones, there is an extensive body of research literature. The available evidence leaves little doubt, as we will see in the following pages, that hormones do play a significant role in human sexual arousal and sexual behavior.

Gonadal Hormones in Male Sexual Behavior A number of experimental investigations have linked androgens, the male sex hormones, with sexual activity. Most of this research has been clinical. Some of the more provocative lines of inquiry include studies of reduced gonadal function, castration, hormone replacement therapy, and androgen-blocking drugs.

Hormones are produced by a variety of glands, including among others the pituitary, the adrenals, the female ovaries, and the male testes, that together make up the human *endocrine system*. There are several diseases of the endocrine system that may impair hormone production in the testes. The result is a state of androgen deprivation, called *hypogonadism*. The effects of hypogonadism indicate the important role of the androgens. If the condition occurs before puberty, maturation of the primary and secondary sex characteristics will be retarded, and the individual may never develop an active sexual interest. If an androgen deficiency occurs after a male reaches adulthood, the results are far more variable. However, in most cases there is some reduction in *libido* (sexual interest) and sexual activity.

The effects of *castration* (removal of the testes) provide further evidence linking androgen with male sexual function. Castration has been practiced since ancient times for a variety of reasons: to prevent sexual activity between harem guards and their charges; to render war captives docile; as part of religious ceremonies (in ancient Egypt, hundreds of young boys would be castrated in a single ceremony); and, after the rise of the church, to preserve the soprano voices of European choirboys.

Castrations are performed today primarily as medical treatment (the operation is called an *orchidectomy*) for such diseases as genital tuberculosis and prostatic cancer. Castrations have also occasionally been performed for legal reasons, either as a method of eugenic selection (to prevent reproduction in, say, a mentally handicapped person) or as an alleged deterrent to sex offenders. The ethical basis of these operations is highly controversial.

Research into the effect of castration has produced somewhat inconsistent findings. One major investigation studied a large group of castrated Norwegian males. It found that a substantial majority of these men showed significantly reduced sexual interest and activity within the first year after the operation (Bremer, 1959). A more recent study of 39 sex offenders in West Germany, who voluntarily agreed to surgical castration while in prison, obtained similar results (Heim, 1981). This offender population, consisting predominantly of rapists and child molesters, was evaluated over a period of several years after release from prison. Sexual arousability and activity were strongly reduced by castration. However, the impact of this surgical procedure was varied. Sixteen of the subjects reported that their sexual behavior was extinguished soon after being castrated. On the other hand, 11 individuals continued to engage in both masturbation and intercourse throughout the follow-up period, although with diminished frequency. Heim concluded that "sexual manifestations caused by castration vary considerably and that castration effects on male sexuality are not predictable with certainty" (p. 19). Other studies have revealed that the effect of castration on sexual desire and erotic functioning in men is highly variable. In one case, a 43-year-old man, castrated 18 years previously, reported having intercourse one to four times weekly (Hamilton, 1943). Still other writers have recorded incidences of continued desire and function for as long as 30 years following castration, without hormone treatment (Ford and Beach, 1951).

In interpreting this evidence, investigators need to take a number of possibilities into account. In cases where sexual activity does diminish after castration, how much of that reduction is attributable to hormone deficit, and how much is psychological? It is reasonable to suspect that psychological inhibition is sometimes a side effect of castration—a result of embarrassment due to a sense of physical mutilation; the self-fulfilling belief in the myth that castration abolishes erectile response; or perhaps a combination of these and other factors.

While our knowledge is still far from complete, the combined evidence from hypogonadism and castration studies supports the contention that androgen influences male sexual behavior, though its impact is variable:

What then can we infer from our knowledge of the effects of castration, testosterone treatment, and clinical disorders about the role of androgen in controlling sexual behavior in normal men? There can be little doubt that androgen (mainly testosterone) plays an important role. However, that role is not absolute. As in carnivores (and to a lesser extent in rodents), some individuals may show only minor impairments for prolonged periods after castration or pathologic changes in testicular function. The deficits, which do occur, are correctable with androgen treatment. Unfortunately, there is little beyond this that can be said. (Bermant and Davidson, 1974, p. 236)

Hormone replacement therapy is sometimes appropriate for hypogonadal or castrated males. This treatment, in which androgen levels are artificially restored in an effort to produce normal functioning, is often effective. Hypogonadal men receiving hormone therapy frequently report increases in libido and sexual activity (Money, 1961). We have less evidence from castration cases. The treatment is often inappropriate when a man has been castrated for medical reasons such as prostatic cancer, where diminished androgen levels are desirable. In any case, the relationship between androgen levels and sexual activity is not absolute. There seems to be an optimal hormone level beyond which increased supplies of androgen do not result in enhanced sexual activity. Furthermore, significant variations in the amount of hormones present may not appreciably alter sexual function. Lloyd (1968) reported variations in blood testosterone levels as great as 100% between men who were exhibiting typical sexual behaviors.

Other findings linking male hormones to sex behavior in men concern the use of drugs to reduce sexual activity. A recently developed class of drugs known as *antiandrogens* has been used experimentally in Europe for the treatment of sexual offenders and individuals reporting extreme sexual activity. The drugs appear to block the action of androgen produced by the testes and adrenal glands. Preliminary findings indicate that antiandrogens may be effective in reducing both sexual interest and activity in humans (Lunde and Hamburg, 1972). However, altering the sex hormones is no guarantee of reduced activity of a sexual offender, particularly when the unwanted acts stem from nonsexual motivations.

Gonadal Hormones in Female Sexual Behavior   Unlike the androgens produced by the testes in men, the evidence suggests that ovarian estrogens play an insignificant role in female sexual motivation and arousal. Data range from studies of postmenopause women (Masters and Johnson, 1966) to studies of women who have had their ovaries removed for medical reasons (Kinsey et al., 1953). Neither change seems to have significant adverse effects on sexual arousal.

Estrogen replacement therapy in women has also shown that this hormone's role in female sexual behavior is minor. Other than facilitating normal menstrual activity and vaginal lubrication, estrogen therapy usually produces little change in sexual interest or activity (Money, 1961). What, then, is the libido hormone in women? As we will see in the next section, androgen seems to be an important factor in sexual motivation and behavior for women, just as it is for men.

Androgen, the Libido Hormone in Both Sexes   The failure to find evidence strongly linking ovarian estrogens to women's sexual behavior induced researchers to look elsewhere. They found that androgens—produced by the cortex of the adrenal glands in both women and men—play an important role in female sexuality.

Salmon and Geist (1943) experimented with the use of both androgen and estrogen in the treatment of women having difficulty reaching orgasm. They found that androgen, and not estrogen, significantly increased erotic arousal and perceived sexual pleasure. The clinical literature on gynecology contains many references to the fact that women undergoing androgen therapy for other problems often report an increase in sexual interest and activity (Carter et al., 1947; Dorfman and Shipley, 1956; Kupperman and Studdiford, 1953).

A reduction in female sexual arousal and response has also been experimentally linked to androgen deprivation. Two research teams reported the results of diminished androgen levels on female sexual response. One study compared the effects of removal of the ovaries with those of an adrenalectomy (removal of the adrenal glands). While sexual activity remained stable in the former case, the adrenalectomy produced profound decreases in sexual desire and behavior (Waxenberg et al., 1959). A related study was done by Schon and Sutherland (1960), who reported similar adverse effects of terminated adrenal activity. A word of caution should be noted about interpreting these findings. It is quite possible that the reduced sexual activity may have also reflected psychological factors. The trauma of the surgery itself and of the disease (often cancer) for which it was prescribed could easily have influenced sexual behavior.

Human sexual behavior is so tremendously individualized that it is difficult to specify the effects of hormones on erotic arousal and expression. Nevertheless, the available data point to androgen as a hormone that facilitates sexual arousal in both women and men.

The Brain

From our experiences, we know that the brain plays an important role in our sexuality. Our thoughts, emotions, and memories are all mediated through its complex mechanisms. Sexual arousal can occur without any sensory stimulation; it can be produced by the process of *fantasy* (in this case, thinking of erotic images or sexual interludes), and some individuals may even reach orgasm during a fantasy experience (Kinsey et al., 1948; 1953).

A variety of events accounts for the manner in which we become aroused and respond to sexual stimuli. Less apparent is the role of individual experience and cultural influence, both of which are mediated by our brains. Clearly, we do not all respond similarly to the same stimuli. Some people may be highly aroused if their partner uses explicit sexual language. Others may find such words to be threatening or a sexual turn-off. Similarly, the smell of genital secretions may be more arousing to many Europeans than to members of our own deodorant-conscious society. The brain is the storehouse of our memories and cultural values, and consequently its influence over our sexual arousability is profound.

Strictly mental events like fantasies are the product of the cerebral cortex, the "gray matter" that controls higher functions like reasoning and language abilities. But the cortex represents only one level of functioning at which the brain influences human sexual arousal and response. At a subcortical level, the *limbic system* seems to play an important part in determining sexual behavior, both in humans and other animals.

Figure 6.1 shows some key structures in the limbic system. These include the cingulate gyrus, the septal area, the amygdala, the hippocampus, and parts of the hypothalamus, which plays a regulating role. There is evidence linking various sites in this system with sexual behavior. For instance, several animal studies have implicated the hypothalamus in sexual functioning. Researchers have reported increased sexual activity in rats, including erections and ejaculations, resulting from stimulation in both anterior and posterior regions of the hypothalamus (Caggiula and Hoebel, 1966; Van Dis and Larsson, 1971; Vaughn and Fisher, 1962). When certain parts of the hypothalamus are surgically destroyed, there may be a dramatic reduction in the sexual behavior of both males and females of several species (Hitt et al., 1970; Sawyer, 1960).

In the 1950s, James Olds conducted a series of experimental investigations of brain stimulation in rats. He implanted electrodes in various regions of their limbic systems and wired the electrodes in a way that allowed the rats to stimulate their own brains by pressing a lever. When the electrodes were placed in the hypothalamus and the septal areas, the rats seemingly could not get enough stimulation. They would press the lever several thousand times per hour, often to the point of exhaustion. These animals were clearly experiencing something akin to intense pleasure, which led Olds to call these regions of the limbic system "pleasure centers" (Olds, 1956). Olds's rats were unable to tell him whether the pleasure they were experiencing was sexual in nature. Subsequent research with humans, outlined in the following paragraphs, is more enlightening.

FIGURE 6.1 THE LIMBIC SYSTEM OF THE HUMAN BRAIN *157*

The limbic system, a region of the brain associated with emotion and motivation, is important in human sexual function. Key structures, shaded in color, include the cingulate gyrus, septal area, portions of the hypothalamus, amygdala, and the hippocampus.

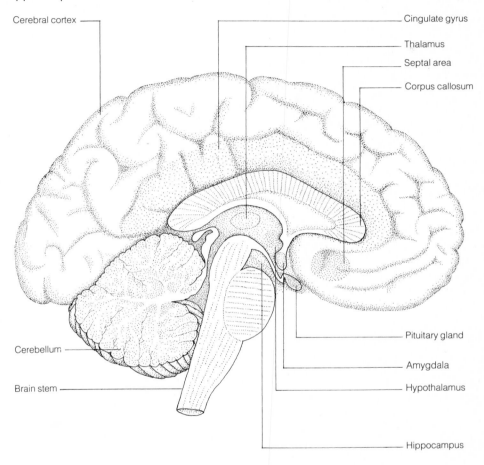

For ethical reasons, few experiments have attempted to study the effects of brain stimulation on humans. However, there have been some instances in which electrical and chemical brain stimulation of humans has been done for therapeutic purposes. Robert Heath, a Tulane University researcher, is one of the pioneers in this area. In the early 1970s, he experimented with limbic system stimulation of a female epileptic and a man troubled with emotional problems. He hypothesized that the pleasure associated with stimulation of these areas would prove to be of therapeutic value to these patients. When stimulation was delivered to the septal area, both individuals reported intense sexual pleasure. The female patient experienced multiple orgasmic response as a direct result of septal area stimulation. Provided with a self-stimulating transistorized device, the male patient stimulated himself incessantly (up to 1500 times per hour). "He protested each time the unit was taken from him, pleading to self-stimulate just a few more times" (p. 6).

In a related investigation, Yale physiologist José Delgado (1969) recorded the following responses of two female patients undergoing brain stimulation during exploration of their epileptic conditions:

[One patient] reported a pleasant tingling sensation in the left side of her body "from my face down to the bottom of my legs." She started giggling and making funny comments, stating that she enjoyed the sensation "very much." Repetition of these stimulations made the patient more communicative and flirtatious, and she ended by openly expressing her desire to marry the therapist.

[A second female patient described] a pleasant sensation of relaxation and considerably increased her verbal output, which took on a more intimate character. This patient openly expressed her fondness for the therapist (who was new to her), kissed his hands, and talked about her immense gratitude for what was being done for her. (p. 145)

It is doubtful that researchers will ever find one specific "sex center" in the brain. However, it is clear that both the cerebral cortex and the limbic system play important roles in initiating, organizing, and controlling human sexual arousal and response. In addition, the brain interprets a variety of sensory inputs that often exert a profound influence upon sexual expression. We will examine this topic in the next section.

The Senses and Sexual Arousal

It has been said that the brain is the most important sense organ for human sexual arousal. This observation implies that any sensory event, if properly interpreted by the psyche, can serve as an effective sexual stimulus. This variety in the sources of erotic stimulation helps to explain the tremendous sexual complexity of humans.

Of the major senses, touch tends to predominate during sexual sharing. However, all of the senses have the potential to become involved, and sights, smells, sounds, and tastes all may be important contributors to erotic arousal. There are no blueprints for the what and how of sensory stimulation. Each of us is unique, with our own individual triggers of arousal. There can be a special joy in discovering these "magic buttons" in ourselves or a sexual partner.

Touch   Stimulation of the various skin surfaces is probably a more frequent source of human sexual arousal than is any other type of sensory stimulus. The nerve endings that respond to touch are distributed unevenly throughout the body, and this explains why certain areas are more sensitive than others. Those locations that are most responsive to tactile pleasuring are commonly referred to as the *erogenous zones*. A distinction is often made between *primary erogenous zones*—those areas that contain dense concentrations of nerve endings—and *secondary erogenous*

zones, which include other areas of the body that have become endowed with erotic significance through sexual conditioning.

A list of primary erogenous zones generally includes the genitals, buttocks, anus, perineum, breasts (particularly the nipples), inner surfaces of the thighs, armpits, navel, neck, ears (especially the lobes), and the mouth (lips, tongue, and the entire oral cavity).*

It is important to remember, however, that just because a given area qualifies as a primary erogenous zone, there is no guarantee that stimulating it will produce arousal in a sexual partner. What is intensely arousing for one may produce no reaction in another; it may even be irritating to someone else.

*Our students typically ask why we leave the feet and hands off this list of primary zones. Actually, we have not yet reached agreement on this issue. Thus, whether or not they are included depends upon who happens to be leading the discussion. It seems contradictory that we classify areas stroked by the hands (genitals and breasts, for instance) as primary arousal zones, while the fingers, which certainly contain an abundance of nerve endings, fail to make the grade. Therefore, if it would make you feel better, add hands to the above list. Feel free to include the feet, too.

The secondary erogenous zones include virtually all other regions of the body. For example, if your lover tenderly kissed and stroked your upper back during each sexual interlude, it is distinctly possible that this area would soon be transformed into a powerful erogenous zone. These secondary locations thus become eroticized because they are touched within the context of sexual intimacies.

While there is no limit to the amount of body surface that can become part of our own private erogenous maps, it seems that women are more likely than men in this society to realize the erotic potentials that exist throughout their bodies. This tentative conclusion is based on a few observations. First, females in our society are touched more than males. This is particularly true during the early formative years. Second, females are also touched more during sexual encounters. Stereotypic gender roles dictate that men are more likely to do the touching, rather than be touched, during sex play. Finally, men are typically more genitally focused than women during sexual interaction.

These are generalized observations and certainly not true for all individuals. Furthermore, we are not suggesting that women are totally free of the burden of bodies made dormant through lack of sensual attention. Many of us, men and women alike, may benefit from exploring the potentials for erotic arousal in the skin surfaces throughout our bodies. A potentially helpful way of doing this is the process of *sensate focus*, which was defined by Masters and Johnson (1970). The process involves a couple sharing the experience of body exploration and pleasuring. Chapter 17 will discuss in detail this and other methods for enhancing our erotic potentials.

Vision   In our society we seem to be preoccupied with visual stimuli. Prime evidence is the importance we often place on physical appearance, including such activities as personal grooming, wearing the right clothes, and the extensive use of cosmetics. Therefore, it is not surprising that vision is second only to touch on the hierarchy of stimuli that most people view as sexually arousing.

The popularity of sexually explicit men's magazines in our society might lead one to assume that the human male is more aroused by visual stimuli than is the female. Early research seemed to support this conclusion. Kinsey found that more men than women reported being sexually excited by visual stimuli such as pin-up erotica and stag shows (Kinsey et al., 1948; 1953). However, this finding reflects several social influences, including the greater cultural inhibitions attached to such behavior in women at the time of his research, plus the simple fact that men had been provided far more opportunities to develop an appetite for such stimuli. This interpretation is supported by recent research, which has demonstrated strong similarities in the responses of males and females to visual erotica (Fisher and Byrne, 1978; Schmidt and Sigusch, 1970). Women in one study actually showed greater pupil dilation (a sign of arousal) when exposed to male pin-ups than did their male counterparts when exposed to female pin-ups (Hess, 1965).

Smell   A person's sexual history and cultural conditioning often influence what smells he or she finds to be arousing. We typically learn through experience to view certain odors as erotic and others as offensive. From this perspective there may be nothing intrinsic to the fragrance of genital secretions that might cause them to be perceived as either arousing or distasteful. We might also argue the contrary—that the smell of genital secretions would be universally exciting to humans were it not that some people learn to view them as offensive. This latter interpretation is supported by the fact that some societies openly recognize the value of genital smells as a sexual stimulant. For example, on the European continent, where the deodorant industry is less pervasive, some women use the natural bouquet of their genital secretions, strategically placed behind an ear or in the nape of the neck, to induce arousal in their sexual partners.

Among other animals, smells are often more important than visual stimuli in eliciting sexual response. The females of many species secrete certain substances, called *pheromones*, during their fertile periods. For any of you who have had a female dog in heat around the house and observed the male dogs coming from miles around to scratch at your door, there can be no doubting the importance of smell in sexual arousal. In spite of the lack of any conclusive evidence, some researchers have suggested that humans may also possess pheromones (Michael et al., 1974; Sokolov et al., 1976). However, the near-obsession people in our society often have with masking natural body odors with armpit and genital sprays makes it very difficult to study this area. Any natural odors designed to trigger arousal are often well disguised. Nevertheless, each person's unique experiences may allow certain smells to acquire erotic significance, as the following anecdotes reveal:

I love the smells after making love. They trigger little flashes of erotic memories and often keep my arousal level in high gear inducing me to go on to additional sexual activities. (Authors' files)

During oral sex the faint odor of musk from my lover's vulva drives me wild with passion. I guess it is all the memories of special pleasures associated with these smells that produces the turn-on. (Authors' files)

In a society that is so concerned about natural odors, it is nice to see that some individuals are able to appreciate the scents associated with sexual sharing and their lover's body.

Taste As with smell, taste seems to play a relatively minor role in human sexual arousal. This is no doubt influenced, at least in part, by an industry that promotes breath mints and flavored vaginal sprays. In addition to making many individuals extremely self-conscious about how they taste or smell, such commercial products may mask any natural tastes that relate to sexual activity. Nevertheless, some people are still able to detect and appreciate certain tastes they learn to associate with sexual sharing:

When I am sucking my man I can taste the salty little drops that come out of his penis just before he comes. I get real excited about that time, because I know he is about to take that sweet ride home. (Authors' files)

I have noticed that my wife often tastes different to me at different times in her cycle. I have asked her about it and she doesn't know why. One thing is a cinch; the taste is always arousing to me. (Authors' files)

Hearing Whether a person makes sounds during sexual sharing is highly variable; so is their partner's response to such verbalizations. Some individuals find words, moans, and orgasmic cries to be highly arousing. Others prefer that their lovers keep silent during sex play. A range of opinions is expressed in the following quotes excerpted from a *Playboy* magazine sex poll:

I love hearing things like, "Open wider," "You're so warm and wet," "Do you want me to come in your mouth?" The more my lover tells me, the more wanted and desirable I feel.

If I want to hear talking while I'm making love, I leave the radio on. My lover's mouth should be busy doing exciting things to my body with lips and tongue.

Silence is so boring, and talking when making love fills the gap. I like practically anything—from "I love the feel of your cock sliding in and out of my pussy" to "What did you think of Woody Allen's latest film?"

The only words I want to hear from him while fucking are, "Let's do it some more." (Smith, *Playboy* Sex Poll, Feb. 1978, pp. 47–50)

Some people may make a conscious effort to suppress spontaneous noises during sex play. If this is a result of the silent, stoical image accepted by many males, it may be exceedingly difficult for men to talk, cry out, or groan during arousal. In one research study, many women reported that their male partner's silence hindered their own sexual arousal (DeMartino, 1970). Female reluctance to emit sounds during sex play may be influenced by the belief that "nice" women are not supposed to be so passionate that they make noises.

In addition to being sexually arousing, talking to each other during a sexual interlude can be informative and helpful ("I like it when you touch me that way," "A little softer," and so on). If you happen to be a person who enjoys noise-making and verbalizations during sex, your partner may respond this way if you give permission beforehand (see Chapter 8).

Sensory stimulation will usually not be effective unless the appropriate emotional conditions are also present. Feelings of trust, of being wanted and cared for, and affection for one's partner often enhance our sexual response; they may actually be necessary ingredients. In contrast, feelings of being used, lack of emotional rapport, or negative emotions like guilt and anxiety often eliminate or restrain our capacity for erotic arousal.

Foods, Chemicals, and Sexual Behavior

Up to this point we have been considering the impact of hormones, brain processes, and sensory inputs on human sexual arousal. There are other factors, though, that may have much to do with a person's arousability in a particular situation. Some of these are real; others, even though imagined, can have a strong impact on a person's sexuality. In the pages that follow, we will examine the effects of a number of products people use to attempt to heighten or reduce sexual arousal.

Aphrodisiacs: Do They Work?   An *aphrodisiac* (named after Aphrodite, the Greek goddess of love and beauty) is a substance that supposedly arouses sexual desire or increases a person's capacity for sexual activities.

Almost from the beginning of time, people have searched for magic potions and other agents able to revive flagging erotic interest or produce Olympic sexual performances. That many have reported finding such sexual stimulants bears testimony, once again, to the powerful role played by the mind in human sexual activity. We will first consider a variety of foods that have been held to possess aphrodisiac qualities, then turn our attention to other alleged stimulants, including alcohol and an assortment of chemical substances.

Foods   Almost any food that resembles the male external genitals has at one time or another been viewed as an aphrodisiac. Many of us have heard the jokes about oysters, although for some a belief in the special properties of this particular shellfish is no joking matter. One wonders to what extent the oyster industry profits from this pervasive myth.

Other foods in this category include bananas, celery, tomatoes, and potatoes. Particularly in Asian countries, the belief that the ground-up horns of animals, such as rhinoceros and reindeer, are powerful sexual stimulants is widespread. Have you ever used the term "horny" to describe a sexual state? Now you know its origin.

A number of drugs are also commonly thought to have aphrodisiac properties. Some of these are discussed in the following section and are summarized in Table 6.1.

Alcohol   More has been written about the supposed stimulant properties of alcohol than any other presumed aphrodisiac substance. In our culture there is widespread belief in the erotic enhancement properties of alcoholic beverages:

I am a great believer in the sexual benefits of drinking wine. After a couple glasses I become a real "hound in bed." I can always tell my wife is in the mood when she brings out a bottle of chilled rosé. (Authors' files)

In a survey of 20,000 middle-class and upper middle-class Americans, 60% of the respondents reported greater sexual pleasure after drinking (Athanasiou et al., 1970). There was a pronounced sex difference, with significantly greater numbers of women reporting this effect. This latter finding may be explained by the impact of alcohol on sexual inhibitions. Far from being a stimulant, alcohol has a depressing effect on higher brain centers, thus reducing cortical inhibitions (such as fear and guilt) that often block sexual expression. Alcohol may also stimulate sexual activity by providing a convenient rationalization for behavior that might normally conflict with an individual's value system ("I just couldn't help myself with my mind fogged by booze"). If our culture produces more sexual inhibitions in females than males—a reasonable assumption held by many—it seems logical that alcohol is more likely to facilitate sexual activity in women than in men.

TABLE 6.1 SOME ALLEGED APHRODISIACS AND THEIR EFFECTS

Name (and Street Name)	Reputed Effect	Actual Effect
1. Alcohol	Enhances arousal; stimulates sexual activity	Can reduce inhibitions to make sexual behaviors less stressful, but is actually a depressant, and in quantity can impair erection ability, arousal, and orgasm
2. Amphetamines ("uppers"; includes benzedrine, dexedrine)	Elevates mood; enhances sexual experience and abilities	Central nervous system stimulants; reduce inhibitions. Long-term use impairs sexual functioning and can reduce vaginal lubrication in women
3. Amyl nitrate ("snappers"; "poppers")	Intensifies orgasms and arousal	Dilates arteries to brain and also to genital area; produces time distortion, warmth in pelvic area. Can produce dizziness, headaches, and fainting
4. Barbiturates ("barbs"; "downers")	Enhances arousal; stimulates sexual activity	Reduces inhibitions in similar fashion to alcohol. Physically addictive, and overdose may produce severe depression and even death due to respiratory failure
5. Cantharides ("Spanish Fly")	Stimulates genital area causing person to desire coitus	Not effective as a sexual stimulant, it acts as a powerful irritant that can cause inflammation to lining of bladder and urethra; can result in permanent tissue damage and even death
6. Cocaine ("coke")	Increases frequency and intensity of orgasm; heightens arousal	Central nervous system stimulant; loosens inhibitions and enhances sense of well-being. Regular use can induce depression and anxiety. Chronic sniffing ("snorting") can produce lesions and perforations of the nasal passage
7. LSD and other psychedelic drugs (mescaline; psilocybin)	Enhances sexual response	No direct physiological enhancement of sexual response; may produce altered perception of sexual activity; frequently associated with unsatisfactory erotic experiences
8. L-dopa	Sexual rejuvenation of older male patients	No documented benefits to sexual ability; occasionally produces a painful condition known as priapism
9. Marijuana	Elevates mood and arousal; stimulates sexual activity	Enhances mood and reduces inhibitions in a way similar to alcohol. May distort time sense with the resulting illusion of prolonged arousal and orgasm

While a drink or two may seem to enhance sexual arousal, consumption of significant amounts of alcohol can have serious negative effects on sexual functioning. Research has demonstrated that with increasing levels of intoxication, both men and women experience reduced sexual arousal (as measured physiologically), decreased pleasurability and intensity of orgasm, and increased difficulty in attaining orgasm

(Briddell and Wilson, 1976; Malatesta et al., 1979; Wilson and Lawson, 1976). One study demonstrated that the amount of androgen present in the blood may be significantly reduced by chronic drinking (Rubin et al., 1976). As discussed earlier, androgen deficits may affect sexual interest in both men and women. Heavy alcohol use may also result in general physical deterioration, a process that commonly reduces a person's interest in and capacity for sexual activity.

Drugs and Other Chemicals   Perhaps the most famous drug considered to be an aphrodisiac is *cantharides*, also known as Spanish fly. This substance is derived from the ground-up bodies of a species of beetle found in southern Europe (Spain and France). Taken internally, it travels to the bladder and is excreted in the urine. It acts as a powerful irritant, causing acute inflammation of the lining of the bladder and urethra as it passes out of the body. This reflex stimulation of genital structures has resulted in cantharides' widespread reputation as an aphrodisiac. In reality, it can be extremely painful to both sexes, producing effects ranging from mild irritation to extensive tissue destruction and even death, depending on the dosage. It is completely useless as a sexual stimulant, and its dangerous side effects make it a substance to be avoided.

Marijuana has also been widely extolled for its sexual enhancement properties. It acts in a way similar to alcohol to reduce inhibitions. In addition, marijuana may increase empathy with others, distort time perception (often with the resulting illusion of prolonged arousal and orgasm), and increase suggestibility—all of which may act independently or in combination to produce a sense of heightened sexual ecstasy. In reality, marijuana possesses no chemical attributes that qualify it as a true sexual stimulant (Mendelson, 1976).

Amphetamines such as benzedrine and dexedrine (commonly known as "uppers") are central nervous system stimulants favored by some for their presumed sexual enhancement properties. Their general effect is to elevate mood, which may in turn act to diminish inhibitions. In addition, amphetamines often energize behavior, producing an increase in confidence. This can lead to a person overestimating his or her sexual prowess.

There is no experimental evidence attributing genuine aphrodisiac properties to amphetamines. It is important to note that these drugs are addictive both physiologically and psychologically and that continued chronic use is known to impair sexual functioning (Kaplan, 1974). Furthermore, amphetamine use often dries the natural secretions of mucous membranes. This may lead to diminished vaginal lubrication and painful intercourse.

Cocaine is a drug extracted from the leaves of the coca shrub. It is occasionally used in medication as a narcotic or local anesthetic. It is also a powerful central nervous system stimulant that has been suggested to be an aphrodisiac. It is usually taken either by injection or sniffing ("snorting"). Some users claim it induces an immediate "orgasm-like rush." Others report that orgasms increase in frequency and intensity while a person is under its influence. However, as with all drugs previously discussed, there is no legitimate biological evidence establishing cocaine as an aphrodisiac. Any reported improvements generally belong to the "loosening of inhibitions" or "enhancement of well-being" categories.

Amyl nitrate, known on the streets as "snappers" or "poppers," is a drug often linked with intensified orgasmic experience. It is commonly used by cardiac patients to prevent heart pain (angina). Inhaled from small ampules which are "popped" open for quick use, it causes a rapid dilation of the arteries that supply the heart muscle and other organs with oxygen. Amyl nitrate also produces a sudden dilation of arteries in the brain, a response that often induces a feeling of giddiness and euphoria. In addition, there is a sense of warmth created in the pelvis and genitals due to dilation of the arteries of the genitourinary tract.

Occasionally, people report that inhaling a "popper" at the moment of orgasm dramatically intensifies and prolongs the experience. However, time is distorted and perceptions altered after inhalation, and it is unlikely that this effect can be attributed to an actual prolongation of orgasm. Furthermore, amyl nitrate is a highly volatile drug that may produce a variety of negative side effects, including severe headaches, dizziness, and fainting. It is hazardous to use such a drug without the supervision of a competent physician.

L-dopa, a drug frequently employed in the treatment of *Parkinson's disease* (a neurological disorder), received considerable publicity a few years ago when researchers reported an apparent sexual rejuvenation in older male patients taking the medication. However, research failed to confirm its suggested aphrodisiac qualities. Occasionally, it has been known to produce *priapism* (prolonged penile erection), a painful condition quite independent of genuine arousal.

Barbiturates (commonly called "barbs" or "downers"), used in the treatment of a variety of mental and physical conditions, may subjectively enhance sexual pleasure in some individuals by lessening inhibitions in a way similar to alcohol.

Finally, most *psychedelic drugs*, including LSD, mescaline, and psilocybin, are not generally linked with enhanced sexual response. Some people have reported very unsatisfactory erotic experiences while under the influence of these drugs.

Androgen is the only chemical substance clearly implicated in the sexual arousal of both men and women. However, as we indicated earlier, androgen does not produce a change in sexual motivation in males unless a condition of prior deficiency exists. In contrast, administration of androgen to hormonally normal women usually increases sexual interest.

In view of the evidence against many of the commonly held beliefs about aphrodisiacs, why do so many people around the world swear by the effects of a little powdered rhino horn, that special meal of oysters and banana salad, or the marijuana cigarette before an evening's dalliance? The answer lies in faith and suggestion—these are the ingredients frequently present when aphrodisiac claims surface. If a person believes something will improve his or her sex life, this faith is often translated into the subjective enhancement of sexual pleasure. From this perspective, literally anything has the potential of serving as a sexual stimulant for a person.

We are not implying here that all alleged aphrodisiacs owe their effects strictly to suggestion. As we have seen, several substances (including alcohol, marijuana, and barbiturates) may increase sexual motivation and arousal by reducing inhibitions. However, their effects are variable and may be greatly influenced by both the particular situation and the attitudes of the person using the drug.

Anaphrodisiacs Several drugs are known to inhibit sexual behavior. Substances that have this effect are called *anaphrodisiacs*.

Tranquilizers, used widely in the treatment of a variety of emotional disorders, have been shown to reduce sexual motivation in some cases. They are occasionally prescribed by physicians for this purpose, though their effects are variable and they may also increase sexual arousal by lessening inhibitions.

Many *antihypertensives*, drugs used for treating high blood pressure, have been experimentally demonstrated to seriously inhibit erection and ejaculation and to reduce the intensity of orgasm in male subjects (Money and Yankowitz, 1967). In an earlier section of this chapter, we noted that certain antiandrogen drugs, which block the effects of testosterone, will retard the sexual interest of both men and women.

Paradoxically, the most widely noted substance used as an anaphrodisiac, *potassium nitrate* (commonly known as saltpeter), is completely ineffective as a sexual deterrent. Many of us have heard the joke about the newlyweds being dosed with saltpeter on their wedding night. In reality, there is no physiological basis for this kind of tale, unless the need for frequent urination can be viewed as a sexual deterrent (potassium nitrate increases urine flow through diuretic action).

Undoubtedly, the most widely used and least recognized anaphrodisiac is *nicotine*. There is evidence that smoking can significantly retard sexual motivation and function by constricting the blood vessels (thereby retarding vasocongestive response of the body to sexual stimulation) and reducing testosterone levels in the blood (Subak-Sharpe, 1974). As noted earlier, alcohol may also impair sexual functioning.

SEXUAL RESPONSE

Human sexual response is a highly individual physical, emotional, and mental process. Nevertheless, there are a number of common physiological changes that allow us to outline some general patterns of the sexual response cycle.

In the years before Masters and Johnson began their research, writers often referred to the various phases of sexual response with terms like "foreplay," "the prelude," "the union" or "communion," and "afterplay." One particularly influential writer, Havelock Ellis (1906), coined the terms "tumescence" and "detumescence" to describe the process whereby blood flows into and out of the pelvic area during sexual arousal and response.

With widespread acceptance of the work of Masters and Johnson (1966), we find that their descriptive language has replaced most of the earlier terminology. However, their work does not stand alone in recent developments in the study of human sexual response. Particularly noteworthy are the views of sex therapist Helen Kaplan (1979). We will briefly outline her ideas before turning to a detailed analysis of Masters and Johnson's work.

Kaplan's Three-Stage Model

Kaplan's model of sexual response, an outgrowth of her extensive experience as a sex therapist, contains three stages: *desire, excitement,* and *orgasm* (see Figure 6.2). She suggests that sexual difficulties tend to fall into one of these three categories and that it

FIGURE 6.2 KAPLAN'S THREE-STAGE MODEL OF THE SEXUAL RESPONSE CYCLE

This model is distinguished by its identification of desire as a prelude to sexual response. (Kaplan, 1979)

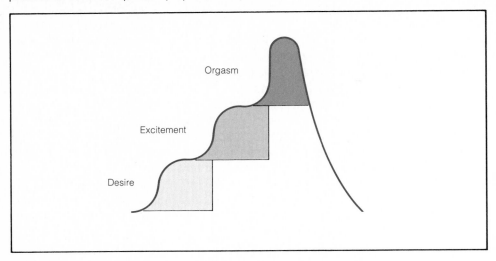

is possible for an individual to have difficulty in one while continuing to function normally in the other two.

One of the most distinctive features of Kaplan's model is that it includes desire as a distinct stage of the sexual response cycle. Many other writers, including Masters and Johnson, do not discuss aspects of sexual response that are separate from genital changes. Kaplan's description of desire as a prelude to physical sexual response corrects this omission and consequently stands as a welcome addition to the literature on sexual response. However, not all sexual expression is preceded by desire for such activity. For example, a couple may agree to engage in sexual sharing even though they may not be feeling sexually inclined at the time. Frequently, these people may find that their bodies begin to respond sexually to the ensuing activity in spite of their lack of initial desire.

Masters and Johnson's Four-Phase Model

Masters and Johnson distinguish four phases in the sexual response patterns of both men and women: *excitement, plateau, orgasm,* and *resolution.* In addition, they include a *refractory period* in the male resolution phase (a recovery stage in which there is a temporary inability to reach orgasm). Figures 6.3 and 6.4 illustrate these four phases of sexual response in men and women. These charts provide basic "maps" of common patterns, but a few cautions to the reader are in order.

First, the simplified nature of these diagrams can easily obscure the richness of individual variation that can and does occur. Masters and Johnson were charting only the physiological responses to sexual stimulation. While our biological reactions may follow a relatively predictable course, there is a tremendous amount of variability in our own subjective responses to sexual arousal. These personal differences are suggested in the several individual reports of arousal, orgasm, and resolution included at later points in this chapter.

A second caution has to do with a too-literal interpretation of the so-called plateau stage of sexual response. Within the behavioral sciences, the term *plateau* is typically used to describe a leveling-off period where no observable changes in behavior can be detected. For example, it might refer to a flat spot in a learning curve where no new behaviors occur for a certain period of time. It has been diagrammed in just this manner in the male chart and in pattern A of the female chart. Actually, the plateau level of sexual arousal involves a powerful surge of sexual tensions that are definitely measurable (for example, as increased heart and breathing rates). Thus, the label of plateau may best be replaced by a more descriptive term such as *charge phase*. This new term is currently being used by some writers in the field.

A third caution warns against a tendency to use charts like these as personal checklists. While we encourage self-references throughout this book, this is one area where a too enthusiastic self-checking can lead to potential problems in the form of "spectatoring." The following quote illustrates:

After learning about the four stages of sexual response in class, I found myself "standing back" and watching my own reactions, wondering if I had passed from excitement into plateau. Also, I began to monitor the responses of my partner, looking for the tell-tale signs that would tell me at what point he was. Suddenly I found myself doing clinical observations rather than allowing myself to fully experience the good feelings. It was a real put-off and I had to force myself to stop being the observer and become more of a participant. (Authors' files)

The descriptions in the following pages should not be viewed as standards for analyzing or intellectualizing your feelings or for evaluating how "normal" your reactions are. We stress that there are many natural variations from these patterns. Perhaps familiarity with these generalized descriptions might help to illuminate some of the complexity of your own responses.

In much of the discussion that follows, we will be looking at the physiological reactions and subjective reports of women and men. Before we become too involved in the several specific processes of sexual response that take place, it is important to note that the basic responses of men and women are very similar—a point that was stressed by Masters and Johnson in their research:

Certainly there are reactions to sexual stimulation that are confined by normal anatomic variation to a single sex. There also are differences in established reactive patterns to sexual stimuli—for example, duration and intensity of response—that usually are sex-linked in character. However, parallels in reactive potential between the two sexes must be underlined. Similarities rather than differences of response have been emphasized by this investigation. (Masters and Johnson, 1966, p. 273)

Masters and Johnson identified three basic patterns in female
sexual response. Pattern A most closely resembles the male
pattern, with the exception of the possibility of one or more
orgasms without dropping below plateau level of sexual arousal.
Variations may include an extended plateau with no orgasm (line
B), or a rapid rise to orgasm (line C) with no definitive plateau and
a very quick resolution. (Masters and Johnson, 1966)

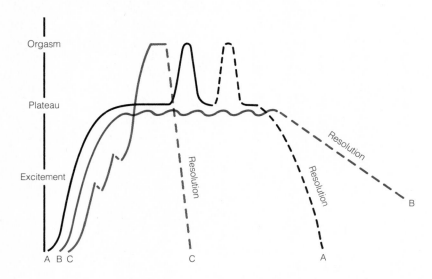

Two fundamental physiological responses to effective sexual stimulation occur in
both women and men. These are *vasocongestion* and *myotonia*. These two basic
reactions are the primary underlying sources for almost all biological responses that
take place during sexual arousal.

   Vasocongestion is the engorgement of blood vessels and a corresponding
increased flow of arterial blood into those tissues of the body that respond to sexual
excitation. Normal flows of blood into organs and tissues are balanced by an equal
outflow through the veins. However, during sexual arousal, the dilation of arteries
increases the inflow beyond the draining capacity of the veins. This results in
widespread vasocongestion in both superficial and deep tissues. The congested areas
that are visible may feel warm and appear swollen and red due to increased blood
content. The most obvious manifestations of this vasocongestive response are the
erection of the penis in men and lubrication of the vagina in women. In addition, other
body areas may become engorged—the labia, testicles, clitoris, nipples, and even the
ear lobes.

   The second basic physiological response is *myotonia*, the increased muscle
tension that occurs throughout the body during sexual arousal. Myotonia is evident in

FIGURE 6.4 MALE SEXUAL RESPONSE CYCLE

171

Only one male response pattern was identified by Masters and Johnson. However, men do report considerable variation in their response patterns. Note the refractory period: males do not have a second orgasm immediately after the first. (Masters and Johnson, 1966)

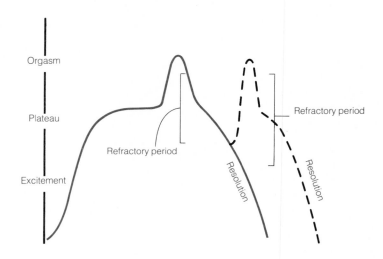

both voluntary flexing and involuntary contractions. Its most dramatic manifestations are facial grimaces, spasmodic contractions of the hands and feet, and the muscular spasms that occur during orgasm.

The phases of the response cycle follow the same general patterns regardless of the method of stimulation. Masturbation, manual stimulation by one's partner, oral pleasuring, penile-vaginal intercourse, dreaming, fantasy, and, in some women, breast stimulation can all result in completion of the response cycle. Often the intensity and rapidity of response vary according to the kind of stimulation.

In the next several pages we outline the major physiological reactions to sexual stimulation occurring during each of the four phases of the sexual response cycle. Subjective reports of several individuals will be included. For each stage, we list reactions common to both sexes and those unique to just one. You will note the strong similarities in the sexual response patterns of men and women. We will discuss some important differences in greater detail at the conclusion of this chapter.

Excitement   The first phase of the sexual response cycle is the excitement phase. As Table 6.2 indicates, it is characterized by a number of common responses, including muscle tension and some increase in the heart rate and blood pressure. In both women and men, several areas of the sexual anatomy become engorged. For example, the clitoris, labia minora, vagina, nipples, penis, and testes all increase in

TABLE 6.2 THE EXCITEMENT PHASE: SEXUAL RESPONSE CYCLE

Reactions Common to Both Sexes	Female Responses	Male Responses
Increased myotonia, particularly in striated muscles of arms and legs. May be some tensing in smooth muscles of abdomen late in phase.	Clitoris swells with blood engorgement. (Change may be very slight to quite noticeable.)	Penis becomes erect. Erection may subside and recur several times.
Moderate increase in heart rate and blood pressure.	Labia majora flatten and separate away from the vaginal opening.	Scrotum elevates; skin thickens and loses its baggy appearance.
Sex flush may appear late in phase. More common in females. Often appears sporadically and seems to be related to intensity of arousal.	Labia minora increase two or three times in size, adding about 1 cm of length to the vagina. The pinkish color begins to deepen.	Testes increase in size and elevate.
Nipple erection (occurs with greater reliability in females).	Lubrication of the vagina begins early in phase. The inner two-thirds lengthens and expands, and the vaginal walls progressively become a deeper purple color.	Cowper's glands may produce some secretions although these are commonly delayed until plateau phase.
	Uterus elevates and becomes engorged with blood, increasing in size up to twice its unstimulated dimensions.	
	Breasts enlarge. Superficial veins become more visible.	

size, and most of them deepen in color. Some responses, such as the appearance of a *sex flush* (a pink or red rash on the chest or breasts), occur among both sexes but are more common with women. Still other responses are specific to just one sex. These are outlined in the table; they are also illustrated in Figures 6.5 through 6.8, which show changes in the sexual anatomy of women and men throughout the phases of the cycle.

The excitement phase may vary in duration from less than a minute to several hours. Both males and females may show considerable variation in the degree of their arousal during this phase. For example, a man's penis may vary from flaccid to semierect to a fully erect state. Similarly, vaginal lubrication in women may vary from minimal to copious.

While the physiological characteristics outlined in the table and figures represent general patterns, different people experience these changes in differing ways. The following two reports give some indication of the subjective variations in how women describe their own feelings during sexual arousal:

Sexual arousal for me is something I look forward to when I realize my husband and I will have sex. His touching, kissing, and loving me in this way brings me to a height of excitement that is incredible. At first I felt selfish about him giving me so much satisfaction through stimulation, but he enjoys it so much, it's a wonderful time. Often we don't have intercourse because we are caught up in the "foreplay" of lovemaking. (Authors' files)

When I am aroused I get warm all over and I like a lot of holding and massaging of other areas of my body besides my genitals. After time passes with that particular stimulation, I prefer more direct manual stroking if orgasm is desired. (Authors' files)

Two men provide their descriptions of sexual arousal in the following accounts:

When I am sexually aroused, my whole body feels energized. Sometimes my mouth gets dry and I may feel a little lightheaded. I want to have all of my body touched and stroked, not just my genitals. I particularly like the sensation of feeling that orgasm is just around the corner, waiting and tantalizing me to begin the final journey. Sometimes a quick rush to climax is nice, but usually I prefer making the arousal period last as long as I can stand it, until my penis feels like it is dying for the final strokes of ecstasy. (Authors' files)

When aroused, I feel very excited and I fantasize a lot. Then all of a sudden, a warm feeling comes over me and it feels like a thousand pleasure pins are being stuck into my loins all at the same time. (Authors' files)

Plateau During the plateau phase, sexual tension continues to accelerate until reaching the extreme level that leads to orgasm. It is difficult to define clearly the point at which a sexually responding individual makes the transition to this phase. Unlike the excitement phase, there is no clear external sign such as lubrication or erection to indicate the onset of the plateau phase. Instead, a number of these signs become more pronounced as they accelerate to peaks in the next phase—hence the alternative term *charge phase* mentioned earlier. Heart rate and blood pressure both continue to rise; breathing grows faster; sex flushes and coloration of the genitals become more noticeable (see Table 6.3). Muscle tension continues to build up and the face, neck, hands, and feet may undergo involuntary contractions and spasms in both the plateau phase and the orgasm phase. Among women, plateau phase is also distinguished by development of the "orgasmic platform" (a term used by Masters and Johnson to describe the markedly increased engorgement of the outer third of the vagina).

The plateau phase is often very brief (typically lasting a few seconds up to several minutes). However, many individuals find that prolonging sexual tensions at this high plateau level produces greater arousal and ultimately more intense orgasms. This is reported in the following subjective accounts:

When I get up there, almost on the verge of coming, I try to hang in as long as possible. If my partner cooperates, stopping or slowing when necessary, I can stay right on the edge for several minutes, sometimes even longer. I know that all it would take is one more stroke and I'm over the top. Sometimes my whole body gets to shaking and quivering and I can feel incredible sensations shooting

FIGURE 6.5 FEMALE EXTERNAL GENITALIA DURING THE SEXUAL RESPONSE CYCLE

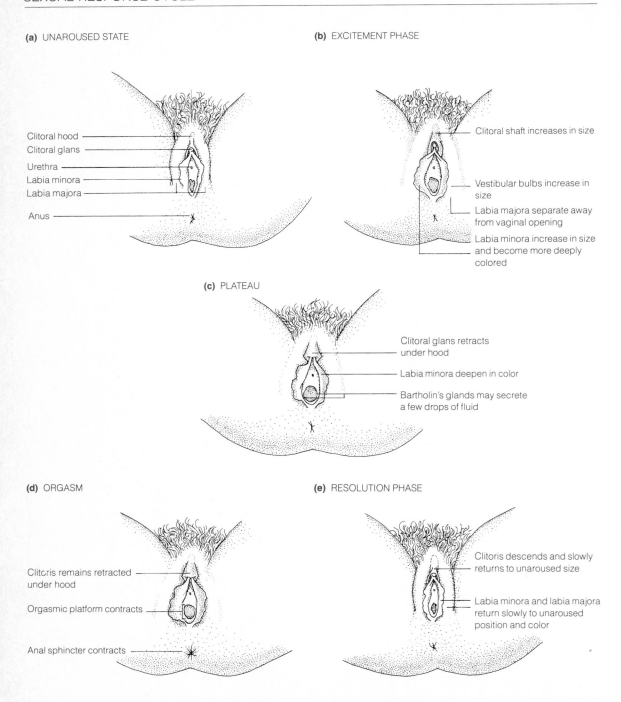

(a) UNAROUSED STATE

Clitoral hood
Clitoral glans
Urethra
Labia minora
Labia majora

Anus

(b) EXCITEMENT PHASE

Clitoral shaft increases in size

Vestibular bulbs increase in size

Labia majora separate away from vaginal opening

Labia minora increase in size and become more deeply colored

(c) PLATEAU

Clitoral glans retracts under hood

Labia minora deepen in color

Bartholin's glands may secrete a few drops of fluid

(d) ORGASM

Clitoris remains retracted under hood

Orgasmic platform contracts

Anal sphincter contracts

(e) RESOLUTION PHASE

Clitoris descends and slowly returns to unaroused size

Labia minora and labia majora return slowly to unaroused position and color

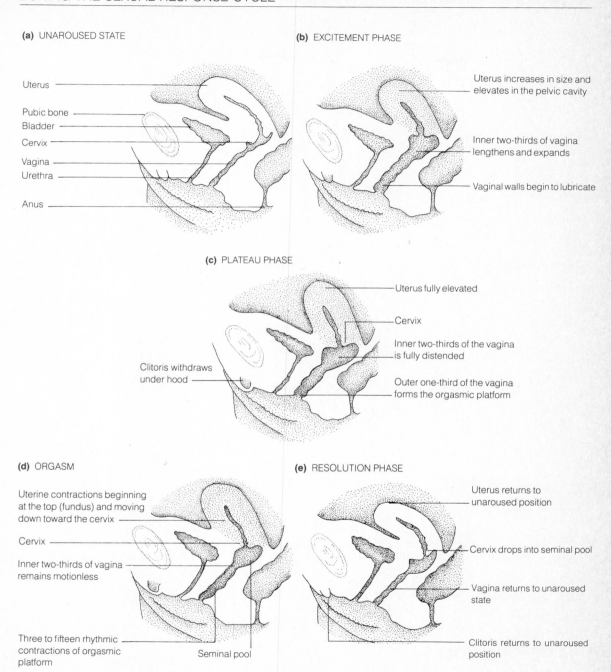

(a) UNAROUSED STATE

Uterus

Pubic bone

Bladder

Cervix

Vagina

Urethra

Anus

(b) EXCITEMENT PHASE

Uterus increases in size and elevates in the pelvic cavity

Inner two-thirds of vagina lengthens and expands

Vaginal walls begin to lubricate

(c) PLATEAU PHASE

Uterus fully elevated

Cervix

Inner two-thirds of the vagina is fully distended

Outer one-third of the vagina forms the orgasmic platform

Clitoris withdraws under hood

(d) ORGASM

Uterine contractions beginning at the top (fundus) and moving down toward the cervix

Cervix

Inner two-thirds of vagina remains motionless

Three to fifteen rhythmic contractions of orgasmic platform

Seminal pool

(e) RESOLUTION PHASE

Uterus returns to unaroused position

Cervix drops into seminal pool

Vagina returns to unaroused state

Clitoris returns to unaroused position

FIGURE 6.7 MALE SEXUAL ANATOMY DURING THE SEXUAL RESPONSE CYCLE

(a) EXCITEMENT PHASE

Full erection (reversible)

Partially aroused

Unaroused state

Testes begin to elevate and engorge

Thickening and tensing of scrotal skin

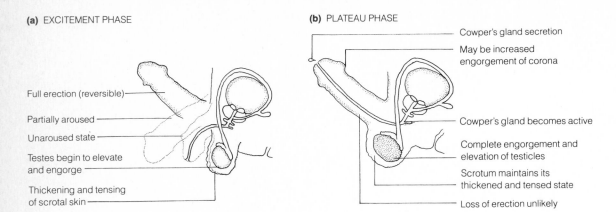

(b) PLATEAU PHASE

Cowper's gland secretion

May be increased engorgement of corona

Cowper's gland becomes active

Complete engorgement and elevation of testicles

Scrotum maintains its thickened and tensed state

Loss of erection unlikely

(c) EMISSION PHASE OF ORGASM

Contractions of ampulla of vas deferens

Internal urethral sphincter contracted

Contractions of seminal vesicle

Urethral bulb expands with seminal fluid

Contractions of prostate gland

External urethral sphincter contracted

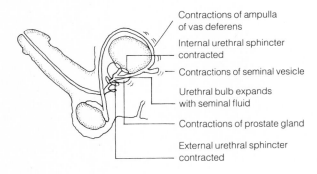

(d) EXPULSION PHASE OF ORGASM

Contractions of penile urethra

Internal urethral sphincter contracted

External urethral sphincter relaxes

Contractions of muscles around base of penis

Contractions of rectal sphincter

(e) RESOLUTION PHASE

First stage of erection loss completed

Unstimulated state (second stage detumescence completed)

Testicles return to unstimulated size

Testes descend

Scrotum thins and resumes wrinkled appearance

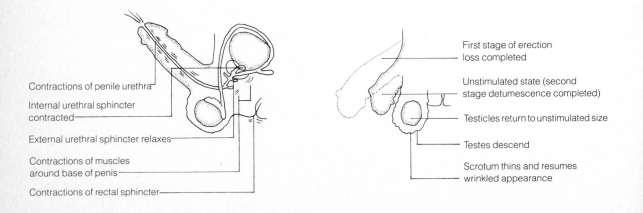

FIGURE 6.8 BREAST CHANGES DURING THE SEXUAL RESPONSE CYCLE   *177*

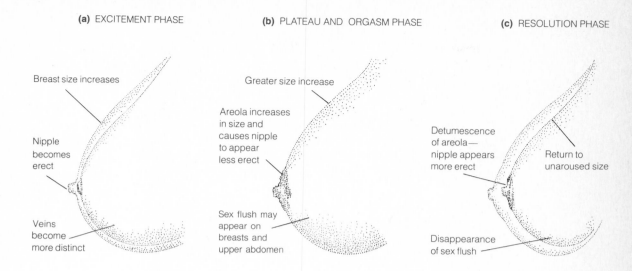

(a) EXCITEMENT PHASE   **(b)** PLATEAU AND ORGASM PHASE   **(c)** RESOLUTION PHASE

Breast size increases

Nipple becomes erect

Veins become more distinct

Greater size increase

Areola increases in size and causes nipple to appear less erect

Sex flush may appear on breasts and upper abdomen

Detumescence of areola— nipple appears more erect

Return to unaroused size

Disappearance of sex flush

TABLE 6.3 THE PLATEAU PHASE: SEXUAL RESPONSE CYCLE

Reactions Common to Both Sexes	Female Responses	Male Responses
Muscle tension becomes quite pronounced throughout the body. There may be grimaces of the face and involuntary muscular contractions in the feet and hands.	Clitoris withdraws under its hood and shortens in length.	Slight increase in engorgement of corona. May be deepening of the reddish-purple color of the glans.
Further increase in heart rate to 100–160 range just prior to orgasm. Blood pressure continues to elevate.	Labia majora undergo no further changes.	Erection is more stable in this stage.
Breathing becomes faster and deeper.	A noticeable intensification of color change in the labia minora called the "sex skin." Become bright red in nulliparous women and deep wine in parous women as orgasm approaches.	Scrotum maintains its thickened and tensed state.
Sex flush becomes more pronounced; may not appear until this phase.	Orgasmic platform develops from further vasocongestion of outer one-third of vagina. Inner two-thirds increases only slightly in width and depth. Lubrication slows considerably, particularly if plateau is extended.	Testicles continue to increase to 150% of unstimulated size and continue to elevate until positioned snugly against the body wall.
Occasionally nipple erection delayed to this stage.	The uterus is fully elevated.	Cowper's glands become active. Secretions may not be present in some men.
	The areola becomes more swollen; may appear that nipple erection has subsided.	

through me like electric charges. The longer I can make this supercharged period last, the better the orgasm. (Authors' files)

When I masturbate, I like to take myself almost to the point of climaxing and then back off. I can tell when orgasm is about to happen because my vagina tightens up around the opening and sometimes I can feel the muscles contract. I love the sensations of balancing myself on the brink, part of me wanting to come and the other part holding out for more. The longer I maintain this delicate balance, the more shattering the climax. Sometimes the pleasure is almost beyond bearing. (Authors' files)

Both of the preceding accounts are by women. Men who wish to delay orgasm may need more frequent interruption of stimulation as plateau phase continues. Nevertheless, it has been our experience that men sometimes report a very different reaction, often alluding to a kind of crisis point, as suggested below:

When I first approach orgasm, it is essential to slow down or stop if I don't want to finish quickly. This is relatively easy during masturbation, but somewhat harder during intercourse. I may have to use this slow-down tactic several times in a short period. However, something then happens to me which is difficult to explain. It's almost like I pass a crisis point where, if I don't come, my staying power gets better. (Authors' files)

This is an interesting phenomenon that may be relatively common judging from the number of our male students who have reported similar experiences. Some women also experience a more intense orgasm when they consciously move in and out of plateau phase. This is sometimes recommended for women who are first learning to have orgasms (Barbach, 1975). We encourage you to experiment with your own (or your partner's) plateau phase to determine the potentials that exist for you.

Orgasm   As effective stimulation continues, many individuals move from plateau to orgasm. This is particularly true for men, who almost always experience orgasm after reaching the plateau level. In contrast, women may obtain plateau levels of arousal without the release of sexual climax. This is often the case during penile-vaginal intercourse, when the man reaches orgasm first or when effective manual or oral stimulation is replaced with penetration as the female approaches orgasm. More will be said about this later.

Orgasm is the shortest phase of the sexual response cycle, typically lasting only a few seconds. Female orgasms often last slightly longer than male orgasms. Table 6.4 summarizes the primary physiological responses during orgasm.

The experience of orgasm can be an intense mixture of sensations that are among the most profoundly satisfying a person may feel. There has been considerable debate about whether women and men experience orgasm differently. This question was evaluated a few years ago in an experimental analysis of orgasm descriptions that were provided by college students (Wiest, 1977). Using a standard psychological rating scale, this researcher found that women's and men's subjective descriptions of orgasm were indistinguishable. Similar results were obtained in an earlier study, when a group of 70 expert judges were unable to reliably distinguish between the written orgasm reports of men and women (Proctor et al., 1974).

Beyond the question of sex differences in orgasmic experiences, it is clear that there is great individual variation in how people, both men and women, describe orgasms. In Box 6.1 some subjective accounts selected from our files illustrate the incredible range of these descriptions. The first one is by a woman and the second by a man. The final three—labeled Reports A, B, and C, respectively—contain no specific references that identify the sex of the describer. Perhaps you would like to try to determine whether they were reported by a male or female. The answers are listed at the back of the chapter under the summary section.

Although the physiology of female orgasmic response can be clearly outlined, as it was in Table 6.4, some past and present issues about its nature need to be discussed. Misinformation about female orgasm has been prevalent in our culture. Freud, writing in the early 1900s, developed a theory of the "vaginal" versus the "clitoral" orgasm, which, although inaccurate, has had a great impact on people's thinking about female sexual response.

Freud viewed the vaginal orgasm as more mature and thus preferable. The physiological basis for this theory was the assumption that the clitoris is a stunted penis. This assumption led to the conclusion that erotic sensations, arousal, and orgasm resulting from direct stimulation of the clitoris were all expressions of "masculine" rather than "feminine" sexuality—and therefore undesirable (Sherfey, 1972). At adolescence, a woman was supposed to transfer her erotic center from the clitoris

TABLE 6.4 THE ORGASM PHASE: SEXUAL RESPONSE CYCLE

Reactions Common to Both Sexes	Female Responses	Male Responses
Reduction in voluntary muscle control. Involuntary muscle spasms throughout body.	Clitoris remains retracted under the hood.	During emission phase, internal secondary sex structures undergo contractions to cause pooling of seminal fluid in urethral bulb.
Blood pressure and heart rate reach highest levels (heart rate may increase to 180 in extreme cases).	No changes in labia majora and labia minora.	
	Orgasmic platform contracts rhythmically 3 to 15 times. First 3 to 6 contractions are intense, spaced at 0.8-second intervals, followed by weaker and slower contractions.	During expulsion phase, semen is expelled by strong, rhythmic contractions of penile urethra and muscles around base of penis. First 2 to 3 contractions are most intense, spaced at 0.8-second intervals, followed by several weaker and slower contractions.
Breathing may reach 40 breaths per minute.		
Sex flush, if present during earlier stages, typically persists through orgasm.	Uterus usually contracts at orgasm.	
No observable changes in the breasts or nipples.	No further changes in breasts or nipples.	
External rectal sphincter muscle contracts involuntarily at 0.8-second intervals.		No observable changes in scrotum, testes, or Cowper's glands.

BOX 6.1 SUBJECTIVE DESCRIPTIONS OF ORGASM*

When I'm about to orgasm, my face feels very hot. I close my eyes and open my mouth. It centers in my clitoris and it feels like electric wires igniting from there and radiating up my torso and down my legs to my feet. I sometimes feel like I need to urinate. My vagina contracts anywhere from 5 to 12 times. My vulva area feels heavy and swollen. There isn't another feeling like it—it's fantastic!

Orgasm for me draws all my energy in towards a core in my body. Then, all of a sudden, there is a release of this energy out through my penis. My body becomes warm and numb before orgasm; after, it gradually relaxes and I feel extremely serene.

Report A. It's like an Almond Joy, "indescribably delicious." The feeling runs from the top of my head to the tips of my toes as I feel a powerful surge of pleasure. It raises me beyond my physical self into another level of consciousness, and yet the feeling seems purely physical. What a paradox! It strokes all over, inside and out. I love it simply because it's mine and mine alone.

Report B. An orgasm to me is like heaven. All my tensions and anxieties are released. You get to the point of no return, and it's like an uncontrollable desire that makes things start happening. I think that sex and orgasm are one of the greatest phenomenons that we have today. It's a great sharing experience for me.

Report C. Having an orgasm is like the ultimate time I have for myself. I am not excluding my partner but it's like I can't hear anything and all I feel is a spectacular release accompanied with more pleasure than I've ever felt doing anything else. (Authors' files)

*For Reports A, B, and C from our files, decide if the subject was male or female. To find the answer, turn to the Summary at the end of this chapter.

to the vagina. If she was not able to do so at this time, psychotherapy was sometimes used to attempt to help her attain vaginal orgasms. Unfortunately, this theory led many women to believe incorrectly that they were sexually maladjusted.

Our modern knowledge about embryology has established the falseness of the theory that the clitoris is a masculine organ, as we have seen in Chapter 2's discussion of the genital differentiation process. In one researcher's words, "to reduce clitoral eroticism to the level of psychopathology because the clitoris is an innately masculine organ . . . must now be considered a travesty of the facts" (Sherfey, 1972, p. 47). Travesty of facts or not, during Freud's time this sexual-center transfer theory was taken so seriously that surgical removal of the clitoris was recommended for little girls who masturbated, to help them later attain "vaginal" orgasms.

Surgical clitoridectomies are no longer performed in our culture. Yet social conditioning, which can be as effective as a scalpel, continues, for Freud had developed an operational definition of female sexual health that is still with us in many respects. For example, a woman's reluctance to ask her partner to manually stimulate her clitoris during coitus (or to do it herself) typifies the learned belief that she "should" experience orgasm from penile stimulation alone. However, cultural conditioning can work two ways: with knowledge and support, a woman can change her attitude about her sexual feelings and behaviors.

Contrary to Freud's theory, the research of Masters and Johnson suggests that there is only one kind of physiological orgasm in females, regardless of the method of stimulation. They state:

From a biologic . . . [and] . . . anatomic point of view, there is absolutely no difference in the responses of the pelvic viscera to effective sexual stimulation, regardless of whether the stimulation occurs as a result of clitoral-body or mons area manipulation, natural or artificial coition, or for that matter, specific stimulation of any other erogenous area of the female body. (1966, p. 66)

While they made no anatomic distinctions between orgasms during coitus and those during noncoital activities, Masters and Johnson did note a difference between the two experiences. They found female orgasms during coitus to be measurably less intense (that is, there were slightly fewer vaginal muscular contractions), a discovery later reflected in the subjective responses of women in *The Hite Report*. In Hite's words, ". . . a clitorally stimulated orgasm without intercourse feels more locally intense, while an orgasm with intercourse feels more diffused throughout the area and/or body" (1976, p. 191).

There is considerable agreement on the existence of the variation described in the above account, and women vary in their preferences for manual or coital orgasms.

Clitoral orgasms (orgasms from direct clitoral stimulation) are stronger and sharper. Sometimes during intercourse I have almost a "missed" feeling. (Hite, 1976, p. 188)

Vaginal orgasms (orgasms from coital stimulation) are deeper, more releasing, more satisfying, better both psychologically and physically. They are like an underground volcano. A manual orgasm is sharper and more piercing, more superficial. (Hite, 1976, p. 190)

As in the other phases in the human sexual response cycle, it is clear that there are wide variations in subjective feelings and preferences in female orgasms.

In the last few years there has been an exciting new development in the study of female sexuality. It has been reported that some women are capable of experiencing orgasm, and perhaps ejaculation, when an area along the anterior wall of their vagina is vigorously stimulated (Addiego et al., 1981; Belzer, 1981; Perry and Whipple, 1981; Sevely and Bennett, 1978). This area has been named the *Grafenberg spot* in honor of Ernest Grafenberg, a gynecologist who first noted the significance of this location within the vagina some 30 years ago (Grafenberg, 1950).

As we saw in Chapter 4, the Grafenberg spot is located about one centimeter beneath the surface of the front or anterior wall of the vagina, somewhat below the cervix, and in line with the urethra (see Figure 6.6a for location of the urethra and its relationship to the vagina). It consists of a system of glands and ducts that surround the urethra. This area is believed to be the female counterpart of the male prostate gland, since it develops from the same embryologic tissue (Belzer, 1981).

The Grafenberg spot may be located by "systematic palpation of the entire anterior wall of the vagina between the posterior side of the pubic bone and the cervix. Two fingers are usually employed, and it is often necessary to press deeply into the tissue to reach the spot" (Perry and Whipple, 1981, p. 29). This exploration may be conducted by a woman's partner, as shown in Figure 6.9. Some women are able to locate their Grafenberg spot through self-exploration.

During initial searching for the sometimes elusive Grafenberg spot, a woman or her partner must rely on the sensations produced by manual stimulation. When the area is located, women report a variety of initial sensations including a slight feeling of discomfort, a brief sensation of needing to urinate, or a pleasurable feeling. After a minute or more of stroking, the sensations usually become more pleasurable and the area may begin to swell to a discernible size. Continued stimulation of the area may result in an orgasm that is often quite intense.

Perhaps the most amazing thing about Grafenberg spot orgasms is that they are sometimes accompanied by the ejaculation of fluid from the urethral opening. Four researchers describe their observation of this event:

With the aid of the subject's husband, four of us (Addiego, Belzer, Perry, and Whipple) were able to observe her response to digital massage of her Grafenberg spot, which led to expulsion of liquid, and reportedly and apparently to orgasm, on several occasions. On none of these occasions did stimulation of the clitoris, direct or otherwise, appear to occur. Orgasmic expulsions occurred after less than a minute of stimulation; they were separated in a multi-orgasmic series by similarly brief periods of time. The urethral area was clearly exposed in bright light, and there was absolutely no doubt that the liquid was expelled from the urethral meatus. Sometimes it exuded from the meatus. At other times it was expelled from one to a few centimeters. On one observed occasion, expulsion was of sufficient force to create a series of wet spots covering a distance of more than a meter (Addiego et al., 1981, p. 17).

Research indicates that the source of this fluid is the "female prostate" discussed earlier. The ducts from this system empty directly into the urethra. In some women, Grafenberg orgasms result in fluid being forced through these ducts and out the urethra. In view of the homologous nature of Grafenberg spot tissue and the male prostate, we might speculate that the female ejaculate is similar to the prostatic component of male seminal fluid. This notion has been supported by one study in which specimens of female ejaculate were chemically analyzed and found to contain high levels of an enzyme, prostatic acid phosphatase (PAP), characteristic of the prostatic component of semen (Addiego et al., 1981). Many women report that the fluid has a mild semenlike scent.

While the existence of Grafenberg spot orgasms, sometimes accompanied by ejaculation, has been reported, our understanding of this phenomenon is far from complete. How common these responses are remains to be determined by additional

FIGURE 6.9 LOCATING THE GRAFENBERG SPOT   *183*

Two fingers are usually employed, and it is often necessary to press deeply into the anterior wall of the vagina to reach the spot.

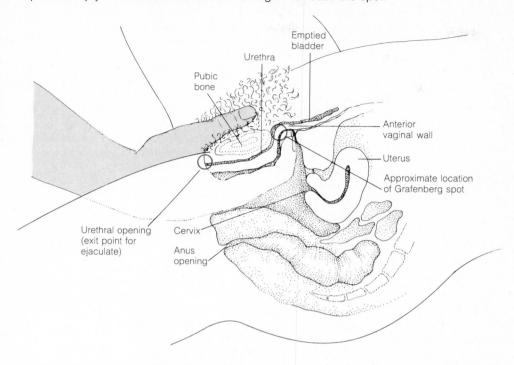

research. Women who want to explore this intriguing new information in relation to their own sexual response are encouraged to do so. However, it may be self-defeating to pursue the pleasures of Grafenberg spot stimulation as a new sexual achievement to be relentlessly pursued.

Resolution   During the final phase of the sexual response cycle, the sexual systems return to their nonexcited state. If no additional stimulation occurs, the resolution begins immediately after orgasm. Some of the changes back to a non-excited state take place rapidly while others occur more slowly. Table 6.5 summarizes the major physiological changes during resolution. Skin coloration subsides quickly; and heart rate, blood pressure, and breathing all become normal almost immediately. Both the clitoris and the penis begin returning to their unstimulated position and appearance immediately, but engorgement dissipates gradually. In men, especially, two stages of erection loss can be identified,with the second much longer than the first. The duration of the resolution phase is often directly influenced by the length of the arousal period prior to orgasm.

The four self-reports on the next page provide some indication of how people vary in their feelings after orgasm. The first two are by females; the second two reports are by males.

TABLE 6.5 THE RESOLUTION PHASE: SEXUAL RESPONSE CYCLE

Reactions Common to Both Sexes	Female Responses	Male Responses
Usually all signs of muscle tension (myotonia) are absent within 5 minutes after orgasm.	Clitoris descends to its overhanging position in 5 to 10 seconds. Engorgement of the shaft and glans takes longer to dissipate, roughly 5 to 30 minutes.	Erection loss occurs in two stages: During first phase, up to 50% of tumescence is lost within a minute or less after orgasm. The second stage is slower, sometimes requiring several minutes or longer for complete detumescence.
Heart rate, blood pressure, and breathing rate begin returning to normal immediately after orgasm.	Labia majora rapidly return to their unaroused size and midline position.	The testes return to their normal size and the scrotal sac to its wrinkled appearance. This return is quite rapid in the majority of men, but is sometimes protracted.
Sex flush, when present, usually disappears quite rapidly.	Labia minora return to normal unstimulated size and lose their "sex skin" coloration within 10 to 15 seconds.	
Nipple erection subsides slowly, often taking as long as one hour. Return to normal state is generally more rapid in females.	Uterus returns to its unstimulated position in the pelvic cavity.	
	Lack of orgasm after obtaining high levels of arousal may dramatically slow resolution. Sexual organs often remain congested, producing pressure which may result in genital and pelvic discomfort.	

After a satisfying experience with my husband I want to be held, as if to finalize and complete our union. Sometimes I like to talk and sometimes I just like to be able to touch him and be touched by his whole body. (Authors' files)

After orgasm I feel very relaxed. My moods do vary—sometimes I'm ready to start all over; other times I can jump up and really get busy; and at other times I just want to sleep. (Authors' files)

After orgasm I feel relaxed and usually very content. Sometimes I feel like sleeping and other times I feel like I want to touch my partner if she is willing. I like to hold her and just be there. (Authors' files)

After orgasm I generally experience a brief period where my sexual interest drops dramatically. While holding and being held is nice, I prefer not to continue any sexual activity, at least not for a few minutes. Usually I feel extremely satiated, similar to the aftermath of dining on a superb meal. Talking and sharing thoughts about the experience is especially pleasant. However, sometimes I like to just roll over and quietly bask in the luxurious afterglow. (Authors' files)

These subjective reports of women and men sound very similar. But there is one significant difference in the response of men and women during this phase—their physiological readiness for further sexual stimulation. After orgasm, the male enters into a *refractory period*—a time when no amount of additional stimulation will result in orgasm. The length of this period ranges from minutes to days, depending on a variety of factors such as the age of the man, the frequency of previous sexual activity, and the degree of his emotional closeness to and sexual desire for his partner. In contrast to men, women experience no equivalent refractory period. They are physiologically capable of returning to another orgasmic peak from anywhere in the resolution phase. However, a woman may or may not desire to do so. There are other differences between men's and women's patterns of sexual response. These, plus a more detailed look at the differences during the resolution phase, will be the subject of the next section.

Some Differences Between the Sexes

The basic similarities of sexual response in men and women are being emphasized more and more by many writers. We see this as a positive trend away from the once-popular notion that great differences exist between the sexes—an opinion that undoubtedly helped create a big market for many love manuals designed to inform readers about the mysteries and complexities of the opposite sex. Now we know that much can be learned about our partners by carefully observing our own sexual patterns. However, some important primary differences remain. In the following pages we will outline and discuss some of them.

Greater Variability in Female Response   One major difference between the sexes is the range of variations in the sexual response cycle. Although the graphs in Figures 6.3 and 6.4 do not reflect individual differences, they do demonstrate a wider range in the female response. One pattern has been outlined for the male and three for the female.

In the female chart, the sexual response pattern represented by line A is most similar to the male pattern. It differs in an important way, though, in its potential for additional orgasms without dropping below the plateau level. Line B represents quite a different female pattern: a smooth advance through excitement to the level of plateau, where the responding woman may remain for some time without experiencing orgasm. The consequent resolution phase is more drawn out. Line C portrays a rapid rise in excitement, followed by one intense orgasm and a quick resolution.

While it appears that women often have more variable sexual response patterns than men, this does not imply that all males experience the response cycle in the same way. Men report considerable variation from the Masters and Johnson standard, including (a) several mild orgasmic peaks followed by ejaculation; (b) prolonged pelvic contractions after the expulsion of semen; and (c) extended periods of intense excitement prior to ejaculation that feel like one long orgasm (Zilbergeld, 1978). In other words, there is no single pattern of sexual response, nor is there one "correct way." All of the patterns and variations—including one person's different reactions to sexual stimuli at different times or situations—are completely normal.

The Male Refractory Period   The presence of a refractory period in the male cycle is certainly one of the most significant differences in sexual response between the sexes. Men typically find that a certain minimum time period must elapse after an orgasm before they may experience another climax. Most women have no such physiologically imposed "shutdown phase."

There is considerable speculation about why only men have a refractory period. Some people believe that the answer to this riddle is somehow connected with the loss of seminal fluid during orgasm. However, no convincing biological evidence is available to support this interpretation, and there is nothing present in the expelled semen to account for an energy drain, marked hormone reduction, or any of the other implied biochemical explanations.

Another explanation of male refractory periods suggests that there may be an evolutionary advantage for them. According to this argument, since women have no sexual shutdown after orgasm, they are able to continue copulatory activity with other males. The resulting increase in numbers of sperm would, this theory holds, increase the probability of impregnation and reproduction of the species. From the point of view of human evolutionary history, the presence of additional seminal fluids perhaps allowed for a natural selection of the fittest sperm (fastest swimmers, longest life, and so forth). Admittedly, the evidence for this theory is tenuous at best, but it is nevertheless a provocative thesis.

Whatever the reason, the refractory period is common not just to human males but to virtually all other animals for which data exist, including rats, dogs, and chimps. It seems plausible that some kind of short-term neurological inhibitory mechanism is triggered by ejaculation. This notion is supported by the recent publication of some fascinating research conducted by three British scientists (Barfield et al., 1975). These researchers speculated that certain chemical pathways between the midbrain and the hypothalamus might have something to do with postorgasm inhibition in males; these pathways are also known to be involved in regulating sleep. To test their hypothesis, the researchers destroyed one specific site (the *ventral medial lemniscus*) along these pathways in rats. For comparative purposes, they surgically eliminated three other areas in hypothalamic and midbrain locations in different rats. Later observations of sexual behavior revealed that the elimination of the ventral medial lemniscus had a dramatic effect on refractory periods, cutting their duration in half.

Other research with rats has provided further evidence implicating the brain in the male refractory period. In two studies large lesions made in an area below the hypothalamus resulted in greatly increased ejaculatory behavior (Heimer and Larson, 1964; Lisk, 1966). In another investigation, it was found that electrical stimulation of the posterior hypothalamus can produce dramatic declines in the intervals between a male rat's copulatory activity (Cagguila, 1970).

Multiple Orgasms   There is a third area of sexual response patterns where some differences between the sexes occur: the ability to experience multiple orgasms. Technically speaking, the term *multiple orgasms* refers to having more than one orgasmic experience within a short time interval.

Although researchers differ in their views of what constitutes a multiple orgasmic experience, for our own purposes, we can say that if a man or woman has two or more sexual climaxes within a short period, that person has experienced multiple orgasms. There is, however, a distinction between males and females that is often obscured by such a definition. It is not uncommon for a woman to have several sequential orgasms, separated in time by the briefest of intervals (perhaps only seconds). In contrast, the spacing of male orgasms is typically more protracted in time.

Public recognition of female capacity for multiple orgasms has only recently emerged. When the Kinsey group published their research data they were widely criticized for this "fantastic tale" of multiple response in women. There is no doubt that many individuals supported Kinsey's finding on the basis of their own experience. Nevertheless, it remained for the pioneer work of Masters and Johnson to firmly establish the legitimacy of this phenomenon.

How many women do experience multiple orgasms? Kinsey (1953) reported that about 14% of his female sample regularly had multiple orgasms. In 1970 a survey of *Psychology Today* readers revealed a 16% figure (Athanasiou et al., 1970). Surveys of our own student population over the years have produced a similar low percentage of women who regularly experience more than one orgasm during a single sexual encounter.

On the surface, it would then appear that the capacity for multiple orgasms is limited to a minority of women. However, the research of Masters and Johnson showed this assumption to be false:

If a female who is capable of having regular orgasms is properly stimulated within a short period after her first climax, she will in most instances be capable of having a second, third, fourth, and even a fifth and a sixth orgasm before she is fully satiated. As contrasted with the male's usual inability to have more than one orgasm in a short period, many females, especially when clitorally stimulated, can regularly have five or six full orgasms within a matter of minutes. (1961, p. 792)

Thus, we find that multiple orgasms are within the capacity of most women, but they are apparently experienced by only a small part of the female population. Why is there a large gap between capacity and experience? The answer may lie in the source of stimulation. The Kinsey report, the *Psychology Today* survey, and our own student surveys mentioned earlier, are all based on orgasm rates during penile-vaginal intercourse. For a variety of reasons—not the least of which is the male tendency to stop after his orgasm—women are not likely to continue sexual activity beyond their initial orgasm when this is experienced during coitus. In sharp contrast, several researchers have demonstrated that women who masturbate and those who relate sexually to other women are considerably more likely both to reach initial orgasm and to continue to additional orgasms (Athanasiou et al., 1970; Masters and Johnson, 1966).

We do not mean to imply by this discussion that all women should be experiencing multiple orgasms. To the contrary, many women may prefer sexual experiences during which they have a single orgasm or perhaps no orgasm at all. Like any of the other responses described here, the data on multiple orgasmic capacities of women is not to be interpreted as the way women "should" respond. This could lead to a new kind of arbitrary sexual standard. The following quotes illustrate this tendency:

When I was growing up, people considered any young, unmarried woman who enjoyed and sought active sexual involvements to be disturbed or promiscuous. Now I am told that I must have several orgasms each time I make love in order to be considered "normal." What a switch in our definitions of normal or healthy—from the straight-laced, noninvolved person to this incredible creature who is supposed to get it off multiply at the drop of a hat. (Authors' files)

Sometimes, men ask me why I don't come more than once. It is as though they want me to perform for them. The truth is one orgasm is all I typically need to be satisfied. Sometimes it is nice not even to worry about having a climax. All this emphasis on producing multiple orgasms is a real put-off to me. (Authors' files)

As suggested earlier, multiple orgasms are considerably less common among males. They are most often reported by very young men, their frequency declining with age. Even at college age it is unusual to find men who routinely experience more than one orgasm during a single sexual encounter. However, we do agree with Alex Comfort (1972) in his assertion that most men are probably more capable of multiple orgasms than they realize. Many have been conditioned by years of masturbation to get it over as quickly as possible ("Hurry up and finish before I am discovered!"). Such a mental set hardly encourages continued experimentation after the initial orgasm. Through experimentation, though, many men make discoveries similar to that described in the following personal reflection of a middle-aged man:

Somehow it never occurred to me that I might continue making love after experiencing orgasm. For thirty years of my life this always signaled endpoint for me. I guess I responded this way for all the reasons you stated in class and a few more you didn't cover. My sweetheart was with me the night you discussed refractory periods. We talked about it all the way home and the next day gave it a try. Man, am I mad at myself now for missing out on something really nice all of these years. I discovered that I could have more than one orgasm in one session, and while it may take me a long time to come again, the getting there is a very nice part. My partner likes it, too! (Authors' files)

Even without a second orgasm, many men may find it pleasurable to continue sexual activity after a climax. However, some people believe it is necessary for a man to achieve orgasm whenever he interacts sexually with his partner. This belief stems from the pervasive myth that sex is not complete for a man unless he reaches "The Big O." This attitude may make it difficult to enjoy activity that does not result in a second climax. Not all males fall victim to this belief, however.

One of the best parts of sex for me is having intercourse again shortly after my first orgasm. I find it is relatively easy to get another erection, even though I seldom experience another climax during the same session. The second time round I can concentrate fully on my partner's reactions without being distracted by my own building excitement. The pace is generally mellow and relaxed and it is a real high for me psychologically. (Authors' files)

Recent evidence suggests that some men may actually be capable of experiencing a series of orgasms in a very short time period. In one study, 13 multi-orgasmic men demonstrated the capacity to experience a series of pre-ejaculatory orgasms culminating in a final orgasm with ejaculation. Physiological measures indicated that the pre-ejaculatory orgasms were indeed genuine. The final orgasm in the series, accompanied by ejaculation, triggered a refractory period (Robbins and Jensen, 1978). This research shows that orgasm and ejaculation in males are not necessarily associated with each other. Furthermore, it suggests that men who learn how to experience orgasm without ejaculation may be able to experience a series of closely timed orgasms in much the same way as women.

There is one final difference between men and women's experiences of multiple orgasms that we should mention here. It has to do with individuals' subjective assessments of sexual climaxes that occur after the first orgasm. Masters and Johnson (1966) found that women who experienced multiple responses in the laboratory reported subsequent orgasms to be more intense and pleasurable than the first. In direct contrast to this, most men who had multiple orgasms in their laboratory reported that the pleasure of the first orgasm was superior. Masters and Johnson interpreted this finding to reflect men's equating seminal fluid volume with superior orgasms, with initial ejaculation producing a larger quantity of semen.

While this finding no doubt reflects the experience of most males, it is important to note that some men report the exact opposite—namely, greater pleasure from subsequent orgasms. Some of the accounts we have heard give credit to increased sensitivity, improved staying power, more control, heightened awareness, and greater appreciation of the partner's response in later orgasms.

In all, multiple orgasms may be seen not as an ultimate goal to be sought above all else but rather as a possible area to explore. A relaxed approach to this possibility may give interested women and men an opportunity to experience more of the range of their sexual potentials.

SUMMARY

THE ROLE OF HORMONES IN SEXUAL AROUSAL

1. While it is difficult to distinguish between the effects of sex hormones and learning experiences, research does indicate that sexual arousal is hormonally influenced. Androgen appears to facilitate sexual desire in women as well as men.

THE BRAIN AND SEXUAL AROUSAL

2. The brain plays an important role in human sexual arousal by mediating our thoughts, emotions, memories, and fantasies.

3. There is evidence linking stimulation and surgical alteration of various brain sites with sexual arousal in both humans and other animals.

4. The limbic system, particularly the hypothalamus and septal area, seems to play an important part in sexual function.

THE SENSES AND SEXUAL AROUSAL

5. The sense of touch tends to predominate in human sexual arousal. Locations on the body that are highly responsive to tactile pleasuring are called erogenous zones. Primary erogenous zones include those areas with dense concentrations of nerve endings. Secondary erogenous zones include other areas of the body that become endowed with erotic significance as the result of sexual conditioning. Sensate focus is an excellent method for getting in touch with the sensual potentials that reside throughout our own bodies and those of partners.

6. Vision is second only to touch on the hierarchy of stimuli that most people find sexually arousing. Recent evidence suggests that women respond as much as men to visual erotica.

7. Our own unique experiences may allow certain smells and tastes to acquire erotic significance. Our culture's obsession with "personal hygiene" items tends to mask natural smells or tastes that relate to sexual activity.

8. Some individuals find sounds during lovemaking to be highly arousing while others prefer that their lovers be silent during love play. In addition to being sexually arousing to some, communication during a sexual interlude can be very informative.

9. Aside from the effects of androgen on females, there is nothing among the ranks of things we eat, drink, or inject that has genuine aphrodisiac qualities. Faith and suggestion account for the apparent successes of a variety of alleged aphrodisiacs.

10. Certain substances are known to have an inhibitory effect upon sexual behavior. These anaphrodisiacs include some tranquilizers, a few antihypertensives, certain antiandrogenic drugs, and nicotine.

KAPLAN'S THREE-STAGE MODEL OF SEXUAL RESPONSE

11. Kaplan's model of sexual response contains three stages: desire, excitement, and orgasm.

12. This model is distinguished by its inclusion of desire as a distinct stage of the sexual response cycle separate from genital changes.

MASTERS AND JOHNSON'S FOUR-PHASE MODEL

13. Masters and Johnson describe four phases in the sexual response patterns of both women and men: excitement, plateau, orgasm, and resolution.

14. During excitement, both sexes experience increased muscle tension, heart rate, and blood pressure. Sex flush and nipple erection often occur, especially among women. Female responses include engorgement of the clitoris, the labia, and the vagina (with vaginal lubrication), elevation and enlargement of the uterus, and breast enlargement. Males experience penile erection, enlargement and elevation of the testes, and sometimes Cowper's glands secretions.

15. The plateau is marked by dramatic accelerations of myotonia, hyperventilation, heart rate, and blood pressure. In females, the clitoris withdraws under its hood, the labia minora deepen in color, the orgasmic platform forms in the vagina, the uterus is fully elevated, and the areolas become swollen. In men, the corona becomes fully engorged, the testicles continue both elevation and enlargement, and the Cowper's glands are active.

16. Orgasm is marked by involuntary muscle spasms throughout the body. Blood pressure, heart rate, and respiration rate peak. Orgasm is slightly longer in duration in females. Male orgasm typically occurs in two stages, emission and expulsion.

17. It is difficult to distinguish between subjective descriptions of female and male orgasms.

18. Masters and Johnson suggest that there is only one kind of physiological orgasm in females, regardless of the method of stimulation.

19. Some women are capable of experiencing orgasm, and perhaps ejaculation, when an area along the anterior wall of their vagina (the Grafenberg spot) is vigorously stimulated.

20. During resolution, sexual systems return to their nonexcited state, a process that may take several hours, depending on a number of factors. Erection loss occurs in two stages, the first very rapid and the second more protracted.

SOME DIFFERENCES BETWEEN THE SEXES

21. Fundamental similarities between sexually responding men and women have been emphasized by many writers. However, certain important primary differences remain.

22. As a group, females demonstrate a wider variability in their sexual response patterns.

23. The presence of a refractory period in only the male cycle is one of the most significant differences between the sexes. While no reason(s) for the existence of this period in men has been clearly demonstrated, there is some evidence that neurological inhibitory mechanisms activated by ejaculation play a role.

24. Multiple orgasms occur with greater frequency in females. They are more likely to be experienced by women while masturbating than during coitus. Recent evidence suggests that some men may actually be capable of experiencing a series of orgasms in a very short time period. Sequential orgasms are generally reported by women to be more intense; men commonly find the opposite to be true.

Answers to Quiz:
  Report A = Male
  Report B = Female
  Report C = Female

SUGGESTED READINGS

Beach, Frank. "Hormonal Control of Sex-Related Behavior." In F. Beach (Ed.), *Human Sexuality in Four Perspectives*. Baltimore: Johns Hopkins Press, 1977 (also available in paperback from same publisher, 1978). A discussion of the effects of sex hormones on the behavior of humans and other animals. Although somewhat technical, this article contains a wealth of relevant facts.

Bermant, Gordon, and Davidson, Julian. *Biological Bases of Sexual Behavior*. New York: Harper & Row, 1974. Contains two excellent chapters dealing with hormonal factors in sexual expression.

Brecher, Ruth, and Brecher, Edward. *An Analysis of Human Sexual Response*. New York: New American Library, 1966. Provides a simplified and accurate reporting of the Masters and Johnson (1966) research findings.

Kaplan, Helen Singer. *Disorders of Sexual Desire*. New York: Brunner/Mazel, 1979. Deals primarily with the treatment of sexual difficulties, particularly problems of desire. It contains excellent information about the effects of a variety of drugs on sexuality.

Masters, William, and Johnson, Virginia. *Human Sexual Response*. Boston: Little, Brown, 1966. A highly technical book outlining the authors' major contributions to the understanding of the physiology of human sexual response. A good source for those readers who desire more detailed information about physiological responses to sexual stimulation.

PART THREE

Sexual Behavior

7

Love and the Development of Sexual Relationships

WHAT IS LOVE?
   Measuring Love
   Jealousy and Love
FALLING IN LOVE: WHY AND WITH WHOM?
LOVE AND SEX
SEX AND RELATIONSHIPS ON YOUR TERMS
   Know What You Want
   Friendships Without Sex
   Saying "Not Yet" to a Sexual Relationship
   Guidelines for "Casual Sex"
   Caring Endings
   Managing Rejection
TYPES OF LOVE
   Passionate Love
   Companionate Love
THE DEVELOPMENT OF INTIMACY
   Self-Love
   The Phases of Relationship
MAINTAINING RELATIONSHIP SATISFACTION
   The Inclusion-Response Foundation
   Individual and Relationship Growth
   Sexual Variety, An Important Ingredient
SUMMARY
SUGGESTED READINGS

Love, intimacy, and sexual relationships are important and complex aspects of people's lives. In this chapter we will examine some of the perspectives and research related to these kinds of interactions, and we will consider a variety of questions. What is love? How does it relate to jealousy? What does research on measuring love and on partner selection tell us? How does sex fit into relationships? Are there different kinds of love? And, finally, what are some factors in developing and maintaining intimacy in a relationship?

WHAT IS LOVE?

Love has intrigued people throughout history. Its joys and sorrows have inspired artists and poets, novelists, filmmakers, and other students of human interaction—indeed, love and its effects are probably one of the most pervasive themes in the art and literature of many cultures. (Box 7.1 offers two contrasting definitions of love.) Each of our own lives has likely been influenced in some significant way by love; our best and worst moments may be tied to a love relationship. Yet, although love is of great concern to humankind, little is conclusively known about it. Interestingly, the merits of research on the subject of love have sometimes evoked controversy. In 1976 the National Science Foundation revoked an $84,000 grant it had awarded for

BOX 7.1 TWO CONTRASTING DEFINITIONS OF LOVE

1. "Love is patient and kind; love is not jealous, or conceited, or proud; love is not ill-mannered, or selfish, or irritable; love does not keep a record of wrongs: love is not happy with evil, but is happy with the truth. Love never gives up: its faith, hope and patience never fail. Love is eternal . . . There are faith, hope and love, these three; but the greatest of these is love." (New Testament; I Corinthians 13)

2. "LOVE is a temporary insanity curable by marriage or by removal of the patient from the influences under which he incurred the disorder. This disease, like caries and many other ailments, is prevalent only among civilized races living under artificial conditions; barbarous nations breathing pure air and eating simple food enjoy immunity from its ravishes." (Ambrose Bierce, *The Devils' Dictionary*, 1943, p. 202)

research on love because of opposition to the proposed study by Senator William Proxmire. Proxmire argued that love is not a science and should remain a mystery. Researchers have continued to explore many aspects of love, however, and in the next section we will examine some of these. We will begin with a look at research related to measuring love and attraction.

Measuring Love

Love is a special kind of attitude with strong emotional and behavioral components. It is also a phenomenon that eludes easy definition or explanation. When asked in one study, two out of three college students were not sure they knew what love was (Kephart, 1967). Given the problematic nature of love, can it be meaningfully measured? Some social scientists have attempted to do so, with interesting results. Perhaps the most ambitious attempt to measure love was undertaken some years ago by psychologist Zick Rubin (1973). On the basis of responses to a questionnaire administered to several hundred dating couples at the University of Michigan, Rubin developed a 13-item measurement device that he called a love scale. On this scale a person is asked to indicate if a particular statement accurately reflects his or her feelings about another person, usually someone of romantic interest.

Love, as measured by Rubin's scale, has three components: attachment, caring, and intimacy. *Attachment* refers to a person's desire for the physical presence and emotional support of the other person. *Caring* refers to an individual's concern for the other's well-being. *Intimacy* is the desire for close, confidential communication with the other.

Some people may argue that it is simply not possible to measure such an unfathomable emotion as love, particularly with a paper-and-pencil measurement device like the love scale. Nevertheless, Rubin did obtain some evidence supporting

the validity of his scale. For example, the scale was used to investigate the popular belief that lovers spend a great deal of time looking into one another's eyes (Rubin, 1970). Couples were observed through a one-way mirror while they waited to participate in a psychological experiment. The findings revealed that "weak lovers" (couples who scored below average on the love scale) made significantly less eye contact than did "strong lovers" whose scores were above average. Another study indicated that the more two people liked each other after an initial meeting the closer they stood together (Byrne et al., 1970).

Jealousy and Love

Many people think that jealousy is a measure of devotion, and conversely, that the absence of jealous feelings implies a lack of love. People will sometimes try to make a partner jealous to assure themselves of their partner's love or as an attempt to increase their partner's attraction to them.

Chapter Seven: Love and the Development of Sexual Relationships

One time when I felt my girlfriend was kind of taking me for granted, I felt neglected so I flirted with another girl at a party. My girlfriend noticed that and became more attentive. Now I will occasionally deliberately flirt with someone else to get her to pay more attention to me. (Authors' files)

However, some writers believe that jealousy is related more to injured pride or fear of losing what one believes he or she controls or possesses than to love. For example, jealousy may be a sign that a person feels inadequate when they find that their lover enjoys the company of someone else.

Not everyone responds to jealousy in the same way and according to one study (Clanton and Smith, 1977) there appear to be some differences in how women and men react. In general, women are more likely to acknowledge jealous feelings, and men are more likely to deny them. A jealous woman will more often focus on the emotional involvement of her partner with another person, whereas a jealous man tends to be concerned with the sexual relationship between his lover and another. Women also often blame themselves as the cause of jealousy, while men typically blame the third party or the woman.

Jealousy is an uncomfortable feeling that can stifle development and pleasure in a relationship. Walster and Walster (1978) offer the following suggestions to people who want to decrease feelings of jealousy. First, find out exactly what it is that makes

Jealousy can generate several feelings—anger, possessiveness, and hurt.

you jealous. Is it a matter of pride? Do you believe that the other person belongs to you like one of your possessions? Does the situation provoking jealousy lead to fears of losing this relationship? Second, it is important to put jealous feelings in perspective. One way is to ask yourself, "What is it that I want to be different?" "What do I really want? Why?" After understanding more fully what it is that really bothers you and leads to feelings of jealousy, the third step is for you and your partner to negotiate agreements or conditions about outside involvements. One student who did this successfully reports:

> My girlfriend and I go to a lot of parties together and have a good time—except for one thing. I find myself feeling jealous when I look across the room and see her talking and laughing with another guy. And then when I'm around her I start putting her down in subtle ways, especially to the guy she's been talking to. She pretty much ignores me when I do that, but I think it could harm our relationship. So I really gave it some thought and realized that I actually don't mind her having fun with other people, in fact it's one of the things I like about her. What I really wanted was for her to pay a little more attention to me at parties and do things like hold my arm or give me a little kiss—little things that told others we were a couple. When I asked her to do those gestures, she was real agreeable and parties have been a lot more fun for us since. (Authors' files)

FALLING IN LOVE: WHY AND WITH WHOM?

What determines why people fall in love and with whom they fall in love? These questions are exceedingly complex. Many of us have learned to expect to fall in love and also to expect a variety of rewards from a loving relationship: emotional support, companionship, and sexual pleasure, for instance. Social pressure may also play a dominant role in falling in love. Most of us receive many messages from friends, family, and society that tell us that falling in love is the appropriate thing to do.

Some writers believe that people fall in love to overcome a sense of aloneness and separateness. Psychoanalyst Erich Fromm (1965) suggested that union with another person is the deepest need of humans. Another psychoanalyst and writer, Rollo May, author of *Love and Will* (1969), also believes that as people experience their own solitariness, they long for the refuge of union with another through love. Others, however, see loneliness as a by-product of our individualistic and highly mobile society rather than as an inherent part of the human condition. This view emphasizes the connectedness that people have with others through all our social relationships, language, and culture, and describes love relationships as one aspect of a person's social network rather than as a cure for the "disease" of loneliness (Solomon, 1981).

For many people, falling in love may serve to justify certain behaviors—for example, being sexual with another or demanding an exclusive relationship. Sometimes when people find themselves responding sexually to someone, they assume they must be in love. Frequently, a person becomes convinced that he or she is in love with another after sharing a pleasant sexual encounter. Later in this chapter we will examine more fully the relationship between love and sex.

200

Just as we know little about why people fall in love, there are no simple answers to explain why they fall in love with those whom they do. There are a number of factors, however, that are often important. One of these is proximity. People often fall in love with individuals they see frequently—in school, at work, at church, or at parties. Another factor is similarity. It has been reported that people who fall in love often have highly similar social backgrounds, sharing like family histories, social class, religion, or other common traits (Rubin, 1973). Commonality of interests also seems to be important to the long term success of a relationship. People who have very similar attitudes and behavioral characteristics frequently become lovers. This does not mean that people necessarily fall in love with individuals who are like them. Frequently, the needs of lovers complement each other. For example, a person who has a need to be assertive and feel in control may enter into a love relationship with someone who prefers a more passive role.

Physical attractiveness also often plays a dominant role in drawing lovers together. In spite of the saying that "beauty is only skin deep," it has been experimentally demonstrated that an individual's physical attractiveness frequently has a dramatic impact on his or her appeal to the opposite sex (Berscheid and Walster, 1974). Physical appearance seems to influence not only "sex appeal" but many aspects of our initial attitudes toward other people. In one study, college students were shown photographs of males and females of differing degrees of physical attractiveness and asked to provide their impression of these people. The researchers reported that the most physically appealing individuals were consistently rated as more interesting, sociable, kind, and sensitive than their less attractive counterparts (Dion et al., 1972).

Although it may be disturbing to discover that the impact of beauty is often more than skin deep, this is most true in the early stages of a relationship: "It seems likely that the impact of physical attractiveness is greatest when we first meet someone. As a relationship progresses, physical attractiveness tends to recede in importance. And we often perceive people whom we love as being beautiful, regardless of what anyone else might think" (McNeil and Rubin, 1977, p. 581).

A person's objective attractiveness appears to be only one factor in how attractive they seem to others. Subjective opinion matters, too, and here situational variables may significantly affect a person's opinion of how attractive or how likeable another person is. One study had two groups of people meet in different rooms where they were given the same photographs of people. They rated how much they thought they would like the people in the photos. One group met in a nicely furnished, pleasant room, and the other met in a dirty, shabbily furnished, messy room. The people in the attractive room were more positive toward the photographs than the group in the unpleasant room (Maslow and Mintz, 1956). Another similar study had a group of strangers meet in a cool comfortable room and others meet in an uncomfortably hot room. In this situation the group in the comfortable room reported liking each other more than the strangers in the uncomfortable room (Griffitt, 1970). Research has also shown that meeting someone while experiencing physiological arousal from fear or anxiety may increase interest in and attraction to the other person (Dutton and Aron, 1974). Pre-existing sexual arousal may also increase subjective attractiveness or interest from one person to another. For example, Stephan et al. (1971) divided men, who were ostensibly coming to a computer dating service to see a photo of their "date," into two groups. While they were waiting, the men in one group were provided with pin-up type magazines, and the other men were given low-key, boring reading material. The men who had been reading sexually suggestive material rated the photograph of their prospective date as more attractive than did the others, although the same photo was given to both groups. Other studies have reported similar results, and this work raises some intriguing possibilities for further research.

LOVE AND SEX

Just what is the connection between love and sex? It is certainly true that couples may engage in sexual relations without being in love with one another. Furthermore, love may exist independently of any sexual attraction or expression. Nevertheless, the feelings of being in love with and sexually attracted to another person are frequently intertwined. The complex interplay of these related mental states gives rise to many familiar questions. For example, does sexual sharing typically deepen a love relationship? Are people more likely to feel they are in love with someone after they have had sex? Is sex without love appropriate? We will attempt to shed some light on these and similar questions in this section.

One study of college students found that women are much more likely than men to report being in love with their partners if they had engaged in coitus than if they had not. Particularly high love scores (as measured by Rubin's love scale) were found among women whose first sexual experiences had been with their current partner. There seemed to be no link between a man's reported love for his partner and whether they had engaged in sexual relations (Peplau et al., 1977).

In response to questionnaires administered in our sexuality classes, women have consistently linked love with sex to a greater extent than men. In a recent survey of several hundred students, roughly 30% of the women indicated that sex was either not enjoyable or totally inappropriate without love. In contrast, only 12% of men indicated the same feelings. However, the majority of these students—70% of the women and 79% of the males—indicated that "love enriches sexual relations but is not necessary for enjoyment."

These findings appear to reflect a double standard that still flourishes in our society. Whereas men have often learned that experiencing sex in a casual relationship is acceptable, women frequently have learned that sexual sharing is appropriate only when one is in love with the other person. It is reasonable to suspect that many women (and, to a lesser extent, men) have attempted to justify their sexual behavior by deciding they are in love. It is likely that some couples even enter into premature commitments (such as going steady, becoming engaged, getting married) to convince themselves of the depth of their love and thus the legitimacy of their sexual involvement.

While many people enjoy sex without love, the activity frequently arouses strong feelings. We are often confronted with the question, "Is it really all right for two people who are not in love to have sex?" There is no absolute answer to such a query. Each of us has our own personal value system that influences the decisions we make for ourselves. Therefore, instead of attempting to answer the question, we will briefly outline a few differing views.

Albert Ellis, in his book *Sex Without Guilt* (1966), suggests that a sexual relationship between individuals who are not in love ought to be both socially and personally acceptable. After providing psychotherapy to individuals and couples for many years, Ellis concludes that sex without love may be quite satisfying, although sex with love is probably more so. In his book, Ellis argues that many people, particularly those who are young, find themselves in a position of desiring sexual intimacy with someone with whom they are not in love. Since people's personalities and past experiences vary widely, and many individuals have little or no capacity for love, these people should not be denied the satisfaction of sexual sharing. Ellis further suggests that imposing a necessary link between sex and love may result in people feeling needlessly guilty about nonloving sexual relations. If business associates, friends, and fishing partners get along excellently without loving each other, why shouldn't sex mates, who may share little else, also experience mutually gratifying encounters?

Rollo May (1969) expresses a different view about sex without authentic love. He observes that there have been significant changes in attitudes since earlier times in our history: "The Victorian person sought to have love without falling into sex; the modern person seeks to have sex without falling into love" (p. 46). May believes that the contemporary preoccupation with technique and performance and a deemphasis on intimacy has resulted in a lack of sexual enjoyment and passion for many people.

Our observations have revealed that many people who embrace the notion that sex and love belong together may nevertheless have sexual relations with someone they do not love. Guilt often results from such encounters, and it may weigh heavily, as revealed in the following account:

I was brought up to believe that sex was something two people shared only after falling in love. I can remember my Mom saying, "Wait until you are in love." Well, I didn't follow her advice. As a matter of fact, my first sexual experience was with a man to whom I was only physically attracted. We had absolutely nothing else in common. The sex was OK but the guilt afterwards was terrible. I thought myself to be emancipated from all that childhood indoctrination. But I wasn't. Even now I am very hesitant to become sexually involved with someone unless I feel strongly affectionate toward him. Intellectually I know this attitude causes me to pass up many opportunities for pleasurable experiences. But I don't like having to deal with the guilt afterwards. (Authors' files)

SEX AND RELATIONSHIPS ON YOUR TERMS

The subject of sex with or without love raises the issue of decision-making regarding sexual relationships. Sexual expression can have many different meanings; for example, sex can be a validation of deep intimacy within a relationship. People can also choose to be sexual as a part of a friendship or as a way of getting to know someone. For some, reproduction may be the primary meaning. Reduction of sexual tension can be a motivation for sex, and sex can also be used as a way of experiencing new feelings, excitement, and risk. It can even be a kind of recreational pastime. People also use sex to try to alleviate feelings of insecurity—to prove their "manhood" or "womanhood" or to please someone or persuade them to care. Some people use sex to experience the power to attract others or to avenge earlier rejections by enticing partners and then turning them down.

Each person has the task of deciding how he or she wants to express sexuality. This important process is complicated by the fact that many of the old rules that have governed sexual relationships are changing, as reflected in these comments of a recently divorced woman:

When I was dating 25 years ago in college, a kiss at the door on a first date was considered to mean I really liked the guy. And I was determined to be a virgin until I got married. These guidelines were held by most of my friends, and I felt a lot of security in them. Now I don't know how to behave. There really don't seem to be any standard rules. It's exciting and frightening to know I can make decisions because I want to. It is also confusing at times, and I sometimes wish the standards I used to know were still common. (Authors' files)

Some people base their decisions on sexuality on clear, pre-existing rules expressed by family, church, or peer group. Many others do not have such specific guidelines or disagree with the values they have been taught. Consequently, these people need to understand their own personal values and develop their own guidelines. The following section discusses some options for establishing guidelines for decisions about sexual expression.

Know What You Want

The first step in integrating sex into your life in a meaningful way is to consider what you want in relationships before initiating sexual involvement with another. This is a variation on the theme "know thyself." Consider the following:

Often when I meet a man for the first time I end up being swept off my feet and into bed. At the time it seems like the thing to do, but afterwards I'm often left confused and a bit empty inside. It's not that I don't like sex. I'm just not sure about what role it should play in my life. (Authors' files)

This woman might be able to reduce the confusion and discomfort she experiences by evaluating her expectations and needs in the area of sexual relationships. An important question for each of us to ask ourselves is "What role do I want relationships and sex to occupy in my life at this time?" The answer to this question will often change over time as a person faces new life situations.

As a part of this self-inventory it might be helpful to consider the following questions:

1. How comfortable am I with some of the contemporary approaches to sex and relationships?

2. Which of the more traditional norms do I value?
3. What are my values as they pertain to sexual relationships and where do they come from—family, church, friends, media, and so forth?

A person can further clarify his or her values in relation to a specific decision about being sexual by asking another question: "Will a decision to engage in a sexual relationship—with this person and at this time—enhance my positive feelings about myself and the other person?" The answer to this question can help a person act in a way that is consistent with his or her value system. It also helps prevent exploitative sexual encounters in which the other person's feelings are not considered.

What if the answer to the previous question is "No"? Then it may be appropriate to think about what kind of relationship, if any, would have the potential for enhancing positive feelings. Perhaps a sexual relationship is not quite right but a nonsexual friendship would be. Or, perhaps a person does not feel ready for a sexual relationship. At this point communication and negotiation are important.

One of the risks of understanding and acting on one's own feelings, desires, and values is that someone else may not see things the same way. Unfortunately, many people have a tendency to believe that such differences mean that either they themselves or the other person is "wrong." However, more often than not, these differences simply indicate that two people do not want the same thing at the same time. Occasionally, a relationship cannot be established without compromising one person's situation or values. When this occurs, one option is to end the relationship. Each person can then seek someone who has more similar perspectives. On other occasions, it may be that clarification, negotiation, and compromise can establish a common bond for a relationship. The following sections will illustrate some options for dealing with several specific relationship situations. Chapter 8 provides additional information on communication in sexual relationships.

Friendships Without Sex

Some people find it very difficult to communicate a desire for friendship without sex, especially when it appears that the other person wants a sexual relationship. The situation is even more formidable when one likes the other person and wants the relationship to continue. One is often concerned that the other person will feel bad or decide to end the relationship. However, most people would probably prefer to be told the truth directly rather than have to decipher the meaning of vague, confusing responses. The following comment is fairly typical of our students:

I hate it when I find myself in a relationship and all I get is the run around. I eventually get the picture when someone else doesn't reciprocate my feelings, but what a waste of time and energy. Why can't they just come out and say what they are feeling? At least I would know where I stand and could act accordingly. (Authors' files)

This person's feeling of frustration is understandable. However, one can attempt to resolve this kind of uncertainty by asking the other person about her or his feelings.

Nonsexual friendships can offer companionship and enjoyment.

The following demonstrates how one student did this:

Jake and I had gone out several times, and initially he acted like he was attracted to me. But then he began to treat me more like a sister. He continued to ask me out, but made no sexual gestures. I finally told him I was confused about how he felt about me. He seemed very concerned about my feelings as he told me that he wanted a friendship with me instead of a romantic relationship. He wasn't sure why, but he had come to realize that's how he felt. I felt disappointed, and it was a little tough on my ego to not be desired sexually, but I decided that a friendship with him would be nice for me. And, several years later, we are still friends. (Authors' files)

Saying "Not Yet" to a Sexual Relationship

One of the benefits of less rigid rules about "proper" sexual behavior is that people may find it easier to set their own pace in sexual relationships. It is common for a person to feel sexual attraction and to desire a sexual relationship with someone—but "not yet." The ability to delay sexual involvement until both people feel ready can do much to enhance the initial experience. Also, waiting until familiarity and trust are established, and making sure that personal values are consistent with the relationship, can enhance positive feelings about oneself.

When sexual attraction exists within a relationship, sex is not necessarily an "either-or" situation. There are progressive stages of intimacy from holding hands to genital contact, and some people move slowly through these steps to savor and grow comfortable with the increasingly intimate contact. Gratification may be greater with a gradual progression toward intimacy than with rushed sexual contact, as the author of the following discovered:

I felt sexually attracted to Mike the first time I met him, but, somehow, almost by mutual instinct, we moved very slowly sexually. We both agreed that was how we wanted it for this relationship. We spent several extremely enjoyable months kissing, touching, holding each other, and even sleeping together before we had intercourse. The entire experience has really changed how I see "fast food sex" and has given new light to the expression, "Haste makes waste." (Authors' files)

Social expectations of "instant sex" can present a challenge to those who want to move gradually into a sexual relationship. There are several things you can do to let another person know that you are not yet ready for sex or that you want the relationship to progress slowly. It is often helpful to begin by indicating that you find the person attractive. You can acknowledge your desire for increased sexual intimacy, but it is equally important to be definite about not yet being ready. Last, letting a partner know what kind of physical contact you desire at a given point in a relationship can help to clarify any confusion about present expectations and reassure the other person.

Guidelines for "Casual Sex"

Sometimes people are interested in a primarily sexual experience. Such encounters are characterized by a lack of deep emotional involvement as well as a focus on sex. The sexual relationship can be brief, or last for an extended period of time. Our students often debate whether sex can be good in this context. Some argue that without some kind of commitment the sex will be less than satisfying. Others maintain that sexual experiences are at their best in this type of situation. Our intent is not to resolve this debate but rather to present some ideas, adapted from *Brief Encounters* (1980), that can help to make casual sexual liaisons self- and other-enhancing experiences.

The basic ingredients of casual sex are two people who are willing to be honest with themselves and each other. The decision to enter into this kind of relationship also needs to be within each individual's value system. Other criteria include:

1. Both partners want to have sex.
2. Neither partner is coercing the other.
3. Both partners are honest with each other that their commitment is limited to mutual enjoyment.
4. Both partners are interested in their own and each other's sexual pleasure and feelings of self-worth.

5. Both partners have taken responsibility to discuss and use any necessary precautions against sexually transmitted diseases or unwanted pregnancy.

Caring Endings

Over the years our sexuality classes have been the scene of many lively discussions of the question "How do you prefer to be informed when someone does not wish to continue a relationship with you?" While students have many different opinions and experiences, the large majority want to be told in a clear, unmistakable manner that their desire for a relationship is not reciprocated by the other. A simple statement like "I appreciate your interest in me but I'm not strongly enough attracted to you to want to pursue a relationship with you" is the kind of ending that most of our students have indicated they would prefer. Most students also report that it would be more difficult to make than to hear such a direct statement; there is rarely an easy way to end a relationship when one person is interested in maintaining it. In general, this kind of situation requires that a person communicate his or her desire to end a relationship in a way that is both effective and compassionate.

Managing Rejection

Fear of rejection can often inhibit people from initiating a relationship or expressing their desires within one. The old adage "Nothing ventured, nothing gained" often does not quell the fears of venturing. One man expresses his concern as follows:

I find it extremely stressful to ask a woman out for the first time. I just can't deal effectively with the prospect of being turned down. I know it's irrational, but when someone says, "No," I have a hard time not feeling real down. (Authors' files)

To many people, a "No" is equivalent to an all-out assault on their sense of self-worth. A person who is rejected may feel unattractive, boring, unsexy, unintelligent, or inherently unlovable. All of us experience rejection at some time, however,

CATHY   **by Cathy Guisewite**

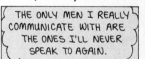

Chapter Seven: Love and the Development of Sexual Relationships

usually because our traits do not match the other person's subjective preferences. The very characteristics that one person finds undesirable may well appeal to another, and the right to choose not to become involved with someone is certainly an option that most people want.

Although rejection can still be a painful experience, there are some strategies for dealing with being turned down. For example, it is important to remember that each of us has self-worth, regardless of whether all people approve of us. Also, defending yourself to someone who has said "No" is not likely to be helpful, since being turned down is usually not a critique but rather an expression of individual preferences. Finally, even though being rejected may appear to be cause for giving up on continued attempts to participate in close relationships, rejection can be avoided completely only if we isolate ourselves from most kinds of social interaction. As one woman states:

I don't like being turned down, but I like being alone even less. Life is full of risks, and the dating game has its share. It might be safer to retreat into a social vacuum and wait for something to happen. But I like making my own choices instead of hoping the right man will ask me. If I'm turned down, someone else always comes along. It's a happy hunting ground out there, filled with all kinds of prospects, some of whom will say yes. (Authors' files)

TYPES OF LOVE

Love takes many forms. Two types that we will focus on in this section are *passionate love* and *companionate love*.

Passionate Love

Passionate love, also known as romantic love or infatuation, is a state of extreme absorption in another. It is characterized by intense feelings of tenderness, elation, anxiety, sexual desire, and ecstasy. Generalized physiological arousal, including increased heart beat, perspiration, blushing, and stomach churning, along with a feeling of great excitement, often accompany this form of love. Strong sexual desire is typically a major component.

Although I had never known him well, I had admired him from a distance for some time. When circumstances threw us together for that day, I felt strongly drawn to him and realized I was really in love with him. Being physically close to him was incredibly intense and I felt as if I could never touch him enough or ever bring our bodies as close together as I yearned to do. (Authors' files)

Intense passionate love typically occurs early in a relationship. It sometimes seems as if the less a person is known, the more intense the passionate love. In passionate love, faults are often overlooked and conflicts are avoided. Logic and reasoned consideration are swept away by the excitement the lover evokes. The object of passionate love may be perceived as providing complete personal fulfillment, a situation that may have unexpected consequences:

Romance is built on a foundation of quicksilver nonlogic. It consists of attributing to the other person—blindly, hopefully, but without much basis in fact—the qualities one wishes him to have, though they may not even be desirable, in actuality. Most people who select mates on the basis of imputed qualities later find themselves disappointed, if the qualities are not present in fact, or discover they are unable to tolerate the implication of the longed-for qualities in actual life. For example, the man who is attracted by his fiancee's cuteness and sexiness may spend tormented hours after they are married worrying about the effect of these very characteristics on other men. It is a dream relationship, an unrealistic relationship with a dream person imagined in terms of one's own needs. (Lederer and Jackson, 1968, p. 439)

Another characteristic of intense passionate love is that it often does not last very long. Love that is based on ignorance about a person's full character is bound to change with increased familiarity. Many couples choose to make some kind of commitment to each other (become engaged, move in together, get married, and so forth) while still fired by the fuel of passionate love, only to feel disillusioned later when ecstasy gives way to routine, and the everyday annoyances and conflicts typical of most ongoing relationships begin to surface. This is the time when the previously infatuated person may begin to have some doubts about his or her partner. Some couples are able to work through this period to ultimately find a solid basis upon which to build a lasting relationship of mutual love. Others discover, often to their dismay, that the only thing they ever really shared was passion.

The frequent confusion at the beginning of a relationship between passionate and companionate love is one reason why a couple may find it helpful to allow their relationship to evolve over a fairly long period of time (months, maybe even years) before committing themselves to major life style changes. They may be able to move beyond the passionate love stage to a point where it is clear whether their relationship has a firm basis for a long term commitment of companionate love.

Unfortunately, many people who experience the lessening of passionate love believe that it is the end of love rather than a possible transition into a different kind of love.

I just don't feel the same excitement and the same passion for my lover as I used to feel. I used to feel overwhelmed waiting for her to meet me. I still look forward to seeing her, but not with breathless anticipation. I guess that I must not be in love anymore. (Authors' files)

On the other hand, some people look forward to a different kind of relationship. Erich Fromm once commented, "Romantic love is a delicious art form but not a durable one. In the end, its most persistent practitioners confess that they would like to escape from its patterned illusion into the next more realistically satisfying stage of an enduring relationship" (1965, p. 252).

Companionate Love

Companionate love describes a kind of love different from passionate love (Walster and Walster, 1978). Companionate love is a less intense emotion. It is characterized by friendly affection and a deep attachment that is based on extensive familiarity with the loved one. It involves a thoughtful appreciation of one's partner. Companionate love often encompasses a tolerance for another's shortcomings along with a desire to overcome difficulties and conflicts in a relationship. This kind of love is committed to ongoing nurturing of a partnership. In short, companionate love is often enduring, while passionate love is almost always transitory.

Sex in a companionate relationship typically reflects the feelings that familiarity provides, mainly security in knowing and understanding what pleases the other. This foundation of knowledge and sexual trust can encourage experimentation and subtle communication. Sexual pleasure in a companionate relationship strengthens the overall bond of the relationship. Although sex in companionate love is usually less exciting than in passionate love, it is often experienced as richer, more meaningful, and deeply satisfying, as the following statement reveals:

> Between my first and second marriage I really enjoyed the excitement of new sexual relationships. The passion and the challenge were all wonderful, especially after so much sexual frustration in my first marriage. Even though I sometimes miss the excitement of those times, I would never trade it for the easy comfort, pleasure, and depth of sexual intimacy I now experience in my 17-year marriage. (Authors' files)

Rollo May stresses the intertwining of love and will as necessary to companionate, or as he calls it, *authentic love. Will* is a decision to care for another person; it is a commitment to involve oneself with the other individual's feelings and to risk being vulnerable in sharing one's own feelings and thoughts. Love is the feelings that nourish that commitment.

Companionate love has also been described as a *mutative relationship* (Goethals, 1980). This notion implies that the two individuals in a love relationship, as well as the relationship itself, continually generate change. This kind of relationship has a dynamic quality that helps satisfy the often contradictory human desires for both security and excitement. The people in mutative relationships grow and change, sometimes in response to individual challenges, sometimes in response to the relationship itself. The partners share a sense of collaboration in their joint life, exhibit a great deal of empathy for each other, and demonstrate a high degree of androgyny. They are sexually exclusive by desire rather than by contractual agreement. Goethals believes that ideal mutative relationships are rare but possible.

Although most relationships begin with a period of passionate love and only later evolve into companionate love, some have the opposite history. Companionate love may develop first in, say, a situation where two people know each other for an extended period as acquaintances, friends, or coworkers. Often an initial sexual attraction is not present or was deemphasized because of circumstances. In these relationships, passionate love is based on familiarity with the other person, rather than on the excitement of the unknown. One woman describes her experience:

Jim and I had been friends for several years before I even became attracted sexually to him. We would occasionally go out to dinner together and I would always enjoy myself. We had a lot of professional interests in common and as I came to know him more fully, I gained a deep appreciation for his personal values and integrity. But he just wasn't my "type." But, one time—I'm not even sure how it happened (I guess we were both horny)—we had sex together. It was nice and comfortable, but not terrific. For some reason, we continued to be sexual and as time passed we have fallen in love, and sex between us as well as our whole relationship continues to be more and more exciting. I never expected it to happen this way. (Authors' files)

THE DEVELOPMENT OF INTIMACY

A question that students often ask and that interests many people is how to maintain intimacy, satisfaction, and sexual enjoyment in a relationship. There are many opinions on this subject and no conclusive answer. This may have to do with the uniqueness of each person; what is satisfaction and intimacy for one person may be dissatisfaction to another. Each person must, in effect, reinvent the wheel and discover for him- or herself how to develop and maintain satisfactory relationships. This section will discuss some ways of thinking about and understanding, developing, and maintaining intimacy.

Self-Love

Satisfying intimacy within a relationship begins with self-love. How can this be? In the context of this chapter, self-love does not mean conceit and lack of consideration of others; these qualities are usually indications of personal insecurities. By self-love we mean the kind of feeling that Leo Buscaglia (1972) describes as a genuine interest, concern, and respect for oneself—the ability to look in the mirror and appreciate the person we see and feel excited about that person's potential.

We believe that positive and accepting feelings toward oneself are a good foundation upon which intimacy in relationships can be built. Certainly a relationship can validate a person's positive feelings about him- or herself, and, at times, help to lessen negative ones. However, when a person is seeking to eradicate a strong negative self-image through a relationship, she or he will likely be disappointed.

A scholar of human development, Erik Erikson (1965), believes that positive self-feelings are a prerequisite to a satisfying relationship. Only as people begin to feel more secure in their own identity are they able to establish intimacy with others, both in friendship and eventually in a love-based, mutually satisfying sex relationship.

The Phases of Relationship

One way of understanding the development of a relationship is to examine different aspects of its growth, or phases; this may also give us some guidelines for maintaining a good relationship. As we discuss the various phases it is important to remember that they are simply a convenient scheme; in reality, a relationship is fluid, dynamic, and frequently unpredictable. We mean to give our readers a framework for thinking about a relationship rather than a prescription for intimacy. Also, this discussion and the following section consider sex as only one part of the total context of a relationship. Let us begin with the first phase, inclusion.

Inclusion   *Inclusion* is when one person extends some kind of invitation to relate, whether it be by eye contact, a smile, or a friendly "Hello." It is the first step that one person takes in meeting another. Many "how-to-pick-up-dates" books specialize in tips for initial inclusion. Often, the signs can be quite subtle.

When I go out dancing alone and want to decide who to ask to dance, I look around the room. When I see a man who returns my glance (especially if he smiles or nods) I'll go over and ask him to dance if he isn't already on his way to ask me. (Authors' files)

Inclusion continues throughout a relationship, and the nature of inclusion behaviors provides the backbone of a positive relationship. A good morning kiss, a smile and hug after a day apart, a sincere "Tell me about your day," a compliment, or an expression of appreciation are some of the kinds of inclusions that can nourish an ongoing relationship.

Response   How one responds to a gesture of inclusion may determine whether a relationship even begins. For example, quickly glancing away from someone's initial eye contact will likely deter any further initiation. However, if one responds in kind and goes a step further with a smile and a greeting, the other person will be more likely to initiate further contact. Positive inclusion and responses are dependent upon each other for the interaction to progress.

As a relationship continues, certain kinds of responses will typically enhance the relationship's growth. These include listening to the other person and understanding his or her point of view, following through with agreements or plans, or being enthusiastic about seeing the other person. Positive and consistent inclusions and responses are the foundation for the next important phases of care, trust, affection, and playfulness. These phases often develop simultaneously as well as build on each other.

Care   Care implies a genuine concern for another's welfare. Care motivates us to consider another person's desires and interests; it creates a desire to please and contribute to another's happiness.

Trust   Trust is a feeling essential to both the ongoing development of a relationship and its satisfactory continuance. It contributes to the belief that each partner will act consistently, in ways that promote the relationship's growth and stability and that affirm each partner. It means that both people trust each other and themselves to be positive and constructive in their inclusions and responses with each other. For example:

I trust my partner to:
Talk to me when she's unhappy about something I've done.
Be concerned about my satisfaction when we make love.
Feel attracted to me when I am naked.
Be honorable and fair.
Take my feelings in consideration.
Use birth control. (Authors' files)

Affection   Affection is characterized by feelings of warmth and attachment. It evokes a desire to be physically close to another, and is often expressed by touches, holding hands, sitting close, hugs, and caresses. Affection can be signalled nonverbally by smiles, winks, and tender looks, and verbally by expressions of appreciation, liking, or loving. The following comment exemplifies a high level of affection within a friendship:

My best friend and I never get together without a hug for a greeting and a goodbye. It's also typical for us to get together at one of our houses for tea, long talks, and foot rubs. (Authors' files)

Playfulness   This is the phase in the development of an intimate relationship in which each person exhibits delight and pleasure in the other. Exhilaration, abandon, and expansive laughter often accompany playfulness, whether it is a parent playing peek-a-boo with a small child or lovers having a pillow fight.

Genitality   As you may have noted, all of the phases described here could characterize a variety of situations, including a good friendship, a parent-child or sibling relationship, or a close mentor-student relationship. The final phase crosses the boundary of sexuality to include genital contact. There may have been varying degrees of sexual feeling in previous phases, but in the genitality phase a person has decided to express feelings by lovemaking.

When people step over the genitality boundary before going through the earlier six phases, they may actually experience a reduction in feelings of emotional closeness. The following account illustrates this:

I had known Chris for some time and thought I was ready to be sexual with him. So, after an evening out together, I asked him if I could stay at his place, and he said "Yes." I felt really aroused as we got in bed. I really enjoyed touching the shapes and textures of his previously unknown-to-me body. As we started to touch each other's genitals, I felt uncomfortable. It seemed that if we were going to proceed in the direction we were headed, we would be going beyond the level of emotional intimacy I felt—in a way, it would be a violation of my feelings. It seemed that I would have to shut out the closeness I felt in order to go further. I had to choose between intimacy and genital contact. Our closeness was more important to me, and I told him that I wanted to know each other more before going further sexually. (Authors' files)

With the foundation of the other six phases, genitality can be the culmination of deep intimacy and emotional closeness. Companionate love is an expression of all of these phases. Fromm (1965) states that the use of the body for the purpose of seeking and expressing satisfaction with one another is what sex truly is and what gives it its most deeply felt meaning. He explains further that sex can be important in two ways, first through initial attraction, and second, by cementing a relationship through the fulfillment and pleasure sex offers.

MAINTAINING RELATIONSHIP SATISFACTION

Human relationships present many, many challenges. To begin, there is the challenge of building a positive relationship with oneself, as described in the section on self-love. There is the additional task of establishing satisfying and enjoyable relationships with

family, peers, teachers, coworkers, employers, and other people within a person's social network. We also have the challenge of developing special, intimate relationships with friends and, when desired, sexual relationships. Finally, many people confront the challenge of maintaining satisfaction and love within an ongoing committed relationship. Commitment in a relationship is often demonstrated by the decision to marry. However, many couples have long-term committed relationships outside of marriage. When we use the word relationship or quote the word marriage, we mean to include both married and nonmarried couples. This section will present some of the factors that may contribute to ongoing relationship satisfaction in general. We will also discuss the value of sexual variety within the sexual relationship.

There are many ingredients in a lasting love relationship. They include self-acceptance and appreciation of one another; commitment and good communication;

realistic expectations; shared interests; and the ability to face conflict effectively (Rosenman, 1979).

These characteristics are not static; they evolve and change over time and influence each other. Often they need to be deliberately cultivated. In contemporary society, the efforts of the partners are probably more important to relationship stability than in the past, when marriage as an institution was sustained more strongly by culture, religion, law, and the extended family (Levinson, 1978).

The Inclusion-Response Foundation

Maintaining positive inclusion and response experiences is crucial to the continued satisfaction of committed couples. The saying, "It's the little things that count" is especially meaningful here. When one partner says to the other, "You don't love me anymore," that often means "You are not doing as many of the behaviors you used to do that I interpret as meaning you love me." The behaviors are often so small that one may not really notice them. However, when couples do fewer things that contribute to their partner's feeling of being loved, or stop doing them, the deficit is often experienced as a lack of love. On the other hand, continuing affectionate and considerate interactions helps maintain a feeling of love. For example:

The kinds of things that enhance my feeling of my partner loving me may seem quite inconsequential, but to me they aren't. When he gets up to greet me when I come home, when he takes my arm crossing the street, when he asks, "Can I help you with that?", when he tells me I look great, when he holds me in the middle of the night, when he thanks me for doing a routine chore—I feel loved by him. Those little things—all added up—make a tremendous difference to me. (Authors' files)

Couples may also find that talking with one another to identify actions that are especially enjoyable and exploring new ideas can be useful. The "Golden Rule" is not always applicable in relationships because people's preferences are often quite different.

Developing enjoyment with and appreciation of one another in nonsexual areas typically enhances sexual interest and interactions. Often, couples report a lack of desire for sexual intimacy when they experience a general lack of intimacy within the relationship. People may make comments like:

I just don't feel like having sex with him when he's been at work all day then comes home and watches TV all night. (Authors' files)

Usually, negative interactions like complaining and blaming also dampen sexual interest. While we cannot discuss general relationship communication tools in this book, we do want to emphasize the important role that effective, positive communication of feelings, appreciations, and requests can have in a relationship. We encourage individuals or couples who want to enhance their skills in this area to use some of the suggested reading sources in this and other chapters.

Growth and change are important in maintaining vitality in a relationship. Each person's growth can provide an opportunity for the other partner to develop new skills within him- or herself in order to appreciate and respond positively to the changes of the beloved. Lovers can draw on emotional, artistic, intellectual, spiritual, and physical dimensions for growth to enrich each other's mutual enjoyment.

At times, this dynamic of growth and change occurs without deliberate effort; at other times it requires direct attention. Couples who maintain satisfactory levels of growth will typically not let love diminish by choosing to withdraw their energy from the relationship at the first sign of strain or boredom. Rather, they will confront the difficulties and attempt to ameliorate them (Csikszentmihalyi, 1980). For example:

My husband and I found it increasingly difficult to have time together because of our busy schedules. And, then, when we were together we felt a little like strangers. So, we decided to structure some time together learning something new. The dancing lessons we took even rekindled some romantic feelings. (Authors' files)

Each person brings her or his strengths and weaknesses into relationships, and a relationship itself has its own combination of strengths and weaknesses. A couple is rarely fully prepared for the myriad of issues that arise from this combination. It is often

An older couple's intimacy and affection develops from years of shared experiences.

helpful to view problems and dissatisfactions as challenges to overcome or differences to accept, rather than as sure signs that the relationship is about to fail. Couples need to be prepared to negotiate and renegotiate what they want out of life and out of their relationship, knowing that the arrangement they work out one day may become untenable the next. At the same time, partners in a committed relationship often recognize that the love they hold for each other means accepting one another as unique human beings. These attitudes give a couple options for shaping a relationship uniquely suited to their individual and collective wants and needs (Walster and Walster, 1978).

The process of being in a committed relationship can itself be a source of growth. Such a relationship can make urgent demands on individuals so that they mature in directions and with a rapidity that would not otherwise occur. The "beneficial trauma" of confronting oneself intensely and learning to accept another deeply as sometimes occurs within an intimate relationship can facilitate individual growth. As Erich Fromm once wrote, "Married lovers grow within love; they develop into better human beings" (1965, p. 288).

Sexual Variety, An Important Ingredient

There is a special little restaurant with great steaks and a cozy, intimate atmosphere that I love to visit once every few months. Good companionship, a favorite bottle of wine, a tasty cut of rare meat, and I am living. Let a friend invite me back the next day, and it is still good, but not quite so stimulating. Given an invitation for a third trip in as many days, and I might just as soon stop off for a McDonald's quarter-pounder. (Authors' files)

There is a message in this personal anecdote. For many people, the desire to seek variety in life's experiences is a very strong motivation. They may acquire an assortment of friends, each providing a unique enrichment to their lives. Likewise, they read different kinds of books, pursue a variety of recreational activities, eat a variety of foods, and take a mixture of classes. They often seek a broad vista of experiences to enrich their lives. Is it not perplexing that many of these same individuals may choose to ignore this motivational thrust in an area of life capable of providing much joy? Consider the following:

Sex for me is dull, boring, and uninspiring routine. My husband likes to "make love" on Saturday night (he is too tired during the week). It's always the same way—a few kisses, some mechanical manipulation of my breasts, and presto, he is in and out and finished. I rarely am satisfied, but I don't even give a damn anymore. Actually I'm glad he finishes quickly. It's never fun to prolong boring things. (Authors' files)

For some readers, particularly those who have never been involved in a long term relationship, it may be difficult to relate to these accounts. However, for others who have been or are presently involved in this kind of relationship, these comments may strike a familiar and distressing chord.

Unfortunately, many individuals enter into a committed relationship thinking that intense sexual excitement will always be a natural occurrence between two people in love. This is not surprising in view of how susceptible we often are to romantic ideas originating in our own fantasies and the pervasive influence of the media. Therefore, it is often difficult to recognize that the heart-pounding joy of initial discovery must eventually be replaced by realistic and committed efforts to maintain the vitality and rewards of a workable relationship. Once a person is committed to a primary partner, and the variety offered by a succession of relationships is no longer available, it may be necessary to seek variety in other ways.

Before going on, we want to emphasize that not every couple feels the need for sexual variety. Many individuals may feel quite comfortable with established routines and have no desire to change them, as expressed in the following:

We settled down into a variation of our own particular pattern, a seldom-deviated-from routine, a practice which *Cosmopolitan* warned was boring, stagnating, and ruinous to a marriage. . . It has taken months, maybe years of persistent trial and error with shyly veiled hints and endless, polite "That was fine, really it was" from both of us before we each discovered what the other enjoyed, responded to, and wanted. Charlie, only slightly less shy than me, knew where I wanted to go and how to get me there, and in turn, over a period of time, I'd been able to reach through his natural reserve to the passionate man underneath. Now we had an intimate knowledge of one another and our own pace, our own rhythm, our own consistent satisfaction, and to hell with the marriage manuals. In bed, at least, we trusted one another. And shared. (Rebeta-Burditt, 1978, p. 288)

However, if you prefer to develop more variety in your sexual relationship, the following paragraphs may be helpful.

Communication is critical. Talk to your partner about your needs and feelings. Share with him or her your desire to try something different. Perhaps some of the guidelines in Chapter 8 will facilitate making requests and exchanging information. You may want to try sharing fantasies and then acting them out.

Avoid the routine of time and place. Make love in unusual places (on the laundry room floor, stretched out on the kitchen counter, alongside a mountain trail) and at extraordinary times ("birdsong in the morning," a "nooner," or in the middle of the night when you wake up feeling sexual).

Some of the most exciting sexual experiences may be those that take place on the spur of the moment with little or no preplanning. It is easy to see how these encounters might occur frequently during courtship days. It is also true that they may become distant memories after couples settle into the demanding daily schedules of living together. Perhaps you may find that striving to maintain this spontaneity will stand you in good stead as your relationship is nurtured over the months or years of your time together.

Do not let questions of what is normal get in the way of an enriched and varied erotic life. Too often, people refrain from experiencing something new because they feel that different activities are "abnormal" or, worse yet, "perverse." In reality, only you can judge what is normal for you. There is a consensus among contemporary writers in the field of human sexuality that any sexual activity is normal, as long as it gives pleasure and is not injurious to either partner.

Related to concerns about what is normal are concerns about frequency. Forget the magazine article that said that couples in your age category are having sex 2.7 times per week. The only right rule for you is to have sex as often as you and your partner desire it.

Finally, lovers sometimes find that books dealing with sexual techniques may be beneficial to their erotic lives. We recommend that you read them together rather than separately. Discussing a particular written suggestion can often open up new vistas of sexual sharing. Such books sometimes provide the necessary approval or justification for trying something new.

We do not mean to imply that all people must have active, varied sex lives to be truly happy. This is not the case. Not all individuals are in need of pursuing more variety in their sex lives. Some may find comfort and contentment in repeating familiar patterns of sexual interaction. Others may consider sex to be relatively unimportant compared with other aspects of their lives and may choose not to exert special efforts in pursuing its pleasures. However, if your sexuality is an important source of pleasure in your life, perhaps our suggestions pertaining to variety may be valuable to you.

SUMMARY

WHAT IS LOVE?

1. Rubin's love scale is a 13-item subjective rating scale that measures some of the components of attachment, caring, and intimacy; studies of eye contact and physical proximity give some support to the validity of the scale.

2. Jealousy may not be a sign of love but an indication of other feelings like fear of losing possession or control of another. Some research indicates that men and women react differently to jealousy.

FALLING IN LOVE: WHY AND WITH WHOM?

3. Many theories exist about why people fall in love, including the need to overcome a sense of aloneness, the desire to justify sexual involvement, or as a consequence of sexual attraction.

4. People tend to fall in love with others with similar backgrounds.

5. Although a person's objective physical attractiveness can be important in attracting another, factors such as an anxiety-producing situation, pleasant surroundings, or preexisting sexual arousal can also enhance interest in another.

LOVE AND SEX

6. There are various perspectives on the question of love and sex. Most students in our surveys report that love enriches sexual relations but is not necessary for enjoyment, although sex without love often produces guilt.

SEX AND RELATIONSHIPS ON YOUR TERMS

7. Deciding one's own values in relation to sexual experiences is especially important today in a time of changing expectations. Asking yourself the question "Will a decision to engage in a sexual relationship—with this person at this time—enhance my positive feelings about myself and the other person?" can help you act in a way that is consistent with your value system.

8. There are many types of relationships: friendships without sex, progressing slowly into a sexual relationship, and having "casual sex" are among the possibilities.

9. You can develop strategies for minimizing the pain of rejection, particularly if you remember that rejection usually occurs because a person's traits do not match another's subjective preferences, not because the person is unworthy.

10. Passionate love is characterized by intense, vibrant feelings.

11. Companionate love is characterized by deep affection and attachment.

THE DEVELOPMENT OF INTIMACY

12. Self-love, positive and accepting feelings towards oneself, are an important foundation for intimacy with others.

13. The phases of a relationship include inclusion, response, care, trust, affection, playfulness, and genitality.

14. Maintaining positive inclusion response experiences is crucial to continued satisfaction in an ongoing relationship.

15. Individual and relationship growth can provide challenges and stimulation to the relationship in order to maintain its vitality.

16. Sexual variety is often an important ingredient in maintaining enjoyable sex in a long term relationship. For some, however, the security of routine is most satisfying.

SUGGESTED READINGS

Bach, George, and Deutsch, Ronald. *Pairing.* New York: Avon, 1970. Written specifically for single people, this book presents ideas about meeting people, choosing partners for positive relationships, and developing intimacy.

Coleman, Emily, and Edwards, Betty. *Brief Encounters.* New York: Anchor, 1980. An indispensable guide for dealing with relationships as a single person, with especially good chapters on the issues of money and sex.

Fromm, Erich. *The Art of Loving.* New York: Bantam, 1963. A classic on the topic of love. Fromm elucidates the power of love to develop human potential within oneself and within a relationship.

Rosenman, Martin. *Loving Styles.* Englewood Cliffs, N. J.: Prentice-Hall, 1979. This book examines what couples can do to help their relationships work better. Contains advice on working out conflict, increasing trust, and keeping a long time relationship fresh.

Singer, Laura. *Stages: The Crises That Shape Your Marriage.* New York: Grosset & Dunlap, 1980. A helpful book that discusses patterns of crisis points in marriage and ideas to deal more effectively with critical stages of marriage.

Walster, Elaine, and Walster, William. *A New Look at Love.* Reading, Mass.: Addison-Wesley, 1978. Discusses questions about love, such as sexual attraction, the dilemma of security versus excitement, and difficulties in love relationships, and reports the latest research findings through case histories and questionnaires.

8

Communication in Sexual Behavior

THE IMPORTANCE OF COMMUNICATION
SOME REASONS WHY SEX TALK IS DIFFICULT
TALKING: GETTING STARTED
   Talking about Talking
   Reading and Discussing
   The Media As a Stimulant
   Sharing Sexual Histories
LISTENING AND FEEDBACK
   Be an Active Listener
   Maintain Eye Contact
   Provide Feedback
   Support Your Partner's Communication Efforts
   Express "Unconditional Positive Regard"
   Use Paraphrasing
DISCOVERING YOUR PARTNER'S NEEDS
   Asking Questions
   Self-Disclosure
   Comparing Notes
   Giving Permission
LEARNING TO MAKE REQUESTS
   Taking Responsibility for Our Own Pleasure
   Making Requests Specific
   Using "I" Language

DELIVERING CRITICISM
   Be Aware of Your Motivation
   Choose the Right Time and Place
   Temper Criticism with Praise
   Nurture Small Steps Toward Change
   Avoid "Why" Questions
   Express Anger Appropriately
NONVERBAL SEXUAL COMMUNICATION
   Facial Expression
   Interpersonal Distance
   Touching
   Sounds
IMPASSES
SUMMARY
SUGGESTED READINGS

*T*his is a chapter about sexual communication, or *sex talk:* the ways people convey their needs and desires to sexual partners. We will consider the reasons why such attempts are sometimes unsuccessful; we will also explore some ways to enhance this aspect of our sexual lives.

THE IMPORTANCE OF COMMUNICATION

Sex talk can contribute greatly to the satisfaction of an intimate relationship. We do not mean that extensive verbal dialogue is essential to all sexual sharing; there are times when spoken communication may be more disruptive than constructive. Nevertheless, couples who consistently elect not to talk about any sexual aspects of their relationships may be denying themselves an opportunity to learn about each other's needs and desires.

Talking about sex is a unique kind of communication that presents a variety of special problems. The presence of warmth, caring, and openness in a relationship is no guarantee that the couple have good sexual communication. Furthermore, even knowledge of effective communication skills is no insurance that a couple will apply them in their relationship. Aside from the fact that it is often particularly difficult to talk about sex, some people may be unmotivated to explore this area with their partners. Sex may seem relatively unimportant to some individuals and therefore not worth any extra effort. Other people may purposely avoid activities designed to improve sexual relations because bad sex may be serving a purpose for them—perhaps to punish, put down, insult, or deprive their partners.

We have seen instances where both members of a couple have all the tools for good communication but are either unable or unwilling to apply them in their relationship. The reasons for this may be far more complex than the possibilities mentioned previously imply. Even when a climate of good will prevails, it is sometimes difficult to establish a satisfying pattern of sexual dialogue. In circumstances such as these, it may be undesirable for the couple to try to resolve all of their communication difficulties strictly on their own. Instead, they should probably seek professional counseling.*

Central to this chapter is our belief that the basis for effective sexual communication is *mutual empathy*—the underlying knowledge that each partner in a relationship cares for the other and knows that care is reciprocated. With this perspective in mind we will discuss a variety of approaches to sex talk that have proved helpful in the lives of many people. We do not claim to have the final word on the many subtle nuances of human communication, nor do we suggest that the ideas offered here will work for everyone. Communication strategies often need to be individually modified; and sometimes differences are so basic that even the best communication cannot ensure a mutually satisfying relationship. We hope, though, that some of these shared experiences and suggestions can be helpful in your own sexual life.

*Chapter 17 provides some guidelines for seeking professional assistance.

SOME REASONS WHY
SEX TALK IS DIFFICULT

Why do so many people find it difficult to talk candidly with their companions about sexual needs? A variety of events and conditions are involved. Some of the most important reasons lie in our socialization; the language available for talk about sex; and the fears many people have about losing spontaneity or expressing too much of themselves.

The manner in which we are reared as children often contributes to later difficulties in talking about sexual needs. Learning to cover our genitals, or to think that eliminative functions are "dirty," or to hide self-pleasuring for fear of adverse reactions all may contribute to a sense of shame and discomfort with the sexual areas and functions of our bodies (see Chapter 13).

A conspiracy of silence about sexual matters exists in many American homes, and it is detrimental in a number of ways. Not talking about sex at home deprives a young child of one valuable source for acquiring a vocabulary with which to communicate about sex later in life. This lack of communication may also convey an implicit message: that sex is not an acceptable topic for conversation. Furthermore, children most effectively acquire communication skills when they are provided with models of verbal interaction followed by the opportunity to express their own thoughts in an accepting atmosphere. None of these elements is typically available in a home where people simply do not talk about sex.

The lack of positive models frequently extends beyond the home. Few individuals have access to classroom or textbook sources that portray how couples talk about sex. Neither peer groups nor the popular media fill the gap by providing realistic or positive information.

Another source of communication difficulty is related to the "socialization by default" that many Americans experience in matters relating to the language of sex. By the time they are grown up and eager to communicate sexual needs and feelings, many individuals don't know how to go about doing it. All the words may have become associated with negative rather than positive emotions. People frequently learn to snigger over taboo sex words or to use them in an angry, aggressive, or insulting manner. Consequently, it can be very uncomfortable for a person to use those same words to describe a sexual activity to someone for whom she or he really cares.

Thus, when we want to begin engaging in sexual communication, we may find ourselves struggling to find the right language for this most intimate kind of dialogue. The range of words commonly used to describe genital anatomy gives some indication of our society's mixed messages about sexuality. Two extremes tend to predominate: street language at one end and clinical terminology at the other, as shown in Table 8.1.

One man's consternation over trying to figure out what words to use for his own genitals is revealed in the following anecdote:

I want to talk with my girlfriend about our sex life. So many times I have made up my mind to do this, but I can't seem to come up with how I should do this. How

TABLE 8.1 SEX LANGUAGE, CLINICAL VS. STREET[a]

Female		Male	
Clinical	**Street**	**Clinical**	**Street**
external genitalia	cunt	external genitalia	equipment
pudendum (Latin meaning "the shamefuls")[b]	snatch pussy	pudendum	pencil and tassles balls and bat
vulva	muff bearded clam beaver hair-pie Happy Valley	penis	cock dick wang prick reamer
vagina	hole quim cockpit	testicles	balls jewels dead meat

[a]Besides the terms listed in this table, euphemistic phrases (such as "privates," "down there," and the "wee-wee" or "pee-pee" words of childhood) can be applicable to either sex.

[b]According to Webster's dictionary, the external genitals of a human being, and especially of a woman.

can I tell her about my body and its needs? What words do I use? Do I say, "I like it best when you caress along the entire length of my penis," or should I say, "It feels good when you touch all of my cock." The first word sounds too clinical but I am afraid the term cock might shock her and put her off. Just what words do lovers use? (Authors' files)

As this man has discovered, our language lacks a comfortable sexual vocabulary. Many of us are not at ease with the words commonly available. We may find them to be either too clinical or too offensive, harsh, or juvenile to use in a caring way. Words like penis and vagina often seem too technical or medical; cock, prick, cunt, and snatch are expressions that are often used aggressively or insultingly. Terms describing sexual activity may create similar problems. Statements like "Let's fuck," while perhaps lovingly delivered and excitedly received by some, may seem too cold, graphic, or aggressive to others. A more scientific description, such as "Let's have sexual intercourse," may seem clumsy and impersonal.

Most of us have also learned while growing up that talking about S-E-X is very different from discussing the afternoon softball game.

When I was in early grade school, an older neighbor girl whispered to me, "You have four children in the family and that means your parents fucked four times." I was quite unfamiliar with slang words; even though I didn't know what it meant, it didn't sound like a very nice thing for *my* parents to have done. I went into the house; my mother took one look at me and asked what was the matter. I said, "What does fuck mean?" My memory from this point is not very clear, but when she recovered from the shock, she tried her best to explain it. The final message I received was not to ask questions about sex. (Authors' files)

Chapter Eight: Communication in Sexual Behavior

Within the context of our culture, it is very "natural"—or at least common—to feel shy or embarrassed when talking about sexuality with friends and lovers. This awkwardness is not entirely unavoidable, though, and people certainly find ways of learning to live with the vocabulary. For example, the context and tone in which sex terms are used may create totally different meanings and reactions, as this woman's comment shows:

I have very different feelings about words depending on how they are used. My lover saying "I love your sweet cunt" is very different from hearing "You stupid cunt." (Authors' files)

Also, some people give their own or their partners' genitals nicknames, such as Fuzzylove, Slurpy, Artesia, Pokey, Peter, or Moby, as an attempt to avoid negative associations with much of the existing terminology.

In the absence of a better language model, each of us may benefit from seeking a vocabulary that is comfortable to use in our intimate relationships. A helpful first step in talking about sex might be to try to determine what words are mutually agreeable. The following anecdote suggests one way of doing this:

Whenever I am with a new person, and our relationship has progressed to the point of having sex, I suggest we play a little game where we try to come up with as many different words as we can to name a specific sexual activity or body part. As we play the game, I ask her which words she likes best, often expressing some of my own preferences. Sometimes I discover words I hadn't even heard before. It is a good way to get relaxed and begin talking about sex. Also, it helps in future discussions because we both have a sense of what words to use. (Authors' file)

In a later portion of this book (Chapter 17) we will explore some of the benefits and joys associated with talking to our lovers while we touch their bodies. We shall see that this is a wonderful time to expand intimacy while learning about each other's needs and preferences. It is a particularly good way to discover what words are mutually acceptable.

Beyond the handicaps imposed by socialization and language limitations, difficulties in sexual communication for some people may also be rooted in fears of too much self-exposure. Any sexual communication involves a certain amount of risk: people place themselves in a position vulnerable to judgment, criticism, and even rejection. The willingness to take risks may be related to the amount of trust that exists within a relationship. In some couples, this mutual trust is lacking, and the potential risks of openly expressing sexual needs are too great to overcome. Other relationships have a high degree of reciprocal caring and trust. Here, the first hesitant steps into sexual dialogue may be considerably easier.

We have outlined some reasons why many people find it difficult to engage in meaningful and effective sexual communication. Despite the difficulties, communication is an important part of sexual sharing, just as it is in other aspects of a relationship. The potential rewards are enhanced sexual experiences and enriched relationships.

TALKING: GETTING STARTED

Many people find it difficult to begin communicating about sex. There are many different ways of breaking the ice, and we will explore a few of them here. These suggestions may be useful, not just at the beginning of a relationship, but throughout its course.

Talking about Talking

When people feel uneasy about a topic, often the best place to start is by talking about talking. Discussing why it is hard to talk about sex can provide a good beginning. Each partner has individual reasons, and understanding those reasons can help set a relationship on a solid foundation. Perhaps you can share experiences about earlier efforts to discuss sex with parents, teachers, doctors, friends, or lovers. It may be helpful to move gradually into the arena of sex talk by directing your initial discussions

A couple's sexual communication is often facilitated by reading
and discussing material that deals with sex.

to nonthreatening, less personal topics (such as new birth-control methods, pornography laws, and so forth). Later, as your mutual degree of comfort with discussing
sexual matters increases, you may be able to talk about more personal feelings and
concerns.

Reading and Discussing

Since many people find that it is easier to read than talk about sex, articles and books
dealing with the subject may provide the stimulus for personal conversations. Partners
may read the material separately, then discuss it together; or a couple can jointly read
and discuss the content and their individual reactions to it. Often, it is easier to make
the transition from a book or article to personal feelings than it is to begin by talking
about highly personal concerns.

The Media As a Stimulant

Another potentially helpful activity is to read a sexy novel together or see an erotic
film. Needless to say, this strategy will not be appropriate for every couple. Some
individuals may be aroused by this activity, while others may find it to be boring,
embarrassing, offensive, or threatening. It may still be a worthwhile experience,

however, in that a couple can later share their feelings about what they saw or read. It may be easy, for instance, to discuss overall reactions to a movie or book (bored? disgusted? excited? aroused?). There may also have been a particular scene that either aroused or offended one person or the other. Comparing reactions can be a helpful way of finding out about a partner's feelings about sexual matters. Also, books and movies may provide ideas for exploring new behaviors. Sometimes an activity is portrayed that one or both partners would like to try.

Sharing Sexual Histories

Another way to start talking is to share sexual histories. There may be many questions that you would feel comfortable discussing with your partner. For instance: how was sex education handled in your home? How did your parents relate to each other—were you aware of any sexuality in their relationship? When did you first learn about sex, and what were your reactions? How did you feel about "making out" for the first time? Many other items could be added to this brief list, depending on the particular feelings or needs of each individual.

LISTENING AND FEEDBACK

Communication, sexual or otherwise, is most successful when it is two-sided, involving both an active listener and an effective communicator. In this section we will focus on the listening side of this process.

From the perspective of the listener, there are a number of strategies that may facilitate communication. Have you ever wondered what special attributes are possessed by those people who seem to draw others to them like metal to a magnet? With some thought you will probably conclude that, among other things, these individuals are often very good listeners. What are the special skills they possess that make us feel they really care about what we have to say? Next time you are with them, observe closely. Make a study of their listening habits. Perhaps your list of good listening traits will include several of the following.

Be an Active Listener

Some people are passive listeners. They may stare blankly into space as their companion talks, perhaps grunting an "uh-huh" now and then. Such responses may make us think that the person is indifferent, even when such is not the case, and we may soon grow tired of trying to share important thoughts with someone who does not seem to be receptive:

When I talk to my husband about anything really important, he just stares at me with a blank expression. It is like I am talking to a piece of stone. I think he hears the message, at least sometimes, but he rarely shows any response. Sometimes I feel like shaking him and screaming "Are you still alive!" Needless to say, I don't try communicating with him very much anymore. (Authors' files)

Chapter Eight: Communication in Sexual Behavior

Being an active listener means really listening to what your partner is saying. You may communicate this by changing facial expressions, nodding your head, asking questions ("Could you give me an example?"), and making brief comments ("I see your point"). Sometimes it may be helpful to reciprocate in the conversation. For example, as your partner relates a feeling or incident, you may be reminded of something in your own life that you would like to share. Making these associations and candidly expressing them to your companion can encourage her or him to continue voicing important concerns.

Maintain Eye Contact

Maintaining eye contact is one of the most vital aspects of good verbal communication. When someone maintains eye contact when we are sharing with them, the message is clear. He or she cares about what we have to say. How different we may feel when the listener gazes around the room, looks out the window, or glances at his or her watch.

> My boyfriend averts his eyes everytime I try to discuss something important about our relationship. I know he cares about me, or at least I think he does. But it sure is disconcerting when he won't look me in the eyes. I know that he is intellectually invested in our relationship but emotionally it seems like he leaves me when his eyes start to wander. (Authors' files)

Our eyes are wondrously expressive of feelings. When we fail to maintain eye contact we deny our partner a valuable source of information about how we are perceiving his or her message.

Provide Feedback

The purpose of communication is to provide a message that has some impact on the listener. However, a message's intent may not always be the same as its impact, for communications are sometimes misunderstood. This is particularly true with a topic like sex, where language is often roundabout or awkward. Therefore, giving your partner some *feedback* or reaction to her or his message can be very helpful. In addition to clarifying how you have perceived your partner's comments, feedback shows unmistakably that you are actively listening.

We may also benefit by asking our partners to provide some response to a message we think is important. A comment like "What are your thoughts about what I have just said?" may encourage feedback that can help you determine the impact of your message on your partner.

Support Your Partner's Communication Efforts

Many of us may feel quite vulnerable when communicating important messages to our partners. Being supported in our efforts can help to alleviate our concerns and encourage us to continue to build communication skills for a viable relationship.

After struggling to voice an important concern, how good it can feel to have a partner say "I really appreciate your sharing your thoughts with me" or "Thanks for caring enough to tell me what was on your mind." Such supportive comments can help to foster mutual empathy while, at the same time, ensuring that our partner will continue to candidly communicate his or her thoughts and feelings.

Express "Unconditional Positive Regard"

The concept of "unconditional positive regard" is borrowed from the immensely popular *Client-Centered Therapy* authored by Carl Rogers (1951). In personal relationships it means conveying to our partners the sense that we will continue to value and care for them regardless of what they do or say. Such unconditional positive regard may encourage a person to talk about even the most embarrassing or potentially painful concerns. The following anecdote reveals one person's response to such a valued attribute:

I know that my wife's love for me is unfaltering and that no matter what I say or reveal, she will continue to care for me. In an earlier marriage, I could never express any serious concerns without my wife getting defensive or just plain mean. As a consequence, I just quit talking about things that really mattered. What a relief it is to be with someone with whom I can express what is on my mind without worrying about the consequences. (Authors' files)

Use Paraphrasing

One way to increase the probability that you and your partner will listen more effectively to each other is to use a technique called *paraphrasing*. This involves a listener summarizing, in his or her own words, the speaker's message. The following dialogue illustrates this technique.

BOB: Mary, I think I would enjoy our relationship more if you were more gentle. Do you understand what I mean?

MARY: I understand. You think I'm an aggressive person.

BOB: That's not quite what I mean. I mean that when you touch me when we make love, I would like you to use a lighter, softer caress.

MARY: Now I think I understand. I always thought you liked me to use firm pressure when I touched you. But now I see that light caressing is what you prefer.

BOB: That is what I meant. Thanks for understanding.

If the paraphrase is not satisfactory, the speaker may choose to express the message in different words. Then the listener can try to paraphrase again. Several attempts may be necessary to clear away discrepancies between the communicator's intent and the listener's interpretation. As time goes by, a couple will typically find that the need to use this approach diminishes as listening skills improve.

DISCOVERING YOUR PARTNER'S NEEDS

Discovering what is pleasurable to a sexual partner is an important part of sexual sharing. Many couples want to know each other's preferences but are uncertain how to find out. In this section we will look at some effective ways of learning about our partner's wants and needs.

Asking Questions

One of the best ways to discover your partner's needs is simply to ask. However, there are several ways of asking: some can be helpful, while others may be ineffective or even counterproductive. We will review a few of the most common ways of asking questions and the effect each is likely to have.

Yes or No Questions   Imagine being asked one or more of the following questions in the context of a sexual interlude with your partner:

1. Was it good for you?
2. Do you like oral sex?
3. Was I gentle enough?
4. Did you come?
5. Do you like it when I stimulate you this way?
6. Do you like being on the bottom?
7. Is it OK if we don't make love tonight?
8. Am I a good lover?

At first glance, these questions may seem reasonably worded. However, they all share one characteristic that may reduce their effectiveness: they are *yes or no questions*. Each asks for a one-word answer, even though people's thoughts and feelings are rarely so simple.

For example, consider Question 2: "Do you like oral sex?" Either answer— "Yes, I do," or "No, I do not"—gives the couple little opportunity to discuss the issue. Certainly, the potential for discussion exists. Nevertheless, in a world where sexual communication is often difficult under the best of circumstances, the asker may get no more than the specific information requested. In some situations, of course, a brief yes or no is all that is necessary. But the person responding may have mixed feelings about oral sex (for example), and the phrasing of the question leads to over-simplification. Open-ended questions or questions that allow statement of a preference can make it easier for the answerer to give accurate replies.

Open-Ended Questions   Some people find that asking *open-ended questions* is a particularly helpful way to discover their companions' desires. This approach places virtually no restrictions on the possible answers that might be given. In a sense, it is like responding to a general essay question on an exam. ("What are some of the important aspects of human sexuality that you have learned thus far this term?") Some examples of open-ended questions are listed on the next page.

1. What things give you the most pleasure when we make love?
2. What aspects of our sexual sharing would you most like to have changed?
3. What parts of your body are most sensitive?
4. What kinds of variations in intercourse positions do you find pleasurable?
5. What is the easiest or most enjoyable way for you to reach orgasm?
6. What are your feelings about oral sex?

A primary advantage of open-ended questions is that they allow your partner freedom to share any feelings or information she or he thinks is relevant. With no limitations or restrictions attached, you may discover much more about your companion.

Open-ended questions can also be valuable in encouraging feedback when you are telling your partner something important. Basically, the technique involves asking for the listener's thoughts along the way, rather than waiting for a response after you have completed a lengthy monologue. Questions like "What do you think about . . . ," "How do you feel about . . . ," or "I sense that you have some feelings about what I am saying" can provide opportunities for expressing important thoughts.

One possible drawback of the open-ended approach is that your partner may not know where to begin when asked such general questions. Consider being asked something like "What aspects of our lovemaking do you like best?" Some people might welcome the unstructured nature of this question. However, others might find it difficult to respond to such a broad query, particularly if they are not accustomed to openly discussing sex. If this is the case, a more structured approach may have a better chance of encouraging talking. There are several ways of doing this; one is the use of either/or questions.

Either/Or Questions The following list gives some examples of *either/or questions:*

1. Would you like the light on when we make love, or shall we turn it off?
2. Am I being gentle enough or too gentle?
3. Is this the way you want to be touched, or should we experiment with a different kind of caress?
4. Would you like to try something different, or shall we stop and just hold each other?
5. Would you like to talk now, or would you prefer we wait for another time?

While either/or questions offer more structure than open-ended questions, they do encourage more participation than simple yes or no queries. People often appreciate the opportunity to consider a few alternatives. The either/or question also shows the questioner's concern about a partner's pleasure. Finally, this kind of question provides the opportunity to discover a little information at a time when a more open-ended question might be overwhelming. However, either/or questions can still be somewhat restrictive. There is always the possibility that individuals will not like either of the choices offered. In this case, the answerer may state another alternative that is preferable.

Besides asking questions, there are other ways of discovering the sexual needs of a partner. We will discuss three communication techniques here: self-disclosure, comparing notes, and giving permission.

Self-Disclosure

Often, direct questions put people on the spot. Whether you have been asked "Do you enjoy oral sex?" or "How do you feel about oral sex?" it may be quite difficult to respond candidly simply because you cannot gauge your companion's feelings on the subject. If the topic has strong emotional overtones, it may be very difficult to reply—no matter how thoughtfully the question has been phrased. It is the content, not the communication technique, that causes the problem.

With potentially loaded topics, a way to broach the subject may be to start with a self-disclosure:

For the longest time, I was reluctant to bring up the topic of oral sex with my lover. We did about everything else, but this was one area we avoided both in action and conversation. I personally was both excited and repelled by the prospect of this kind of sex. I didn't have the slightest idea what she felt about it. I was afraid to bring it up for fear she would think I was some kind of pervert. Eventually, I could no longer tolerate not knowing her feelings about what might be incredibly erotic. I brought it up by first talking about my mixed emotions, like feeling that maybe it wasn't natural but at the same time really wanting to try it out. As it turned out she had been having similar feelings but was afraid to bring them up because of how I might react. Afterwards, we laughed about how we had both been afraid to break the ice. Once we could talk freely about our feelings, it was easy to add this form of stimulation to our sex life. (Authors' files)

Personal disclosures require some give-and-take. It is much easier to share feelings about strongly emotional topics when a partner is willing to make similar disclosures. Admittedly, such an approach may have risks, and occasionally one can feel vulnerable sharing personal thoughts and feelings. Nevertheless, the increased possibility for open, honest dialogue may be worth any discomfort a person may feel about making the first disclosure.

A form of self-disclosure that some people find exciting and informative involves telling their partner about personal fantasies, as revealed in the following anecdote:

I had this sexual fantasy that kept going through my mind. I would imagine coming home after a long, hard day of classes and being met by my partner, who would proceed to take me into the bedroom and remove all my clothes. He would then pick me up and carry me into the bathroom where a tub full of hot water and bubbles awaited. The fantasy would end with us making passionate love in the bathtub with bubbles popping off around us. Finally, I shared my fantasy with him. Guess what happened when I came home after the next long day? It was even better than I had imagined! (Authors' files)

Understandably, many people might be concerned about the potentially adverse effects of such highly personal communication. Certain precautions may help to reduce the possibility of an unpleasant outcome.

Sharing is usually most successful when it is mutual rather than unilateral. If your partner is unwilling to engage in such talk, at least for the present, it would be wise to respect this wish. Sometimes starting out with very mild fantasies can help to desensitize fears and embarrassment and allow you to gauge the impact of such sharing on your partner and yourself. If you sense that your companion is feeling uncomfortable, it may be best not to press. It is probably advisable to avoid altogether any fantasies that you anticipate will be shocking to your companion. Fantasies that involve other lovers may be particularly threatening.

Comparing Notes

Many couples, while planning an evening out, consider it natural to discuss each other's preferences: "Do you like the symphony, theater, movies?" "How close do you like to sit?" "Do you prefer steak or seafood?" Afterwards, they may candidly discuss the evening's events: "The orchestra was great." "I think the balcony seats would be better next time." "Boy, I wouldn't order the scampi again."

Admittedly, it may be a big step from this to discussing sexual preferences and making these same kinds of evaluations about the sexual areas of a relationship. Nevertheless, people do engage in this type of sexual dialogue. Some people feel comfortable discussing sexual preferences with a new lover before progressing to lovemaking. They may talk about what areas of their bodies are most responsive, how they like to be touched, what intercourse positions are particularly desirable, the easiest or most satisfying way to reach orgasm, time and location preferences, special turn-ons and turn-offs, and a variety of other likes and dislikes.

The appeal of this open, frank approach is that it allows a couple to focus on particularly pleasurable activities rather than discovering them by slow trial-and-error efforts. However, some people may feel that preparatory dialogues are far too clinical, perhaps even robbing the sexual experience of the excitement of experimentation and mutual discovery. Furthermore, what some people find to be desirable may vary so much with different partners that they may find it difficult to assess specific preferences in advance.

Couples may also find it helpful to share feelings after a sexual encounter. They may offer reactions about what was good and what could be better. They may use this time to reinforce the things they found particularly satisfying in their partner's lovemaking ("I loved the way you touched me with your hands"). A mutual feedback session can be extremely informative; it can also contribute to a deeper intimacy between two people.

Giving Permission

Discovering your partner's needs can be made immeasurably easier by the practice we call *giving permission*. Basically, it means providing verbal encouragement and reassurance. One partner tells the other that it is OK to talk about certain specific feelings or needs—in fact, that he or she wants very much to know how the other feels about the subject:

HE: I'm not sure how you like me to touch you when we make love.

SHE: Any way you want to is good.

HE: Well, it would be good to know what you like best, and you can help me by saying what feels good while I touch you.

Many of us have had experiences where we have felt rebuffed in our efforts to communicate our needs to others. It is no wonder people often remain silent even when they want to share personal feelings. Giving and receiving permission to express needs freely can contribute to the exchange of valuable information.

LEARNING TO MAKE REQUESTS

People are not mind readers. Nevertheless, many lovers seem to assume that their partners know (perhaps by intuition?) just what they need. People who approach sex with this attitude are not taking full responsibility for their own sexual pleasure. If sexual encounters are not satisfactory, it may be convenient to blame the other— "You don't care about my needs"—when in all probability it was one's own reluctance to express those needs that lay at the root of the problem. Expecting another person to somehow know what we want without having been informed places a heavy burden on a partner. The alternative is to speak up and say what you want. While many people think they "shouldn't have to ask," in fact, asking can be an affirmative, responsible action that is helpful to the partner and at the same time leads to an important interaction.

Taking Responsibility for Our Own Pleasure

When two people are really in harmony with each other, you don't have to talk about your sexual wants. Each will sense and respond to the other's desires. Talking just tends to spoil these special magical moments. (Authors' files)

What this person speaks of seems to exist more in the fantasyland of idealized sex than in the real world. As we noted earlier, most people are not mind readers, and intuition leaves much to be desired as a substitute for genuine communication. In fact, a person who expects another to know his or her needs by intuition is placing an unfair burden upon the other. The message seems to be that "It's not my function to let you know my needs but rather it's your role to know what they are"; and, by inference, "If my needs are not fulfilled it is your fault and not mine." Needless to say, this is a potentially destructive approach to sexual sharing that may lead to casting blame, misunderstandings, and unsatisfactory sex.

In a similar vein, some individuals may take too much responsibility for their partner's sexual pleasure. This behavior pattern may also be counterproductive. In

effect, the person says, "It is my job to sexually satisfy you. I will make all the decisions and assume responsibility for your pleasure." Even in the best of circumstances, this can be a heavy burden. A person so intent on figuring out and fulfilling the needs of a partner may find that his or her own needs are largely overlooked. Furthermore, such a take-charge attitude encourages passivity and undermines a partner's resolve to assume responsibility for her or his own satisfaction.

In summary, the best way for us to get our needs met is to speak up with our requests. Two individuals willing to communicate their desires and take responsibility for their own pleasure create an excellent framework for effective, fulfilling sexual sharing.

Of course, even with the strongest resolve, many of us may still find it difficult to ask our partner for a particular kind of stimulation during sexual sharing. There may be several reasons for this reluctance, not the least of which is the fear that our partner may be offended or threatened by our boldness. This is shown in the following account:

I know what I need in a sexual relationship, but how do I get this message across to my partner? I'm afraid if I were to come right out and state my requests he would feel inadequate—like why didn't he think of it without me needing to tell him? But the truth of the matter is he usually doesn't come up with it on his own. So what do I do?—keep my mouth shut and hope he will eventually figure it out or do I state specifically what I would like with the possibility of turning him off by being too demanding? At this point in my life I generally opt for the former. Obviously, it is easier and less risky to say nothing. But I'm not sure I can go on much longer with my needs not being met. (Authors' files)

In thinking about this account, one fact stands out. If this woman had been encouraged by her partner to share her sexual needs, much of her frustration might have been alleviated. However, the reality is that often we are not provided with a clear mandate to reveal our special needs. Do we then remain silent, or should we trust our lover to be accepting of our self-revelations? One woman states her experience with assuming responsibility for her own pleasure:

For much of my life sex has been a hit-or-miss proposition with the miss part predominating. Only recently have I discovered how to change this pattern. I know what I need sexually to be satisfied. I am very good at giving myself pleasure. Finally, it occurred to me how futile it was to hope that my partners would somehow automatically possess this knowledge that took me years to discover for myself. I decided that the better I could express myself about my sexual needs, the greater the likelihood they would be fulfilled. Assuming this responsibility for my own pleasure was a big step that I took with a great deal of hesitancy and anxiety. But I have been pleasantly surprised by most of my subsequent lovers' reactions. They are usually quite relieved to have the guesswork taken out of our sexual experiences. One man praised me for my openness and confided that my willingness to tell him what I wanted relieved him of one of his greatest concerns, namely not knowing what his partner desired from him during sex. (Authors' files)

Taking control of our own sexual lives and freely expressing our needs to partners can be a liberating experience, infinitely preferable to blind trust in their ability to sense these needs without clear, verbal direction.

Deciding to assume responsibility for one's own satisfaction is an important step. Just as important are the methods a person selects for expressing his or her needs. The way a request is made has a decided effect on the reaction it draws. Some suggestions are listed in the next two sections.

Making Requests Specific

The more specific a request, the more likely it is to be understood and heeded. This is a fact frequently noted by social psychologists and communication specialists. Nevertheless, many of us neglect to apply this sound principle to our sexual sharing. Lovers often ask for changes in the sexual aspects of their relationships in the vaguest of language. It can be quite uncomfortable, even anxiety provoking, to be on the receiving end of an ill-defined request. Just what do we do in response? Probably very little, if anything.

The key to preventing unnecessary stress for both partners lies in delivering requests in as clear and concise a manner as possible. Thus, an alternative to the vague request "I'd like you to try touching me differently" might be something like "I would like you to touch me gently around my clitoris but not directly on it." Other examples of specific requests include:

1. I would like you to spend more time touching and caressing me all over before we have intercourse.
2. I would like to be on top this time. It's real good for me and I love being able to watch you respond.
3. I like having my frenum stimulated during oral sex. If you would run your tongue back and forth over it I'll tell you if I want it harder or softer.
4. I would like you to continue with your kisses and caresses after penetration because it makes intercourse so much better for me.
5. I would really like you to stroke my penis with your hand.

Using "I" Language

Many counselors encourage their clients to use "I" language when stating their needs to others. This forthright approach will more often bring the desired response than will a more general statement. For example, saying "I would like to be on top" is considerably more likely to produce that result than a less direct statement such as "What would you think about changing positions?"

Many people find it difficult to ask for what they want in such clear, unequivocal language. Saying "I want . . . " may seem to some to be selfish. However, there is a difference between being self-centered and recognizing that "I am as important as others in my life and my needs are worthy of being met." Individuals who experience gratification of their own needs are often able to give much of themselves to others. Conversely, the philosophy of "never put myself first" may ultimately produce so much frustration and resentment that a person may be left with few positive feelings to share.

Expressing requests directly may not always be effective. Some people may want to make all the decisions during sex, and they may not take kindly to requests from their partners during lovemaking. To them, a partner's assertiveness may be offensive. You may want to determine if this is your companion's attitude before an encounter, thereby avoiding an awkward situation later on. One way to do this is to ask the open-ended question "How do you feel about asking for things during lovemaking?" Or, you may choose to wait and find out during sex play. At any rate, if a person appears closed to this approach, you may wish to reevaluate your strategy. Perhaps making your needs known at some time other than during sexual interaction may give your partner a more relaxed opportunity to consider your desires.

DELIVERING CRITICISM

Contrary to the popular romantic image, no two people can fill all of each other's needs all of the time. It seems inevitable that sometimes in an intimate relationship people will need to register some complaints and request changes. This is not an easy process for caring individuals whose involvement is characterized by mutual empathy. When the criticism pertains to the emotionally intense area of sexual sharing, it may be doubly difficult. Consequently, partners will want to think carefully about appropriate strategies and potential obstacles to accomplishing this delicate task. Perhaps the best place for one to begin, before verbalizing a complaint to his or her partner, is to first examine the motivations underlying the need to criticize.

Be Aware of Your Motivation

The way criticism is offered may depend largely on the motive of the critic. Consider the following two anecdotes:

My husband is a lousy lover. He doesn't know the first thing about how to turn me on and when I tell him I don't get any pleasure out of our sex life, he just clams up. I don't know what's the matter with him but it sure burns me up. (Authors' files)

A couple of years ago I found out that my wife was involved in an affair with a man she works with. She claimed he was kind and gentle and that she couldn't help being attracted to him. Faced with my ultimatum she changed jobs and stopped seeing him (I think). Since that time our sex life has been a real bust. She seems to lack enthusiasm and we engage in sex much less frequently. Sometimes I think her having sex with the other guy has ruined our sex life. Maybe she thinks he was better than me. When I confront her with my dissatisfaction with her lack of enthusiasm she gets upset and we usually end up having a fight. (Authors' files)

It seems clear that these individuals' motivations for delivering criticism are not based on a caring desire to make their respective relationships better. In the first example the aim of the woman appears to be to hurt or humiliate her husband. The man in the second anecdote seems to be motivated by a desire for revenge. If the aim is to hurt, humiliate, blame, ridicule, or get even, it is likely that criticizing a partner will prove to be far more destructive than constructive.

In this book we are concerned with constructive criticism that is prompted by a genuine desire for necessary change. It is not always easy to criticize effectively while maintaining an emphasis on sharing and building a sense of togetherness in a relationship. There are, however, certain strategies that can help you to maintain empathy in a confrontational situation. One important consideration is picking the right time and place.

Choose the Right Time and Place

Whenever my lover brings up something that is bothering her about our sex life, it inevitably is just after we have made love. Here I am, relaxed, holding her in my arms, thinking good thoughts, and she destroys the mood with some criticism. It's not that I don't want her to express her concerns. But her timing is terrible. The last thing I want to hear after lovemaking is that it could have been better. (Authors' files)

Choosing the right time and place for expressing sexual concerns can facilitate communication.

This man's dismay is obvious. His partner's decision to voice her concerns during the afterglow of lovemaking, while understandable, worked against her purpose. He may have felt vulnerable and he clearly resented having his good mood broken by the prospect of potentially difficult conversation. Of course, other couples may find this to be a time when they are exceedingly close to each other and thus a good atmosphere in which to air concerns.

Many people, like the woman in the previous example, never choose the best time to confront their lover. Rather, the time chooses them. They jump right in when the problem is uppermost in their minds. There are some benefits to dealing with an issue immediately. However, such people may also be feeling disappointed, resentful, or angry, and these negative emotions, when running full tide, may get in the way of constructive interaction. Avoid registering complaints when anger is at its peak. Even with the best intentions of making your criticism constructive, anger has a way of disrupting a search for solutions. Sometimes it may be necessary to express anger, and we will consider this process at the end of this section.

In most cases it is unwise to tackle a problem when either you or your partner has limited time or is tired, stressed, preoccupied, or under the influence of drugs or

242

alcohol. Rather, try to select an interval when you have plenty of time and are both relaxed and feeling close to each other.

A pragmatic approach to the problem of timing is to simply ask your lover. "I really value our sexual sharing, but there are some concerns I would like to talk over with you. Is this a good time or would you rather we talk later?" Be prepared for some anxiety induced stalling. If your partner is hesitant to talk now, support her or his right to pick another time or place. However, it is important to agree on a time, particularly if you sense your partner might prefer to let the matter go.

Choosing the right place for expressing sexual concerns can be as important as timing. Some people may find that sitting around the kitchen table, sharing a pot of coffee, is a more comfortable setting than the place where they make love, while others might prefer the familiarity of their bed. A walk through a park or a quiet drive in the country, far removed from the potential interferences of a busy life style, may prove best for you. Try to sense your partner's needs. At what time and where is she or he most likely to be receptive to your requests for change?

Picking the right time and place to deliver criticism does not ensure a harmonious outcome, but it certainly improves the prospects of your partner responding favorably to your message. Using some other constructive strategies can also increase the likelihood of beneficial interaction. One of these is to combine criticism with praise.

Temper Criticism with Praise

This strategy is based largely on common sense. All of us tend to respond well to compliments, while harsh criticism, untempered by praise, is difficult to accept. The gentler approach of combining criticism with praise is a good way to reduce the negative impact of a complaint. It also gives the person who has been criticized a broader perspective from which to evaluate the criticism and reduces the likelihood that he or she will respond in a defensive or angry manner. Consider how you might react differently to the following criticisms based on whether or not they are accompanied by praise:

Criticism Alone	Criticism + Praise
1. When we make love you seem so inhibited.	I appreciate the way you respond to me when we make love and I think it could be even better if you would take the initiative sometimes. Does this seem like a reasonable request?
2. I really am getting tired of your turning off the lights every time we make love.	I enjoy hearing and feeling you react when we make love. I would also like to see you respond and this is not possible when you turn off the lights. How would you feel about leaving them on sometimes?

3. I think our lovemaking is much too infrequent. It almost seems like sex is not as important to you as it is to me.

Having sex gives me a great deal of pleasure and I value sharing it with you. My concern is that it doesn't happen as frequently as I would like. What are your thoughts about this?

Sadly, just about all of us have been on the receiving end of criticisms like those in the left column. Common reactions are anger, feeling humiliated, anxiety about our competency as lovers, and resentment. While some people may respond to such harsh complaints with a resolve to make things better, it is more likely that the opposite will occur. On the other hand, affirmative criticism, like the examples in the right column, is more likely to encourage efforts to change.

There is a good deal of wisdom in the adage "People are usually more motivated to make a good thing better than to make a bad thing good." The point of this saying applies as much to sexual sharing as to any other area of human interaction. Recently one of us was approached by a woman complaining that her husband was often too rough with her during love play. She was reluctant to discuss her concern with her husband for fear that he would feel put down or angered. She also had mixed feelings about her husband's roughness—it was part of the unbridled enthusiasm with which he related to her sexually, a zestiness she very much enjoyed. On those rare occasions when he did take the time to be gentle with her, she was very pleased. Now, the problem: how could she tell him she didn't like his roughness while at the same time assuring that he would maintain his enthusiasm and not feel angry or inept?

What she finally told him was essentially what she had expressed in seeking advice. Sometimes it was terrific when he was gentle. She loved being pursued with enthusiasm and vigor. It could be even better if he would include more gentleness in their lovemaking. Although he was somewhat surprised and dismayed over his inability to detect her needs, her husband's response was quite positive. What do you suppose his reaction might have been had she coldly complained, "Do you have to be so rough when we make love?"

It is also a good idea to ask for feedback when delivering criticisms. Regardless of how much warmth and humanity we put into this difficult process, there is always the possibility that our partners may become silent or change the subject. Asking them to talk about their reaction to our request for change helps to reduce these prospects. (Note that in the previous list, all "Criticism + Praise" examples ended with requests for feedback.)

Nurture Small Steps Toward Change

Complete behavioral changes rarely occur immediately following criticism—no matter how positively stated. Rather, they must be patiently nurtured, with each small step along the way properly acknowledged with words of appreciation. In the example of the woman wanting more gentleness from her husband, it would have been unreasonable for her to assume that once she expressed her criticism, her partner would completely change his ways. In fact, what occurred was a noticeable but minimal effort to be less vigorous in the next sexual encounter. Soon the old patterns ingrained over many years took over again.

Backsliding is natural and predictable and, like other unwanted behaviors, it requires tact. Have you ever heard the words "I see you didn't pay a bit of attention to what I said"? Such a negative reaction could easily cool your desire to follow through with change. It is far more encouraging and reassuring to be on the receiving end of a message like the one delivered by the wife to her "trying to be more gentle" husband: "I really appreciate the time you took to be gentle when we made love. It means a great deal that you care about my needs." With such a caring and supportive reaction, few people are likely to stick to the same old behavior.

Avoid "Why" Questions

People frequently use "why" questions as thinly veiled efforts to criticize or attack their partners while avoiding full responsibility for what is said. Have you ever been asked any of the following?

1. Why don't you make love to me more frequently?
2. Why don't you show more interest in me?
3. Why don't you get turned on by me anymore?
4. Why can't you be more loving toward me?
5. Why are you so lazy?

Such queries have no place in a loving relationship. They are hurtful and destructive. Rather than representing simple requests for information, they are typically used to convey hidden messages of anger that people are unwilling to own honestly. These are hit-and-run tactics that give pain and seldom induce positive changes. Get rid of them. They cannot help us register constructive criticism.

Express Anger Appropriately

Earlier in this chapter we noted that it is wise to avoid confronting our partners when anger is riding high. However, there will probably be times when each of us feels compelled to express these feelings. If so, certain guiding principles may help defuse a potentially explosive situation.

Avoid focusing your anger on the character of your partner ("You are an insensitive person"). Instead, try directing your anger toward his or her behaviors ("Sometimes when you don't listen to my concerns I feel like they are unimportant to you and I feel angry"). At the same time, express appreciation for your partner as a person ("You are very important to me and I don't like feeling this way"). This acknowledges that we can be both angered by our partners' behaviors and feel loving toward them as people at the same time—an often overlooked but important truth.

Anger is probably best expressed with clear, honest "I statements" rather than with accusatory and potentially inflammatory "you statements." Consider the following:

"I Statements"	"You Statements"
1. I feel ignored.	You don't give a damn about me.
2. I don't like being blamed.	You always blame me for our problems.
3. I am upset.	You make me upset.
4. I am angry.	You make me angry.
5. I feel unloved.	You don't love me.
6. I don't feel important to you.	You treat me like I am unimportant to you.

"I statements" are self-revelations that express how we feel without placing blame or attacking our partner's character. In contrast, "you statements" frequently are interpreted as attacks on the character of the other person and attempts to fix blame.

Finally, if we become angry with our partner it is because we choose to respond with anger. Another cannot make us angry, although it certainly may seem that way at times. We have control over our own responses. Instead of getting angry, we might choose from a variety of responses including humor, silence, submission, withdrawal, or caring confrontation. The last possibility is clearly the best bet for positive change. All too often we allow ourselves to be victimized by our emotions rather than taking control of how we respond. As long as we continue to control the sentences running through our minds, we have the opportunity to harness anger and engage in constructive, caring confrontation.

NONVERBAL SEXUAL COMMUNICATION

Sexual communication is not confined exclusively to words. Sometimes a touch or smile may convey a great deal of information. Tone of voice, gestures, facial expression, and changes in breathing may also be important elements of the communication process:

I can usually tell when my sweetheart is in the mood for some loving. There is a certain softness about her face and a huskiness which comes into her voice. She touches me more with her hands and it almost seems like she presents her body as more open and vulnerable. Believe me, there is some truth to all this stuff about body language. She rarely needs to verbalize her desire for sex because I usually get the message. (Authors' files)

Sometimes when I want my lover to touch me in a certain place, I move that portion of my body closer to his hands or just shift my position to make the area more accessible. Occasionally, I will guide his hand with mine to show him just what kind of stimulation I want. (Authors' files)

These examples reveal some of the varieties of nonverbal communication that may have particular significance for our sexuality. In this section we will direct our attention to four important components of nonverbal sexual communication: facial expression, interpersonal distance, touching, and sounds.

Facial Expression

Facial expressions often communicate the type of feelings a person is experiencing. While there is certainly variation in people's expressions, most of us have learned to identify particular emotions from facial expression with a high degree of accuracy. The rapport and intimacy between lovers may further increase the accuracy of this yardstick.

A look into the face of our lover during sexual sharing will often give us a quick reading of his or her pleasure quotient. If we see a look of complete rapture, we will likely continue providing the same type of stimulation. However, if the look conveys something less than ecstasy, we may decide to try something different or perhaps encourage our partner to provide some verbal direction.

Facial expressions can also provide helpful cues when talking over sexual concerns with a partner. If his or her face reflects anger, anxiety, or some other disruptive emotion, it might be wise to deal with this emotion immediately ("I sense that you are angry with me. Would you like to talk about your feelings?"). Conversely, a face that mirrors interest, enthusiasm, or appreciation can encourage us to continue expressing a particular feeling or concern. It is also a good idea to be aware of the nonverbal messages you are giving your partner when she or he is sharing thoughts or feelings with you. Sometimes we may inadvertently shut down potentially helpful dialogue by setting our jaw or frowning at an inappropriate time.

Interpersonal Distance

Social psychologists and communication specialists have much to say about *personal space*. In essence, this idea suggests that each of us tends to maintain differing degrees of interpersonal distance between ourselves and the people we have contact with, depending on the nature of our relationship with them (actual or desired). It follows that the intimate space to which we admit close friends and lovers restricts contact much less than the distance we maintain between ourselves and the general public.

It is instructive to watch what takes place between people meeting each other at places like singles bars and parties. Consider the following:

When I meet someone I am attracted to I pay close attention to body language. If they seem uneasy or retreat when I move closer, it is a pretty good indication my interest is not reciprocated. (Authors' files)

When a person attempts to decrease interpersonal distance it is generally interpreted as a nonverbal sign that she or he is interested, attracted, or desirous of more intimate contact. A person's withdrawal from another's efforts to establish greater body closeness is usually interpreted as lack of interest or a gentle kind of rejection.

Lovers, whose interpersonal distance is generally at a minimum, may use these cues to signal desire for intimacy. When your lover moves in close, making his or her body available for your touches or caresses, the message of desired physical intimacy (not necessarily sex) is quite apparent. Similarly, when he or she curls up on the other side of the bed, it may be a way of saying "Please don't come too close tonight."

Touching

Touch is a powerful vehicle for nonverbal sexual communication between lovers. Hands can convey special messages. For example, increasing or decreasing the tempo with which a lover's back is kneaded may signal a desire for more or less intense reciprocated stimulation. Reaching out and pulling someone closer can indicate desire and readiness for more intimate contact.

Touch is a powerful vehicle for nonverbal sexual communication.

Touch can also defuse anger, heal rifts, and close the gap between temporarily alienated lovers. As one man states:

I have found that a gentle touch, lovingly administered to my partner, does wonders in bringing us back together after we have exchanged angry words. Touching her is my way of reestablishing connection. (Authors' files)

In the early stages of a developing relationship, touch can also be used to express a desire for more intimate involvement.

When I meet a man and find myself attracted to him, I use touch to convey my feelings. Touching him on the arm to emphasize a point or letting my fingers lightly graze across his hand on the table generally lets my feelings be known. (Authors' files)

We can be thankful for the delights that touch can bring us. Sounds can also be powerful vehicles for nonverbal sexual communication.

Sounds

Whether people make sounds during sexual sharing is highly variable. Many individuals find increased breathing, moans, groans, and orgasmic cries to be extremely arousing. Also, such sounds can be helpful indicators of how a partner is responding to lovemaking. Some people find the absence of sounds to be quite frustrating.

My man rarely makes any sounds when we make love. I find this to be very disturbing. In fact it is a real turn-off. Sometimes I can't even tell if he has come or not. If he wasn't moving I'd think I was making love to a corpse. (Authors' files)

Some people make a conscious effort to suppress spontaneous noises during sex play. In doing so they deprive themselves of a potentially powerful and enjoyable form of nonverbal sexual communication. Not uncommonly, their imposed silence also hinders their partner's sexual arousal as the foregoing example illustrates.

In this section we have acknowledged that not everything has to be spoken between lovers. However, facial expression, interpersonal distance, touching, and sounds cannot convey all of our complex needs and emotions in a close relationship: words are needed, too. One writer observes, "As a supplement to verbal communication, acts and gestures are fine. As a substitute, they don't quite make it" (Zilbergeld, 1978, p. 158).

IMPASSES

Candid communication between caring and supportive partners often leads to changes that are mutually gratifying. However, even an ample supply of openness, candor, support, and understanding cannot assure a meeting of the minds on all issues. Impasses may be reached. Your partner may simply not want to try a new coital position. Or, your suggestion to incorporate a vibrator into shared sex play may be just a bit too threatening. Perhaps the two of you cannot agree on the question of other relationships.

What does one do when communication results in a standoff? Continued discussion may be helpful. However, it is self-deceiving to assume that talk, even the most open and compassionate, will always lead to desired changes.

Sometimes it is useful to try to put yourself in your partner's shoes. Try to see things from the other person's perspective. If you have some difficulty with this, ask your companion for help ("I am having some trouble seeing this from your perspective—can you help me out?"). If you can understand his or her point, by all means say so. Indicating that you see how reasonable the other's viewpoint must seem is a process called *validating* (Gottman et al., 1976). Validating does not mean that you will give up your own position. You are not saying "I am wrong and you are right." Quite the contrary, you are simply admitting that another point of view may make sense, given some assumptions that you may not share with your partner. Sometimes, this process of trying to see the validity of another viewpoint may lead to new perspectives that can end the deadlock. However, if you continue to disagree after this effort, it may be easier to accept the idea that you can both be right.

At a time of impasse it may also be beneficial for a couple to take a break from each other for awhile. Sometimes forced continuation of a discussion, particularly when emotions are strong, is counterproductive. Scheduling another time to talk can be a good tactic. Perhaps in the future, after each has had the opportunity to privately consider the other's feelings, it may be possible to readdress the issue with more tangible results.

Sometimes people cannot or will not change, often for justifiable reasons. Certainly all of us covet the individual freedoms that allow us the right to refuse to do something we consider undesirable. Granting these same rights to those close to us is an important ingredient in a relationship characterized by mutual respect.

Failure to reach a solution to an impasse is not necessarily cause for despair. At least a problem has been brought out into the open and the couple has discussed a sensitive issue. Possibly they have also increased their understanding of each other and the level of intimacy between them. In the event that unresolved impasses threaten to erode a relationship, professional counseling may be desirable (see Chapter 17 for guidelines for counselor selection).

SUMMARY

THE IMPORTANCE OF COMMUNICATION

1. Sexual communication often contributes positively to the contentment and enjoyment of a sexual relationship; infrequent or ineffective sex talk is a common reason why many people feel dissatisfied with their sexual lives.

2. An excellent basis for effective sexual communication is mutual empathy—the underlying knowledge that each partner in a relationship cares for the other and knows that care is reciprocated.

WHY SEX TALK IS DIFFICULT

3. Childhood training, which often creates a sense of discomfort with sexual matters, may contribute to later difficulties in engaging in sex talk.

4. Our language is characterized by a conspicuous absence of an effective, comfortable sexual vocabulary.

5. Some people object to sex talk on the grounds that it disrupts spontaneity or that it may place one in a position of increased vulnerability to judgment, criticism, or rejection.

TALKING: GETTING STARTED

6. It is often difficult to start talking about sex. Some suggestions for doing this include talking about talking; reading about sex, then discussing the material; seeing movies or reading explicit novels; and sharing sexual histories.

LISTENING AND FEEDBACK

7. Communication is most successful with an active listener and an effective communicator.

8. The listener may facilitate communication by maintaining eye contact with the speaker, providing some feedback or reaction to the message, expressing appreciation for communication efforts, maintaining an attitude of unconditional positive regard, and by the effective use of paraphrasing.

DISCOVERING YOUR PARTNER'S NEEDS

9. Efforts to seek information from sexual partners are often hindered by the use of yes/no questions, which encourage limited replies. Effective alternatives may be open-ended queries or either/or questions.

10. Self-disclosure may make it easier for a partner to communicate his or her own needs. Sharing fantasies, beginning with mild fantasies, may be a particularly valuable kind of exchange.

11. Comparing notes about sexual needs, preferences, and reactions, either before or after a sexual encounter, may be beneficial.

12. Giving permission encourages partners to share feelings freely.

LEARNING TO MAKE REQUESTS

13. Making requests is facilitated by (a) making sure requests are specific and (b) using "I" language.

DELIVERING CRITICISM

14. It is important to carefully select the right time and place for expressing sexual concerns. Avoid registering complaints when anger is at its peak.

15. Criticism is generally most effective when tempered with praise. People are usually more motivated to make a good thing better than a bad thing good.

16. It is beneficial to reward each small step in the process of changing undesirable behavior.

17. "Why" questions have no place in the process of registering constructive criticisms.

18. It is wise to direct anger toward behavior rather than toward a person's character. Anger is probably best expressed with clear, honest "I statements," not with accusatory "you statements."

NONVERBAL SEXUAL COMMUNICATION

19. Sexual communication is not confined to words alone. Facial expression, interpersonal distance, eye contact, touching, and sounds also convey a great deal of information.

20. The value of nonverbal communication lies primarily in its ability to supplement—not to replace—verbal exchanges.

IMPASSES

21. Sex talk, no matter how candid and compassionate, does not always lead to solutions.

22. Trying to see things from a partner's perspective may be beneficial when deadlocks occur.

23. When impasses occur, it may be helpful to temporarily suspend the discussion, during which time each person privately ponders the issue at hand.

Alberti, Robert, and Emmors, Michael. *Your Perfect Right: A Guide to Assertive Behavior*, 3rd ed. San Luis Obispo, Calif.: Impact Publications, 1978. Contains excellent suggestions for how to be assertive while communicating with others, without being exploitative or overpowering.

Brenton, Myron. *Sex Talk*. Greenwich, Conn.: Fawcett Publications, 1973. Provides some good ideas for improving sexual communication between partners and between parents and children.

Gottman, John; Notarius, Cliff; Gonso, Jonni; Markman, Howard. *A Couples' Guide to Communication*. Champaign, Ill.: Research Press, 1976. This book, while not focused on sex talk per se, provides some excellent suggestions for enhancing couple communication. Includes such topics as hidden agendas, negotiating agreements, listening, getting through a crisis, and so forth.

Langer, Ellen, and Dweck, Carol. *Personal Politics: The Psychology of Making It*. Englewood Cliffs, N.J.: Prentice-Hall, 1973. A well-written book containing some valuable strategies for improving interpersonal communication, several of which may be applied directly to the sexual aspects of human relationships.

9

Sexual Behavior Patterns

CELIBACY
MASTURBATION
    Perspectives on Masturbation
    Purposes of Masturbation
    Masturbation through the Life Cycle
    Self-Pleasuring Techniques
EROTIC FANTASY AND DREAMS
SHARED TOUCHING
    Manual Stimulation of the Female Genitals
    Manual Stimulation of the Male Genitals
ORAL-GENITAL STIMULATION
ANAL STIMULATION
COITUS AND COITAL POSITIONS
    Man Above, Face-to-Face
    Woman Above, Face-to-Face
    Side Position, Face-to-Face
    Rear-Entry Position
SEXUAL ADJUSTMENT AND DISABILITY
    Stereotypes about Sexuality and Disability
    Body Image
    Sexuality and Medical and Institutional Care
    Spinal Cord Injury
    Cerebral Palsy
    Blindness and Deafness
    Developmental Disabilities
SUMMARY
SUGGESTED READINGS

*P*eople express their sexuality in many ways. The emotions they attach to sexual behavior also vary widely. In this chapter we will define and explain a number of types of sexual expression, looking first at individuals and then considering couples. Some of the feelings and attitudes people have about these specific behaviors will also be discussed. Celibacy, the first topic we will consider, may not commonly be thought of as a form of sexual expression. However, celibacy represents a conscious decision not to engage in genital sexual behavior, and this decision in itself is an expression of one's sexuality.

CELIBACY

A physically mature person who chooses not to engage in genital sexual behavior is said to be *celibate*. This person has the capacity for sexual expression, but he or she has made a decision not to engage in certain overt sexual behaviors. There are two degrees of celibacy. In *complete celibacy* a person neither masturbates nor has interpersonal sexual contact. If a person is *partially celibate*, he or she engages in masturbation but not sexual contact with another person.

Celibacy is most commonly thought of in connection with religious devotion: joining a religious order or becoming a priest or nun often includes a vow of celibacy. But individuals may choose celibacy for other reasons as well. The following statements reflect a variety of decisions to be celibate:

I had painfully ended a long-term marriage. Celibacy was a good option for me because I needed time of my own to resolve my feelings about my ex-wife. I wasn't ready for another relationship and I do not like casual sex. (Authors' files)

I've been working on a very important project for several months. Sexual relationships seem to have a way of becoming complicated and time-consuming. Since deciding to be celibate, I've established some good friendships and have had more time and energy for my project. (Authors' files)

Many factors may lead a person to be celibate. Hygiene or health considerations such as recurring vaginal infections or concerns about sexually transmitted diseases may prompt a decision to stop having sexual intercourse. Some people choose to be celibate until marriage because of religious or moral beliefs. Some people maintain celibacy until their personal criteria for what they consider to be a good sexual relationship have been met. Others may choose celibacy because they have experienced confusion or disappointment in past sexual relationships, and they want to spend some time establishing relationships without the sometimes complicating factor of sexual interaction. At times a person can be so caught up in other aspects of life that sex is not a priority (Laws and Schwartz, 1977).

Some people find that a period of celibacy can be quite rewarding. There is often a refocusing on oneself: exploring self-pleasuring; learning to value one's aloneness, autonomy, and privacy; or giving priority to work and nonsexual relationship commitments. Friendships may gain new dimensions and fulfillment. The following comment provides an example:

When I began to be celibate, I really missed affectionate physical contact that had been part of sex. So I began hugging, doing massage, and even sleeping—and I mean *just* sleeping—together in an affectionate way with good friends. (Authors' files)

Many people do not choose to be celibate, however, for despite its rewards for some individuals, it also has a number of disadvantages. These can include lack of physical affection and loneliness for sexual intimacy. Coming out of a period of celibacy may be difficult, too, for re-establishing sexual relationships can be awkward and frightening. This is not made easier by the fact that today many people may not be accepting or supportive of the idea of celibacy or of virginity. The historical ideal that people should not be sexual except for procreation has been replaced by an expectation that individuals should freely and frequently express their sexuality. Rollo May observes that "Our contemporary Puritan holds that it is immoral not to express your libido" (1969, p. 45). It is interesting that of the many options that exist for self-expression, celibacy is one choice that people sometimes have considerable trouble understanding. However, both virginity and celibacy can be reasoned and personally valuable choices.

MASTURBATION

In this text, the term *masturbation* is used to describe self-stimulation of one's genitals for sexual pleasure. We will discuss some perspectives on and purposes of masturbation, patterns of self-stimulation through the life cycle, and specific techniques used in masturbation.

Perspectives on Masturbation

Masturbation has been a source of social concern and censure throughout Judeo-Christian history. This state of affairs has resulted in both misinformation and considerable personal shame and fear. Many of the negative attitudes toward masturbation are rooted in the early Judeo-Christian view that procreation was the only legitimate purpose of sexual behavior. Since masturbation obviously could not result in conception, it was condemned. The "evils" of masturbation received a great deal of publicity in the name of science during the mid-eighteenth century, due largely to the writings of a European physician named Tissot. He wrote vividly about the mind- and body-damaging effects of "self-abuse." This view of masturbation became part of social and medical attitudes, as illustrated in one 1918 American volume then described as an "encyclopedia of health and home" (Wood and Ruddock). An excerpt from that publication appears in Box 9.1. These false beliefs about masturbation may be one reason why earlier generations of men in Kinsey's study reported less masturbation and more concern about it than did later generations (Downey, 1980).

Freud and most other early psychoanalysts recognized that masturbation does not harm physical health and saw it as normal during childhood. However, they

BOX 9.1 MASTURBATION: AN HISTORICAL OPINION

There are various names given to the unnatural and degrading vice of producing venereal excitement by the hand, or other means, generally resulting in a discharge of semen in the male and a corresponding emission in the female. Unfortunately, it is a vice by no means uncommon among the youth of both sexes, and is frequently continued into riper years.

Symptoms—The following are some of the symptoms of those who are addicted to the habit: . . . becoming timid and bashful, and shunning the society of the opposite sex; the face is apt to be pale and often a bluish or purplish streak under the eyes, while the eyes themselves look dull and languid and the edges of the eyelids often become red and sore: the person can not look anyone steadily in the face, but will drop the eyes or turn away from your gaze as if guilty of something mean.

The health soon becomes noticeably impaired; there will be general debility, a slowness of growth, weakness in the lower limbs, nervousness and unsteadiness of the hands, loss of memory, and inability to study or learn, restless disposition, weak eyes and loss of sight, headache and inability to sleep or wakefulness. Next come sore eyes, blindness, stupidity, consumption, spinal affection, emaciation, involuntary seminal emissions, loss of all energy or spirit, insanity and idiocy—the hopeless ruin of both body and mind . . .

The subject is an important one. Few, perhaps, ever think, or ever know, how many of the unfortunate inmates of our lunatic asylums have been sent there by this dreadful vice. Were the whole truth upon this subject known, it would alarm parents, as well as the guilty victims of the vice, more even than the dread of the cholera or smallpox . . .

Source: *Vitalogy*, described as an "encyclopedia of health and home" (Wood and Ruddock 1918, p. 812).

believed that masturbation in adulthood could result in "immature" sexual development and in the inability to form good sexual relationships.

Contemporary views reflect conflicting beliefs about masturbation, and much of the traditional condemnation still exists. In 1976 the Vatican issued a "Declaration on Certain Questions Concerning Sexual Ethics," which described masturbation as an "intrinsically and seriously disordered act."

On the other hand, many writers today view masturbation as a positive aspect of sexuality. For example, Betty Dodson, author of *Liberating Masturbation*, states:

Masturbation, of course, is our first natural sexual activity. It's the way we discover our eroticism, the way we learn to respond sexually, the way we learn to love ourselves and build self-esteem. Sexual skill and the ability to respond are not "natural" in our society. Doing what "comes naturally" for us is to be sexually inhibited. Sex is like any other skill—it has to be learned and practiced. When a woman masturbates, she

*"**Now** they tell us masturbation is harmless!"*

learns to like her own genitals, to enjoy sex and orgasm, and furthermore, to become proficient and independent about it. (1974, p. 13)

Purposes of Masturbation

People masturbate for a variety of reasons. Not the least of these is the pleasure of arousal and orgasm. In one study (Clifford, 1978), college women reported that experiencing pleasurable sensations and physical release of sexual tension were their primary motives for masturbation. At certain times the satisfaction from an autoerotic session may be more rewarding than an interpersonal sexual encounter, as the following quote illustrates:

I had always assumed that masturbation was a second-best sexual expression. One time, after reflecting back on the previous day's activities of a really enjoyable morning masturbatory experience and an unsatisfying experience that evening with a partner, I realized that first- and second-rate was very relative. (Authors' files)

Furthermore, some people find that the independent sexual release available through masturbation can help them make better decisions about relating sexually with other people. Within a relationship, too, masturbation can help to even out the effects of dissimilar sexual interest. Masturbation can be a shared experience:

When I am feeling sexual and my partner is not, he holds me and kisses me while I masturbate. Also, sometimes after making love I like to touch myself while he embraces me. It is so much better than sneaking off to the bathroom alone. (Authors' files)

Beyond these reasons, some people find masturbation to be valuable as a means of self-exploration. Sex educator Eleanor Hamilton recommends masturbation to adolescents as a way to release tension and to become "pleasantly at home with your own sexual organs" (1978, p.33). Indeed, people can learn a great deal about their sexual responses from masturbation. One woman describes how she used self-stimulation to explore her responses to stimulation of the Grafenberg spot:

When I first heard about female ejaculation at orgasm, I thought it was the ridiculous resurgence of an old myth. Then I started thinking more carefully about some of my own sexual experiences. I remembered times during intercourse when I was on top and my vagina felt especially good, and my partner's pubic area would be very wet with a fluid, thinner than the viscous wetness of my usual secretions. I also remembered a time I would rather have forgotten; the time I had an especially intense orgasm during oral sex, and my lover told me I had peed in his mouth. After that, whenever I felt that same unique, intense feeling building up I would back off from it. So after hearing about the Grafenberg spot I decided to experiment on my own. I stroked the top of my vagina and did find an especially sensitive spot; initially it was even a little unpleasant. However, as I continued massaging that particular spot it felt better and better. Succulent is the word that keeps coming to mind to describe it. In contrast to my usual arousal pattern of my vaginal muscles contracting, kind of pulling in, they relaxed and felt like they were pushing outward. I had an orgasm from vigorously stroking the spot, but no ejaculation. I continued to experiment and massaged my "spot" every day. It seemed to become more sensitive. After about two weeks I had an intensely pleasurable orgasm and ejaculated. It felt very similar to those earlier experiences that I had not clearly understood. The fluid had a faint semenlike smell that wasn't at all like urine. (Authors' files)

Self-stimulation is often helpful for anorgasmic women learning to have orgasms and for men experimenting with their response patterns to increase ejaculatory control (see Chapter 17). Finally, some people find masturbation to be an aid to inducing sleep at night, for the same generalized feelings of relaxation that often follow a sexual encounter can also accompany self-pleasuring.

While masturbation is a widely existing practice that is being recognized more and more as a normal activity, guilt about masturbation is still common:

Every time before I would masturbate I would pray and say "I promise, God, this will be the last time." (Authors' files)

Most people have "done it," but many people *feel* uncomfortable about masturbating. At the same time, it is possible to feel uneasy about *not* doing it, too!

I was with a group of friends who started talking and joking about masturbation. I knew what they were talking about, but I had never done it. I didn't want to say so, though. (Authors' files)

Most people who masturbate probably view the behavior with a mix of pleasure and a socialized sense of uneasiness or guilt. Box 9.2, a contemporary account of masturbation, illustrates these mixed feelings.

Another common concern about masturbation is "doing it too much." Even in writings where masturbation is said to be "normal," masturbating "to excess" is often presented as a problem. A definition of excess rarely follows. If a person were masturbating so much that it significantly interfered with daily life, there might be cause for concern. However, in that case masturbation would be a manifestation of the problem rather than the problem itself. For example, someone who is experiencing intense emotional anxiety may use masturbation as an attempt to release the anxiety or as a form of self-comforting. The problem is the source of the anxiety rather than the masturbation.

Masturbation through the Life Cycle

Masturbation often continues as part of a person's sexual expression throughout his or her life. It is normal for infants to touch their genitals and respond pleasurably to self-stimulation. Most children soon learn, though, to be secretive about masturbation. Few receive permission for or information about self-stimulation from their parents. On the contrary, parents may not address the topic at all or may express direct disapproval by a look, a slap, or moving the child's hands away from his or her genitals. In some cases parents punish or chastise the child severely. One woman reports:

When I was about eight years old my mother caught me masturbating in bed. She told me that I was a very bad girl and made me sleep in the hallway that night. The next weekend we had our aunt and uncle over for supper, and she told everyone at the dinner table what I had done. (Authors' files)

Children who experience no direct disapproval from their parents or others will usually learn quickly that masturbation must be done in secret and kept private, as reflected by the following comment:

BOX 9.2 MASTURBATION: A CONTEMPORARY ACCOUNT

Masturbation has become a central unifying experience in my daily routine. I trudge up to my room at the end of a typically frazzled, emotionally draining day and pour out my frustrations and joys into my journal . . . Then, removing my clothes, I slowly begin pulling together alienated and scattered fragments. From dance and yoga I've learned to stretch out the tenseness in my head, shoulders, back, legs, hips, and toes. Flexing, extending, relaxing, breathing deeply and rhythmically, I stand, sit, lie on the carpet or pillows. I create a space for myself the way I would for a special lover. Music, candles, incense. I will perhaps find myself dancing in my nakedness in front of the mirror or rubbing all over my body with oil—belly, nipples, navel, toes, armpits, face, neck, arms, legs. My noisy mind begins to quiet as I slip into the totality of my body. In time, even though I may not have felt sexual tension earlier, my penis becomes erect. Often I sit crosslegged in front of the mirror next to my bed, singing and swaying, feeling rushes of sexual excitement all through my body . . . I cover my penis with oil and softly, gently, stroke it . . . I take time, half an hour to an hour. I release tension through body movement and massage, not orgasm, which allows a more relaxed orgasm, an extended orgasm. I bring myself to the point of orgasm and back off. I continue to make love following orgasm . . . I discover new sensations— foods, colors, clothes, chanting, hyperventilating, drugs, showers and hot baths . . .

Did (this description of masturbation) embarrass you? It was scary to write. Masturbation has been a continuous sexual involvement for thirteen years of my life, yet I choke on the word. For years I would "jerk off" under the covers, light off, touching only my penis, not moving or breathing, deathly afraid of discovery. This guilt and fear which most of us feel to some degree, is rooted in four thousand years of patriarchal, religious, medical, and social prejudice which identifies masturbation as "self-abuse" and "immature." Even my liberal friends think of it as a substitute for the real thing or an indication that "something's wrong with your sex life" . . . Sometimes I fear that men discovering sexual self-awareness will just perform better, and will succeed in taking but not giving love. But somehow, in my experience, self-love removes the desperate orgasm hunger that blinds us, that pushes us to be insensitive and oppress people. We become less horny and so become more insistent that lovemaking be something else: emotional, sharing, communicative, spontaneous. And we can see more clearly our real needs for sensual contact, trust, responsiveness, companionship, and commitment. Moving aware from fantasies and orgasm-erection brings me closer to making love with friends even though they don't fit my fantasy "type." I can trust them to be affectionate, receptive and honest, to help me transcend the burning fear of "impotence" or the explosive letdown of releasing horniness. (Bevson, 1975, p. 41)

I didn't even know there was a word to describe what I was doing when I touched myself. I don't even remember being told not to, but somehow I knew I had to be very careful not to be caught. (Authors' files)

The perception that masturbation must be kept secret can produce feelings of guilt and shame and make it difficult for a child to ask clarifying, and potentially useful, questions about masturbation.

During adolescence the number of boys who masturbate increases dramatically. Kinsey's figures estimated that only 21% of 12-year-old boys masturbated, compared with 82% of 15-year-old boys (1948). Corresponding statistics for girls were much lower: an initial 12% at 12 years of age, increasing only to 20% by the age of 15 (1953). More recent statistics have higher percentages for both boys and girls, but there is still a wide discrepancy between the sexes (Hunt, 1974). The precise reasons why masturbation is more common among males are unknown. One factor may be that young boys are taught to hold their penises during toilet training, thus receiving some degree of encouragement to touch themselves. Girls, however, learn to use toilet tissue to wipe their genitals, and this may make it less likely for girls to discover the pleasurable sensations in their genitals.

During adolescence social expectations for gender role stereotyped behavior often become stronger and more rigid, and these stereotypes may also contribute to lower masturbation rates among females. Masturbation is a direct statement of desire for one's own sexual pleasure and orgasm. It does not conform to gender role stereotypes in which males obtain sexual satisfaction and females provide it. The lower percentage of adolescent girls who masturbate may also reflect the idea that "good girls" are not sexual. From these perspectives, masturbation does not fit into the expectations that females often learn to have about sex. In contrast, the value of sex for pleasure and release of sexual tension meshes more closely with stereotypical male attitudes about sexuality. Adolescent males are probably more likely to experience peer support for masturbation, and it is not uncommon for boys to show each other how to masturbate. For females, however, the situation is often quite different; some women in Kinsey's study masturbated for the first time only after their partners manually stimulated them. A more recent study also found that approximately 20% of women learned to masturbate by copying their partner's petting technique (Clifford, 1978).

In adulthood, the majority of men and women, both married and unmarried, masturbate on occasion. Women tend to masturbate more after they reach their 20's, and Kinsey hypothesized that this phenomenon was due to increased erotic responsiveness, opportunities for learning about the possibility of self-stimulation through sex play with a partner, and a reduction in learned sexual inhibitions.

It is common for people to continue masturbation even when involved in a committed relationship. Hunt's 1974 survey reported that 72% of young husbands and 68% of young wives (in their 20's and early 30's) masturbate on the average two times and one time per month, respectively. However, masturbation is often not considered appropriate if a person has a sexual partner. Some people believe that they should not engage in a sexual activity that excludes their partner or that experiencing sexual pleasure by masturbation deprives their partner of pleasure.

Others mistakenly interpret their desire to masturbate as a sign that there is something wrong with their relationship. But unless it interferes with enjoyable sexual sharing in a relationship, masturbation can be considered a normal part of each partner's sexual repertoire.

During the adult years individuals who are not in a sexual relationship may use masturbation as a primary sexual outlet. Among older people, masturbation may be particularly valuable as a way of continuing sexual expression when a partner is not available due to illness, absence, death, or divorce.

Self-Pleasuring Techniques

This section offers descriptions of self-pleasuring techniques. Self-exploration exercises can help a person become more aware of genital and whole-body sensations, and readers who would like to experiment with some or all of the steps are invited to do so. It is not unusual for someone first trying self-pleasuring to feel anxious. If this happens to you, two suggestions may be helpful. First, focus for a minute on physical relaxation: take a few slow breaths, extending your belly outward as you inhale. Another way to relax yourself is to tense a body part, like the hands and arms, for a few seconds and then release it. Second, try to clear your mind of thoughts related to the "rightness" or "wrongness" of self-pleasuring, and allow yourself to concentrate instead on the positive physical sensations that can come from self-stimulation.

Since the genitals are only one part of the body, we suggest involving the entire anatomy in the self-exam to explore one's sensuality as well as specific structures.

A relaxed bath can be a way to get in touch with one's sensuality.

Both men and women often report that their sexual feelings are enhanced by learning to be less genitally focused and more in touch with the sensual potentials that exist throughout their bodies.

Set aside a block of time (at least one hour for the entire exercise) when you will have privacy. Allow several minutes for your mind to quiet down from the noisy clatter of the day. A good way to begin is with a relaxing bath or shower. You can start the self-exploration while bathing, washing with soap-covered, slippery hands in an unhurried manner. Towel off leisurely and then explore all areas of your body with your fingertips, gently touching and stroking the skin of your face, arms, legs, stomach, and feet.

As you are touching, focus on the various textures and shapes. Compare the sensations when you have your eyes open or closed. You may wish to experiment with using a body lotion, oil, or powder. After the gentle stroking try firmer, massaging pressures, paying extra attention to areas that are tense. You might like to allow yourself some pleasurable fantasies during this time. Notice whether your breathing is relaxed; let it be deep and slow. When you have completed this part, notice how you feel.

For the next step, we recommend that you return to the genital self-examination exercises in Chapters 4 and 5. Once you have completed the exploration, continue experimenting with various kinds of pressure and stroking. Pay attention to what feels good. The following paragraphs are descriptions of ways of touching that some people use during masturbation.

Specific techniques for masturbation vary. Males commonly grasp the penile shaft with one hand, as shown in Figure 9.1. Up-and-down motions of differing

FIGURE 9.1 MALE MASTURBATION

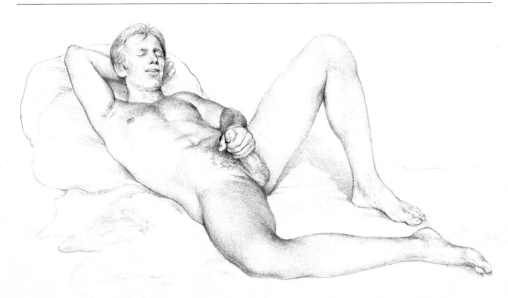

FIGURE 9.2 FEMALE MASTURBATION 263

pressures and tempos provide stimulation. A man may also stroke the glans and frenum or caress or tug the scrotum. Or, rather than using his hands, he may rub his penis against a mattress or a pillow.

Women enjoy a variety of stimulation techniques. Typically, the hand provides circular, back-and-forth, or up-and-down movements of the mons and clitoral area (Figure 9.2). The glans is rarely stimulated directly, although it may be touched rhythmically when covered by the hood. Some women thrust their clitoral area against an object such as bedding or a pillow. Others masturbate by pressing the thighs together and tensing the *pubococcygeal, or PC, muscles.* This is one of several muscles that underlie the vulva structures. Contrary to what is often portrayed in pornography, few women use vaginal insertion to produce orgasm during masturbation. Only 1.5% of women in Hite's survey (1976) used vaginal insertion of a finger or phallic-shaped object; over half of this small group had also used prior clitoral stimulation.

Individuals and couples also use vibrators for added enjoyment or variation. Although some men enjoy using a vibrator on their genitals, women tend to be greater enthusiasts of this technical advancement. To use a vibrator for sexual pleasure, experimentation is in order. Placing it on different areas of the body or genitals will indicate what is particularly arousing. Moving the pelvis or the vibrator may or may not enhance enjoyment.

There are several different types of vibrators available, as shown in Figure 9.3, and people's preferences vary. The phallic-shaped, battery-operated ones usually have less intense vibrations. These vibrators do not require an electrical outlet, and they are also the least expensive type of vibrator.

Electric vibrators are either held in the hand or strapped to the back of the hand. Two basic kinds of hand-held vibrators are the wand-shaped and the multiple-attachment type, both of which usually have two speeds. A variety of shapes of attachments come with the vibrator unit. One brand has a special clitoral attachment. Electric vibrators should never be used in or around water, as lethal electric shock may result.

Hand-strapped vibrators attach to the back of the hand and cause the fingers to vibrate. The vibrations transmitted this way are generally less intense than with hand-held vibrators, and some people prefer this. In addition, some prefer receiving indirect stimulation, through their own or partner's fingers, to direct application of the

FIGURE 9.3 VIBRATORS

Four types of vibrators: (a) phallic-shaped with batteries, (b) wand-shaped, (c) hand strap, and (d) hand-held with attachments.

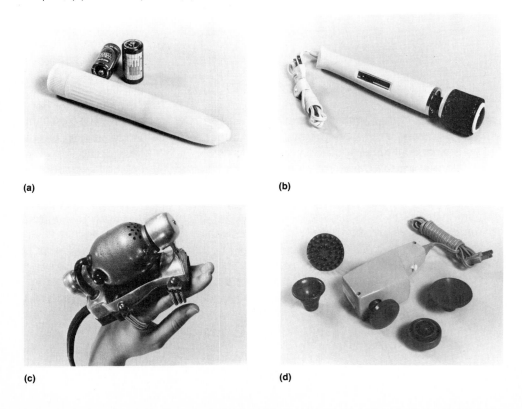

(a)

(b)

(c)

(d)

vibrator to their genitals. However, the hand attached to the vibrator can become numb or uncomfortable.

The recent development of detachable, hand-held pulsating shower heads has added another alternative. Some women have long known that a stream of water over their genitals is very arousing.

Vibrators are available in department and hardware stores, by mail order, and in adult bookstores. If possible, compare different models for strength of vibrations and ease in handling. Vibrators with more than one speed are most likely to meet individual needs. You may find that you sometimes prefer different intensities of vibrations.*

Although masturbation has value for many people in varied situations, it is not desired by everyone. Sometimes, in our attempts to help people who would like to eradicate their negative feelings about self-stimulation, it may sound as if the message is that people *should* masturbate. This is not the case, however. Masturbation is an option for sexual expression—not a mandate.

EROTIC FANTASY AND DREAMS

Besides masturbation, other common forms of solitary sexual experience occur within a person's mind, either with or without accompanying sexual behavior. These are erotic fantasies and dreams. Fantasies are mental experiences that may arise from our imagination or be stimulated by books, drawings, or photographs.

Erotic fantasies are common. In the Kinsey studies, 84% of men and 67% of women reported having sexual fantasies. People fantasize during masturbation, during sexual encounters with a partner, or in nonsexual situations. Fantasies vary considerably and can range from nonexplicit romantic images to quite graphic representations of a real or imagined experience. Research on fantasy content reveals this diversity. According to Hunt's (1974) survey, the most common fantasy for both men and women was to imagine having intercourse with a loved partner. Sex with a stranger was also common for both but more typical for males. Other fantasies included sexual encounters with several people of the other gender, being forced to have sex, forcing someone into sex, and sexual experiences with a same-gender partner. As we might expect with male-female sex role socialization, males in the Hunt study were more likely to fantasize being the aggressor and females were more likely to imagine being the subject of aggression in their fantasy roles. For some, however, the reverse was true. Fantasies seem to be limited only by our imaginations, as Box 9.3 shows.

In a comparison of erotic fantasy content of homosexual and heterosexual men and women, Masters and Johnson (1979) obtained some interesting findings. They examined the type and frequency of fantasy in sexually functional heterosexual males, heterosexual females, homosexual males, and homosexual females. In general,

*An excellent book on vibrators is *Good Vibrations* by Joanie Blank (Burlingame, Calif.: Down There Press, 1976).

Sexual fantasies and erotic dreams take many forms. This is a detail from "The Garden of Delights" by Hieronymous Bosch.

women (both homosexual and heterosexual) reported having a more active fantasy life than both groups of males. Interestingly, fantasies about cross-preference sexual interaction were common in all groups—that is, homosexual men and women imagined heterosexual contact and heterosexual men and women fantasized homosexual experiences.

Erotic fantasies can serve many functions. First of all, they can be a source of pleasure. Erotic thoughts typically serve to enhance sexual arousal during masturbation or partner sexual activities. Vividly visualizing touches or the stimulated area can help amplify the sensations from sexual stimulation. Fantasies can also be a way to mentally rehearse and anticipate new sexual experiences. For example, fantasizing about initiating sex may help a person more comfortably initiate when the situation warrants.

Erotic fantasies can also be an alternative to personally unacceptable behaviors and expand one's erotic experiences by imagination alone. The fact that a sexual activity in a fantasy is "forbidden" may make it more exciting. In a fantasy, a person can engage in lustful group sex, cross-preference sexual liaisons, brief sexual encounters with strangers, erotic relations with people in one's life, incestuous experi-

BOX 9.3 SEXUAL FANTASIES

As the following student descriptions show, men and women have a tremendous variety of sexual fantasies.

Women's Fantasies During Masturbation

"My 'ever patient lover' walks up behind me and caresses my hair, back, buttocks, and then gently wraps his arms around me fondling my breasts, belly, and vulva. He then lays me down, telling me what we're going to do—sometimes tying my legs apart. Then I use my vibrator and imagine him entering me and bringing me to orgasm."

"I walk into a male locker room and tell them to drop their shorts. I proceed to suck them off one by one. All the others are watching and panting in anticipation. When I am done with all of them, I take off my clothes, and they all begin to kiss me and touch me very slowly. I get hotter and hotter and we all end up in a sweaty orgy."

"I fantasize about being seduced by another woman. Although I've never had an affair with another woman, it really makes me sexually excited to think of oral sex being performed on me or vice versa."

Men's Fantasies During Masturbation

"I usually think of some woman (no one that I know), blond, beautiful, lowering herself onto me, letting me eat her out in a 69. Often times a strong and bearded man is involved and gives me oral stimulation at the same time the woman is kissing me or letting me eat her."

"My favorite fantasy is to imagine myself with two women friends, who begin the sexual interlude by making love to each other as I observe. As their excitement heightens I join in, and we do every imaginable act together."

"I fantasize about being with a close friend, usually in a nice outdoor setting—park, woods, or beach. We're always alone. We begin by cuddling and then go down with a kind of innocence."

"Most generally I visualize a woman, usually dark haired with light skin color. She is on her belly with her ass raised and moaning. I enter her and aggressively take her as she screams."

Women's Fantasies During Sex with a Partner

"When my partner and I make love I let my mind leave all other thoughts behind and totally experience and feel what is happening. All aromas become much more noticeable and pleasurable. The warmth increases and I imagine my lover and I suspended in mist upon a bed of clouds. Our bodies come closer together in my mind as arousal increases, and at the moment of orgasm it is as if we were mentally and physically one. I caress my lover's body but it is as if it were part of my own."

Continued on next page

BOX 9.3 CONTINUED

"When having intercourse with my husband of 17 years I often fantasize that I am taking a young virgin male to bed for his first time. I show him what I want done to me just the way I like it while at the same time giving this poor young boy an experience he will long remember."

"My biggest fantasy with my partner is that I have just met him. We sorta look at each other up and down and say, 'I'd like to fuck your brains out' and we go to a hotel and do just that. When I fantasize this with my partner I seem to lose some of my inhibitions and get a little more wild."

Men's Fantasies During Sex with a Partner

"I close my eyes and picture my partner's body and feel senses like softness, moistures, and sounds develop a rhythm."

"The fantasy that reoccurs most when I am making love is a visualization of being on an isolated tropic beach. The warm sun is baking our bodies golden brown. The rhythmic pounding of the waves eliminates all tensions and worries. My partner and I are one."

"I fantasize about a young woman in knee socks and high heels and nothing else."

ences, forcing someone or being forced to have sex, sex with animals, and other variations of sexual activities without actually doing them. Fantasies about being forced to have sex can serve various purposes. One may be the erotic feelings accompanying the thought of arousing uncontrollable lust in another. For men, these fantasies may offer an alternative to the stereotypical male role of initiator. For women, who often learn to have mixed feelings about being sexual, this type of fantasy offers sexual adventures free from the responsibility of a personal choice. Enjoyment of forced sex fantasies does *not* mean women really want to be raped. A woman is in charge of her fantasies, but as a victim of sexual aggression she is not in control.

Fantasy can also be a substitute for action. For example, in a sexually exclusive relationship people can fantasize about past relationships or others to whom they feel attracted even though they are committed to a single sexual partner.

Some people may decide to incorporate a particular fantasy into their sexual behavior. Acting out a fantasy can be pleasurable; on the other hand, if a fantasy is counter to one's value system or has possible negative consequences, a person should seriously consider the advantages and disadvantages of doing so. For some people fantasies are more exciting when they remain imaginary and are a disappointment in actual practice.

Some couples find that telling each other their fantasies is erotic; others prefer to keep them private. Whether to share a fantasy with a partner is a difficult question; a lover might feel upset about fantasies involving other people or behaviors that would be objectionable to them. A thorough understanding of one's partner will help a person make the decision about what to reveal.

Most people draw a distinct boundary between their fantasy world and the real world. For example, a woman may enjoy fantasizing about having intercourse with her partner's best friend but would not really act in this way. For people who experience guilt over their fantasies, it is important to remember that thinking is not the same as doing. As long as people feel able not to act on a fantasy that would hurt themselves or others, they probably do not need to be concerned.

In rare cases, fantasy may contribute to a person acting in a harmful way to others. This is of particular concern with people who may sexually molest children or sexually assault adults. A person who thinks that he or she is in danger of committing such an act should seek professional psychological assistance. See Chapter 20 for further information about fantasy and sexual offenders.

Sexually explicit films or books are sometimes used to enhance erotic fantasies and sexual arousal. One study (Heiman, 1980) reports that women in an experimental laboratory setting expressed more subjective and physiological arousal from erotic audio tapes and readings than from self-generated fantasy.

Another form of imaginary sexual activity often takes place without a person's conscious direction. Erotic dreams and occasionally orgasm may occur during sleep. Almost all of the male subjects and two-thirds of the females in Kinsey's two studies reported experiencing erotic dreams. Individuals may waken during such a dream and notice signs of sexual arousal—erection, vaginal lubrication, or pelvic movements. If orgasm occurs, males usually notice the ejaculate (hence the label "wet dreams"). Female orgasm may be more difficult to determine, due to the absence of such a visible sign. As with other dreams, the content of erotic dreams may be logical or quite nonsensical. Explicit sexual expression in the dreams varies widely, too, from common sexual activities to behaviors considered to be taboo. Both conscious fantasy and erotic dreams can be ways to express and explore dimensions of experiences and feelings.

Up to this point in the chapter, we have been looking at ways that people express themselves or find sexual outlets as individuals. However, many of the sexual behaviors with which we are concerned in this book take place as interactions between people.

In the sections that follow, we will discuss some of the more common forms of shared sexual behaviors. The sequence in which they are presented does not mean that such a progression is "best" or necessary in a particular sexual encounter. For example, a heterosexual couple may desire oral-genital stimulation after coitus rather than before. Also, one complete sexual experience may consist of one or more sexual activities. With the exception of coitus, the discussions of touching, oral-genital and anal stimulation are directed toward all individuals, regardless of their sexual orientation.

Although the following sections include discussions of sexual technique, a technique is not able to stand on its own; it is part of the framework of the relationship in which it occurs. Feelings, desires, and attitudes strongly influence choices about sexual activity. Sensitivity to a person's sexual needs will help develop shared pleasure and arousal more effectively than any specific technique. Mutual consent is an important aspect of a sexual relationship, and sexual activities that both partners are willing to engage in are likely to provide a couple with enjoyable sexual experiences. Open communication can greatly help couples establish their unique and changing preferences.

SHARED TOUCHING

i like my body when it is with your
body. It is so quite new a thing.
Muscles better and nerves more.
i like your body. i like what it does,
i like its hows. i like to feel the spine
of your body and its bones, and the trembling
-firm-smooth ness and which i will
again and again and again
kiss, i like kissing this and that of you,
i like, slowly stroking the, shocking fuzz
of your electric fur, and what-is-it comes
over parting flesh. . . . And eyes big love-crumbs,

and possibly i like the thrill

of under me you so quite new*

Touch is one of the first and most important senses that we experience when we emerge into this world. Infants who have been fed but deprived of this basic stimulation have died for lack of it. Touch also forms the cornerstone of sexuality shared with another. In Masters and Johnson's evaluation:

Touch is an end in itself. It is a primary form of communication, a silent voice that avoids the pitfall of words while expressing the feelings of the moment. It bridges the physical separateness from which no human being is spared, literally establishing a sense of solidarity between two individuals. Touching is sensual pleasure, exploring the textures of skin, the suppleness of muscle, the contours of the body, with no further goal than enjoyment of tactile perceptions. (1976, p. 253)

Touch does not need to be directed at an erogenous area of the body to be sexual. The entire body surface is a sensory organ and touching—almost anywhere— can enhance intimacy and sexual arousal. It is important to remember that partners

*Reprinted from *Tulips & Chimneys* by e. e. cummings, by permission of Liveright Publishing Corporation. Copyright 1923, 1925 and renewed 1951, 1953 by e. e. cummings. Copyright © 1973, 1976 by the Trustees for the e.e. cummings Trust. Copyright © 1973, 1976 by George James Firmage.

Sensual touching can be pleasurable to both the giver and the receiver.

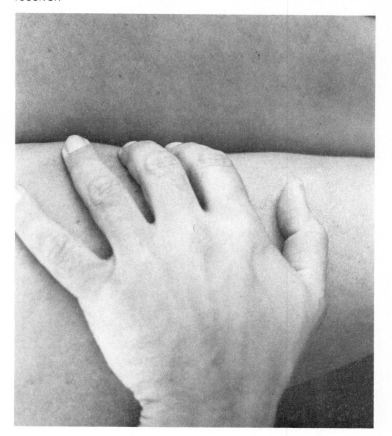

may like different kinds of touching. It may be helpful for couples to openly discuss their preferences to avoid the frustration when one partner touches the other in the way that the former would like instead of the way the latter would enjoy.

Shere Hite advocates a redefinition of sexuality and touching:

All the kinds of physical intimacy that were channeled into our one mechanical definition of sex can now be reallowed, and rediffused throughout our lives, including simple forms of touching and warm body contact. There need not be a sharp distinction between sexual touching and friendship. Just as women described "arousal" as one of the best parts of sex, and just as they described closeness as the most pleasurable aspect of intercourse, so intense physical intimacy can be one of the most satisfying activities possible—in and of itself . . . Sex is intimate physical contact for pleasure, to share pleasure with another person (or just alone). (1976, p. 527)

Masters and Johnson's *sensate focus* exercises described in Chapter 17 give an opportunity to explore and experience the pleasurable sensations from giving and receiving touching.

While the entire body responds to touching, some specific areas are, of course, more receptive to sexual feelings than others. Preferences vary from one person to another. Many men and women report breast stimulation (especially of the nipple) to be arousing; others find it unenjoyable or unpleasant. A few women reach orgasm from breast stimulation alone (Masters and Johnson, 1966). The size of the breasts is not related to how erotically sensitive they are. Some women's breasts become more sensitive, even tender, during certain times of their cycles. A woman may find that a firm touch that had been highly arousing one week feels uncomfortable and harsh the next week. Once again, ongoing communication is important.

Genital stimulation is often highly pleasurable to women and men. Many people's first experience with manual genital stimulation comes from masturbation, and this self-knowledge can form the basis of further learning with a partner. People who have not previously masturbated can explore and learn what is enjoyable with each other. Either one partner can touch the other or they can explore each others' sensations simultaneously. Manual stimulation can provide pleasure or orgasm, or it can be a step towards other activities.

Manual Stimulation of the Female Genitals

The vulva tissues are delicate and sensitive. If there is not enough lubrication to make the vulva slippery, it can become easily irritated. A lubricant such as K-Y Jelly, a lotion without alcohol, or saliva can be used to moisten the fingers and vulva.

There is great variation from one woman to another in the kind of touches that create arousal. Even the same woman may vary in her preference from one moment to another. Gentle or firm movements on different areas of the vulva may be desired. Direct stimulation of the clitoris may be uncomfortable for some women; touches above or along the sides may be preferable. Insertion of a finger into the vagina may enhance arousal. Anal stimulation is erotic to some women but not to others. It is important not to touch the vulva or vagina with the same finger used for anal stimulation because bacteria that are normal in the rectum can cause infections if introduced into the vagina.

Manual Stimulation of the Male Genitals

Men also have individual preferences for manual stimulation, and as with women, the pace of the movements may vary as arousal increases. Gentle or firm stroking of the penile shaft and glans and light touches or tugging on the scrotum may be desired. Occasionally, some men experience uncomfortable sensitivity of the penile glans when it is touched immediately following orgasm. Some men find that lubrication with a lotion or saliva increases pleasure. With heterosexual couples, if intercourse might follow, the lotion should be nonirritating to the woman's genital tissues. Some men also enjoy manual stimulation or penetration of the anus.

Both the mouth and genitals are primary biological erogenous zones, areas of the body generously endowed with sensory nerve endings. Therefore, couples who are psychologically comfortable with oral-genital stimulation often find both giving and receiving to be highly pleasurable. Oral-genital contact is used to produce pleasure, arousal, or orgasm. As one woman states:

At first, I was very uncomfortable with the idea of oral sex. After some explanations and some showing by my partner, I realized that maybe this wasn't so bad after all. In fact, for the first time in my life, I reached orgasm. (Authors' files)

Oral-genital stimulation can be done individually (by one partner to the other) or simultaneously. Some people prefer oral sex individually because they can focus on either giving or receiving. Others especially enjoy the mutuality of simultaneous oral-genital stimulation. Simultaneous stimulation is sometimes referred to as "69" because of the body position suggested by the numbers (see Figure 9.4). A variety of body positions can be used; lying side by side, using a thigh for a pillow, is another option. As arousal becomes intense during mutual oral-genital stimulation, partners need to be careful not to suck or bite too hard.

Some people may have reservations concerning oral-genital stimulation. These views or preferences come from a number of sources. As we have seen, sexual behaviors that do not have the potential of resulting in a socially sanctioned pregnancy within marriage have been historically labeled immoral, and many people believe that oral sex is wrong. This notion of immorality has been institutionalized into law, and sexual behaviors other than coitus are still illegal in many states.

Other reservations have to do with the belief that oral-genital stimulation is unsanitary or that genitals are unattractive. It may be difficult for someone who has a

FIGURE 9.4 SIMULTANEOUS ORAL-GENITAL STIMULATION IN THE "69" POSITION

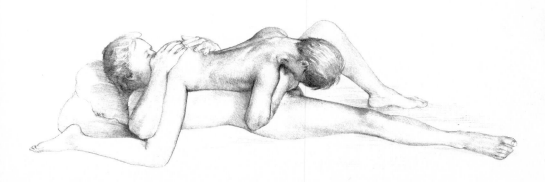

negative image of his penis or her vulva to feel comfortable with receiving oral sex. Many people have also acquired the attitude that the genitals are "dirty," since the urinary openings and the anus are close to the genitals. However, routine thorough washing of the genitals with soap and water is adequate for cleanliness.

Other reasons some people object to oral sex stem from the belief that it is a "homosexual act"—even when experienced by heterosexual couples. Although many homosexual people do engage in oral sex, the activity is not homosexual by nature. Rather, its "homosexuality" or "heterosexuality" depends on the sexes of the partners involved.

Despite these negative attitudes, oral-genital contact is quite common and has become even more so in recent years. In this period, too, it seems to have gained more acceptance throughout a cross-section of educational levels. Kinsey's research in the late forties and early fifties revealed that 60% of college-educated couples, 20% of high-school-educated couples, and 10% of grade-school-educated couples had experienced oral-genital stimulation as part of their marital sex. Hunt's 1974 investigations indicated that by the 1970s, 90% of married couples under 25 years of age— regardless of educational level—had experienced oral-genital sex. While it is likely that these different figures reflect a degree of sample bias (as we described in Chapter 3), it also seems probable that oral-genital contact is gaining more widespread acceptance and practice.

Different terminology is used to distinguish oral-genital stimulation of women from that of men. *Cunnilingus* (Latin meaning: *cunnus*, "vulva"; and *lingere*, "to lick") is oral stimulation of the vulva—the clitoris, labia minora, vestibule, and vaginal opening. Many women find the warmth, softness, and moistness of the partner's lips and tongue to be highly pleasurable and effective in producing sexual arousal or orgasm. Variations of stimulation include rapid or slow circular or back-and-forth tongue movement on the clitoral area, sucking the clitoris or minor lips, and thrusting the tongue into the vaginal opening. Some women are especially aroused by simultaneous manual stimulation of the vagina and oral stimulation of the clitoral area.

Fellatio (Latin meaning: *fillare*, "to suck") is oral stimulation of the penis and scrotum. Both of Kinsey's studies found that, in heterosexual couples, women were less likely to stimulate their partners orally than the reverse. Options for stimulation include gently or vigorously licking and sucking the glans, the frenum, and the penile shaft, and licking or enclosing a testicle in the mouth. Some men enjoy combined oral stimulation of the glans and manual stroking of the penile shaft, testicles, or anus.

Couples differ in their preference for including ejaculation into the mouth as a part of male oral stimulation. Many find it acceptable and some find it exciting; others do not. Occasionally, a couple avoids fellatio entirely because the partner wants to avoid ejaculation into his or her mouth. In this case, the couple can agree beforehand that the man will indicate when he is close to orgasm and other stimulation can then be used. For couples who are comfortable with ejaculation into the mouth, the ejaculate can be swallowed or not according to one's preference. In either case, it is usually best for the partner who is doing the oral stimulation to control the movements. During oral sex the man's partner can grasp the penis below his or her lips with the hand to prevent the penis from going further into the mouth than is comfortable.

This will help avoid difficulty with a gagging reflex. Also, vigorous thrusting may result in lacerations of the partner's lips as he or she attempts to protect the penis from the teeth.

ANAL STIMULATION

Like oral-genital stimulation, anal stimulation may be thought by some to be a "homosexual" act. However, penile penetration of the anus is practiced by both heterosexual and male homosexual couples; so is the use of small phallic-shaped vibrators for anal insertion. The anus has dense supplies of nerve endings that can respond erotically. Some women report orgasmic response from anal intercourse (Masters and Johnson, 1970), and heterosexual or homosexual men often achieve orgasm from stimulation during penetration.

Individuals or couples may also use anal stimulation for additional arousal and variety. Manually stroking the outside of the anal opening or inserting one or more fingers into the anus can be very pleasurable for some people during masturbation or partner sex. Others may engage in oral-anal stimulation, called *analingus* or "rimming." Hunt's (1974) survey reported that various forms of anal stimulation had been used, at least experimentally, by many of his respondents. Over half of the men and women under 35 in his sample had experienced manual-anal stimulation, and over a quarter had experienced oral-anal contact. Approximately 25% of married couples under 35 reported that they used anal intercourse occasionally.

Besides the sphincter muscle, the anus is composed of delicate tissues, and some special care needs to be taken in anal stimulation. A nonirritating lubricant and gentle penetration are necessary to avoid discomfort or injury to these tissues. It is helpful to use lubrication on both the anus and the penis or object being inserted. The partner receiving anal insertion can bear down (as with a bowel movement) to relax the sphincter. The partner inserting needs to go slowly and gently, keeping the penis or object tilted to follow the direction of the colon (Morin, 1981). Heterosexual couples should never have vaginal intercourse directly following anal intercourse, since bacteria that are normal in the anus often cause vaginal infections. To prevent vaginal infections from this source, a couple may choose to use a condom during anal intercourse. Alternatively, the penis should be washed thoroughly after anal intercourse. Bacteria may, however, remain harbored in the penile urethra. Another alternative is for vaginal intercourse to precede anal intercourse.

If a person chooses to engage in analingus, there are some important health risks to consider. Various types of intestinal infections, hepatitis, and sexually transmitted diseases can be contracted or spread through oral-anal contact.

COITUS AND COITAL POSITIONS

There are a wide range of positions a couple may choose for penile-vaginal intercourse, or coitus. Many people may have a favored position, yet enjoy others. A

There are a great variety of intercourse positions.

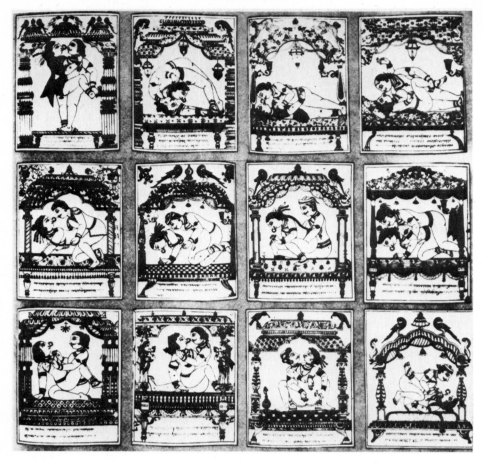

30-year-old man states:

Different intercourse positions usually express and evoke particular emotions for me. Being on top I enjoy feeling aggressive;.when on the bottom I experience a special kind of receptive sensuality. In the side-by-side position I easily feel gentle and intimate. I like sharing all these dimensions of myself with my lover. (Authors' files)

In the pages that follow, we will describe some of the basic coital positions and their potential advantages and disadvantages. These are meant only as general descriptions, not inflexible guidelines. As in all areas of sexuality, individual preferences vary. Furthermore, the desirability of a particular position may change with health, age, weight, pregnancy, or different partners. Therefore, the points in our discussion of potential advantages and disadvantages will not be true for everyone.

We can make one other general statement about coitus. Beyond technique, cooperation and consideration are important, particularly at certain times. Some couples may find that mutual cooperation during *intromission* (entry of the penis into the vagina) is helpful. Often the woman can best guide her partner's penis into her vagina by moving her body or using her hand. If his penis slips out of the vagina, which can occur fairly easily in some positions, a helping hand will most likely be welcome. Furthermore, both nonverbal and verbal communication about preferences of position, tempo, and movement can enhance pleasure and arousal of both partners. Coitus can also occur with or without orgasm for one or both partners.

Man Above, Face-to-Face

The most familiar coital position in our society, sometimes known as the "missionary position," is with the man above and the couple facing each other (Figure 9.5). There are several potential advantages of this position. First of all, the man is typically the more active partner in our society, and many couples are most comfortable with the man having the initiative. In this position, he has maximum freedom and control over coital movements. Kinsey's research in the late 1940s indicated that a large majority of males predominantly or exclusively experienced coitus in this position.

Closeness of upper bodies and opportunity for kissing and eye contact can also enhance this position. The woman's hands are free to manually caress and hold her partner. If the man is raised on his hands, she can stimulate her clitoris. This is also a good position for maintaining penetration after ejaculation. If a pregnancy is desired, this position improves the possibility of conception (as will be discussed in more detail in Chapter 12).

The position also has disadvantages. The man usually supports his weight on his knees and hands or elbows, a position that is both physically tiring and limiting to his ability to caress his partner. Also, the strain of both supporting himself and actively

FIGURE 9.5 MAN-ABOVE, FACE-TO-FACE, INTERCOURSE POSITION

moving increases muscle tension, and this may hasten ejaculation. He may find it more difficult to control his orgasm and prolong intercourse. For this reason, most sex therapists working with men who want to establish ejaculatory control suggest positions other than man-above.

This position is also limiting for the woman, whose control over her own pelvic movements is often restricted. It may be more difficult for her to experience the pressures and movements that are most arousing to her. If her partner is much heavier than she, his weight may be uncomfortable. Also, she has little control over penetration, and deep penetration is uncomfortable for some women. Finally, this position is a poor one during pregnancy once the woman's abdomen has enlarged, as pressure on the abdomen will be uncomfortable.

Woman Above, Face-to-Face

An alternative to the man-above position is for the woman to be on top. As Figure 9.6 shows, she may either be prone or sitting upright. Some of the advantages of either of these positions are the converse of when the man is on top. The woman can control the tempo, direction, and depth of movement. Many women find pressure against their partner's pubic bone stimulating, and this position allows for the woman to adjust her body to provide the kind of pubic bone contact that is especially arousing to her. Her partner can assume a more receptive role. These combined factors are the reasons that most sex therapists ask heterosexual clients to use this position as an aid to modifying a variety of difficulties.

Apparently, "primitive" humans were aware of what sex therapists know. The woman-above position is common in prehistoric drawings that show intercourse scenes. In Kinsey's survey (1948), this position was reported to be used occasionally, with frequency varying somewhat according to education level. Thirty-five percent of college-educated men, 28% of high-school-educated men, and 17% of grade-school-educated men reported having used this position. The use of the woman-above position has been increasing, as indicated by Kinsey's 1953 findings that 35% of women born before 1900 and 52% born after 1900 had used it frequently. In 1974 Morton Hunt found that nearly three-quarters of married couples reported using this position occasionally.

Particularly when the woman is sitting upright, the position has another advantage besides those mentioned in that the woman or her partner can stimulate her clitoris. A vibrator can also be used. When she is sitting upright, the woman is free to touch her partner; and whether she is prone or sitting, the man's hands are free to caress much of her body. When she is prone, full-body contact can be enjoyable. It is a good position for looking at and talking to each other.

One of the disadvantages of the woman-above position is that one or both partners may be uncomfortable with the woman assuming a more active role. The woman may also find this position tiring. If the male attempts to maintain a very active role, he may find the muscle tension created by moving both his body and hers results in his orgasm occurring sooner than desired. Finally, even if both partners are comfortable with this position, the woman may need some time at first to experiment and learn how to move her pelvis.

FIGURE 9.6 TWO VARIATIONS OF THE WOMAN-ABOVE POSITION   279

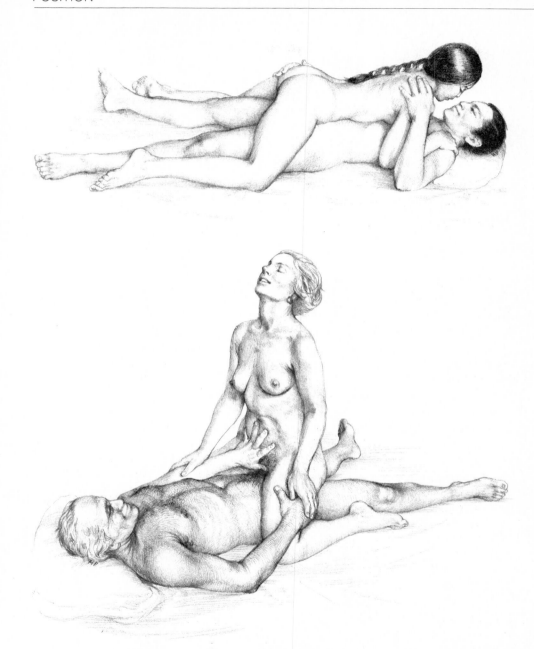

FIGURE 9.7 FACE-TO-FACE SIDE INTERCOURSE POSITION

Side Position, Face-to-Face

In this position, both partners face each other, but they lie on their sides (see Figure 9.7). One of the primary advantages of this position is that neither partner must support the other's weight. Each has one hand available to caress and fondle the partner, and manual clitoral stimulation can be included. This is typically a relaxed, unhurried position; talking, looking at each other, even sipping some wine are all options. Intercourse can often be prolonged due to the relaxed nature and mutual control over pelvic movements. If desired, a couple can remain intertwined after completing intercourse and fall asleep in each other's arms. This can be a good position in late pregnancy because depth of penetration can be easily regulated and there is no extra pressure on the woman's abdomen.

A possible disadvantage of the face-to-face side position is difficulty with intromission. For this reason, some couples prefer to begin in either the woman- or man-above position, then roll over to the side position. Another disadvantage is that it is not a good position for vigorous pelvic thrusting, due to the limited mobility of both partners. Also, it may be difficult to make the kind of pubic bone contact that is often arousing for the woman.

In their treatment program for couples with sexual difficulties, Masters and Johnson make extensive use of the lateral coital position, a variation of the side position. It is different, however, in that the woman lies slightly on top of the man and her bottom leg is inside of his legs. This position has the advantages of the side position, with the additional opportunity for more vigorous thrusting if desired. It is also a restful position for prolonged intercourse. In follow-up studies, 75% of Masters and Johnson's clients report continued frequent use of this position (1970).

Rear-Entry Position

One of the potential advantages of a rear-entry intercourse position is the number of possible variations. Depending on the option selected, intercourse can be vigorous or relaxed. The woman's clitoris can be easily stimulated by herself or her partner. She can also stroke his scrotum. The side-by-side, back-to-belly variation shown in Figure 9.8 can be a good position during pregnancy. In the kneeling position, where the woman is on her knees and the man enters from behind, the man has considerable ease of penetration.

One common objection to rear-entry coitus is the feeling of lack of intimacy without face-to-face contact. Others believe it is "animalistic," because animals copulate in a similar position. Furthermore, it is sometimes associated with anal intercourse which, as we have discussed, has negative overtones for some people.

SEXUAL ADJUSTMENT AND DISABILITY

People with various disabilities often have special needs in relation to their sexual behavior. This section will discuss some of the special needs in sexual adjustment of people with spinal injuries, cerebral palsy, blindness, deafness, and developmental disabilities. (The sexual impact of illnesses like diabetes, arthritis, heart attack, and multiple sclerosis will be discussed in the sexual problems chapter.) First we will examine some of the issues that people with disabilities have in common about their sexuality.

Stereotypes about Sexuality and Disability

Myths about the sexual nature and abilities of disabled persons are something that most people with disabilities must confront. These myths often have their basis in the notion, common in our society, that the only people who have the right to be sexual are those who are young and beautiful. "Barbie and Ken" doll-type images are constantly portrayed in the popular media. People who are obese, old, or do not conform to the current standards of sexual attractiveness are usually presented as asexual or ludicrous. This narrow stereotype has been particularly damaging to physically or mentally disabled individuals. In one writer's words: "Society has placed an added handicap on the already handicapped person by helping to deny two basic needs—a realistic and positive identity as a sexual being, and the opportunity for sexual expression and fulfilling sexual relationships" (Bidgood, 1974, p.1). The belief that people with certain kinds of disabilities are not sexual beings is an important myth for both able-bodied and disabled persons to examine and reject.

The stereotype of the asexual disabled may be based on incorrect assumptions about some of the sexual limitations that certain kinds of disabilities present. These assumptions commonly focus on lack of genital sensation or ability for erection, orgasm, or ejaculation; inability to have penile-vaginal intercourse or to use the male-on-top position; or the presence of bowel and bladder apparatus or braces and prostheses that may be believed to preclude satisfactory sexual relations. Infertility as a result of disability may also be interpreted as a loss of sexuality. However, as stressed throughout this text, sexuality is integral to all of us—regardless of whether erection, intercourse, orgasm, or pregnancy can occur and in spite of crutches, braces, or wheelchairs. A person is a sexual being no matter what her or his physical appearance or level of functioning is.

Certainly the limitations and special circumstances that disabilities present are often a challenge for sexual adjustment. Special information and teaching tools may be needed for appropriate sex education. Good communication within relationships is especially important because a nondisabled partner is unlikely to know what the disabled partner can or cannot do. Disabled people can greatly benefit from flexibility in sexual roles and innovation in sexual technique. As a woman with cerebral palsy explains:

My disability kind of makes things more interesting. We have to try harder and I think we get more out of it because we do. We both have to be very conscious of each other—we have to take time. That makes us less selfish and more considerate of each other which helps the relationship in other areas beside sexuality. (Shaul et al., 1978, p. 5)

This kind of exploration, experimentation, communication, and learning together are ways of relating that can contribute to pleasure and intimacy in relationships of nondisabled couples, too.

A disability does not eliminate the human need and capacity for shared intimacy.

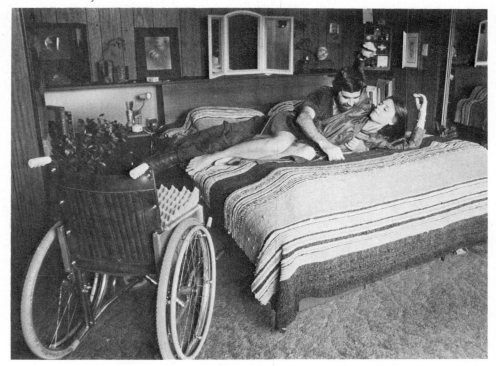

Body Image

Physical disabilities often affect a person's body image. Accepting and positive feelings about one's physical self are an important part of sexuality; a good body image contributes to a person's perception of him- or herself as a sexual, and sexually attractive, individual. People who believe that they are unattractive may avoid social situations or feel inadequate in a sexual relationship. Body image also influences how much attention a person pays to grooming and other aspects of personal physical care. A positive body image can contribute to how lovable and worthwhile one feels and what kinds of relationships a person chooses.

For individuals with physical disabilities and limitations, developing a positive body image may be difficult. It can be emotionally painful to compare one's body to nondisabled people or to oneself prior to becoming ill or injured. Frustration over impaired mobility and physical abilities for recreation, self-care, and work per-formance can generate resentment and anger towards one's body. These feelings can be exacerbated by juxtaposing media images of attractiveness and one's scars from injuries or surgery, lack of muscle tone from paralysis, or involuntary muscle spasms from neurological damage. Yet these characteristics are very much a part of a person and need to be accepted along with his or her other attributes. As one person who had polio noted:

Before my disability I was very active. I figure skated, danced, played the piano. After I was disabled, it changed my body so much. Well, it happened at 17 and was quite a shock . . . at the present time I'm working on trying to accept my body and to be more aware of it. It is really part of my self-image. Sometimes I'd like to put it [my body] out there somewhere and act as if it's not part of me, but I'm working to admit that it's there and trying to include it as part of me. (Shaul et al., 1978, pp. 6–7)

Body image often can be improved for both disabled and nondisabled people. Many people have negative feelings about their bodies, and all of us will confront body image changes caused by wrinkles, gray hair, or reduced physical speed or agility due to the aging process. The suggestions for helping disabled individuals improve their body image can be helpful for others, as well. These include:

1. Using a mirror and noting your positive features and thinking about how they can be enhanced.
2. Exploring and becoming acquainted with features or body parts you consider less attractive.
3. Putting up photographs of yourself that you like.
4. Saying out loud to the mirror the next time you go to extra effort to look good, "I look great today."
5. Pampering your body with relaxing baths, fragrances, backrubs, a new haircut and clothes.
6. Asking people what they find physically attractive about you.
7. Developing your physical potential with exercise and diet.
8. Talking with other people with disabilities to help overcome a sense of isolation.
9. Shopping for prostheses or braces where the sales people are concerned with appearance as well as function.
10. Paying attention to the ways you've grown and improved. (Shaul et al., 1978)

Sometimes a person will face the difficulties of body image changes from a disability with previously unknown reserves of emotional strength. Meeting such a challenge can promote a re-evaluation of personal values and priorities. A young woman who broke her neck in a car accident reports:

I went through enormous personal changes after my accident. I had been working as a model prior to my accident and was very sought after socially, mainly because of my physical attractiveness. I didn't really reach out to others to get to know them; I always got enough attention by being pretty. But after my accident, with my hair shaved for the halo-type metal band that screwed into my skull and attached to a shoulder-neck brace, I wasn't very pretty. I had to learn to reach out to others to help them feel comfortable with me so that I wouldn't be so alone and lonely. It has been the most valuable, and most difficult, experience in my life. (Authors' files)

Most individuals with a disability will have contact with medical or institutional care. Helping professionals may pay attention to reproductive concerns of disabled people but ignore the emotional and social effects of a disability on sexuality. They sometimes mistakenly assume that they should not talk about sexuality with disabled patients to avoid adding to their problems and anxieties. Although those responsible for health care of the disabled have become more sensitive to their patients' needs in this area, there is still a great need for sexuality education for the staff and clients in these settings. Perhaps most important for disabled persons are opportunities to explore options for self and interpersonal sexual expression within their capabilities. One writer clearly outlines some of the issues and decisions about sexuality and disabled individuals.

Slowly, as society is coming to grips with its own sexuality . . . we are beginning to realize fully that all human beings are sexual by nature from the moment of birth to the moment of death, including those who by birth, accident or disease live in deformed or crippled bodies or possess incomplete faculties. "Privacy rooms" are beginning to appear in institutional settings. In the Netherlands, in England, and in Cincinnati, Ohio, apartment units designed for handicapped couples have been built and are staffed by professionals. Various non-marital heterosexual and homosexual relationships are being tolerated, and eventually accepted among handicapped couples. In a few institutions, those individuals too handicapped even to masturbate are having masturbation prescribed and provided. Interest in sex education programs for the handicapped is increasing greatly as this acceptance of them grows, and as the options for them broaden. (Bidgood, 1974, p. 14)

The next sections briefly describe several disabilities and their possible impact on sexuality. We will also discuss some of the relevant sexual adjustment needs.

Spinal Cord Injury

People with spinal cord injuries (SCI) have reduced motor control and sensation because the damage to the spinal cord obstructs the pathway between the body and brain. The parts of the body that are paralyzed vary according to the location of the injury. A person can be *paraplegic* (loss of feeling and voluntary muscle function of the trunk and legs) or *quadraplegic* (loss of feeling and voluntary muscle function of the arms or hands, as well as of the trunk or legs). Injuries lower on the spine result in paraplegia, and higher injuries cause quadraplegia.

In an SCI person the ability for arousal and orgasm may be hampered; this varies according to the specific injury. Some men and women are able to experience arousal or orgasm from physical stimulation and others are not. An SCI person may or may not be able to feel the sensations of arousal that he or she experiences. Some SCI individuals report that the sensations they experience change or increase slightly over time.

Lack of erection in the SCI male usually requires some sexual adjustments, and experimentation with positions that work for each couple is important. A couple can use the "stuffing technique" when erection does not occur (Mooney et al., 1975). This is a method in which the woman uses her fingers to stuff the flaccid penis into her vagina to experience intravaginal sensations of the penis. Surgically inserted implants are sometimes used to make the penis erect. However, SCI males and their partners often re-evaluate the importance of penile-vaginal intercourse and develop other viable options for pleasure, such as manual and oral stimulation or the use of vibrators.

Much of the professional and personal sexual education for SCI individuals and couples consists of redefining and expanding sexual expression. For example, genital sensations may be very slight or nonexistent, but other areas of the body may increase in sexual responsiveness and may cause intense pleasure. The book *Sexual Options for Paraplegics and Quadraplegics* describes techniques to increase feelings of pleasure.

Sensory amplification, the method used by some disabled men and women to achieve the most pleasure and satisfaction from a sensory input, is the act of thinking about a physical stimulus, concentrating on it, and amplifying the sensation in your mind to an intense degree. Thus, it is possible to achieve a higher level of satisfaction and possibly a mental orgasm. Some who have lost physical sensation in the genital area substitute or transfer a sensation to an area of the body that has retained some feeling, such as the inside of an arm, the neck, breasts, buttocks, or around the anal area. By transposing these sensations mentally, or by using your imagination to create a fantasy, you may find intense satisfaction. (Mooney et al., 1975, p. 5)

Observing one's partner's responses to sexual pleasure can heighten the satisfaction and enjoyment of a spinal cord-injured partner. Some disabled people have developed the ability to "feel" what their partners are feeling and share intensely in their excitement (Mooney et al., 1975). Most spinal cord-injured people have able-bodied partners who can enhance the sexual relationship by taking an active role in sex play.

Cerebral Palsy

Cerebral Palsy (CP) is caused by damage to the brain before or during birth or during early childhood and is manifested by mild to severe lack of muscular control. Involuntary muscle movements may disrupt speech, facial expressions, balance, and body movement. Involuntary, severe muscle contractions may cause limbs to jerk or assume awkward positions. A person's intelligence may or may not be affected. Unfortunately, it is often mistakenly assumed that people with CP are mentally handicapped because of their physical difficulty in communicating.

Genital sensation is unaffected by CP. Spasticity and deformity of arms and hands may make masturbation difficult or impossible without assistance, and the same problems in the hips and knees may make certain intercourse positions painful or difficult. Anxiety or sexual arousal may also stimulate an increase in involuntary muscle movements. (Shaul et al., 1978)

The sexual adjustment of a person with Cerebral Palsy is contingent, to a large degree, upon what is physically possible and the extent of environmental support for social contacts and privacy. People with CP and spinal cord injuries may require the help of someone who can assist in preparation and positioning for sexual relations.

The excellent film *Like Other People* shows the intimate relationship of a young couple, both of whom have CP. They live in an apartment within an English institution and take great pleasure in being as independent as possible. The camera catches their enjoyment in each other, cooking simple meals, spending an evening listening to music and typing poetry, helping each other bathe with care, tenderness, and playfulness, and cuddling in bed with a good night kiss.

Blindness and Deafness

The sensory losses of blindness and deafness can affect a person's sexuality in several ways. A woman with visual impairment comments:

When I am trying to meet a person for the first time, I do not have access to eye contact. For example, I can't flirt with my eyes . . . A new experience I had last year was being in a hot tub for the first time with three friends. I was really looking forward to this experience. I would have liked being able to see the other bodies, but I could not. I mentioned this to my boyfriend afterward. So the next time we did this, he described these people to me in graphic detail: "Her nipples point up; he's got a roll around his middle; he's got a large penis . . . it makes mine look like . . ." His descriptions really made the experience fun for me. (Straw, 1981, pp. 37–38)

A great deal of information and many attitudes and social interaction skills are acquired by seeing or hearing others, and visual or hearing deficits can impair this learning process. Deafness or blindness that occurs in adolescence or adulthood may cause depression, lowered self-esteem, and social withdrawal during the adjustment period. If the sensory losses are a result of disease, the disease itself may have deleterious effects on sexual functioning. In themselves, blindness and deafness do not appear to physically impair sexual interest or response.

Sex education for sight- or hearing-impaired children requires special methods. Children who are blind can especially benefit from the use of anatomical models that they can explore through touch. In Scandinavia, live models have been used to help educate blind children about sexual anatomy (Helsinga et al., 1974). Learning words and their meanings is an enormous challenge for a deaf person, and sex education materials must be geared for appropriate learning levels. One sex education program for deaf children found that the adolescents were experientially naive but very interested in sex (Sarlin and Altshuler, 1968).

Developmental Disabilities

Developmentally disabled people have below average intellectual functioning. A person with an IQ of below 70 is usually classified as developmentally disabled. Such people have, however, a broad range of learning capabilities that vary from one person to the next. The ability to meet age-appropriate standards of independence and responsibilities depends somewhat on intelligence, but with repetition and guidance many people with intellectual deficits can learn adaptive behaviors related to daily living and to sexuality.

Unfortunately, there are strong stereotypes that imply that developmentally disabled people are unable to learn and are either asexual or unable to control their sexual impulses. More often than not, developmentally disabled people have not had adequate learning opportunities because parents or health-care providers have attempted to deny or repress any sexual expression and have not provided adequate teaching of appropriate sexual behavior. The result is a lack of effective social-sexual skills.

Sex education is particularly important for both developmentally disabled people and their families. Sexual development of the developmentally disabled follows the typical patterns (initial involvement with masturbation followed by heterosexual and/or homosexual exploration), but with a lag in time compared with nondisabled children. A crucial point in sex education is that developmentally disabled people have a basic right to sexual expression. Thorough teaching of important areas of responsibility including self-care, menstrual hygiene, use of contraceptives, and appropriateness of time and place is essential. The idea that masturbation is normal needs to be taught to developmentally disabled people, their parents, and health-care professionals (Kolodny et al., 1979). Judgment in social situations is also a part of sex education.

In institutional settings where privacy is at a minimum, "appropriateness" in terms of privacy for sexual activities should be liberally defined. The bathroom, bedroom, or secluded outdoor places can be considered appropriate for masturbation or intimacy with others. The developmentally disabled share the usual human interest and desire for closeness, affection, and physical contact, and institutions need to be sensitive to this aspect of their residents' lives. (Johnson, 1971)

SUMMARY

CELIBACY

1. The choice not to engage in genital sexual interaction is defined as celibacy. Celibacy can be complete (no masturbation or interpersonal sexual contact) or partial (masturbation included).

MASTURBATION

2. Masturbation is self-stimulation of the genitals, intended to produce sexual pleasure.

3. Past attitudes toward masturbation have been highly condemnatory. However, the meaning and purposes of masturbation are currently being more positively re-evaluated.

4. Masturbation is an activity that is continuous throughout the life cycle, although its frequency varies with age and sex.

EROTIC FANTASY AND DREAMS

5. Erotic fantasies can serve to enhance sexual arousal; erotic dreams often accompany sexual arousal and orgasm during sleep.

SHARED TOUCHING

6. The entire body's surface is a sensory organ, and touch is a basic form of communication and shared intimacy.

7. Breast stimulation is arousing to most men and women, but some people find it unenjoyable.

8. Preferences as to the tempo, pressure, and location of manual genital stimulation vary from person to person. A lubricant, a nonirritating lotion, or saliva may enhance pleasure.

ORAL-GENITAL STIMULATION

9. Oral-genital contact has become more common in recent years. Concerns about oral-genital stimulation usually stem from ideas that it is immoral, unsanitary, or a homosexual act.

10. Cunnilingus is oral stimulation of the vulva and fellatio is oral stimulation of the male genitals.

ANAL STIMULATION

11. Anal stimulation is engaged in by couples for arousal, orgasm, and variety. Careful hygiene is advised to avoid introducing anal bacteria into the vagina.

COITUS AND COITAL POSITIONS

12. The diversity of coital positions offers potential variety during intercourse. The man above, woman above, side-by-side, and rear entry are common positions.

SEXUAL ADJUSTMENT AND DISABILITY

13. A disability may influence the ways in which a person expresses his or her sexuality, but does not alter the inherent sexual nature of the person.

14. Development of a positive body image can be an important component of sexuality for a physically disabled individual.

15. Institutional care does not generally allow for the sexual needs of disabled residents, although the situation is slowly improving.

SUGGESTED READINGS

Comfort, Alex. *The Joy of Sex: A Gourmet Guide to Love Making*. New York: Simon & Schuster, 1974. A well-illustrated adult "sex education" guide to erotic techniques, described in intimate detail with an emphasis on enhancing pleasure.

Friday, Nancy. *My Secret Garden*. New York: Simon & Schuster, 1973. A collection of women's sexual fantasies that reflects the diversity among women.

Friday, Nancy. *Men In Love*. New York: Delacorte, 1980. A collection of men's sexual fantasies and interpretations of their meaning.

Mooney, Thomas. *Sexual Options for Paraplegics and Quadraplegics*. Boston: Little, Brown, 1975. A nontechnical and explicit book written for spine-injured persons to help them deal with the impact of the injury on their sexuality.

Morin, Jack. *Anal Pleasure and Health*. Burlingame, Calif.: Down There, 1981. An excellent book for people who wish to know and understand more about arousal from anal stimulation.

10

Homosexuality

A CONTINUUM OF SEXUAL ORIENTATIONS
   Defining Bisexuality
SOCIETAL ATTITUDES
   Homophobia
"CAUSES" OF HOMOSEXUALITY
   Psychosocial Theories
   Biological Theories
LIFE STYLES
   Homosexual Relationships
   Sexual Expression
   "Coming Out"
GAY RIGHTS AND ANTIGAY RIGHTS
SUMMARY
SUGGESTED READINGS

Most people think of homosexuality as sexual contact between individuals of the same sex. However, this definition is not quite complete. It does not take into account two important dimensions—the context within which the sexual activity is experienced and the feelings and perceptions of the people involved. Nor does it encompass all of the meanings of the term *homosexual,* which can refer to (a) sexual behavior, (b) emotional affiliation, and (c) a definition of self. The following definition incorporates a broader spectrum of elements: A homosexual person is an individual "whose primary erotic, psychological, emotional, and social interest is in a member of the same sex, even though that interest may not be overtly expressed" (Martin and Lyon, 1972, p. 1).

A homosexual person's gender identity agrees with his or her biological sex. That is, a homosexual person perceives him- or herself as male or female, respectively, and feels attraction toward a same-sex person.

A word commonly used for homosexual is *gay.* Gay was initially used as a code word between homosexuals, and it has moved into popular usage to describe men, women, and social concerns related to homosexual orientation. Gay women are often referred to as lesbians. Pejorative words like faggot, fairy, homo, queer, lezzie, or dyke have traditionally been used to demean homosexuality. However, within certain gay subcultures, gay people use these terms with each other in a positive or humorous way.

A CONTINUUM OF SEXUAL ORIENTATIONS

Homosexuality, bisexuality, and heterosexuality are words that label *sexual orientation*—that is, to which of the sexes an individual is attracted. Thus, attraction to same-sex partners is a homosexual orientation, and attraction to other-sex partners is a heterosexual orientation. Bisexuality refers to attraction to both same- and other-sex partners. Since sexual orientation is only one aspect of an individual's life, this text will use these three terms as descriptive adjectives rather than as nouns that label one's total identity.

In our society, we tend to make clear-cut distinctions between homosexuality and heterosexuality. Actually, the delineation is not so precise. A relatively small percentage of people consider themselves to be exclusively homosexual; a greater number think of themselves as exclusively heterosexual. These groups represent the opposite ends of a broad spectrum. Between them exist varying degrees of preference and experience.

Figure 10.1 shows a seven-point continuum Kinsey devised in his analysis of sexual orientations in American society (1948). The scale ranges from 0 (exclusive contact and erotic attraction to the other sex) to 6 (exclusive contact and attraction to the same sex). Category 3 represents equal homosexual and heterosexual attraction and experience; in between are varying degrees of homosexual and heterosexual orientation.

How many people in our society fall into the homosexual category on the continuum? According to the Kinsey data, the exclusively homosexual category comprised 2% of women and 4% of men. Although this percentage of people who

FIGURE 10.1 CONTINUUM OF SEXUAL ORIENTATION

Adapted from Kinsey et al., 1948, p. 638.

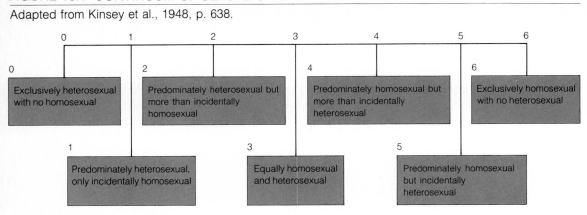

identified themselves as having had exclusively homosexual experiences appears small, slightly less than 3% of the 200-million population in the United States would be six million people. Some gay-rights advocates believe that the actual number of predominantly homosexual people is 10% of the population, or 20 million people. This higher estimate is based partly on the assumption that social pressures cause many homosexual people to conceal their orientation (a behavior that is commonly known as being "in the closet"). This can be done in a number of ways, including having heterosexual experiences. Social pressure for heterosexual conformity often results in homosexual individuals' dating, having sexual experiences with, and marrying partners of the other sex.

Between the extreme points on the continuum are many individuals who have experienced sexual contact with or been attracted to people of the same sex. Kinsey's estimate of this group's number was quite high: 37% of males and 13% of females in his research population reported having had overt homosexual experiences at some point in their lives, and even more had experienced erotic psychological responses to the same sex.

Kinsey's estimates were made some time ago, and they have come in for some criticism since then. It has been suggested that the study's sample techniques (for example, making interview contacts in gay bars) produced an inflated estimate of the number of homosexual people in our society. Hunt's more recent report (1974) revealed a somewhat lower incidence of homosexuality among his respondents, who were contacted by telephone. However, Hunt has criticized his own study for being somewhat underweighted with homosexual people. He has suggested adjusting his data upward and Kinsey's data downward to arrive at what may be more accurate figures. The revised estimates after this adjustment are that approximately 2% of men and 1% of women are exclusively homosexual; about 75% of men and 85% of women are exclusively heterosexual; and roughly 23% of men and 14% of women have both types of experience.

In interpreting the continuum shown in Figure 10.1 we want to caution against too broad a use of the term *bisexual*. There is a tendency to use behavior as the only criterion for sexual orientation and to use *bisexual* as a catch-all to describe the considerable number of people who fall between exclusive heterosexuality or homosexuality. This grouping fails to take into account the context within which the sexual experiences occur and the feelings and thoughts of the individuals involved. It is the context, not the contact, that may be most significant. Bisexuality can be considered as a behavior or as an identity, and the two are not always the same. As one bisexual woman states:

My dreams and fantasies could remain bisexual; I could continue to be sometimes equally attracted to the male and female star at the movies; still, the world would define me, not by my own sexuality, but by my lover's gender. (Orlando 1978, p. 60)

If bisexuality is defined as an erotic attraction toward both men and women, many situations where bisexual behavior is exhibited would not be considered to represent bisexuality. For example, there are a number of homosexual people who maintain a facade of heterosexuality by marrying, but who continue to have brief, clandestine homosexual contacts. These individuals have sexual contact with both sexes, but their feelings are homosexual. In a similar sense, some prostitutes or male hustlers may do business with either sex and yet be involved in only heterosexual or homosexual relationships in their personal lives. Other individuals may engage in bisexual behavior exclusively in group-sex situations but never in one-to-one relationships.

There are situations, too, where partners of the preferred sex are unavailable, and this may result in other kinds of sexual contacts. Transitory homosexual behavior occurs in same-sex boarding schools and in prisons, yet the individuals resume heterosexual relationships when the opportunity is once again available. Finally, some people may experience attractions to both sexes but have never had sexual encounters with both sexes. These individuals may define themselves as bisexuals, even though they have had contact with only one sex. In all, bisexual behavior does not always mean that a person is truly bisexual.

Sexual orientation is often viewed as an either-or situation. Self-identified bisexual individuals are often pressured by heterosexual or homosexual people to make up their minds. However, there appears to be an increasing openness to bisexual life styles and identity.

SOCIETAL ATTITUDES

Cross-cultural attitudes towards homosexuality have varied considerably, as described in more detail in Chapters 1 and 22. A number of research studies of other cultures have revealed widespread acceptance of homosexuality. One survey of 190 societies found that two-thirds of them considered homosexuality socially acceptable for certain individuals or on specific occasions (Ford and Beach, 1951). Homosexuality has been widely accepted in many earlier cultures. For example, over half of 225 Native American tribes accepted male homosexuality, and 17% accepted female homosexuality (Pomeroy, 1965). With the exception of ceremonial heterosexual contacts, homosexuality was the primary form of sexual expression among a group of eastern Peruvian native males (Schneebaum, 1975). In ancient Greece, homosexual relationships between men were believed to be a superior intellectual and spiritual expression of love, whereas heterosexuality provided the more pragmatic benefits of children and a family unit.

In our own Judeo-Christian tradition, homosexuality has been viewed far more negatively. Many religious scholars believe that the condemnation of homosexuality stems from a reformation movement beginning in the seventh century B.C., through which Jewish religious leaders wanted to develop a distinct, closed community that was different from others of the time. Homosexual activities were a part of the religious services of many groups of people, including the Jewish people, in that era. Rejecting religious rituals involving homosexual activities that had been previously considered sacred was one way of establishing the uniqueness of a religion. Homosexual behaviors were then condemned as a form of idolatry, or pagan worship (Kosnik et al., 1977). Strong prohibitive biblical scriptures were written. For example, "You shall not lie with a man as one lies with a female, it is an abomination" (Leviticus 18:22).

In the Judeo-Christian tradition, the purpose of sexual interaction is procreation, not pleasure. Nonprocreative sexual behavior, whether practiced by homosexual or heterosexual individuals, was viewed as immoral within this philosophical framework:

St. Thomas [Aquinas] treats of homosexual acts in connection with the sins against temperance, specifically lust . . . His judgment is predicated on the Stoic assumption that any pursuit of sexual pleasure outside of the purpose of all sexual acts, namely procreation, offends against nature and reason. (Kosnik et al., 1977, p. 198)

A prominent modern historian (Boswell, 1980) states that there has been more widespread and vehement intolerance toward gay people during the first half of the twentieth century than at any other time in Western history. He also maintains that religious belief was not the cause of intolerance, but that biblical strictures have been employed selectively in Christian countries to justify personal and popular prejudice.

The religious mandates of morality often become translated into law. In the United States today it is not illegal to be a homosexual person, but sexual acts other than heterosexual coitus are still illegal in many states. The illegal status of homosexual acts and the social stigma attached to homosexuality often make the homosexual person wary of law enforcement personnel or agencies. If a homosexual person is a victim of an assault, homicide, robbery, or other crime related to his or her sexual orientation, the incident may be concealed out of fear of legal reprisal or indifferent prosecution. In the past few years some states have begun to replace these antiquated laws with statutes that legalize all private sexual behaviors between consenting adults.

In recent years there has been a shift in attitudes toward homosexuality. The belief that homosexuality is immoral has been replaced to some degree by a belief that individuals with same-sex orientation are mentally ill. The notion that homosexuality is a sickness is still common. In a survey conducted in the 1970s, the majority of respondents believed that homosexual people were sexually abnormal, perverted, and/or mentally ill (Weinberg and Williams, 1976).

The medical and psychological professions have used drastic treatments in attempting to cure the "illness" of homosexuality. Surgical procedures such as castration were performed in the 1800s. Lobotomy (brain surgery that severs nerve fibers in the frontal lobe of the brain) was performed as late as 1951. Psychotherapy, drugs, hormones, hypnosis, shock treatments, and aversion therapy (pairing nausea-inducing drugs or electric shock with homosexual stimuli) have been used (Katz, 1976).

Actually, much of current research contradicts the notion that homosexual people are mentally ill; the first major research to compare the adjustment of nonpatient heterosexual and homosexual individuals found no significant differences between the two groups (Hooker, 1967). Further research has supported these findings. Bell and Weinberg summarize that ". . . homosexual adults who have come to terms with their homosexuality, who do not regret their sexual orientation and who can function effectively sexually and socially, are no more distressed psychologically than are heterosexual men and women" (1978, p. 216).

Attitudes toward homosexuality continue to change. For example, about 50% of Hunt's respondents thought that homosexual acts between consenting adults should be legal (1974). Many churches have endorsed gay rights legislation. Also, in 1973 the American Psychiatric Association, after great internal conflict, removed homosexuality per se from the category of a mental disorder. In 1975 the American Psychological Association urged ". . . all mental health professionals to take the lead in removing the stigma of mental illness that has long been associated with a homosexual orientation" (American Psychological Association press release, January 24, 1975).

Homophobia

Some of society's negative attitudes stem from what Weinberg (1973) labels *homophobia*. Homophobia is defined as irrational fears of homosexuality in others, the fear of homosexual feelings within oneself, or self-loathing because of one's homosexuality. It stems from ignorance and popular myths that give rise to homosexual prejudice. Box 10.1 illustrates one scale that has been used to measure homophobic tendencies. Perhaps you may want to use this scale to examine your own attitudes.

The recent recognition and discussion of homophobia represents a significant shift in the view of homosexuality. Traditionally, homosexuality has been examined in order to look for the causes and expression of this "difficulty." An exploration of homophobia implies that homophobic attitudes are the problem, rather than the sexual orientation itself. However, fear of homosexuality still characterizes the majority, and it is not typically classified as a problem (Weinberg, 1973).

Homophobia can be exhibited in many ways, both subtle (even unconscious) and pronounced. Telling "queer" jokes and belittling homosexuality expresses an element of hostility that is often part of the homophobic attitude. This hostility can be overt, and people who are suspected of being homosexual are sometimes subjected to verbal or physical assault:

BOX 10.1 THE HOMOPHOBIC SCALE

A researcher has developed the following scale to identify homophobia. Respondents answer yes in agreement or no in disagreement to the following statements:

1. Homosexuals should be locked up to protect society.
2. It would be upsetting for me to find out I was alone with a homosexual.
3. Homosexuals should be allowed to hold government positions.
4. I would not want to be a member of an organization which had any homosexuals in its membership.
5. I find the thought of homosexual acts disgusting.
6. If laws against homosexuality were eliminated, the proportion of homosexuals in the population would probably remain the same.
7. A homosexual could be a good President of the United States.
8. I would be afraid for a child of mine to have a teacher who was homosexual.
9. If a homosexual sat next to me on a bus, I would get nervous.

The key for interpreting responses appears in the Summary at the end of this chapter. (Smith 1973, pp. 129–30)

The group I ran around with in high school used to drive downtown to where the gay bars were, pick up a swishy-looking one, beat him up, and dump him back on the street. (Authors' files)

Many psychologists believe that such aggression toward homosexuality is an attempt to deny or suppress homosexual feelings in oneself.

Another expression of homophobia may be the careful avoidance of any behavior that might be interpreted as homosexual. In this sense, homophobia can restrict the lives of heterosexual people. For example, manual-genital or oral-genital contact with an opposite-sex partner might be avoided if a person believes that these activities are inherently homosexual. During lovemaking, sexual receptivity in men and vigorous assertiveness in women may be viewed as threatening if these behaviors are believed to demonstrate homosexual tendencies. Same-sex friends or family members may refrain from spontaneous embraces; wearing "unfeminine" or "un-masculine" clothing may be shunned; or a woman may decide not to march in a women's movement demonstration because she fears being called a lesbian.

Any gender role reversal can be perceived as threatening. According to some research (MacDonald and Games, 1974), homophobia may be related to rigid gender role stereotypes. This study found a correlation between attitudes about gender roles and attitudes toward homosexuality, with respondents who supported rigid gender role stereotypes having more negative feelings about homosexuality than other respondents. Bell, Weinberg, and Hammersmith (1981) discuss the idea that homo-sexuality confronts people with their ability to tolerate diversity in gender roles:

In a society such as ours a special loathing is reserved for any male who appears to have forfeited the privileges and responsibilities associated with upholding the conventional imagery of males. The spectre of a group of males living outside the strict confines of "masculinity" can appear as a threat to men who are not entirely certain about their own maleness and thus heighten whatever antagonisms are expressed toward those who do not follow male "rules." Similarly, to the degree that lesbianism is associated with the rejection of traditionally "feminine" roles and responsibilities, heterosexual women may feel threatened by those who do not join their ranks. (p. 221)

Homophobic attitudes can change over time, with experience or deliberate thought. One of our students describes this process:

My own reaction to learning that one of my fraternity brothers was gay was discomfort. I increasingly avoided him. I am sorry now that I didn't confront myself as to why I felt that way at that time. I had an opportunity to explore a part of myself with another person whom I cared about. I was homophobic. And because I didn't deal with that then, the process of resolving it psychologically took a long time for me. It also kept me from developing a closeness with my other men friends, which I regret since many of them are now gone. I lost something in those relationships simply because I was afraid that by being physically and emotionally close to another man meant that I, too, was homosexual.

As with everybody, ideas and concepts change. I gradually became aware of myself and comfortable with my own heterosexuality. I finally began to explore why I felt so uncomfortable touching or being touched by another man. Not consciously, perhaps, I began exploring the idea of touching with others who I was comfortable with. And it worked.

Today I think nothing of hugging or otherwise showing a person, male or female, that I care about them. I can do it without threatening their sexuality or worrying about my own. I am no longer threatened or frightened by physical closeness from another man, even if I know his preference is other men. I am secure enough to deal with that honestly. (Authors' files)

"CAUSES" OF HOMOSEXUALITY

What determines sexual orientation? A variety of theories have attempted to explain the origins of homosexuality. Considerable research has been done over the years, but there are still no definitive scientific answers. In the next few pages, we will look at common notions about the causes of homosexuality and evaluate some of the research that has attempted to substantiate these theories.

Bell, Weinberg, and Hammersmith (1981) have done the most comprehensive study to date about the development of sexual orientation. They used a sample of 979 homosexual people matched to a control group of 477 heterosexual people. All research subjects were asked questions about their childhood, adolescence, and sexual practices during four-hour face-to-face interviews. The researchers then used sophisticated statistical techniques to analyze causal factors in the development of homosexuality or heterosexuality. This research will be cited frequently throughout this section because of its excellent methodology.

Psychosocial Theories

Some of the theories about the development of a homosexual orientation relate to life incidences, parenting patterns, or psychological attributes of the individual. Unhappy heterosexual experiences or the inability to attract partners of the other sex are sometimes believed to cause a person to become homosexual. The statements, "All a lesbian needs is a good lay" or "He just needs to meet the right woman" reflect this type of idea. These kinds of beliefs may attach particularly to lesbian behavior because of the societal tendency to define female sexuality in relation to the male. It is often assumed that lesbianism is due to resentment, dislike, fear, or distrust of men rather than attraction toward women. The absence of logic in this argument is clear if we turn the argument around to say that female heterosexuality is caused by a dislike and fear of women. Actually, research indicates that up to 70% of lesbians have had sexual experiences with men, and many report having enjoyed them. However, they prefer to be sexual with women (Klaich, 1974; Martin and Lyon, 1972). Furthermore, Bell and his colleagues' analysis of their data indicates that "homosexual orientation among females reflects neither a lack of heterosexual experience nor a history of particularly unpleasant heterosexual experiences" (1981, p. 176).

Their data also found that the homosexual and heterosexual groups did not differ in the frequency of dating during high school. This refutes the belief that lack of heterosexual opportunity causes homosexuality. The male and female homosexual groups did tend, however, to feel differently about dating than the heterosexual groups; fewer homosexual subjects reported that they enjoyed dating. Their feelings likely indicated less interest in heterosexuality. For example, although the homosexual males dated as much as the heterosexual males in the study, they tended to have fewer sexual encounters with females and to have engaged in fewer types of heterosexual activities such as manual stimulation of genitals, oral-genital sex, or intercourse. The data suggest "that unless heterosexual encounters appeal to one's deepest sexual feeling, there is likely to be little about them that one would experience as positive reinforcement for sexual relationships with members of the opposite sex" (p. 108).

Another myth that is shown to be false by the Bell et al. study is that young men and women become homosexual because they have been "seduced" by older homosexuals. Their data indicate that most homosexual males and females had their first homosexual encounter with someone, usually a friend or acquaintance, about the same age as themselves. In fact, homosexual individuals were less likely than heterosexual individuals to have initial sexual encounters with a stranger or an adult.

Some people may believe that homosexuality can be "caught" from someone else. People seem especially concerned about the influence of homosexual teachers; they are fearful that exposure to a homosexual teacher, especially a well-liked and respected teacher, will cause students to model after him or her and become homosexual. However, a homosexual orientation appears to be established even before school age, and modeling is not a relevant factor (Marmor, 1980).

Another prevalent theory concerning the "cause" of homosexuality has to do with certain patterns in a person's family background. Speculation about environmental causes of homosexuality can be found in the literature of psychoanalysis. Psychoanalytic theory implicated both childhood experiences and relationships with parents. Freud (1905) maintained that the relationship with one's father and mother was a crucial factor in the development of homosexuality. He believed that men and women were innately bisexual, but with "normal" developmental experiences, passed through a "homoerotic" phase in the process of establishing a heterosexual orientation. However, he thought that people could become "fixated" at the homosexual phase if certain kinds of life experiences occurred, especially if a male had a poor relationship with his father and an overly close relationship with his mother. Later clinical research attempted to confirm these hypotheses. A study by Irving Bieber (1962), for instance, compared homosexual and heterosexual men who were undergoing psychoanalysis. Bieber's data indicated that certain patterns were frequently found in the family backgrounds of homosexual clients—most typically, a dominant and overprotective mother and a passive and detached father.

Another study gave some support to Bieber's finding. It compared homosexual and heterosexual men who had lost one or both parents before the age of 15. More of the homosexual group reported that their mothers had been overcontrolling or that their fathers had been emotionally distant toward them (Saghir and Robins, 1973).

The belief that certain childhood factors are the critical determinants in the development of a homosexual orientation has not been clearly established. For example, many homosexual people do not have a family background of a dominant mother and emotionally detached father, just as many heterosexual people have been reared in families where such patterns prevailed. Bell and his colleagues (1981) reported some interesting findings on the role of family patterns in the development of sexual orientation. Although there was some evidence that male homosexuality was related to poor father-son relationships, they state that the traditional psychoanalytic model of the impact of parents is exaggerated. On the basis of their findings, no particular phenomenon of family life can be singled out as "especially consequential for either homosexual or heterosexual development" (p. 190). These researchers also stress the variations in patterns of homosexual development.

Implicit in many psychosocial explanations of homosexuality is the assumption that homosexuality is a less permanent condition than heterosexuality and that it may "right itself" under favorable circumstances. This view was examined in a study that compared attitudinal differences about sexuality between white, middle-class homosexual and heterosexual males (Lumby, 1976). While the heterosexual group was confident that they would not change their sexual orientation, they were less certain that homosexuality was as stable a characteristic. In the researcher's words, "This difference may reflect the common heterosexual optimism that it is still possible to 'convert the sexual deviate'" (p. 46). The use of different types of therapy to try to change homosexual orientation also indicates the belief of professionals that sexual orientation can be altered.

Some therapists provide therapeutic intervention for homosexual and bisexual people who are highly distressed by their orientation and want to develop a heterosexual preference. Masters and Johnson have done some preliminary work in this area, described in their recent publication, *Homosexuality in Perspective* (1979). However, Masters and Johnson have come under heavy criticism for their claim of converting "homosexuals" to heterosexual functioning and for their research reporting and methodology (Barlow et al., 1980; Zilbergeld and Evans, 1980; Bell et al., 1981). For example, many of the subjects may have been incorrectly labeled as homosexual individuals when they were, in fact, bisexual or heterosexual people who had turned to homosexual behavior due to sexual problems in heterosexual relationships. Most therapists agree that exclusive homosexuality is extremely difficult, if not impossible, to change to functional and satisfactory heterosexuality. It is usually much easier to successfully treat sexual problems than to change a person's sexual orientation.

Due partly to recent research—and due also to the removal of homosexuality from the category of mental illness by the American Psychiatric and Psychological Associations—many therapists and counselors have changed the focus of therapy. Rather than making the assumption that the homosexual client's sexual orientation must be "cured," therapists have made it an objective of treatment with homosexual patients to assist them to love, live, and work in a society that harbors considerable hostility toward them (Milligan, 1975). This change in therapeutic practice is significant, in that it defines the problem as society's negativity toward homosexuality, rather than homosexuality itself.

Biological Theories

Researchers have looked into a number of areas in an effort to establish physiological reasons why some people are homosexual and others are not. One biological theory centers on the possibility of a genetic factor. Is there something in a person's genetic inheritance that influences or determines homosexuality? One study (Kallman, 1952a and 1952b) tried to answer this question by comparing sexual orientations in both fraternal and identical sets of twins. In all cases, the twins had been reared together, so they had minimal differences in prenatal and postnatal environments. The primary difference between the two groups lay in the genetic inheritance, which was identical in one group but not in the other. Kallman reported a 100% *concordance* (the percentage frequency of both twins showing the trait) for homosexuality in the identical twins group. In marked contrast, the sets of fraternal twins manifested a concordance rate of only 12%.

Kallman's findings are intriguing, but they have been criticized because of the sources of his twin sets. (He had to rely on correctional, psychiatric, and charitable organizations for many of his subjects.) Also, since the time of his study, other research has failed to duplicate his conclusions (Heston and Shields, 1968). There is no convincing evidence to date that hereditary factors directly determine sexual orientation as heterosexual, bisexual, or homosexual (Money, 1981).

Other researchers have studied hormonal imbalances, both before birth and during adulthood, to see if they might be a cause of homosexuality. Some writers speculate that prenatal hormone imbalances can alter the masculine and feminine development of the fetal brain and that this may contribute to a homosexual orientation (Murphy and Fain, 1978). They base their speculations primarily on other research into the effects of prenatal androgen deficiency in animals (Dörner, 1976; Money and Ehrhardt, 1972). This research demonstrates that female mating behavior can be produced in male animals as a consequence of experimentally induced androgen deficiency during prenatal development. The researchers speculate that there is a critical period in which the fetus is particularly sensitive to levels of sex hormones and hypothesize that a prenatal androgen deficiency in human males could contribute to homosexuality. However, it is highly questionable to draw conclusions about humans from animal studies. The relevance of these data for sexual orientation in humans—a much more complex phenomenon than mating behavior in animals— is as yet unknown. Dörner and his associates (1975) also did some research with humans that uncovered differences in the ways homosexual and heterosexual males' hormones respond to injections of estrogen. They believe that this work supports the theory of prenatal hormonal influences.

Although Bell and his co-workers (1981) did not do any hormonal studies, they believe that their research also suggests biological causes, especially for Kinsey category 6 homosexuality. They write that, in general, homosexuality "is a pattern of feelings and reactions within the child that cannot be traced back to a single social or psychological root" (p. 192) and that "a boy or girl is predisposed to be homosexual or heterosexual, and during childhood and adolescence this basic sexual orientation begins to become evident" (p. 187).

These researchers believe that evidence for a biological predisposition for homosexuality is the strong link between adult homosexuality and *gender non-conformity* as a child. Gender nonconformity is a variable the researchers used that measured the extent to which the research subjects conformed to stereotypic notions of masculinity or femininity during childhood. Respondents were asked their own perceptions of how masculine or feminine they were as children and how much they enjoyed conventional boys' or girls' activities (see Box 10.2 for examples of responses). Both male and female homosexuals were more likely to experience far-ranging and deep-seated gender nonconformity than were heterosexuals; one-half of homosexual males and one-fourth of heterosexual males did not conform to a typical "masculine" identity pattern, and about four-fifths of homosexual females and two-thirds of heterosexual females were not highly "feminine" during childhood. Gender nonconformity in homosexual persons also occurs in societies other than the United States. A comparative study of males in the United States, Guatemala, and Brazil indicated that gender nonconformity related to childhood toy and activity interests and sexual interest in other boys were behavioral indicators of adult homosexual orientation (Whitam, 1980). Bell and his colleagues speculate that "if there is a biological basis for homosexuality, it probably accounts for gender nonconformity as well as for sexual orientation" (p. 217).

Other researchers have speculated that hormone levels in adults may contribute to homosexuality. Some have compared hormone levels in adult homosexual men and women with those in heterosexual adults. Here, too, the data have been contradictory (Meyer-Bahlburg, 1977; Tourney, 1980). Some studies report that

BOX 10.2 EXAMPLES OF CHILDHOOD GENDER NONCONFORMITY REPORTED BY HOMOSEXUAL ADULTS

In What Ways Do You Think You Were Different From Other Boys Your Age?

"I wanted no involvement in sports where you have to prove your strength. I hated physical education and sports."

"I remember writing a good composition and having the guys put it down. They said it was like a girl's, so I suppressed my writing and creative talents."

"I wasn't as aggressive as other boys, not as active as they were, not rambunctious and boisterous."

"I just didn't feel I was like other boys. I was very fond of pretty things like ribbons and flowers and music."

"I was more emotional. I was too 'goody-goody' to be one of the boys."

In What Ways Do You Think You Were Different From Other Girls Your Age?

"I played outdoors more. I was much more of a tomboy. For example, I disturbed the Brownie meeting by bringing along some of my boyfriends."

"I didn't like girls' things such as sewing parties or paper dolls."

"To me, girls' activities were nonsense."

"I still liked to wear pants."

"Girls my age were so feminine and pretty, and I was so horsey. I wanted to be feminine but hated frills."

"I didn't express myself the way other girls would. For example, I never showed my feelings. I wasn't emotional."

(Bell et al., 1981)

---

homosexual males have less androgen than heterosexual males; others indicate just the opposite; and still others reveal no difference. There have been only a few studies exploring hormone levels in lesbians and, just as in male homosexual studies, the results have been inconsistent (Gaitwell et al., 1977; Griffiths et al., 1974; Loraine et al., 1971). One researcher suggests that future research needs to control for the many variables operating in this experimental area (Tourney, 1980). These include establishing adequate criteria for selection of subjects, the use of control subjects matched for age, sex, education, and other factors, and compiling thorough sexual histories of those being studied. More comprehensive studies may clarify some of the conflicting reports of the relationship of hormones in adults to homosexuality.

However, even if a consistent pattern of hormonal differences were found in adult homosexuals versus heterosexuals, it would remain unknown if the differences were a cause or a result of sexual orientation. Testosterone levels are sensitive to a number of variables, including general health, diet, drug use, marijuana use, cigarette smoking, sexual activity, and physical and emotional stress (Marmor, 1980). Many of these variables can be controlled for in careful research. However, it is important to note that the stress and anxiety many homosexual individuals experience as a result of societal oppression may itself have an impact on hormone levels.

The question of biological causation of homosexuality raises some important issues. On one hand, if homosexuality were found to be biologically based, the assumption that homosexuality is "unnatural" would be challenged, because something biologically innate is natural for that person. Parents who have blamed themselves or have been blamed by others for causing what they view as an aberration could be relieved of their guilt. Society's expectations for gender role behaviors might become more flexible given the acceptance of biologically based gender nonconformity. From the opposite perspective, if homosexuality were shown to be biologically caused and homosexuals were labeled as biologically "defective," attempts to use biology to "prevent" homosexuality might be implemented through such procedures as fetal monitoring and medical intervention related to prenatal hormone levels (Bell et al., 1981). In the past, although the data were inconsistent regarding hormone imbalance and homosexuality, medical interventions such as hormone therapy (consisting of androgen supplements) were used during the 1930s and 1940s to attempt to cure male homosexuality. Such efforts, while they sometimes increased sexual interest, did not result in significant changes in sexual orientation (Money and Ehrhardt, 1972). It appears that scientific knowledge does not necessarily resolve the issue of societal acceptance of homosexuality.

In conclusion, more research is beginning to suggest that there is a biological predisposition to exclusive homosexuality (Kinsey 6). However, the causes of sexual orientation in general, and homosexuality specifically, remain speculative at this point. It appears to be more appropriate to think of the continuum of sexual orientation as influenced by a variety of psychosocial and biological factors that may be unique for each person, rather than thinking in terms of a single causative factor for sexual orientation.

LIFE STYLES

As we have discussed in the preceding section, people whose sexual orientation is homosexual cannot clearly be distinguished from heterosexual people by hormonal balance or mental health. This leads to another observation: that homosexual life styles are as varied as heterosexual life styles. All social classes, occupations, races, religions, and political persuasions are represented. The only elements homosexual people necessarily have in common are their desire for emotional and sexual fulfillment with someone of the same sex and their shared experience of oppression from a hostile social environment.

Despite this variety of life styles, stereotypes exist. Many of these concern the physical appearance of homosexual individuals. It is true that there are some homosexual people who dress and act according to commonly held stereotypes. Characteristics often associated with an identifiable homosexual man include exaggerated "feminine" gestures, tight and flashy clothing, and earrings; in contrast, the image of a stereotypically recognizable lesbian consists of such attributes as short hair and highly "masculine" clothing and gestures. Although the incidence of people who fit the stereotypes is small, the stereotypes persist. This is in part because people who believe that homosexual individuals look a certain way notice and categorize (sometimes erroneously) those who seem to fit the image. The fact that many homosexual people may not fit the stereotype at all often goes unnoticed.

A criticism sometimes leveled against homosexual individuals who are open about their orientation is that they are flaunting their sexuality. A gay man dressed in tight pants, walking with a sensuous wiggle, carrying a shoulder bag, and wearing earrings may be regarded as exhibitionistic or a public menace. In many places, he may also be subject to physical assault. It is interesting to note that a heterosexual woman can usually dress and move in such a manner without being accused of flaunting her sexuality. As one writer stated, "Gay people whose mannerisms are stereotyped are implicitly rejecting the ascription of gender roles and asserting their right to be feminine or masculine irrespective of their genitals. Their 'crime' is simply that they reject heterosexual stereotypes" (Milligan, 1975, p. 100).

Beyond the way a person (homosexual or heterosexual) dresses, there are a number of far more basic elements of a homosexual life style. We will look briefly at some of these in the next few pages.

Homosexual Relationships

It is sometimes mistakenly thought that homosexual couples always enact the stereo-typical active "male" or passive "female" roles. This notion stems in part from the pervasive heterosexual model of relationships. Because this model of male-female role playing has historically been the predominant one in our culture, both het-erosexual and homosexual intimate relationships have typically been patterned after it. However, options for more egalitarian relationships have increased in recent years, and these are being followed by both heterosexual and homosexual couples. In this regard, a homosexual relationship may well be the more flexible in our society. Some adults state that they have made a conscious decision to follow their homosexual rather than heterosexual feelings, partly because of their belief that more equal relationships are possible between same-sex than other-sex partners.

One research study (Peplau, 1981) that compared characteristics of homosexual and heterosexual relationships found major differences in gender roles. The study reported that heterosexual couples were likely to adhere more closely to traditional gender role expectations than were homosexual couples. Most of the homosexual relationships studied resembled "best friendships" combined with romantic and erotic attraction. The researcher suggests that studies of homosexual couples can provide insights and models for heterosexual couples who are trying to establish more egalitarian relationships.

There are some differences between homosexual men and women in their number of sexual partners. Lesbian women are likely to have had fewer than 10 sexual partners. Homosexual men are more often involved in casual sexual en-counters with sometimes hundreds of partners (Bell and Weinberg, 1978; Kinsey, 1948). These encounters are sometimes exceedingly brief, occurring in public restrooms or in film booths in pornography shops. This difference may reflect traditional gender role definitions. Males learn initially to be interested in sex; females learn initially to be interested in love.

These differences in numbers of sexual partners of homosexual men and women has been also attributed to the greater tendency of males in general to separate sex from affection, to estimate their personal worth on the basis of how much sex they have, and to view fidelity as an undesirable restriction upon their freedom and independence. (Bell and Weinberg, 1978, p. 101)

In one study (Peplau, 1981) homosexual women differed from homosexual men in the extent to which they associated love with sex. Most of the lesbians waited to have sex with a partner until they had developed emotional intimacy. Although 46% of gay men had become friends with their partner before having sex, they were more likely than lesbians to have had sexual experiences with casual acquaintances or men whom they had just met. Gay men were also much more likely to have sexual experiences with others than their primary partner than were lesbians or heterosexual women and men. What explains the less sexual exclusiveness among gay men? Peplau suggests that the gender role socialization of males places more emphasis and gives more permission for casual sex for males than for females. Heterosexual relationships are, to some extent, a compromise between the male and female gender role expectations. However, with gay relationships, this particular compromise is not typically as necessary, and casual sex outside of an intimate relationship can more easily occur.

However, sexual involvement with many partners is not universal among homosexual men. Many men feel no urge for such multiple relationships, and others have decided that they do not adequately meet their needs. Some men want to have a strong emotional relationship before becoming sexually involved. And for some men, being involved in an ongoing relationship eliminates sexual interest in other men (Tripp, 1975). In some cases the growing desire of homosexual men to modify the definition of masculinity has encouraged them to develop committed, multi-dimensional relationships rather than pursuing casual sexual encounters.

Although marriage between two people of the same sex is not legally recognized by any state, many homosexual couples share significant one-to-one relationships. Half of the lesbians and one-quarter of the homosexual men in Bell and Weinberg's study were in primary relationships. Lesbian pairs are more likely than male homosexual couples to share a household, perhaps due in part to less suspicion aroused by such a living arrangement. The great majority of homosexual couples who live together do not divide tasks according to sex role expectations (Bell and Weinberg, 1978). The Metropolitan Community Church, which primarily serves gay people, performs holy unions (this term is used because marriage is a legal contract) that provide the spiritual significance of marriage for homosexual couples.

Bell and Weinberg's 1978 research concluded that homosexual relationships and life styles could be classified into five basic categories which reflect the many variations in homosexuality. Seventy-one percent of the homosexual people fit into these five groups; the remaining 29% were too diverse to be easily grouped.

306

A holy union performed by the Metropolitan Community Church in Honolulu, Hawaii.

1. *Close-coupled:* People in this group had a close bond within a relationship. They were less likely to seek partners outside the relationship and tended to look to each other for sexual and interpersonal satisfaction. They reported having gratifying sexual lives and had the smallest amount of sexual problems of any group. They were unlikely to regret being homosexual and had rarely experienced difficulties in their jobs or outside lives because of being homosexual. The close-coupled men and women were the happiest and least lonely of any group. Using a heterosexual framework, one might call them "happily married." About 28% of lesbians and 10% of gay males were close-coupled.

2. *Open-coupled:* Open-coupled individuals were living with a primary partner and also sought and engaged in numerous extrarelationship sexual experiences. Open-coupled individuals reported broad sexual repertoires, but the men had concerns about getting their partners to meet their sexual requests, and the women worried about their partners wanting to do unwelcome sexual activities. This life style also appeared to be more difficult and less satisfying for females than for males who engaged in it. About 17% of lesbians and 18% of gay men were open-coupled.

3. *Functionals:* People in this group were "single" and reported more sexual activity with a greater number of partners than did any other group. They reported being more interested in sex than other groups and had few, if any, sexual problems. They also appeared uninterested in establishing a committed relationship. These individuals were highly involved in the gay world and were the least likely to regret being homosexual. They were also likely to have had contact with the legal system for

a "homosexual" offense. Approximately 10% of lesbians and 15% of gay men fit into this category.

4. *Dysfunctionals:* Individuals in this group were regretful about their homosexuality and reported more sexual problems than any other group. Their overall psychological adjustment was poor, and they encountered many difficulties and dissatisfactions in daily living. About 5% of lesbians and 12% of male homosexuals fit into this group.

5. *Asexuals:* People in this group tended not to be involved with others. They reported less interest in sex, fewer sex partners, and more narrow sexual repertoires than other groups. They typically spent leisure time alone and described themselves as lonely, but were not interested in becoming involved with others. About 11% of lesbians and 16% of male homosexuals were in this category.

Other research (Peplau, 1981) has examined characteristics of homosexual love relationships. This study found many similarities between homosexual and heterosexual relationships and reported that most differences in relationships have more to do with whether the partners are men or women, rather than homosexual or heterosexual. Matched samples (overrepresented by young, well-educated, middle-class whites) of homosexual females and males and heterosexual females and males all indicated that "being able to talk about my most intimate feelings" with a partner was most important in a love relationship. Using Rubin's love scale (discussed in Chapter 7), Peplau found no differences in the depth of love and liking experienced by homosexual or heterosexual individuals in the study. The research also found that partners in a love relationship, regardless of sexual orientation, must deal with and attempt to reconcile desires for togetherness and independence. For many individuals, these desires were not mutually exclusive; some people wanted both a secure love relationship and meaningful activities and friendships separate from the relationship.

Responses from homosexual and heterosexual women were different in some ways than those from homosexual and heterosexual men. Women placed greater importance on emotional expressiveness within a relationship than did men. Women also gave higher ratings to the importance of having an egalitarian relationship and having similar attitudes and political beliefs.

Sexual Expression

Homosexual individuals who are in sexual relationships engage in sexual behaviors similar to those of heterosexual persons, with the exception of penile-vaginal intercourse. Touching, kissing, manual-genital stimulation, oral-genital contact, and anal stimulation are techniques that are used during sexual interactions. Younger homosexual people are typically more likely to have experienced a greater variety of sexual behaviors than older people (Bell and Weinberg, 1978), as is the case with the heterosexual population.

Sexual Behaviors among Women Several misconceptions exist regarding lesbian sexual expression. One is the notion that sex between women is unsatisfactory. For example, one sex book states, "One vagina plus one vagina equals zero" (Reuben, 1969, p. 269). This implies that sexual relating between women is

unsatisfactory because a penis is lacking. However, in terms of orgasm from sexual encounters, Kinsey's 1953 study indicated that lesbian women had orgasms in a greater percentage of sexual encounters than did heterosexual married women. After five years of marriage, 55% of heterosexual women had orgasms in 60–100% of sexual contacts. After five years of homosexual experience, 78% of homosexual women had orgasms in 60–100% of their sexual encounters. Kinsey has suggested these results may be due to better understanding of sexual and psychological response between members of the same sex than between those of the opposite sex. Hite (1976) states that greater sexual satisfaction between women may occur because "lesbian sexual relations tend to be longer and involve more all-over body sensuality" (p. 413).

Another mistaken belief is that dildoes (penis-shaped devices) are used extensively among lesbians. However, only 2% of the homosexual women in Hunt's 1974 survey had ever used a dildo. Manual stimulation, oral contact, and rubbing genitals together or against the partner's body are included in lesbian sexual behaviors (Hite, 1976; Hunt, 1974; Kinsey, 1953).

It may be more difficult for lesbians to initiate a sexual relationship than for either heterosexual or male homosexual persons. One explanation for this is that society conditions women to respond to sexual initiation rather than to take the lead. Without the familiar cues of "being pursued," women may not even be aware of a mutual attraction; both are waiting for the other person to take a first step to demonstrate interest. Consequently, the sexual relationship may not even begin (Schwartz and Blumstein, 1973).

Sexual Behaviors among Men Contrary to the stereotype that sexual experiences between men are completely genitally focused, extragenital eroticisms and affection are important aspects of the sexual contact between many homosexual men:

No doubt most people will always conceive of male sexuality in general, and male homosexuality in particular, in terms of phallic actions. Certainly this focus invites the kinds of misconceptions which, in turn, tend to obscure the meaning homosexuality has for those who practice it . . . These and similar ideas have led to a widely held impression that homosexual practices lack precisely those kinds of affection which, in fact, are usually the main motives behind them. (Tripp, 1975, p. 102)

Hugging, kissing, and total-body caressing are important, as one homosexual man clearly states:

One of the best parts of making love is the time we spend holding each other, touching each other's faces and looking into the other's eyes. (Authors' files)

Anal intercourse is often thought to be the most prevalent sexual behavior between homosexual men. However, the Bell and Weinberg study (1978) found that fellatio is the most common mode of expression. Partner manual stimulation is the next most common, and anal intercourse is least common. Almost all of the homosexual men in the study had used a considerable variety of sexual techniques.

"Coming Out"

The extent to which a homosexual person decides to be secretive or open about his or her sexual orientation has a significant effect on the person's life style. There are various degrees of being "in the closet," and there are several steps in the process of *coming out*—acknowledging, accepting, and openly expressing one's homosexuality. Although these decisons are unique to each individual and situation, there are often some common components.

Self-Acknowledgment   Very "closeted" homosexual persons may attempt to suppress their sexual orientation from even their own awareness. These persons may actively seek sexual encounters with the opposite sex, and it is not uncommon for them to marry in an attempt to convince themselves of their "normalcy." Some of the homosexual people who have previously been married (one-third of women and one-fifth of men in the Bell and Weinberg study) may have done so to avoid openly confronting their sexual orientation. As one man, now openly homosexual, states:

As I look back now, I can see that my playboy life style was really an attempt to convince myself that the nagging attraction I felt for John was just a good friendship. It was as if I thought I could change my feelings by having sex with enough women. (Authors' files)

A woman in her thirties, recently divorced, explains:

The stronger I experienced feelings for Alice, the more I pressured my boyfriend to set the date for our wedding. For the first few years and two babies it seemed to work; I was living the life that I had grown up to expect. (Authors' files)

The initial step in coming out is usually a person's realization that she or he feels different from the surrounding heterosexual model. Some people report knowing they were homosexual when they were small children. Others realize during adolescence that something is missing in their heterosexual involvements.

Not just when, but how a person becomes aware of being homosexual varies from one person to another. It is not unusual for people to engage in explicit sexual behavior with same-sex partners without thinking of themselves as homosexual. For others, the initial homosexual experience represents the acknowledgment of this orientation.

Self-Acceptance   Accepting one's homosexuality is the next important step after realizing it. Self-acceptance is often difficult, for it involves overcoming the internalized negative societal view of homosexuality (Weinberg, 1973). The term *gay* is commonly used to describe homosexual people who see their homosexuality as a positive part of their identity.

Initially a homosexual person often has difficulty from the pervasive condemnatory attitudes toward homosexuality. Like the prejudiced heterosexual, his early impressions about homosexuality came from the culture around him. As a child he heard the same nasty references to homosexuals. He has heard them called "queers," seen them portrayed as dissolute and sad, on stage and screen, in novels, in newspaper articles. His own attitude toward homosexuality has evolved out of a context almost wholly derogatory. His prejudice against himself is an almost exact parallel to the prejudice against homosexuals held in the larger culture. (Weinberg, 1973, p. 74)

Disclosure   Related to acknowledgment and self-acceptance is the decision to be secretive or open. Deciding to remain in the closet may erode a person's pride and self-respect. Concealment can intensify social isolation and personal loneliness; it also inhibits participation in any gay rights activities. The illusion of security gained by concealment can also be jeopardized by discovery at any time (Milligan, 1975). *Passing* is a term sometimes used for maintaining the false image of heterosexuality. Passing as heterosexual is usually quite easy, since most people have learned to assume everyone is heterosexual:

Heterosexuals have an amazing capacity for blindness, or perhaps they refuse to notice it in the way any polite person might refuse to notice another's dandruff. If I had to give an award to the blindest heterosexual I've known it would be a tough decision. The prize might go to a friend of mine for twelve years now, who stayed with my lover and me for a week, during which time we were openly affectionate, and upon leaving told me how wonderfully I got on with a roommate. Only in 1976 when she announced her marriage—a year after it had happened—and told me that I was probably the last to know of it—I told her "You're probably the last person to know I'm gay." (Jay, 1978, p. 29)

Being homosexual usually requires a lifelong process of decision-making about whether to be in or out of the closet as new relationships and situations unfold. The significance of this is sometimes not understood by heterosexuals, as exemplified by the quote on the next page.

I don't see any reason why they have to tell anyone. They can just lead their lives without making such a big deal out of it. (Authors' files)

In most daily interactions, sexual orientation is irrelevant. However, imagine being a closeted homosexual person listening to a friend tell a "queer" joke, being asked "When are you going to settle down and get married?" or being invited to an office party for couples. In one writer's words, "Because of its devalued status, affirmation of homosexuality (or disclaiming it) becomes a more significant act than the same would be for a heterosexual, with significant consequences for a lifestyle" (Gagnon, 1977, p. 248).

With some exceptions, the more within "the system" a person is or desires to be, the more risk there is in not concealing one's sexual orientation. Jobs, social position, and friends may all be placed in jeopardy. Bell and Weinberg (1978) confirm this notion with their findings that relatively overt homosexual men and women are more likely to have lower social status (less education and income) than those who remain covert. The conservativeness of the surrounding community may further affect one's decisions.

Coming out may be a particularly difficult issue for homosexual adults who are parents. Approximately 60% of homosexual men and women who have been married have at least one child (Bell and Weinberg, 1978). The difficulties met by a gay parent in attempting to attain custody or visitation rights may be severe. It is not unusual for gay parents to lose either right exclusively on the basis of their sexual orientation, regardless of their fitness as parents. Yet there are some courts that hold that homosexuality itself is not proof of unfitness. The pattern of decisions at this time is arbitrary and uncertain (Stevens, 1978).

Telling the Family   The decision and process of coming out to one's family and friends is a particularly significant step, as the following account by a 35-year-old man illustrates:

Most of my vacation at home went well, but the ending was indeed difficult. Gay people kept cropping up in conversation. My mother was very down on them (us), and I of course was disagreeing with her. Finally she asked me if I was "one of them." I responded that I was. It was very difficult for her to deal with. She asked a lot of questions which I answered as calmly, honestly, and rationally as I could. We spent a rather strained day together. It was so painful for me to see her suffering so much heartache over this, and not even having a clue that the issue is the oppression of gay people. I just wish my mother didn't have to suffer so much from all this. I feel very down on our society. (Authors' files)

Because telling the family is so difficult, many homosexual people do not do so. Approximately half of the respondents in the Bell and Weinberg survey believed that their parents did not know about their homosexuality; fathers were somewhat less likely to know than mothers.

Each person decides if, when, and how to come out (unless it is discovered by accident). For those who decide to disclose their sexual orientation to their parents,

BOX 10.3 "DEAR ABBY"

Dear Abby: Some time ago you made the statement in your column that lesbians are born, not made.

Abby, I have a beautiful, talented 30-year-old daughter who is a lesbian, and I have always blamed myself for that. When she was little, she hated dresses, so I let her wear blue jeans and T-shirts just like her brothers wore. I didn't think a thing of it at the time, but now I realize I helped to make a tomboy out of her. I blame myself for not insisting that she dress and act like a girl instead of putting her in boys' clothes and encouraging her to play boys' games with her brothers and their friends.

So, my question is, if I didn't contribute to the way she turned out, how in the world did it happen?—Puzzled in Hope, Ark.

Dear Puzzled: Don't blame yourself. Millions of little girls are tomboys and prefer jeans to dresses, yet the vast majority of them do not become lesbians. The causes of lesbianism, like those of male homosexuality, are complex and not fully understood, but there is growing evidence that many lesbians are born with a predisposition in that direction.

The important thing to remember is that sexual preference is not a matter of choice; it is determined at a very early age. Children who grow up to be homosexuals need their parents' love and understanding no less than other children do. In fact, they need it more.

Weinberg (1973) offers some suggestions, qualified with the statement that none are universally applicable. In the following list, the term *parents* can be translated to brothers, sisters, or friends:

1. Initiating discussions about homosexuality in general may help a gay person to test parents' openness. It may also provide the opportunity to give information to them about homosexuality.
2. Literature about homosexuality may also be helpful in facilitating their comfort and knowledge.*
3. In telling parents about being homosexual, avoiding both blame and apologies can help maintain the dignity of both parties.
4. The person should make explicit the goodwill and desire for increased closeness that has motivated the disclosure.
5. Some parents may initially react explosively. It may be best to end the discussion at this point to give parents a chance to think it over. If parents become

*The books *A Family Matter, A Parents' Guide to Homosexuality* by Charles Silverstein, or *Loving Someone Gay* by Don Clark, may help to increase both communication and understanding.

vindictive, the person may decide to remove himself or herself from the relationship until the parents indicate a willingness to resume communication.

Weinberg also offers some suggestions for parents whose child has told them about being homosexual. Given the negative cultural stereotypes about homosexuality, it is understandable that a parent, sibling, or friend may have difficulty accepting the news calmly. Weinberg suggests that the parents keep in mind that the son or daughter is exactly the same person they have known and loved. The only difference is that she or he is being more honest than before. Parents who have severed their relationship with a homosexual son or daughter can decide to attempt to reestablish the relationship. Box 10.4 is a letter from a gay son, and it addresses many of these issues.

Involvement in the Gay Community   Involvement with homosexual people as a group may be another step in coming out. Weinberg describes issues such as "[w]hether to ridicule homosexuals. Whether to disparage other people called deviates by society. Whether to avoid homosexuals who are outspoken, who are gay and proud, or to join them. Whether to join the gay liberation movement" (1973, p. 87).

Some aspects of homosexual life styles may center around various gay subcultures. In larger cities, gay bars and cafes cater to different groups or clientele. As with heterosexual bars, these gathering places range from low-key socializing spots to establishments with reputations for casual pickups. Lesbian women are far less likely to "cruise" in search of casual encounters than are homosexual males. However, many homosexual men do not cruise either. Particularly in past years, homosexual bars, as well as certain recreational areas, restaurants, or steam baths, served an important function—often they were the only place where the patrons could drop the facade of heterosexuality. In recent years, this need has diminished to some extent. Gay people have helped to found service organizations, educational centers, and professional organizations. Religious organizations for gay people, such as the Metropolitan Community Church, and denominational groups, including Dignity for Roman Catholics and Integrity for Episcopalians, have been established. In addition, political interest groups such as gay rights organizations have also formed. Since its beginning in the 1960s, the growing gay rights movement has provided support for many homosexual men and women to be more open about their sexual orientation. The following section describes some of these activities.

GAY RIGHTS AND ANTIGAY RIGHTS

In the 1950s some organizations for gay people were established, in spite of the very conservative atmosphere of the times. The Mattachine Society had chapters in many cities which provided a national network for support and communication among homosexuals. The Daughters of Bilitis, an organization of lesbians, also published a journal called *The Ladder,* which contained fiction, poetry, and political articles. The goals of both organizations were to educate homosexual and heterosexual persons

BOX 10.4 A LETTER FROM A GAY MAN TO HIS PARENTS WHO WERE RECENTLY TOLD OF HIS SEXUAL ORIENTATION BY HIS ANGRY EX-WIFE

Dear Mom and Dad,

Hi! I hope that all is well with you.

Well, I was waiting to tell you about my sexuality—waiting for a time when it would be best for you to deal with it. But now that it is out in the open I'm happy that I can share that part of my life with you. My relationship with Bob is a big part of what is positive in my life, so not being able to share that has really been difficult for me.

I would hope that my sharing this with you will bring us closer together. I would like to do anything I can to help you understand me and to understand what it's like to be gay. Please realize that you are in no way responsible for my sexual preference. What you did or didn't do as parents is not what determined my sexuality. I want to be absolutely clear—you are not to "blame," it is not your "fault"—it's just part of who I am and it is a beautiful part of me. So do not feel guilty. Besides, accepting my feelings has made me truly happy for the first time in my life. My being gay is not a tragedy—it's just part of who I am.

I know that my preference to be in a relationship with a man is going to be difficult for you to understand and difficult to accept. There is a lot of social pressure and programming against it. For that reason I had a hard time accepting it myself. I tried to deny it, in fact, for 29 years. I didn't want to disappoint you as parents and I wanted to be "normal" and accepted by those around me. As I said, it was not easy to accept the social context, but I firmly believe, deep in my heart and soul, that being with another man is going to make me happy and fulfilled (it has already).

My feelings for a man are deeper, more beautiful and more intense than anything I have felt with a woman. How can it be wrong if it fills me full of joy and happiness? How can it be wrong when being with a man is just so comfortable and easy?

How can it be wrong? Because Anita Bryant says so? Because the Catholic Church says so? Because ignorant people who know nothing about it and are afraid of looking at their own sexuality say so? *Who has the right* to tell me that my feelings are wrong?

I hope you can accept my relationship because it is the most important aspect of my life—that love and caring form a base for everything else that I do. I would very much like you to share my life and I hope that you can see that I'm still the same person that you have always loved and cared about. I definitely do not want to be in the position of having to choose between your approval and my happiness—because from my perspective, the choice would be an obvious but unfortunate one.

Also, please try to react out of love, not fear, guilt or sadness. I tried to write this letter from my heart and I hope that you will receive it in the same spirit in which it was written.

I love you very much,

Don   (Authors' files)

about homosexuality, increase understanding of homosexuality, and eliminate discriminatory laws toward homosexual individuals (Katz, 1976).

During the 1960s many people began to question traditional aspects of American life in all areas including the sexual. In this atmosphere more gay people began to respond to social and political changes and to question and challenge the social problems they faced. The symbolic birth of gay activism occurred in 1969 in New York City. As was common practice, police raided a gay bar, the Stonewall. However, this time people in the bar resisted and fought back. A riot followed and did not end until the next day. The Stonewall incident acted as a catalyst for the formation of gay rights groups, and various activities, such as Gay Pride Week, are held in yearly commemoration of the Stonewall riot (Hankel and Cunningham, 1979).

Since the early 1970s, groups have worked to end various kinds of discrimination against homosexual people. Some organizations have lobbied for more accurate coverage of homosexual life styles in the media. Gay people have organized to confront prejudice within their own professions. The National Gay Task Force was founded in 1973 to work with homosexual men and women around the country to help achieve legal rights.

The gay rights movement has been primarily concerned with areas of legislation related to consensual sex laws and civil rights laws. Both of these areas are seen as essential to providing homosexual people the same legal protection enjoyed by heterosexual people. The desired legislation aims to prevent harassment and discrimination based on sexual orientation. The movement's central philosophy is that private consensual sexual expression is not a matter of legal concern, nor is it adequate reason to deny or rescind housing or employment.

Many states have passed legislation legalizing private sexual behavior between consenting adults. However, sexual behaviors such as oral-genital contact, manual-genital stimulation, and anal intercourse are still illegal in many states, whether performed by same- or other-sex partners. These laws are most commonly enforced against homosexual men. Some states have meted out life imprisonment to convicted homosexual "offenders." *Entrapment,* the practice of undercover police enticing propositions from homosexual men, is a major source of arrests.

A major legislative goal of gay rights advocates is an amendment to the 1964 Civil Rights Act that would broaden it to include "affectional or sexual preference" along with race, creed, color, and sex. This would make it illegal to discriminate in housing, employment, and public accommodations on the grounds of sexual orientation. Such a bill was introduced into Congress in 1975, but the legislation has not yet been passed, nor has such civil rights legislation passed in any state legislatures. However, some local governments have adopted laws prohibiting discrimination on the basis of sexual orientation. Additionally, several large private corporations and the Federal Civil Service Commission have established equal opportunity employment in regard to homosexuality. This means that it is illegal for an employer to discriminate against anyone in hiring or firing based exclusively on their sexual orientation.

These gains have been countered by antigay rights forces. The backlash was well underway by 1977 when a successful attempt was made to revoke the Dade County, Florida, ordinance prohibiting discrimination based on sexual orientation.

Entertainer Anita Bryant played the central role in revoking the legislation. In mid-1977 she formed the Save Our Children (since changed to Protect America's Children) organization to overturn the previously approved ordinance. The following paragraphs will compare some of the claims of opponents and advocates of gay rights.

Opponents to gay rights typically believe that homosexuality is a sin. Does the belief that homosexual behaviors are "sinful" provide grounds for discriminatory laws against homosexuals? This question represents another basic issue. As discussed at the beginning of this chapter, the biblical condemnation of homosexuality stems from a unique historical context. The implications of these prohibitions for today's world are questioned by religious scholars:

There is no doubt that the Old Testament condemns homosexual practice with the utmost severity. The reason for the condemnation, however, and the severity of the punishment cannot be appreciated apart from the historical background that gave rise to them. Simply citing verses from the Bible outside of their historical context and then blithely applying them to homosexuals today does grave injustice both to scripture and to people who have already suffered a great deal from the travesty of biblical interpretation. (Kosnik et al., 1977, p. 188)

If the religious beliefs of some were codified into law for all, then eating pork, drinking coffee, and driving a car would be illegal. "Those who argue that our law is based on the Judeo-Christian ethic sometimes are highly selective in their application of biblical sanctions" (The Portland Town Council, 1976, p. 13).

The gay rights position maintains that the United States Constitution upholds the separation of church and state. A crucial point is that civil rights legislation provides legal protection in housing, employment, and public accommodations—not necessarily moral sanction for homosexuality. The American Civil Liberties Union stated in 1975: "Homosexuals are entitled to the same rights, liberties, lack of harassment, and protections as are other citizens" (The Portland Town Council, 1976).

Another basic issue has concerned the reputed dangers of permitting homosexual people to work in jobs as teachers, childcare providers, or other positions where they would have contact with children. Beliefs that many homosexual adults sexually molest children formed the basis for objections to the Miami ordinance's prohibitions against employment discrimination. Antigay groups are afraid that contact between homosexual persons and children might result in "recruitment" of children into homosexuality. As a Save Our Children ad proclaimed, "The recruitment of children is absolutely necessary for the survival and growth of homosexuality—for since homosexuals cannot reproduce, they must recruit, must freshen their ranks" (*Miami Herald*, March 30, 1977).

These conclusions are erroneous on several points. First, as will be discussed in Chapter 20, child molestation is done primarily by heterosexual male adults who are family members or friends of the children. That children be protected from sexual abuse is a concern shared by homosexual and heterosexual adults. Civil rights antidiscriminatory employment protection for homosexual teachers absolutely does not give them any more rights than heterosexual teachers to make sexual advances to students.

Second, it is untrue that homosexual people attempt to increase their numbers by "recruitment." Even if they did, sexual orientation is a phenomenon much too complex to be readily changed by overt sexual seduction or indirect example. In fact, recent preliminary research indicates that even children who live with a homosexual parent are not likely to adopt a homosexual orientation (Green, 1978).

Antigay sentiment can escalate to drastic proportions. For example, several weeks after the Dade County ordinance prohibiting discrimination based on sexual orientation was revoked, several people murdered a homosexual man in San Francisco by repeatedly stabbing him in the chest as they shouted "faggot! faggot!" They reported that their only motive for committing the crime was that the victim was gay. Furthermore, many cities are reporting an increase in physical assaults on gays and others "suspected" of being gay. Events like these indicate a pathological fear and hatred of homosexuality and deepen the commitment of gays and others sympathetic to their concerns to eradicate the attitudes that contribute to such violence. The National Gay Task Force has started a major project to monitor and document violence against homosexuals. They plan to utilize the data as a tool for civil rights advocacy and to help reduce gay victimization (Gurel, 1982).

The struggle for gay rights is far from ending. Both gay rights supporters and antigay rights groups are attempting to pass or restrict antidiscriminatory legislation in various places throughout the country. It is our hope that gay civil rights and consensual adult legislation will prevail, and that homosexual Americans will be freer to live, work, and contribute to society.

SUMMARY

1. The term *homosexual* can be an objective or subjective appraisal of sexual behavior, emotional affiliation, and/or self-definition.

A CONTINUUM OF SEXUAL ORIENTATIONS

2. Kinsey's seven-point continuum ranges from exclusive heterosexuality to exclusive homosexuality.

3. Kinsey based his ratings on a combination of overt sexual behaviors and erotic attractions.

4. Based on methodological adjustments between Kinsey and Hunt, approximately 2% of men and 1% of women are exclusively homosexual; about 23% of men and 14% of women have both homosexual and heterosexual experiences; and roughly 75% of men and 85% of women are exclusively heterosexual.

5. Bisexuality can be characterized by overt behaviors and/or erotic responses to both males and females. As with heterosexuality and homosexuality, a clear-cut definition is difficult to establish.

SOCIETAL ATTITUDES

6. Cross-cultural attitudes toward homosexuality vary from condemnation to acceptance; negative attitudes toward homosexuality still predominate in our society.

7. Homophobia is the irrational fear of homosexuality, the fear of homosexual feelings within oneself, or self-loathing because of one's own homosexuality.

"CAUSES" OF HOMOSEXUALITY

8. There are a number of psychosocial and biological theories that attempt to explain the "cause" of homosexuality. Some of the psychosocial theories relate to parenting patterns, life experiences, or the psychological attributes of the person. Theories of biological causation look to genetic causation or prenatal or adult hormone differences.

9. Various "treatments" have been used to attempt to change homosexual orientation to heterosexual. Such attempts in the past have not

been particularly successful, and much controversy surrounds current therapy designed to develop heterosexual functioning in homosexually oriented individuals.

10. Sexual orientation, regardless of where it falls on the continuum of heterosexuality and homosexuality, is formed from a composite of inconsistent and undetermined elements.

LIFE STYLES

11. Contrary to popular stereotypes, homosexual individuals exhibit a wide variety of life styles.

12. As gender role stereotyping has decreased, many homosexual and heterosexual couples have developed more egalitarian relationships. Some of the differences reported between homosexual men and women may be attributed to general gender role differences between men and women.

13. Bell and Weinberg classified homosexual relationships and life styles into five basic categories including close-coupled, open-coupled, functionals, dysfunctionals, and asexuals.

14. "Coming out" or being "in the closet" often has a significant impact on a homosexual person's life style.

15. The steps of coming out involve recognizing one's homosexual orientation, deciding how to view oneself, and being open about one's homosexuality.

GAY RIGHTS AND ANTIGAY RIGHTS

16. Gay rights activists have been promoting legislation relating to consensual sex laws and civil rights laws. These activities have met with opposition from various individuals and groups.

Key to Box 10.1 "The Homophobic Scale": According to Smith, yes responses to questions 1, 2, 4, 5, 8 and 9 and no responses to questions 3, 6 and 7 indicate homophobic attitudes.

SUGGESTED READINGS

Bell, Alan; Weinberg, Martin; and Hammersmith, Sue. *Sexual Preference: Its Development in Men and Women.* Bloomington: Indiana University Press, 1981. An ambitious and readable study about the development of sexual orientation. An excellent, informative resource.

Boswell, John. *Christianity, Social Tolerance, and Homosexuality.* Chicago: University of Chicago Press, 1980. Winner of the 1981 American Book Award for History, this scholarly book studies the history of attitudes toward homosexuality in Western Europe from the beginning of the Christian era to the fourteenth century.

Califia, Pat. *Sapphistry: The Book of Lesbian Sexuality.* Tallahassee, Fla.: Naiad Press, 1980. A nonjudgmental account of the diversity of sexual relations possible between women with an emphasis on sharing and communication of sexual desire.

Hanckel, Frances, and Cunningham, John. *A Way of Love, A Way of Life.* New York: Lothrop, Lee & Shepard, 1979. This book is written to inform people, especially young people, about what it means to be gay. It discusses how young people who are gay can know that they are, how to develop positive attitudes about themselves, how to tell family and friends, where to go for help, the history of gay rights, and variations in life styles.

Orlando. "Bisexuality: A Choice Not an Echo?" *Ms.*, October 1978. A personal exploration of the discovery of bisexuality.

Reid, John. *The Best Little Boy in the World.* New York: Balantine, 1973. An autobiographical novel with a happy ending of the story of one man's coming-out process.

Resources

The National Gay Task Force, 80 Fifth Avenue, New York, N.Y. 10011. (212)741-1010. They will provide information about social, political, and educational organizations in a particular locale.

Parents and Friends of Lesbians and Gays (Parents FLAG), P.O. Box 24565, Los Angeles, CA 90024. This group provides support and counseling for parents and public education on gay rights.

PART FOUR

*Sexuality and the
Life Cycle*

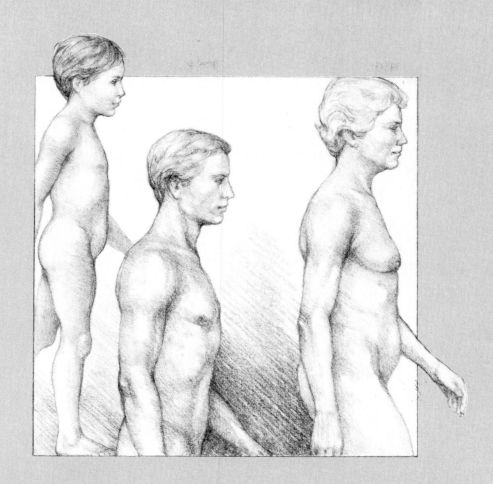

11

Contraception

HISTORICAL AND SOCIAL PERSPECTIVES
    Birth Control in the United States
    Birth Control As a Contemporary Issue
SHARED RESPONSIBILITY
CURRENTLY AVAILABLE METHODS
    A Comparison of the Most Commonly Used Methods
    Oral Contraceptives
    Intrauterine Devices
    Diaphragms
    Cervical Caps
    Vaginal Spermicides
    Condoms
    Methods Based on the Menstrual Cycle
    Other Methods
    Postcoital Contraception
INDUCED ABORTION
    Right-to-Life Versus Prochoice
    Medical Procedures for Abortion
    Pregnancy Risk-Taking and Abortion
STERILIZATION
    Female Sterilization
    Male Sterilization
NEW DIRECTIONS IN CONTRACEPTION
    New Directions for Men
    New Directions for Women
SUMMARY
SUGGESTED READINGS

*O*ur knowledge of humankind's concern with controlling conception goes back to the beginning of recorded history. In ancient Egypt, dried crocodile dung was soaked in sour milk and placed by the cervix to prevent conception. In sixth-century Greece, eating the uterus, testicle, or hoof paring of a mule was recommended. If an unwanted pregnancy did occur, infanticide (killing of newborn children) was practiced by the Greeks and Romans. In more recent historical times, the eighteenth-century Italian adventurer Giovanni Casanova was noted for his animal membrane condoms tied with a ribbon at the base of the penis. In seventeenth-century Western Europe, condoms, withdrawal of the penis from the vagina before ejaculation, and sponges soaked in a variety of solutions and inserted into the vagina were used.

Birth Control in the United States

Although we may take for granted the variety of birth control methods available today in the United States, this phenomenon is quite recent in our history. Through the years, both the methods available and the laws concerning their use have been restrictive. In the 1870s, Anthony Comstock, then secretary of the New York Society for the Suppression of Vice, succeeded in having national laws enacted which prohibited disseminating contraceptive information through the United States mail on the basis that such information was obscene. (The laws became known as the Comstock Laws.) At that time, the only "official," legitimate form of birth control was abstinence, and reproduction was the only acceptable reason for sexual intercourse. The view that contraception other than abstinence or the rhythm method is sinful is still held by some orthodox and fundamentalist religious leaders. However, many contemporary religions favor the use of contraceptives.

Margaret Sanger was the person most instrumental in promoting the changes in birth control legislation and availability in the United States. She opened an illegal clinic in 1915 where women could obtain and learn to use the diaphragms she had shipped from Europe. She also published birth control information in her newspaper, *The Woman Rebel.* As a result, Sanger was arraigned for violating the Comstock Laws. She fled to Europe to avoid certain prosecution, but later returned to initiate birth control hormone research, a project financed by her wealthy friend, Katherine Dexter McCormack. These women wanted to develop a reliable method by which women could control their own fertility. In 1960, after limited testing and research in Puerto Rico, the first birth control pills came on the United States market.

It was not until 1966 that the last major law regulating the sale of contraceptives was revoked. Laws governing contraceptive availability continue to change. Currently, some states are liberalizing laws on dispensing contraceptives to adolescents without parental consent or displaying condoms and foam in pharmacies on open shelves rather than behind the counter. On the other hand, controversy continues on the national level about whether to require parental notification when minors receive contraceptive services from government-funded organizations. Even today the availability and acceptability of contraception is still a contested issue.

326

Margaret Sanger helped make birth control available for American women.

Birth Control As a Contemporary Issue

In recent years, the availability and use of reliable birth control has been seen as increasingly desirable for a variety of reasons. There has been a growing emphasis on couples and individuals having planned and wanted children. Many couples who want children wait for some years to better establish their relationship and their financial stability. Birth control also enables couples and individuals to limit the size of their families.

The use of birth control can also contribute to the physical health of the mother. Pregnancy itself has health risks, and spacing pregnancies usually means better health for the mother and child. In some cases, birth control is used to avoid the possibility of bearing children with hereditary diseases and birth defects.

Women who want to combine a career and parenthood can better do so with birth control. Women who have a career and want no children rely on birth control to provide them with this option. Furthermore, both men and women who choose not to be parents can accomplish this with greater ease since the development of more effective birth control methods.

The world's population growth is another concern that plays a part in some people's decision to limit their family size. The world's natural resources are not unlimited, and a continually increasing population may precipitate a crisis. For these reasons, population control through the use of birth control is seen by some people as a social necessity.

Objections to contraception often stem from religious mandate. The official doctrine of the Roman Catholic church, as well as some other religions, holds that use of means other than abstinence and methods based on the menstrual cycle is against God's will and therefore immoral. However, there is great diversity of views among leaders of the church. For example, a study commissioned by the Catholic Theological Society of America states, "The mere fact that a couple is using artificial means of birth control cannot provide a sufficient basis to make a judgment about the morality or immorality of their married life and sexual expression" (Kosnik et al., 1977, p. 127). Also, the discrepancy between doctrine and practice is wide. The majority of church members use some kind of artificial contraception. In fact, the difference between Catholic and non-Catholic use of contraceptive devices is minimal. As of 1975, about 76% of married Catholic women under 45 and about 80% of married non-Catholic women of the same age group used some kind of contraceptive method (Westoff and Jones, 1977).

SHARED RESPONSIBILITY

In promoting the pill, it was Margaret Sanger's idea to give women control over their own fertility. However, control does not necessarily mean total responsibility by the woman. There are reasons why it may not be wise for a man to assume that the woman has "taken care of herself." Many women do not regularly practice birth control, especially if they are not engaged in a long term relationship, or the woman may be using a method incorrectly. If there is any uncertainty about using birth control, the relationship may suffer. Decisions about an unwanted pregnancy are not easy, and fear of pregnancy can negatively affect both partners' sexual experience.

Sharing the responsibility of contraception can enhance a relationship. Talking about birth control can be a good way to practice discussing personal and sexual topics. A relationship in which a man takes an active interest in contraception is less likely to be affected by resentments women often feel for men who, by ignoring the issue, put the entire responsibility for contraception on them. As one writer states, "Taking care of business before you get down to pleasure often enhances lovemaking by reducing stress and building trust" (Castleman, 1980a). For these reasons, we recommend that responsibility for birth control be shared.

The first step in sharing contraceptive responsibility may simply be for either partner to ask the other about birth control before the first time they have intercourse.

Would you be more careful if it were you that got pregnant?

In our experience talking with students and clients, this initial question is rarely asked. (See Chapter 13 for further discussion of nonuse of contraception.) An openness on the part of the male partner to using condoms or noncoital sexual activities as the method of choice or as a backup or temporary method is one way to share responsibility for birth control. Most birth control clinics offer classes that are open to partners. Reading about and discussing the various alternatives and choosing the one that seems best is an important way for both partners to be involved. The man can also participate by accompanying his partner when a medical exam is needed. Some physicians or nurse practitioners are comfortable with the woman's partner being present during the exam. Expenses for both the birth control method and the exam can also be shared. Further suggestions for sharing responsibility will be included in the following section on specific methods. We believe that sharing the responsibility for birth control can help provide both better sexual relationships and improved contraceptive effectiveness.

CURRENTLY AVAILABLE METHODS

There are a variety of forms of birth control. However, a perfect method that is 100% effective, reversible, has no side effects, and that is usable by either sex is not available now or in the foreseeable future. Each of the methods currently available has advantages and disadvantages with regard to effectiveness, safety, and convenience. It is a good idea to be familiar with the various methods available because most people will use several of them at some time in their active sexual lives.

A Comparison of the Most Commonly Used Methods

How do people go about choosing a method of birth control? A number of criteria are important, including convenience, safety, expense, and effectiveness. Details relating to specific birth control methods will be discussed later in this section. Here, we will present only a brief comparison.

Convenience   What is convenient or easy to use for one person may be seen as inconvenient or difficult by another, depending upon a number of factors. Because the decision is so subjective, we will discuss ways of using each contraceptive in the following pages to permit readers to judge for themselves.

Safety   Every method of contraception has health risks. Some of the dangers are directly due to the method, and others are due to failure of the method and resulting birth complications. One study compared the annual risk of death of women from control methods and from births following contraceptive failures in the United States and Britain (Tietze et al., 1977). The major findings were that barrier methods (condom and diaphragm), with therapeutic abortion backup, are the safest methods of reversible fertility control. Method- and/or birth-associated deaths for barrier methods, the IUD, and the pill increase as a woman becomes older. The most important point is that the overall risk to life is very small. There is one exception: women over 40 years of age who smoke cigarettes and use the pill have an increased risk of death.

Method Expense   There are several factors involved in comparing costs of different contraceptives, and these make direct comparisons difficult. Pills, IUDs, and diaphragms require examinations by a health-care specialist, whereas foam and condoms do not. Yet a woman needs to have yearly or biannual Pap smears even when she is not using a prescription method of birth control. When a method causes side effects or is personally unsatisfactory, visits to the doctor for problems with the method will add expense. Frequency of intercourse will affect how expensive some methods are. For example, foam and condoms would cost less per month with infrequent intercourse. Finally, the emotional and financial expense of an unplanned pregnancy is related to user and method effectiveness.

Planned Parenthood clinics and government-sponsored clinics often provide exams on a sliding fee schedule based on a person's ability to pay. At a private physician's office the cost of an exam and Pap smear is usually in the range of $25 to $50. An IUD insertion adds $40 to $80 to this fee; a diaphragm fitting is an additional $10 to $20. Since fees vary, it may be useful to call various health-care providers for estimates.

Pharmacy expenses are also a consideration. Birth control pills average about $8 to $12 per monthly packet. The diaphragm itself costs about $8, and each application of cream or jelly about 40¢. A cervical cap costs about $10. Depending on the brand, foam averages 35¢ to 40¢ per application. Spermicidal suppositories are about 45¢ each. Condoms, which are sold by threes or dozens, range from 65¢ to over $1.25 each. Methods based on the menstrual cycle, such as the ovulation method, cost nothing once the individual has become educated in how to use the method.

Contraceptive Effectiveness   Several variables influence the effectiveness of birth control. For example, the theoretical effectiveness of a method does not take into account human error. Physician mistakes (such as improper IUD insertion or poor fitting of diaphragm, discussed later in this chapter), lack of user knowledge of correct method use, negative attitudes about using the method, an uninvolved partner, forgetfulness, or deciding "this time it won't matter" greatly increase the chances of pregnancy. Contraceptive effectiveness is often examined in the framework of how many women out of 100 would get pregnant in a year's time using a particular method. Table 11.1 compares theoretical effectiveness with actual failure rates, for 100 women in a year, for several of the most commonly used methods. As Box 11.1 suggests, many couples may want to use backup methods to provide greater protection under certain circumstances.

In addition, many factors influence people in their decisions about whether to use a birth control method and which methods to use. As we discuss a number of commonly used methods in the paragraphs that follow, we will present more specific information on how to use each method, how it works, how a couple may share responsibility, and the potential advantages and disadvantages of each option.

Oral Contraceptives

There are two basic types of oral contraceptives currently on the market, the combination pill and progestin-only pill (sometimes called the mini-pill). The *combination pill* contains two hormones, synthetic estrogen and progestin. It is the most commonly used oral contraceptive in the United States, and has been on the market since the early 1960s. There are more than twenty different varieties which contain varying amounts and ratios of the two hormones.

The *progestin-only pill* contains only 0.35 mg of progestin (a progesterone-like substance)—about one-third of the amount in an average-strength combination pill. No estrogen is contained in the progestin-only pill. This pill has been on the market since 1973.

TABLE 11.1 BIRTH CONTROL METHOD EFFECTIVENESS. Theoretical and actual use rates. Number of pregnancies during the first year of use per 100 nonsterile women initiating method.

Method	Used correctly and consistently	Average U.S. experience among 100 women who wanted no more children
Abstinence from intercourse	0	?
Tubal ligation	0.04	0.04
Vasectomy	0.15	0.15+
Combination pills	0.34	4–10
Progestin-only pills	1–1.5	5–10
IUD	1–3	5
Foam and condom	less than 1	5
Condom	3	10
Diaphragm and spermicide[a]	3	17
Cervical cap	?	7–8
Foam	3	22
Spermicidal suppositories	3	20–25
Withdrawal	9	20–25
Fertility awareness		
Calendar only	13	21
Basal body temperature only	7	20
Cervical mucus only	2	25
Douching	?	40
No method	90	90

[a]A study of diaphragm effectiveness in 1976 at the Sanger Bureau reported an *actual use* failure rate of two women out of 100. The majority of women were under 30 years of age and unmarried. The high contraceptive success of these diaphragm users was likely due to careful fitting and thorough education in correct use of the diaphragm (Hatcher et al., 1980).
Source: Adapted from Hatcher et al., 1980, p. 4.

How Pills Work The combination pill prevents conception primarily by inhibiting ovulation. Estrogen in the pill affects the hypothalamus and inhibits the release of pituitary hormones, LH and FSH, that would otherwise begin the chain of events that culminates in ovulation (see Chapter 4). The progesterone in the pill provides secondary contraceptive protection by thickening and chemically altering the cervical mucus so that it is more hostile to sperm and hampers its ability to travel through the mucus into the uterus. Progesterone also causes changes in the lining of the uterus, making it less receptive to implantation. In addition, progesterone may inhibit ovula-

BOX 11.1 USING BACKUP METHODS TO INCREASE CONTRACEPTIVE EFFECTIVENESS

There are a number of circumstances where a couple may need or want to use more than one method to ensure effective contraception. Some examples of these circumstances include:

- During the first cycle of the pill.
- For the remainder of the cycle after forgetting to take one or more birth control pills.
- The first month after changing to a new brand of pills.
- During the initial one to three months after IUD insertion.
- When taking antibiotics or aspirin and using an IUD. It is suspected by some that aspirin and antibiotics may

lower IUD effectiveness (Boston Women's Health Book Collective, 1976).

- When first learning to use a diaphragm.
- When the couple desires to increase the effectiveness of one method (for instance, using foam and condoms together creates a very effective contraceptive protection).

Abstinence from intercourse and use of condoms, foam, or a diaphragm are possible backup methods that can be combined in many ways with other birth control methods for extra contraceptive protection.

tion by mildly disturbing hypothalamic-pituitary-ovarian function (Hatcher et al., 1980).

The progestin-only pill works somewhat differently than the combination pill. It is believed that most women who take the progestin-only pill continue to ovulate at least occasionally. The primary effect of this pill is to alter the mucus in the cervix to a thick and tacky consistency that effectively blocks sperm from entering the uterus. As with the combination pill, secondary contraceptive effects may be provided by alterations in the uterine endometrial lining that make it unreceptive to implantation.

How to Use the Pill A woman who chooses to use the birth control pill typically begins her first packet on the fifth day after the onset of menstruation. For most effective protection, a woman should complete one cycle on the pill before completely relying on it for contraception. Currently, most packets contain 28 pills: 21 hormone pills and seven inert "reminder pills." With this kind of packet, a woman takes a tablet each day and begins a new packet after finishing the last one. She will usually have a menstrual-like flow that results from the hormone withdrawal after the second or third day with no hormone supplements. Some packets have 21 hormone pills and no reminder pills. To use these, a woman takes no pills for seven days and must remember to start the cycle again.

With the progestin-only pill, a woman takes one on the first (instead of the fifth) day of her menstrual period. She continues taking a pill every day, even during menstruation. There are no inert pills.

Forgetting pills reduces the potential effectiveness of this method; taking the pill at approximately the same time each day maximizes it. Since the pills maintain a particular hormone level in the body, missing one or more pills can alter the hormone level and allow ovulation to occur. A woman must take a missed pill as soon as she remembers it; she then takes the next pill at the regular time. When more than one pill is forgotten, it is best for a woman to consult her health-care practitioner. When this happens, a woman should use a backup method such as foam or condoms for the remainder of her cycle.

Potential Advantages of Oral Contraceptives   Birth control pills have several advantages. They can be taken at a time of day separate from sexual activity, a factor many people believe helps to maintain sexual spontaneity. If the combination pill is used correctly, it is a highly effective method, as Table 11.1 shows. Furthermore, some women who experience breast enlargement from the pill consider this to be a positive side effect. Acne is often improved by taking oral contraceptives. The pill also often eliminates mittelschmerz (pain at ovulation) and reduces menstrual cramps and the amount and duration of the flow. Iron deficiency anemia is decreased in pill users. Oral contraceptives can be effective in treating endometriosis or cysts of the ovary, and may decrease the incidence of benign breast lumps, rheumatoid arthritis, and uterine and breast cancer in users compared with nonusers of the pill (Hatcher et al., 1980; Kols et al., 1982). A woman who is pleased with this method states:

I really like the pill I'm taking. My periods are light and the bad cramps I used to have are gone. I hadn't been using anything before taking the pill. It's a tremendous relief to make love and not be afraid of getting pregnant. (Authors' files)

These advantages explain, in part, why the combination pill is more commonly used than any other temporary method of birth control. The pill is currently used by 5 to 8 million women in the United States (Hatcher et al., 1980).

The progestin-only pill has the advantage that it eliminates estrogen-related side effects and reduces the likelihood of progestin-related problems because of the low progestin dosage (Nelson, 1973). Adverse reactions to the combination pill, including carbohydrate metabolism alterations, yeast infections, nausea, weight gain, acne, and depression, may be reduced by switching to this type of pill, and it is often recommended for women over 35 or for very young, sexually active women.

Cautions in Using Oral Contraceptives   A woman should have a complete medical and family history taken before using oral contraceptives. A physical exam (including a Pap smear, blood pressure, urinalysis, a gonorrhea culture, and breast and pelvic exams) is needed before starting pills and at least once a year while taking them. In fact, all women should have routine yearly breast, Pap, and pelvic exams regardless of whether they use pills.

Women vary in their responses to different pill hormone combinations. Some of the side effects such as nausea, fluid retention, increased appetite, acne, depression, spotting, or lack of "menstruation" (withdrawal bleeding), can be eliminated by a change in the type of pill. Generally, a woman will be given a type of pill that will work well with her and that has the lowest practical hormonal potency to reduce the possibility of side effects.

Some women are much less prone to experience problems with the pill than are others. Women who are most likely to have no serious problems with the pill are under 30, are nonsmokers and of normal weight, have regular menstrual cycles, and have a medical history with no contraindications for the pill. For most healthy young women, the benefits of oral contraceptives outweigh the risks (Ory et al., 1980).

Potential Disadvantages of Oral Contraceptives Because the hormones in birth control pills circulate in the bloodstream through the entire body, there are a variety of potential side effects. Much is yet unknown, and the risks and rewards of oral contraception remain controversial. It is not wise to consider the pill to be completely harmless as some do. A nurse practitioner reports:

It's frightening to me to realize that many women on the pill don't consider it to be medication. When I take their medical histories and ask if they are taking any medications, they say "no" or ask, "Does aspirin count?" When I later ask if they have ever taken birth control pills, they answer, "Yes, I'm taking them now." (Authors' files)

We will look first at some of the problems that have been associated with the estrogen-progestin pill, then examine possible side effects of the progestin-only pill.

The combination pill has been associated with an increased risk of blood clots in users (Seaman and Seaman, 1978). If a clot forms and travels to the lung or the brain, it can cause crippling or death. The symptoms of a blood clot may include severe leg or chest pains, coughing up blood, breathing difficulty, severe headache or vomiting, dizziness, fainting, disturbances of vision or speech, and weakness or numbness of an arm or leg. If a woman using an oral contraceptive experiences one or more of these symptoms, she should obtain immediate medical attention. Women who are immobilized or confined to a wheelchair are often advised against using the pill because poor circulation (sometimes related to lack of physical activity) can increase the potential for developing blood clots. Research indicates that the risk of a fatal blood clot is 15 times greater during pregnancy than with the pill. However, it is also important to compare side effects of the pill to risks from other methods of birth control. Pregnancy is not the only other option.

Another risk associated with the combination pill is increased likelihood of heart attacks, particularly for women over 40. For this reason, the U.S. Food and Drug Administration (FDA) has urged physicians not to prescribe the pill to women past 40 years of age. The risks are especially high for women over 40 who smoke cigarettes.

Some research indicates that women who have used oral contraceptives for more than 10 years continue to be more susceptible to heart attack even after discontinuing the pill (Slone et al., 1981).

High blood pressure (hypertension) is another potential risk of taking the pill. One in 20 pill users develops this complication. Pill-related high blood pressure can be reversed by discontinuing use. Periodic blood pressure measurements are important in pill users, and women who already have high blood pressure are usually advised to use another form of contraception.

The FDA has also listed an increased risk of noncancerous liver tumors as a potential side effect of oral contraceptives. These tumors are very rare but can be fatal. Women 27 years and older who have used oral contraceptives with a high hormonal potency for seven years or more run the greatest risk of developing liver tumors (Centers for Disease Control Morbidity and Mortality Report, September 1977). Other researchers have found some oral contraceptive-associated liver tumors to be cancerous (Neuberger, 1980).

The relationship of the pill to cancer is not yet clearly understood. At the present time, there is no evidence that the pill causes cancer of the breasts, uterus, or ovaries (Vessey, 1976). In fact, there is some indication that combination pills with higher ratios of progesterones to estrogens may provide some protection against cancer of the lining of the uterus (Hulka et al., 1982). A World Health Organization (WHO) study of the effects of the pill on the development of cervical cancer reported no clearcut results (World Health Organization Scientific Group, 1978). However, once cancer of the breasts or uterus develops, estrogen can speed its growth.

In some women the pill affects carbohydrate metabolism. These changes may lead to a prediabetic or diabetic condition or may aggravate already existing diabetes. A careful medical history taken when birth control pills are first prescribed may reveal the need for glucose tolerance testing. Some women experience an increase in vaginal discharge as a side effect of the pill. The pill does alter the chemical balance of the vagina, and this causes women to develop yeast infections more easily.

Since the pill works primarily by inhibiting ovulation, a woman's ovaries do not produce mature ova during the time she uses it. After a woman has stopped the medication, it may take time for her ovaries to resume normal functioning. Unfortunately, birth control pills have been prescribed to "regulate menstruation" in women with infrequent periods. In those women who were not ovulating regularly, the suppression of this function by the pill may worsen their problem with irregular ovulation. The progestin-only pill may be an alternative because most women continue to ovulate while taking it.

The pill may also be related to emotional changes, although it is difficult to establish a definitive cause for any emotional state. Many women, however, see a correlation between their moods and use of oral contraceptives. Some studies have shown an increase in depression in women on the pill (Lewis and Hoghughi, 1969); since depression can affect all aspects of a woman's life, it is not to be taken lightly. A woman who suspects her depression may be pill-related can use another method for a time and observe any changes in her mood.

Many women take the pill to increase their enjoyment and the spontaneity of their sexual expression. Hatcher et al. (1980) note that women on the pill usually experience an increase in sexual desire. However, Seaman and Seaman (1978) suggest that a decrease in sexual motivation is more common than an increase. A decline in sexual interest may be influenced by a variety of side effects, including frequent yeast infections, a reduction of vaginal lubrication, and depression. Hormonal and other psychological factors may also contribute.

There are still other potential adverse effects. First, use of oral contraceptives for two or more years doubles the risk of developing gall bladder disease (Boston Collaborative Drug Surveillance Program, 1973), as well as an increase in bladder and kidney infections. Some conditions—including migraine headaches, asthma, epilepsy, and cardiac or kidney dysfunction—may be aggravated by the fluid retention that accompanies the pill. (When these conditions are related to hormone imbalance, however, the pill is sometimes used to alleviate the difficulty.) The hormones in the pill can also alter the way in which the body assimilates vitamins and minerals that are essential for optimal health. Finally, the increase in estrogen from the pill or pregnancy will stop the long bone growth in a woman who has not reached her full height. The progestin-only pill does not have this last side effect.

There are a number of contradictions in oral contraceptive research (Ory et al., 1980). The authors of this summary study cite a lack of confirmation for several side effects, including impaired fertility and an increase in diabetes, gall bladder disease, and urinary tract infections. They also suggest that past research findings may overstate the risks for today's young women for two reasons. First, the pills used in the 1960s and early 1970s usually had higher doses of estrogen than do pills today. Higher levels of estrogen are linked with increased risk of most side effects. Second, most of the studies have been done with women older than 25, and the results may, to some extent, reflect that influence.

While the reduced amount of hormones in the progestin-only pill causes this medication to have fewer potential side effects, some disadvantages are associated with it, too. Irregular and "breakthrough" bleeding (a light flow between menstrual periods) happens more frequently with the progestin-only pill than with the combination pill. However, the bleeding irregularities usually diminish in two to three months, as they do with the combination pill.

Also, "some of the side effects seen with the combination pill are reported for the progestin-only pill . . . [These include] changes in weight, . . . change in cervical secretion, jaundice, allergic skin rash, chloasma (darkened skin on the face), depression, gastrointestinal disturbances and breast changes" (Boston Women's Health Book Collective, 1976). The progestin-only pill is probably safer in terms of serious side effects than the combination pill, but there are no long term studies that prove this.

Serious problems associated with the pill can be summarized by the acronym ACHES (Table 11.2).

Sharing Responsibility   The woman's partner can share in the responsibility of oral contraceptive use by understanding the manifestations and consequences of potential side effects and sharing the expense of the exam and pills. He can also use condoms as a backup method for the rest of the cycle if the woman forgets one or more pills or during the initial month of pill use, when the risk of pregnancy is higher. Sharing responsibility may be more important with the progestin-only pill than with

TABLE 11.2 REMEMBER "ACHES" FOR THE PILL. Women who use the pill and their partners need to know the signs of serious problems from the pill. The acronym ACHES spells it out. A woman who develops any of these problems should contact her health-care practitioner.

Acronym	Five signals	Possible problem
A	Abdominal pain (severe)	Gallbladder disease, liver tumor, blood clot
C	Chest pain (severe) or shortness of breath	Blood clot in lungs or heart attack
H	Headaches (severe)	Stroke, high blood pressure, or migraine headache
E	Eye problems: blurred vision, flashing lights, or blindness	Stroke, high blood pressure, or temporary vascular problems of many possible sites
S	Severe leg pain (calf or thigh)	Blood clot in legs

Source: Hatcher et al., 1980.

the combination pill, as the progestin-only pill is slightly less effective (see Table 11.1). Condoms and noncoital sexual sharing, as well as the use of a diaphragm and foam, can help ensure contraception during the mid-cycle ovulation phase.

A Comment on Oral Contraceptives   The long list of potential side effects of oral contraceptives makes it difficult to not sound alarmist. However, informed choice is dependent on thorough information and weighing the alternatives. Much remains to be learned about the effects of oral contraceptives, and studies are still contradictory.

Many informed women continue to choose the pill as their best contraceptive alternative. The physical risks associated with the pill are still less than with pregnancy. However, since the pill can aggravate some medical problems, a woman with a history of certain conditions should use a different method of contraception. These conditions include blood clots, strokes, circulation problems, heart problems, jaundice, cancer of the breast or uterus, and undiagnosed genital bleeding. In addition, a woman who currently has a liver disease, who suspects or knows she is pregnant, who is nursing her child, or who is 40 years of age or older should not take the pill.

Finally, women who should weigh the potential risks most carefully and use the pill only under close medical supervision are those who have problems with migraine headaches, depression, high blood pressure, epilepsy, diabetes or prediabetes symptoms, asthma, and varicose veins (Boston Women's Health Book Collective, 1976).

Intrauterine Devices

Intrauterine devices, commonly referred to as *IUDs*, are small plastic objects that are inserted into the uterus through the vaginal canal and cervical os. Although IUDs did not become widely available until the 1960s, people have used the technique of inserting an object into the uterus to prevent pregnancy for a long time. For example,

Middle Eastern camel drivers would insert a smooth stone into female camels' uteri so they wouldn't become pregnant during desert crossings.

Contemporary IUDs are made in different shapes and sizes, as shown in Figure 11.1. All are made of flexible plastic; the CU 7 (Copper 7) and the Copper T have copper wire wrapped around portions of them. The Progestasert T has slow-releasing progesterone embedded in the plastic. Most IUDs have fine plastic threads attached to them; the ends are cut to hang slightly out of the cervix into the vagina (Figure 11.2).

How the IUD Works   Exactly how an IUD works has not been scientifically established. The most widely held theory suggests that the uterine lining is slightly irritated and inflamed due to the presence of this foreign object, and as a result the fertilized ovum does not implant. The IUD also alters the delicate timing of ovum transport through the tubes. The copper wire on some IUDs allegedly increases effectiveness, again in some unknown way. The progesterone in Progestasert T may have some of the contraceptive effects of the progestin-only birth control pill.

How to Use the IUD   The IUD is inserted by a trained health-care professional using sterile instruments. Most IUDs come with an inserter. The inserter and IUD are introduced through the os and into the uterus. The inserter is then withdrawn, leaving the IUD in place, as shown in Figure 11.2. It is preferable that a woman be menstruating when her IUD is inserted to ensure that she is not pregnant. (Also, the os is slightly dilated at this time, which facilitates insertion and reduces discomfort.) A woman should be screened for gonorrhea before inserting an IUD, since the procedure may cause the bacteria to be pushed farther into the uterus. The Progestasert T needs to be replaced yearly because the progesterone gradually loses its effectiveness. An IUD with copper on it should be replaced every three to five years. Barring complications, other IUDs can stay in place until a pregnancy or alternate method of contraception is desired. IUDs should be removed when a woman reaches menopause and stops menstruating (Hatcher et al., 1980).

Shared Responsibility   A backup method such as foam, condoms, or the diaphragm is recommended for the first one to three months after an IUD has been inserted. Some women and their partners choose to continue to use a backup method each month during the fertile mid-cycle.

While a woman is using an IUD, she or her partner needs to check each month after her menstrual period to see that the string is the same length as when inserted. To do this, she or he reaches into the vagina with a finger and finds the cervix. If the cervix is far back in the vagina and difficult to reach, she can squat or bear down to make it more accessible. The string should be felt in the middle of the cervix, protruding out of the small indentation in the center. Occasionally, it curls up in the os and cannot be felt, but any time a woman or her partner cannot find it, she needs to check with her health-care specialist. She should also seek attention if the string seems longer or the plastic protrudes out of the os. This probably means that the IUD is not in place correctly.

FIGURE 11.1 VARIOUS TYPES OF INTRAUTERINE DEVICES

(a) Progestasert T.   (b) Copper T.   (c) Copper 7.   (d) Lippies loop.

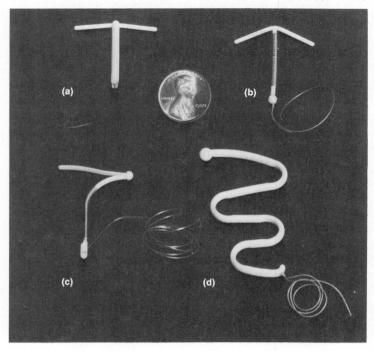

FIGURE 11.2 INTRAUTERINE DEVICE IN THE UTERUS

The IUD is inserted into the uterus and the string hangs out of the cervical os.

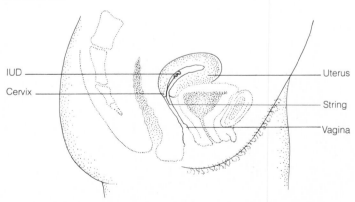

Potential Advantages of the IUD   The primary advantage to the IUD is that when it is in place, the woman has contraceptive protection with little inconvenience beyond the monthly checking of the string. In one woman's words:

> The IUD insertion was uncomfortable to me and my periods are now longer, but all I have to do is to check the IUD string once a month instead of taking a pill every day or using the diaphragm each time. (Authors' files)

The IUD allows uninterrupted sexual interaction. Beyond the initial cost for the exam and insertion, there are no further supplies to be purchased. Although an IUD cannot be inserted until two to three months after childbirth, it does not interfere with nursing once it is in place. Some women who experience initial discomfort after the insertion find that this decreases in a month or two.

Potential Disadvantages of the IUD   Discomfort, cramping, bleeding, or pain may occur during insertion. The discomfort or bleeding sometimes continues for a few days and occasionally much longer. Approximately 15% of IUD users have them removed because of bleeding or spotting (Hatcher et al., 1980). Women who keep their IUDs typically experience an increase in menstrual cramps and have a longer and heavier menstrual flow. Other women may have intermittent cramps and bleeding throughout their cycle. Anemia (lack of iron in the blood) is common among IUD users, as the following account illustrates:

> I thought the IUD would be a great method, but I had such bad cramping and heavy bleeding intermittently during the three months before I had it removed, I was rarely in the mood for sex. I also became anemic and had to take iron for awhile. (Authors' files)

The Progestasert T usually diminishes bleeding by half of the regular menstrual flow (Hatcher et al., 1980).

From 5% to 20% of users will expel their IUD within the first year following insertion (Hatcher et al., 1980). The uterus reacts to the IUD as a foreign body, contracting and sometimes pushing it out. This is most likely to occur during menstruation, so a woman needs to check her tampons or sanitary napkins before disposing of them. Also, during intercourse her partner might feel the IUD protruding out of the cervix. It is wise to check the string several times a month at first, because if the IUD is either incorrectly positioned in the uterus or is expelled, the woman will not be protected against an undesired pregnancy.

As discussed in Chapter 4, the multidirectional muscles of the uterus are interwoven. In rare cases, the IUD breaks through the uterine wall. This perforation can partially extend through the wall, or the IUD can slip completely through the uterus into the abdominal cavity. When this occurs, surgery may be necessary to remove it. Occasionally (although rarely) a woman may require a hysterectomy as a result of this type of complication. If an IUD string seems to become shorter, this may be an indication that the IUD is perforating, and the woman should seek immediate medical attention.

Another significant disadvantage associated with the IUD is that it increases a woman's chances of uterine infection. The infection can occur at insertion if bacteria are introduced into the sterile environment of the uterus. The string of the IUD is also sometimes suspected of providing an entryway for bacteria. An IUD is likely to aggravate a gonorrhea infection and make treatment more difficult. Most physicians recommend removal of an IUD when a woman is being treated for a uterine infection.

Pelvic inflammatory disease (PID) is also more common among women with IUDs. One of the complications associated with PID is partial or complete blockage of the fallopian tubes and a resultant increased chance of ectopic pregnancy. It is believed that the overall rate of ectopic pregnancies is higher for women who use the IUD than for those who do not (Hatcher et al., 1980). Recent studies indicate that the incidence of ectopic pregnancy is higher with the Progestasert IUD than with other types (FDA Bulletin, 1978–9). Tubal blockage from PID can also be a contributing factor in infertility.

Other problems may occur if a woman becomes pregnant with an IUD in place. Her chances of a miscarriage in the first six months of pregnancy are two to three times higher than those of a woman who had been using other methods or no contraception when she conceived (Harlap et al., 1980). After some reports of deaths of pregnant IUD users in 1974, removal of the IUD when a woman becomes pregnant is now usually recommended. It is thought that during pregnancy as the uterus enlarges, the string in the vagina is drawn into the uterus and carries bacteria with it. The string may also act as a wick for bacteria, facilitating the spread of any infectious organisms. Due to the increased blood flow in the tissues of the uterus during pregnancy, such an infection travels rapidly through the woman's bloodstream and may cause death within 24 to 48 hours. The Dalkon Shield was implicated in 13 deaths involving pregnancy, and it was taken off the market. However, some deaths occurred with other IUDs as well (Seaman and Seaman, 1978). If an IUD is removed during the first three months of pregnancy, the risk of a subsequent miscarriage is increased only slightly over no IUD use (Foreman et al., 1981).

TABLE 11.3 REMEMBER "PAINS" FOR THE IUD. Women who use the IUD and their partners need to know the signs of serious problems from the IUD. The acronym PAINS spells it out. A woman who develops any of these problems should contact her health-care practitioner.

Acronym	Five signals
P	Period late, no period
A	Abdominal pain
I	Increased temperature, fever, chills
N	Nasty discharge, foul discharge
S	Spotting, bleeding, heavy periods, clots

Source: Hatcher et al., 1980.

Finally, a number of previous or current conditions seem to be related to heightened risks in using an IUD. A woman should consult a health-care practitioner if any of these conditions apply to her: a history of or active PID or gonorrhea; current or suspected pregnancy; or current conditions such as endometriosis, anemia, heavy menstrual flow or cramping, a very small or malformed uterus, heart disease, or the use of anticoagulants (Boston Women's Health Book Collective, 1976).

Serious problems associated with the IUD can be summarized by the acronym PAINS (Table 11.3). Besides the IUD and the pill, a number of other methods are available that may have fewer potential complications for some women. We will look at these in the paragraphs that follow.

Diaphragms

The *diaphragm* is a round, soft latex dome with a thin flexible spring around the rim (see Figure 11.3). It is inserted into the vagina with a spermicidal contraceptive cream or jelly that comes in a tube. The diaphragm rim fits from in back of the cervix to forward underneath and behind the pubic bone, as shown in Figure 11.4. Some women's cervixes are located farther back in the vagina, and others are closer to the opening. Therefore, diaphragms vary in size from 2 to 4 inches in diameter to fit each individual correctly. Diaphragms are also made with different kinds of springs: the coil spring, the flat spring, or the arcing spring. Some women find one style easier to insert and better fitting than another. For example, the arcing spring may stay in place better than a coil spring for a woman with reduced vaginal muscle tone.

How the Diaphragm Works   The cervix lies within the dome of the diaphragm, which covers it. When the diaphragm is used with the cream or jelly, it provides a chemical as well as mechanical barrier to prevent sperm from entering the cervix and uterus.

How to Use the Diaphragm   The diaphragm must be fitted by a skilled practitioner. (After pills and IUDs came onto the market in the 1960s, some medical schools stopped teaching how to fit diaphragms.) A size estimate is made during the pelvic exam; then different sizes and types are inserted until the best fit is found. It is very important that the examiner thoroughly instructs the woman on how to insert and care for her diaphragm. Then the woman practices inserting it herself in the examination room until she is able to do so. The examiner makes a final check to see if she has correctly learned the insertion technique.

Figure 11.4 shows how to use the diaphragm. First, a tablespoon of the cream or jelly (available at pharmacies without a prescription) is put into the cup of the diaphragm. Some of the spermicide should also be spread around the inside of the rim. The sides of the rim are then squeezed together with one hand, while the other hand opens the inner lips of the vulva. Some women prefer to use the plastic diaphragm introducers, while others find these more difficult than manual insertion. The diaphragm is then pushed into the vagina, with the cream side facing upwards. The woman may be standing, lying, or squatting.

FIGURE 11.3 DIAPHRAGM AND CONTRACEPTIVE CREAM OR JELLY

The diaphragm is made of a soft latex dome on a coil spring and is used with contraceptive cream or jelly.

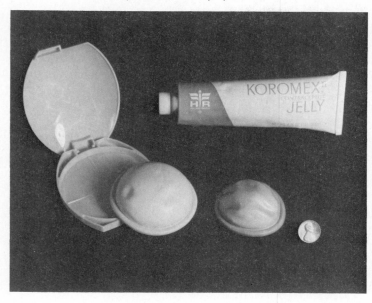

FIGURE 11.4 INSERTION AND CHECKING OF DIAPHRAGM

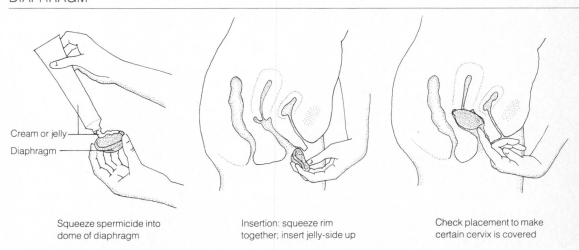

Cream or jelly —
Diaphragm —

Squeeze spermicide into dome of diaphragm

Insertion: squeeze rim together; insert jelly-side up

Check placement to make certain cervix is covered

344

After the diaphragm is inserted, it is important for the woman or her partner to feel it with the fingers to determine if the cervix is covered by the diaphragm dome. Occasionally, the back rim lodges in front of the cervix, so that it offers no contraceptive protection. When the diaphragm is placed correctly, it rarely can be felt by the woman or her partner during intercourse.

Some sources state that the diaphragm can be inserted up to six hours prior to intercourse; others recommend no more than two hours prior without an additional application of spermicide. The shorter time span may afford better protection. The diaphragm can also be inserted just before intercourse. Some women prefer to insert the diaphragm ahead of time in privacy, while others share this experience with their partner. As one explains:

I have had a traditional repulsion of "just-before" birth control devices such as condoms and diaphragms. However, with my present partner the use of the diaphragm is part of sexual excitement for us. We usually become quite stimulated before reaching for the good old jelly and diaphragm, and then I continue with manual clitoral stimulation while she inserts the device. I have also learned to put it in while she continues to stimulate herself and me at the same time. Also, any leftover jelly works nicely as a lubricant. The pause between being ready for intercourse and actually doing it seems to heighten the whole thing. (Authors' files)

The diaphragm should remain in the vagina for at least six hours following intercourse to assure that the spermicide has killed all the sperm in the vaginal folds. It is important not to douche during this time. If intercourse occurs again before six hours elapse, the diaphragm can be left in place, but additional cream or jelly needs to be inserted. Reusable plastic applicators can be purchased with the creams and jellies.

To remove the diaphragm, a finger is inserted into the vagina under the front rim of the diaphragm. Squatting or bearing down may make it easier to find the rim. After a slight pull with one finger to break the air seal, it is easier to grasp the rim with two fingers to pull it out. After removal, the diaphragm should be washed with a mild soap and warm water. Then it should be carefully and thoroughly dried, dusted with cornstarch, and returned to its plastic case.

A well cared-for diaphragm can last for several years. It should remain soft, flexible, and free of defects. To make certain of this, the woman should check it periodically. Any tiny leaks can be detected by placing water in the dome. The diaphragm should also be brought along when a woman has her yearly Pap smear so that its fit and condition may be evaluated. A different diaphragm may be needed after a pregnancy (including an aborted pregnancy) or a weight loss or gain of 10 pounds or more.

A most important point in using the diaphragm is to have it available. It simply will not do a woman any good at home in a drawer when she is at the beach for the weekend. Depending on a woman's life style, the best place for it may be in her purse, bedroom, bathroom—wherever is most convenient for her situation. Some women prefer to own two diaphragms to assure availability.

Part Four: Sexuality and the Life Cycle

Shared Responsibility   As the earlier anecdote indicates, inserting the diaphragm can be a shared experience. A woman's partner can learn to insert the diaphragm in the examination room if the health-care practitioner agrees, or later, from the woman herself. Checking to see if it is in correctly and helping remove it can also be a mutual responsibility. Both remembering to use the diaphragm and a commitment to do so are very important.

Potential Advantages of the Diaphragm   The recent resurgence of the diaphragm is most likely due to concern about pill and IUD side effects, coupled with reports of high rates of contraceptive effectiveness with diaphragm use. In studies where women are thoroughly instructed in the use and care of their diaphragms, effectiveness is roughly comparable to the pill and IUD (see footnote, Table 11.1). The largest recent examination of diaphragm effectiveness also reported that 80% of the women who began using the diaphragm were still doing so at the end of one year (Lane et al., 1976). Most importantly, there are no potentially dangerous side effects comparable to those encountered when using pills and IUDs.

Through learning to use the diaphragm a woman may become more knowledgeable and comfortable with her body. She may also find it helpful in making decisions about relating sexually with others. For example:

Since I've been using the diaphragm, I've moved more slowly into sexual relations. I want to discuss my method with a new partner before we have intercourse. When I'm feeling like I'm not comfortable enough to talk about birth control, I'm not ready to have intercourse. (Authors' files)

Some people think that there may be some additional positive side effects to proper use of the diaphragm. It is speculated that some spermicidal jellies and creams may promote vaginal health and decrease the incidence of vaginal infections. There is also some evidence that certain contraceptive creams, jellies, and foams may help prevent gonorrhea (Singh et al., 1972).

Potential Disadvantages of the Diaphragm   The diaphragm is not without disadvantages, however. Some people may find it is inconvenient, that using the diaphragm interrupts spontaneity, or that the cream or jelly is messy. The cream or jelly can also interfere with oral-genital sex. However, a couple can engage in oral-genital contact before inserting the diaphragm, or the woman's partner can focus stimulation on the clitoral rather than vaginal area. Occasionally, women or their partners experience irritation from a particular cream or jelly. Usually, switching to a different brand will take care of any difficulty. In rare instances, a woman is allergic to the latex of the diaphragm. Using a plastic type of diaphragm instead can eliminate this problem.

Poor diaphragm fit may occasionally cause problems. Since diaphragms are fitted when a woman is not sexually aroused, they may not fit as well during sexual arousal due to the vaginal expansion that occurs. The penis may then be placed between the diaphragm and cervix. This is most likely to happen during position changes, with reinsertion of the penis, and in the woman-on-top position. The cream or jelly will still provide some contraceptive protection if this occurs. If either partner feels the diaphragm during intercourse, she or he should check to see if it is correctly in place. Some women report bladder discomfort, urethral irritation, or recurrent cystitis from rim pressure. Using another diaphragm size or rim type may eliminate these difficulties (Hatcher et al., 1980). A few women with certain pelvic structure problems, like marked loss of vaginal muscle tone and support, cannot effectively use the diaphragm.

Cervical Caps

The *cervical cap* is a thimble-shaped cup made of rubber or plastic (Figure 11.5). The cap is like a miniature diaphragm that comes in different sizes, but fits only over the cervix. Although it can be used alone, it is usually recommended that a spermicide be used with the cap (Cappiello and Grainger-Harrison, 1981).

Different versions of the cervical cap have been used for centuries. In ancient Sumatra women molded opium to fit over their cervixes. In the Orient an oiled, silky paper called *musgami* was made into cup shapes to be used in the same manner. European women melted beeswax into cervical discs. In eighteenth-century Europe Casanova promoted the idea of using a squeezed-out lemon half to cover the cervix. The modern cervical cap was developed in 1838 by a German gynecologist who took a wax impression of each patient's cervix and made custom cervical caps out of rubber (Seaman and Seaman, 1978).

The cervical cap is widely used in Europe today, but it is relatively unknown in the United States. The cervical cap is not recognized by the FDA as a birth control method, and, perhaps as a result, there has been little research done on it. Some writers believe that research and development of the cervical cap has lagged because it is not as profitable for drug companies as other contraceptive methods as it does not require yearly replacement (Seaman and Seaman, 1978). However, some health clinics and physicians are distributing cervical caps, and in early 1981 the FDA began to study this method's contraceptive effectiveness (Cappiello and Grainger-Harrison, 1981). There is also some current research on devising caps with one-way valves to allow for discharge of cervical secretions and menstrual flow (Arthur, 1980; Goepp, 1982).

How to Use the Cervical Cap The cervical cap comes in different sizes and must be individually fitted by a skilled practitioner. When a woman uses the cap, she or her partner fills it one- to two-thirds full of spermicide. The cap is inserted by folding its edges together and sliding it into the vagina along the vaginal floor. The cup is then pressed onto the cervix. The woman or her partner then sweeps a finger around the cap to see if the cervix is covered and depresses the dome of the cap to feel the cervix through the rubber. A woman can usually reach her cervix more easily if she is in a squatting or upright sitting position. The cap can be inserted hours or minutes before intercourse. It should not be removed for at least six hours following intercourse and douching should be avoided during this period. Pulling on one side of the rim will

FIGURE 11.5 CERVICAL CAPS

347

break the suction to permit easy removal of the cap from the vagina. After removal, the cap should be washed with warm water and soap and dried.

Shared Responsibility A woman's partner can learn to insert, remove, and care for the cervical cap. He can also help her to remember to use it.

Potential Advantages of the Cervical Cap A major advantage of the cervical cap is the lack of side effects. Another is its low cost. Women who cannot use the diaphragm because of pelvic structure problems or loss of vaginal muscle tone or support can often use this method. The cap can be left in place longer than the diaphragm and is less expensive because it requires less spermicide.

Potential Disadvantages of the Cervical Cap A woman who has distortions of her cervix from cysts or lacerations is usually an unsuitable candidate for cervical cap use. Currently available caps will fit only 60%–75% of women (Cappiello and Grainger-Harrison, 1981). The cap is usually more difficult to learn to use than the diaphragm, and for some people it is uncomfortable to wear. There is some concern that wearing the cap for prolonged periods may cause problems by damaging the cervix or interrupting the normal discharge of secretions from the cervix, although there are no clear data on this matter. Currently, two major disadvantages of the cervical cap are the difficulty in obtaining one and the lack of scientific research on the utility of this method.

Vaginal Spermicides

There are several types of *vaginal spermicides*. The most widely used, commonly called foam, is a white substance that looks like shaving cream. It comes in pressurized cans and has a plastic applicator (Figure 11.6). Foam is available in pharmacies without a prescription. (Feminine hygiene products, although often displayed along with various brands of foam, are *not* contraceptives.) A new type of vaginal spermicide, a vaginal suppository, was introduced to American markets in 1977. It has an oval shape and contains the same spermicidal chemical found in foam (Figure 11.6). The third kind of vaginal spermicide consists of contraceptive creams and jellies. Although some of these are made to be used without a diaphragm, they are not as effective as foams or suppositories and are often not recommended for use without a diaphragm. Therefore, we will not discuss them further in this section.

How Spermicides Work Foam, suppositories, creams, and jellies contain a spermicide, a chemical which kills sperm. When foam is inserted with the applicator, it rapidly covers the vaginal walls and the cervical os. By contrast, contraceptive vaginal suppositories take about 20 minutes to dissolve and cover the walls. One brand of suppositories, Encare, effervesces and creates a foam inside the vagina. Other brands melt.

How to Use Vaginal Spermicides Some brands of foam come with an applicator that can be filled ahead of time; others are "prefilled." For maximum effectiveness, foam should be inserted into the vagina no more than a half-hour before intercourse and preferably as close to intercourse as possible. First, the can should be shaken well to mix the spermicide. Depending on the brand, the applicator on the top of the can is either pressed or tilted. The foam then enters the applicator, pushing the plunger upwards. It is a good idea to have an extra can on hand in case one becomes empty.

To insert the foam, the woman first lies down. The vaginal lips can be opened with one hand and the applicator inserted with the other, in the same way that tampons are inserted (aiming towards the small of the back). Once the tip of the applicator is well inside the vagina, the plunger is pushed to deposit the foam by the cervix (Figure 11.7). The foam quickly disperses to cover the vaginal walls. If intercourse is delayed beyond a half hour, another application should be inserted prior to coitus.

Proper use of the spermicidal vaginal suppository is somewhat different from that of foam. The suppository must be inserted at least 10 minutes before intercourse to allow it to dissolve in the warmth and moisture of the vagina. It should be placed at the back of the vagina by the cervix rather than at the vaginal opening. The couple must either have intercourse within an hour of inserting the suppository or insert another 10 minutes before intercourse.

As with spermicides used with the diaphragm, another application of foam or another suppository is necessary with each further act of intercourse. If a woman douches, she needs to wait eight hours after intercourse to assure that the spermicide has killed the sperm. It is probably better to shower than take a bath to prevent the spermicide from being rinsed out of the vagina.

FIGURE 11.6 VAGINAL SPERMICIDES

349

Vaginal spermicides are available in pharmacies (without a prescription). (a) Foam and applicator. (b) Suppositories.

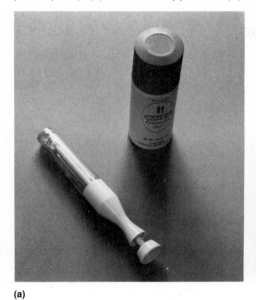

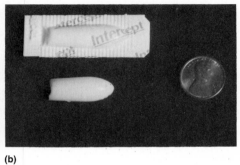

(a)

(b)

FIGURE 11.7 INSERTION OF FOAM

The filled applicator is inserted into the vagina and the foam is deposited at the back of the vaginal canal.

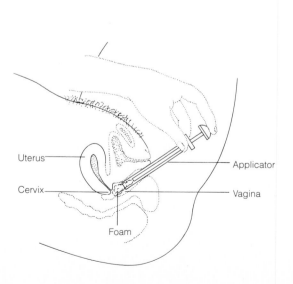

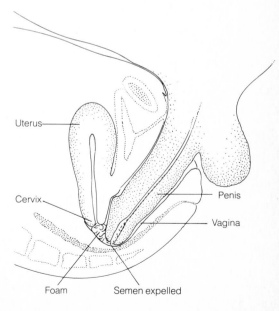

Shared Responsibility   Purchasing the spermicide, remembering to use it, and inserting it can all be shared by a partner. Using condoms along with foam or suppositories, particulary during ovulation, will increase the overall contraceptive effectiveness.

Potential Advantages of Vaginal Spermicides   Since spermicides are available in pharmacies, this method does not require a visit to a physician's office. It also has no known dangerous side effects to the woman, and some couples welcome the additional lubrication spermicides provide. As with the diaphragm cream or jelly, spermicidal foam and suppositories may give some protection against vaginal infections and venereal disease. The suppository has the advantage of being small and convenient to use.

Potential Disadvantages of Vaginal Spermicides   Occasionally, a woman or her partner may report irritation of genital tissues from the foam or suppositories. Changing brands will often alleviate this difficulty, but in some cases any brand causes discomfort. Some of the suppositories may not dissolve completely and feel gritty. Some women or couples dislike the additional lubrication during intercourse or the postcoital discharge following intercourse. Because of the unpleasant taste, using vaginal spermicides may limit couples who engage in cunnilingus after intercourse. (A couple can still have oral sex before inserting the foam or suppositories.) These products may also have a soaplike scent that is disagreeable to some users. Also, some people believe that inserting foam or suppositories, even though the procedure takes only about 30 seconds, interrupts spontaneity. One specific disadvantage of the spermicidal suppositories is that their contraceptive effectiveness has not been thoroughly established.

There is some preliminary indication of a link between the use of vaginal spermicides during or after conception and miscarriages and congenital disorders in infants. Jick et al. (1981) found that women who had used vaginal spermicides (including foam, cream, and jelly) prior to conception had 1.8 times as many miscarriages that required hospitalization as other women. Also, more than twice as many infants born of women who used vaginal spermicides had major congenital anomalies as other infants. The researchers speculate that these problems could occur in several ways. The spermicides could damage sperm which, if one fertilized an ovum, could produce abnormalities. Chemicals from the spermicide could also be absorbed into the bloodstream and damage the ovum prior to conception or, if spermicides were used following conception, the embryo itself could be damaged. These writers emphasize that these results are tentative until confirmed by other data.

Condoms

Condoms, also called "safes," prophylactics, and rubbers, are currently the only temporary method of birth control available for men. A condom is a sheath that fits over the erect penis and is made of thin surgical latex or sheep membrane. Condoms are available without prescription at pharmacies, family-planning clinics, by mail

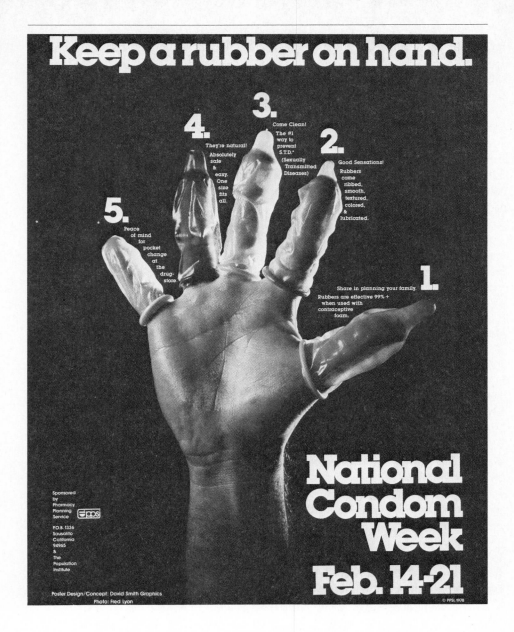

Keep a rubber on hand.

4.
They're natural!
Absolutely
safe
&
easy.
One
size
fits
all.

3.
Come Clean!
The #1
way to
prevent
S.T.D.*
(Sexually
Transmitted
Diseases)

2.
Good Sensations!
Rubbers
come
ribbed,
smooth,
textured,
colored,
&
lubricated.

5.
Peace
of mind
for
pocket
change
at
the
drug-
store.

Share in planning your family. **1.**
Rubbers are effective 99%+
when used with
contraceptive
foam.

Sponsored
by
Pharmacy
Planning
Service ☐pps

P.O.B. 1336
Sausalito
California
94965
&
The
Population
Institute

Poster Design/Concept: David Smith Graphics
Photo: Fred Lyon

**National
Condom
Week
Feb. 14-21**

© PPSI, 1978

order, and, in some areas, in vending machines. Recent changes in the laws of some states have made condoms more accessible by placing them on drugstore shelves rather than behind the counter, much to the relief of some customers:

The rubber-buying scene in the movie *Summer of '42* was hilariously similar to the first time I bought rubbers in our local small pharmacy: waiting until no one else was in the store, trying to look casual, and really not knowing how to ask for them. (Authors' files)

Chapter Eleven: Contraception

In the past, laws regarding condom use for contraception have been very restrictive. Their sale for contraceptive use was made illegal by most state legislatures beginning in 1868, and by Congress in 1873. Many of the laws also made it a criminal offense for one person to inform another of the condoms' utility in pregnancy prevention. These laws have all changed and anticondom laws have been declared unconstitutional. However, until a few years ago many condom packages still bore a label: "Sold only for the prevention of disease" ("Condoms," 1979).

Most condoms are packaged—rolled up and wrapped in foil or plastic—and come lubricated or nonlubricated. There is less chance of the condom breaking if it is lubricated, and some men report less reduction of penile sensation during intercourse with lubricated condoms. The sheep membrane, natural skin condoms are more expensive but often interfere less with sensation than do the latex ones. Some condoms have a small nipple on the end, called a reservoir tip, and others have a contoured shape or textured surface (Figure 11.8). They have an average shelf life of about two years, although not all packages are dated. Condoms should not be stored in hot places like the glove compartment of a car or a back pocket because the heat can deteriorate the latex.

How the Condom Works When used properly, both the ejaculate and the fluid from Cowper's glands secretions are contained within the tip of the condom. Therefore, sperm are inside the condom rather than the vagina.

How to Use the Condom Most condoms are packaged rolled up. Correct use includes unrolling the condom down over the erect penis before any contact with the vulva. Sperm in the Cowper's gland secretions or in the ejaculate can travel from outside of the labia to the inside of the vagina. For maximum comfort and sensation, an uncircumcized man can retract the foreskin before rolling the condom over the penis. With plain-ended condoms, without the reservoir tip, the end needs to be twisted before rolling the condom down over the penis (Figure 11.9). This leaves some room at the end for the ejaculate and reduces the chances of the condom breaking. If a condom breaks or slips off, contraceptive foam, cream, or jelly should be inserted into the vagina immediately.

If the condom is nonlubricated, some vaginal secretion, saliva, or K-Y jelly needs to be put on the outside of the condom before intromission. After ejaculation, due to detumescence of the penis, it is important for the condom to be held at the base of the penis before withdrawing it out of the vagina. Otherwise it may slip off and spill semen inside the vagina.

The first time I used a rubber, I relaxed inside her after I came, holding her for a while. Then I withdrew, leaving the rubber behind. My first thought was, "Oh, no, it's dissolved." I reached inside her vagina and found the rubber. We used some foam right away but were nervous until her next period started. (Authors' files)

Condoms are best disposed of in the garbage rather than the toilet because they have been known to clog plumbing.

FIGURE 11.8 CONDOMS353

FIGURE 11.8 CONDOMS

(a) Unrolled condom with plain end. (b) Unrolled condom with reservoir tip.

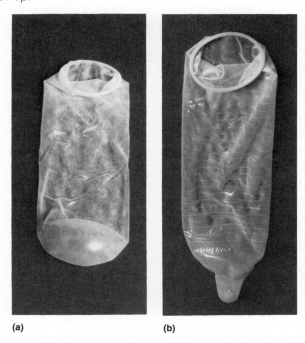

(a)   **(b)**

FIGURE 11.9 CORRECT USE OF PLAIN-END CONDOM

The end of a plain-end condom needs to be twisted as it is rolled onto the penis in order to leave space at the tip.

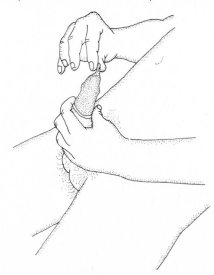

Shared Responsibility   The woman partner can share the responsibility of this method of birth control by helping pay for the condoms, remembering to use them, putting them on, or holding on to the base after ejaculation before her partner withdraws. Women who want their prospective partners to use condoms may wish to carry them, since there is no guarantee that the man will be prepared.

Potential Advantages of Condoms   Condoms are available without prescription. There are no harmful side effects associated with their use. If condoms are not the primary method of birth control, they are useful as a backup. Some men prefer the slightly lessened sensation because they find that the duration of intercourse before ejaculation is prolonged. Since the semen is contained inside the condom, some women appreciate its tidiness.

I really like the juiciness of sex when I can bathe afterwards, but when we go camping and don't have a stream or shower handy, my husband uses condoms so it's not as messy. (Authors' files)

Condoms provide protection from contracting and spreading sexually transmitted diseases and vaginal infections. For this reason, venereal disease experts advocate their use for both heterosexual couples and homosexual men who have more than one sexual partner.

Potential Disadvantages of Condoms   Unless putting on the condom is incorporated as part of sexual interaction, it can interrupt spontaneity. Reduced penile sensitivity is seen as a disadvantage by some. Condoms can break or slip off, but this is not usual.

Methods Based on the Menstrual Cycle

The birth control methods we have already discussed require use of pills or devices. Some of these methods have side effects in some users. There may be health risks in the pill and the IUD. Other methods that we have looked at—condoms, foam, the diaphragm—have fewer side effects, but they require that the couple use them each time they have intercourse.

Many couples are interested in a birth control method that has no side effects, is inexpensive, and does not interrupt spontaneity during sexual interaction. In the next paragraphs, we will look at some methods of birth control based on the menstrual cycle, which may answer some of these couples' needs. These methods are sometimes referred to as natural family planning or fertility awareness methods. A fertile woman's body reveals subtle and overt signs of cyclic fertility that can be used both to help prevent and plan conception. The three methods—mucus, calendar, and basal body temperature—can be most effective when used together.

Mucus Method   The *mucus method*, also called the ovulation method, is based on the cyclic changes of the cervical mucus. These natural changes, if carefully observed, will reveal periods of fertility in the woman's cycle. To use this method, a woman learns to read the amounts and textures of vaginal secretions and to maintain a daily chart of the changes. A woman reads her mucus by wiping herself every time she goes to the bathroom and observing the secretions on the tissue. After menstruation there are usually some "dry days" when there is no vaginal discharge on the vulva. When a yellow or white sticky discharge begins, the fertile time is considered to have started. Unprotected coitus should be avoided. (Some ovulation method teachers say that abstinence from intercourse is preferable.) Several days later the ovulatory mucus appears. It is clear, stringy, and stretchy in consistency, similar to egg white. A drop of this mucus will stretch from an open thumb and forefinger. A vaginal feeling of wetness and lubrication accompanies this discharge. Its chemical balance and texture facilitate the entry of sperm into the uterus. Four days after the ovulatory mucus begins and a cloudy discharge resumes, it is considered safe to resume unprotected intercourse. The fertile period usually totals nine to 15 days out of each cycle. The temperature method is often combined with the mucus method to pinpoint the time of ovulation.

Many cities have classes in this method offered at a hospital or clinic. Each woman's mucus patterns may vary, and a class is the best way to learn to interpret the changes. The *Atlas of the Ovulation Method* by Billings et al. (1974) contains detailed information.

The Calendar Method With the *calendar method*, also called the rhythm method, a woman estimates the calendar time during her cycle when she is ovulating and fertile. To do this she keeps a chart, preferably for one year, of the length of her cycles. (She cannot be using oral contraceptives during this time, for they impose a cycle that may not be the same as the woman's own cycle.) The first day of menstruation is counted as day number one. The woman counts the number of days of her cycle, the last day being the one before the onset of menstruation. To determine the high risk days, she subtracts 18 from the number of days of her shortest cycle. For example, if her shortest cycle was 26 days, day number 8 would be the first high risk day when nonprotected coitus would be avoided. To estimate when nonprotected coitus could resume, she subtracts 10 from the number of days in her longest cycle. For example, if her longest cycle is 32 days, she would resume intercourse on day 22. In this fashion, she avoids coitus without birth control protection during the mid-cycle ovulation. The pattern for this woman would be either to abstain from coitus or use a barrier method from days 8 through 22. Forms of lovemaking other than intercourse can continue during the high risk days.

The Basal Body Temperature Method Another way of estimating high fertility days is through temperature. Immediately prior to ovulation, the *basal body temperature* (BBT, the body temperature at the resting state upon waking in the morning) drops slightly. After ovulation, the corpus luteum releases more progesterone, which causes the body temperature to rise slightly (0.2°–0.6°) (Figure 11.10). These temperature changes are slight, and a thermometer with easy-to-read gradations must be used.

FIGURE 11.10 BASAL BODY TEMPERATURE DURING A MODEL MENSTRUAL CYCLE

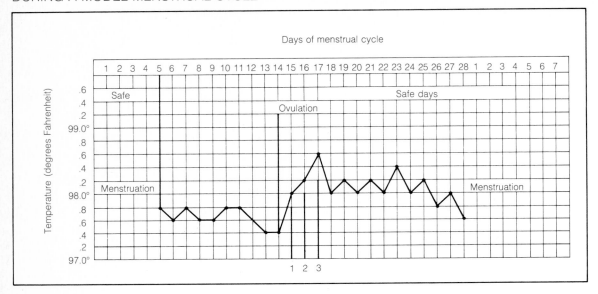

Shared Responsibility   The man can share in these methods by learning to recognize the mucus changes, helping to chart menstrual cycles, and reminding his partner to take morning temperatures. If the couple does not abstain from coitus during the fertile days, he can participate in the use of a barrier method. (However, it is usually recommended that the couple not use foam or diaphragms with the mucus method because they interfere with interpreting the mucus.) For those who abstain from coitus, mutual cooperation and sexual experimentation can greatly enhance the use of these methods.

Potential Advantages of Menstrual Cycle-Based Methods   A major advantage is that there are no side effects from these methods and that they are free or very inexpensive. Some women and their partners report increased comfort and appreciation of their bodies' cycles and processes. The fertile days, if abstinence from penile-vaginal intercourse is chosen, can provide time and motivation for noncoital sexual relating. Knowledge of cyclic changes can also help a couple to plan a pregnancy. Also, these methods are acceptable to some religious groups that oppose other contraceptive methods.

Potential Disadvantages of Menstrual Cycle-Based Methods   Learning to accurately detect the mucus and temperature changes involves practice, and with all of these methods a couple must keep records for several cycles before beginning to rely on them for contraception. The charting must be done diligently for increased accuracy; considerable commitment is essential to maintain daily observation and charting. These methods are more difficult for women who have irregular cycles, and some women are unable to clearly see mucus and temperature patterns. Also, vaginal infections, semen, and contraceptive foams, jellies, and creams make it more difficult to accurately interpret mucus.

While temperature changes are often good indicators of change in cycle, this method is fallible. Slight temperature variations can result from many conditions—a low-grade infection or cold, unrestful sleep, and so forth. Also, because sperm can remain alive in the fallopian tubes up to 72 hours, the preovulation temperature drop does not occur far enough ahead of time to safely avoid coitus. Although the temperature method is more effective in preventing an undesired pregnancy than no method, it is quite unreliable.

Even after careful arithmetic, the calendar method is very unreliable. Although ovulation usually occurs about 14 days before the onset of menstruation, even with a woman who ordinarily has regular cycles, the timing of ovulation and menstruation may vary due to factors such as illness, fatigue, or excitement. For a woman who routinely or periodically has irregular cycles, the calendar method is even less safe and requires longer abstention from coitus.

All these methods may also restrict spontaneity of intercourse and ejaculation during fertile times. Finally, present research indicates that these methods are considerably less effective than most others (Hatcher et al., 1980).

Other Methods

There are other methods of birth control that are less commonly used than the ones we have been discussing. Some of them are mentioned here, partly because they are often used both as birth control methods and as backups for other methods; and partly because people may have misconceptions about their effectiveness. We will discuss withdrawal, douching, and abstinence.

Withdrawal   The practice of the man removing his penis from the vagina just prior to ejaculation is known as *withdrawal*. The oft-unfulfilled hope is that there will be no sperm present to fertilize an ovum. However, withdrawal is not very effective. The pre-ejaculatory Cowper's gland secretions may contain sperm that can fertilize the egg, and it may be difficult for the man to judge exactly when he must withdraw. His tendency is likely to be to remain inside the vagina as long as possible, and this may be too long. Both partners may experience pleasure-destroying anxiety about whether he will withdraw in time. Furthermore, even withdrawal before ejaculation is not insurance against pregnancy. If sperm are deposited on the labia after withdrawal, they can swim into the vagina.

Douching   *Douching* after intercourse as a method of birth control is very ineffective. After ejaculation, some of the sperm are inside the uterus in a matter of minutes. It is also thought that the movement of the water from douching may help some sperm reach the opening of the cervix. Furthermore, frequent douching can irritate vaginal tissues.

Abstinence from Coitus   The voluntary avoidance of coitus is a 100% effective method of birth control. The rhythm, ovulation, or temperature method, combined with abstinence, is currently the only method of birth control sanctioned by the Catholic church. Individuals or couples abstain from intercourse for a variety of reasons, and they may still engage in self-stimulation and partner noncoital sexual interaction. As a man in his mid-20s states:

Right now in this relationship I'm very sexual; I'm just not "intercoursal." (Authors' files)

Postcoital Contraception

Women or couples may seek some kind of postcoital contraception following unprotected mid-cycle intercourse. The risk of pregnancy from unprotected mid-cycle intercourse ranges up to 30% (Hatcher et al., 1980). For contraception after intercourse, administration of high levels of hormones and insertion of an IUD are the methods most commonly used.

Diethylstilbestrol   Diethylstilbestrol *(DES)* is a synthetic estrogen often called the "morning-after pill." A woman has to begin the drug within 72 hours following intercourse, and she usually takes it for five days. The medication is a massive dose of estrogen and often causes nausea and vomiting. In 1975 the FDA approved DES as an emergency postcoital contraceptive. However, there is a great deal of controversy regarding its effectiveness and safety. DES was prescribed extensively from 1950–69 to pregnant women to prevent spontaneous abortion. Some daughters who were exposed in utero to DES have developed cancer of the vagina during adolescence and early adulthood, and some of the sons have developed abnormalities of sperm and the testes. For these reasons, if DES does not prevent the pregnancy, the FDA recommends that a woman consider an abortion. There is currently no evidence that postcoital use of DES contributes to cancer risk in the user. However, many writers see DES as an unattractive option because of the possible risks (Hatcher et al., 1978).

Progestins or Estrogen-Progestin   Some research has been done on using progestin or estrogen-progestin combinations for postcoital contraception. The drug is taken within 72 hours following intercourse, and the dosage is usually much smaller than with DES. Theoretically, these drugs are safer than DES; however, there are no conclusive data. If a woman uses any kind of morning-after pill, she must be aware of and watch for symptoms (Hatcher et al., 1980).

Morning-After IUD Insertion   Inserting an IUD within 24 hours following unprotected mid-cycle intercourse can prevent pregnancy. The Copper-7's effectiveness for this purpose has been demonstrated. Other IUDs inserted after intercourse are believed to prevent pregnancy, but as of yet, there are no published reports of their use in this manner. IUDs are believed to work by preventing implantation of the fertilized ovum, and they can be kept as an ongoing method. An IUD should not be used as morning-after protection if there has been a high risk of exposure to a sexually transmitted disease.

Shared Responsibility   The partner can help with postcoital contraception in several ways. He can be aware of the options and risks of the various methods or be willing to help find the necessary information. He can be supportive and encourage the woman to obtain immediate medical advice. He can also help in planning future contraceptive protection for his partner and himself.

The methods we have been discussing are all intended to prevent pregnancy. Sometimes an unwanted pregnancy does occur, however, either with or without birth control precautions. In this case, women or couples may decide to seek an abortion.

INDUCED ABORTION

Abortion, also a medical term for spontaneous miscarriage, is most commonly thought of as the induced removal of a fetus. Induced abortion continues to be a controversial issue in the United States and other countries. Beliefs regarding the beginning of life, the reproductive choice of women, and the quality of life influence the stand one takes regarding elective termination of pregnancy.

Laws regulating abortion continue to change. Abortion early in pregnancy was legal in ancient China and Europe. In the thirteenth century, St. Thomas Aquinas delineated the Catholic church's view that the fetus developed a soul 40 days after conception for males and 90 days for females. Abortion after ensoulment (development of the soul) became a serious crime. Early American common law allowed abortion until fetal movement or quickening was felt by the pregnant woman. Quickening usually occurs during the fourth or fifth month after conception.

In the late 1860s, Pope Pius IX decreed abortion a sin. In the United States during the Civil War era of the 1860s, abortion became illegal except when medically necessary to save the woman's life. Some of the reasons given for making abortion illegal included the high mortality rate from abortion due to scarcity of antiseptics and to crude abortion procedures. Also, population growth was seen by some decision-makers as important to the country's developing economy (Lader, 1966).

In contemporary times before abortion became legal again, women desperate to terminate their unwanted pregnancies sought illegal abortions or attempted to abort themselves. Women with money could fly to Europe or Japan or persuade an American physician to perform an abortion. Low-income women often resorted to unskilled, unsanitary, medically unsafe procedures. By 1967, due to the advocacy of women and men who organized to lobby for change, a few states began altering their abortion laws. In 1973, the Supreme Court legalized a woman's right to decide to terminate her pregnancy before the fetus has reached the age of viability. *Viability* is defined as the fetus's ability to survive independently of the woman's body. This usually occurs by the sixth or seventh month of pregnancy, but most abortions are done before the third month.

The legalization of abortion in 1973 has not been the end of the story. Legislation in the late 1970s greatly curtailed the availability of medically safe abortions to low-income women. In July 1977, the Hyde Amendment was passed and the Supreme Court ruled to prohibit federal Medicaid funds for abortions. (Medicaid is a state and federal joint program to provide payment of medical services for low-income citizens.) The Court also established that states are not required to provide Medicaid funds for the purpose of elective pregnancy termination. Before this legislation, one-third of the approximately one million annual abortions had been paid for by Medicaid. Many of the low-income women who carry their unwanted pregnancies to term and do not give the child out for adoption will have larger families, making it more difficult for them to break out of the cycle of poverty. While low-income women may not have the financial resources to choose a medical abortion, middle and upper income women are able to continue to obtain medically safe abortions.

Right-to-Life Versus Prochoice

Currently, abortion is a major social and political issue in the United States, characterized by highly polarized opinions for and against. The right-to-life advocates argue that life begins at conception and abortion is immoral. They wish to re-establish national legislation to make abortion illegal and to establish the "constitutional rights" of the unborn fetus. Although a recent Associated Press NBC News poll (October 5, 1981) revealed that 78% of people questioned believed abortion was a decision to be made by the woman and her physician, and 66% opposed an amendment to the Constitution that would make abortion illegal, the right-to-life minority is waging an active battle against legal and available abortion.

Prochoice advocates see abortions as a social necessity, due to imperfect and sometimes unavailable birth control methods and lack of education. They want abortion to be an option for women who are faced with the dilemma of an unwanted pregnancy and who decide that terminating it is their best alternative. Prochoice forces support a woman's choice not to have an abortion if she so desires, but they are strongly opposed to right-to-life legislation restricting others' choices. Many prestigious organizations have made public statements opposing right-to-life bills, including the National Academy of Sciences, the American Public Health Association, the American Medical Association, and the American College of Obstetricians and Gynecologists.

One study examined recent trends in abortion attitudes and differences and found that people who approve of legally available abortions are more likely to support civil liberties and women's rights. People who disapprove of legal abortion are more likely to have strongly committed Catholic and fundamentalist Protestant affiliations (Granberg and Granberg, 1980).

Medical Procedures for Abortion

There are several different abortion procedures used at different stages of pregnancy. The most common are the *suction curettage, D and E, prostaglandin induction*, and *saline injection*. The suction curettage is usually done from seven through 13 weeks after the last menstrual period. With suction curettage the cervical os is usually dilated

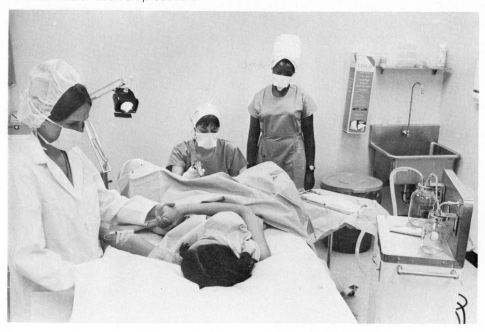

by graduated metal dilators or a small cylinder of seaweed stem *(Laminaria digitata)* inserted hours earlier. The laminaria slowly expands as it absorbs cervical moisture, and it gently opens the os. This gradual expansion reduces the chance of cervical trauma. During the abortion, a small plastic tube is inserted into the uterus. The tube is attached to a vacuum aspirator, which draws the fetal tissue, placenta, and built-up uterine lining out of the uterus. The suction curettage is done by physicians at clinics or hospitals, and the procedure takes about 10 minutes. However, admission, preparation, counseling, and recovery take longer. A local anesthetic may be used. There are minor risks of uterine infection or perforation, hemorrhage, or incomplete removal of the uterine contents. If a pregnancy progresses past approximately 12 weeks, the suction curettage procedure can no longer be performed as safely. The uterine walls have become thinner and perforation and bleeding are more likely.

D and E, or dilation and evacuation, is used commonly between 13 to 15 weeks of pregnancy. A combination of suction equipment, special forceps, and a curette (a metal instrument used to scrape the walls of the uterus) is used. General anesthesia is usually required and the cervix is dilated wider than with suction curettage (Hatcher et al., 1980). Since all of the abortion procedures performed after 13 weeks are riskier and more complicated, they are usually done in hospitals.

Prostaglandins (a type of human hormone) are currently among the most commonly used compounds to induce termination of second trimester pregnancies. (They are also sometimes used to induce full term labor.) The appropriate type of prostaglandin can be introduced into the vagina as a suppository or into the amniotic sac by inserting a needle through the abdominal wall. These hormones cause uterine contractions, and the fetus and placenta are usually expelled within 24 hours (Embrey, 1977).

Similar to intra-amniotic prostaglandin injections, two other methods for pregnancy termination after 13 weeks are the saline and urea injection procedures, in which either a saline or urea solution is injected into the amniotic cavity. These procedures kill the fetus and cause contractions to begin; a miscarriage is the result. An increasing number of abortions after 13 weeks are being performed by combined use of two or three of these substances (Hatcher et al., 1980).

Shared Responsibility   There are several ways in which a couple can share responsibility for abortion. First, the man can help his partner clarify her feelings and can express his own in the decisions to be made about an unwanted pregnancy. The decision-making process begins when a woman discovers that she is pregnant. After she has confirmed her suspicions with a pregnancy test, the woman will have to decide whether to carry the pregnancy and keep the child, to give it up for adoption, or to have an abortion. Important topics for a couple to discuss include each person's life situation at the time; their feelings about the pregnancy, possible choices, and each other; and their future plans as individuals and as a couple. If the couple disagrees on what to do, it is our opinion that the final decision rests with the woman. Also, male partners do not have a legal right to demand or deny abortion for the woman.

Once the woman has made a decision for abortion, the man can help pay medical expenses and accompany her to the clinic or hospital. According to several studies, about three-fourths of male partners of pregnant women agreed to the abortion decision and helped pay for the procedure (Pfuhl, 1978; Shostak, 1979). The man can also be understanding about not having intercourse for at least the week following the abortion and can help in planning effective postabortion contraception. Since the abortion process is likely to evoke some difficult emotions, the couple may find it useful to continue to talk with each other about their reactions.

Potential Advantages of Abortion   The most important advantage of abortion is that it is the only procedure that can terminate an unwanted pregnancy. It allows a woman the choice of having a child because she truly wants and is able to care for one. For many women, abortion eliminates the severe stress of an unwanted pregnancy (David, 1973), and most women report a sense of relief (Freeman et al., 1980). Another advantage is that the medical risks involved in abortion, especially early abortion, are minimal.

Potential Disadvantages of Abortion   A woman will usually experience bleeding and cramps for the first two weeks following an abortion. During this time, she should use sanitary pads instead of tampons to help protect against infection. She should not douche for at least a week for the same reason.

Some medical complications can result from abortion. Infection, intrauterine blood clots, cervical or uterine trauma, excessive bleeding, incomplete abortion, or continued pregnancy are some of the short term problems that can occur. Generally, research data about long term medical complications following abortion is inconclusive and contradictory (Hatcher et al., 1980), but research does indicate that having two or more abortions may lead to a higher incidence of miscarriages in subsequent pregnancies (Levin et al., 1980; Madore et al., 1981).

Abortion is usually a difficult decision for a woman and her partner to make. It means weighing and examining highly personal values and priorities. When made, the decision is usually the "best of the bad alternatives." Even if the pregnancy is unwanted, the woman and/or man may feel loss and sadness. They may also feel regret, depression, anxiety, guilt, or anger about the abortion or what led to needing to have the abortion. Research indicates that women who have abortions usually experience emotional distress before and after abortion, which tends to disappear within several months. Women who have repeat abortions experience higher emotional distress in interpersonal relationships than do women with a first abortion (Freeman et al., 1980).

A great many factors can affect the woman and/or man's emotional response to the abortion. The reactions of close friends and family, the attitude of the medical staff and physician performing the abortion, the individuals' values about abortion, the voluntariness or pressure from others about the decision, the nature and strength of the relationship of the woman and her partner all can contribute to positive or negative reactions. One study has found that support from partners, friends, and families was the most important variable in the degree of anxiety and depression women felt before and after abortion (Moseley et al., 1981).

The timing of the abortion may also be important; early abortions are medically, and usually emotionally, much easier than later abortions. A woman who has had a legal abortion is also less likely to be as upset as with an illegal, clandestine abortion.

Pregnancy Risk-Taking and Abortion

In many cases an unwanted pregnancy is clearly a matter of contraceptive failure. A woman and her partner can face a situation in which they have used an effective method of birth control correctly and consistently and the woman still became pregnant. For other women or couples seeking abortions, contraceptive risk-taking can be common.

To better understand the issues in unwanted pregnancies not related to method failure, one researcher (Luker, 1975) studied 500 women who had abortions. Luker's research showed that there can be various kinds of "costs" to contraceptive use. Some women stop using a method because they fear side effects. Obtaining birth control from a pharmacy or health-care practitioner can mean acknowledging one's intent to engage in or continue nonmarital intercourse, which may conflict with one's value system, cause guilt, and result in risk-taking. Actively seeking and using contraception is also contrary to the traditional role of female passivity. Pregnancy prevention may interfere with romantic passion, and, in some cases, a woman may fear alienating her partner by asking for cooperation in contraceptive planning and implementation. Using drugs and alcohol also increases the chances of risk-taking unless a woman uses the pill or IUD.

"Getting away with" contraceptive risk-taking often increases carelessness (Luker, 1975). For example, the couple who does not use the diaphragm on a few occasions during one month without a pregnancy resulting is likely to increase nonuse the following month. People also have a tendency to focus on present and obvious costs rather than on possible future costs.

In some cases lack of information about contraceptive methods results in risk-taking. Although the majority of women in Luker's (1975) study had previously demonstrated contraceptive skills, they began to do more contraceptive risk-taking, either believing that they were unlikely to become pregnant or because they placed a higher value on pregnancy. Two-thirds of the women interviewed reported that a gynecologist had told them that they would have difficulty becoming pregnant, and many consequently were not as careful with birth control.

Some women may take contraceptive risks because of the high social value placed on pregnancy. Pregnancy connotes fertility, womanhood, and adulthood in our society and is, accordingly, often considered a measure of a woman's worth. Pregnancy can also be a bargaining chip for marriage, or be used to test or coerce a man's commitment to a relationship or parenthood, or to prevent an impending breakup. Pregnancy can be a plea for help or an attempt to punish someone—usually the woman's parents. Life transitions may also affect risk-taking—the mother who has just sent her last child off to school or the woman past 30 who has never been pregnant may become more careless in contraceptive use (Luker, 1975).

Repeat Abortions   Although there is limited data about women who have had more than one abortion, the available research findings are interesting. First, the data indicate that contraceptive method failure is a major contributor to repeat abortions. Other reasons may include high levels of risk-taking and nonuse of contraception because of fears about side effects, actual medical problems, and lack of supplies (Gibb and Millard, 1981; Howe et al., 1979; Paxter et al., 1973).

STERILIZATION

One other method of contraception has become common in recent years, due to improved surgical techniques and increasing societal acceptance. *Sterilization* is the most effective method of birth control, and its safety and permanence appeal to many who desire no more children or prefer to remain childless. Many surveys indicate that sterilization is the most commonly used method of fertility control for married couples over 30 years of age (Hatcher et al., 1980). Although there is some research being conducted on ways of restoring fertility and reversing sterilization, at present the procedures involve complicated surgery and their effectiveness is not guaranteed. Therefore, sterilization is usually recommended only to those who desire a permanent method of birth control. Because sterilization is best considered as permanent, a person should carefully explore his or her situation and feelings before deciding on the procedure. Questions to consider include: Are there any circumstances under which I would want (more) children (for example, if my child dies or if I begin a new relationship)? Is my sense of masculinity or femininity tied to my fertility? What are my alternatives to sterilization? In the following paragraphs, we will look at the procedures for sterilization of females and males.

Female Sterilization

In recent years female sterilization has become a relatively safe, simple, and inexpensive procedure. Sterilization can be accomplished by a variety of techniques using small incisions and often only localized anesthesia.

Tubal ligation (cutting the tubes) can be done in several ways. The most common procedure, called *laparoscopy*, is shown in Figure 11.11. One or two small incisions are made in the abdomen, usually at the navel and slightly below the pubic hair line. A narrow, lighted viewing instrument called a laparoscope is inserted into the abdomen to locate the fallopian tubes. The tubes are then tied off, cut, or cauterized to block passage of sperm. Other methods have also been developed to block the tubes. The use of a band or a clip on the tubes is sometimes employed instead of removing a segment of the tube (Brenner, 1981; Penfield, 1981). The ligated (cut) or blocked tubes prevent the sperm and egg from meeting and uniting in the tube, and pregnancy is prevented. The incisions are generally so small that bandaids rather than stitches are used after surgery. Sometimes the incision is made through the back of the vaginal wall, and the procedure is called a *culpotomy*.

Sterilization acts only as a roadblock in the tubes. It does not further affect the woman's reproductive and sexual system. Her hormonal levels remain the same, and

FIGURE 11.11 FEMALE STERILIZATION BY LAPAROSCOPIC LIGATION

The tubes are located by the laparoscope.

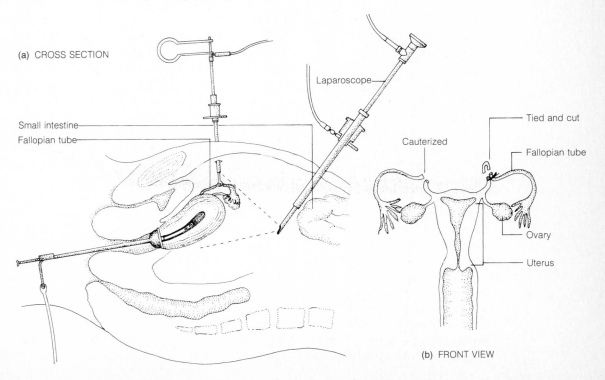

(a) CROSS SECTION

Laparoscope

Small intestine

Fallopian tube

Tied and cut

Cauterized

Fallopian tube

Ovary

Uterus

(b) FRONT VIEW

the timing of menopause will not be altered. Her sexuality will not be physiologically changed, but she may find her interest and arousal increase because she no longer is concerned with pregnancy or birth control methods. The released egg will simply degenerate, as do millions of other cells daily, and be carried away by the body's circulatory system.

Following a tubal ligation, a woman should usually wait to resume normal activities for two to three days or until she feels comfortable doing so. She should avoid strenuous lifting for about a week. She can resume sexual intercourse when it is comfortable.

Some discomfort or complications can occur from female sterilization. A woman may experience some pain at the site of the incision, and, if the tubes are sealed by burning, other tissue in the pelvic cavity may be accidently burned. Postsurgical bleeding is also a possible complication. To minimize the possibility of complications, it is important for a woman to choose a doctor who is experienced in sterilization procedures.

Surgical reversal of female sterilization is sometimes successful. Rates of post-surgery pregnancy vary from about 40% to 80% in various studies, but information about the selection of patients for the reconstructive surgery is often omitted in these accounts. One researcher found that women were most likely to have successful reversal if the previous sterilization procedure had removed or blocked only a small portion of the tube on the end close to the uterus (Henderson, 1981).

Male Sterilization

Vasectomy is a minor surgical procedure that involves cutting and tying the vas deferens, the two sperm-carrying ducts. The operation is typically performed in a physician's office. Under a local anesthetic, a small incision is made in the scrotal sac, well above the testicle. The vas is lifted out, and a small segment is removed. The free ends are tied off, clipped, or cauterized to prevent rejoining. After repeating the procedure on the opposite side, the incisions are closed and the operation is completed, usually in less than 20 minutes (Figure 11.12).

Because a significant amount of sperm is stored beyond the site of the incision, a man remains fertile for some time after the operation. Studies have shown that sperm may be present in the first 10 to 20 postoperative ejaculations. Therefore, effective alternative methods of birth control should be employed until semen analysis reveals no sperm present in the seminal fluid. Many physicians recommend two consecutive negative evaluations before engaging in unprotected intercourse. Generally, these checks occur six to eight weeks after the operation. In rare cases the two free ends of the severed vas grow back together (this is called *recanalization*), and once in a very great while a man will be found who has more than one vas on one or both sides.

Unlike castration, vasectomy does not alter continued testicular production of male sex hormones and their absorption into the bloodstream. A vasectomized man will also continue to produce sperm that are absorbed and eliminated by his body. His ejaculations will contain almost as much semen after the operation as before, since sperm from the testes constitutes less than 10% of the total ejaculate. The characteristic odor and consistency of the semen will also remain the same.

FIGURE 11.12 VASECTOMY

The procedure for male sterilization by vasectomy is demonstrated in steps 1–5.

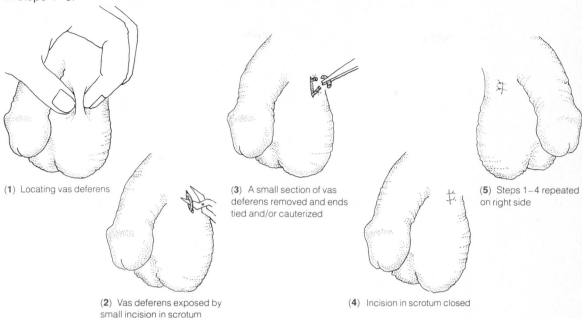

(**1**) Locating vas deferens

(**2**) Vas deferens exposed by small incision in scrotum

(**3**) A small section of vas deferens removed and ends tied and/or cauterized

(**4**) Incision in scrotum closed

(**5**) Steps 1–4 repeated on right side

Most men report that vasectomy does not affect their sexual functioning (Russell, 1961). Some report improvements, often due to greater spontaneity of sexual expression and less fear of impregnating their partners. A few report a reduction in sexual desire, which may be related to concerns about their continued masculinity.

At present there are no known physical side effects of vasectomy that compromise its value as a permanent method of contraceptive control. There may be some short term postoperative problems like swelling or inflammation in the region of the surgery.

Successful reversal of vasectomy is still unlikely. With selected patients and experienced microsurgeons, the chances of reconnecting the vas have increased (Hatcher et al., 1980). However, the major problem complicating *vasovasectomy* (vasectomy reversal surgery) is reduced fertility following reconnection. After vasovasectomy many men have lower sperm counts and/or reduced sperm motility. Another factor in reduced post-vasovasectomy fertility may be the antisperm antibodies that develop in some men (Smith and Paulson, 1980). The most important measurement of vasovasectomy success is subsequent pregnancy; various studies report a pregnancy rate of from 35% to 71% using current techniques of vasovasectomy (Martin, 1981).

Long term effects are more difficult to evaluate. Long range studies are necessary to find out if men experience any medical difficulties years after having a vasectomy.

The spectrum of choices available for family planning has increased markedly in the past few decades. As we have seen in this chapter, however, there are still potential health hazards or inconveniences associated with available methods. A great deal of research is being done to improve safety, reliability, and convenience of birth control. We will look at some projected improvements for both men and women.

New Directions for Men

Presently, male contraception is limited to condoms, vasectomy, and the highly unreliable withdrawal method. However, there are some research efforts currently underway that suggest other methods may be available in the future. These efforts have concentrated on the development of a male "pill" that would work by inhibiting sperm production, motility, or maturation (Linde et al., 1981).

Some years ago it was shown that the conventional estrogen-progesterone female birth control pill will induce temporary sterility in men by curtailing sperm production. This effect was presumed to result from suppression of pituitary go-nadotropins, the mechanism whereby the pill induces temporary sterility in women. Unfortunately, men often reported markedly reduced sex interest while taking the pill, a fact that seriously limited its practicality. The idea of giving men a contraceptive pill that will cause modified hormone levels still holds some promise, and research with various substances is under way (Nieschlag et al., 1981).

A gonadotropin-releasing hormone inhibitor (LHRH agonist) is currently under study as a male contraceptive. LHRH agonist has been shown to reduce the number and motility of sperm in men who received daily injections of the substance. Testosterone levels also dropped, and inability to achieve an erection occurred in more than half of the men in the study. This side effect disappeared after stopping treatment. Further research is being done to see whether testosterone combined with LHRH agonist could be effective in maintaining sexual functioning while producing temporary infertility (Linde et al., 1981).

Another substance under research as a male contraception is *gossypol*, a compound derived from the seeds, stems, or roots of cotton plants. Gossypol was first identified as an antifertility agent in China. Investigators found that there was an extremely low birthrate in an area where the local people used cottonseed oil for cooking. Clinical trials in China began in 1972, and more than 10,000 men have been studied. Among the first 400 men who received the drug for six months to four years, gossypol was reported to be 99.89% effective. Gossypol apparently inhibits enzyme activity necessary for sperm production and reduces sperm count dramatically, but does not affect either sex hormone levels or sexual interest and functioning. Some of the side effects reported included transient weakness, an increase or decrease in appetite, gastrointestinal disturbances, and a small incidence of decreased sexual interest and functioning (Nieschlag et al., 1981). Although there have been several births of healthy babies from wives of men who stopped taking gossypol (Maugh, 1981), recovery of complete sperm counts did not occur in 25% of the 2000 men who were followed up after stopping gossypol (Nieschlag et al., 1981). A great deal of further research is needed to determine the safety of gossypol as a contraceptive agent.

Many scientists are concerned about the potential long range effect of hormone-based contraceptives for males. One concern is the possibility that complications associated with the female pill may also occur in men. Furthermore, it is feared that the hormones might produce genetic damage, and that fertilization by any sperm that might still be produced could result in fetal abnormalities.

Several researchers are considering the possibility of developing a vaccine to immunize a man against his own sperm. The idea would be to introduce a substance into the male system that would induce him to develop antibodies against his sperm cells. There has even been some effort to develop an antisperm vaccine for women. However, there are still some unresolved problems with this approach, including possible genetic damage and unhealthy reactions of body tissue to the vaccine.

In all of these developments there is one issue that is seldom discussed: the question of how many women will be willing to risk a possible pregnancy in an encounter with a man who says he is "on the pill." This would likely be more of a problem in a first encounter than in a long term relationship. The following commentary indicates one woman's attitude:

I would never trust a man who told me he was fixed or taking some kind of drug to make him infertile. I have too much at stake. My experience has been that men rarely take responsibility for birth control. They certainly don't like using rubbers. Maybe he would say he was OK just so he didn't have to use a condom. Until I have a permanent partner I can trust, or physicians start tattooing a man when he has been fixed or on some pill, I'll make certain that I am protected. (Authors' files)

This is an important consideration, and one that will no doubt become a major issue in the event that new forms of male contraception become a reality. As long as women continue to bear the primary responsibility for dealing with undesired pregnancies, some will undoubtedly be reluctant to shift the entire responsibility for conception control onto an unseen procedure or drug used by their male partners.

New Directions for Women

An array of contraceptive methods for women are currently under experimentation. All of the hormonal methods have potential side effects similar to the pill, but these vary with the manner of administration. Injections of progesterone, given every three months, are used in many countries. Also, a time-release capsule containing progesterone embedded in a woman's arm or leg can remain effective for years. The capsule can be removed if a woman desires a pregnancy before the capsule loses its effectiveness. There is still the possibility of infertility after using these two methods. Another device is a "vaginal ring." Somewhat like a diaphragm ring, a new one is inserted once a month, and it slowly releases low doses of progesterone. The hormone is absorbed into the bloodstream through the vaginal mucosa. As mentioned earlier, another possibility is a vaccination to develop a woman's immunity to her partner's sperm. This method is still in the experimental stages, and effective reversal of the immunity has not yet been firmly established. The use of a luteinizing hormone-releasing factor inhibitor (LFR agonist) as a method of contraception is also under study. Injections of LFR agonist for three successive days beginning with the first day of menstruation has been shown to induce a chain of hormonal events that results in inadequate maturation of the ovarian follicle and the lining of the uterus. Both of these effects would act to prevent conception. It may also be possible to use LFR agonist in a birth control pill taken monthly at the beginning of menstruation (Sheehan et al., 1982).

Two new types of barrier-method contraceptives are also being explored. One is the use of gossypol as a vaginal spermicide. However, the effects of gossypol on the male and female genitals are unknown and must be carefully researched (Tatum and Connell-Tatum, 1981). The other method under study is the *collagen sponge*. This highly resilient and liquid-absorbent sponge is a cylindrical cup that is used in a similar way to the diaphragm. It is inserted either manually or with an applicator. It expands in the space around the cervix and acts as a mechanical barrier to prevent the entry of sperm into the opening of the cervix. Spermicide can also be embedded within the sponge to provide higher contraceptive effectiveness. As with other new methods, the safety and effectiveness of the sponge needs to be established (Chvapil and Droegemueller, 1981).

SUMMARY

HISTORICAL AND SOCIAL PERSPECTIVES

1. From the beginning of recorded history, humankind has been concerned with birth control.

2. Margaret Sanger opened the first birth control clinics in the United States at a time when it was illegal to provide birth control information and devices.

SHARED RESPONSIBILITY

3. The male partner can share contraceptive responsibility by being informed, asking a new partner about birth control, accompanying his partner to her exam, using condoms and/or coital abstinence when desired, and/or sharing the expense of the exam and method.

CURRENTLY AVAILABLE METHODS

4. Comparison of relative convenience, safety, cost, and effectiveness may influence the choice of contraception.

5. Two types of oral contraceptives are currently available. The combination pill contains both estrogen and progestin. The progestin-only pill consists of a low dosage of progestin only.

6. Potential advantages of the combination pill include high effectiveness, reduction of menstrual flow and cramps, and its lack of interference with sexual activity.

7. The potential advantage of the progestin-only pill is the reduced chance of harmful side effects.

8. Some of the potential disadvantages of the combination pill include possible side effects such as blood clots, increased probability of heart attack, high blood pressure, liver disease, diabetes, more rapid growth of cancer of the breast and uterus, fetal abnormalities, infertility, depression, and reduced sexual interest. Potential disadvantages of the progestin-only pill include irregular bleeding and possibility of additional side effects.

9. Several types of IUDs are currently on the market. Potential advantages include uninterrupted

sexual interaction and simplicity of use. Potential disadvantages include increased cramping and bleeding, spontaneous expulsion, uterine perforation, tissue changes and infection, and pregnancy complications.

10. Diaphragm use is currently increasing. Potential advantages include lack of side effects, high effectiveness with knowledgeable and consistent use, and possible promotion of vaginal health. Some potential disadvantages are interruption of sexual activity, irritation from the cream or jelly, and possible misplacement during insertion or intercourse.

11. The cervical cap is not widely available in the United States. Some women who have problems fitting the diaphragm can use the cervical cap, but cervical caps will not fit all women.

12. Foam and vaginal suppositories are available without a prescription. Potential advantages are lack of serious side effects, added lubrication, and promotion of vaginal health. Potential disadvantages include irritation of genital tissues and interruption of sexual activity.

13. Condoms are available in a variety of styles. Potential advantages include protection from venereal diseases, improved ejaculatory control, and ready availability as a backup method. Potential disadvantages include interruption of sexual activity and reduced penile sensation.

14. The mucus, calendar, and basal body temperature methods help in planning coital activity to avoid a woman's fertile period.

15. Neither douching nor the withdrawal method are reliable for contraception.

16. Postcoital contraception may be used following unprotected mid-cycle intercourse. Various types of hormones, including DES, and morning-after IUD insertion are the available methods.

INDUCED ABORTION

17. Abortion is a controversial issue in the United States today. Suction curretage, D and E, intra-amniotic injections, and intravaginal suppositories of prostaglandins are the medical techniques used for pregnancy termination.

18. Contraceptive risk-taking sometimes precedes an unplanned pregnancy and consequent abortion. There are different kinds of "costs" and "benefits" to contraceptive use for each woman and each relationship.

STERILIZATION

19. At this time, sterilization should be considered as permanent, and such a decision should be carefully evaluated.

20. Tubal ligation is the sterilization procedure most commonly done for women. It does not alter her hormone levels, menstrual cycle, or menopause.

21. Vasectomy, the sterilization procedure for men, is not effective for birth control immediately after surgery because sperm remain in the vas deferens above the incision. The majority of men report that vasectomy does not affect their sexual functioning.

NEW DIRECTIONS IN CONTRACEPTION

22. Possible contraceptive methods for men for the future include several options for a male pill or a sperm-immunization vaccine.

23. Possible contraceptive methods for women in the future include several hormonal alternatives, a vaginal ring, and new barrier methods.

SUGGESTED READINGS

"Condoms." *Consumer Reports*, October 1979. An article that describes and compares different brands of condoms and thoroughly discusses various advantages and disadvantages reported by their survey.

Cooke, Cynthia, and Dworkin, Susan. *The Ms. Guide to a Woman's Health*. New York: Anchor, 1979. An up-to-date guide to a woman's health. Includes section on contraception and other concerns.

Hatcher, Robert et al. *Contraceptive Technology: 1980–1981*. New York: Irvington, 1980. A comprehensive, up-to-date book about birth control, which includes a section about birth control and nutrition. A must for anyone who wants the latest information about the technology and effects of contraception.

Levin, Marshall. "Let George Do It: Male Contraception." *Ms.*, January 1976. A very readable article containing good, practical information about three common male-oriented contraceptive methods—withdrawal, the condom, and vasectomy.

Seaman, Barbara, and Seaman, Gideon. *Women and the Crisis in Sex Hormones*. New York: Bantam, 1978. A highly critical view of the contraceptive industry and the medical profession's practices related to the risks of birth control.

12

Conceiving Children: Process and Choice

PARENTHOOD AS AN OPTION
BECOMING PREGNANT
  Infertility
  Enhancing the Possibility of Conception
  Alternatives to Couple-Intercourse for Conception
  Preconceptual Sex Determination
  Pregnancy Detection
  Spontaneous Abortion
A HEALTHY PREGNANCY
  Fetal Development
  Prenatal Care
  Amniocentesis
  Pregnancy after 35
THE EXPERIENCE OF PREGNANCY
  The Woman's Experience
  The Man's Experience
  Sexual Interaction During Pregnancy
CHILDBIRTH
  Stages of Childbirth
  Childbirth Practices: Past and Present
  Birthplace Alternatives
  Medical Interventions: Pros and Cons
POSTPARTUM
  Parent-Child Contact
  Breast Feeding
  Sexual Interaction after Childbirth
SUMMARY
SUGGESTED READINGS

*T*his chapter is about the important decision of whether to become a parent and about the processes of conception, pregnancy, and birth and some of the emotions that accompany them, from the points of view of the mother and the involved father. The discussions that follow are not intended to be complete, but are meant to give an overview of a number of processes and options. We encourage people who desire further information on one or more topics to seek more extensive references or to consult a physician. As a starting point, we will look at the option of parenthood and some of the alternatives that are available for people who want to become mothers and fathers.

PARENTHOOD AS AN OPTION

Parenthood is changing in contemporary American society, both in the degree of choice adults have about becoming parents and with regard to the definition of parenthood itself. Until recently, highly effective birth control methods were not available and parenthood was an expected consequence of marriage. Today, however, adults have more choice about becoming parents. Couples may make conscious decisions about when or whether they would like to have children. One result of this freedom of choice is that an increasing number of married people are deciding not to have children at all.

However, people who choose child-free marriage often experience external pressure about their decision. *Pronatalism* is a word used to describe policies and attitudes that encourage parenthood for all couples. Childless married couples are routinely asked questions like "When are you going to start your family?" or "You're *not* going to have children? Why aren't you?" (Rarely when someone says they *are* planning to have children does someone ask "Why?") Other manifestations of pronatalism are commonly held stereotypes about people, especially women, who choose not to be parents. Many women have learned to believe that motherhood is essential to their personal fulfillment and that they are selfish or "unnatural" if they choose not to be mothers. One study of college students and their parents indicates that these stereotypes may be becoming less prevalent. Only 22% of people surveyed agreed that having babies was totally fulfilling for women, and 88% disagreed that women who do not want children are selfish or unnatural. However, males were more likely than females to endorse stereotypical attitudes about women and motherhood (Hare-Mustin and Broderick, 1979). If these differences in attitude between males and females are common to the general population, they may be a source of relationship conflict when choices about parenting are made. The unfortunate consequence of pronatalism may be that individuals or couples who really do not desire children have them anyway and then find that this negatively affects the quality of their own and their children's lives. In other cases, couples who have children without fully desiring them discover enjoyment and fulfillment in their parenting roles.

Couples who decide to be child-free may do so before or after marriage. One study found that one-third of 52 voluntarily childless couples had made agreements not to have children prior to marriage (Veevers, 1973). The other two-thirds of couples remained childless after a series of postponements and a later decision. Initially, women in these marriages did not have strong feelings about parenthood and assumed that they eventually would have one or two children. However, unlike many other couples, these people used contraception conscientiously and continuously during the early years of marriage. At some point, the couples openly acknowledged the possibility that they might choose to remain child-free and began to examine the pros and cons of bringing children into their lives and relationships. The couples in this study made the decision to remain child-free and appeared contented with the implications of their choice.

Since parenthood is much more of a choice today than in the past, many people are taking the time to carefully consider the question of child-free living versus parenthood. Many individuals and couples are ambivalent about these alternatives. There are gains and losses with each choice, and, regardless of the one selected, there is a large element of chance in what the actual, rather than the predicted or assumed, consequences of such a decision will be.

There are many potential advantages to being child-free. Child-free individuals and couples have much more time for themselves and do not have worries about providing for the physical and psychological needs of children. Child-free people can continue more spontaneous recreational, social, and work life patterns. There is usually more time and energy for companionship and intimacy in an adult relationship. People without children can more fully pursue careers and may experience a great deal of challenge and fulfillment in their professional lives. There is often less stress on marriages, and some studies show that marriages without children are happier and more satisfying than marriages with children (Campbell, 1975). Nonparents also have more financial resources available to them.

There are, however, many potential advantages to having children. Children themselves give and receive love, and their presence may enhance the love between couples as they share in the experiences of raising their offspring. Managing the challenge of parenthood can also be a source of self-esteem and give a sense of accomplishment. Parenthood is often an opportunity for discovering new and untapped dimensions of oneself that can give one's life greater meaning and satisfaction. Many parents say that they have become better people through parenthood. Children offer ongoing stimulation and change as they develop through childhood and may also provide financial or emotional support in the parents' old age (Mayleas, 1980).

The potential rewards of a particular decision may be romanticized or unrealistic for a given person or couple. There are no guarantees that the benefits of children or child-free living will meet one's expectations. For example, children may not provide companionship in a parent's old age, or a career may be much less personally rewarding than anticipated. Still, it is important to assess the choice of parenthood because it is a permanent and major life decision. Box 12.1 presents some important considerations for people making decisions about having children. There are no "right" or "wrong" answers; these questions are merely a tool to help you explore your feelings about parenthood. And since we all change, your feelings about parenthood may very well change during your life.

Although more people today are deciding to be child-free, there has also been

BOX 12.1 ARE WE PARENT MATERIAL? (OR, AM I? IN THE CASE OF SINGLE PARENTHOOD)

1. Are my partner and I willing to devote at least 18 years of our lives to being responsible for a child?
2. How would a child affect our growth and development as individuals and as a couple? How would a child affect our careers, education, social life, recreational interests, and privacy?
3. Do my partner and I understand each other's feelings about religion, careers, family, child-raising, future goals? Will children fit into these feelings, hopes, and plans?

4. Could we give a child a good home? Is our relationship basically happy and strong?
5. Do we like children? Do we enjoy activities that children can do?
6. How would we feel if our child's ideas and values turn out to be different from our own?
7. Do I expect a child to make up for happiness I feel is missing from my life?

(Adapted from a pamphlet by the National Alliance for Optional Parenthood.)

an increase in the number of couples and single women who are having children outside of legal marriage. Unmarried women, including lesbians, sometimes choose to become pregnant and have children by means of artificial insemination. Most unmarried mothers now keep their infants (Boston Women's Health Book Collective, 1976). Other couples or single men and women are bringing nonbiologically related children into their homes to form or enlarge their families. This may be done in a variety of ways. In adoption, a child becomes the legal daughter or son of one or two adults. A recently available option is subsidized adoption, legal adoption with continued partial government financial aid to the child. This takes place when legislated funds are made available to help families who desire to adopt "hard-to-place" (older or handicapped) children but who have limited financial resources to meet the special needs of the children (Watson, 1972). Another option besides adoption is to provide homes for foster children. Foster children usually have legal (biological) parents, but for various reasons their home environment is temporarily unavailable or unacceptable.

There are many reasons why adults may want to raise children who are not biologically their own. They may be partly motivated by a concern with overpopulation and a desire to give homeless children love and security. Another frequent reason may be that a couple is unable to have children due to infertility or medical problems. Currently, potential parents of healthy newborn infants outnumber the babies who are available for adoption. However, children or adolescents who are older, handicapped, or previous foster children are being placed more and more frequently in adoptive homes (Benet, 1976).

We have seen that there are a number of options for becoming parents without experiencing the process of pregnancy and childbirth. Most people who have children, however, are biological parents. In the remainder of this chapter, we will look at some of the developments, experiences, and feelings that are involved in the physiological process of becoming parents, starting with becoming pregnant. This may be difficult for some couples, for a number of reasons.

Infertility

It has been estimated that as many as 10%–15% of the couples who want to be parents are unable to conceive. If attempts at impregnation are unsuccessful after a reasonable period of time (usually a year), a physician should be consulted. Since approximately 40% of infertility cases result from male factors, it is important that both the female and male partners be evaluated (Speroff et al., 1978). The causes of infertility are sometimes difficult to determine and rectify (10%–20% of couples will not have a diagnosable cause for their infertility). Couples who seek help are often under tremendous psychological stress and their sexual relationships may be disrupted. In this section, we will look briefly at some common causes of female and male infertility.

Female Infertility   A woman may have difficulty conceiving or be unable to conceive for a number of reasons. Failure to ovulate at regular intervals is quite common. Basal body temperature charts, hormonal tests, and endometrial biopsies are used to document ovulation. A lack of ovulation may be caused by a variety of factors, including hormone imbalances, severe vitamin deficiencies, metabolic disturbances, poor nutrition, genetic factors, emotional stress, or medical conditions. A variety of so-called "fertility drugs" are sometimes used to stimulate ovulation. These drugs are often successful in accomplishing their purpose. However, they may produce certain undesirable side effects, including multiple births.

In instances where tests indicate the woman is ovulating and the man is producing adequate numbers of viable sperm, the next step is a postcoital test to ensure that the sperm remain viable and motile in the cervical mucus. Some women produce cervical mucus that impedes the passage of sperm into the uterus. In such cases, several months of using condoms or abstaining from intercourse may reduce the level of sperm antibodies in the mucus sufficiently to allow fertilization (Fraser et al., 1980; Speroff et al., 1978).

Infections of the uterus, vagina, fallopian tubes, or ovaries and growths in the uterus or tubes may all prevent fertilization. Scar tissue in or around the ovaries can also obstruct passage of the egg and sperm. The *hysterosalpingogram* is a procedure in which dye is injected through the cervix into the uterus and tubes to test for tubal obstructions. The path of the dye can be traced in an X-ray, permitting a physician to determine if a blockage exists. A woman may also have a *diagnostic laporoscopy* where a small telescope is inserted through an incision in the navel to look at the external surface of the uterus, tubes, ovaries, and pelvic cavity for evidence of problems that may be remedied by medication or surgery.

Male Infertility   Other than the relatively rare condition of ejaculatory inhibition (see Chapter 16), causes of infertility in men are usually related to low sperm count or, less frequently, to abnormal sperm (sperm cells that do not propel themselves with sufficient vigor). Infectious diseases of the testes, particularly mumps, may reduce sperm output. Infectious diseases of other areas of the male reproductive tract can alter sperm production, transport, and viability. Environmental toxins may also produce reduced sperm counts and abnormal sperm cells (Castleman, 1980b).

Another cause of male sterility may be undescended testes. If this condition is not corrected before puberty, sperm will be less likely to mature because of the higher temperatures within the abdomen. Hormone deficiencies may also result in an inadequate number of sperm cells in the semen. This situation can sometimes be remedied by hormone therapy.

Discovery or treatment of male infertility is sometimes hampered by psychological factors. Some men are quite reluctant to subject themselves to fertility evaluation. The following account reveals one possible motivation for this reluctance:

My wife and I have been trying to have a baby for over a year without success. Both physicians she has seen have assured her that nothing is wrong with her reproductive system. The doctors want me to come in for a checkup. What if they find out I'm not making enough sperm? There is nothing wrong with my drive or capabilities. Somehow, the idea of a low sperm count suggests I am sexually inadequate. How can a man with a high sex drive be shooting blanks? (Authors' files)

It is not uncommon for a man to relate his masculinity or virility to his ability to produce babies. However, it is uncommon to find a relationship between capacity for sexual response and production of sperm. Male sterility can occur among men who are highly sexually active as well as among individuals with infrequent outlets. Occasionally, however, low sperm count and reduced sexual interest may both stem from the same cause, insufficient hormone output.

Infertility and Sexuality   Couples may experience various reactions to their difficulty or inability to become pregnant, and problems with infertility can have profoundly negative effects on a couple's sexual functioning (Menning, 1979). When a couple is first informed of their infertility, they may deny it or downplay their desire to have children. As knowledge of their infertility becomes more evident, the couple may feel a great sense of isolation from others during social discussions of pregnancy, childbirth, and childrearing. As one woman who has been unable to conceive states:

Coffee breaks at work are the worst times; everyone brings out their pictures of their kids and discusses their latest trials and tribulations. I can't help feeling like there's something wrong with me for not being able to get pregnant. When one of the women complains about having problems with something like childcare, I just want to shout at her and tell her how lucky she is to be able to have such a "problem." (Authors' files)

Couples may also become isolated from each other and believe that the partner does not really understand. Each may feel inadequate about his or her masculinity or femininity due to problems with conceiving. Each may feel anger and guilt and wonder "Why me?" Finally, the couple may feel grief over the loss of potential biological children, the pregnancy experience, and the option to conceive. Intercourse itself may evoke these uncomfortable feelings and become an emotionally painful rather than pleasurable experience.

Also, the medical procedures used in fertility diagnosis and treatment are often disruptive to the couple's sexual spontaneity. Sex can become very stressful and mechanical. Taking basal body temperature and timing intercourse according to ovulation can create tremendous sexual performance anxiety that can interfere with sexual arousal and response. This kind of "sex on demand" pressure is especially intense for a man when he must masturbate into a jar or special condom to produce semen for sperm count or artificial insemination and when postcoital evaluations of the sperm's ability to enter the cervical mucus are necessary (Debrovner and Shubin-Stein, 1976).

Because of these psychological and sexual stresses, health-care practitioners who work with infertility problems need to be sensitive to and skilled in helping affected couples. The nationwide organization, *Resolve* (P.O. Box 474, Belmont, MA 02178) offers support groups, counseling, and referrals for people with infertility problems.

Enhancing the Possibility of Conception

If a couple is having difficulty conceiving a child, both partners should be medically evaluated. Before extensive medical evaluation and treatment is begun, a couple may be told to follow certain steps to maximize the possibility of conception. Modifying both coital position and the timing of coitus can sometimes increase the chances of fertilization. The recommendations that follow may be helpful for couples who are trying to become pregnant.

A woman's position during intercourse can affect the likelihood of conception. Ideally, her position should take advantage of the seminal pool that collects in the ballooned inner portion of a sexually stimulated vagina (see Chapter 6). For most women, the best position is to lie on the back, with knees drawn up. This allows the cervix to dip down into the pool of semen. Some fertility counselors recommend placing a pillow under the woman's buttocks. The added elevation helps prevent semen from escaping out of the vagina. For a woman with a severely retroflexed (backward-tipped) uterus, where the cervix is on a straight line with the vagina rather than at right angles to it, it may be best to use the knee-chest position for coitus. The woman kneels face down, supporting her weight on her elbows and knees, as the man enters from behind. This position allows gravity to help keep the semen in the vagina.

In both cases, when the man's orgasm is imminent, he should penetrate as deeply as is comfortable to his partner and stop moving once he has begun expelling seminal fluid. After ejaculation, he should make no further movements other than a careful withdrawal of his penis (additional movements may disperse the seminal pool). The woman should remain in her position for a few minutes.

Picking the right time to have coitus is also important in increasing the probability of conception. While it is difficult to predict the exact time of ovulation, several methods permit a reasonable approximation. Perhaps the best is the mucus method discussed in the previous chapter, where the couple times coital activity according to the fertile period in the woman's menstrual cycle. Body temperature and the principles of the calendar method may also be used in estimating ovulation time.

In cases where low sperm count is suspected, the optimal frequency of ejaculation during intercourse to achieve pregnancy is usually every other day during the week of ovulation (Speroff et al., 1978). In such circumstances it would be important for a couple to chart the woman's cycle so that they can reasonably estimate, in advance, her most fertile time. A man with a borderline sperm count might also want to avoid taking hot baths and wearing tight clothing and undershorts, since these and similar environments expose the testicles to higher than normal temperatures.

Alternatives to Couple-Intercourse for Conception

In recent years various alternatives have been developed to help overcome the problem of infertility. Artificial insemination is one option to be considered in cases of an abnormality related to sperm motility. In this procedure, semen from a woman's partner is mechanically introduced into her vagina or cervix by a health-care practitioner. If the man is not producing adequate viable sperm, or if a woman does not have a partner, artificial insemination with a donor's semen is another option.

Various procedures to allow a woman who cannot conceive through intercourse or artificial insemination to have a child are also being developed. The world's first "test-tube baby," born in England in 1978, provided impetus to research in this area. In this method, mature eggs are removed from the ovary and are fertilized in a laboratory dish by the sperm of the woman's husband. One fertilized egg is then introduced into the woman's uterus and, if the procedure is successful, will develop just as if the process of fertilization and implantation had occurred normally. Another method under study for women with blocked tubes is called *low tubal ovum transfer.* To date, this procedure has been tested only with primates. It involves using a laparoscope to remove a mature egg from the ovary. The egg is then inserted by a syringe into a fallopian tube on the uterus side of the blocked area. Another method being tested with primates, *embryo transfer,* also called *artificial embryonation,* may be a future possibility for women who are unable to produce an egg due to diseased or removed ovaries. This procedure is the reverse of donor artificial insemination, in that the egg comes from a woman other than the one who will carry the pregnancy. In embryo transfer a volunteer female donor would be artificially inseminated by the sperm of the infertile woman's husband. Approximately five days following fertilization the tiny embryo would be removed from the woman donor and transferred surgically into the uterus of the mother-to-be who then carries the pregnancy. At present, these techniques are quite experimental and success rates are low. However, they do provide hope for infertile individuals and couples in the future.

Surrogate mothers are women who are willing to be artificially inseminated by the male partner of a childless couple, carry the pregnancy to term, deliver the child, and give it to the couple for adoption. This is sometimes done anonymously through a health-care practitioner or privately by arrangement between the woman and the couple. There are many problematic legal ramifications to surrogate motherhood, especially when the surrogate mother is paid for her services.

Preconceptual Sex Determination

The desire to predetermine the sex of a child has existed since ancient times. Superstitions, including beliefs that if a man wears a hat during intercourse he will father a male child or that hanging his trousers on the left bedpost will produce a girl, are part of our folk culture. In contemporary times, an obstetrician-gynecologist, Dr. Landrum Shettles (1972), basing his techniques on the premise that female-producing sperm travel slower, live longer, and survive better in the acid pH of the vagina than do male-producing sperm, reported that a precoital baking soda and water douche and intercourse with deep vaginal penetration near ovulation would increase chances of conceiving a boy. Conversely, douching with vinegar and water prior to inter-course, shallow penetration, and intercourse two to three days prior to ovulation would increase the chances of a girl. However, other researchers have not found these approaches to be as reliable as has Shettles (Karp, 1980).

Some researchers are experimenting with techniques to separate Y- from X-bearing sperm in ejaculates. The male- or female-producing sperm would then be introduced into the vagina by artificial insemination. The most promising method for obtaining viable, undamaged, and well-separated sperm samples is to induce sperm migration through progressively denser solutions of albumen (egg white). However, this procedure yields only Y-bearing sperm, and its effectiveness is not yet conclusively established (Karp, 1980).

If preconceptual sex selection became effective and easy, what would the impact be on society? An imbalance in sex ratios, probably in favor of males, might result. The overall birth rate could also be reduced, because parents would no longer continue having more children than they would otherwise in hope of conceiving a child of the desired sex. The potential societal impact of scientific developments in human reproduction is well illustrated by preconceptual sex determination.

Other researchers contend that a woman can preselect the sex of her child by taking mineral supplements and regulating her diet beginning one and one-half menstrual cycles preceding conception. According to this method, a woman who wants to conceive a girl should eat foods rich in calcium and magnesium such as milk, cheese, nuts, beans, and cereals; a woman who wants a boy should eat foods rich in potassium and sodium such as meat, fish, vegetables, chocolate, and salt. The researchers claim an 80% success rate but are not certain by what mechanism the preselection occurs (Stolkowski and Choukroun, 1981).

Pregnancy Detection

The initial signs of pregnancy may provoke feelings ranging from joy to dread, depending on the woman's desire to be pregnant and a variety of surrounding circumstances. Although some women may have either a light blood flow or "spotting" (irregular bleeding) after conception, usually the first indication of pregnancy is the absence of the menstrual period at the expected time. Breast tenderness, nausea, vomiting, or other nonspecific symptoms (such as tiredness or change in appetite) may also accompany pregnancy in the first weeks or months.

Any or all of these clues may cause a woman to suspect she is pregnant. Urine tests and pelvic exams are medical techniques used to make the determination with a greater degree of certainty. The urine of a pregnant woman contains a hormone, *human chorionic gonadotropin* (HCG), secreted by the *trophoblast cells* of the placenta. HCG is detectable in a testing solution about a month after conception or two weeks after the expected date of menstrual onset. Recently, sensitive blood assays for HCG have become available that can detect pregnancy by about 10 days after conception. Also, around the sixth week after conception, a softening of the uterus can be felt by an experienced practitioner doing a pelvic exam (see Figure 12.1).

Spontaneous Abortion

Even when pregnancy has been confirmed, complications may prevent full-term development of the fetus. Sometimes, genetic or physical defects in a fetus will cause *spontaneous abortion,* or miscarriage, to occur, thus terminating a pregnancy. Although the exact frequency of spontaneous abortion is unknown, it is estimated that

FIGURE 12.1 PELVIC EXAM PREGNANCY DETECTION

One sign of pregnancy is a softening of the uterus.

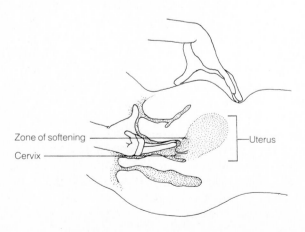

10%–40% of pregnancies end in miscarriage. The majority of these occur within the first trimester.

Early miscarriages may appear as a heavier than usual menstrual flow; later ones may involve uncomfortable cramping and profuse bleeding. Fortunately for women who desire a child, one miscarriage rarely means a later pregnancy will be unsuccessful. While miscarriage may not be preventable in many cases, there are a number of things a woman can do to have the healthiest possible pregnancy.

A HEALTHY PREGNANCY

Once a woman becomes pregnant, her own health care plays an important part in the development of a healthy fetus. Countless books have been written about pregnancy and prenatal care (a few are listed in the Suggested Readings); we will mention only a few important points here.

Fetal Development

The nine-month span of pregnancy is customarily divided into three three-month segments called *trimesters*. Characteristic changes occur in each trimester.

As with all mammals, humans begin as a zygote (a united sperm cell and ovum), which develops into the multicelled blastocyst that implants on the wall of the uterus about a week after fertilization (see Figure 12.2). Growth progresses steadily. By 9 to 10 weeks after the last menstrual period, the fetal heartbeat can be heard with a special stethoscope known as the *Doppler*. By the second month from the time of conception, the fetus is a small (1/12 inch in length) grayish shape, as shown in Figure 12.3. During this same month, the spinal canal and rudimentary arms and legs form, as do the beginnings of recognizable eyes, fingers, and toes. During the third month, internal organs such as the liver, kidneys, intestines, and lungs begin limited functioning in the 3-inch fetus.

The second trimester begins with the fourth month of pregnancy (see Figure 12.4). By now, the sex of the fetus can often be distinguished. External body parts, including fingernails, eyebrows, and eyelashes, are clearly formed. The fetus's skin is covered by fine, downlike hair. Future development will primarily consist of growth in size and refinement of the features that already exist. Fetal movements can be felt by the end of the fourth month, and the heartbeat can be heard slightly later with a regular stethoscope. Weight has increased to one pound by the end of the fifth month. Head hair may appear at this time, and subcutaneous fat develops. By the end of the second trimester, the fetus has opened its eyes.

In the third trimester, the fetus continues to grow and develop the size and strength it will need to live on its own, apart from the mother's warmth and sustenance. It increases in weight from four pounds in the seventh month to an average of seven pounds at birth. The downlike hair covering its body disappears, and head hair continues growing. The skin becomes smooth rather than wrinkled. It is covered with a protective waxy substance, the *vernix caseosa*.

FIGURE 12.2 FROM OVULATION TO IMPLANTATION

(a) The egg travels into the tube where fertilization occurs. The fertilized ovum divides as it travels toward the uterus where it implants on the wall. (b) Sea urchin ovum being fertilized by sperm.

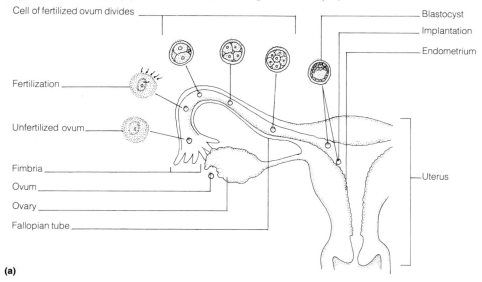

Cell of fertilized ovum divides

Fertilization

Unfertilized ovum

Fimbria

Ovum

Ovary

Fallopian tube

Blastocyst

Implantation

Endometrium

Uterus

(a)

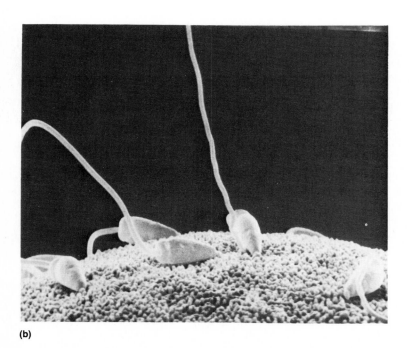

(b)

FIGURE 12.3 FETUS AT TWO MONTHS

The spinal canal and rudimentary arms and legs form by two months.

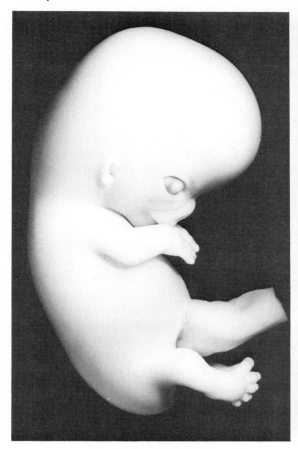

FIGURE 12.4 FETUS AT FOUR MONTHS

External body parts are clearly formed by four months.

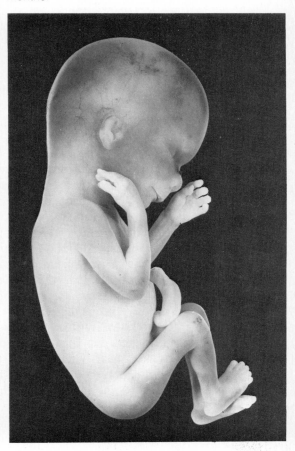

Prenatal Care

The developments just described take place in most pregnancies. Occasionally, however, something may go wrong. The fetus may not develop normally, or the pregnancy may terminate early, as we discussed previously. The causes may be genetic and unpreventable; but the mother's own health and nutrition are also crucial in providing the best environment for fetal development. This is one reason why it is important for a woman to have a complete physical examination before becoming pregnant. She also needs to have a test to determine her immunity to rubella (German measles), a disease which may cause severe fetal defects if the mother contracts it while she is pregnant.

Thorough prenatal care is essential for promoting the health of both the mother and the fetus. Components of optimal prenatal care include good nutrition, general good health, adequate rest, routine health care, exercise, and childbirth education. Early in the pregnancy, the woman, her partner, and her health-care practitioner should discuss the health needs of both the mother and the developing fetus; they can also begin to make plans for the birth.

As women have increasingly taken up athletic activities, many have questions about the effects on pregnancy. Although moderate exercise is commonly recommended as an important part of a healthy pregnancy, there are few studies about intensive athletic training and pregnancy. According to Shanegold (1980b), there is no evidence to suggest that athletes have more pregnancy complications than the general population. Shanegold believes that it is "reasonable for a pregnant woman to continue any activity she practices before pregnancy at the same level of exertion. It is also probably reasonable for pregnant women to avoid exercising to the point of exhaustion, in order to avoid potential risk to the fetus" (p. 335).

The fetus is dependent upon the mother for nutrients, oxygen, and waste elimination, as substances pass through the cell walls of the *placenta* (a disc-shaped organ attached to the wall of the uterus, shown in Figure 12.5). The fetus is joined to the placenta by the umbilical cord. The fetal blood circulates independently within the closed system of the fetus and the inner part of the placenta. Maternal blood flows in the uterine walls and uterine side of the placenta. Fetal and maternal blood do not intermingle. All exchanges between the fetal and maternal blood systems occur by absorption through the cell walls. Nutrients and oxygen from the maternal blood pass through the cell walls into the fetal circulatory system. Carbon dioxide and waste products from the fetus pass through the cell walls, to be removed by the maternal circulation.

Although the placental barrier is able to prevent some kinds of bacteria from passing into the fetal blood system, many bacteria do cross through the placenta. Furthermore, many substances ingested by the mother easily cross through the placenta and can be damaging to the developing fetus. Certain medications, drugs, alcohol, and tobacco are all potentially dangerous, and there have been a number of tragic situations where children have been damaged by medications taken by their mothers during pregnancy. For example, the drug *thalidomide,* prescribed as a sedative to pregnant women during the early 1960s, was absorbed into the circulatory systems of fetuses, causing severe deformities to the extremities. Also, as we noted earlier, in the last few years some daughters and sons of women who took diethylstilbestrol (DES) while pregnant have developed cancer of the vagina or testicle. Tetracycline, a frequently used antibiotic, can damage an infant's teeth and cause stunted bone growth if it is taken during pregnancy. In animal studies, even nonprescription drugs such as aspirin have been implicated in fetal abnormalities.

Other substances known to cause harm to the mother also pose serious hazards to a developing fetus. The infants of mothers who regularly use an addictive drug such as heroin, codeine, morphine, or opium during pregnancy are often born addicted. Withdrawal from the drug can be fatal to a newborn infant, so the drug must often be continued until the infant is strong enough to be taken off it. Another health hazard for

FIGURE 12.5 THE PLACENTA ATTACHED TO THE UTERINE WALL

The placenta exchanges nutrients, oxygen, and waste products between the maternal and fetal circulatory systems.

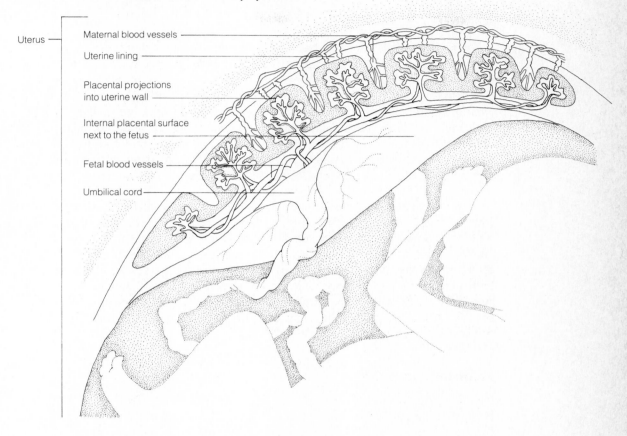

Uterus

Maternal blood vessels

Uterine lining

Placental projections into uterine wall

Internal placental surface next to the fetus

Fetal blood vessels

Umbilical cord

the fetus is cigarette smoking. Maternal smoking increases the chances of spontaneous abortion and pregnancy complications that can result in fetal or infant death. Smoking reduces the amount of oxygen in the bloodstream, and this may adversely affect the fetus by slowing its growth. Infants of mothers who smoked during pregnancy often weigh less and are in poorer general condition than infants of nonsmoking mothers. Heavy alcohol use, too, has been linked to increased spontaneous abortion, infant congenital heart defects, poor intellectual development, and other physical mal-formations. It may be that even moderate drinking can create alcohol dependency in the infant.

The extent of our knowledge about the effect of most of the drugs and other substances consumed by pregnant women is very limited; little is known of the exact risk of a given drug taken during pregnancy. What we do know at this point is that we are learning of more and more potential hazards. For this reason, *no* drugs should be used during pregnancy unless they are absolutely necessary and are taken under close medical supervision.

Amniocentesis

If a woman and her physician have some reason to suspect that there may be fetal abnormalities, a reliable and accurate test known as *amniocentesis* (an "amniotic tap") can help establish whether a problem exists. The test is done during the fourteenth to sixteenth week of pregnancy. The procedure consists of inserting a needle through the woman's abdominal wall and into the uterine cavity to draw out a sample of the *amniotic fluid* (fluid surrounding the fetus). Cells from the fluid are cultured for chromosomal analysis and the fluid is tested in procedures that take two to three weeks to produce results. A variety of birth defects can be detected by this means. Although amniocentesis cannot detect all fetal abnormalities, the number is increasing as techniques become more sophisticated.

Circumstances in which amniocentesis may be of benefit include: maternal age over 35 years, a parent with a chromosomal defect, a previous child with Down's syndrome, a previous child with certain defects of the spine or spinal cord, or a familial background that suggests a significant risk of other chromosome abnormality-related disorders that can be detected in utero. If the test results reveal a serious untreatable birth defect, the parents can have the pregnancy terminated. Amniocentesis itself involves some risks, including damage to the fetus, induced miscarriage, and infection; for this reason the procedure is not used unless there is a serious likelihood of a problem.

Pregnancy after 35

Increasing numbers of women are deciding to have children after 35 years of age. Projections for the 1980s indicate that the percentage of births to women 35 years and older will increase by 37% (Adams et al., 1982). In some cases couples are waiting until later in life to have their first children, while in others the woman deliberately delays childbearing for career or other reasons (Howley, 1981).

There are some greater risks to the fetus and mother with pregnancy in increased age. The rate of fetal chromosomal abnormalities rises with maternal age: the estimated rate of these types of fetal defects per 1000 women rises from 2.6 up to age 30, 5.6 at age 35, 15.8 at age 40, to 53.7 at age 45 (Hook, 1981). The most common chromosome abnormality, *Down's syndrome,* results in impaired intellectual functioning and various physical defects. Women 35 and older may also be more likely to experience pregnancy and delivery complications. However, medical advances have greatly reduced the risks of childbearing after 35, and for women between 35 and 44 years, prenatal diagnosis, such as amniocentesis, and elective abortion reduce the risk of bearing an infant with a severe birth defect to a level comparable with that for younger women (Goldberg et al., 1979). Furthermore, with careful monitoring and management of pregnancy and labor, risks to the newborn and mother can be reduced almost to the level of the younger population (Kujansuu et al., 1981).

Another concern that women and their partners have when they consider postponing having a child until the woman is past her 20s is that her ability to become pregnant may be lessened. Current research indicates that as women become older, they have a slightly increased chance of infertility. However, "for the majority of women who want to postpone childbearing until they have completed their education and established themselves in a career, the risks they are running may be quite small compared with the benefits" (Bongaarts, 1982, p. 78).

THE EXPERIENCE OF PREGNANCY

Pregnancy is a unique and significant experience for both the woman and her partner, especially if he is involved throughout the pregnancy. In the following paragraphs, we will look at the experience and the impact it may have on the woman and the man.

The Woman's Experience

Each woman has different emotional and physical reactions to pregnancy, and the same woman may react differently to different pregnancies. Factors influencing a woman's emotional reactions can include how the decision for pregnancy was made, current and impending life style changes, her relationship with others, her financial resources, and her self-image. The woman's acquired attitudes and knowledge about childbearing and her hopes and fears about parenthood will also contribute to her experience.

Women sometimes feel they should experience only positive emotions when they are pregnant. However, the physical, emotional, and situational aspects of a pregnancy often elicit an array of contradictory emotions, including joy, depression, excitement, impatience, and fear. As one writer states:

That calm, sure, unambivalent woman who moved through the pages of the manuals I read seemed as unlike me as an astronaut. Nothing, to be sure, had prepared me for the intensity of relationship already existing between me and a creature I had carried in my body and now held in my arms and fed from my breasts. Throughout pregnancy and nursing, women are urged to relax, to mime the serenity of madonnas. No one mentions the psychic crisis of bearing a first child, the excitation of long-buried feelings about one's own mother, the sense of confused power and powerlessness, of being taken over on the one hand and of touching new physical and psychic potentialities on the other, a heightened sensibility which can be exhilarating, bewildering, and exhausting. No one mentions the strangeness of attraction—which can be as single-minded and overwhelming as the early days of a love affair—to a being so tiny, so dependent, so folded-in to itself—who is, and yet is not, part of oneself. (Rich, 1976, p. 36)

The marked physical changes that occur also have a significant effect on the experience of pregnancy. Several changes take place during the early stages of the

first trimester (first three months). Menstruation ceases. As the milk glands in the breasts develop, the breasts increase in size. The nipples and areola usually become darker in color. Nausea, sometimes called "morning sickness," may occur. Many women experience a marked increase in tiredness:

I'm ordinarily a very energetic woman but during the first two months of my pregnancy, I couldn't get enough sleep. This meant a drastic change in my daily routine. (Authors' files)

Vaginal secretions may change or increase. Urination may be more frequent and bowel movements more irregular. These physical changes may pass unnoticed, however, for there will be little or no increase in the size of the woman's abdomen during these first three months.

In the second trimester, there are more outward signs of pregnancy. The waistline thickens and the belly begins to protrude. For some women, looking pregnant provides a sense of confirmation:

Even though I knew I was pregnant, I somehow really didn't believe it until my stomach started to grow. (Authors' files)

Fetal movements may be felt in the fourth or fifth month. First trimester nausea and tiredness usually disappear by now, and a woman may experience heightened feelings of well-being. The breasts may begin to secrete thin yellowish fluid called *colostrum.*

During the last three months, the uterus and abdomen increase in size (see Figure 12.6). The muscles of the uterus occasionally contract painlessly. The enlarged uterus produces pressure on the woman's stomach, intestines, and bladder. This may cause discomfort, indigestion, and frequent urination. Fetal movements can be seen and felt from the outside of the abdomen.

Fatherhood does not involve the same physical experiences as does maternity (although occasionally, a "pregnant father" may report psychosympathetic symptoms such as the nausea or tiredness his partner is experiencing). However, the experiences of pregnancy and birth are often profound for the father.

The Man's Experience

Significant changes have occurred in the last several decades in the role of the woman's partner during pregnancy, childbirth, and childrearing. Pregnancy, once seen as predominantly the woman's domain, is now commonly viewed as an experience to share with one's partner:

For many couples the proposition is now *our* pregnancy and birth. With the advent of the Lamaze method and the prepared natural-childbirth movement, the man became more intimately involved in the pregnancy and childbirth experience. He attended pregnancy and childbirth classes, and even watched childbirth films. He became an

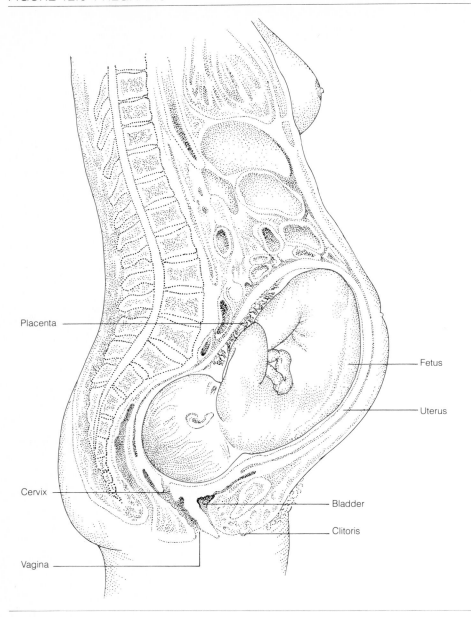

Placenta

Fetus

Uterus

Cervix

Bladder

Clitoris

Vagina

aide in the process, helping with breathing exercises, listening to little heartbeats, learning to comfort and cope with the experience of the woman. There is no question that this movement brought the male closer to the pregnancy and birth experience in some cases. For that special group there is a very real sense of "our pregnancy and birth" which represents a substantial departure from the traditional involvement of the male. (Dailey, 1978, p. 43)

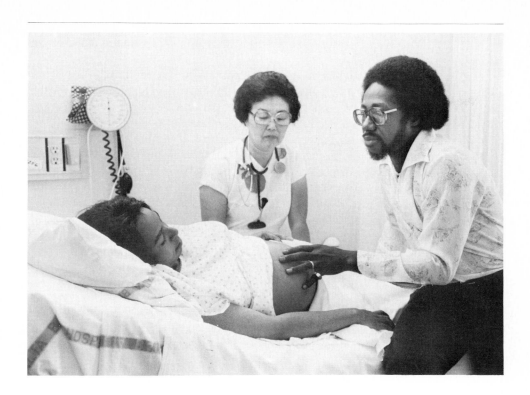

The author of the preceding quote is describing some of the unique emotional experiences of the male in what he terms the "male pregnancy." Like the woman, her partner often reacts with a great deal of ambivalence. He may feel ecstatic, but he may also be fearful about the pregnancy or the woman's safety. He may feel especially tender toward his partner, and he may become more solicitous. At the same time he may feel a sense of separateness from the woman because of the physical changes only she is experiencing. He may be proud at the prospect of becoming a father, but he may question his parenting ability and may feel concern over the impending increase in responsibility. In all, the "pregnant male" has special needs, as does his partner, and in Dailey's view, it is important that the woman be aware of these needs and be willing to respond to them. This "two-way" support and comfort can enhance "[t]he level of sharing, support, and mutuality. . . and for many parents, the notion of 'our' child seems much more real" (Dailey, 1978, p. 44).

Sexual Interaction During Pregnancy

During pregnancy it may be necessary for·a couple to modify intercourse positions. The side-by-side, woman-on-top, and rear-entry positions are generally more comfortable than the man-on-top position as pregnancy progresses. Oral and manual genital stimulation as well as total body touching and holding can continue as usual. In fact, pregnancy is a time when a couple may explore and develop these dimensions more fully; even if coitus is not advised, intimacy, eroticism, and sexual satisfaction can continue.

A woman's sexual interest and responsiveness may change through the course of her pregnancy. In limited studies, Masters and Johnson report no increase in sexual desire and activity during the first trimester (Masters and Johnson, 1966). Nausea, breast tenderness, and fatigue may inhibit sexual interest during this time. However, they report that increased sexual tension and response is common for some women during the second trimester. Some women may experience orgasm for the first time and others develop a multiorgasmic response. This change in sexual response may be due to the increases in pelvic vascularity during pregnancy and the resulting inten-sification of sexual vasocongestion. During this time the duration and intensity of orgasmic contractions are increased and resolution is slowed. During the third tri-mester, a decrease in sexual interest may occur.

Most other studies confirm the third trimester decline in sexual interest and activity reported by Masters and Johnson. However, other research that examined the influence of pregnancy on sexuality did not show a second trimester increase for most women; on the contrary, the study reported that the level of sexual interest and activity declined progressively over the pregnancy (Calhoun et al., 1981). Some of the most common reasons women gave for decreasing sexual activity during pregnancy included physical discomfort, feelings of physical unattractiveness, and fear of injuring the unborn child.

There is currently disagreement in the medical community about the safety of intercourse late in pregnancy. Some evidence suggests that sexual intercourse during the last weeks of pregnancy may be related to greater fetal distress and to greater frequency of infections of amniotic fluid (Naeye, 1979). On the other hand, Masters and Johnson state that ". . . frequently, blanket medical interdiction of coital activity for arbitrarily established periods of time both before and after delivery has done far more harm than good" (1966, p. 168). They believe that sexual intercourse may be continued as desired until the onset of labor, with some exceptions; no coital contact should take place if spotting, or vaginal or abdominal pain occur, or if the amniotic sac ("water bag") breaks. As with many other areas of sexual health care, a woman, her partner, and her health-care practitioner can make an informed decision.

CHILDBIRTH

The full term of pregnancy usually lasts about nine months, although there is some variation in length. Some women may have pregnancies that are longer; others may give birth to fully developed infants up to a few weeks before the nine-month term is over. There is a good deal of variation in the experience of childbirth also, depending on a score of factors; the woman's physiology, her emotional state, the baby's size and position, and the kind of childbirth practices (discussed later in this section) all play an important part. Despite the variations, there are three generally recognizable stages in the process of childbirth.

A woman can often tell that labor has begun when regular contractions of the uterus begin. Another indication of beginning *first-stage labor* may be the "bloody show" (discharge of the mucous plug from the cervix). The amniotic sac may rupture in the first stage of labor, an occurrence sometimes called "breaking the bag of waters."

Before the first stage begins, the cervix usually will have already *effaced* (flattened and thinned) and dilated slightly. It continues to dilate throughout first stage, and it is the extent of dilation that defines the early, late, and "transition" phases of first-stage labor. The cervix is dilated up to five centimeters during early first phase; five to eight centimeters in late; and eight to 10 during the final or transition phase of the first stage. Each phase becomes shorter and the contractions become stronger; transition is usually the most intense. First stage is the longest of the three stages, usually lasting 10–16 hours for the first childbirth, and 4–8 hours in subsequent deliveries (see Figure 12.7).

The *second stage* begins when the cervix is fully dilated and the infant descends further into the vaginal birth canal, usually head first (as in [b] of Figure 12.7). The second stage often lasts from a half hour to two hours—although it may be much

FIGURE 12.7 THREE STAGES OF CHILDBIRTH

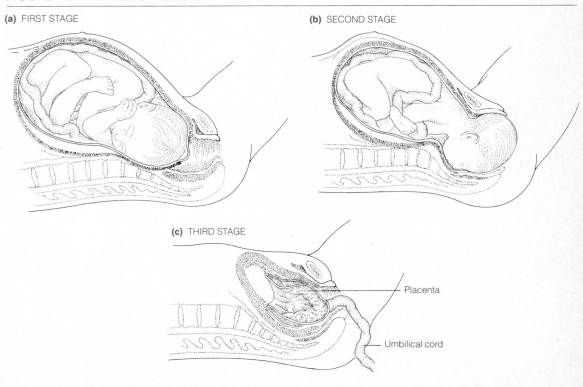

(a) FIRST STAGE

(b) SECOND STAGE

(c) THIRD STAGE

— Placenta

— Umbilical cord

shorter or longer. During this time, the woman can actively push to help the baby out, and many women report their active pushing to be the best part of labor:

I knew what "labor" meant when I was finally ready to push. I have never worked so hard, so willingly. (Authors' files)

The second stage ends when the infant is born.

The *third stage* of labor consists of the delivery of the placenta, shown in (c) of Figure 12.7. With one or two more uterine contractions, the placenta usually separates from the uterine wall and comes out of the vagina, generally within a half hour after the baby is born. The placenta is also called the *afterbirth*.

Childbirth Practices: Past and Present

In Europe before the 1600s, women usually gave birth in their own homes, assisted by a birth attendant, a woman called a *midwife*. Childbirth generally took place with the woman in a sitting or squatting position that permitted gravity to help the child exit from the birth canal.

This practice began to change during the 1600s, however, when male "physicians" (often students, barbers, butchers, and hog gelders) began replacing midwives. Many women then went to hospitals in large cities. These hospitals were primarily charity institutions where souls could be saved as people died. There was no knowledge of the principles by which infectious diseases spread, and laboring women would be examined by the unwashed hands of a "physician"—who may have just examined someone with syphilis, cholera, smallpox, typhoid, or perhaps had recently completed dissecting a diseased cadaver. Sometimes entire wards of new mothers died from infections spread in this way. In the mid-1800s, a physician in Vienna discovered the link between childbirth fever and the infected hands of examiners. Even with minimal changes in hygienic procedures, childbirth fever deaths were eliminated in his hospital within a year (Arms, 1975).

However, other developments began that reinforced the notion that birth was painful and dangerous, necessitating extensive medical intervention. The supine position, anesthesia, and forceps all came into common use in the mid-1800s.

Louis XIV initiated the use of the supine position. He found it sexually arousing to hide behind a screen and watch his various mistresses give birth. Louis had the court physician convince women to lie on their backs on a table, in full view of the hidden king, rather than sitting as they had previously done (a position which obstructed his view). The supine position then became fashionable and was widely adopted. Similarly, when Queen Victoria was convinced to use chloroform during birth, anesthesia became popular. Most of the opposition for its use came from religious leaders who said it was God's will for women to suffer in childbirth (Arms, 1975).

By the mid-1800s, forceps and the supine position had a counteracting relationship. Forceps (tongs applied to the sides of the baby's head) speeded delivery and the supine position slowed it down. The woman lying on her back works against gravity rather than with it, losing its natural assistance during delivery. The supine position also puts pressure on the blood vessels, which may slow the return of blood to the heart and thereby decrease blood availability to other organs, including the uterus. The reduction of blood flow can cause fetal distress.

By the 1900s, even uncomplicated childbirth was treated as risky, requiring hospitalization, various anesthetics, instruments, and machines. Technically trained medical practitioners offered a new sanitized, mechanized, controlled, physically and emotionally detached birth. Although many of the technical advancements can be helpful and frequently life-saving in problem situations, their routine use in problem-free births and possible resulting complications are now being criticized (Arms, 1975). Today, obstetric technology is still an available option in cases where complications arise, but there are also many alternatives that can make problem-free childbirth simpler, less expensive, and, for some individuals, more pleasant.

The best-known advocates of contemporary childbirth alternatives are Grantly Dick-Read and Bernard Lamaze, who began presenting their ideas about childbirth in the late 1930s and early 1940s. Basically, they felt that certain attitudes and practices could help make childbirth a better experience. Dick-Read believed that most of the pain during childbirth stemmed from the muscle tension caused by fear. In an effort to reduce anxiety, he advocated education about the birth process and relaxation with calm, consistent support during a woman's labor. The Lamaze philosophy is similar. The method consists of learning to voluntarily relax abdominal and perineal muscles and to use breathing exercises to dissociate the involuntary labor contractions from pain sensations. Both of these methods are incorporated into childbirth education classes throughout the United States.

Although sometimes referred to as "natural" childbirth, *prepared childbirth* is a more appropriate label for the Dick-Read and Lamaze methods. A woman and her partner are indeed preparing themselves. An additional benefit of prepared childbirth is the company and support of the labor coach, often the woman's partner. It has only been recently that husbands and trained labor coaches have been commonly allowed in the delivery room.

Another birth technique has been developed by a French physician, Frederick LeBoyer (1975). Instead of the parents' preparation, it focuses primarily on the birth experience of the infant. The LeBoyer techniques can be suitable for hospital, home, or clinic delivery. (In anticipation of possible policy conflicts, permission and arrangements should be made beforehand with a hospital.)

LeBoyer's basic philosophy is that the newborn's transition from the inner world of the uterus to the outer world should be made as nontraumatic as possible. Techniques such as lowered lights and hushed voices to greet the emerging infant, immediate skin contact on the mother's belly, not cutting the umbilical cord until after it has stopped pulsing, and a body temperature water bath all attempt to soothe the senses of the newborn and reduce the shock of birth. How effective these techniques are is undetermined. However, some studies indicate the one-, two-, and three-year-old children of the lower-middle-income women arbitrarily assigned to LeBoyer for delivery have higher scores on a psychomotor function test, have walked earlier, and have had fewer toilet-training, eating, sleeping, or digestive disorders than non-LeBoyer-born children in a matched group (*Behavior Today,* 1976).

Newborn in LeBoyer's warm water bath.

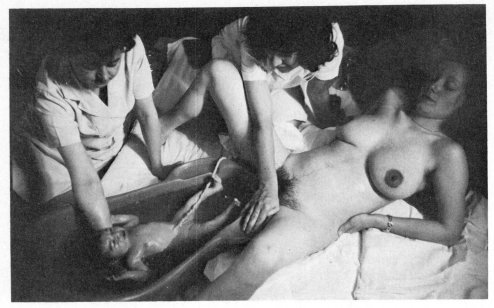

Birthplace Alternatives

Along with more options for childbirth practices have been new options for places where childbirth occurs. Not many years ago having a baby meant a stay at the hospital. But in the last few years, the alternatives for location of labor and delivery facilities have increased greatly and include birthing clinics and private homes as well as hospitals. Each birthplace is unique in terms of what it offers the parents and the infant.

Birthing Clinics Birthing clinics or centers are beginning to appear in the United States. Some are adjoined to hospitals and others are separate organizations. The birthing-clinic rooms are furnished more like a home than a hospital, and the pregnant woman can arrange to have family members and friends with her. Women and their chosen attendants have the use of a room throughout labor and delivery, and some emergency medical equipment is available. A woman who delivered her second child in such a setting reports her experience:

I was delighted to learn about the family-oriented maternity center. When labor began, my husband and three-year-old girl drove there and moved into our room. At first, between contractions, I would go to the communal kitchen to make some tea or to the playroom to chat with my daughter. When Jason was born, my family, a long-time woman friend, and the doctor were all there. The doctor was supportive, yet he never interfered with my previously clarified wishes. Knowing that emergency equipment was readily available helped me to be even more relaxed. (Authors' files)

The birth of a child in an alternative birthing center within a hospital.

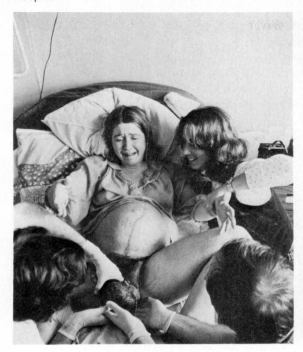

Home Birth　Home birth has become more common over the last few years. Between 1972 and 1975, the number of out-of-hospital births increased by 60% (Maynard, 1977). With precautions—careful prenatal screening for complications, thorough preparations, a skilled attendant, and available emergency transportation— home birth may be safe. However, it may still be difficult to find doctors or midwives who will deliver at home. Midwives are illegal in some states, and in some cases doctors who do home deliveries may have their hospital privileges revoked. The primary advantages of home birth are the familiar surroundings, the ability to make decisions about delivery, the initial contact with the newborn independent of institutional policies, the involvement of other children or friends, the limited exposure of the newborn to strangers, and the reduced cost. To many people, the relaxed home setting is particularly valuable:

When my contractions began, I called the midwife, my mother, and my husband to come over to the house. Supplies were already on hand. When my contractions stopped for a while, my husband and I curled up and took a nap while the others visited in the living room. The delivery went fine. I was glad I had taken the prepared childbirth classes and learned the breathing to help me over the rough spots. Afterwards, as I was lying in my husband's arms holding our new baby I felt—at home. (Authors' files)

The greatest risks with a home birth are that life-saving emergency equipment is not readily available and that emergencies are not always predictable.

Hospital Births   The hospital setting provides emergency medical care should birth complications arise. The hospital is the appropriate place for delivery in any high risk pregnancy. Conditions that raise the risk of complication include premature labor; the infant in other than the head-first presentation; blood incompatibility between mother and fetus; *toxemia* (water retention and high blood pressure are early symptoms—the condition may result in convulsions if untreated); *placenta previa* (the placenta positioned over the cervical opening); multiple births; five or more previous deliveries; too small a pelvis; illness; or advanced age (Boston Women's Health Book Collective, 1976). Competent and thorough prenatal screening can detect most of these complications.

Most pregnancies can be delivered normally with no medical interventions. However, some women welcome extensive medical intervention in a hospital delivery:

I want to have my second child the way I had my first. General anesthesia when things get rough—then I wake up as if nothing happened and see my beautiful baby, all clean and dressed in, hopefully, her new clothes. I don't understand women who want to go through all that work, panting, and pain when the doctor can simply take care of it all. (Authors' files)

Other women and their partners want to be actively involved throughout the birth experience, and this can often be possible in a hospital setting. Hospitals have grown more receptive to individualized birth in recent years, and many hospitals now have birthing rooms which have a homelike atmosphere. Participation of partner, labor coach, and others; nondrug deliveries; delivery techniques such as LeBoyer; and immediate postdelivery maternal-infant physical contact are increasingly available:

My husband and I had a great deal of privacy during labor. We had consulted with our doctor prior to delivery. She agreed to use no medications unless I agreed, and to let me use the sitting-up and holding-my-knees position during second-stage pushing. We also used LeBoyer's water bath. It really felt like *our* delivery rather than "being delivered." (Authors' files)

Regulations vary among physicians and hospitals, so that experiences such as the one just described are not always permitted. Therefore, it is important to discuss and agree on childbirth plans with the practitioner before the time of delivery.

Medical Interventions: Pros and Cons

Women and their partners should be aware of possible benefits and side effects of medical procedures used during childbirth. Often an initial minor intervention will result in other procedures becoming necessary. Furthermore, there is some evidence that the receptivity and contact between the parent and child immediately after delivery may have an effect on the formation of their relationship: "Today scientists are beginning to report evidence that supports what many women have felt for generations: that where and under what conditions a woman gives birth greatly affects the course of her labor, the normalcy of her delivery, the health of her baby, and the lifelong relationship of mother and child" (Arms, 1975). Drugs, fetal heart monitors, forceps, cesarean section, and episiotomies are common medical interventions whose advantages and disadvantages need to be evaluated carefully.

Most drugs given to the woman during childbirth cross the placental barrier. As a result, they can affect not only the mother, but also the fetus during labor and often after delivery. Research indicates that drugs can slow, lengthen, or stop labor; cause maternal convulsions and lowered blood pressure; eliminate the urge to push during second stage labor; and affect fetal heart rate and oxygen supply (Bonica, 1972; Brazelton, 1973; Scanlon, 1974). Newborn sucking behavior, responsiveness to cuddling, muscular, visual, and neural development have been shown to be retarded by the use of certain obstetrical medications (Kron et al., 1966; Scanlon, 1974). Drugs may inhibit the newborn's responsiveness to its parents, which may negatively affect the parent-child attachment.

In addition to the administration of drugs, other procedures have been frequently used during deliveries. An *episiotomy,* an incision in the perineum from the vagina toward the anus, is often made in hospital deliveries. The rationale for episiotomies is that they reduce the pressure on the infant's head, and they also help prevent vaginal tearing, which is more difficult to suture than a straight incision and often heals less well. Episiotomies also are thought to help preserve pelvic muscle tone and support. While the procedure is common in the United States, it is not considered necessary in most other societies. Only 8% of birthing women in Holland have episiotomies. Relaxation, proper breathing and pushing, physician patience, manual stretching of the perineum, and freedom of leg movement can eliminate the need for many routine incisions.

Forceps, shaped like salad tongs, fit alongside the baby's head and are used to assist the infant out of the birth canal. Forceps are often used after analgesics and anesthetics have reduced the strength of uterine contractions. Careful use of forceps is justified with certain complications but not with routine normal deliveries, for they pose some risks of injury to the woman and baby.

A *cesarean section,* in which the baby is removed through an incision made in the abdominal wall and uterus, can be life-saving surgery for the mother and child. Cesarean birth may be recommended in a variety of situations, including a fetal head that is too large for the mother's pelvic structure, maternal illness (including herpes in the vaginal tract), birth complications like breech-fetal position (feet or bottom, instead of head, first coming out of the uterus), and many others. Mothers who do have a cesarean section often have a spinal anesthetic and are awake to greet their infant when she or he is delivered. A woman may have more than one baby by cesarean section. Also, many women can have subsequent vaginal deliveries, depending on the circumstances of the earlier cesarean section(s) and the subsequent delivery (Lavin et al., 1982; Saldana et al., 1979).

402

The percentage of cesarean sections performed in U. S. hospitals has increased dramatically over the last 10 years. In 1970, approximately 6% of births were cesarean deliveries; in 1976 this figure doubled to almost 12%. Some large teaching hospitals reported rates of 16%–20% for cesarean section births (Larned, 1978). The increase in the incidence of cesarean sections has evoked controversy. While some maintain that the increase reflects better use of medical technology in the management of childbirth, others believe that cesarean deliveries are aggressive medical interventions that are being too readily used.

POSTPARTUM

The first several weeks following birth are referred to as the *postpartum* period. It is a time of both physical and psychological adjustment for each family member and is likely to be a time of intensified emotional highs and lows. Understanding that these feelings are a common response to adjustments to the new family member may help new parents cope with the stresses involved. Combined with the excitement and pleasures of the arrival of the long-awaited infant are often other feelings. The mother may experience what is described as "postpartum blues," during which she may cry easily and feel fearful or sad. Such reactions may be partly due to the sudden physical and hormonal changes following delivery.

The new baby also affects the roles and interactions of all the members of the family. The mother and father may experience an increased closeness to each other as well as some problematic feelings. New fathers sometimes feel jealous of the relationship between the mother and child. Both the man and woman may want extra emotional support from the other, but each may have less than usual to give. The time and energy demands of caring for an infant can contribute to weariness and stress—feelings that may be compounded by the impact of the responsibility of caring for this new addition for the next 20 years. Brothers and sisters may also be affected, as they often have some negative feelings about the attention given the new family member.

Each of these feelings and concerns gradually tends to lessen as the family makes adjustments to new roles and expectations. Often, too, the adjustment is easier when family members have accurate expectations (or previous experience) to prepare them for the demands as well as the pleasure of the new arrival.

Parent-Child Contact

Not just the first weeks after birth but also the first few minutes after birth may be a very important period. There has been a growing interest and concern about the parent-child contact that takes place following birth and the impact that this contact has on parent-child attachment. The reciprocal attachment may influence the developing child's behavior and may help the parent make the adjustment to the nurturing role, providing motivation to meet the insistent demands of a helpless infant.

Some hospitals are changing the traditional postpartum separation of infant and mother. In others, however, standard procedure is similar to the following description:

Many men share in caring for their children.

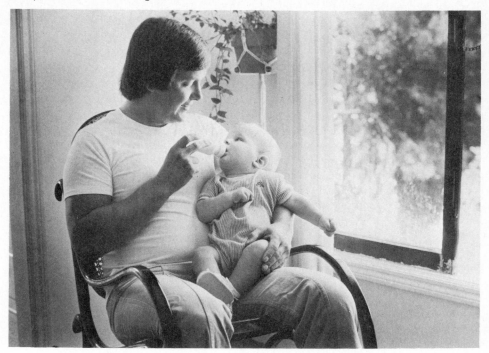

In many hospitals, the newborn, after the cord is tied, is given to a nurse. She takes him to a table where a radiant heat panel avoids chilling his wet skin. A footprint is taken so no confusion is possible later on. Soon the baby, wrapped in a blanket, is brought to the mother. In some places, a 5–10 minute visit is allowed, but in others the nurse merely shows the baby to her. Then the child is taken to the nursery, washed, weighed and placed in a crib—alone again. (Spezzano and Waterman, 1977, p. 110)

One study compared groups of infant-mother pairs where different amounts of contact were experienced (Klaus and Kennel, 1976). Some mothers were given more contact with their newborns both immediately after birth and during their hospital stay than is the usual hospital procedure. These extended-contact mothers consequently engaged in more holding, fondling, kissing, eye contact, talking to the infant, and successful and lengthy breast feeding than other mothers. These infants were found to cry less and to smile and laugh more. At five years of age, the children of extended-contact mothers had significantly higher IQs and more advanced scores on language tests than children who were treated according to standard hospital procedures. In this same study, fathers who were asked to establish eye contact for one hour during the first day of life and to dress their children twice a day during the hospital stay also demonstrated an increase in their caretaker role at home.

Attachment depends, in part, on complex interactions between parent and child which begin immediately after birth. The mother, when she is alert during delivery, often wants to have the closest possible contact with her newborn. The immediate interaction can be a profound experience that initiates a "series of reciprocal interactions" (Klaus and Kennel, 1976, p.11). The timing of the initial close physical contact appears to be important to the infant, also:

> Right after a drug-free, uncomplicated delivery, the baby is quite alert—even more so than he will be later on. Evidence shows that he responds to a moving face and to sounds near his ear. If the corner of his mouth is touched, he reflexively turns his head to that side and starts to suck. Rub his palm, especially between thumb and forefinger, and he will hold on to whatever is tickling him. His senses and reflexes mark him as a responsive human being in need of human contact, and the contact he needs is right there—mother. She has the rhythmic heartbeat he is accustomed to, eyes to look at, a warm body to touch, breasts to suck. (Spezzano and Waterman, 1977, p. 110)

The father can also provide this kind of contact. Therefore, the maximum potential for parent-child attachment depends partly on an environment that encourages physical closeness of the parents and child.

Once again, prospective parents who are informed about the choices can discuss their needs with the physician before the delivery. Even in cases of cesarean section or with premature babies who must be in incubators, adjustment of hospital routines can sometimes be made to maximize parent-child contact, if the parents wish.

Breast Feeding

Closely related to the concern with postpartum contact is the renewed interest in breast feeding over the last several years. La Leche League, 9616 Minneapolis Avenue, Franklin Park, IL 60131, is an organization that promotes breast feeding.

Production of breast milk does not take place as soon as the infant is born. Right after delivery, the breasts produce a yellowish liquid called *colostrum*, which contains antibodies and protein. Lactation or milk production begins about one to three days after delivery. Pituitary hormones stimulate milk production in the breasts in response to the stimulation of the infant suckling the nipple. If a new mother does not begin or continue to nurse, milk production subsides within a matter of days.

Nursing may temporarily inhibit ovulation. However, it is highly unreliable as a method of birth control. Birth control pills should not be used during nursing because the hormones (as well as other drugs) are transmitted to the infant in the mother's milk.

For women who decide to nurse, breast feeding is another opportunity for close physical contact. It also has other advantages. It provides the infant with a digestible food filled with antibodies and immunity-producing substances. Nursing also induces uterine contractions that help speed the return of the uterus to its pre-pregnancy size. Nursing can be an emotional and sensual experience for the mother. Sexual interest

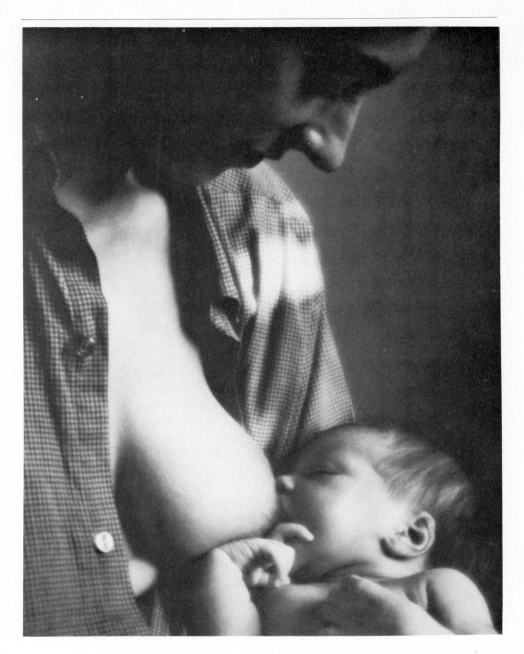

often returns more rapidly in women who breast feed than in those who bottle feed (Masters and Johnson, 1966).

However, nursing has some disadvantages as well. The nursing mother's genitals may be oversensitive and become sore from intercourse because of the reduction of estrogen that nursing creates (estrogen conditions and maintains vulvar tissue) (Murray, 1976). Her breasts may also be tender and sore. Milk may be ejected involuntarily from her nipples during sexual excitement and be a source of embarrassment. Also, the tasks of caring for a baby and the physical demands of producing milk may leave the woman with little extra energy for sexual activities.

Some mothers may have negative feelings about breast feeding. Many women feel ambivalent about this activity, perhaps partly because of our society's emphasis on breasts as sex symbols. Furthermore, some mothers' life styles may be too disrupted by the sole feeding responsibility of nursing. It is often easier to share childcare responsibilities by bottle feeding rather than nursing, and fathers can take a greater role by holding and feeding the infant. Also, some women have to return to work shortly after childbearing and are not available to nurse their babies. As in other areas, breast feeding is a matter of exploration and personal preference.

Sexual Interaction after Childbirth

In the past, many physicians prohibited intercourse until six weeks after delivery. Currently, couples are commonly advised that intercourse can resume after the flow of a reddish uterine discharge (called *lochia*) has stopped and after episiotomy incisions or vaginal tears have healed (Masters and Johnson, 1966). After a cesarean section the couple needs to wait until the incision has healed enough for intercourse to occur without discomfort. It is important to note that other sexual and affectionate relations can be shared while waiting.

Couples may delay resuming intercourse after childbirth for a variety of reasons (Calhoun et al., 1981). Fatigue, tension, and physical discomfort of breasts or at the episiotomy site may be factors, along with anxiety about painful intercourse or about displeasing a partner because of a more relaxed vaginal opening. Along with specific problems or concerns, couples whose sexual activity has been disrupted by pregnancy and birth may feel "out of practice" with their sexual relationship. It is often helpful for couples to slowly resume sexual activity in an explorative manner as if they were first initiating a sexual relationship (Murray, 1976).

Once intercourse is resumed, contraception is necessary for as long as the couple wants to avoid another pregnancy. Ovulation may be delayed, especially if the mother is nursing, but accurately predicting when ovulation will occur is difficult.

SUMMARY

PARENTHOOD AS AN OPTION

1. Increased numbers of couples are choosing not to be parents and others are adopting children or providing homes for foster children.

BECOMING PREGNANT

2. Failure to ovulate and blockage of the fallopian tubes are typical causes of female infertility, and low sperm count is the most common cause of male infertility.

3. The emotional stress and the disruption of a couple's sexual relationship from infertility can result in sexual difficulties.

4. The man-above intercourse position, deep penetration at ejaculation, and staying still after ejaculation may enhance chances of conception.

5. Techniques for predetermining the sex of a child are not absolutely effective.

6. The first tentative sign of a pregnancy is a missed menstrual period. Urine tests and pelvic exams are used to determine pregnancy.

7. Spontaneous abortion, or miscarriage, sometimes occurs during pregnancy. Often the aborted tissues are abnormal.

A HEALTHY PREGNANCY

8. Pregnancy is divided into three trimesters, each of which is marked by fetal changes.

9. Nutrients, oxygen, and waste exchange between the woman and fetus occurs through the placental cell walls. Substances harmful to the fetus can pass through the placenta.

10. In amniocentesis, cells and the amniotic fluid are examined to detect an ever-increasing number of birth defects.

11. More women are having children after age 35. These women have slightly decreased fertility and somewhat more risk of conceiving a fetus with abnormalities and of having pregnancy and delivery complications. However, with careful monitoring of pregnancy and childbirth, risks are reduced almost to the level of younger women.

THE EXPERIENCE OF PREGNANCY

12. Some first trimester physical changes include cessation of menstruation, tiredness, and breast size increase. In the second trimester, the woman's belly begins to protrude; fetal movements may be felt. By the third trimester the abdomen is enlarged and fetal movements are pronounced.

13. Men have become increasingly involved in the prenatal, childbirth, and childrearing processes.

14. Although modifications of sexual interaction may be indicated during pregnancy, sensual and sexual interaction, with few exceptions, may continue as desired.

CHILDBIRTH

15. Indications of first-stage labor are regular contractions of the uterus, discharge of the mucous plug, rupture of the amniotic sac, and cervical effacement and dilation up to five centimeters.

16. Second-stage labor is the descent of the infant further into the birth canal. The second stage ends with birth and the placenta is delivered in the third stage.

17. Prepared childbirth, popularized by Bernard Lamaze and Grantly Dick-Read, and LeBoyer birth techniques have changed childbirth practices.

18. The birthing clinic combines a home setting and limited emergency backup equipment.

19. Home births are becoming more common. A woman or couple have maximum control of the birth experience in the home, yet medical emergency backup equipment is not available.

20. Hospital delivery procedures have become more flexible for noncomplicated deliveries and provide the safest place for problem deliveries.

21. Medical interventions during birth (drugs, forceps, cesarean section, and episiotomies) can be helpful in the delivery process, but many people believe that they are overused.

POSTPARTUM

22. Extended postdelivery parent-child contact may positively influence the quality of the relationship.

23. Breast feeding is regaining popularity in the United States. There are advantages and disadvantages to breast or bottle feeding.

24. Intercourse after childbirth can usually resume once the flow of lochia has stopped and any vaginal tears or the episiotomy incision have healed.

SUGGESTED READINGS

Ehrenreich, Barbara, and English, Deirdre. *Witches, Midwives, and Nurses: A History of Women Healers.* Old Westbury, N. Y.: Feminist Press, 1973. A fascinating history of women healers.

Hannon, Sharron. *Childbirth.* New York: M. Evans, 1980. A consumers' guide to options of childbirth. Contains information on and resources for genetic counseling, exercising, budgeting, birthplace alternatives, and sex during pregnancy, among others.

408   LeBoyer, Frederick. *Birth without Violence.* New York: Knopf, 1975. A compelling and poetic book that emphasizes providing comfort for the newborn's transition into the world.

Lynn, David. *The Father: His Role in Child Development.* Monterey, Calif.: Brooks/Cole, 1974. This insightful book examines and encourages the father-child relationship and explores the contemporary transitions in relationships between mothers, fathers, and children.

Rubin, Sylvia. *It's Not Too Late for a Baby.* Englewood Cliffs, N. J.: Prentice-Hall, 1980. A practical guide to childbirth for the expectant parent over the age of 35. Includes a section on fathers over 35; has illustrative case examples.

Resources

International Childbirth Education Association, P.O. Box 20048, Minneapolis, MN 55420

National Association of Parents and Professionals for Safe Alternatives in Childbirth, P.O. Box 267, Marble Hill, MO 63764

American College of Nurse-Midwives, 1012 14th NW Suite 801, Washington, DC 20005

National Alliance for Optional Parenthood, 2010 Massachusetts Ave., NW, Washington, DC 20036.

13

Sexuality During Childhood and Adolescence

SEXUAL BEHAVIOR IN CHILDHOOD
THE PHYSICAL CHANGES OF ADOLESCENCE
SEXUAL BEHAVIOR DURING ADOLESCENCE
    The Double Standard
    Virginity or "Sexual Liberation"?
    Masturbation
    Petting
    Ongoing Sexual Relationships
    Sexual Intercourse
    Homosexuality
SOME KEY INFLUENCES ON PSYCHOSEXUAL DEVELOPMENT
    Dirty Diapers, Going Potty, and Related Issues
    Reactions to Masturbation
    Positive Models
    The Question of Nudity
    Independency Issues
    Privacy Concerns
SEX EDUCATION
ANDROGYNOUS CHILD-REARING AND SEXUALITY
SUMMARY
SUGGESTED READINGS

*I*n many Western societies, including the United States, it has been traditional to view childhood as a time when sexuality remains unexpressed and adolescence as a time when sexuality needs to be restrained. These viewpoints no doubt reflect, at least in part, the sex-for-procreation philosophy that has long influenced American sexual attitudes and behaviors. The opinion that adolescent sexual behavior should be curtailed continues to receive considerable support. However, with the widespread circulation of the research findings of Alfred Kinsey and other distinguished investigators, the false assumption that childhood is a period of sexual dormancy is gradually eroding. In fact, it is now widely recognized that infants of both sexes are born with the capacity for sexual pleasure and response.

Signs of sexual arousal in infants and children, such as penile erection, vaginal lubrication, and pelvic thrusting, are often misinterpreted or unacknowledged. However, careful observers may note these indications of sexuality in the very young. In some cases, both male and female infants have been observed experiencing what appears to be an orgasm. The infant, of course, cannot offer spoken confirmation of the sexual nature of such reactions. However, the behavior is so remarkably similar to that exhibited by sexually responding adults that little doubt exists about its nature. The following two quotations are offered as evidence for this conclusion:

Orgasm has been observed in boys of every age from 5 months to adolescence. Orgasm is in our records for a female babe of 4 months. The orgasm in an infant or other young male is, except for the lack of an ejaculation, a striking duplicate of orgasm in an older adult. The behavior involves a series of gradual physiologic changes, the development of rhythmic body movements with distinct penis throbs and pelvic thrusts, an obvious change in sensory capacities, a final tension of muscles, especially of the abdomen, hips, and back, a sudden release with convulsions, including rhythmic anal contractions—followed by the disappearance of all symptoms. A fretful babe quiets down under the initial sexual stimulation, is distracted from other activities, begins rhythmic pelvic thrusts, becomes tense as climax approaches, is thrown into convulsive action, often with violent arm and leg movements, sometimes with weeping at the moment of climax. After climax the child loses erection quickly and subsides into the calm and peace that typically follows adult orgasm. It may be some time before erection can be induced again after such an experience. There are observations of 16 males up to 11 months of age, with such typical orgasm reached in 7 cases. In 5 cases of young pre-adolescents, observations were continued over months or years, until the individuals were old enough to make it certain that true orgasm was involved and in all of these cases the later reactions were so similar to the earlier behavior that there could be no doubt of the orgastic nature of the first experience. (Kinsey et al., 1948, p. 177)

The typical reactions of a small girl in orgasm, seen by an intelligent mother who had frequently observed her three-year-old in masturbation, were described as follows; "Lying face down on the bed, with her knees drawn up, she started rhythmic pelvic thrusts, about one second or less apart. The thrusts were primarily pelvic, with the legs tensed in a fixed position. The forward components of the thrusts were in a smooth and perfect rhythm which was unbroken except for momentary pauses during which the genitalia were readjusted against the doll on which they were pressed; the return from each thrust was convulsive, jerky. There were 44 thrusts in unbroken rhythm, a slight momentary pause, 87 thrusts followed by a slight momentary pause, concentration and intense breathing with abrupt jerks as orgasm approached. She was completely oblivious to everything during these later stages of the activity. Her eyes were glassy and fixed in a vacant stare. There was noticeable relief and relaxation after orgasm. A second series of reactions began two minutes later with series of 48, 18, and 57 thrusts, with slight momentary pauses between each series. With the mounting tensions, there were audible gasps, but immediately following the cessation of pelvic thrusts there was complete relaxation and only desultory movements thereafter."

   We have similar records of observations made by some of our other subjects on a total of 7 pre-adolescent girls and 27 pre-adolescent boys under four years of age. These data indicate that the capacity to respond to the point of orgasm is certainly present in at least some young children, both female and male. (Kinsey et al., 1953, pp. 104–105)

   Considering the preverbal nature of infants, it is impossible to determine what such early sexual experiences mean to them. Nevertheless, it is reasonably certain that these activities are gratifying. Many infants of both sexes engage quite naturally in self-pleasuring unless such behavior produces strong negative responses from parents or other childcare agents.

   As this information demonstrates, sexuality cannot accurately be viewed as something that remains dormant during the early years of life. Rather, a variety of behaviors and body functions, including sexual eroticism, develop during infancy and childhood. In some ways, sexuality may be especially important during this period, as many experiences during these formative years may have great impact on the later expression of adult sexuality. In the opening section of this chapter we will briefly outline some typical sexual behaviors during childhood.

SEXUAL BEHAVIOR IN CHILDHOOD

People show considerable variation in their sexual development during childhood, and many diverse influences are involved. Despite these differences, however, certain common features in the developmental sequence tend to emerge. In the next few pages we will briefly outline some of these typical behaviors, keeping in mind that each person's unique sexual history may differ from one or more of the following points. As you consider this information, it is also important to realize that most of the data about childhood sexual behavior is based on the recollections of adults who are asked to recall their childhood experiences. As we noted in Chapter 3, it may be quite difficult to accurately remember some facts, particularly if they are based on experiences occurring many years earlier.

   In the first few years of life, many girls and boys discover the pleasures of genital stimulation. This activity often involves rubbing the genital area against an object such as a doll or pillow. With the development of coordinated hand movements, manual stimulation may become a preferred method for producing sexual pleasure. In all probability, such activity is more likely to be observed in children raised in home environments where adults hold permissive attitudes toward genital touching.

The inclinations we have as adults toward sharing sexual intimacies seem to be related to our childhood experiences of warm, pleasurable contact with others, particularly parents.

A child may also learn to express his or her affectionate and erotic feelings through other activities like kissing and hugging. The responses the child receives for these expressions of intimacy may have a strong influence on the manner in which he or she expresses sexuality in later years. The inclinations we have as adults toward giving and receiving affection seem to be related to our early opportunities for warm, pleasurable contact with significant others, particularly parents. A number of researchers believe that children who are deprived of "contact comfort" (being touched and held) during the first months and years of life may have difficulty establishing intimate relationships later in their lives (Harlow and Harlow, 1962; Money, 1980; Montagu and Matson, 1979; Trause et al., 1977).

In addition to self-stimulation, prepubertal children often engage in play that may be viewed as sexual in nature. Such play takes place with friends or siblings of the same or the other sex. It may occur as early as the age of two or three, but it is more likely to take place between the ages of four and seven. Kinsey (1948, 1953) reported that 45% of the females and 57% of the males in his sample indicated having these experiences by age 12. In a more recent survey, parents of six- and seven-year-old children reported that 83% of their sons and 76% of their daughters had participated in some sex play with friends or siblings (Kolodny, 1980). The activities may range from exhibition and inspection of genitals, often under the guise of "playing doctor," to simulating intercourse by rubbing genital regions together. While most adults, particularly parents, tend to react to the apparent sexual nature of this play, for many children the play aspects of the interaction may be far more significant than any sexual overtones:

While adults may react to the apparent sexual nature of this interaction, many children find its play aspects to be more important than any sexual overtones.

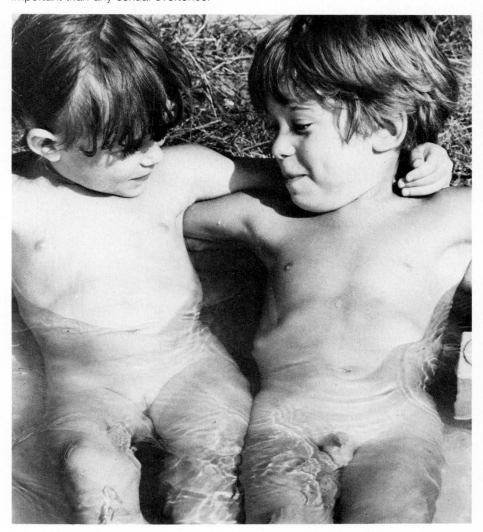

The sexual nature of these games is not always understood by the child and even when the small boy lies on the top of the small girl and makes what may resemble copulatory movement, there is often no realization that genital contact might be made, or that there might be an erotic reward in such activity. (Kinsey et al., 1953, p. 108)

When we think of preadolescent activities that look sexual—we, as adults, looking back on it, or as parents looking at it in our children—we respond to the sexual aspect; the sex is very important; the play is unimportant. To the child, however, the balance is exactly the opposite. The play is the major part; whatever sex might be in

Childhood curiosity about sexuality takes many forms.

it, is mainly interesting because it is forbidden, like mommy's jewel box or daddy's tool chest. (Gagnon, 1977, p. 85)

As this last quote suggests, curiosity about what is forbidden probably plays an important role in encouraging early sexual exploration. Curiosity about the sexual equipment of others, particularly the other sex, is quite normal. Many day-care and nursery schools now have bathrooms open to both sexes so that children can learn about sexual differences in a natural, everyday way.

Besides showing interest in sexual behaviors, many children in the five-to-seven age range begin to act in ways that mirror the predominant heterosexual marriage script in our society. This is apparent in the practice of "playing house," which is typical of children of this age (Broderick, 1966). Some of the sex play described earlier occurs within the context of this activity.

By the time children reach the age of eight or nine, there is a pronounced tendency for boys and girls to begin to play separately, although romantic interest in the other sex may exist at the same time. Furthermore, in spite of an apparent decline in sex play with others, curiosity about sexual matters remains high. This is an age when many questions about reproduction and sexuality may be asked.

Most 10- and 11-year-olds are keenly interested in body changes, particularly those involving the genitals and secondary sex characteristics. They often wait in eager anticipation for these signs of approaching adolescence. Many prepubescent children may become extremely self-conscious about their bodies and may be quite reticent about exposing them to the view of others. Segregation from the other sex is still the general rule and children of this age often strongly protest any suggestions of romantic interest in the other gender. Nonetheless, most girls and boys of this age have already decided they want to get married (Broderick, 1971).

Sex play with friends of the same sex is common during the late childhood years. In fact, during this time when the segregation of the sexes is particularly strong, homosexual activity is probably more common than heterosexual encounters (Comfort, 1963). In one survey of 432 Caucasian children, conducted by Kinsey, 52% of males and 35% of females reported homosexual experiences prior to puberty (Elias and Gebhard, 1969). In most instances, these childhood homosexual encounters are of a brief, transitory nature, soon replaced by the heterosexual courting of adolescence. Parents who become aware of these behaviors are cautioned against responding in an overly negative fashion and/or labeling such activity as homosexual in the adult sense (Gadpaille, 1975).

Masturbation is one of the most common sexual expressions during the childhood years. In Kinsey's study of children, 30% of the females and 56% of the males reported masturbating prior to adolescence (Elias and Gebhard, 1969). In a more recent survey, two-thirds of the male respondents and one-third of the females reported having masturbated by the age of 13 (Hunt, 1974). For both sexes, masturbation is the most frequent source of preadolescent orgasm (Kinsey et al., 1948 and 1953). Most boys learn about it from friends, and some may even receive instruction in the particulars of self-stimulation, as the following account indicates:

My introduction to the fine art of masturbation was provided by an older buddy. One day in his basement, while changing from wet swim suits, he asked me if I had ever "jerked off." Well, I hadn't and he proceeded to soap up his penis and demonstrate his technique. When I tried it, the sensations were very good but, unlike my friend, nothing came out of my penis. He told me to keep practicing and I did. Several months later I had my first ejaculation. (Authors' files)

In contrast to males, most young girls do not discuss masturbation with friends. Consequently, discovery of this activity is predominantly a solitary and often accidental event:

I discovered the delights of masturbation when I was about eight years old. My mother always encouraged me to thoroughly wash my "privates." One day in the tub I decided to make them "squeaky clean." I slid my bottom under the faucet and directed a stream of warm water over my vulva. Wow! That was one kind of washing I really liked. In short order I experienced my first orgasm. I didn't even know what you called it, but the sensations were great. I soon improvised all kinds of ways to squirt water over my clitoris. I never told anyone about my "discovery," but continued masturbating regularly with this water-spray technique. Today I have no problem understanding the popularity of hand-held water massagers. (Authors' files)

As these accounts and the preceding discussion have indicated, self-discovery and peer interactions are very important during childhood development of sexuality. These factors continue to be influential during the adolescent years, as we shall discover in subsequent portions of this chapter. But first we will turn our attention to the physical changes that accompany the onset of adolescence.

THE PHYSICAL CHANGES OF ADOLESCENCE

Adolescence is a time of dramatic physiological changes and social role development. In Western societies it is the transition between childhood and adulthood that typically spans the period from 12 to 20 years of age. Most of the major physical changes of adolescence take place during the first few years of this period. However, important and often profound changes in behavior and role expectations occur throughout this phase of life. By cross-cultural standards, adolescence in our society is rather extended. In many other cultures (and in Western society in preindustrial times) adult roles are assumed at a much earlier age. Rather than undergoing the protracted period of child-adult status that we know, the child is often initiated into adulthood once puberty is reached.

Puberty (Latin *pubescere*, to be covered with hair) is a term frequently used to describe the period of rapid physical changes in early adolescence. Before puberty, boys and girls have been growing taller and stronger. The onset of puberty is approximately two years earlier for girls than for boys. It is not known what mechanism triggers the chain of developments that follow. We do know that the hypothalamus plays a part (Katchadourian, 1977). In general, when a child is between the ages of eight and 14 years old, the hypothalamus increases secretions that cause the pituitary to release greater amounts of *gonadotropins* into the bloodstream. The gonadotropins, hormones that stimulate activity in the gonads, are chemically identical in men and women. However, in males they cause the testes to increase testosterone production; in females, they act on the ovaries to produce elevated estrogen levels.

At this point, external signs of characteristic male and female sexual maturation differentiation begin to be manifested in response to higher levels of the male and female hormones. The resulting development of breasts, facial, body, and pubic hair, and deepened voice are called *secondary sex characteristics*. Growth of pubic hair in both sexes and breast budding (slight protuberance under the nipple) in girls are usually the earliest signs of puberty. A growth spurt also follows. This spurt eventually terminates, again under the influence of the sex hormones, which send signals to close the ends of the long bones. The growth spurt usually occurs earlier in females than males (on the average, age 12 versus 14) and often results in girls being taller than boys during early adolescence (Marshall, 1977). External genitals also undergo enlargement; the penis and testes increase in size in the male, and the labia become enlarged in the female.

Under the influence of hormone stimulation the internal organs of the male and female also develop during puberty. In girls, the vaginal walls become thicker and the uterus becomes larger and more muscular. The vaginal pH environment changes from alkaline to acidic as vaginal and cervical secretions increase in response to the changing hormone status. Menstruation begins; the first menstrual period is called *menarche*. Initial menstrual periods may be irregular and occur without ovulation.

Most girls begin menstruating around 12 or 13, but there is widespread variation in the age of menarche. Research suggests that menarche may be triggered when a certain minimum percentage of body fat is present (Frisch and McArthur, 1974). At the onset of puberty the average ratio of lean to fatty tissue in females is 5 to 1 (that is, approximately one-sixth of the total body weight is fat). At menarche it is about 3 to 1 (about one-fourth of body weight is fat). In support of the suggested connection between body fat and menarche, research has revealed that female athletes and ballet dancers, who often engage in prolonged and strenuous training, frequently experience delayed menarche or interrupted menstruation (Frisch et al., 1980). Presumably, this results from an underdevelopment or reduction in body fat.

In boys, the prostate gland and seminal vesicles increase noticeably in size during this time. Although boys may experience orgasms throughout childhood, ejaculation is not possible until the prostate and seminal vesicles begin functioning under the influence of increasing testosterone levels. The first ejaculation occurs typically a year after the growth spurt has begun, usually around age 13 or 14, but, as with menstruation, the timing is highly variable. Kinsey (1948) reported that, in two out of three boys, initial ejaculation occurred during masturbation. There appears to be a period of early adolescent infertility in girls and boys following initial menstruation and ejaculation. However, this should not be depended upon for birth control.

Voice changes caused by growth of the voice box (larynx), occur in both sexes but are more dramatic in boys, who often experience an awkward time when their speech alternates between low and high pitched. Facial hair in boys and axillary (underarm) hair in both sexes usually appears approximately two years after growth of pubic hair. Increased activity of oil-secreting glands in the skin can cause facial blemishes, or acne.

Many of these physical developments may be sources of concern or pride to the adolescent and his or her family and friends. Feeling self-conscious is a common reaction, and individuals who mature early or late often feel particularly self-conscious:

I was the first one to get hair on my chest. At first I would cut it off so I wasn't different from everyone else in the shower room. (Authors' files)

All my friends had started menstruating a long time before and I still had not. I started wearing pads and a belt once a month so I wouldn't feel so out-of-it. (Authors' files)

The physical changes we have been describing are quite dramatic and rapid. Quite suddenly the body that one has been living in for years undergoes mysterious changes that are often disconcerting:

If given the chance, I would *never* repeat my early teen years. My body was so unpredictable. At the most inopportune moments my voice was cracking, my penis was erect, or a pimple was popping out on my face. Sometimes, all these things would happen at the same time! (Authors' files)

These physical changes do not go unnoticed by adolescent peers. Boy-girl friendships often change and adolescents are likely to become—at least temporarily—

more *homosocial*, relating socially primarily with members of the same sex. A young woman clarifies:

When I was growing up a neighbor boy and I were best buddies. We spent our summers exploring nearby fields, wrestling, and building a great tree house. When I started developing breasts, it all changed and we didn't seem to know how to talk to each other any more. (Authors' files)

Adolescent relationships often do not remain homosocial for very long. The period of adolescence is marked not only by physical changes, but also by important behavioral changes. In the following pages, we will look at some important areas of adolescent sexual behavior.

SEXUAL BEHAVIOR DURING ADOLESCENCE

Adolescence is a period of exploration, when sexual behavior—both self-stimulation and partner-shared—generally increases. While much of teenage sexuality represents a progression from childhood behaviors, a new significance is attached to sexual expression. There are several areas of sexual behavior where important developments take place during adolescence. We will look at a few specific behaviors, including masturbation, petting, development of on-going relationships, intercourse, pregnancy and the use of birth control methods, and homosexuality. In most areas of adolescent sexuality, the male-female double standard is a pervasive influence. We will look at this issue before turning to specific behaviors.

The Double Standard

Although children have been learning gender role stereotypes since infancy, the stress on gender role differentiation often increases during adolescence. One way that the gender role expectations for males and females are revealed is through the double standard. As we will see in Chapter 16, the double standard has profound effects on both male and female sexuality throughout our lives. The sexually emerging adolescent receives the full brunt of this polarizing societal belief.

For males, the focus of sexuality may be sexual conquest. Young men who are nonexploitative or inexperienced are often labeled with highly negative terms like "sissy." On the other hand, peers often provide social reinforcement for stereotypical "masculine" attitudes and behaviors; for example, approval is given to aggressive and independent behavior. For some young men, telling their peers about their sexual encounters is more important than the sexual act itself. As one young man states:

My own self-image was at stake. There I was—good looking, humorous, athletic, liked to party—but still a virgin. Everybody just assumed that I was an expert at making love. I played this role and, without a doubt, always implied, "Yes, we did and boy was it fun." (Authors' files)

For females, the message and the expectations are often very different. The following account illustrates one woman's view of both sides of the double standard:

It always seemed so strange, how society encouraged virginity in girls but it was OK for boys to lose theirs. I came from a large family, my brother being the oldest, and we girls followed him. I can remember when word got around how much of a playboy my brother was (he was about 18). My parents were not upset, but rather seemed kind of tickled. When we girls were ready to go out, our parents became suspicious. I can always remember how I felt and how if I ever became a parent I wouldn't allow such an inequality and emphasis on female virginity to take place. (Authors' files)

Many girls face a dilemma. They may learn to appear "sexy" to attract males, yet they often experience ambivalence about overt sexual behavior. A young woman expresses this feeling:

Going out with boys is hard for me when it comes to making a decision about sex. I'm afraid if I don't hold out long enough they'll think I'm easy and if I wait too long they'll lose interest. (Authors' files)

The dilemma often encompasses far more than sexual behavior. Girls may begin to define their worth by their boyfriends' accomplishments rather than their own. Wearing the quarterback's letter jacket may bring a girl infinitely more status than wearing one of her own. Her abilities may even be seen as liabilities rather than assets. She may be concerned, for example, about getting better grades than her boyfriend.

While the influence of the double standard is clearly diminishing in many people's lives, these different evaluations and expectations for boys' and girls' sexual behavior have hardly disappeared, and they are still institutionalized in the juvenile justice system. Adolescent women are confined more frequently than young men for *status offenses*, noncriminal offenses for which an adult would not be arrested. These include running away from home, "incorrigibility," and promiscuity. Of those boys and girls who are arrested, nearly 75% of girls compared with 30% of boys are arrested for status offenses. Furthermore, boys are not brought to court for promiscuity, but girls are (Milton et al., 1977).

Virginity or "Sexual Liberation"?

While the double standard is still influential, both males and females today are also affected by another societal influence—the increase in permissive attitudes toward sex. This greater tolerance for and increased expectation of sexual behavior sometimes goes by the label *sexual liberation*. A dimension of this so-called liberation is the considerable pressure many adolescents feel to be sexually active. While peers are most often the source of this pressure, parents may even attempt to "push" their adolescent children into sexual activity (Anthony et al., 1982). Teenagers who resist being pressured into becoming sexually experienced run the risk of being labeled "up-tight," moralistic, or old-fashioned. Furthermore, teenagers who respond to these pressures by becoming sexually active may feel anxious, confused, guilty, or inadequate as lovers (Luloff, 1978).

As a result of these new expectations, boys and girls in some schools or peer groups see virginity as something to be eliminated as soon as possible. This pressure, however, varies according to place and time:

My older sister says she used to lie to her friends and say she was a virgin to protect her reputation. It is just the opposite for me. I lie to my friends claiming I'm not a virgin. (Authors' files)

In view of these kinds of pressures, how appropriate is the term sexual liberation? It is our belief that true liberation means a promotion of choice rather than coercion to say yes instead of no to sexual intercourse or other activities. Given the current emphasis in some peer groups to have intercourse, saying no is often difficult.

However, many adolescents have not experienced intercourse. In Sorenson's 1973 study of 13–19-year-old teenagers, 55% of females and 41% of males had not had intercourse. Other studies have produced varying findings, as Table 13.1 shows later in this chapter. These statistics indicate that many adolescents are remaining virgins. Major reasons given by adolescents who have not experienced sexual intercourse include (a) not being ready for it, (b) not having met a girl or boy they would like to have sex with, and (c) not having met a girl or boy who wants to have sex with them (Sorenson, 1973).

Masturbation

Although a significant number of adolescents do not experience sexual intercourse by the age of 19, many masturbate. As we saw earlier in this chapter, masturbation is a common sexual expression during childhood. During adolescence the behavior tends to increase in frequency. Studies indicate that by the time they have reached the end of adolescence, almost all males and two-thirds of females have masturbated to orgasm (Hunt, 1974; Sorenson, 1973). A recent survey of 580 women revealed that approximately three out of four had masturbated sometime during their adolescence, a result that suggests an upward trend in the incidence of masturbation among teenage women (Kolodny, 1980). Although masturbation is the primary sexual expression for many adolescents, approximately half of those who do masturbate experience anxiety about doing so (Hass, 1979; Sorenson, 1973). Chapter 9 gives further details about this behavior and the mixed feelings many people have about it.

Masturbation can serve as an important avenue for sexual expression during the adolescent years. In addition to providing an always available outlet for sexual tension, self-stimulation is an excellent way to learn about one's body and its sexual potential. Teenagers can experiment with different ways of pleasuring themselves, thereby increasing their self-knowledge. This information may later prove helpful during sexual sharing with another. In fact, many sex therapists believe that people who do not masturbate during adolescence may be omitting an important element in their sexual development.

Petting

Another form of noncoital sexual expression provides an important way for many couples to relate to one another, often as an alternative to intercourse.

My fiancee and I agreed that it was important for both of us to remain virgin before marriage. Neither of us felt it was a particular hardship to wait until we were married to experience coitus. Instead, we engaged in lots of necking and heavy petting, often to orgasm. (Authors' files)

Petting refers to erotic physical contact, which may include kissing, holding, touching, manual stimulation, or oral-genital stimulation—but which does not include coitus. "Necking," "making out," "messing around" are other expressions for petting. Even very "heavy" petting is a common activity among teenagers. According to the 1974 Hunt survey, during adolescence approximately one-half of girls and two-thirds of boys have experienced some type of petting to the point of orgasm.

"How far to go" in petting is often an issue. It can become a contest between the young man and woman, he trying to proceed as far as possible and she attempting to go only as far as is "respectable." Since "love" often motivates or justifies sexual behavior for girls, his saying "I love you" may be used as a ploy to engage in further sexual behaviors.

However, petting is often not so narrowly goal oriented, and it may provide a form of sexual expression that offers both members of a couple the highly valued factors of safety and enjoyment. Petting can be an opportunity for young people to experience sexual sharing while technically remaining virgins. The steps from holding hands to genital stimulation can progress with increasing emotional intimacy. Through petting adolescents begin to learn, within the context of an interpersonal relationship, about their own and their partner's sexual responses. They can develop a repertoire of pleasurable sexual behaviors without the risk of pregnancy, as the following account shows:

One boy I went out with in high school and I had a great understanding. We both knew we were not ready for intercourse. Because of this mutual decision—and our mutual affection—we felt very free to experiment together and spent most of our dates making out for hours. (Authors' files)

This account illustrates not just the function petting serves as a sexual outlet but also the importance of a partner relationship in adolescent sexual behavior.

Ongoing Sexual Relationships

Despite the lingering double standard, data indicate that early petting and intercourse experiences are now more likely to be shared within the context of an ongoing relationship than was the case in Kinsey's time (Hunt, 1974; Kinsey, 1948, 1953; Sorenson, 1973). Prostitutes and impersonal relationships made up a significant number of initial sexual encounters for males in the Kinsey sample (Kinsey, 1948). By the time of the Hunt study (1974), the number of males having such first experiences had decreased.

One major study (Sorenson, 1973) revealed that many adolescents (40% of nonvirgin adolescents) are involved in one-to-one, sexually exclusive relationships. Slightly over half of these relationships continue for one year or more. There is also some indication of differences in monogamous as compared with nonmonogamous relationships. Adolescents in monogamous pairs are more likely to use contraceptives consistently than are nonmonogamous young people. Also, approximately half of the monogamous females report usually or always having an orgasm as compared to 29% of nonmonogamous females. These data suggest that many adolescents are expressing their sexuality within a framework of developing intimacy.

Many adolescents form caring relationships with each other.

Sexual Intercourse

Before beginning to discuss adolescent coital behavior, it is worthwhile to note a basic point of semantics that places some limitations on our interpretations of data.

A frequently quoted statistic in sex research is the number of people in a given category who have engaged in "premarital sex." As a statistic in sex surveys, *premarital sex* is defined as penile-vaginal intercourse that takes place between a couple before they are married. For two reasons, however, the term is somewhat misleading. First, as a measure that is frequently used to indicate the changing sexual or moral values of American youth, it excludes a broad array of noncoital heterosexual and homosexual activities. We saw in the previous discussion that petting can include extensive noncoital types of sexual contact, and that it often produces orgasm. For some people, maintaining virginity prior to marriage may not reflect a lack of sexual activity.

Second, the term has connotations that may seem highly inappropriate to some people:

I really hate those survey questions that ask, "Have you engaged in premarital coitus?" What about those of us who plan to remain single? Does this mean we will be engaging in premarital sex all of our lives? I object to the connotation that marriage is the ultimate state that all are supposed to evolve into. (Authors' files)

In spite of these limitations of the term premarital sex, most of the statistics we have are based on this measure. We will now turn to some of the available data on sexual intercourse during adolescence; then we will look at two related areas, adolescent pregnancy and the use of contraceptives.

Incidence of "Premarital Sex"   Kinsey's 1953 data revealed that half of the women in his sample had experienced coitus before marriage. (This statistic includes women whose initial coital experience occurred after adolescence but before marriage.) Social class, as determined by educational level, did not significantly influence this statistic. Slightly over half of these women had had premarital coitus with only one partner, typically the man they married. This percentage of women who experience premarital coitus with only one partner appears to have remained constant into the 1970s (Hunt, 1974).

Kinsey's findings revealed that a major change in the sexual activity of young women occurred in the 1920s. Less than one-quarter of the women in his sample who had married prior to 1920 had had intercourse before marriage. In sharp contrast, about half of those married after 1920 had experienced premarital coitus. These figures remained fairly constant until the middle 1960s, when another significant increase occurred (Cannon and Long, 1971).

As one might anticipate, there were higher premarital coital rates among men than among women in Kinsey's surveys. Approximately three out of four males in his total sample stated that they had participated in sex before marriage. The frequency of this behavior was significantly related to education, with 67% college-educated, 84% high school-educated, and 98% elementary-educated men reporting premarital coitus. Besides being more likely to have premarital intercourse than the women in the

	Females	Males
Kinsey (1948, 1953)	20%	45%
Sorenson (1973)	45%	59%
Zelnik and Kantner (1977)	55%	No males in survey
Zelnik and Kantner (1980)	69%	77%

sample, Kinsey's male respondents also reported, on the average, having a greater number of partners. However, in contrast to the women in his sample, there was no significant correlation between men's premarital coital rates and the decade in which they were born.

In spite of the fact that no contemporary studies match the scope and comprehensiveness of Kinsey's efforts, there is evidence of significant increases in the sexual activity of unmarried adolescent females in recent years. All of the data presented here are drawn from studies discussed in some detail in Chapter 3. A revealing comparison can be made between the Kinsey findings and the results of three more contemporary studies, Sorenson's 1973 work and the 1976 and 1979 surveys of Zelnick and Kantner, reported in 1977 and 1980, respectively (see Table 13.1). All three of these investigations employed good methodology, and the Zelnik and Kantner surveys came reasonably close to utilizing probability samples. However, the extent of nonrespondent bias is unknown in all of these studies.

Sorenson's study was a national survey of adolescent sexual behavior in the early 1970s, and, as the table shows, it found that 45% of the females reported having premarital coitus by age 19. The more recent national surveys conducted by Zelnik and Kantner reported that 55% of unmarried women in their national sample had experienced intercourse by age 19, a figure that increased to 69% in their 1979 sample. By sharp contrast, Kinsey's earlier sample revealed that slightly less than 20% of women reported premarital coitus by age 19. Thus, the more recent surveys by Sorenson and Zelnick and Kantner demonstrate pronounced increases in premarital coital rates of American adolescent women.

Throughout the 1960s, when the percentage of adolescent women who had experienced premarital coital activity was increasing, the male rates showed little change from the earlier Kinsey figures (Davis, 1971). However, in the 1970s there has been some evidence of a significant increase in the incidence of coitus among young, unmarried males. In Sorenson's national sample, 59% of adolescent males reported experiencing premarital intercourse by age 19 as compared with 45% from the Kinsey survey. More recently, the 1979 survey by Zelnick and Kantner reported that 77% of adolescent males in their sample had experienced intercourse by age 19. Overall, these data on males do not show increases as dramatic as the comparable figures for adolescent women. However, these statistics do reveal a marked upward trend in the incidence of premarital intercourse among adolescent males. It is particularly interesting to note the apparent convergence in the corresponding rates for adolescent men and women over the last 30 to 40 years (male rates more than double female rates in

Kinsey's studies versus a mere 8 percentage points separating males and females in Zelnick and Kantner's 1979 survey population). If this trend continues we might anticipate that parity between the sexes will be achieved sometime during the 1980s.

In broad terms, we can briefly summarize the major changes in adolescent coital activities in the last three decades as follows. First, there has been an increase in the percentages of both young men and women who have experienced coitus. Second, these increases have been considerably more pronounced in females. Finally, there are still fewer women than men who have "premarital sex." However, this difference between the sexes would appear to be diminishing at a very rapid rate.

Changes other than an increase in rates of intercourse have also occurred in adolescent sexual activity. Specific sexual behaviors of adolescents appear to reflect increased societal acceptance of a greater variety of sexual expression. In comparison with Kinsey's statistics of the late forties and early fifties, a fairly comprehensive study in the early seventies indicated an increase in oral-genital stimulation, duration of both noncoital and coital contact, and variety of coital positions (Hunt, 1974).

Adolescent Pregnancy   As premarital intercourse has become more common in the United States, the rate of adolescent pregnancy has increased sharply and has become a matter of urgent social concern. There are approximately 700,000 adolescent pregnancies each year. These result in 300,000 abortions; 200,000 out-of-marriage births; 100,000 marriages; and 100,000 miscarriages each year (Byrne, 1977). Ten percent of all female adolescents, and 23% of those who reported being nonvirgin, report having been pregnant at least once (Sorenson, 1973).

These statistics represent a great amount of personal disruption and adversity. A pregnant adolescent is four to five times more likely to have pregnancy complications than a woman in her 20s. Furthermore, the younger the adolescent is, the higher is the risk (La Barre, 1969). Biological immaturity and poor access to or use of prenatal health care contribute to such difficulties. Most unmarried adolescent mothers (87%) now keep their babies. Eight percent place their children for formal adoption, and 5 percent place the child themselves, usually with relatives (Alan Guttmacher Institute, 1976).

Pregnancy and the decision to keep one's child appear to have a significant impact on the adolescent's educational and financial resources. Eight out of ten adolescents who give birth between the ages of 15 and 17 drop out of high school. Ninety percent of mothers who gave birth at those ages are unemployed; 72% are receiving welfare (Delatiner, 1978). A low education level and limited employment skills severely limit future economic independence.

Use of Contraceptives   Despite the economic, life-style, and emotional stress pregnancy often brings and the availability of birth control today, contraceptive use is not widespread among nonvirgin adolescents. One study indicated that only about 20% of teenagers who have experienced sexual intercourse use a birth control method regularly (Byrne, 1977). In another survey, 55% reported that neither partner used contraceptives the first time intercourse occurred; another 13% were not sure if their partner used a method (Sorenson, 1973). The age of a woman when she first has intercourse has been related to current contraceptive use. One study by the American Public Health Association indicated that women who were 15 years old or younger at first intercourse are less reliable contraceptive users than women who were 16 years or older at initial coitus (Cvetkovich et al., 1978).

Recently 1200 teenage women were surveyed during their first visit to one of a varied group of family-planning clinics in eight American cities (Zabin and Clark, 1981). These were women who had never before been pregnant or sought professional birth control help. Thirty-six percent of these respondents indicated they came to the clinic because they suspected a pregnancy. Only 14% sought birth control information before their first experience with intercourse. The remaining 50% visited the clinic some time after they became sexually active (most waited a year or more). Fear that parents would find out about their sexual activity was a major reason these women reported for delaying their visit to a clinic. This finding is particularly significant in view of the recent effort, at the federal level, to enact legislation that would require government-funded family-planning agencies to notify parents if their minor-age children receive prescription contraceptives.

Another reason birth control methods are avoided is that the use of contraception implies an acknowledgement that one is planning to have intercourse. Some young people's attitudes reflect the value that the teenage woman who does it without contraceptive evidence of premeditation is more "moral" than the young woman who assumes responsibility for her sexual activity and uses birth control. This theme emerges in the responses we received from high school students who were asked, "Why would a high school-age woman who didn't want to become pregnant not use birth control?"

She may feel guilty about planning ahead about sex.

She feels guilty. If she uses birth control, then she is admitting she is having sex.

Maybe people would think of her as a big sleeze if the word got out that she was on the pill or something.

Because she wants to consider it making love. (Authors' files)

In a major study, additional reasons given by adolescent girls for not using contraception included a belief that they would not get pregnant from unprotected intercourse ("It can't happen to me") because, for example, they were too young, they did not have intercourse often enough, or they used the rhythm method (Zelnik and Kanter, 1977).

Male attitudes about contraception are also important for the practice and effectiveness of birth control. Adolescent boys often consider birth control to be the girl's responsibility. In our own student surveys we asked, "Why would a high school-age man who did not want to be a father have sexual intercourse and not use a condom?" Responses included:

He may have thought that it was the girl's problem, not his.

Maybe he wanted to get the girl pregnant because she made him mad at her by flirting with another guy.

He probably didn't want it to seem planned.

Because he didn't like the feeling of the rubber.

It was too much of a hassle using it.

Embarrassed about putting them on. (Authors' files)

Opponents of contraceptive education for adolescents often believe that widespread knowledge about birth control methods will encourage sexual behavior. By not providing adolescents with contraceptive information, they hope to prevent adolescent sexual intercourse from occurring. However, research indicates that lack of knowledge about birth control does not deter young people from experiencing intercourse (Commission on Population Growth and the American Future, 1972).

Homosexuality

The 1973 Sorenson research indicated that about 6% of adolescent females and 11% of adolescent males in the study group had experienced same-sex contact during their adolescent years. The great majority of these contacts took place between peers. These data, or the behaviors they describe, do not entirely reflect a person's later orientation. Same-sex sexual contact with the intent of sexual arousal can be either experimental and transitory or an expression of a lifelong sexual orientation. As we saw in Chapter 10, many homosexual individuals do not act on their sexual feelings until adulthood, and many people with heterosexual orientations have one or more early homosexual experiences.

Some people, however, do define themselves as homosexual during adolescence. This realization may create severe problems for the young person. It may begin with an awareness of having different feelings about sexual attractions than those commonly verbalized by peers. Often a person will have a homosexual experience before she or he either applies a label of homosexuality to the behavior or understands its significance. Not being "part of the crowd" can be emotionally painful. It may be very difficult for young people to find confidants with whom they can share their concern or find guidance. Parents, ministers, doctors, or teachers often are unable to offer constructive help or personal support:

Since most school counselors are heterosexual and relatively few have been formally sensitized to homosexuality, they can relate to the problems of acne-prone, obese, or other physically problem-stricken youths who feel socially ostracized, but when confronted by a young person acknowledging her/his homosexuality, few counselors know what to say. Most gay high schoolers at present would hesitate even to confide, knowing that homophobic school officials might contact homophobic parents and start a personally disastrous chain of events. (Portland Town Council, 1976, p. 57)

The adolescent's problem is further complicated by the fact that homosexual organizations, although designed to provide assistance and support, are often reluctant to offer help to underage people because of possible legal action for "contributing to the delinquency of a minor" (Martin and Lyon, 1972). Still, as with many of the other areas of sexuality discussed in this chapter, homosexual expression is gaining more widespread acceptance in many areas of society. Hopefully, this acceptance will help make this time of life easier for adolescents with homosexual orientations.

SOME KEY INFLUENCES ON PSYCHOSEXUAL DEVELOPMENT

We began this chapter with a look at sexual behavior in childhood and adolescence, including the physical changes that take place as a person begins to mature sexually. In this section we will retrace our steps, considering some of the important psychological and social influences on a person's sexual development, beginning with early childhood.

Of the variety of factors and conditions that are influential in shaping early psychosexual development, parenting and family practices appear to be of great importance. In the pages that follow, a considerable portion of our discussion will be directed toward the potential impact of these influences upon the sexual development of children. Some of our discussion is based on established facts. Other observations are anecdotal or speculative in nature, drawn primarily from interactions with our own children and from the experiences of friends, colleagues, and students who also share the common bond of concerned parents. We will look closely at a few important areas: toilet practices, adult reactions to children's masturbation, the modeling parents provide through their own behaviors, the treatment of nudity, independency issues, and privacy concerns.

Dirty Diapers, Going Potty, and Related Issues

An influential area in which adults may mold children's attitudes about sexuality is treatment of eliminative functions. Have you ever watched a parent changing a diaper with a disgusted expression on his or her face or perhaps gagging? Were you ever scolded for relieving yourself behind a bush because you played one minute too long? Or were words like "stinky," "messy," or "ugh" ever used when there was a setback in your toilet-training program?

We can only guess the impact of such reactions on an infant or toddler. Certainly, however, it does not promote the development of positive feelings about the natural eliminative functions of the genitals. It might possibly even be one factor in the development of an association between discomfort with elimination and with later sexual functioning. (Other factors are also involved, however, and undoubtedly, many people who have had these experiences in their infancy do nevertheless function in a sexually healthy manner as adults.)

Home environments that treat eliminative functions as secretive or dirty may foster feelings of discomfort with the body and its natural processes. Furthermore, there is the possibility that children raised in such surroundings may learn to associate the guilt, shame, or embarrassment connected with genital elimination to genital sex. These are some of the reasons why it may be helpful for parents to create a relaxed and open atmosphere in the area of toilet practices.

Reactions to Masturbation

A second, often important influence on developing sexuality is parental reaction to self-pleasuring. In our society, comments about masturbation that pass from parent to child are typically either nonexistent or negative. Think back to your youth. Did your parents ever express to you that they accepted this activity? Or, did you have an intuitive sense that your parents were comfortable with self-pleasuring in their children? Probably not. Most often, a verbal message to "stop doing that," a disapproving look, or a slap on the hand are the responses children receive to masturbation. These gestures may be noted even by a young child who does not yet have language capabilities.

In writing about the issue of early alienation from such an important part of our bodies as our genitals, the words of Mary Calderone, executive director of Sex Information and Education Council of the United States, come to our minds. "We should see this [genital fondling] as normal and human. The body of a child belongs to him or her and each should have the right to experience pleasure with it" (Portland lecture, 1978). In many children's and parents' lives, though, there is probably much confusion and anxiety surrounding this very natural form of sexual expression.

How can adults convey their acceptance of masturbation? One way to begin is by not reacting negatively to the genital fondling that is typical of infants and young children. Later, as we respond to children's questions about their bodies, it may be desirable to mention the potential for pleasure that exists in their genital anatomy ("It feels good when you touch it"). Respecting privacy—for example, knocking before entering a child's room—is another way to foster comfort with this very personal activity. Perhaps you may feel comfortable with making specific accepting responses to self-pleasuring activity in your children, as did the parents in the following accounts:

One day my seven-year-old son joined me on the couch to watch a football game. He was still in the process of toweling off from a shower. While appearing to be engrossed in the activity on the screen, I noticed one hand was busy stroking his penis. Suddenly his eyes caught mine observing him. An uneasy grin crossed his face. I wasn't sure how to respond so I simply stated, "It feels good, doesn't it?" He didn't say anything, nor did he continue touching himself but his smile grew a little wider. I must admit I had some initial hesitancy in openly indicating my approval for such behavior. I was afraid he might begin openly masturbating in the presence of others. However, my fears were demonstrated to be groundless in that he continues to be quite private about such activity. It is gratifying to know that he can experience the pleasures of his body without the unpleasant guilt feelings that his father grew up with. (Authors' files)

The first time my 10-year-old daughter and I took a shower together, after purchasing a hand-held water massager, I told her it felt good when directed toward her vulva. While I only spoke about this potential, feeling uncomfortable about conducting an actual demonstration, the message seemed to sink in, judging from the long showers she often took from that date forward. (Authors' files)

431

Many parents are reluctant to openly express their acceptance of masturbation, afraid that their children, armed with this parental stamp of approval, will go off to some cloistered area and masturbate away the hours. While this is an understandable concern, available evidence does not suggest that this is likely. Children have many other activities that also occupy their time.

Another concern, voiced in the first anecdote, is that children will begin masturbating openly in front of others if they are aware that their parents accept such behavior. This also is a reasonable concern. Very few of us would be enthusiastic about needing to deal with Johnny or Suzie masturbating in front of Grandma. However, children are generally aware enough of social expectations to maintain a high degree of privacy in something as emotionally laden and personal as self-pleasuring. They are typically much more capable of making important discriminations than parents sometimes acknowledge. In the event that children do masturbate in the presence of others, it would seem reasonable for parents to voice their concerns, taking care to label the choice of location and not the activity as inappropriate.

Most children masturbate. Telling them to stop this behavior will rarely eliminate it, even if such requests are backed with threats of punishment or claims of mental or physical deterioration. Rather, these negative responses will most likely succeed only in greatly magnifying the guilt and anxiety associated with such behavior.

Positive Models

Most adult behavior is strongly influenced by models identified with or emulated during the growing-up process (Bandura and Walters, 1963). We need only observe the little girl combing her hair like mother or the young boy imitating his father's walk to sense how powerful this modeling process is. The question for us is, where does a child find positive models for caring, nonexploitive, joyful sexual interaction? Not typically in the popular media. (When is the last time you saw a movie or read a novel that made you feel good about the potential for genuine joy in intimate relationships?) The peer group often leaves something to be desired, with its rudimentary or inaccurate knowledge, its tendency toward sexism and narrow views of morality, and its often competitive view of sexual interaction ("How many times have you 'scored'?" "How many invitations did you get to the dance?") What then is left as a potential source for positive models? One answer is the relationships between adults who are significant in a child's life.

Among American parents there seems to be a marked reluctance to reveal to children the sensual or intimate aspects of the parents' relationship. Parents may show this in several ways: by hiding spontaneous displays of affection for one's partner, refraining from talking about loving each other in front of the children, or avoiding acting "turned on" unless alone with one's mate. This reluctance to display such natural feelings and behaviors may stem from attitudes such as discomfort with

432   Parents may provide their children with positive models of shared
sensual intimacies.

sexuality in general, concern that such displays will lead to embarrassing questions,
and worry that children may learn about sexual experimentation too early in life.
Thus, these potentially positive models may be unavailable to children, as they
perhaps were to their parents and their parents' parents.

How many of us grew up with a realization that our parents were sexual and that
they were still "doing it"? Student surveys in our classroom indicate that very few
respond affirmatively to this question. Consider the following account:

One day when I was 15, my Mom phoned me at home and asked if I would
gather some information contained in papers located in her bedroom chest of
drawers. This was her private space that I had never before invaded. But with
permission, I proceeded to look for the papers. During the course of my
explorations I was amazed and horrified to discover a box of condoms. I couldn't
believe she and Dad were still doing it. However, I opened it up and found some
were missing. Then I knew for sure! (Authors' files)

We wonder what the world would be like if such a discovery failed to produce surprise in the majority of developing children. Why not allow them to witness desire, caring, and sharing between adults? To the extent that parents' relationships are characterized by mutual caring and warmth, what better model can be made available to them?

For parents who feel comfortable about expressing affection in front of their children, what limits are there to such expression? The major concern here is the potential damaging impact of observing parents engaged in sexual contact, particularly coitus. Some writers, particularly those of a psychoanalytic orientation, have expressed concern about such a practice, stating that severe psychological trauma may result in children who see their parents having sex. The following experience exemplifies this fear:

When I was still a little girl, I guess about 10 or 11, I walked in on my Mom and Dad while they were having intercourse. They failed to hear me enter and I didn't announce my presence. Something was going on that I didn't understand, but I knew it made me feel real uncomfortable. It seemed like Dad was hurting Mom, banging up and down on top of her, and from the look on her face, it certainly didn't seem like she was enjoying it. And yet, something about the scene kept me from asking what was going on. Instead, I quietly slipped out being careful not to let them know they had been observed. I was bothered by my memory of this experience for a long time after. I guess the hardest part was not having anyone to talk to about what I had seen and wondering if Dad always hurt my mother when they went into their bedroom to be alone. (Authors' files)

Here the child had misinterpreted the sexual activity as aggressive and abusive behavior on the part of her father. The misunderstanding was complicated by the fact that there was enough ambiguity in the situation that the girl was unwilling to ask her parents about what she had seen. This is the potential problem in a child surreptitiously observing parents involved in sex play. We wonder how much of this child's bewilderment stemmed from a general lack of knowledge about sexuality. It seems less likely that such confusion and discomfort would exist in a young person whose parents regularly maintained open communication about sexual or intimate matters.

We are not advocating exposing children to the sexual play of their parents. Such a decision is a highly individual matter, with many ramifications. Neither are we suggesting that such an experience is inevitably damaging. The following report of a woman in one of our sexuality classes is relevant to this issue:

I live in a tiny apartment with my six-year-old son and my lover. It offers virtually no privacy, consisting of one large room with pull down beds and a small bathroom. We can't afford anything bigger since we are both going to school. It really presented problems when it came to lovemaking. It was always at night after my son was asleep and then we had to be careful about the sounds we made. Finally, we got tired of the lack of spontaneity and limited nature of our responses. One morning, while my boy was watching TV, we decided to have sex. Halfway through he came over and stood by the bed and watched us moving under the covers for a few moments. Finally he said, "What are you doing?" I answered, "Making love." His response to this was, "Oh," followed by watching for a couple more minutes and then back to the TV set. It just wasn't any big deal for him. However, later he did ask me some questions which I thought was real good in that it started us talking about sex. (Authors' files)

Many people would not be comfortable with the explicitness of this scene. However, direct observation is not the only vehicle through which parents may model positive aspects of sexuality to their children. Consider the following scenario. It is a lazy Saturday afternoon, and parents and children have spent time together having lunch and working in the yard. Mom and Dad are unashamedly expressing mutual affection, periodically kissing and hugging, clearly taking pleasure in each other's company. Eventually they slip off to their bedroom, making no effort to conceal their excitement and anticipation from the children. Later they return, arm in arm, contentment mirrored in their faces. With repeated exposure to such scenes the children are likely to realize that their parents are sexual, and furthermore, that such activity brings them great pleasure and happiness. The children will also have the somewhat unique opportunity to observe such behavior in a caring, nonexploitive, and joyful relationship. The many benefits that may result from such early modeling are well worth considering before parents elect to bar their children from all awareness of intimate or sexual aspects of their relationship.

Frequently, we are asked by single parents if it is healthy to reveal to their children that they are sharing an intimate relationship with someone they regularly see. There are factors here that are not present in the intact nuclear family situation. It is possible that children may feel quite uncomfortable with their parent's relationship with someone other than the original spouse. This may involve feelings of loyalty to the parent no longer present, a sense of betrayal, or even the futility that results when hope for a reconciliation is shattered. Nevertheless, it is possible that surreptitious behavior, in some circumstances at least, may be more damaging than open and honest acknowledgement of feelings. Consider the following experience:

After I was divorced from my husband I felt very uncomfortable displaying any affection for my men friends in the presence of my children. It was very awkward to have them over to the house. The kids never said anything, but I always felt they were disapproving of me becoming involved with men other than their father. When I met the man I am with now it became a real problem. While he and I prefer not to marry, at least in the immediate future, we have made a personal commitment to each other. I love him very much and the kids seem to enjoy his company. It was very hard having him over for dinner and treating him like a casual friend rather than the man I dearly love. On those rare occasions when we spent an entire night together, it was always at his place after making up some trumped-up excuse. Finally, it all came to a head one evening when my 16-year-old got up in the middle of the night and discovered us making love in front of the fireplace. It was terrible. I was so shook up I didn't know what to say. He just went back to bed without saying anything. The next day I mustered up my courage to ask him what he thought about last night. He simply said, "Mom, I think it's great that you two get it on together. Me and the rest of the kids have always thought it was kind of silly you pretended you didn't have something going." I didn't say much of anything, but believe me it was a relief to know that I didn't have to go on acting out some charade. (Authors' files)

Clearly, a great deal of individual discretion is necessary in deciding whether (and how much) children should know about a sexual relationship; specific family circumstances and the nature of the outside relationship are important considerations. Children do not always react as reasonably as did the son in the preceding account. Occasionally, a child will emotionally pressure his or her single parent into curtailing, if not totally eliminating, all involvement with potential significant others. This highly undesirable behavior is revealed in the following anecdote:

Whenever I have a male friend over, my little boy undergoes a personality change. He becomes sullen, belligerent, and verbally abusive. I am at my wits' end trying to deal with such behavior. Under any other circumstance he is a beautiful person, sweet, attentive, and very helpful. It's getting so that I just avoid dating so that I don't have to deal with his strange and unpleasant behavior. (Authors' files)

We suggest that this child's behavior is not so strange—particularly in view of the fact that it proved successful in curtailing his mother's relationships with other men. Not uncommonly, scenarios like these are enacted in the lives of divorced, widowed, or separated parents. Many factors may be operating. The child or children may have a strong desire to occupy a position of sole preeminence in the life of the parent with whom they are living. Resistance to the "intrusion" of another important person may also involve elements of jealousy, loyalty to the parent no longer present, or fear that the new relationship will only be transitory and that the loss will be repeated. When a child has concerns like these, it may be helpful to acknowledge them and attempt to open lines of communication. However, it seems unnecessary for single parents to restrict their pursuit of new relationships even if their children resist such activities. As long as the young people receive a fair share of loving attention, the parent need not feel uncomfortable about satisfying his or her own relationship needs.

The Question of Nudity

Related to modeling is the manner in which nudity is treated in the household. Over the years we have asked thousands of human sexuality students the question, "Did you feel comfortable with nudity around the home while you were growing up?" In a class of 75, the number of hands raised often can be counted on the fingers of one hand. Consider the following accounts:

I can remember accidentally walking in on my father when he was shaving, naked as a jaybird. His response was off the wall. I got the message loud and clear that there was something wrong about a little girl seeing her father naked. My mother was quite prudish too as I think back on it. I didn't see another adult male naked, I mean close up so I could really look him over, until I was involved in my first heavy sex experience. (Authors' files)

As early as I can remember, we kids were told to always lock the bathroom door when showering or taking care of nature's calling. We were in real trouble if we forgot to knock when someone else was using the john. They didn't even like the sounds. We flushed the toilet so someone else would not hear the pee hit the pot. It's crazy, but I'm still compulsive about flushing at the strategic moment. (Authors' files)

These accounts are typical of many stories related to us. To the extent that the home environments of our students are reasonably representative of cultural values about nudity, it would seem that the majority of us either were or are exposed to at least some family taboos in this area. Do you remember being told to cover up? What was it that you were supposed to cover? Your neck, face, feet, or arms? More likely, it was the "down-theres." Somehow it was okay to expose the rest of the body, but for many of us the genitals (and breasts for girls) needed to be covered up at all times, even in the privacy of our own homes.

What kind of message does this convey? For many of us, the taboo against self-exposure became translated into a sense of shame or discomfort about these areas of our bodies. Certainly we do not compulsively cover up that which is healthy and acceptable. Therefore, by implication, there must be something basically unpleasant or dirty about our genital anatomy. Later in life, when we become aware that sexual expression is often related to these hidden unmentionables, it is easy to see how sexuality becomes, by association, "dirty" or something of which to be ashamed.

It is not uncommon for people to feel anxious during the early stages of sexual intimacies with others. These feelings may stem from many factors—performance anxiety, guilt, conflict, and, for some, basic discomfort with their own bodies. It is difficult to feel good about exposing parts of our anatomy that we have been told to cover up since we could barely walk. A person can feel incredibly vulnerable in such a circumstance with the old associations ("it's dirty," "cover up," "lock the door," "flush the toilet") clanging away in his or her head like alarm bells.

Acquiring good feelings about nudity, and particularly one's own sexual anatomy, can contribute to an overall positive sexual awareness. Parents who feel at ease with nudity within the home can help foster these same feelings in their children by exhibiting an open comfort with their own bodies and those of their children. A variety of activities shared by a family—bathing together, dressing together, skinny-dipping in a mountain lake—may encourage the process whereby young family members acquire more positive body images. Consider the following:

Some of our most joyous family times were those spent crowded together, all four of us, in one large shower or bathtub. We talked, and joked, and just felt good together. Our nakedness was a natural thing, so common as to be undeserving of mention. (Authors' files)

Understandably, many parents may find it difficult to implement these suggestions about nudity, particularly if their own experiences make such activities seem inappropriate or uncomfortable. We are not suggesting that lack of open nudity around the house will inevitably be detrimental to the sexual development of a child.

Growing up in a family that is at ease with nudity may contribute to a positive sexual awareness.

In fact, parents who try to be open about nudity when they are not personally convinced of its appropriateness may inadvertently communicate this discomfort to their children. There are alternatives. Parents who wish to maintain privacy about their own bodies can avoid directing negative comments toward their children who, for example, may forget to dress completely before entering the family room. Acceptance of nudity does not necessarily imply open display. This is a matter of individual choice.

Independency Issues

Late childhood and most of adolescence is a time of life characterized by a great deal of ambivalence or confusion about appropriate behavior. One important consequence of this is that the child-parent relationship is often stressful during adolescence.

Children are neither entirely dependent nor entirely independent, yet often they want to be both:

I used to harass my mother to let me do things I was really a little afraid of doing. Although I would feel inner relief when she said no, I would belligerently tell her how mean she was. (Authors' files)

When dependency versus independency conflicts increase, tension within the family often rises. Culturally defined "adult" behaviors, such as driving, drinking, smoking, and sexual intercourse are sometimes used by adolescents as symbols of maturity or as a form of rebellion against parental authority.

Parents (or other caretakers of adolescents) may greet their children's sexual maturation with a mixture of emotions, including avoidance, ambivalence, concern, and pride. At the same time, they may have dilemmas about their own role, for as their children change and become more independent, the nature of the parent-child relationship and of their adolescents' needs also changes.

One of the most difficult problems for parents is how to help adolescents make decisions about sexual matters. Parents are often caught in conflicts between attitudes toward their own sexuality and social pressures they and the adolescents experience. There is a sharp discrepancy between the societal ideal of sex within marriage and the societal reality of adolescent sexual behavior. These two factors are typically not easy to reconcile, even by the most concerned and caring adults. Furthermore, many adults understandably experience an uncomfortable gap between their intellectual ideas and their emotional reactions to their children's sexuality. For example:

I told my daughter that when she decided she was ready to have intercourse to let me know and we would make arrangements for birth control. Well, several years later she said it was time. I couldn't help it—I became upset with her. (Authors' files)

Many adults express the desire to help their children be positive and comfortable with their sexuality. However, as the foregoing account illustrates, parents are often in a confusing double bind. The traditional role of the parent in our society has been to suppress and control children's sexuality rather than to encourage overt sexual expression. Even talking about sex may be believed to precipitate adolescent sexual activity. And so, although parents may want to encourage open communication and positive feelings, they may feel inhibited by dominant societal attitudes and their own family backgrounds.

Privacy Concerns

Another issue that is often troublesome to parents concerns privacy, which may take on a new meaning with the onset of adolescence. During childhood, one's bedroom is often a special place to take friends. At the onset of sexual maturity, however, many parents may become uncomfortable with allowing this same privacy to the adolescent. They may perhaps make the bedroom off limits to other-sex friends, out of fear that such privacy may now be interpreted by their children as a license to engage in intercourse. The adolescent, however, may perceive an entirely different message, welcoming the security offered by the home setting:

While I was growing up, my Mom and Dad always allowed me to entertain friends of both sexes in my room. The neat thing was that they didn't eliminate this opportunity when I started dating. It was OK to have my boyfriends in the bedroom with me, and with the door closed. Most of the time we just watched TV, talked, or listened to my stereo. Sometimes we did a little heavy necking and petting. As crazy as it may sound, it was great knowing my Mom was just a few steps away if things got a little out of hand. Also, I think it encouraged my boyfriends to be a little more responsible. None of that back seat scene and being pressured into something I didn't want. I love my Mom and Dad for treating me like an adult, someone capable of making responsible choices. (Authors' files)

A variety of choices relate to the issue of privacy in the home: whether guests are allowed when parents are not home (if so, it may be wise to ask that the friend's parents are informed), or only when adults are at home; the hours of visiting; or use of another room, like the den, instead of the bedroom. Other rules may seem appropriate in a particular family.

SEX EDUCATION

Today many parents want to provide some input into the sexual education of their children. Societal values about sex are rapidly changing and we are all exposed to an abundance of contrasting opinions. How much should children see, or how much should they be told? Many parents—even some of those who are comfortable with their own sexuality—have difficulty judging the "best" way to act and react toward their children's sexuality.

Perhaps the information that we offer in the following paragraphs will help to modify some of this uncertainty. We do not profess to have the last word on raising sexually healthy children, so we advise you to read this material with a critical eye. Along the way, however, you may acquire some new insights that will aid in your efforts to provide meaningful sex education for your children, either now or in the future.

We are often asked the question "When should we start telling our kids about sex?" One answer to this inquiry is "When the child begins to ask the questions." It seems typical for children to inquire about sex along with the myriad of other questions they ask about the world around them. Research indicates that by about age four, most children begin asking questions about how babies are made (Martinson, 1980). What is more natural than a query about where you came from? Yet this curiosity is often stopped short by parental response. A flushed face and a few stammering words, a cursory "Wait till your mother (or father) comes home to ask that question," or "You're not old enough to learn about such things" are a few of the common ways communication in this vital area is blocked before it has a chance to begin. Putting questions off at this early age means that you may be confronted with the potentially awkward task of starting a dialogue on sexual matters at a later point in your children's development.

Earlier, we discussed the value of parental modeling. One important application of this principle is for parents to include information about sex (when appropriate) in everyday conversations that their children either observe or participate in. Accomplishing this with a sense of ease and naturalness may increase the comfort with which the children introduce their own questions or observations about sex.

If a child's questions either do not arise spontaneously or get sidetracked at an early age, there may be a point when you as a parent will feel it is important to begin to talk about sexuality. Perhaps a good starting point is to share your true feelings with your child—that possibly you are a bit uneasy about discussing sex with them or that maybe you are confused about some of your own beliefs or feelings. There is something very human about a parent who can express his or her own indecision or vulnerability to a child. This may be all you will say during this initial effort, simply indicating your feelings and leaving the door open to future discussions. An incubation period is often valuable, allowing a child to reassess her or his interpretation of your willingness to talk about sexuality. If no questions follow this first effort, it might be wise to select a specific area for discussion. Some suggested open-ended questions for a not too stressful beginning might be (a) How do you feel about the changes in your body? (b) What are some of the things that the kids at school say about sex? and (c) What are your feelings about birth control? Is it "proper"? Who should be responsible, male or female or both?

Understandably, parents sometimes have a tendency to overload a child who asks a question expecting a relatively brief, straightforward answer. For example, when a five-year-old inquires "Where did I come from?" he or she is probably not asking for a detailed treatise on the physiology of sexual intercourse and conception. In such cases it may be more helpful to just briefly discuss the basics of sexual intercourse, perhaps including the idea of potential pleasure in such sharing. When young children want more information, they will probably ask for it, provided an adult has been responsive to their initial questions.

Some parents may feel that it is inappropriate to tell their children that sexual interaction is pleasurable. Others may conclude that there is value in discussing the joy of sex with their offspring, as revealed in the following account:

One evening, while sitting on my daughter's bed and discussing the day's events, she expressed some concern over her next-door playmate's announcement that her father was going to purchase a stud horse. Apparently, she had been told to have me build a higher fence to protect her mare. She asked why this was necessary. Actually, she knew all about horses mating as evidenced by her quick acknowledgment of my brief explanation. However, such commentary on my part did produce the following inquiry, "Do you and Mom do that?" to which I replied, "Yes." "Do my uncle and aunt do that?" Again the affirmative response which produced the final pronouncement, "I don't think I'll get married." Clearly, she was experiencing some strong ambivalence about what this sexual behavior meant to her. It seemed of critical importance to make one more statement, namely that not only did we do this, but that it is a beautiful and pleasurable kind of sharing and lots of fun! (Authors' files)

Reluctance to express the message that sex can be enjoyable may stem from parents' concern that their children will rush right out to find out what kind of good times they have been missing. However, there is little evidence to support such apprehension. On the other hand, there are many unhappy lovers striving to overcome early messages about the dirtiness and immorality of sex.

There are some topics that may never get discussed, at least not at the proper time, unless parents are willing to take the initiative. We are referring to certain aspects of sexual maturing that may not be considered by the child until he or she experiences them. These include menstruation, first ejaculation, and nocturnal orgasms. The desirability of discussing with daughters the implications of their first periods, well in advance of the event, has been well documented. Nevertheless, a majority of women students in our classes have consistently commented that they knew little or nothing about menstruation until they were either given sketchy accounts by peers or faced with the actual occurrence of their first period. It is also typical for males to be unaware of their potential for ejaculating when masturbating. Experience with first menstruation or ejaculation can come as quite a shock to the unprepared, as revealed in the following two anecdotes:

I hadn't even heard of menstruation when I first started bleeding. No one was home. I was so frightened I called an ambulance. (Authors' files)

I remember well the first time I ejaculated during masturbation. At first I couldn't believe it when something shot out of my penis. The only thing I could figure is that I had whipped up my urine. However, considering earlier lectures from my mother about the evils of "playing with yourself," I was afraid that God was punishing me for my sinful behavior. (Authors' files)

It is important that youngsters be aware of these impending changes before they actually happen. Some parents may find it relatively easy to discuss menstruation, while they may find it quite difficult to discuss nighttime orgasms or first ejaculations because of their associations with sexual activity. However, discussion of these events may also provide an opportunity to talk about self-pleasuring. Females also may experience nighttime orgasms. The fact that girls have no seminal traces to deal with in the morning does not eliminate possible confusion or guilt over the meaning of these occurrences.

When I was a little girl I began to have these incredibly erotic dreams that sometimes produced indescribably good sensations. Looking back on it now, I realize these were my first experiences with nighttime orgasms. At the time I thought it was awful to have such good feelings connected with such wicked thoughts. I wish someone had told me then that my experiences were normal. It certainly would have eliminated a lot of unnecessary anxiety. (Authors' files)

Most young people prefer their mothers or fathers to be the primary source of sex information. Yet in most cases, this information does not come from parents. In one study, friends were reported to be the principal source for 67% of adolescent males and 59% of adolescent females (Commission on Obscenity and Pornography, 1970). In another study, over 70% of adolescents reported that their parents did not talk to them about sex (Sorenson, 1973). The gap created by lack of information in the home is likely to be filled with incorrect information from peers and other sources. Unfortunately, peers often provide inaccurate information that can be dangerous (for example, that a girl will not get pregnant if she only has intercourse "now and then"). Peers may also encourage traditional gender role behavior and often put inappropriate pressure on each other to become sexually active. The issue facing parents is whether they want to become actively involved in their children's sex education, thereby minimizing some of these potential pitfalls faced by children and adolescents who must turn to their peers for sex information.

Parents may hesitate to discuss sex with their children because they are concerned that such communication may encourage early sexual experimentation. However, there is no evidence that sex education leads to sexual activity. This inaccurate but understandable assumption may stem, at least in part, from the tendency of adults to overestimate teenagers' interest in sex. The truth is that there are many things that adolescents typically consider to be more important issues in their lives. In a recent nationwide survey of teens (Norman and Harris, 1981), 13- to 18-year-olds ranked sex seventh in a list of major concerns behind school, parents, money, friends, siblings, and drinking or drugs. In another survey, in which teenagers ranked six activities in order of importance—sex, doing well in school, athletics, friendships with their own sex, friendships with the other sex, and romantic involvement with someone—girls ranked sex last and boys put it fourth on the list (Hass, 1979).

In response to both the frequent lack of information from the home and the inaccuracy of much of the information that comes from peers, other social institutions are attempting to provide sex education. Some schools have included sex education as part of the curriculum, although the quality and extent of these programs varies considerably from place to place.

A 1977 Gallup poll revealed that 77% of the respondents approved of sex education in the schools. Nevertheless, school sex education programs are often hampered by pressures brought to bear by well-organized and highly vocal minorities. In response to these pressures, some school systems completely omit sex education from their curriculums. Others attempt to avert controversy by only allowing discussion of certain "safe" topics such as reproduction and anatomy. As a consequence, some important areas for discussion, such as making responsible sexual decisions, preventing pregnancies, and relationship processes and values, are entirely overlooked. There is evidence that parental support of school sex education is most likely to be offered for programs that they believe will help to prevent "inappropriate" sexual behavior by stressing the dangers of sexually transmitted diseases and unwanted pregnancies (Roberts et al., 1978). This scare-tactic approach often does little more than create scepticism about the reliability of any sexual information coming from adults. Furthermore, fear of pregnancy or diseases is typically ineffective in deterring young people from sexual activity. School sex education is further limited by the fact that it is typically provided during the late stages of high school at a time when more than half of the students have already begun sexual experimentation (Zellman and Goodchilds, 1982).

In some communities churches have begun to provide programs that far surpass the scope and depth of sex education offered through public schools. One excellent program, "About Your Sexuality," developed by the Unitarian church, presents sex as a positive and enriching aspect of one's life.

Individuals who are pondering whether it would be beneficial to discuss sexuality with their children might wish to consider the following information. The World Health Organization has stated that sexual ignorance is a major cause of "sexual mis-adventures" (Calderone, 1965). These "misadventures" may include such things as unwanted pregnancies, exploitive relationships, contracting sexually transmitted diseases, and nonfulfilling sexual experiences. Several studies have also revealed a connection between lack of education and venereal disease (Deschin, 1963; Levine, 1970). Our experiences, and those of other therapists and educators, have demonstrated the strong relationship that often exists between lack of knowledge of sexual matters and sexual maladjustment.

On the brighter side, researchers have shown that providing people with factual sex information contributes positively to their psychological and sexual adjustment (McCary and Flake, 1971; Wright and McCary, 1969). Furthermore, studies indicate that young people whose parents play a major role in their sex education are not as likely to engage in early sexual activity as are their less-informed counterparts (Lewis, 1973). One survey of 600 teenagers indicated that if a young person obtained "sex knowledge from parents or adults with whom a positive identification exists, there appeared to be less tendency toward involvement in promiscuity" (Deschin, 1963). Thus, in sharp contrast to what many believe, it seems that talking with our children about sex is more likely to discourage rather than encourage premature or irresponsible sexual involvement with others.

ANDROGYNOUS CHILD-REARING AND SEXUALITY

The idea of raising children in an androgynous fashion has much to offer to parents anxious to minimize the limiting influence of gender-role expectations in the lives of their children. As discussed in Chapter 2, the term androgyny is used to describe flexibility in gender roles. In this sense, androgynous child-rearing means raising a child in a way that encourages selection of whatever feminine or masculine behaviors feel good to him or her.

On numerous occasions in this text we have expressed our belief that strict adherence to stereotypic gender roles may have a detrimental effect upon sexual functioning. The examples are many, ranging from the man who is unable to express emotion and tenderness because it is not "masculine" to the woman who has great difficulty communicating her sexual needs because she has been conditioned to be passive. Many parents may wish to counteract these limiting influences by the manner in which they rear their children. Perhaps such things as reassuring little boys that it is

People who do not conform to traditional role stereotypes have
more alternatives available to them.

okay to cry and reinforcing girls for expressions of appropriate assertiveness will help
to offset the impact of rigid gender roles.

Encouraging a child to develop as a human being first and a male or female
second is a developmental goal that is receiving increasing support in our society.
Those inclined to agree with the philosophy and intent of this evolving concept of
androgyny may find the most fertile ground for its implementation in the home
environment.

One of the truly striking aspects of a gender role-dominated society is that boys
and girls grow up playing primarily with same-sex peers. Little girls get together to see
who has the latest Barbie doll fashions and boys shoot each other with mock guns.
Other than dating in adolescence, this same-sex pairing generally holds up throughout
the developmental years. There may be many effects of this sex segregation, not the
least of which is the awkwardness and lack of spontaneity that characterizes many
man-woman relationships. The segregation may often seem to be self-imposed (girls
frequently do not *want* to play with boys and vice versa). However, a contributing
factor may sometimes be adult approval of sex-specific play activities. Many now
believe that it is acceptable for boys to play with dolls and girls to push trucks through
dirt piles. Would children play so consistently in same-sex groups if these activities
were encouraged more?

Besides the socialization that occurs in encouraging or discouraging types of
play, parental modeling is also an important influence in raising children in an
androgynous fashion. Parents who feel comfortable sharing childcare and housework
can provide models of androgynous behavior for their developing children. It may be

Parents can provide models of nonstereotyped behavior for their developing children.

particularly valuable to engage in behaviors that are markedly different from traditional gender-role stereotypes. For example, Dad may cook dinner or change diapers, while Mom works late at the office, changes the oil in the car, and so on.

We believe that people raised in an androgynous fashion may enjoy freedom to behave sensitively and sensibly, and that by lifting restrictive notions about "acting like a lady" or "being a man," adults can encourage their children to have a broader outlook. This potential reflects one of the possible values of this alternative approach to parenting.

SUMMARY

1. The traditional view of infancy and childhood as a time when sexuality remains unexpressed is not supported by research findings.

2. Infants of both sexes are born with the capacity for sexual pleasure and response, and some experience observable orgasm.

SEXUAL BEHAVIOR IN CHILDHOOD

3. Self-administered genital stimulation is common among boys and girls during the first two years of life.

4. Sex play with other children, which may occur as early as the age of two or three, increases in frequency during the five-to-seven age range.

5. Segregation of the sexes becomes pronounced by the age of eight or nine. However, romantic interest in the other sex and curiosity about sexual matters are typically quite high during this stage of development.

6. The ages of 10 and 11 are marked by keen interest in body changes, continued segregation of the sexes, and a substantial incidence of homosexual encounters.

7. Masturbation is one of the most common sexual expressions during the childhood years. It is the most frequent source of preadolescent orgasm for both sexes.

THE PHYSICAL CHANGES OF ADOLESCENCE

8. Puberty refers to the physical changes that occur in response to increased hormones. These physical developments include maturation of the reproductive organs and consequent menstruation in girls and ejaculation in boys.

SEXUAL BEHAVIOR DURING ADOLESCENCE

9. The double standard often pressures males to view sex as a conquest and places females in a double bind about saying yes or no.

10. The number of adolescents who masturbate increases between the ages of 13 and 19.

11. Petting is a common sexual behavior among adolescents. One-half of adolescent girls and two-thirds of adolescent boys have engaged in petting to the point of orgasm.

12. Adolescent sexual expression is today more likely to take place within the context of an ongoing monogamous relationship than during Kinsey's time.

13. A significant increase in the number of both young men and women who experience intercourse by age 19 has occurred since Kinsey's research was conducted. These increases have been considerably more pronounced in females.

14. One in 10 adolescent females becomes pregnant by the age of 19. Pregnancy usually compounds social, medical, educational, and financial difficulties.

15. Despite the complications of pregnancy and the availability of birth control, the majority of adolescents who have intercourse do not regularly use contraceptives.

16. Homosexual experiences during adolescence can be experimental or an expression of permanent sexual orientation.

SOME KEY INFLUENCES ON PSYCHOSEXUAL DEVELOPMENT

17. Negative feelings about one's own sexual anatomy may stem from adverse parental reactions to eliminative functions and punitive or disapproving responses to early genital fondling.

18. Much of the anxiety children experience over their masturbation practices is related to real or imagined parental disapproval. Expressing acceptance of masturbation, while unlikely to appreciably increase its incidence, may allow a child to feel less guilty and more comfortable with this form of self-discovery.

19. Many parents are reticent about revealing to their children the sensual/intimate aspects of their relationship. This is an area that merits careful consideration, in that parents can often provide a far more positive model of caring, nonexploitive sharing than is typically offered by a young person's peer group or the popular media.

20. Many individuals acquire a sense of shame or uneasiness about the genital areas of their bodies, feelings that may be fostered by a lack of comfort with nudity around the home.

21. Dependency versus independency conflicts between parents and children often become pronounced during adolescence. Parents may find it particularly difficult to encourage adolescents to make independent decisions pertaining to sexual expression.

22. Another issue that is often troublesome to parents concerns privacy, which may take on a new meaning with the onset of adolescence. Many parents may be uncomfortable about granting privacy to teenage children who bring their other-sex friends home.

SEX EDUCATION

23. One answer to the question of when to start discussing sex with our children is "When they start asking questions." If communication does not

spontaneously occur, it may be helpful for parents to initiate dialogue, perhaps by simply sharing their true feelings or asking nonstressful, open-ended questions.

24. Some important topics—particularly menstruation, first ejaculation, and nocturnal orgasms—are rarely discussed unless parents take the initiative.

25. Although the majority of adolescents prefer their parents to be the primary source of sex information, evidence indicates that peers are considerably more likely than parents to provide this information, often in a biased and inaccurate manner.

26. Several studies have revealed a connection between sexual "misadventures" and an inadequate sex education. Furthermore, research indicates that individuals who receive factual sex education, in contrast to their uninformed counterparts, demonstrate better psychological and sexual adjustment and a reduced tendency to engage in premature or irresponsible sexual activity with others.

ANDROGYNOUS CHILD-REARING AND SEXUALITY

27. In addition to encouraging a child to develop his or her potential, androgynous child-rearing practices help to break down the stereotypic gender roles that often have a negative effect upon sexual functioning.

SUGGESTED READINGS

Anthony, James; Green, Richard; and Kolodny, Robert. *Childhood Sexuality.* Boston: Little, Brown, 1982. Provides up-to-date and comprehensive information about childhood and adolescent sexuality.

Calderone, Mary, and Johnson, Eric. *The Family Book about Sexuality.* New York: Harper & Row, 1981. This excellent book, helpful for both parents and children, offers practical advice and valuable insights into childhood sexuality.

Comfort, Alex, and Comfort, Jane. *The Facts of Love.* New York: Ballantine, 1979. A supportive, realistic guide for young people that covers such topics as physical development, sexual activity, peer pressure, ethical issues, and responsible decision making.

Gordon, Sol. *Let's Make Sex a Household Word: A Guide for Parents and Children.* New York: Day, 1975. Contains some valuable information for all readers who are interested in sex education in the home.

Hanckel, Frances, and Cunningham, John. *A Way of Love, A Way of Life.* New York: Lothrop, Lee and Shepard, 1979. A sensitive, thoughtful book that gives young people information about what it means to be homosexual.

Pogrebin, Letty. *Growing Up Free: Raising Your Child in the '80s.* New York: McGraw-Hill, 1980. An important source of information for parents who wish to raise their children in an androgynous fashion.

14

Sexuality and the Adult Years

SINGLE LIVING

COHABITATION

    Personal Reasons for Living Together

    The Social Impact of Living Together

MARRIAGE

    Changing Expectations and Marital Patterns

    Why Do People Marry?

    Sexual Behavior within Marriage

RELATIONSHIP CONTRACTS

EXTRAMARITAL RELATIONSHIPS

    Nonconsensual Extramarital Relationships

    Consensual Extramarital Relationships

DIVORCE

    Interpreting Divorce Statistics

    Adjusting to Divorce

WIDOWHOOD

SUMMARY

SUGGESTED READINGS

*R*elationships occupy a position of considerable significance in many adults' lives. An individual's relationship status—as single, married, or living with someone— becomes an important social concern, as well as an important element in that person's self-identity. The nature of a person's relationship status may also have considerable influence on the kinds of sexual interactions he or she experiences during the adult years. This chapter will examine several alternatives for adult life styles and intimate relationships, many of which have been undergoing transition in recent years.

SINGLE LIVING

Increasing numbers of people in our society live alone. This increase is most pronounced among people in their 20s and early 30s. For example, a comparison of 1970 and 1980 census figures reveals that the percentage of men in the 20 to 24 age range who were single increased from 55% in 1970 to 69% in 1980. Comparable figures for women demonstrated an increase from 36% to 50%. Overall, it appears that single adults constitute more than 22% of the total number of American households. Approximately one-third of these individuals have never married.

These figures seem to represent a shift in adult living patterns. In the past, a far smaller percentage of adults either divorced or remained unmarried. A combination of factors contribute to the increasing numbers of single adults; these include people marrying at a later age, a slight increase in the numbers of those who never marry, more women placing career objectives ahead of marriage, rising divorce rates, and a decline in remarriage rates (Glick and Norton, 1979). The figures also reflect what may be a change in societal attitudes. Until recently in the United States, a stigma was often attached to remaining single. This stigma attached itself particularly to women, as terms such as "old maid" and "spinster" indicate. (Single men would most likely be referred to by the less negative term "bachelor.") Today these terms are heard less frequently, and it is quite possible that remaining single, either as an option to first marriage or following termination of a marriage, will play an increasingly prominent role in American culture. If this happens, we may also witness a reduction in the number of people who marry primarily for convention's sake or to avoid the negative perception of the single state. Nevertheless, single life is still often seen as the period before, in-between, or after marriage.

Single living encompasses a range of sexual life styles and differing levels of personal satisfaction. Some people who live alone remain celibate by choice or because of lack of available partners. Others may be involved in a long-term, sexually exclusive relationship with one partner. Some practice serial monogamy and move through a succession of sexually exclusive relationships. Still others prefer concurrent sexual and emotional involvements with a number of different partners. Some single people develop a primary relationship with one partner and have occasional sex with others. Many single individuals who are sexually active with a variety of partners express satisfaction with the freedom they have to explore emotional or intimate relationships with different people without disapproval from a primary partner (Libby, 1977; Stein, 1976). However, there is evidence that with the passing years some singles find that their enthusiasm for their "play the field" life style is replaced by a desire to find a more permanent relationship (Jacoby, 1974).

Meeting people for prospective social contacts, sexual partners, or marriage is often important to single people. Singles bars or apartment complexes often serve this purpose, especially among middle- and upper-income, urban, unmarried individuals. Singles bars may also offer people an opportunity to enjoy socializing and to overcome boredom and loneliness. However, the singles bar atmosphere may provoke anxieties, prompt people to assume roles they are not comfortable with, and generally increase feelings of alienation and isolation (Allon and Fishel, 1979). People who dislike the "heavy hustle" scene and superficiality that sometimes characterize such places may prefer to develop contacts through common activities of interest or through work, friends, or family.

Single living is becoming more acceptable in our society. However, the majority of people still choose to enter into a longer term relationship with a partner—even though it may not be a lifelong bond. There are several ways of defining a long-term sexual relationship, and we examine these various options in most of the remainder of this chapter.

Many cities have singles bars.

COHABITATION

When I was a college student in the early 1960s, the possibility of living with someone dear to me, without the sanctity of marriage, simply never entered my mind. When I met a very special person and found myself wishing for the intimacy of sharing a home together, marriage was my only option. Although we were sexual prior to marriage, there were no occasions when we even took a weekend trip together. The topic of unmarrieds living together was never discussed, although I did occasionally hear a hushed reference to someone "living in sin." (Authors' files)

This account reflects a prevalent societal attitude toward *cohabitation* (living together in a sexual relationship without being married), and this attitude has only recently begun to undergo change. In the past few decades, there has been a significant increase in both the number of people choosing this living arrangement and societal acceptance of what was at one time an unconventional practice. Census figures reveal that the number of unmarried couples living together in the United States rose by more than 700% from 1960 to 1970. In the period from 1970 to 1980 these figures rose another 300% to a point where there were approximately 1.6 million cohabiting heterosexual couples in the U.S. Even older people seem to be embracing this life style with increasing frequency. According to one estimate, more than 350,000 people over 55 live together without marriage (Glick and Spanier, 1980). It appears that cohabitation is now well established as a social phenomenon. In 1980 the U.S. Census Bureau formally acknowledged living together by announcing a new category: POSSLQ ("person of opposite sex sharing living quarters").

This dramatic increase has been attributed to American youth's growing inclination to question traditional mores, particularly those pertaining to the value of marriage. These questioning attitudes are supported by an expanding societal awareness that sexuality is an important part of a person's life and that marriage is not the only life style that legitimizes sexual relations. In addition, some social theorists have pointed to the increased availability and variety of birth control methods as influencing people's decision to live together outside of matrimony. Beyond these factors, there are a number of personal reasons why people choose to live together as a temporary or permanent alternative to marriage. We will look at some of them before examining the impact of this trend on the more traditional life style of marriage.

Personal Reasons for Living Together

There are several reasons why a couple may choose to live together. Many people are waiting longer to get married and delaying having their first child, factors that increase the attractiveness of cohabitation as a life style option. Older people may elect to cohabit because they simply cannot afford marriage. (If a widow remarries she may lose half or all of her Social Security pension, but if she cohabits with her male partner the two can pool their incomes without suffering a financial loss.)

Another important factor influencing the decision to live together is the desire for sexual fulfillment. In a study of college students who were living together (Macklin,

1976), 96% of respondents reported having sexually satisfying relationships. Some sexual difficulties were acknowledged, however. The most common of these were differing degrees of sexual interest, fear of pregnancy, and occasional failure to reach orgasm. It appears that most cohabiting couples, particularly young adults, prefer to have a sexually exclusive relationship (Macklin, 1978).

The sexual involvement of couples living together is only one element of the desire to share a home with a partner. Other reasons for choosing this life style may include desire for a meaningful relationship, need for companionship, an attempt to secure more intimacy and emotional security, and dissatisfaction with the "dating game." For many cohabitants, living together provides an opportunity to determine their suitability for a long-term commitment before entering into the more binding partnership of marriage (Clarke, 1978). However, marriage is usually not the initial goal at the time a couple enters into a cohabitation relationship, and most individuals do not believe that a long-term commitment is necessary to begin a living-together relationship (Macklin, 1976 and 1978).

Many couples prefer the relative informality of cohabitation arrangements to the more official aspects of a marriage. They appreciate the sense of living together because they want to, not as a result of the binding power of a legal contract, as the following account demonstrates:

I object to people constantly asking us when we are going to get married. We live together because it feels good and because it seems like a reasonable thing to do. Neither one of us have any intention of ever getting married, to each other or to anyone else. We have been together for over two years and plan to continue

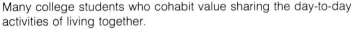

Many college students who cohabit value sharing the day-to-day activities of living together.

for a long time. One thing is certain. We are together because we want to be, not because we are in some kind of "training for marriage." (Authors' files)

The informality of living together may have other advantages. A couple may not feel as pressured to take on the new and demanding roles of wife and husband. As a result, the relationship is less likely to produce the sort of "identity crisis" that may follow as a person tries to live up to social expectations attached to these roles. A third perceived advantage may be that if the relationship is not satisfactory, the stigma of failure is less than with a divorce. This does not necessarily mean that it is easy to break up after living together. Terminating such a relationship can be very traumatic.

While living together offers some advantages to many couples, it also poses certain unique problems. Many of these problems stem from lack of social acceptance for this arrangement. Disapproval on the part of parents and other family members can sometimes be severe—a situation that can place considerable emotional strain on one or both partners. There may also be difficulties in obtaining and holding jobs. Some employers may be reluctant to employ people who live in "questionable circumstances." Some couples may also have difficulty in renting or buying property, although this problem is becoming less common. Owning property does present other potential difficulties, however. Who owns the property and financial assets the couple may have shared? Without a clear written contract, legal rights upon dissolution of the partnership are less clear than with a divorce. Death of one or both partners can result in legal confusion as well as emotional trauma. Again, unless the couple has had the foresight to write a contract, there is no clearly established legal definition of partnership rights.

In addition to social disapproval and possible legal difficulties, there may also be financial disadvantages to living together. For instance, unmarried couples often receive discriminatory treatment under the tax laws. Despite the potential disadvantages, however, the practice of living together is a growing trend. In the next few paragraphs, we will look at the impact of this trend.

The Social Impact of Living Together

It is still too early to assess what impact the experience of living together may have on relationship satisfaction, the stability of partnerships, and the marriage institution itself. There are those who view cohabitation as a clear sign of moral decay. Others applaud the advent of a new alternative to the narrow restrictions of a life script that defines marriage as the only legitimate mode for commitment and the sharing of day-to-day living.

A question arising from the increase in the number of couples choosing cohabitation is whether such experiences have any measurable effect upon the longevity and happiness of any subsequent marriages. There is evidence that living-together arrangements are considerably more transitory than marriages (Glick and Spanier, 1980). However, cohabitators seem to find as much satisfaction in their relationships as do marrieds (Yllo, 1978). But what about the impact of cohabitation on marriage? At present, with very little available evidence, there are two opposing hypotheses. One holds that positive benefits will prevail, with happier and more stable marriages emerging as a result of living together. Trial experiences can allow a person to better identify his or her own needs and expectations within the context of the struggles and joys of an everyday relationship. In this view, such arrangements provide the couple an opportunity to explore their compatibility before making a long-term commitment.

The opposing hypothesis suggests that living together will have an overall negative impact upon the institution of marriage, particularly its long-term stability. The belief is that when people who are living together are faced with conflict, they may find it easier to end the relationship than to exert effort to resolve the problems. A marriage relationship often carries with it a greater commitment to solving problems, in part because termination of marriage carries with it legal complications and social stigma. The concern is that once the pattern of breaking up has been established, people will be more likely to respond to marital conflict in the same way. The following account expresses the basic rationale behind this view:

> Many times during our marriage I have thought seriously about leaving. I am quite certain, had it not been for the moral commitment of the marriage contract and the legal and family hassles I could expect from divorce, our marriage would have ended long ago. It may sound strange, based on what I just said, but I am thankful that being married helped to keep us together. It takes one heck of a lot of work to make a marriage work. My guess is that people who just live together have much less incentive to struggle to keep things good. I'm glad I am still married. We have something really worth holding onto. (Authors' files)

It is possible that neither of these opposing hypotheses is correct. Cohabitation may have no demonstrable effect upon the longevity or satisfaction of any subsequent marriage. There is some limited evidence that supports this contention. In one study, couples who had cohabited before marriage were just as likely to divorce as those who did not (Newcomb and Bentler, 1980). Another study reported that couples who had cohabited and then married were no more satisfied with their marriage than couples who had not lived together before marriage (Jacques and Chason, 1979).

Perhaps further research will clarify the impact, if any, of cohabitation on marriage. One thing we can say with some confidence. People do not appear to be permanently substituting living-together arrangements for marriage (Macklin, 1980). In spite of the rapidly changing societal mores pertaining to human relationships and sexual expression, Census Bureau statistics reveal that about nine out of every ten adults in the United States marry, some more than once. Statistics released in 1981 by the National Center for Health Statistics show six consecutive years (1976–1981) of growth in the number of marriages in America. A closer look at the institution of marriage may provide some insight into its continuing appeal.

MARRIAGE

Marriage is an institution that is found in virtually every society. It has traditionally served several functions, both personal and social. It provides societies with stable family units that help to perpetuate social norms, as children are typically taught society's rules and expectations by parents or kinship groups. In many cultures, marriage defines inheritance rights to family property. Marriage performs an important function by structuring an economic partnership that ties child support and subsistence tasks into one family unit. Marriage regulates sexual behavior to maintain the family line. It also serves the important personal function of providing a framework for the social and emotional support needs of humans.

Although marriage is integral to most cultures, it assumes many different forms. Our society has defined its own marriage ideal. Within this ideal, we can isolate a number of elements that many people take for granted—for instance, legality, permanence, heterosexuality, sexual exclusivity, emotional exclusivity, and number of people. But the elements that are traditional to marriage in our society are not necessarily the same in other societies. For example, some societies may have marriages between one man and several women (polygamy); others (although far less frequently) have recognized unions between one woman and several men (polyandry).

In our own society, there are several modifications of the marriage ideal, although changing one element is still often seen as a radical departure from the norm. Yet even when one element is changed, other elements of a partner relationship are often expected to remain the same. For example, the extramarital sexual behavior known as "swinging" (discussed later in this chapter) theoretically alters only the sexual exclusivity of the marriage ideal. Other elements, including emotional exclusivity, are expected to remain constant in the relationship. Likewise, a couple living together often adheres to virtually all aspects of the marriage ideal except for its legal sanction. (In this case, even legality is granted in many states, where the relationship becomes a common-law marriage after a certain number of years.) The same assumptions sometimes hold true when the element of gender is changed. Some homosexual couples want their unions to be legally recognized marriages. In spite of the fact that homosexual marriages are not accepted as legal by the judicial system, some couples nevertheless have wedding ceremonies and adopt the marriage ideal for their relationships.

Changing Expectations and Marital Patterns

The institution of marriage has been both condemned and venerated in contemporary America. Currently, a large discrepancy exists between the American marriage ideal and actual marriage practices. Cohabitation, high divorce rates, widespread extramarital sexual involvements, the increasing popularity of personalized relationship contracts are all developments that are antithetical to the traditional ideal of marriage.

Some of the reasons for contradictions between the ideal and actual marriage practices have to do with changes that have been taking place, both in expectations for marriage and in the social framework of marriage. Historically, the function of marriage has been to provide a stable economic unit in which to raise children. People who did not want to have children were often admonished not to marry (Ritter, 1919). In many societies, and in some groups within our own society in the past, marriages were arranged through contracts between parents; "romance" was not expected to play a part. Today, however, most people expect more from marriage, as they seek fulfillment for their social, emotional, financial, and sexual needs—all within the marriage relationship. "Happiness" itself is sometimes thought to be an automatic outcome of marriage. These are high expectations, and they are difficult to meet. As one observer states, "Marriage was not designed as a mechanism for providing friendship, erotic experience, romantic love, personal fulfillment, continuous lay psychotherapy or recreation" (Cadwallader, 1975, p. 134). However, many modern couples expect a satisfactory degree of these benefits from the marital relationship.

At the same time that people's expectations for marriage have increased, our society's supportive network for marriage has decreased. Extended families and small communities have become less prevalent, and many married couples are isolated from their families and neighbors. In effect, this places further demands on the marriage to meet a variety of human needs, for there is often no place else to turn to for such things as childcare assistance, emotional support, and financial or housework help. Another development that is influencing marital patterns is increased longevity. "Till death do us part" now means many more years than it did in the past. This raises the question of how long even the best marriage can be expected to fulfill all of these functions.

At a personal level, courtship experiences before marriage also contribute to the discrepancy between expectations and reality. Dating rarely offers a couple the kinds of experiences that would enable them to draw a realistic picture of the marriage relationship or learn the skills that may help resolve later difficulties. Both partners frequently present their more likeable, sociable side. The focus of their time together is usually on pleasurable activities, with day-to-day problems kept separate from their interactions. The fairy-tale ending to their courtship—"they married and lived happily ever after"—is often difficult to achieve. While the challenges of sharing everyday life can provide enrichment and meaning to some couples, the lack of preparedness may be cause for disillusionment for others.

There are many things a couple can do that may help prepare them for the experience of marriage. Some couples make an effort to talk about such things as finances, children, and daily tasks that frequently are basic to disagreements. They may plan the handling of finances for shared activities or a vacation. They may also decide to divide living expenses equally or on a percentage basis relative to their respective incomes.

Desires and decisions about children may be discussed—whether each person wants children, how many, and when. If neither partner has children at the time, they may want to make arrangements to share volunteer childcare work or babysitting for friends to help them assess and discuss their childrearing attitudes. The logistics of responsibility for caring for their own children may be planned.

Some couples may work on a cooperative project or share homemaking activities. Building something together, organizing a party, trading work days at each other's houses, or cooking meals for each other are samples of activities that may help couples learn more about how well they can work together.

Situations in which the pair discovers problems can make the couple aware of what differences they bring into the marriage. A "good marriage" is not necessarily a problem-free marriage but rather a relationship in which two people are committed to working with the problems that invariably arise.

Marriage is a traditional and deeply ingrained institution in American society.

Why Do People Marry?

While both individual and societal expectations have undergone important changes, marriage remains a dominant life style in our culture. Certainly, the majority of Americans marry, some several times. The fact that marriage is such a traditional and deeply ingrained institution in American society at least partly answers the question "Why do people marry?" The following list includes some additional reasons people often give for entering wedlock:

1. Marriage can provide a feeling of permanence in one's life and a very reassuring sense of belonging and being needed.
2. The closeness and trust engendered by marriage may lead to richer relationships and deeper caring.
3. Sexual interaction is legally and socially sanctioned in marriage.
4. Being married reduces the energy spent in the pursuit of potential intimate partners.

5. With the greater familiarity provided by marriage, people may develop better understanding of each other's needs and thus a more harmonious relationship.
6. There are some monetary and legal advantages granted married people under present legal codes.

Marriage itself has not remained the same in the face of changing expectations and needs, and there is a growing interest in making the most of the institution in a changing society. The popularity of "marital enrichment" programs is one indication of the desire of many couples to improve their relationships. The aim of these programs is usually to teach the couple to be more responsive and accepting of each other's needs, to improve communication, and to deepen intimacy (Koch and Koch, 1976). Other couples seek professional counseling to improve the manner in which they relate to each other. The large number of "make your marriage better" books and magazine articles also reflect the importance placed on "good" marriages. Sexual behavior has also changed within the marriage structure, and this is another area that has come under professional scrutiny.

Sexual Behavior within Marriage

Contemporary developments and changes in sexual mores and behavior are often discussed in the context of unmarried or extramarital activities. However, the greatest impact of increased sexual liberalization may be on the marital relationship itself. As compared with the people in Kinsey's research groups, contemporary American married men and women appear to be engaging in sexual intercourse more often, experiencing a wider repertoire of sexual behaviors, and enjoying sexual interaction more.

Several studies, most notably Morton Hunt's nationwide survey (1974), reveal that the average duration of precoital activity has increased, with more people focusing on enjoyment of the activities themselves rather than viewing them as preparation for coitus. Oral stimulation of the breasts and manual stimulation of the penis has increased; so has oral-genital contact, both fellatio and cunnilingus. For example, only 15% of high school-educated married men in Kinsey's sample reported engaging in cunnilingus, a figure which increased to 56% of all married men in Hunt's sample and 70% of working-class men in a more recent study (Rubin, 1976).

Married couples' experiences with coitus also seem to have changed over the years. Today's couples report using a wider variety of intercourse positions, and the average duration of coitus was reported by Hunt (1974) to be five times longer than the two-minute average reported in Kinsey's 1948 study. The average frequency of marital coitus also appears to have increased to approximately two or three times per week for couples in their 20s and 30s, a frequency that gradually declines with increasing age (Pietropinto and Simenauer, 1979; Trussel and Westoff, 1980). Decreasing coital frequency does not necessarily imply reduced sexual satisfaction. Some couples find that the quality of their sexual sharing improves with the increased knowledge of each other gained from years spent together. Some may even find that they have intercourse more often as their sexual adjustment improves with the passing years.

A number of studies have attempted to assess satisfaction with marital sex and to isolate some of the factors that contribute to sexual fulfillment within marriage. Three-fifths of the married women and two-thirds of married men in the Hunt (1974) sample reported that marital sex was very pleasurable. Sixty-seven percent of the women in the *Redbook* survey indicated that marital sex was good or very good (Tavris and Sadd, 1977).

Redbook women who either always or never initiated sex were the least sexually satisfied respondents in this survey. This suggests that mutuality in initiating sex may be an important contributor to women's happiness with marital sex. It also appears that women who take an active role during sexual sharing are more likely to be pleased with their sex lives than those who assume a more passive role (Tavris and Sadd, 1977). Research also suggests a positive correlation between marital happiness and female orgasm. In one survey of over 1000 women, orgasm frequency was considerably higher among those women reporting marital happiness than in those who indicated they were unhappily married (Gebhard, 1966). There is evidence that orgasm frequency is increasing among married women (Hunt, 1974; Pietropinto and Simenauer, 1979; Tavris and Sadd, 1977).

It appears that good communication contributes greatly to sexual satisfaction within marriage. Eighty-eight percent of the *Redbook* women who reported always discussing their sexual feelings with their partners described their sex lives as good or very good. In contrast, only 30% of women who reported never discussing sex with their partners described their sex lives as good or very good (Tavris and Sadd, 1977).

Morton Hunt's (1974) research indicates that a positive relationship exists between subjective ratings of sexual pleasure and emotional closeness within marriage. Couples who rated their marriage as very close emotionally almost always rated marital coitus in the year preceding the study as highly pleasurable, while three-fifths of women and two-fifths of men who rated their marriages "not close" considered marital coitus to be unpleasant or not pleasant enough. (This still indicates that for two-fifths of women and three-fifths of men in this study, sexual pleasure was present despite a lack of emotional closeness.)

The *Redbook* survey also suggests an apparent relationship between women's subjective assessments of the quality of their marriages and the degree of satisfaction in their sex lives. Eighty percent of women who reported happy marriages also said their sex life was good. On the other hand, 70% of women reporting poor marriages indicated that sex was poor (Tavris and Sadd, 1977).

After reviewing the information just presented, one might be tempted to conclude that all is well with marital sex. However, we caution against such a generalization. One of the shortcomings of much of the available data is that it is generally collected from people involved in intact marriages as opposed to those whose marriages have ended. This is an important biasing influence that quite possibly leads to a more positive image of marital sexual satisfaction than is justified. Furthermore, most studies focus on the frequencies of certain behaviors and attitudes rather than how people feel about various aspects of their marriages, including sex. One notable exception is the work of sociologist Lillian Rubin (1976). She interviewed 50 working-class and 25 professional middle-class couples living in the San Francisco Bay area. Her interviews explored not only how her respondents behaved sexually, but, perhaps more important, how they felt about sex in their marriages. Each of the 75 couples in her study population reported some problems in sexual adjustment. Masters and Johnson (1970) also state that marital sexual problems are quite common, and they estimate that approximately half of all American married couples experience difficulties with sexual adjustment.

A number of factors may interfere with marital sexual enjoyment. When people marry, their relationship often changes. They suddenly find themselves confronted with a new set of role expectations. They are no longer just friends and lovers but also husband and wife, and the romance of the former condition may be replaced by stress from role adjustments to the latter. They no longer have the independence of living separately, and day to day togetherness may erode their sense of individuality and autonomy. Unfortunately, many people are less motivated to maintain personal attractiveness once they have secured a marriage partner; being overweight, out of shape, and poorly groomed may reduce one's sexual attractiveness and pleasure during sexual activity. People often get caught up in a "rat race" life style that can seriously erode the quality of marital sex. Holding down a job, doing laundry, fixing the lawn mower, socializing with two sets of relatives and friends, and countless other tasks can reduce the time a couple has for intimate sharing. Couples who become parents may discover that children can place unexpected strains on their relationship as well as interfering with their privacy and spontaneity. Finally, boredom can be a devitalizing factor. Sex may become routine and predictable. The discussion in Chapter 7 on maintaining relationship satisfaction may be helpful in enhancing sexual enjoyment in marriages and other long-term relationships.

RELATIONSHIP CONTRACTS

Another contemporary development is the use of relationship contracts to define particular aspects of both marital and nonmarital relationships. A *relationship contract* is a mutually agreed-upon set of rules, plans, or philosophies related to the relationship, and it can be either written or verbal. Some contracts may include legal documentation that spells out particular points.

Developing an individualized contract can be potentially useful to the couple. Such a contract might include the woman's right to use her maiden name if they marry; an agreement about the children's names; decisions concerning reproduction, such as method of birth control and number and timing of natural, adoptive, or foster children; husband's advance permission for an abortion; childrearing practices; divisions of labor for housework or other work; financial arrangements; living location and decision-making process for moving; agreements and commitments regarding sexual, social, and emotional exclusivity or nonexclusivity; and any other issues of importance to an individual couple (Edmiston, 1972). One person expressed the following feelings about writing a contract: "What we are really doing in thrashing out a contract is finding out where we stand on issues, clearing up all the murky, unexamined areas of conflict, and unflinchingly facing up to our differences" (Edmiston, 1972, p. 67). Many couples who implement individualized contracts renew, revise, or amend them on an ongoing basis to fit the changing needs of the relationship.

EXTRAMARITAL RELATIONSHIPS

The term *extramarital relationship* is a label for sexual interaction experienced by a married person with someone other than his or her spouse. The term is a general one that makes no distinction among the many ways in which extramarital sexuality occurs. It can be clandestine; it can also be an open agreement between the married couple. The extramarital relationship may be a casual encounter, or it may involve deep emotional commitment. The relationship may last for a brief or extended time period. Sometimes this form of sexual sharing occurs within the context of an alternative life style, as in the case of group marriages. The following discussions will examine extramarital relationships, both nonconsensual and consensual.

Nonconsensual Extramarital Relationships

In *nonconsensual extramarital sex*, the married person engages in an outside sexual relationship without the consent or knowledge of his or her spouse. This form of behavior has been given many labels, including "cheating," adultery, infidelity, having an affair, and "fooling around."

Why do people enter into nonconsensual relationships? The reasons are varied and complex. Sometimes, extramarital relationships are motivated by a desire for excitement and variety. The person may have no particular complaints about the marital relationship but wants to enrich or broaden his or her own emotional or sexual life with extramarital encounters. In other cases, people may be highly dissatisfied with their marriage. If emotional needs are not being met within the marriage, having an "illicit lover" may seem particularly inviting. Occasionally, the reason for outside involvements may be the unavailability of sex within the primary bond. A lengthy separation, a debilitating illness, or an inability or unwillingness of the partner to relate sexually, for instance, may all contribute to a person deciding to look elsewhere for sexual fulfillment. An affair may also be motivated by a desire for revenge. In such instances, the offending party may be quite indiscreet, to insure that the "wronged" spouse will discover the infidelity.

It is difficult to estimate the incidence of extramarital sexual involvements. Kinsey's surveys reported that approximately half of the men and a quarter of the women in his samples admitted to experiencing extramarital sexual intercourse at least once by age 40. The term *admitted* is a significant qualifier. Many writers and researchers believe that a considerable number of people are reluctant to acknowledge this kind of behavior, which may contribute to low estimates of its prevalence. This speculation receives some support from a survey of 750 individuals undergoing psychotherapy (Greene et al., 1974). Thirty percent of the sample initially admitted to having experienced extramarital involvements. After a period of extensive psychotherapy, however, an additional 30% revealed previous affairs. Furthermore, many sex surveys fail to distinguish between consensual and nonconsensual relationships—although it is reasonable to assume that the substantial majority of extramarital sexual contacts are nonconsensual. In Hunt's 1974 study, only one in five spouses whose partners had had such contacts had been told of the occurrence by their partner.

There is considerable difference of opinion about whether extramarital sex is becoming more frequent. Hunt found very little evidence of an upturn in this activity since Kinsey's surveys. However, he did find evidence of a shift in this behavior pattern. His study showed a significant increase occurring in one subgroup of his sample: women aged 18 to 24 were three times as likely to have experienced extramarital sex as women of the same age in Kinsey's study population. This apparent shift in the sexual practices of young married women was also indicated in another survey (Athanasiou et al., 1970). More recent evidence suggests that middle-aged women may be just as likely as their husbands to have extramarital sexual relationships (Fuchs, 1978; Wolfe, 1980). It would appear that the double standard of adult marital infidelity that was clearly evident in Kinsey's time has begun to erode.

It is quite possible that future sex surveys will reveal pronounced increases in extramarital sexual activity. This prediction is based on the many social changes evident in contemporary American life. For instance, greater mobility has increased people's opportunities to establish relationships away from home. Another factor is the increased number of women in the work force—a trend that has also served to increase the potential for sexual contacts and close daily relationships between men and women. A third factor is the increased availability of effective birth control, which has had the effect of making extramarital sex less a potential hazard than it once was. Another change, greater societal acceptance of nonprocreative sexual expression, has probably also contributed to more relaxed attitudes toward sexual behavior in general, as has a fifth factor—the general decline in religious commitment in our society. Kinsey's statistics suggest a correlation between religious involvement and marital sexual exclusivity. Kinsey also found a positive correlation between premarital and extramarital coitus among both sexes in his sample groups. In view of the discussion in Chapter 13 of rising premarital coital activity in the United States, and assuming that the relationship between premarital and extramarital coitus still holds, it seems likely that this is a sixth factor that will contribute to further increases in extramarital activity.

The effects of extramarital sex on a marriage vary. When secret involvements are discovered, the "betrayed" spouse may feel devastated. He or she may experience a variety of emotions, including feelings of inadequacy and rejection, extreme anger, resentment, shame, and jealousy. This last emotion can be very difficult to deal with, particularly when one partner has remained faithful while the other "cheated." Jealousy may emerge from a sense of betrayal—the belief that the spouse is giving away something that belongs exclusively to the other partner. Also involved may be the fear that another person will usurp one's position of preeminence in the life of the spouse. Particularly for men, part of sexual jealousy may stem from a sense of ownership. However, the discovery of infidelity does not necessarily erode the quality of a marriage. In some cases it motivates a couple to search for sources of discord in their relationship, a process that may ultimately lead to an improved marriage.

Kinsey attempted to determine the impact of extramarital involvements on a marriage. There were several hundred divorced men and women in both his study samples whose earlier marriages included extramarital sex (either by self, by the spouse, or by both), and he asked them about its effect. The question was posed in two ways. When asked, "Did *your* extramarital intercourse figure in your divorce?" 61% of both sexes reported it had "no effect at all." However, when they were asked, "Did your *spouse's* extramarital intercourse have any effect on your divorce?" they answered quite differently. In fact, it was viewed as a very important factor by both sexes, particularly men. Seventy-five percent of women and 83% of men stated it had either a "moderate" or "major" effect. None of the respondents indicated it had no effect at all (1948; 1953).

Consensual Extramarital Relationships

This category includes marriages where both partners are informed about and supportive of sexual involvements outside their primary marriage bond. These mutually agreed-upon experiences, often called *consensual extramarital involvements*, may be primarily emotional, primarily sexual, or they may involve the couple's whole life style. There are indications of increasing societal tolerance of this type of extramarital sexual activity. A number of organizations have emerged that facilitate the movement of people into such experiences or life styles. This is a significant difference from the traditional covertness of extramarital sexual experiences, and in effect it gives some societal legitimacy to nonmonogamy. A variety of arrangements fall under the category of consensual extramarital involvements. We will examine three: open marriage, swinging, and group marriage.

Open Marriage   The concept of *open marriage* received widespread public attention with the 1972 publication of George and Nena O'Neill's book *Open Marriage*. For many people who are not aware of the broad scope of this concept, open marriage has become synonymous with consensual sexual involvements. However, this is an incomplete view of the open marriage idea. The essence of the O'Neills' thesis is that one relationship is unlikely to fulfill a person's total intimacy needs throughout the adult years. The concept of open marriage is people allowing each other the freedom to have intimate emotional relationships with members of either sex without compromising their primary relationship. These intimacies do not necessarily include sexual sharing. This is a matter for an individual couple to determine.

Those who support open marriage believe that it is confining to limit emotional or sexual sharing to only one person. Some have even argued that it is "essentially absurd to expect that all physical sexual expression for a fifty-year period will be confined to the marriage partner" (Roy and Roy, 1973, p. 144). Other advocates of open marriage are committed to sexual exclusivity, but they find it stressful to avoid nonsexual intimacies with individuals other than their spouse. As the following anecdotes reveal, a marriage relationship that is too "closed" can have a confining and potentially negative effect:

When I married my husband it was with the intention of being totally faithful to him. I couldn't imagine myself wanting sex with another man. However, I was unprepared for the jealous way he reacts to anybody I show an interest in. If I talk too long to another man at a party he comes unglued. He doesn't even like me to spend time with my girlfriends, and I lie to him on those rare occasions I go out to lunch or shopping with a friend. I long for the companionship of others. I still love my husband, but sometimes I just need to be close to someone else. Sometimes I think his extreme possessiveness will be the end of us. (Authors' files).

In my job I form close working relationships with both men and women. A couple of the women have become very dear friends. I wish I could feel comfortable taking them out to lunch on occasion or having them call me at home like good friends do. But my wife raises hell even when their names come up in conversation. I guess she thinks being friends and crawling into bed go hand-in-hand. (Authors' files)

Open Marriage maintains that people who are allowed the freedom to form close, meaningful relationships with others are often able to bring more contentment and satisfaction to the primary relationship with their spouse. As an alternative to the resentment and frustration evident in the preceding accounts, open marriages attempt to foster mutual trust, support, and appreciation. *Eternity*, a poem by William Blake, perhaps captures the essence of loving with open arms:

> He who binds to himself a joy,
> Does that winged life destroy,
> But he who kisses the joy as it flies
> Lives in eternity's sunrise.

Swinging *Swinging* refers to a form of consensual extramarital sex that a married couple shares. Both husband and wife participate simultaneously and in the same location, and this distinguishes swinging from the extramarital sexual contact that might occur in an open marriage, where mutual participation is not usual. This activity has been labeled as "wife-swapping" in the past. However, this term came into disrepute among swingers because of its implications of male property rights. Most participants object to labeling this activity as extramarital sex. Since they do it together, it is not considered extra to, but rather part of, their marriage. Furthermore, many believe it to be far more acceptable morally than a secretive affair. In the words of one male swinger, "The hypocrisy that you find in the country club set—where everybody knows that everyone is balling everyone else, but it's clandestine—simply doesn't exist here" (Lewis, 1971, p. 33).

Much of the data about swingers comes from four major studies. These are the research by Bartell (1970), by Smith and Smith (1970), by Palson and Palson (1972), and by Gilmartin (1977). Together, these works provide a composite picture of typical swingers, who tend to be middle-class and upper middle-class, Caucasian, politically conservative, and generally indistinguishable from the general population of middle America. The reasons most commonly given for becoming involved in swinging were boredom with their partner and a desire to introduce excitement into their sex lives.

There are a number of ways a couple may "swing." They may get together for weekends with a few like-minded couples, or they may visit local nightclubs known to cater to such activities. Swinging may also involve more formal prearrangements, including highly organized club activities. Most participants carefully avoid emotional involvements with their sexual partners. For them, swinging is "designed to make extramarital sex safe for marriage by defusing emotional involvement and exclusivity" (Gagnon, 1977, p. 230).

The general prohibition against emotional involvement ultimately leads to boredom for some individuals:

At first swinging was a real high. The sex was much better than I expected. Some of the men I encountered were really expert lovers, at least from a technique point of view. But, as the initial excitement wore off, the whole scene became jaded. Finally, I realized that instead of standing around making meaningless small talk, as is typical of cocktail parties, we were lying around and engaging in meaningless screwing. I got out and I can't say that I miss it. (Authors' files)

Swinging seems to affect individuals and couples in a variety of ways, however. Some suggest that it improves the sexual aspects of the marriage, increases togetherness, and broadens social horizons. Gilmartin (1977) reported that the swingers in his research population, compared with a matched control group of nonswingers, had sex more often with their spouse, were slightly more happily married, and generally seemed to be less bored. However, swinging is not without potential hazards. Some of its participants report extreme sexual performance pressures (this is particularly true of men), guilt, jealousy, and feeling threatened. It appears that swinging does not maintain its appeal for very long; most couples terminate their participation after a brief period of experimentation (Murstein, 1978).

Group Marriage   *Group marriage* refers to a living and sharing arrangement where several people live together with commitment to each other. Each member of the group maintains what are considered marriage-type relationships with more than one other person. Usually three or four people enter into such a group relationship, but sometimes there is a larger membership. Some of the people may be legally married to each other. (This activity may not be accurately classified as extramarital sex if none of the participants is married.)

There is very little available information about this rare social phenomenon. The most frequently quoted source is one in-depth study of slightly more than 100 group marriages (Constantine and Constantine, 1973). These writers outline a number of factors that lead individuals to enter such expanded family groups. For some, the primary advantage lies in having more people to relate to intellectually, socially, emotionally, and sexually. Many participants in group marriages want the unique opportunities for personal growth offered by close, intimate contact with a group of like-minded companions. Others believe that children profit from having more siblings and parent models with whom to interact. (Most of the children included in group marriages were born into nuclear families before their parents formed a multilateral marriage.) Other benefits to group marriage may come from pooling economic resources.

Group marriages face the challenge of working out daily living arrangements and interpersonal relationships among several people.

Not uncommonly, couples who enter into group marriages have had a prior pattern of consensual extramarital sex. Each partner may have experienced periodic outside involvements with the consent of his or her spouse, or perhaps these experiences have been shared in the past by participating in swinging. However, the couple may have been dissatisfied with the emotional and relational limitations of such arrangements.

The realities of group marriage are not always consistent with the expectations of participating members (Constantine and Constantine, 1973; Salsberg, 1973). Conflicts may emerge in a number of areas: differing life styles, privacy, division of labor, childrearing practices, financial arrangements, and other issues. The difficulties encountered when living with one other person are compounded in group marriages. Not infrequently, jealousy becomes a disruptive influence. Not all members may be in equal demand for emotional or sexual sharing. Some groups seek to avoid this potential difficulty by setting up sleeping together on a rotational basis. However, the resulting lack of spontaneity may also be a problem.

Most participants in group marriages see their involvement as a positive experience. However, many of these evaluations are obtained in retrospect. Most group marriages have a short life span, generally lasting for a few months to a few years (Macklin, 1980; See, 1975).

DIVORCE

We have just seen that today different people may interpret marriage in a variety of ways, according to particular needs. Despite this increased flexibility, however, there are a growing number of marriages that are ending in divorce. Rising divorce rates are a common topic in the popular media, and they are often presented as a sign of societal rejection of the institution of marriage. This interpretation is not necessarily accurate. Available divorce statistics are not an entirely reliable indicator of the current state of American marriage.

Interpreting Divorce Statistics

There are several factors that have some bearing on the way we interpret divorce statistics. Many states in this country have not adopted uniform standards for divorce record-keeping (Glick and Norton, 1971), so that records may reflect variable data collection procedures. Also, there have been many recent legal changes. The rise in divorce rates may reflect the increased ease of legally obtaining a marital dissolution more than a rise in dissatisfaction with marriage itself. Obtaining a legal divorce has become a simpler, less expensive process in recent years. Furthermore, a significant percentage of the divorce rate is composed of people who have had more than one marriage and divorce. Therefore, a higher percentage of first marriages remain intact than a quick glance at the statistics indicates.

[© Engleman (Rothco)]

"Playing house is old-fashioned . . .
let's play divorce!"

TABLE 14.1 NUMBER AND RATIO OF DIVORCES TO MARRIAGES, 1950, 1977, AND 1981

	1950	Ratio	1977	Ratio	1981	Ratio
Number of divorces	385,000	1	1,097,000	1	1,200,000	1
Number of marriages	1,667,000	4	2,176,000	2	2,400,000	2

Sources: U.S. Bureau of the Census, 1978, and National Center for Health Statistics, 1982.

Research does show that the proportion of marriages ending in divorce has increased dramatically since the 1950s. In Table 14.1 we can see that the ratio of divorce to marriage was 1 to 4 in 1950. By 1977, the ratio had changed to one divorce to every two marriages. More recent statistics reveal that there were approximately 1.2 million divorces and 2.4 million marriages in 1981, still a ratio of 1 to 2. However, the number of divorces may reflect dissatisfaction with a particular marriage, rather than with marriage itself. Approximately four out of five divorced men and women remarry (Glick, 1975). In a summary of studies of remarriages, 70%–80% of the individuals reported marital happiness (Murstein, 1974).

Adjusting to Divorce

Although the chain of events leading to marriage is individual, most people marry with the hope that the relationship will last. Divorce often represents loss of this hope and other losses as well: one's spouse, children, life style, the security of familiarity, and often part of one's identity. Many people who terminate nonmarital intimate relationships also share this experience.

The loss a person feels in divorce is often comparable to the sense of loss when a loved one dies. In both cases, the person undergoes a grieving process. There are important differences, however. When the grief is caused by death, there are rituals and social support available which may be helpful to the survivor. In contrast, there are no recognized grief rituals to help the divorced person. Initially, a person may experience shock: "This cannot be happening to me." Disorganization may follow, a sense that one's entire world has turned upside down. Volatile emotions may unexpectedly surface. Feelings of guilt may become strong. Loneliness is common. Finally (usually not until after several months or a year), a sense of relief and acceptance may come (Krantzler, 1974). If after several months of separation a person is not developing a sense of acceptance, professional help may be needed. Although many of the feelings triggered by divorce are uncomfortable, even painful, they can be steps toward resolving the loss so that a person will be able to reestablish intimate relationships. Grieving can lead to healing.

Separation and divorce represent a major life transition. Even in a mutually agreed-upon, friendly termination of a legal marriage, many significant life style changes usually occur. The newly single person often faces adjustments in social and sexual relationships, financial and living arrangements, and, if applicable, parenting roles. Extensive changes such as these, even if accompanied by the relief of ending an undesirable situation, typically cause stress. Of course, many divorces are not peaceful agreements but rather conflicts full of bitter contention. A person's self-confidence may also be negatively affected if the divorced individual believes he or she has "failed" in the marriage.

Other difficulties may arise with the change of status from being married to being single. Many married people have established friendships and social relationships as couples rather than as individuals, and the divorced person may feel awkward being alone with others in pairs. At the same time, other couples may not be comfortable including a single person in their activities. The sense of security or belonging that often accompanies being in an established pair is replaced by sudden autonomy. People who become divorced often need to find new groups of other single people to establish social contacts. Many cities have organizations where single people can meet and form new friendships.

There is a potential for personal growth in the adjustment process that accompanies divorce. Many people experience a sense of autonomy for the first time in their lives. Others find that being single presents opportunities to experience more fully dimensions of themselves that had been submerged in their identity within a couple. Learning to reach out to others for emotional support can help diminish feelings of aloneness. Divorce can offer an opportunity to reassess oneself and one's past, a process that may lead to the evolution of a new life. One person describes the experience as very positive:

Today I look back on the last three years as the most personally enriching period in my life. Through a painful emotional crisis, I have become a happier and stronger person than I was before. I learned that what I went through was what all divorced people, men and women, go through to a greater or lesser degree—first a recognition that a relationship has died, then a period of mourning, and finally a slow, painful emotional readjustment to the facts of single life. I experienced the pitfalls along the way—the wallowing in self-pity, the refusal to let go of the old relationship, the repetition of old ways of relating to new people, the confusion of past emotions with present reality—and I emerged the better for it. (Krantzler, 1975, p. 30)

Making the transition from marital to postmarital sexual relationships often presents a challenge to divorced individuals. The newly divorced person may experience considerable ambivalence about intimacy. Feelings of anger, rejection, or fear remaining from the trauma of the divorce may inhibit openness to intimate relationships. To protect themselves from emotional vulnerability, some people may withdraw from potential sexual relationships. Others may react by seeking many superficial sexual encounters.

Despite problems often encountered in establishing sexual expression in a nonmarital context, Morton Hunt's research revealed considerable sexual satisfaction and activity among the divorced people in his volunteer subject group (1974). Specific data on the sexual activity of divorced men indicated a slightly higher frequency of coitus than for married men of the same age, while the rate for divorced women as compared with married women of the same age was approximately the same. In this same study, divorced respondents reported greater participation in noncoital sexual activities and more variety in intercourse positions than did married respondents. There is also evidence that divorced women may be more orgasmic in their post-marital relationships than in their previous marriages (Gebhard, 1970). In one national survey it was reported that a majority of divorced individuals become sexually active within the first year following break-up of their marriages (Hunt and Hunt, 1977).

WIDOWHOOD

Most marriages end with one partner's death. Although a spouse can die during early or middle adult years, widowhood usually occurs later in life. In most cases, it is the man who dies first, a tendency that has become more pronounced during this century. The ratio of widows to widowers has increased from less than 2-to-1 in the early 1900s to 5-to-1 in the 1970s (Hoult et al., 1978).

In one national survey widowhood is different in some ways from that of divorce. Widowed people typically do not have the sense of having failed at marriage. In addition, the anger and resentment that often help to ease the emotional separation after a divorce is frequently lacking when a partner dies. The grief may be more intense, and the quality of the emotional bond to the deceased mate is often quite high. For some people, this emotional tie remains so strong that other potential relationships appear dim by comparison.

In many cases, the life style adjustments and the grieving process described in our discussion of divorce are experienced, often to a greater degree, by widowers and widows. Further information on widowhood is included in the following chapter's discussion of aging and sexuality.

SUMMARY

SINGLE LIVING

1. Although single living is often seen as a transition period before, in-between, or after marriage, some people choose it as a permanent life style.

COHABITATION

2. The number of couples who live together has increased by 1000% from 1960 to 1980.

3. Research indicates that most college students who cohabit do not have plans to marry when they first enter into this arrangement.

4. The possible effect of cohabitation on subsequent marriage stability is unknown at present.

MARRIAGE

5. The primary elements in the marriage ideal of our society are a permanent and exclusive legal relationship between two heterosexual adults.

6. The reasons people give for entering marriage vary widely and may include one or more of the following: a desire to achieve a sense of permanence and belonging; a response to social pressures to conform and be traditional; as a means to obtain legally and socially sanctioned sexual interaction; as a way to develop a closer and deeper relationship; and because of the monetary and legal advantages granted to married people.

7. Recent changes in sexual behaviors can be observed within the marital relationship. Married couples are engaging in a wider variety of sexual behaviors and experiencing coitus more often and with greater duration than in the past.

RELATIONSHIP CONTRACTS

8. Individualized contracts attempt to outline mutually agreed-upon rules, plans, or philosophies related to the relationship.

EXTRAMARITAL RELATIONSHIPS

9. Nonconsensual extramarital relationships occur without the partner's knowledge or consent.

10. Kinsey found that approximately 50% of married males and 25% of married females had experienced sexual intercourse outside the marriage by age 40.

11. The most notable increase in extramarital sexual intercourse in current studies is among women under age 25.

12. Consensual extramarital relationships occur with the spouse's knowledge and agreement. Examples of these involvements include open marriage, swinging, and group marriage.

13. The open marriage concept can include a combination of emotional, social, and sexual components in the extramarital relationship.

14. Swinging is structured to facilitate sexual expression and inhibit emotional involvement between the participants.

15. Group marriage is seen by participants as a commitment to live as if the several people involved were married to each other.

DIVORCE

16. The ratio of divorces to marriages has increased from 1 to 4 (1950) to 1 to 2 (1981).

17. Divorce typically involves many emotional, sexual, interpersonal, and life style changes and adjustments.

WIDOWHOOD

18. Most marriages end by the death of one partner. The ratio of widows to widowers is now close to 5 to 1.

Colgrove, Melba; Bloomfield, Harold; and McWilliams, Peter. *How To Survive the Loss of A Love*. New York: Bantam, 1977. A sensitive, warm, and practical book that can assist people in the process of emotional healing after experiencing loss.

Hoult, Thomas; Henze, Lura; and Hudson, John. *Courtship and Marriage in America: A Text with Adapted Readings*. Boston: Little, Brown, 1978. This text explores many aspects of human relationships during courtship and marriage from a historical and contemporary perspective.

Krantzler, Mel. *Creative Divorce*. New York: Signet, 1975. This book views divorce as an opportunity for personal growth and learning. It also gives readers support during the difficulties usually accompanying divorce.

Masters, William, and Johnson, Virginia. *The Pleasure Bond*. New York: Bantam, 1976. An exploration of the meaning of sexual exclusivity in a marital relationship and of the ways in which it serves to solidify the bond between the couple.

Scanzoni, John. *Sexual Bargaining: Power Politics in the American Marriage*. Englewood Cliffs, New Jersey: Prentice-Hall, 1972. A thought-provoking look at contemporary marriage. Author Scanzoni refutes the notion that marriage is a dying institution and examines the potentially positive outcomes of marital conflict arising from women seeking equality within the marital partnership.

Singer, Laura. *Stages: The Crises That Shape Your Marriage*. New York: Grosset & Dunlap, 1980. This book discusses the evolving pattern of predictable crisis points in marriage and provides positive suggestions to help resolve problems.

Smith, James, and Smith, Lynn (Eds). *Beyond Monogamy*. Baltimore: Johns Hopkins University Press, 1974. A collection of articles that seeks to understand nonmonogamous styles of marriage.

15

Sexuality and Aging

SEXUALITY IN THE LATER YEARS: EXAMINING THE MYTHS
   The Double Standard of Aging
   Sexuality and Aging in Nursing Homes
PHYSIOSEXUAL CHANGES AND SEXUAL RESPONSE: THE OLDER FEMALE
   Estrogen Replacement Therapy
   The Sexual Response Cycle of the Older Female
PHYSIOSEXUAL CHANGES AND SEXUAL RESPONSE: THE OLDER MALE
   The Prostate Gland
   The Sexual Response Cycle of the Older Male
MAXIMIZING SEXUAL FUNCTIONING IN THE LATER YEARS
   Potential Problems and What to Do About Them
   Sexual Expression in the Later Years
SUMMARY
SUGGESTED READINGS

During the young adult years, the prospect of altered sexual expression with aging may seem remote and unimportant. However, in the later years of life, most people begin to note that certain changes are taking place in their sexual response patterns. Some women and men who understand the nature of these variations may accept them with equanimity. Others will observe them with alarm and perhaps even respond with deep concern. Both sexes may begin to worry about the possibilities of being rejected or of developing difficulties with sexual functioning.

An important source of the confusion, frustration, and perhaps outrage many aging people feel is the prevailing notion that old age is a sexless time. In this chapter, we will examine some facts about aging and sexuality to see how much basis there is for this potentially harmful myth.

SEXUALITY IN THE LATER YEARS: EXAMINING THE MYTHS

Some people begin to deny their sexuality as they grow older. This change in sexual identity often starts at about age 50, or some time thereafter, and it may occur as part of an overall identity shift that takes place to a greater or lesser degree when a person realizes he or she is growing old.

Why is aging in our society often associated with sexlessness? There are a number of reasons. Part of the answer is that American culture is still influenced by the philosophy that equates sexuality exclusively with procreation. For older people, whose prospects for having babies are either nonexistent or unrealistic, this viewpoint offers little beyond self-denial.

Society also suppresses sexuality in its older members by disproportionately focusing on youth. The media usually link love, sex, and romance together with the implicit assumption that all three belong exclusively to the young. There is also a pervasive, often unspoken assumption in American society that it is not quite acceptable for older people to have sexual needs. In all probability, attitudes like these at least partly account for the infrequency with which older couples publicly display expressions of affection such as hugging, kissing, or holding hands.

With such widespread denial of the validity of sexual expression in the "golden years," it is not surprising that many individuals are confused about aging and sexuality. Unfortunately, some older people may accept the cultural mandate for a sexless old age and, as a result, may actively suppress their natural urges. Others may not deny their continued sexuality as they grow older, but they may feel conflict or be concerned that they are either morally decadent or physically abnormal (Rubin, 1965).

In examining the myth of sexless old age, two notable societal phenomena merit some special attention. These are, first, the double standard as it relates to the aging process and, second, the manner in which nursing homes deal with the sexual needs of their residents.

The need for affection and sexual intimacy extends to older years; and this can be a time of sharing and closeness.

The Double Standard of Aging

In this text, we have discussed the double standard as it relates to male and female sexual expression during adolescence and adulthood. The same assumptions and prejudices implicit in the double standard continue into old age, imposing a particular burden on women.

Although a woman's erotic and orgasmic capabilities continue after menopause, it is not uncommon for her to be considered past her "sexual prime" relatively early in the aging process. For example, *Playboy* magazine printed an article entitled "The Mystique of the Older Woman" (May 1977), where the average age of the 12 women discussed was 33.

Women are considered to be less sexually attractive as they grow older. The cultural image of an erotically appealing woman is commonly equated with youth, as exemplified by the statement of a 30-year-old man who told one of the authors with delight about the woman he had started seeing. "She's 22," he said, "but she has the body of a 16-year-old." As a woman grows further away from this nubile image, she is usually considered less and less attractive. So, in our society, even young girls are sometimes told not to frown ("You'll get wrinkles"); and cosmetics, specially designed clothing, and even surgery are often used to maintain a youthful appearance for as long as possible.

In contrast, the physical and sexual attractiveness of men is often considered to be enhanced by the aging process. Gray hair and facial wrinkles may be thought to look "distinguished" on men—signs of accumulated life experience and wisdom. Likewise, while the professional achievements of women may be perceived as threatening to a potential male partner, it is relatively common for a man's sexual attractiveness to be closely associated with his achievements and social status, both of which may increase with age.

The pairings of powerful, older men and young, beautiful women reflect this double standard of aging. The marriage of a 60-year-old man and a 20-year-old woman would probably generate a much smaller reaction than if the sexes were reversed—a situation that was portrayed in the 1972 film *Harold and Maude*. In reality, such pairings almost never occur.

One research study (Stimson et al., 1981) suggests that there are male-female differences in the aspects of sexuality that contribute to a general feeling of well-being among the aged. For the older man, pride in his sexual performance and attractiveness to the opposite sex appeared to be crucial to his general feeling of well-being. In contrast, sexual performance did not seem related to general feelings of well-being for the older woman. However, feeling sexually attractive to the other sex was important; when the older woman no longer felt attractive, her general feelings of well-being decreased. Given that attractiveness in women is often equated with youthfulness, the older woman can be negatively affected by this narrow concept of beauty.

It is our opinion that exaggerated attempts at remaining perpetually youthful are both a losing battle and a denial of a woman's full humanity. Susan Sontag presents an alternative:

Women have another option. They can aspire to be wise, not merely nice; to be competent, not merely helpful; to be strong, not merely graceful; to be ambitious for themselves, not merely themselves in relation to men and children. They can let themselves age naturally and without embarrassment, actively protesting and disobeying the conventions that stem from this society's double standard about aging. Instead of being girls, girls as long as possible, who then age humiliatingly into middle-aged women and then obscenely into old women, they can become women much earlier—and remain active adults, enjoying the long, erotic career of which women are capable, for longer. Women should allow their faces to show the lives they have lived. (Sontag, 1972, p. 38)

Sexuality and Aging in Nursing Homes

The double standard, especially as it relates to aging, has been so ingrained in our social traditions that until recently it has rarely been questioned. In the past decade, however, the treatment that older people receive in some nursing homes has come under increasing public scrutiny. Nursing homes have been criticized for their insensitivity to the human rights of aged individuals; our concern here is with antisexual prejudice and practices, which are clearly demonstrated in many nursing home facilities. For example, researchers often find that administrators and personnel in senior facilities resist programs having to do with sexuality (Starr and Weiner, 1981). Of the 5% of the population over 65 who live in nursing homes at a given time, many are denied the adult rights of sexual opportunity and privacy. One writer describes the situation:

Their environment is almost totally desexualized. It is considered progress when dining room or recreation halls and residential wings are not sex-segregated. Privacy is virtually nonexistent . . . [O]nly a minority of institutions make an effort to provide areas where a couple can be alone to talk, much less to court. Even married couples may be separated; some state institutions segregate them or permit the sexes to mix only under "supervision." If only one spouse is in a home, the other seldom has the right to privacy during a visit. (Lobsenz, 1974, p. 30)

These problems can be especially acute for older homosexual partners. Antihomosexual prejudice may make it extremely difficult for a gay person to express affection and to be involved with his or her lover or friend in hospital or nursing home settings. Even nursing homes that allow conjugal visits for their heterosexual residents are unlikely to do this for a homosexual couple (Kimmel, 1978).

Because older people are often assumed not to be sexual, medications are sometimes prescribed without consideration of their effects on sexuality. Some tranquilizers, antidepressants, and high blood pressure and arthritis medications can have an inhibiting effect on sexual interest and arousal. In cases where drug therapy is indicated, these factors should be discussed with each person and adjustments made. It is also desirable for older people to be thoroughly educated about the potential effects on sexuality of suggested surgeries, particularly those that involve the reproductive organs (Page, 1977).

Some relatives of nursing home residents and the staffs of such facilities help to perpetuate difficulties like those just outlined, perhaps in part because of their own lack of knowledge or discomfort about sexuality and aging. Concerned individuals, progressive nursing-home personnel, and organizations such as the Gray Panthers and Services to Ongoing Mature Aging are beginning to have some effect on restrictive practices in nursing homes. Staff education, programs on sexuality for the residents, private lounges, and acceptance of affectional and sexual rights of residents are important elements of care in these facilities. Perhaps as these alternatives are made increasingly available, they will help maintain the important option of sexual expression for the aged who are in institutions.

We have been looking at some of the elements of myths about sexuality and aging that have had particularly oppressive impact on some older people. One of the foundations of these myths is a widespread ignorance of the facts about sexual functioning in aged people. The remainder of this chapter will examine some of the physiosexual changes and altered sexual responses that take place as part of the aging process.

PHYSIOSEXUAL CHANGES AND SEXUAL RESPONSE: THE OLDER FEMALE

There is widespread misinformation about the physiosexual changes that accompany menopause. Menopause is *not* what David Reuben describes in *Everything You Always Wanted to Know About Sex:*

Increased facial hair, deepened voice, obesity, and decline of breasts and female genitalia all contribute to a masculine appearance. Coarsened features, enlargement of the clitoris, and gradual baldness complete the tragic picture. Not really a man but no longer a functional woman, these individuals live in a world of intersex. (1969, p. 365)

Menopause is the point along the aging process in women that is marked by the cessation of menstruation. It occurs as a result of certain physiological changes that take place at around 45–50 years of age. Although the pituitary continues to secrete follicle-stimulating hormone (FSH), the ovaries cease production of mature ova. Ovarian estrogen output also slows down, although the adrenals, liver, and adipose (fat) tissue produce some estrogen after menopause (Mosher and Whelan, 1981).

The cessation of menstruation and fertility do not physiologically lower sexual desire and response. In fact, the altered ratio of hormones and elimination of fear of pregnancy may sometimes increase sexual interest. Although the role of hormones and sexual motivation is not yet thoroughly understood, Kaplan states that "[f]rom a purely physiologic standpoint, libido should theoretically increase at menopause, because the action of the woman's androgens, which is not materially affected by menopause, is now unopposed by estrogen" (1974, p. 111).

During menopause women may experience some physical symptoms other than cessation of menstruation. However, only about one-quarter of all women seek medical consultation due to difficulties related to menopause (Novak et al., 1970). For many, the "event" is surprisingly uneventful:

After hearing comments for years about how menopause was so traumatic, I was ready for the worst. I was sure surprised when I realized I had hardly noticed it happening. (Authors' files)

Women who do experience problems report symptoms such as changes in vaginal tissues, menstrual irregularities, headaches, insomnia, and "hot flashes." Hot flashes may occur sporadically, and there is a physiological explanation for them. Hormones influence the vasomotor system, so that as hormone levels fluctuate during menopause, the diameter of the blood vessels may change. Rapid dilation of the vessels may cause a woman to experience a momentary rush of heat, typically in the face. The sensation can be quite disconcerting. Hot flashes can occur several times a day and during sleep; they will usually cease within two years. About 10% to 20% of women report extreme discomfort from hot flashes (Seaman and Seaman, 1978).

Changes in the vaginal tissues are also hormonally caused. They result from a decrease in circulating hormones. The vaginal mucosa becomes thinner and changes to a lighter pinkish color. Both the length and width of the vagina decrease, and these changes contribute to the diminished expansive ability of the inner vagina during sexual arousal. There may also be diminished lubrication during sexual response. Both of these changes can result in uncomfortable or painful intercourse.

Estrogen Replacement Therapy

Medical treatment of menopause and its symptoms is controversial. *Estrogen replacement therapy* (ERT) has been used for the last 50 years to restore the hormone balance. The peak year for ERT sales was 1975; more than 8 million women were using estrogens at that time. Currently, fewer than 2 million postmenopausal women are taking ERT (Mosher and Whelan, 1981). This decrease is due to public and professional disagreement over the risks and benefits of ERT, which is the focus of much debate. Proponents of routine and continual use of estrogen believe menopause is a deficiency condition that is appropriately treated indefinitely by ERT. Others maintain that the premenopausal level of estrogen necessary for reproductive functioning is not essential or desirable once a woman's fertility cycles are ended (Seaman and Seaman, 1978). As stated in a gynecology text, "Many [women] require only reassurance and education, and in only a comparatively small proportion is endocrine therapy necessary" (Novak et al., 1970, p. 633).

ERT can effectively alleviate the two menopausal difficulties of hot flashes and drying of vaginal tissues (Mosher and Whelan, 1981). However, it will not delay the natural aging process, and it is not without risks. Research shows that women who receive long-term (more than 5 years) ERT for menopausal symptoms are more likely to develop gallstones (Boston Collaborative Drug Surveillance Program, 1974). Recent studies indicate that women who receive ERT may be up to 30 times more likely to develop cancer of the endometrium (Jick et al., 1980). The risk of this type of cancer increases with extended use of ERT, as well as when higher doses of estrogen are prescribed (Antunes et al., 1979).

The number of endometrial cancer cases reached a peak in 1975, and much of this increase has been attributed to greater use of ERT. Estimates suggest that ERT was responsible for over 15,000 cases of endometrial cancer from 1971 to 1975. These figures represent "one of the largest epidemics of *iatrogenic* [physician-induced] *disease* that has ever occurred in this country" (Jick et al., 1980, p. 264). The incidence of endometrial cancer began to fall in 1976 when estrogen sales declined.

There may also be a link between ERT and breast cancer. Although the causes of cancer are difficult to determine because the disease may manifest itself years after the contributing factors occurred, a study released in August 1976 indicated a correlation between ERT and breast cancer. Regardless of the length of time of ERT use, within 15 years after beginning hormone treatments, twice as many treated women had breast cancer as those who had never undergone estrogen replacement therapy (Hoover et al., 1976).

The current research suggests that a menopausal woman may wish to carefully evaluate the potential benefits and risks of ERT against the symptoms of hormone deficiency. Thorough discussions with one's physician are recommended. When ERT is determined to be appropriate, low-dose, short-term treatment is generally advisable.

There are some alternatives to ERT. Continued frequent sexual activity helps maintain vaginal lubrication during sexual arousal. Creams containing estrogen can be inserted directly into the vagina, and these can sometimes replace estrogen pills to counteract the drying of vaginal tissues. Although some of the locally applied estrogen will be absorbed into the bloodstream, the amount is less than with oral estrogen. Physical exercise, good nutrition, and food supplements can also sometimes alleviate some menopausal symptoms (Ritz, 1981).

Other physiosexual changes that occur as a woman grows older will be described in the following discussion of the sexual response cycle of the older female.

The Sexual Response Cycle of the Older Female

Prior to Masters and Johnson's (1966) research, the sexual response cycle of menopausal and postmenopausal women had not been studied. Sixty-one women between the ages of 41 and 78 were in Masters and Johnson's research population. In the following paragraphs we will contrast the sexual response cycles of these postmenopausal women with patterns that typically occur in premenopausal women, as described in Chapter 6. For the most part, the changes that accompany aging have to do with somewhat decreased intensity rather than with significant alterations of response.

Excitement Phase The first physiological response to sexual arousal, vaginal lubrication, typically begins more slowly in an older woman. Instead of 10–30 seconds, it may take several minutes or longer before vaginal lubrication is observed. In most cases, the amount of lubrication is also reduced. However, neither the slowing of the response nor the reduction in lubrication are necessary accompaniments of aging. The Masters and Johnson group included three subjects who had maintained active sexual involvement throughout their adult years and had rapid, full lubrication.

Other characteristic changes of excitement phase, such as the sex flush and expansion of vagina, are often less pronounced than in earlier years. Clitoral sensitivity and nipple erection remain the same.

Plateau Phase During the plateau phase, the vaginal orgasmic platform develops and the uterus elevates. In a postmenopausal woman, these changes occur to a somewhat lesser degree than before menopause. However, the vaginal opening is constricted to the same degree as with a younger woman, and the clitoris withdraws under the hood as before.

Orgasm Phase   Contractions of the orgasmic platform and the uterus continue to occur at orgasm, although the number of these contractions is typically reduced in an older woman. In some women, the uterine contractions that take place at orgasm may be painful. This typically results from a hormone deficit or imbalance, a condition that can usually be corrected by providing a proper balance of both estrogen and progesterone. The capacity for multiple orgasms continues, and several of the older women in the Masters and Johnson study experienced multiple orgasmic response.

Orgasm appears to be an important aspect of sexual activity to older women. One survey (Starr and Weiner, 1981) found that 69% of women aged 60 to 91 listed "orgasm" first in reponse to the question "What do you consider a good sexual experience?" Only 17% of the women answered "intercourse" to this same question. Additionally, "orgasm" was the most frequent response to the question "What in the sex act is most important to you?" Compared with when they were younger, 65% of the women reported that the frequency of orgasm was the same, and 20% said it was increased. About 14% reported that they now experienced orgasms less often, but only 1.5% of the sample said they never experienced orgasm.

Resolution Phase   Resolution phase typically occurs more rapidly in post-menopausal women. Labia color change, vaginal expansion, orgasmic platform formation, and clitoral retraction all disappear soon after orgasm. This is most likely due to the overall reduced amount of pelvic vasocongestion during arousal.

In summary, complete sexual response can continue throughout a woman's lifetime. As Masters and Johnson state, "The aging human female is fully capable of sexual performance at orgasmic response levels, particularly if she is exposed to regularity of effective sexual stimulation" (1970, p. 238). What happens to male physiosexual functioning and sexual response in the later years? We now turn to an examination of that question.

PHYSIOSEXUAL CHANGES AND SEXUAL RESPONSE: THE OLDER MALE

As a man grows older, certain physiosexual changes occur that are in large part related to decreased production of testosterone. In most men, the male hormones reach their peak level sometime between the ages of 17 and 20. The output then steadily but slowly declines until around age 60, at which time it stabilizes. The hormone level remains relatively constant thereafter.

With aging, a man may note several changes in his sexual anatomy or functioning. The size and firmness of his testicles diminishes somewhat. This is a normal change in body anatomy that is unlikely to impair his ability to function sexually. There is also a thickening and gradual degeneration of the seminiferous tubules, and this generally results in reduced sperm production. However, many men retain their fertility well into the older years. There are numerous recorded cases of men older than 80 who have fathered children.

The Prostate Gland

One of the most common physiosexual changes encountered by men during the aging process involves the prostate gland. This structure produces the major portion of the fluids contained in the ejaculate. Inflammation of the prostate, a condition known as *prostatitis,* is a difficulty that may be experienced by young and old alike, but it is considerably more common in the aging male. In most cases it results from a bacterial or viral infection, although occasionally it may be attributed to a disruption in the usual pattern of sexual behavior (either an increase or decrease in frequency). Some common symptoms of prostatitis include pain in the pelvic area, backache, urinary complications, and occasionally a cloudy discharge from the penis. In the case of a bacterial infection, medical treatment generally involves the administration of antibiotics. Nonbacterial prostatitis often responds to prostatic massage (the physician inserts a finger into the rectum and presses rhythmically against the prostate).

Also, as men grow older the prostate gland tends to increase in size, a condition called benign prostatic hypertrophy. The enlarged prostate tends to put pressure on the urethra and decreases urine flow (Ritz, 1981).

It is not uncommon for aging men to develop benign or malignant tumors of the prostate. Early detection of prostatic cancer is important to its successful treatment. Therefore, it is good preventive practice for all men past the age of 40 to have yearly prostate evaluations.

The usual treatment for prostate cancer is surgical removal of the entire gland (*prostatectomy*) or treatment with female sex hormones (Kolodny et al., 1979; Ritz, 1981). These treatments may contribute to a variety of problems in sexual functioning. Hormone treatments sometimes result in difficulty achieving an erection. Surgically removing portions of the prostate via the urethral tract damages the urethral sphincter valves, and this can result in retrograde ejaculation. This produces sterility, although in some cases, artificial insemination is successfully performed with sperm removed from the man's urine. Most types of surgeries for prostate problems are followed by a low incidence of erectile problems, but with radical surgical procedures for prostate cancer, loss of erectile ability is common (Kolodny et al., 1979).

Besides the physiosexual changes caused by prostate gland changes, other variations in orgasmic and erectile function may also accompany the male aging process. We will look at some of these changes in the following section.

The Sexual Response Cycle of the Older Male

Masters and Johnson studied 39 men between the ages of 51 and 89 and found that, as with the female, most changes in the sexual response cycle involve alterations in the intensity and duration of response.

Excitement Phase During youth, many males are capable of achieving an erection in a few seconds. This ability is typically altered with the aging process. Instead of eight or 10 seconds, a man may now require several minutes of effective stimulation to develop an erect penis. More direct stimulation may also be desirable or necessary. This slowed rate of erectile response may cause alarm, stimulating the potency fears that some men experience:

I guess it was the little things adding up that finally made me realize it was taking me longer to get a hard on—the fact that I could go to bed with an extremely desirable woman and still be flaccid; that kissing and hugging often wasn't enough to get me started. At first I was real shook up at this discovery, thinking that maybe I would lose my potency. However, I received some good advice from my physician who assured me that while things may slow down a bit, they continue to remain functional. (Authors' files)

Fortunately, this man received good advice. Others, fearful they will ultimately lose their erectile function, may develop such anxiety that their fears become reality. However, most men retain their erectile capacities throughout their lifetimes. The slowed rate of obtaining an erection is a natural occurrence within the aging process. When understood in perspective, this altered pattern has little or no effect on the enjoyment of sexual expression.

One change in the excitement phase is often interpreted as a positive event by the older male. This is the fact that it is often possible to maintain an erection for a protracted period of time before reaching orgasm (Masters and Johnson, 1966). Many men appreciate this prolonged opportunity to enjoy other sensations of sexual response besides ejaculation.

Plateau Phase Older men do not typically experience as much myotonia (muscle tension) during plateau phase as when they were younger. The testes may not elevate as close to the perineum. Complete penile erection is frequently not obtained until late in the plateau phase, just prior to orgasm.

One result of these changes is that the older man is often able to prolong the plateau phase much longer than he did when younger, which may significantly enhance his pleasure. When he engages in intercourse, his partner also may appreciate his greater ejaculatory control.

Orgasm Phase Most aging males continue to experience considerable pleasure from their orgasmic responses. In fact, about 73% of older men in one study reported that orgasm was "very important" in their sexual experiences (Starr and Weiner, 1981). However, they may note a decline in intensity. Frequently absent are the sensations of ejaculatory inevitability that correspond with the emission phase of ejaculation. The number of muscular contractions occurring during the expulsion stage are typically reduced and so is the force of ejaculation. The seminal fluid is usually less copious and somewhat thinner in consistency.

Resolution Phase   Resolution typically occurs more rapidly in older men. Loss of erection is usually quite rapid, perhaps bypassing altogether the two stages of penile detumescence characteristic of younger men. The testicles generally descend immediately after ejaculation.

While resolution becomes faster with aging, the refractory period between orgasm and the next excitement phase gradually lengthens. Men may begin to notice this as early as their 30's or 40's. Often by age 60, the refractory period may last for several hours and even days in some cases. Some men may be quite philosophical about this increased time span between ejaculations. As one 70-year-old man stated:

I can still shoot just as good—it just takes me longer to reload. (Authors' files)

MAXIMIZING SEXUAL FUNCTIONING IN THE LATER YEARS

As the preceding discussion of sexual responses indicates, most people retain the capacity for sexual expression throughout their lives. However, it is important to distinguish between the capacity and the desire for sexual expression. Although the capacity is typically retained, some individuals or couples may not wish to maintain or renew sexual activity in their later years. Therefore, the following information is primarily directed toward those who are interested in continued sexual expression.

Potential Problems and What to Do About Them

There are certain conditions, other than those discussed earlier, that may reduce the pleasures of sex in the later years. A brief discussion of these potential deterrents, and some ways of minimizing them, may help older people to better enjoy their sexuality.

Like all physical expressions, sexual activity may become increasingly fatiguing to the person who allows his or her physical condition to markedly deteriorate through lack of exercise. Consequently, maintaining a regular program of physical activity (walking, jogging, swimming, and so forth) may enhance erotic abilities in addition to contributing to one's general health.

Related to the value of maintaining physical exercise are the known benefits of sexual regularity. Masters and Johnson maintain that regularity of sexual expression throughout the adult years (whether by masturbation or activity with a partner) is a crucial factor in maintaining satisfactory sexual functioning beyond one's youth and middle age: "Even more necessary for maintained sexual capacity and effective sexual performance is the opportunity for regularity of sexual expression" (1966, p. 240).

This conclusion is supported by data from Kinsey's studies (1948 and 1953) that reveal a close correlation between sexual activity levels in the earlier years and those in the later years. Another researcher's work corroborated Kinsey's findings and found that the differences between men in levels of sexual activity before middle age tended to be maintained as the men grew older (Martin, 1981). These findings do not necessarily demonstrate a direct cause-and-effect relationship; it may simply be that

As one grows older, an active physical life can contribute to self-satisfaction.

those people with the strongest sex interest in their youth maintain that interest into old age. However, some theorists believe that regular functioning of the sex organs is a key factor that directly affects sexual ability in the later years. According to their argument, regularity helps maintain sexual vigor by preventing the deterioration of the sex organs with aging (Rubin, 1965).

Overindulgence in food or drink has frequently been linked with declining sexuality. Overeating may become a major problem in older individuals who often slip into a sedentary life style. In previous portions of this text, we have pointed out the potentially adverse effects of excessive alcohol consumption. Moderation in both eating and drinking can indirectly contribute to healthier sexual functioning.

The monotony of a repetitious sexual relationship, often exaggerated after long years of living with the same person, may also significantly reduce an older couple's sexual ardor. The need for experimentation and variety may be particularly important at this time. Certainly, not all long-term couples report problems with boredom. For some, who may have grown to understand and adjust to each other's needs over the years, familiarity may breed contentment.

Sexual Expression in the Later Years

As we grow older, all of us will experience some physical changes that will affect our sexual functioning. However, it is unlikely that these natural alterations will eliminate our capacity to maintain a rewarding and satisfying sex life. If we are aware of and accepting of these changes, the aging process will probably only mark another stage in our development as sexual beings.

The options for sexual expression may also change in the later years. Men die an average of eight years earlier than women, and women accustomed to expressing their sexuality exclusively within a marriage may find themselves suddenly alone. Furthermore, older males without partners often seek younger female companions, whereas women are less likely to be involved with younger men.

For some older women and men, widowed or divorced, masturbation can become or continue to be a form of sexual release and expression. A study of 800 people between 60 and 91 years of age reports that women are becoming more accepting of masturbation as a means of sexual expression (Starr and Weiner, 1981). As a woman of 60 states:

I thought my life was over when my husband of 35 years died two years ago. I have learned so much in that time. I learned to masturbate. I had my first orgasm. I had an "affair." I have established intimate relationships with women for the first time in my life. And most of all, I have survived. (Authors' files)

Being married is no guarantee of the availability of a satisfying sexual relationship. One partner's sexual interest may lag behind the other's. A woman who finds that her sexual needs are more demanding than those of her male partner may find it quite difficult to seek more frequent sexual activity with her partner, particularly if a pattern of male initiation has long been established. A misunderstanding about altered patterns of sexual response may give rise to difficulties. A woman may misinterpret the slower erectile and ejaculation response of her male partner as being signs of waning interest or rejection. Similarly, a man may believe that reduced vaginal lubrication is an indication that his female lover is less aroused by him.

On the other hand, both well-established and new relationships may blossom during the later years. The opportunities for sexual expression in a relationship are often increased as pressures from work, children, and fulfilling life's goals may be reduced and more time is made available for sharing with a partner. Couples may increasingly emphasize quality rather than quantity of sexual experience. For example, one study found that for younger men the amount of sexual activity they engaged in was an important aspect of their social confidence. However, for older men the quality of their sexual activity was the most crucial factor (Stimpson et al., 1981). A small study on older gay men found this same trend. Most of the homosexual respondents indicated that sex was less frequent than when they were younger, but half felt that it was more satisfying than before. As one 63-year-old man said, "Less accent on the genitals, more on the total person now" (Kimmel, 1978, p. 199).

Intimacy, a lifelong need, may find new and deeper dimensions in later years. Some people find their sex lives markedly improved by the greater opportunities to explore relaxed and prolonged lovemaking. A few may even have more frequent sexual encounters, as revealed in one survey of people more than 65 years old (Pfeiffer, 1975). For others, genital sexual activity may become less frequent, but interest, pleasure, and frequency of nonintercourse sexual activity like caressing, embracing, and kissing may remain stable or increase (Foster, 1979). As a 73-year-old man expressed:

I don't know if I'm oversexed, but I'm a lover. I like to pet, kiss, hug. I have more fun out of loving somebody I love than the ultimate end. You know, some people want sex and forget the rest of it—the hugging and the petting—and I think that's wrong. People say, "What will happen to me when I get older?" Well, I'm still alive! (Vinick, 1978, p. 362)

Older people may redefine their sexual and affectional relationships. Nonsexual friendships with either sex can offer affectionate physical contact, emotional closeness, intellectual stimulation, and opportunities for socializing. People of two or more generations may live together or an unmarried couple may share a household. Sexual relationships with same-sex partners may be explored. Remarriage may also be an option; each year there are more than 35,000 marriages in the United States in which one of the partners is 65 or older (Vinick, 1978).

Most people who regularly play golf, hike, fish, or till a garden during their youth will continue to do so in their later years, although often with somewhat reduced vigor. Far from developing a total incapacity for these activities, older people may simply pursue them at a more leisurely pace. The same can be true of one's sexuality, particularly if misconceptions and anxieties are avoided or resolved.

Nonsexual friendships often provide affection and closeness.

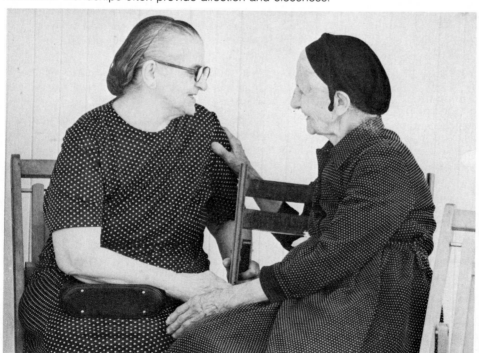

SUMMARY

SEXUALITY IN THE LATER YEARS: EXAMINING THE MYTHS

1. American culture continues to be influenced by the philosophy that equates sexual expression with procreation and youth.

2. The double standard of aging often affects both sexes but may impose a particular burden on women.

3. Antisexual prejudice against older people is particularly pronounced in some nursing home facilities.

PHYSIOSEXUAL CHANGES AND SEXUAL RESPONSE: THE OLDER FEMALE

4. Menopause is the cessation of menstruation and signals the end of female fertility. The level of estrogen output is reduced by the end of menopause.

5. Some women experience menopause-related symptoms such as hot flashes, menstrual irregularity, headaches, insomnia, and changes in the vaginal tissues.

6. Estrogen replacement therapy (ERT) is a medical treatment for menopausal symptoms. Potential side effects necessitate careful use of this medication.

7. With aging a woman typically requires more time to achieve vaginal lubrication.

8. The sexual response cycle of the older woman is also characterized by less vaginal expansion, reduced sex flush, diminished orgasmic intensity, and a more rapid resolution. The capacity for multiple orgasmic response is typically maintained.

PHYSIOSEXUAL CHANGES AND SEXUAL RESPONSE: THE OLDER MALE

9. After early adulthood, testosterone production declines steadily until approximately age 60. Many physiosexual changes in the aging male result from this decreased hormone output.

10. Common physiosexual changes in the older male include reduction in the size and firmness of the testicles, lowered sperm production, and difficulties with the prostate gland.

11. The older male typically requires longer periods of time to achieve erection and reach orgasm. Greater ejaculatory control may be beneficial to both his partner and himself.

12. The sexual response cycle of the aging male is also characterized by less myotonia, reduced orgasm intensity, more rapid resolution, and longer refractory periods.

MAXIMIZING SEXUAL FUNCTIONING IN THE LATER YEARS

13. Continued physical exercise may help to maintain sexual functioning, and evidence suggests that regularity of sexual expression throughout the adult years may be another crucial factor.

14. Overindulgence in food or drink has frequently been linked with declining sexuality in the later years.

15. Boredom with a repetitious sexual relationship may also inhibit sexual ardor in older couples. However, routine and familiarity may also bring contentment.

16. It is unlikely that the physiosexual changes of aging alone will eliminate one's capacity to maintain a satisfying sex life.

17. The options for sexual expression may change in the older years, as many individuals find themselves without a sexual partner. Masturbation may serve as one alternative.

18. Sexual relationships may improve during the later years when individuals focus on intimacy and redefine their sexual and affectional relationships.

Butler, Robert, and Lewis, Myrna. *Sex After Sixty: A Guide for Men and Women for Their Later Years.* New York: Harper and Row, 1976. Extensive, down-to-earth health and living adjustment information related to sexuality. Many useful suggestions within a context of individual differences with encouragement for personal and relationship growth.

Dickenson, Peter. *The Fires of Autumn.* New York: Drake, 1974. A folksy, sexual permission-giving book. Life style alternatives are explored within a historical, present-day, and future context.

Sontag, Susan. "The Double Standard of Aging." *Saturday Review,* September 23, 1972, 23-25. A strong indictment of the double standard of aging and its effects on women.

Starr, Bernard, and Weiner, Marcella. *The Starr-Weiner Report on Sex and Sexuality in the Mature Years.* New York: Stein and Day, 1981. An informative report on the personal responses to questions about sexuality of more than 800 people between the ages of 60 and 91.

Troll, Lillian; Israel, Joan; and Israel, Kenneth (Eds.). *Looking Ahead, A Woman's Guide to the Problems and Joys of Growing Older.* Englewood Cliffs, N.J.: Prentice-Hall, 1977. An up-to-date volume that combines theoretical, professional, and personal perspectives of aging. This is one of the few books that deals with other than middle-class women.

PART FIVE

Sexual Problems

16

The Nature and Origins of Sexual Difficulties

ORIGINS OF SEXUAL DIFFICULTIES
  Cultural Influences
  Personal Factors
  Interpersonal Factors
  Organic Factors
DESIRE PHASE DIFFICULTIES
  Inhibited Sexual Desire
  Sexual Aversion
AROUSAL DIFFICULTIES
  Inhibition of Vaginal Lubrication
  Erectile Inhibition
ORGASM DIFFICULTIES
  Anorgasmia
  Rapid Ejaculation
  Ejaculatory Inhibition
  Faking Orgasms
VAGINISMUS
SUMMARY
SUGGESTED READINGS

*T*he next three chapters are concerned with some of the difficulties that can hinder sexual functioning and some ways of preventing or resolving these difficulties. This chapter looks at a number of relatively common sexual problems and the factors that frequently contribute to them. First, we discuss some common origins—cultural, personal, interpersonal, and physiological. Then we look at a number of specific problems related to sexual desire, arousal, and orgasm. The next chapter outlines several ways for enhancing sexuality and overcoming specific difficulties. In Chapter 18, we will turn our attention to understanding and preventing sexually transmitted diseases.

ORIGINS OF SEXUAL DIFFICULTIES

What are the causes of sexual difficulties? This may sound like a simple question, but finding origins to sexual problems is often complex. There are several reasons for this. First of all, even when a sexual difficulty has been clearly identified, it is often hard to isolate the specific causes, because many varied influences and experiences contribute to sexual feelings and behavior. Second, it is difficult to identify a clear and consistent cause-and-effect relationship, because the experiences that contribute to a specific sexual difficulty in one person may produce no such effects in another individual. Finally, people who do not demonstrate any specific, objectively measurable sexual difficulty may still experience dissatisfaction with their sexuality.

The following paragraphs will examine several factors, each of which can either interfere with sexuality or enhance it. We hope that a clearer understanding of the events that shape sexuality will lead to increased satisfaction, communication, and pleasure. Cultural, personal, interpersonal, and organic factors can each contribute to sexual difficulties. Significant interaction between these areas also occurs. Therefore, the separate categories of factors that we describe in the following pages may be somewhat arbitrary.

In reading this chapter, it is important to remember that sexual satisfaction is a subjective perception. One person or couple could experience some of the problems described in this chapter, and yet be satisfied with their sexual lives. In fact, some research has indicated that, of the happily married couples studied, many experienced sexual problems with arousal and orgasm but felt very positive about their sexual relations and marriages (Frank et al., 1978).

Cultural Influences

Culture strongly influences both the way we feel about our sexuality and the way we express it. At times, because cultural influences are so pervasive, it is easy to think of them as innate or "natural" rather than learned. Yet, in another time or culture, a quite different sexual behavior or attitude may be viewed as the norm. These cross-cultural inconsistencies clearly reveal the powerful shaping impact that society has upon sexuality. The following sections will examine some issues in Western society—and particularly in the United States—that influence our sexuality and may contribute to sexual problems in some people.

Negative Childhood Learning   We learn many of our basic, important attitudes about sexuality during childhood. The views of some people are strongly influenced by our cultural legacy that sex is sinful. It has been widely reported by a variety of therapist researchers that severe religious orthodoxy that equates sex with sin is an element common to the backgrounds of some sexually troubled people.

A child may or may not be directly told that sex is shameful or sinful, but the groundwork of such a belief can be laid in other ways. Helen Singer Kaplan describes some aspects of childhood sexuality and the response it often evokes in our society:

> Infants seem to crave erotic pleasure. Babies of both genders tend to touch their genitals and express joy when their genitals are stimulated in the course of diapering and bathing, and both little boys and girls stimulate their penis or clitoris as soon as they acquire the necessary motor coordination. At the same time, sexual expression is, in our society, systematically followed by disapproval and punishment and denial. (1974, p. 147)

The resulting lesson is that sexual pleasure from touching one's genitals is bad, provoking guilt feelings about sexual stimulation. Conflict about erotic pleasure may thus be initiated early in a person's life. Kaplan summarizes: "The interaction between the child's developing sexual urges and the experiences of growing up in our sexually alienating society probably produces some measure of sexual conflict in all of us" (Kaplan, 1974, p. 145).

Not only do children often learn that it is wrong to touch their genitals; they may also learn that their genitals are "down there" and somehow dirty. Rather than understanding that their sexual anatomy is one more part of their body to learn about and explore, they may begin to have strong negative feelings about their genitals. This can carry over to adult life and influence feelings towards self-exploration and sharing one's body with another person.

The availability of accurate and appropriate information about sexuality can influence sexual attitudes and behaviors. Boys generally acquire more knowledge, but not necessarily good feelings, about their sex organs than do girls. It is quite typical, for example, for a girl not to learn she has a clitoris, as the following report illustrates:

> It wasn't until the first time that a man touched my clitoris with his hand that I knew I had anything down there so special. This new knowledge really paid off when I realized I could do for myself what he had done to me. (Authors' files)

Children begin early on to develop a sense of whether it is acceptable to ask questions about sex. Schools and parents typically contribute only in a limited way to a child's understanding of sex, and by and large peers are the most frequent providers of sexual information (Hunt, 1974). Unfortunately, much of the information a child receives from his or her friends is incorrect. Also, since sexuality is an emotionally laden topic, many young people learn *not* to talk about sex. It is no wonder that by the time people reach adulthood, sharing needs and discussing information about sex is often difficult.

The manner in which others react to childhood genital exploration may affect how children learn to feel about their sexual anatomy.

While growing up, we learn important lessons about human relationships. We observe and integrate the models we see around us. During this time we are also forming our sense of self. Both of these elements, the sense of self and relationships with others, contribute to the meaning and expression of sexuality. As children we often had limited choices about what we learned. However, this learning and development continues throughout our lives, and as adults we are more able to choose what information and experiences are valuable to us.

The Double Standard   The expression *double standard* refers to our society's expectations and beliefs about male and female sexual expression. Standards for males and females are sometimes polar opposites, and this can create difficulty for each sex. Furthermore, many double-standard beliefs and practices are the source of much mistrust, misunderstanding, and conflict within relationships.

Although the rigidity of the double standard appears to be lessening somewhat, some cultural expectations for women are still quite prevalent in our society. For example, women are expected to appear attractive and "sexy" while carefully controlling their sexual behavior, and virginity and sexual inexperience are valued. Labels such as "loose," "easy," or "promiscuous" imply overstepping acceptable, although often arbitrary, limits of sexual behavior. As we saw in Chapter 2, women may learn that it is more appropriate to respond sexually than it is to initiate sexual behavior. Furthermore, women often are responsible for controlling sexual advances made by men, who, they are told, "are only after one thing." Being on the defensive can have additional negative effects. As the Boston Women's Health Book Collective describes it, women ". . . are always so busy setting limits and holding off this powerful sexuality coming from [men] that [they] never get a chance to explore [their own sexuality]" (173, p. 26).

In spite of the change in societal views, the notion that "good" women do not enjoy sex still lingers. Masters and Johnson noted that "[s]ociocultural influence more often than not places a woman in a position in which she must adapt, sublimate, inhibit or even distort her natural capacity to function sexually. . . . Herein lies a major source of woman's sexual dysfunction" (1970, p. 218). The "good girl" facade and pervasive cultural repression of female sexuality affects most girls and women to some degree—both those with and without definable sexual problems.

In our more recent history, marriage gives permission for female sexual responsiveness. The contradictory message is, "Sex is dirty, save it for someone you love." However, as many women find, such a rapid transition from sexual repression to responsiveness is not easy to make:

I dutifully followed the expectation to be chaste until marriage. However, a 15-minute ceremony did not make me instantly sexually responsive. My inhibition was a great disappointment to my husband and myself. (Authors' files)

The male side of the double standard is also a function of cultural expectations. Men frequently learn that sexual conquest is a measure of "manliness"; as a result, they should be interested in enticing as many women as they can into sexual relationships. According to this image, a man is supposed to be always ready for sex:

Erotic materials portray men as always wanting and always ready to have sex, the only problem being how to get enough of it. We have accepted this rule for ourselves and most of us believe that we should always be capable of responding sexually, regardless of the time and place, our feelings about ourselves and our partners, or any other factors. We have thus accepted the status of machines, performing whenever the right button is pushed. (Zilbergeld, 1978, p. 41)

As a result of these expectations, men have often assumed that intercourse was primarily for their own pleasure and sexual release. This was true especially in the past. However, today men frequently feel responsible for the woman's sexual pleasure as well.

These cultural expectations can produce discomfort, frustration, and resentment for men as well as for women. Often a man may feel overburdened by his responsibility for sexual activity. At times, his feeling that he must perform and the resulting lack of spontaneity may obliterate his sexual arousal and pleasure. His sense of

Differing expectations can lead to difficulties in intimate relationships.

responsibility for the success of the sexual relationship may also result in psychological distress if his partner has a sexual problem. One research study (Derogatis et al., 1977) that examined psychological distress in couples in which one of the partners had a diagnosed sexual problem found some gender differences in the reactions of the other partners. Men partners without sexual problems indicated more feelings of depression, anxiety, and self-deprecation than did women partners without sexual problems. In fact, the former demonstrated as much psychological distress as did male subjects with diagnosed sexual problems. In contrast, women partners without sexual problems had significantly lower levels of psychological problems than did women with sexual problems.

The following accounts typify some of the ways in which the double standard influences sexuality. The first is by a woman who wishes to assume more responsibility in initiating relationships; the second, by a woman who is now openly a lesbian and regrets her delayed learning of sexual assertiveness; and the last, by a man now in his 30's.

I've really been struggling with being able to ask a man for the first date. I worry that if I take the first step he's going to think that I'm ready to go to bed without any further question. And if I make the first move to be affectionate, I'm sure he'll make that same false assumption. I feel like if I initiate a kiss, I have to first say,

"Look, this does not mean I want to have intercourse, it just means I want to kiss you." (Authors' files)

My lover and I spent about six months pretending to be straight (heterosexual) and avoiding any discussion of our attraction to each other when we were first roommates. I would lie in bed at night fantasizing about her, feeling certain I couldn't express my feelings to her. I guess it's amazing it only took us six months to come out to each other. Six very long and wasted months. (Authors' files)

When I think about what sex was like for me as a young man, I cringe. I concentrated so much on attempting physically and verbally to coerce my date to "go further" that I really didn't experience sensual pleasure. I was always thinking about my next move rather than enjoying what was happening. (Authors' files)

A Narrow Definition of Sexuality   Besides early socialization experiences and continuing exposure to the double standard, popular opinions about the appropriateness of sexual behaviors also influence our expressions of sexuality. Although attitudes about what is "normal" appear to have changed in recent years, certain assumptions still strongly affect sexual expression.

The notion that "real sex" equals penile-vaginal intercourse is pervasive in our society, and this assumption can significantly affect erotic behavior. Less than 5% of respondents to Hite's survey (1976) described their patterns of sexual encounters as something other than the standard one of (a) foreplay, (b) penetration, (c) thrusting, and (d) orgasm, especially male orgasm (lesbian responses excepted).

Certainly coitus is a viable option. However, it is one alternative—rather than the only, most important, or best avenue for experiencing sexual pleasure. A strong inclination to view coitus as synonymous with sex can place burdensome and anxiety-provoking expectations on intercourse. It can also lead people to overlook other sensual enjoyments in relating sexually. In Zilbergeld's words, "Many men, when asked how it felt to touch their partners or be touched by them, have said that they didn't know because they were so busy thinking about getting to intercourse. In this way we (men) rob ourselves of pleasure and of fully experiencing the stimulation necessary for an enjoyable sexual response" (1978, p. 45).

The sex-equals-coitus model in heterosexual relating may greatly reduce the eroticism of the experience for both people. Nevertheless, the stimulation of the penis provided by the vaginal walls is likely to be adequate for inducing male orgasm. The problem may be greater for women, who are less likely to experience orgasm from intercourse alone. Therefore, this model is one in which many women are left with the specific sexual dissatisfaction of not experiencing orgasm with a partner. This important topic will be discussed in a later section dealing with female orgasm difficulties.

Goal Orientation   There has been a wide variety of goals prescribed for sexuality throughout history. Certainly a common one has been reproduction. Another is the man's biological release, with the woman providing it as her duty. Once pleasure began to be considered a legitimate aspect of sexual contact, the simultaneous orgasm became the pinnacle of achievement. As women are increasingly viewed as sexual beings, "vaginal" orgasms and, currently, multiple orgasms may be seen as essential to sexual experience. Contemporary magazines and sex manuals provide the latest in acrobatic positions, techniques, and gadgets. The "modern" message about sexuality often appears to be "Sex is OK for both males and females, and you better be good at it" (LoPiccolo and Heiman, 1978, p. 56). It sometimes seems as if the pursuit of bigger, better, and more orgasms has become a consuming American pastime—and shame on the couple who used only one intercourse position last time! As Philip Slater (1973) in his article "Sexual Adequacy in America" aptly states:

Discussions of sexuality in America have always centered on the orgasm rather than pleasure in general. This seems to be another example of our tendency to focus on the *product* of any activity at the expense of the *process*. It may seem odd to refer to orgasms as a product, but this is the tone taken in such discussions. Most sex manuals give the impression that the partners in lovemaking are performing some sort of task; by dint of great cooperative effort and technical skill (primarily the man's), an orgasm (primarily the woman's, which masculine mystification has made problematic) is ultimately produced. The bigger the orgasm, the more "successful" the task performance. (p. 19)

We do not intend to demean sexual exploration and variety. Nor, by any means, do we mean to criticize the orgasm. We do believe, however, that arbitrary definitions of sexuality that impose external standards for measuring "success" or "failure" reduce the opportunity for individuals and couples to determine what is satisfactory based on their own feelings.

Personal Factors

Beyond the cultural setting and the influence it has on sexual feelings and expression, sexual difficulties may also stem from other factors. Each of us is a unique, complex, and interrelated blend of biological, cultural, and emotional elements. Our sexuality is an expression of all of these aspects of ourselves that begin forming in childhood and continue to develop throughout our lives.

Personal factors are important, for human reactions to life experiences are highly variable. Two individuals may respond in totally different ways to the same situation. It is in this light that we present a discussion of some of the personal influences that help mold an individual's sexual expression and satisfaction.

Sexual Knowledge and Attitudes   The knowledge and attitudes we acquire about sex have a direct influence on our sexual options. For example, if a woman knows about the function of her clitoris in her sexual arousal and believes her own sexual gratification is important, she will most likely have experiences different from a woman who has neither this knowledge nor this belief. Even education and social class have an impact on sexual attitudes and behaviors. For example, Kinsey's study found that the higher the educational and occupational level, the greater was the tendency to use a variety of noncoital stimulation and intercourse positions (Kinsey et al., 1948 and 1953). In certain cases where difficulties are based on ignorance or misunderstanding, accurate information can sometimes alleviate sexual dissatisfaction.

Self-concept   Self-concept is a term that refers to the feelings and attitudes we have about ourselves. These feelings influence the kinds of decisions we make about expressing our sexuality. For example, one man may decline a sexual proposition because he lacks confidence. Another man's reasons for saying no in the same situation may be based on an entirely different attitude; for example, he may have found casual sexual encounters to be unrewarding.

Sexual difficulties may often be tied to problems of self-concept. Some studies have found that men and women with sexual problems are likely to have more feelings of depression and anxiety and to have less self-confidence than men and women without sexual problems (Clement and Pfafflin, 1980; Derogatis et al., 1979). In addition, women who report disliking themselves indicate that they experience less sexual satisfaction than do women who have more positive feelings about themselves (Frank et al., 1979).

Self-concept combined with social skills also affects the ease or difficulty with which people begin, maintain, and end relationships. People often feel more at ease relating to others (sexually and socially) after having had some experience and having gained a sense of confidence in their own feelings and abilities.

Emotional Difficulties   Often related to poor self-concept are personal emotional difficulties, such as anxiety or depression. These difficulties can be a response to a current situation or they may stem from unresolved past events. Whatever the source, emotional states have a strong impact on sexuality. However, once again this impact is relative to the individual. One person who is feeling a generalized kind of anxiety may respond by becoming exceptionally sexually active. Another may withdraw from sexual encounters in an attempt to reduce anxiety or as a reaction to his or her emotional state.

Discomfort with certain emotions can also affect sexuality. Two important factors related to sexual expression are a person's feelings about intimacy and lessening of control. The desire for intimacy, and apprehension about it, can significantly influence sexual encounters. An individual who experiences intimacy in a sexual relationship as threatening may have considerable sexual difficulty (Kaplan, 1979). On the other hand, being sexual with someone does not result in automatic intimacy. In fact, sexual encounters can be used to increase or decrease interpersonal closeness. For example, people can use their sexuality to increase warmth and involvement with another person or to express hostility and rejection. The second factor mentioned, the issue of control, also frequently contributes to the quality of a sexual experience. Arousal is usually accompanied by a reduction in control. For some people, this experience may provoke some anxiety, and they may inhibit their sexual response by maintaining control over their arousal.

Sexual Victimization   A traumatic sexual experience, such as rape or incest, may contribute to sexual difficulties. One study of 83 female sexual assault victims found that 56% experienced sexual problems as a result of the assault; fear of sex and lack of desire or arousal were the most frequently mentioned problems. Incest victims commonly reported never having experienced orgasm (Becker et al., 1982). Another study found that 71% of rape victims had decreased sexual activity four to six years after the assault (Burgess and Holmstrom, 1979).

Interpersonal Factors

Besides personal feelings and attitudes, there are a variety of interpersonal factors that can strongly influence the satisfaction or dissatisfaction couples experience from a sexual relationship. These factors often vary according to the couple and their particular circumstances. For example, one couple may find that an argument typically ends with passionate lovemaking, whereas another couple moves to separate bedrooms for a week after a disagreement.

According to the popular media, it would almost seem that our sexuality is separate from the context in which we express it. An abundance of movies, magazines, and novels perpetuates the belief that if we are "sexually liberated" we can turn ourselves on and off regardless of our feelings of the moment. It is sometimes jarring to realize that as real people, we cannot always relate this way. A lack of trust, dislike of a partner, boredom, fear, or rejection can easily lead to sexual dissatisfaction or disinterest. The dynamics of a whole relationship are highly significant in determining sexual satisfaction or dissatisfaction, and this fact is reflected in the strong emphasis in

sex therapy on working with the couple rather than the individual. Relationship problems, as an aspect of sexual functioning, appear to have become more severe over the last decade. For example, a sex therapy clinic that has used the same assessment technique to measure marital distress reports an increase in general relationship distress in the couples coming to the clinic for relationship/sexual therapy (LoPiccolo, 1980b). In many cases, a sexual difficulty is a symptom of a more general relationship problem.

How a person reacts to a partner's sexual problem can be extremely important. For example, demanding and critical responses to a lover's sexual difficulty may magnify the problem by increasing anxiety. Likewise, a sexual problem may become worse when one partner mistakenly interprets the sexual difficulty of the other to mean he or she "doesn't love me" or has a negative evaluation of his or her sex appeal or ability. As we will see in Chapter 17, an informed and caring response to a partner's difficulties may produce quite different results.

Many relationship issues can affect sexual satisfaction. Among the more important are ineffective communication, fear of pregnancy, and sexual orientation.

Ineffective Communication   Ineffective communication can contribute to and perpetuate sexual dissatisfaction. As we discussed in Chapter 8, verbal communication between partners is a basic tool for learning about needs and sharing desires. Without effective communication couples must base their sexual encounters on assumptions, past experiences, and wishful thinking—all of which may be inappropriate in the immediate situation.

A frequent source of communication problems is stereotyped gender roles—in particular, the myth that ". . . sex is exclusively the man's responsibility and that sexual assertiveness in a woman is 'unfeminine' " (Kaplan, 1974, p. 350). A woman who believes that it is not her "place" to tell her partner that she is or is not in the mood to make love, or that she would like another kind of stimulation (or any other sex-related desire), may find that their relationship becomes increasingly frustrating, simply because her partner does not know what she wants. How could he?

For many reasons—stereotyped gender roles, stereotyped images of romance, misplaced assumptions about the other person—couples sometimes operate under the belief that communication is unnecessary in a good sexual relationship. However, communicating sexual needs is often the first step in having them met. Communication is also the basis for the negotiation often necessary to reach compromises over individual differences.

Fears about Pregnancy   The fear of an unwanted pregnancy may interfere with coital enjoyment in a heterosexual relationship. A 100% effective temporary method of birth control is simply not available at this time. The reality is that unless one of the partners is surgically sterilized, there is a risk of impregnation, however small, in heterosexual intercourse.

Anxiety related to pregnancy may also stem from not using some method of birth control when a woman first begins to experience coitus. Studies indicate that a significant percentage of women have their first coital experiences without the protection of any reliable birth control method (Sorenson, 1973). A worker in a family-planning birth control clinic states:

It is very unusual to see a teenage woman come in for birth control advice *before* experiencing coitus. Typically she had been coitally active from several months to several years before assuming responsibility for contraception. (Authors' files)

If a couple uses no birth control, this may result in a pairing of intercourse with thoughts such as "I sure hope I don't get pregnant." It is not easy to enjoy sex with that concern in the back of one's mind.

An unwanted pregnancy has historically been the "punishment" for nonmarital sexual intercourse. If a woman experiences guilt about being sexual, it follows that she might expect consequences for her "transgression." Sometimes women may believe that simply being aroused or pleasured sexually can result in pregnancy:

When I was in high school, I would spend long hours making out. We wouldn't even touch each other's genitals. Although I *knew* how women got pregnant, and that I hadn't done what was necessary for a pregnancy to occur, I still worried that I might get pregnant, simply because I had been turned on. (Authors' files)

The relationship between pregnancy anxiety and arousal can sometimes be seen in women who are completely freed from the possibility of pregnancy through sterilization or menopause. It is not at all uncommon for sexual activity and desire to increase at this point.

On the other hand, fears about not being able to become pregnant can create sexual difficulties. Many couples who want to conceive and have difficulties with infertility often find that their sexual relationship becomes anxiety-ridden, especially if they have to modify and regulate the timing and pattern of sexual interaction to enhance the possibility of conception.

Sexual Orientation Another reason why a woman or man may not experience sexual satisfaction in a heterosexual relationship can be a preference to be involved with individuals of the same sex. It is understandable that a person with a homosexual orientation experiences sexual difficulty or a lack of satisfaction in heterosexual relations. Sexual difficulties with heterosexual partners are most likely to be considered problems by homosexual people who are attempting to conceal their orientation by relating sexually to partners of the other sex or by people who want to change their orientation to heterosexual. Although some progress has been made by gay rights groups, it is not accurate to state that a homosexual life style is accepted by our society. Following one's homosexual inclinations still involves severe societal pressures and repercussions, and many homosexual people attempt to "stay in the closet" and relate heterosexually in spite of their desire not to do so. Other individuals have a commitment and desire for the heterosexual relationships (often marriage) to continue and to be sexually fulfilling. Sex therapists are increasingly attempting to provide services for individuals and couples to resolve these complex difficulties (Gochros, 1978; Masters and Johnson, 1979).

Organic Factors

Organic or physiological conditions are estimated to be the primary cause of a sexual problem in 10%–20% of cases (Kolodny et al., 1979; Munjack and Oziel, 1980). In other situations, physiological factors contribute to a problem. Various illnesses, drugs, and physical problems—many of them seemingly unrelated to sexuality—can result in pain or discomfort during intercourse and can influence sexual interest, arousal, or orgasmic response. A person's psychological reaction to an organic disorder can often magnify or lessen its effect upon his or her sexual functioning. Consulting a physician may provide useful information about necessary sexual adjustments and options for people with temporary or permanent organic problems.

Illness   Illnesses and diseases of the neurological, endocrine, and vascular systems can interfere with sexual functioning. An illness that is painful or debilitating may inhibit sexual interest, or the illness itself may affect physiological sexual response. Surgical or medical treatments can also physically or emotionally impair sexual functioning. For example, people who undergo renal dialysis may have significant difficulty with sexual response.

Multiple sclerosis (M.S.) is a neurological disease of the brain and spinal cord, in which damage occurs to the covering of nerve fibers; vision, sensation, and voluntary movement are affected. The person with M.S. may experience reduction or loss of genital sensation, arousal, and orgasm, as well as uncomfortable hypersensitivity to genital stimulation.

Nerve damage or circulatory problems from diabetes can also cause sexual problems. Many diabetic men experience difficulty or inability in having an erection, and a few diabetic men ejaculate into the bladder. Women with diabetes may experience an absence of or decrease in the frequency of orgasm.

Rheumatoid arthritis is a progressive, systemic disease that results in inflammation of the joints. Chronic inflammation can cause pain, destruction of the joint, or reduced joint mobility. Nerves and muscle tissue surrounding the affected joints are also often damaged. Rheumatoid arthritis does not directly impair sexual response, but chronic pain and fatigue may lessen a person's sexual interest. Pain or deformities in the hands may also make masturbation difficult or impossible without assistance. Arthritic impairment of hips, knees, arms, and hands may interfere with certain intercourse positions.

Sexual problems following a heart attack are usually due to anxiety and misinformation rather than to organic causes. A person may be worried that sexual excitement will bring on another heart attack and consequently be fearful of and avoid sexual activity. The actual exertion of the heart during intercourse with a long term partner for a middle-aged married man is about the same as climbing two flights of stairs. Many physicians recommend that a person resume sexual activity with their usual partner once they are able to climb two flights of stairs comfortably (Wagner and Sevarajan, 1979). It is essential for a person who has had a heart attack to consult with his or her physician regarding the heart and sexual activity to secure individualized, accurate information.

In some cases, medication will cause sexual problems. For example, certain drugs used to treat gastrointestinal problems, some drugs prescribed for high blood pressure, and some medications used for psychiatric disorders may impair vaso-congestive and orgasmic response. Barbiturates and narcotics (heroin, morphine, codeine, and methadone) depress the central nervous system and can inhibit sexual response, and chronic alcohol abuse results in physiological disturbances that can cause a variety of sexual difficulties. Estrogen, sometimes used to treat prostate cancer or as replacement therapy after menopause, often decreases sexual interest. Birth control pills may also decrease sexual interest and arousal in some women.

It is important to remember that physiological factors can cause or contribute to sexual problems. We advise people who are concerned about a sexual problem to consult their physicians, especially if they have unsuccessfully attempted to resolve their difficulties by some of the methods described in these chapters. A sex therapist may also help direct a person to health-care facilities where he or she may obtain the appropriate exams and screening tests.

It may be desirable to have a general physical and a gynecological or urological exam to help rule out organic factors in sexual difficulties. Tests for diabetes, hormone problems, or other illnesses may be indicated, and special procedures have been developed to evaluate physical factors in erection problems. Instruments designed to measure penile blood pressure or thermography (measuring body heat of areas of the penis) can help evaluate possible vascular problems (Langone, 1981; Tordjman et al., 1980). A *nocturnal penile tumescence* (NPT) test can also be performed to help assess physiological erectile capability, although results of this procedure are not always conclusive and research on its effectiveness as a diagnostic tool is continuing (Hatch, 1981).

Painful Intercourse in Women The medical term for painful intercourse is *dyspareunia*. Experiencing pain with intercourse is very likely to affect a woman's sexual arousal. Coital discomfort stems from a variety of causes, and for this reason it is important for the woman to determine specifically where the pain is. Discomfort at the vaginal entrance or inside the vaginal walls is commonly due to a lack of adequate lubrication. Typically, this occurs because a woman has been insufficiently aroused. There are many reasons why a woman may not become aroused—a lack of effective stimulation, the myriad of cultural inhibitions that affect sexual responsiveness, or possibly relationship difficulties with her partner. Physiological causes, such as im-balance or insufficient amount of hormones, may also reduce lubrication. The use of a lubricating jelly may provide a temporary solution so that intercourse can take place comfortably, but this may bring only short term relief. It would no doubt be better if the woman could discover the cause of her discomfort, and then take steps to remedy the situation. A woman can consult a physician for help with physiological causes of this difficulty.

There are also a variety of other causes for vaginal discomfort during inter-course. Yeast, bacteria, and trichomoniasis infections cause inflammations of the vaginal walls and may result in painful intercourse. This is a circular problem: intercourse with insufficient lubrication irritates the walls and increases the possibility of vaginal infections. Foam, contraceptive cream or jelly, condoms, and diaphragms may irritate the vaginas of some women. Pain at the opening of the vagina may also be attributed to an intact hymen, a Bartholin's gland infection, or scar tissue at the opening.

Another area where there may be discomfort is the clitoral glans. Occasionally, smegma collects under the clitoral hood and may cause distress when the hood is moved during sexual stimulation. Gentle washing of the clitoris and hood may help prevent this.

Pain deep in the pelvis during coital thrusting may be due to jarring of the ovaries or stretching of the uterine ligaments. A woman may experience this type of discomfort only in certain positions or at certain times. Some women report that it only occurs around the time they are ovulating. Avoiding positions or movements that aggravate the pain is the first solution, and if a woman has more control of the pelvic movements during coitus, she may feel more secure in having intercourse and avoiding pain. If the discomfort is difficult to remedy, a physician should probably be consulted, for pain during intercourse can also be caused by medical problems.

Another source of deep pelvic pain is *endometriosis*, a condition in which tissue that normally grows on the walls of the uterus implants on various parts of the abdominal cavity. The endometrial tissue can prevent the internal organs from moving freely, resulting in pain during coitus. Birth control pills are sometimes prescribed to control the buildup of tissue during the monthly cycle.

Infections in the uterus, such as gonorrhea, may also result in painful intercourse. In fact, pelvic pain may often be the first physical symptom noticed by a woman who has gonorrhea. If the infection has caused considerable scar tissue to develop, surgical treatment may be necessary. Childbirth and rape may tear the ligaments that hold the uterus in the pelvic cavity; this may also result in pain during coitus. Surgery can relieve this difficulty partially or completely.

Painful Intercourse in Men   Dyspareunia in men is unusual, but it does occur. If the foreskin of an uncircumcised male is too tight, he may experience pain during sexual arousal and difficulty reaching orgasm. In such circumstances, minor surgery may be called for. Inadequate hygiene of an uncircumcised penis can result in the accumulation of smegma or infections beneath the foreskin, causing irritation of the glans during sexual stimulation. This problem may be prevented by routinely pulling back the foreskin and washing the glans area. Another possible source of pain or discomfort is *Peyronies disease*, where fibrous tissue and calcium deposits may develop in the space above and between the cavernous bodies of the penis. Medical treatments can sometimes be effective in treating this condition. Finally, infections of the urethra, bladder, and the prostate gland or seminal vesicles may induce burning, itching, or pain during or after ejaculation (Masters and Johnson, 1970). Proper medical attention can generally alleviate this source of discomfort during coitus.

DESIRE PHASE DIFFICULTIES

In the preceding pages, we have looked at a number of factors that may influence sexual functioning and cause difficulties. The remainder of this chapter deals with some of the specific problems people encounter. We will treat these problems according to whether they have to do with desire, arousal, or orgasm phases of sexual response. In reality, there is a considerable amount of overlap between them. Problems with desire and arousal also affect orgasm, and orgasm difficulties can easily have an impact on a person's interest and ability to become aroused.

The following types of sexual problems can vary in duration and focus from person to person. A specific difficulty can be of lifelong duration (primary) or occur after a certain time (secondary). Individuals may experience the problem in all situations with all partners (global) or exclusively in a specific situation or with one partner (situational) (Kaplan, 1977; LoPiccolo, 1980a).

Inhibited Sexual Desire

Inhibited sexual desire (ISD) is a common sexual difficulty experienced by both men and women. Kaplan (1979) describes it as a lack of "sexual appetite." ISD is characterized by a lack of interest in initiation and participation in sexual fantasy and activity. Inhibited sexual desire can be distinct from arousal and orgasm difficulties. In fact, some people who are uninterested in sex become aroused and experience orgasm when they engage in a sexual encounter. Others may experience pleasure from touching and physical closeness but have no desire for erotic excitement. Still others with inhibited sexual desire feel tension and anxiety with physical and sexual contact and do not experience arousal and orgasm.

Primary ISD is rare. People with this condition did not masturbate or exhibit sexual curiosity in childhood, and as adults they do not develop interest in sexual fantasy, sexual activity, or the sexual aspects of a relationship. More commonly, however, people develop secondary inhibited sexual desire at a specific point in their lives. In other cases, a person may experience ISD in a particular situation, such as with a spouse but not with masturbation or with a lover.

A precise definition of inhibited sexual desire is difficult to establish. First of all, there is great variety in the level of sexual desire from person to person. Second, lack of desire is a realistic response to many situations; when a sexual situation or partner is negative or disadvantageous, sexual interest normally diminishes. For example, it would be adaptive to lose sexual interest in a person one does not like, a partner with poor hygiene, or someone who is verbally or physically abusive (Kaplan, 1979). In general, inhibited sexual desire is most commonly presented as a problem when it causes distress in a relationship.

Common psychological and physiological factors associated with ISD are depression, severe stress, low testosterone levels, and certain drugs and illnesses. A marked decrease in or absence of sexual interest often accompanies depression. Severe life problems such as death in the family, divorce, or extreme family or work difficulties can create stress that results in lack of sexual interest, as can personal illness (Kaplan, 1979). Insufficient testosterone levels from surgical removal of testosterone-producing glands or medications that counter the action of testosterone can also reduce sexual desire. Other factors that negatively affect desire include narcotics, high doses of sedatives or alcohol, and certain high blood pressure medications.

Inhibited sexual desire sometimes occurs following prolonged frustration from lack of arousal and orgasm. By not being interested and avoiding sexual activity, the person protects him- or herself from experiencing embarrassment or a sense of failure from unsatisfying sexual experiences. For some couples, hostility or lack of trust or respect in a relationship may inhibit sexual desire. It is usually difficult to feel desire for someone who arouses strong negative feelings. The following anecdote describes this common situation:

> Over the years of our marriage my sexual desire for my wife has diminished gradually to the point that it is presently almost nonexistent. There have been too many disputes over how we raise the children, too many insensitive comments, too many demands, not enough freedom to be my own person. When I look at her I have to acknowledge that she is a remarkably beautiful woman, just as lovely as the day I was first attracted to her. I certainly feel no physical repulsion to her body. I guess it would be more accurate to say that I simply no longer have sexual feelings for her. One feeling I do have plenty of is hostility. I suspect it is this largely suppressed anger that has been the killer of my sexual interest. I wonder what it would be like if we could go back to the early years of our marriage when there were no children and the conflicts were few and the loving was good. (Authors' files)

One partner consciously or unconsciously may even use his or her lack of sexual interest and receptivity to punish or "get back at" the other. A person who is frequently pressured into engaging in sex or feels guilty about saying no may become less and less interested and feel increasingly diminished desire (Kolodny et al., 1979).

Some of the anxieties and conflicts that form the basis for ISD may be more complex. Some people may unconsciously be so fearful of sexual pleasure or intimacy that they prevent themselves from feeling sexual desire. They may have developed a "turn off" mechanism, described by Kaplan:

> Most of the patients I have studied tend to suppress their desire by evoking negative thoughts or by allowing spontaneously emerging negative thoughts to intrude when they have a sexual opportunity. They have learned to put themselves into negative emotional states . . . In this manner they make themselves angry, fearful, or distracted, and so tap into the natural physiologic inhibitory mechanisms which suppress sexual desire. (1979, p. 83)

Kaplan further explains that people are usually not aware of the active role they play in creating their inhibitions. Their lack of desire appears to emerge automatically and involuntarily, and they do not realize that they have control over the focus of their thoughts.

Some people with ISD either do not perceive or misperceive internal and external cues associated with sexual arousal. They may not have learned to notice their own genital sensations of arousal or to generate interest and arousal within themselves. They also tend not to notice the potential sexual nature of situations or to consider themselves as sexual people (LoPiccolo, 1980a).

Sexual aversion is characterized by extreme, irrational fear of sexual activity. Even the thought of sexual contact can result in intense anxiety. A person who experiences sexual aversion may exhibit physiological symptoms of sweating, increased heartbeat, nausea, or diarrhea as a consequence of their psychological fear. Both men and women experience sexual aversion, but it is more common among women (Kolodny et al., 1979).

Several factors appear frequently in the histories of people with sexual aversion. Severely negative parental sexual attitudes or a history of childhood sexual trauma, such as incest or sexual assault, are common. A pattern of constant pressuring, coercion, or bargaining for sex in a relationship can also precede the development of sexual aversion. Repeated unsuccessful attempts to please a sexual partner or "working at sex" to overcome a sexual difficulty may generate intense anxiety about sexual relations. Anxiety about unresolved conflicts in sexual identity or orientation may surface in anticipation of a sexual experience and also create intense fear (Kolodny et al., 1979).

AROUSAL DIFFICULTIES

Both men and women experience difficulties in sexual arousal. We will focus here on lack of vaginal lubrication in women and inability to secure or maintain an erection in men. These respective difficulties are particular to just one sex, but in many cases the reader may note similarities between the sexes in the origins of these conditions.

Inhibition of Vaginal Lubrication

As we saw in Chapters 4 and 6, vaginal lubrication is a woman's first physiological response to sexual arousal. The inhibition of lubrication is labeled as *general sexual dysfunction* by Kaplan (1974). Kaplan compares the lack of lubrication in a woman to the lack of erection in a man because in both cases sufficient vasocongestion does not occur. However, it is our opinion that the label "general sexual dysfunction" connotes that all aspects of a woman's sexuality are dysfunctional. Since she remains a sexual person, whether or not she experiences lubrication, and may enjoy touching and closeness, we prefer to use terms such as lack of lubrication or *inhibition of vaginal lubrication* to describe this situation.

For some women, inhibited lubrication is only an occasional problem. They become sufficiently aroused to experience lubrication in certain situations but not in others. Other women have never experienced vaginal lubrication during a sexual encounter. Biological factors, including low estrogen levels, can be a factor in lack of lubrication, and nonphysiological factors, such as the effects of years of learning not to experience sexual arousal, frequently contribute to this difficulty. Feelings of apathy, anger, or fear may also inhibit arousal and lubrication.

Lack of lubrication in a particular situation does not necessarily mean something is wrong. Vaginal lubrication frequently decreases during prolonged coitus. This may be due to lengthy stages of plateau levels of arousal (during the plateau phase, lubrication typically decreases). Or it may be the result of exclusive coital stimulation that may not be stimulating enough to induce continued lubrication. In the latter case, if continued sexual contact is desired, simultaneous manual stimulation of the clitoris or other parts of the body or changing to noncoital activities may increase lubrication.

Erectile Inhibition

The term most commonly applied to male erection difficulty is *impotence.* The origin of this word suggests the primary reason for our opposition to its use. It comes from a Latin word that, literally translated, means "without power." The implication is that a man without an erection is without power or potency as a lover. It is likely that a man who experiences lack of erection as a problem is often deeply anguished; the implication that a man is without value as a lover unless he is capable of penile erection contributes to this distress. As the following account indicates, however, this can be far from reality:

I met a man once whose erectile capacity was completely destroyed by a cord injury in the precise region of the lower spine where erectile function is controlled. While he couldn't get it up, he certainly had no trouble getting it on! I've often wondered if his acquired status of highly desired lover had something to do with his discovery that erections are not essential to meaningful sexual interaction. (Authors' files)

Instead of the term impotence, we will use the more descriptive phrase *erectile inhibition,* which adequately describes a major male difficulty without the implications just mentioned.

Erectile inhibition problems may be broadly classified into two types. Men with *primary erectile inhibition* have attempted but never experienced maintained penetration (either vaginally or anally) with a sexual partner during their entire lives, although they may routinely experience nighttime erections and have erections during masturbation.

The label *secondary erectile inhibition* is applied to the man who has previously had erections with his partner(s), but finds himself presently unable to consistently experience a functional erection. This condition is far more prevalent than primary erectile difficulty (Kaplan, 1974). It is common for men to occasionally be unable to achieve or maintain an erection due to minor factors like fatigue or stress. Masters and Johnson state that if a man is unable to have an erection in 25% or more of his sexual experiences, this label is appropriate for him. We believe that the percentage is not as important as whether the individual or couple sees this occurrence as a problem.

The underlying factors in erectile inhibition are many. Frequently, erectile problems are due to a combination of organic and psychogenic factors. Biological factors which may contribute to erectile difficulty include the effects of certain drugs (for example, alcohol, narcotics, amphetamines, and some prescription medications), severe diabetes, and a wide variety of anatomic, endocrine, vascular, cardiorespiratory, and infectious conditions (Kaplan, 1974; Masters and Johnson, 1970). A hormonal deficiency or imbalance can result in inability to attain erection. Erection difficulties can also occur as a result of medical problems that affect blood flow into the penis and constriction of penile venous system arteries and sphincters (Tordjam et al., 1980; Wagner et al., 1982).

Fatigue, worry, and relationship conflict typically produce only transitory episodes of erectile inhibition. However, occasionally these experiences may produce such concern and anxiety that they develop into a pattern. His own anxiety, his partner's response, or the combination of the two turn a transitory difficulty into a serious problem for an individual or a couple. The composite case presented in Box 16.1, drawn from several such cases we have dealt with over the years, illustrates some of the ways psychological factors can escalate a situational difficulty.

Another common precursor to secondary erectile inhibition is a history of rapid ejaculation (described at the end of this chapter). If a man has developed a lot of anxiety about ejaculating too soon, he may become very susceptible to erection difficulties.

Occasionally, a traumatic first sexual experience can cause erectile inhibition. A response from a man's partner that he interprets as an attack on his self-worth may be particularly damaging. The following account illustrates this situation:

I was with this woman for the first time. Other than being a little nervous, I was really looking forward to a good time. When I took my clothes off my penis was still soft (the room was cold!). She said, "Where is it!" Well, let me tell you, she didn't see much that night. Neither did anyone else for quite awhile. It even took a long time for me to feel comfortable again about undressing in full view of my partner. (Authors' files)

ORGASM DIFFICULTIES

The problems we have been discussing have primarily been ones of desire and arousal. Some other sexual difficulties specifically affect orgasmic response, and a variety of different problems are reported by both men and women. Some of these are either the infrequency of orgasms or their total absence. Others involve reaching orgasm too rapidly, or have to do with delayed climaxes. Sometimes a partner may fake orgasm to conceal its absence.

Anorgasmia

The term *frigidity* has been used as a general, descriptive label for female sexual problems including lack of interest, arousal, or orgasm. It is both imprecise and pejorative, mistakenly implying that women with these difficulties are totally sexually unresponsive and emotionally cold or unloving. Many sexuality educators and therapists now use the word *anorgasmia*, meaning the absence of orgasm.

Women who do not achieve orgasm may experience arousal, lubrication, and enjoyment from sexual contact. However, their sexual response does not increase to the point of experiencing orgasm. Some women who do not have orgasms enjoy

BOX 16.1 A CASE STUDY IN PSYCHOLOGICALLY BASED ERECTILE INHIBITION

The following case is a composite of several actual situations described to the authors by students and clients. At the end are some questions that may prove helpful as you analyze both the source(s) and potential remedies for the difficulties encountered by this hypothetical couple.

Bill and Karen attended a party, during the course of which she became quite angry over his lack of attention. As the evening wore on, her anger mounted, ultimately resulting in an argument with Bill. On the drive home, neither talked. Both felt somewhat responsible, but neither was willing to apologize. Bill was actually feeling some guilt over his actions and was determined to make up in bed. At the same time, he was still angry at Karen. He brought these conflicting feelings to bed with him and was unable to get an erection. Now Karen became openly angry and suggested that Bill's present ineptness, together with his earlier indifference at the party, clearly indicated a lack of caring on his part. He feebly assured her that such was not the case, that he was just tired, and that everything would be back to normal the next time. But would it really be fine the next time? This question bothered him as he lay awake long after Karen had fallen asleep by his side.

Next day he could think of little else. "I have got to make it right tonight—must show her that I still care." However, as the evening approached, his anxiety mounted. By the time he was driving home, the pressure was really intense. He stopped at Joe's Bar for a drink or two to soothe his growing fears. Finally, after an evening spent trying to appear casual and collected on the outside, while inwardly worried and apprehensive, it was time for bed—time for him to function as a lover.

Instead of being spontaneously swept away by the passions of lovemaking, his mind remained focused on his penis, willing it to respond and to become erect. He had now become a spectator to his own performance, cursing his flaccid penis, sick with frustration and concern over Karen's response to his repeated failure. Unexpectedly, but perhaps more damaging, her reaction was not overtly accusatory. Rather she simply withdrew in brooding silence, leaving him alone with his acute misery. At this point, he was on the merry-go-round of the failure-fear-failure syndrome.

Some questions for analysis:

1. What does this case illustrate about the relationship between emotional conflicts and sexual sharing?
2. In what ways do you think Bill and Karen's expectations of love and intimacy may have contributed to the development of their shared problem?
3. How might this situation have been averted?
4. What do you think Bill and Karen could do to resolve their sexual problem?

sexual encounters. Many others are highly disappointed and distressed. They view their lack of orgasm as failure, and the lack of physical release from orgasm results in experiences that are less and less enjoyable.

Anorgasmia can be primary, secondary, situational, or coital. A woman who has *primary anorgasmia* has never experienced orgasm by masturbation or with a partner. *Secondary anorgasmia* refers to a woman who has previously experienced orgasm but no longer does so. A woman who has *situational anorgasmia* experiences orgasm rarely or in some situations but not in others; for example, where a woman is orgasmic with masturbation but not with a partner. *Coital anorgasmia* refers to women who are orgasmic with manual or oral partner stimulation but not during intercourse.

It is rare for anorgasmia to be due to physiological causes. However, conditions that impair the vascular system or nerve supply of the genital area can inhibit orgasmic response. Disorders of the endocrine system or chronic illnesses can also interfere with arousal and orgasm.

Primary anorgasmia is quite common; surveys indicate that approximately 10% of adult women in the United States have never experienced orgasm by any means of self- or partner stimulation (Hite, 1976; Kaplan, 1974; Kinsey, 1953). This 1-out-of-10 figure is especially noteworthy when compared with the number of men who have never experienced orgasm in their lifetime. Because it is assumed that males have orgasms, the question is rarely even asked. Nevertheless, some men are totally nonorgasmic, although the incidence is extremely rare.

There are some indications that the number of primary anorgasmic women is decreasing, and some sex therapy clinics are seeing a smaller percentage of women with primary anorgasmia as their presenting problem (LoPiccolo, 1980b). This apparent decrease may be due to the accessibility of excellent self-help books for women who want to learn to experience orgasm.

Women with primary anorgasmia often lack knowledge of their sexual response patterns that others have learned through self-stimulation. Few of these women masturbate. Lacking masturbation experiences, a woman misses a potentially important opportunity to learn about and become comfortable with her orgasmic response. Most men have had these initial learning experiences provided by self-stimulation.

The absence of routine orgasm during coitus without additional manual-clitoral stimulation is not an unusual pattern for many women. The Hite Report (1976) asked women if they routinely experienced orgasm during coitus without simultaneous manual stimulation of the clitoral area; only 30% responded that they did. Another study found that less than half—44%—of 141 women attending human sexuality workshops usually or always experienced orgasm during intercourse without simultaneous manual clitoral stimulation (Ellison, 1980). Kaplan states, "There are millions of women who are sexually responsive, and often multiply orgasmic, but who cannot have an orgasm during intercourse unless they receive simultaneous clitoral stimulation" (1974, p. 397). The reason for this, as we have seen in Chapter 4, is that for many women the indirect clitoral stimulation during coitus is less effective than direct manual or oral stimulation of the clitoral area.

During coitus, the clitoris may be stimulated indirectly in two ways. First, coital thrusting can create tension of the labia minora which extends to the clitoral hood.

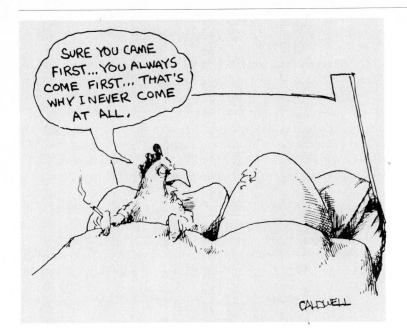

Clitoral stimulation thereby occurs from pressure and movement of the hood (Masters and Johnson, 1966). Second, pressure on the mons and clitoral area from the partner's pubic bone may provide stimulation (Hite, 1976; Masters and Johnson, 1966). Although this indirect clitoral stimulation is often not sufficiently intense to result in orgasm, most women, as indicated in *The Hite Report*, report intercourse to be highly enjoyable and desirable.

   The Hite Report does raise an important question about a definition of sexuality that says women must have orgasms during intercourse. In her view, we should not be asking why women aren't having orgasms from intercourse, "... but rather: Why have we insisted women should orgasm from intercourse? And why have women found it necessary to try everything in the book, from exercises to extensive analysis to sex therapy to make it happen?" (Hite, 1976, p. 236). Once again, this issue reflects the sex-equals-coitus model of sexuality, which is inadequate in indicating how to provide effective stimulation for female orgasmic release.

   Unfortunately, many women believe there is something wrong with them for not responding to such a model—even though it does not fully take into account their physiological needs. The painfully asked question, "I come when he touches me but not when he's inside me. What's wrong with me?" is very common. Women who require clitoral stimulation to reach orgasm may feel pressured to fake climax at the "appropriate" moment. In addition, they may be reluctant to ask for or engage in manual stimulation or to request noncoital stimulation after their partner ejaculates.

   Besides lack of clitoral stimulation, insufficient duration of coitus is another factor that may contribute to lack of orgasm during intercourse. This is especially true if a woman's partner has difficulty with controlling his ejaculation. Worry about whether coitus will last long enough can also inhibit arousal. Given the nature of the direct stimulation of the penis on the vaginal walls versus the indirect clitoral stimulation from the hood and pubic bone pressure, it is logical that, unless modifications are incorporated, the male will often reach orgasm more rapidly than his partner.

A less frequently expressed difficulty is the lack of orgasm from manual or oral stimulation by a partner. Some women prefer and respond more readily to stimulation from intercourse, and the internal stretching and pressure sensations from intercourse can trigger orgasm (Ellison, 1980). On the other hand, lack of orgasm from partner manual or oral stimulation can be rooted in negative attitudes about self-stimulation that affect feelings about noncoital stimulation from sexual partners.

Another frequent factor in nonorgasmic response with a partner may be ineffective sexual techniques; many women have not requested or received effective stimulation by a partner. Lack of self- or partner stimulation is not always the cause, however, and supplying stimulation does not always solve what may be a more complex problem. Experiencing orgasm usually involves a lessening of conscious control. Feelings of anxiety, fear, anger, or guilt about her sexual expression, situation, or relationship can interfere with a woman's willingness to "let go," and this can inhibit orgasmic response. The woman may be ambivalent about the relationship or have negative feelings about her partner. A woman who does not want to lose control of her feelings or behavior in front of her partner may consent to sexual interaction while simultaneously saying no to orgasm. Performance pressure to have an orgasm can also interfere with her arousal; anxiety about having an orgasm may diminish the pleasurable sensations that create it.

Rapid Ejaculation

An orgasm difficulty that is common to men is *rapid ejaculation*. We define rapid ejaculation as consistently reaching orgasm so quickly that it either significantly lowers subjective enjoyment of the experience and/or impairs a partner's gratification. This definition eliminates arbitrary time "goals," takes into account the partner's pleasure, and views the person's own subjective needs as an important determinant of what constitutes reaching orgasm too fast. While it is true that most people encounter this common problem during heterosexual coitus, too-rapid climax is sometimes a difficulty in homosexual relationships or noncoital heterosexual activity. Thus, speed of response may be considered an issue whenever people, including women, reach orgasm sooner than they want to during sexual activity.

While there are no statistics establishing exactly how many people experience premature orgasm, it is an extremely common problem among men in our society. Masters and Johnson state that it is the most prevalent sexual problem of men, estimating that millions are troubled by it. In anonymous surveys of students enrolled in our human sexuality classes over the last several years, we have consistently found that less than 25% of men report that premature ejaculation is never a problem. One-quarter of our male students report it to be an ongoing difficulty, and the other 50% is distributed between these two extremes. Comparable data obtained from our women students reveal that approximately 32% reach orgasm sooner than desired at least occasionally, with 8% reporting it to be a common occurrence.

Biological factors, such as an overly sensitive penile glans, are rarely the primary cause of this difficulty. However, a low amount of vaginal lubrication can increase friction of the penis during intercourse and cause rapid ejaculation (Steege, 1981). Men with rapid ejaculation often have fewer orgasms in a given time period and may ejaculate at a lower level of arousal than men who do not experience rapid ejaculation (LoPiccolo, 1980b). Usually, past experiences are more likely to contribute to the pattern of rapid ejaculation—for instance, striving to reach orgasm quickly to alleviate anxiety or to demonstrate sexual prowess.

In our society, early sexual experiences—both coital and noncoital—are frequently anxiety producing and thus completed as quickly as possible. For many men, self-stimulation is not a relaxed, leisurely episode of discovery and delight but is often a brief and furtive experience designed solely to release sexual tension:

Masturbation for me consisted of jerking off in the shower as fast as possible (no lock on bathroom door) or under the covers at night, holding my breath and making certain no weird groans signaled my solitary vice. (Authors' files)

Perhaps less significant, but by no means uncommon, is the adolescent male practice of group masturbation, often referred to graphically as a "circle jerk." Typically, several friends get together to see who can ejaculate first. After "Ready, set, go," the quickest finisher wins. Such experiences may provide peer-group esteem for a person who is able to ejaculate rapidly.

Young people often have their first sexual encounters in an atmosphere that is not at all conducive to relaxed exploration. It has been reported that an individual's first heterosexual coital experience takes place most commonly in either the home or the back seat of an automobile. Both settings can establish patterns of anxious and pressured sexual expression. A typical scene in the home might involve a young couple ostensibly watching Johnny Carson, while furtively having intercourse on the living room sofa, one ear listening for the sounds of distant stirring (what a time for Dad to decide to have a late night ham sandwich!). The back seat of a car is often no better. Consider the following account:

When I was young, the logical choice of locations for sexual intimacy was the local lovers' lane, a tall butte in the middle of suburbia we called "the rock." The county sheriff's department took their role as protectors of the public morality quite seriously, patrolling this area with precision regularity, every 7 to 10 minutes as I recall. The criterion for not being hassled was two or more heads visible. Quite obviously, one's capacity for relaxed sharing was seriously damaged by such close scrutiny unless he or she was content to restrict the evening's activities to stargazing! (Authors' files)

Situations like these may have powerful conditioning effects since the sexual activity often generates anxiety over possible discovery. The completion of intercourse (typically, the male's ejaculation), aside from any sexual pleasure accompanying it, is reinforcement in itself: the sooner ejaculation occurs, the quicker will be the relief from the unpleasant state of anxiety. Such early experiences may establish a strong tendency toward rapid ejaculation and this inclination can be quite difficult to overcome later on in life.

Any one or a combination of the situations just outlined may lead to prematurity difficulties, and anxiety may further strengthen the pattern. This is particularly true in situations where the individual or couple attempt changes that result only in additional, frequently magnified, failures. The consequent anxiety often promotes muscle tension (myotonia) which tends to hasten orgasm.

Rapid Orgasm in Women Women, too, may be troubled by rapid orgasms. The problem of female prematurity has not received a great deal of attention, but conversations with colleagues, students, and friends have convinced us that some women do have concerns about too-rapid orgasms. This may present a difficulty, especially when the woman reaches orgasm before her partner and does not want to continue (women sometimes find that their clitoris or vulva becomes extremely sensitive after orgasms).

More commonly, female prematurity may happen when a woman feels the pressure to experience orgasm sooner than she desires:

Sometimes when we make love, with him using his mouth to pleasure me, and I'm really getting into it, bang, he wants me to come just like that! I mean, sometimes I just want to lay back, fantasizing and enjoying, making it last and last: When he says 'What's the matter, what am I doing wrong?' it really ruins it for me. He's not doing anything wrong with his mouth. It's the head trip he is laying on me—like I've got to produce the big O instantly or his ego or masculinity will be threatened. All I want to do is enjoy for awhile. Is that asking too much? Why does lovemaking have to be so product-oriented? (Authors' files)

Unlike rapid ejaculation, we have found that often only the woman is aware of and concerned about her prematurity. Considering the emphasis on sexual performance in our society, it is unlikely that female orgasm, regardless of the speed with which it occurs, would be viewed with concern by most male partners. Quite the contrary, as the preceding account illustrates, a man might even view his partner's rapid orgasm as a sign of his skill as a sexual partner.

Ejaculatory Inhibition

Ejaculatory inhibition, sometimes called retarded ejaculation, generally refers to the inability of a man to ejaculate during coitus. Unlike premature ejaculation, it is a relatively uncommon condition. However, some clinicians think that mild forms of this difficulty may actually be quite prevalent (Kaplan, 1974).

Most men who are troubled by retarded ejaculation are able to reach orgasm by masturbation or by manual or oral stimulation by their partner. In some cases, however, a man may not ejaculate at all during a sexual encounter, as revealed in the following account.

I began a sexual relationship several months ago with a man who has a problem I've never before encountered. He has no difficulty getting an erection. In fact, he usually seems real excited when we make love. But he never comes. The first time I thought it was great—he seemed to be able to go on forever. But, after awhile it started getting to me. I've tried everything—going down on him, using my hand, stroking his scrotum when he is inside me—nothing works. He doesn't want to talk about it, but I sense he is as frustrated as I am, maybe more. Once I got him to admit he climaxes when he masturbates. Why can't he come with me? (Authors' files)

Many researchers and therapists distinguish between primary and secondary ejaculatory inhibition. Primary ejaculatory inhibition includes men who have never been able to experience intravaginal ejaculation. Most of these are capable of ejaculation, outside the vagina through stimulation by a partner, or through masturbation. However, there are extremely rare cases of men who have never experienced ejaculation in their entire lives (Kaplan, 1974).

When retarded ejaculation develops in a man who has a past history of normal ejaculatory functioning, it is classified as *secondary ejaculatory inhibition*. A variation of this is *partial ejaculation*. Here, the man experiences the sensations of ejaculatory inevitability but fails to have the strong muscle contractions and intense pleasure associated with the expulsion stage of orgasm. Instead of spurting out, the semen seeps from the penis during such a "half" orgasm. Chronic partial ejaculation is very rare. However, many men report having this experience occasionally, particularly when they are tired or under stress. Sometimes when a man is trying to delay ejaculation he will go "one stroke too far" and experience a seeping emission rather than a full orgasm.

Ejaculatory inhibition may be related to a variety of factors. In isolated cases, the problem is associated with a physical condition. Disease may cause damage to the neurological structures that coordinate ejaculation, and certain prescription drugs used in the treatment of emotional problems or hypertension have occasionally been known to induce retarded ejaculation.

Far more frequently, ejaculatory inhibition has a psychological cause. Some of the more common psychological factors are guilt over sexual activities (often stemming from strict religious training), conflict with a partner, fear of the partner's pregnancy, and lack of interest in or dislike for a partner. Masters and Johnson (1970) report instances in which men dislike their partners so much that they attempt to frustrate them by withholding their ejaculate. If the couple is involved in a high-conflict relationship (particularly one in which the man often feels overpowered or dominated), his retarded ejaculation may represent an act of defiance or rebellion in the power struggle.

Occasionally, retarded ejaculation may be traced to a particularly traumatic event early in a man's sexual development. For example, he might have suffered severe punishment at the hands of a parent after being discovered masturbating, or perhaps he had been acutely embarrassed when intercourse in a car was interrupted by a law officer's spotlight. The ejaculatory response may also be inhibited later on by association with a psychologically painful experience. Masters and Johnson (1970) report one case in which a man discovered his wife having intercourse with her clandestine lover. His first view of the scene was seminal fluid dripping out of her vagina. While the marriage was maintained, the man was no longer able to ejaculate intravaginally. Apparently, he felt that his wife's vagina had been made unclean by the other man's semen, and he could not tolerate the thought of allowing his seminal fluid to mix, even symbolically, with her lover's ejaculate.

Faking Orgasms

A final orgasmic difficulty we will discuss is *faking orgasms*, pretending to experience orgasm without actually doing so. This kind of sexual deception is typically discussed in reference to women, and it happens quite often. According to a recent survey of female students in our sexuality classes, 62% have faked an orgasm at some time. This statistic is comparable to Hite's 1976 findings.

Unlike some of the other difficulties discussed in this chapter, faking orgasm reflects a conscious decision. A person is often motivated to engage in such deception by pressures to perform that are either real or imagined, as the following brief comments reveal (all are statements made by women):

> He feels badly if I don't have an orgasm during intercourse, so I fake it, even though I have real ones from oral sex. (Authors' files)

> I get tired of intercourse after a certain period, and there he is, still pumping away, determined not to stop until I come, so I pretend to climax. (Authors' files)

> I don't know my partner well enough to tell her what I like, but I don't want her to think it's her fault that I don't come. (Authors' files)

> I figure if I don't have orgasms with him, he'll go find someone who does. (Authors' files)

> I started our sexual relationship faking, and I don't know how to stop. (Authors' files)

Although some women may find faking orgasm to be an acceptable solution in their individual situation, others find that faking itself becomes troublesome, as in the last of the preceding comments.

In recent years we have heard an increasing number of reports of men faking orgasms. Some of this behavior may be related to feeling pressured to reveal virility through multiple orgasmic responses, as revealed in the following account:

> Sometimes when I am having sex I feel like my partner wants me to perform like an orgasm machine, pumping them out in rapid succession, both hers and mine. Recently, I was with a woman who kept asking, "Has it happened for you, yet?"—and this after I had already come once and was doing good just to get it up again. Occasionally, in these situations I just fake it. I figure since I've come once already, she won't know the difference. Also, it is hard for me to admit that one or maybe two orgasms is all that I can produce in a given session. (Authors' files)

Chapter Sixteen: The Nature and Origins of Sexual Difficulties

Occasionally, a man who has difficulty with ejaculatory inhibition may fake orgasms in an attempt to hide the problem from his partner. This creates another problem in itself, however, for ". . . if their deception is to be successful, they must either forego orgasm altogether or masturbate in solitude later, after their wives are asleep" (Kaplan, 1974, p. 320).

There is often a vicious circle involved in faking orgasms. The person's partner is likely not to know that his or her partner has pretended to climax. Consequently, the deceived partner continues to do what he or she has been led to believe is effective and the other partner continues to fake to prevent discovery of the deception. This makes it more difficult for the couple to talk about and to discover what is gratifying to both of them.

How to best change this pattern of interaction is a matter of personal decision. Some people may not want to change, because faking orgasms serves a purpose in a relationship. For those who do, it would be helpful to communicate sexual needs rather than succumbing to the initial pressures to deceive. Once established, however, a pattern of deception may be quite difficult to break. A person faced with this situation might decide to discontinue faking orgasms without discussing the decision with his or her partner. Under such circumstances, some of the procedures for enhancing sexual pleasure outlined in the next chapter might prove helpful. Another alternative would be to inform one's partner of such past activity and to discuss the reasons why pretending to climax seemed necessary. Some of the communication strategies outlined in Chapter 8 may help this process along. Maybe some specific difficulties will surface as the motivation for deception (such as female orgasm problems, retarded ejaculation, and so forth). It may be helpful or perhaps necessary to engage a counselor to help communicate with a partner; this may also facilitate efforts to establish more rewarding sexual behaviors.

VAGINISMUS

Vaginismus is characterized by strong involuntary contractions of the muscles in the outer third of the vagina (see Figure 16.1). The contraction can be so strong that attempts at inserting a penis into the vagina are very painful to the woman. A woman with vaginismus will usually experience this same contracting spasm during a pelvic exam. Even the insertion of a finger into her vagina can cause great discomfort.

Masters and Johnson (1970) state that vaginismus is often linked with chronic painful intercourse, repeated erectile difficulties of a woman's partner, strong orthodox religious taboos about sex, a homosexual orientation, past physical or sexual assault, or feelings of hostility or fear toward a partner. It is important to note that although a woman who experiences vaginismus can learn to prevent the contractions, she does not consciously will them to occur. Rather, they are a conditioned, involuntary response to fearful, painful, or conflicted situations or feelings. When a woman experiences physical pain from vaginismus, she will probably be anxious about pain occurring the next time she attempts intercourse. Her apprehensions will increase the

FIGURE 16.1 CONSTRICTION OF VAGINAL MUSCLES
DURING VAGINISMUS

521

Vaginismus, characterized by strong involuntary contractions of the
muscles in the outer third of the vagina, is a relatively uncommon
sexual difficulty.

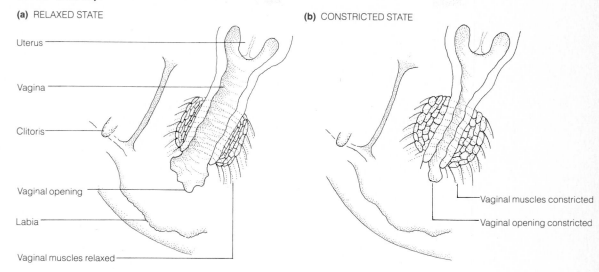

(a) RELAXED STATE   **(b)** CONSTRICTED STATE

Uterus

Vagina

Clitoris

Vaginal opening

Labia

Vaginal muscles relaxed

Vaginal muscles constricted

Vaginal opening constricted

likelihood of involuntary muscle contractions, and when her expectations are once
again met, she will be even more anxious on subsequent occasions.

The incidence of vaginismus is believed to be very low. Some women who
experience vaginismus are sexually responsive and orgasmic with manual and oral
stimulation. However, since to most couples coitus is a highly important aspect of their
sexual relationship, this difficulty typically causes great concern.

The preceding discussions have outlined a picture of some of the reasons people
encounter dissatisfactions, problems, or discomfort in what can be an experience of
great pleasure and joy. It remains for us to explore ways of preventing or overcoming
these difficulties. This will be our focus in the next chapter.

SUMMARY

ORIGINS OF SEXUAL DIFFICULTIES

1. Cross-cultural variations in sexual attitudes and
behaviors reflect the powerful impact of culture and
society on sexuality.

2. The acquired attitude of sex-as-sin and negative
feelings about one's genitals can be detrimental to
acceptance of one's body and sexual feelings.

3. The double standard prescribes opposite
expectations of sexual behavior for males and
females.

4. The cultural notion that "real sex" equals coitus
often limits the erotic potential of sexual interaction.

5. A goal orientation toward sexual expression can
increase performance pressure.

6. Sexual knowledge, self-concept, and emotional difficulties are personal factors that may affect the motivations and decisions individuals make regarding their sexuality.

7. Ineffective communication can often inhibit sexual satisfaction.

8. Factors such as fear of pregnancy or a homosexual orientation can negatively affect heterosexual experiences.

9. Illnesses, drugs, and painful intercourse are organic difficulties that can interfere with sexual response.

DESIRE PHASE DIFFICULTIES

10. Inhibited sexual desire (ISD) is characterized by a lack of interest in sexual fantasy and activity. ISD sometimes stems from fear of sexual intimacy.

11. Sexual aversion is an extreme irrational fear of sexual activity.

AROUSAL DIFFICULTIES

12. A lack of vaginal lubrication indicates an inhibition of the vasocongestive response.

13. Erectile inhibition can be primary (never having completed vaginal or anal penetration) or secondary (previously able to attain and maintain erections).

ORGASM DIFFICULTIES

14. A primary anorgasmic woman has never experienced orgasm by any means of self- or partner stimulation.

15. The term secondary anorgasmia refers to a woman who has experienced orgasm but no longer does so.

16. Situational anorgasmia describes a woman who can experience orgasm in one situation but not another, such as during masturbation but not with a partner.

17. Coital anorgasmia refers to women who have orgasm with their partners but not during intercourse. Coitus primarily provides indirect clitoral stimulation and for many women is not sufficient to result in orgasm.

18. This text defines rapid ejaculation as reaching orgasm so quickly as to significantly reduce enjoyment of the experience or to interfere with the partner's gratification.

19. Many men establish patterns of ejaculating rapidly from hurried masturbation, "circle jerks," and furtive sexual experiences.

20. Ejaculatory inhibition is the inability of a man to ejaculate (usually during coitus).

21. Both men and women fake orgasm. Pretending may perpetuate ineffective patterns of relating.

VAGINISMUS

22. Vaginismus is an involuntary contraction of the outer vaginal muscles.

Belliveau, Fred, and Richter, Lin. *Understanding Human Sexual Inadequacy*. New York: Bantam, 1970. A conversationally written analysis of Masters and Johnson's work with sexual problems.

Hite, Shere. *The Hite Report*. New York: Dell, 1976. A compilation of 3019 women's responses to open-ended questions about female sexuality and Hite's analysis of the information. The book illuminates many of the struggles and joys women experience in dealing with their sexuality.

Slater, Phillip. "Sexual Adequacy in America." *Intellectual Digest*, November 1973. An excellent article that points out how our society places more importance on orgasm than on pleasure and the difficulties this emphasis presents.

Zilbergeld, Bernie. *Male Sexuality: A Guide to Sexual Fulfillment*. Boston: Little, Brown, 1978. An exceptionally well-written and informative treatment of male sexuality including such topics as sexual functioning, self-awareness, and overcoming difficulties.

17

Increasing Sexual Satisfaction

THE PLISSIT MODEL OF SEX THERAPY
    Permission
    Limited Information
    Specific Suggestions
    Intensive Therapy
SELF-KNOWLEDGE
    Self-Awareness
    Self-Stimulation
SHARING WITH A PARTNER
    Communicating Feelings and Problems
    Sensate Focus
    Active-Receptive Communication Exercise
    Self-Stimulation with a Partner Present
SPECIFIC SUGGESTIONS FOR WOMEN
    Becoming Orgasmic: Strategies for Women
    Experiencing Orgasm with a Partner
    Dealing with Vaginismus
SPECIFIC SUGGESTIONS FOR MEN
    Lasting Longer
    Dealing with Erectile Difficulties
    Reducing Ejaculatory Inhibition
TREATMENT FOR INHIBITED SEXUAL DESIRE
GUIDELINES FOR SEEKING PROFESSIONAL ASSISTANCE
    Selecting a Therapist
    Fees and Ethics
SUMMARY
SUGGESTED READINGS

*T*his chapter focuses on approaches in sex therapy and methods for increasing sexual satisfaction. The activities we discuss may be pursued individually or by a couple; they range from expanding self-knowledge to sharing more effectively with a partner. Much of what follows embraces our belief that all of us have the potential for self-help. The various suggestions offered here have proved helpful in the lives of many people. However, the same techniques do not work for everyone and exercises often need to be individually modified. Furthermore, professional help may be called for in those cases where individual efforts, couple efforts, or both do not produce the desired results. Recognizing that counseling is sometimes necessary to promote change, we have included guidelines for seeking sex therapy in the last section of this chapter.

THE PLISSIT MODEL OF SEX THERAPY

There are many approaches to sex therapy. However, most sex therapies have several elements in common. The PLISSIT model of sex therapy (Annon, 1974) specifies four levels of treatment; each successive level provides increasingly in-depth therapy. PLISSIT is an acronym for permission, limited information, specific suggestions, and intensive therapy.

Although PLISSIT describes formal levels of sex therapy, many people find similar kinds of help in informal ways. A trusted friend saying, "I feel the same way, too," a lover enjoying our body in spite of our insecurities about size or shape, a television interview with someone in a situation similar to ours, or books we read at the "right time" can give us needed permission and useful information and suggestions.

Permission

A therapist can play an important role in reassuring clients that thoughts, feelings, fantasies, desires, and behaviors that enhance their satisfaction and do not have potentially negative consequences are normal. Helping individuals and couples to appreciate their unique patterns and desires instead of comparing themselves with friends or national averages of frequency is sometimes all the help they need. Another aspect of this level of therapy is giving people permission *not* to engage in certain behaviors unless they choose to do so. For example, a therapist can support a person's desire to set limits about sexual relationships, not have orgasms with *every* sexual encounter, or not engage in an undesired sexual activity.

Limited Information

In the limited information level of treatment a therapist provides the client with information that is specific to his or her sexual concern. A person can use information, as well as permission, to change thoughts and feelings that impede his or her sexual satisfaction. Information that helps a person to view sexuality as positive and to think, talk, and fantasize about sex is a major component in treatment of many sexual problems. Factual information about concerns with penis size, clitoral sensitivity, or effects of medications on sexual response can alleviate anxiety and problems related to lack of knowledge.

Specific Suggestions

Specific suggestions are the activities and steps that therapists recommend to clients to help them reach a goal. Many of the suggestions in this chapter are similar to techniques that a sex therapist would use in treatment. Most are designed to reduce or eliminate anxiety, enhance communication, and to teach new, arousal-enhancing behaviors. Self-stimulation techniques, sensate focus, and the squeeze technique described later in this chapter are examples of specific suggestions common in sex therapy. A therapist may also suggest that a client read books that give permission, information, and specific suggestions. In fact, some therapists ask potential clients to read certain books before their first therapy appointment. In some cases, an appropriate book can help resolve problems so that therapy is no longer needed. In others, it can enhance the therapy process (McGovern, 1982).

Intensive Therapy

If a client's problem has not been resolved by the first three therapy levels, intensive therapy may be required. According to Annon (1974), intensive therapy is needed in about one out of 10 sexual problem cases. These are likely to be situations in which personal emotional difficulties or significant relationship problems interfere with sexual expression.

Let us now look at some of the methods for enhancing sexual satisfaction. As we noted, many of these are similar to techniques used in the course of sex therapy. They can also be used on one's own to enhance sexual awareness and satisfaction and to add variety to a sexual relationship.

SELF-KNOWLEDGE

During childhood the sexual development of many people may be influenced by the effects of negative conditioning, limiting attitudes, and a lack of self-exploration. All of these factors can hinder sexual enjoyment or functioning. Increased self-knowledge may help to modify some of these negative preconceptions and feelings. With this in mind we briefly outline procedures for improving awareness of your body and of activities that provide the most pleasurable stimulation.

Self-Awareness

People who know themselves—their sexual feelings, their needs, and how their bodies respond—are often better able to share this valuable information with a partner than are those who are unaware of their sexual needs and potentials. A good way to increase comfort with and knowledge about our sexuality is to become

well-acquainted with our sexual anatomy. It is not unusual for women to report having never looked at their own vulvas. While men may not feel quite so alienated from their bodies, many are not comfortable with their genital structures. The following anecdotes reveal the extent of this lack of knowledge and negative feelings that some people experience:

The first time I looked at my vulva, I was about nine years old. I was sitting on my bed, looking at the different parts and trying to make sense out of what it was all for, when I saw this shiny little bump. My first thought was that I had a growth that was probably cancer. After I touched it for a while, I decided it couldn't be cancer because it felt so *good!* (Authors' files)

I find it very difficult to undress in the presence of my lover. I guess this has a lot to do with how I feel about my body. Everytime I look at my genitals in the mirror I think "My God, how ridiculous they look. Here is this funny little shriveled up thing hanging between my legs." It doesn't look much better when erect. I can't remember when I first got the idea my genitals were dirty. I even perfected a technique where I could unzip and whip it out without touching the nasty little thing. (Authors' files)

We strongly recommend becoming familiar with your genitals by looking and touching as a process for increasing comfort with your body. It can be helpful to include all areas of your anatomy, not just the genital region. Examine yourself visually and experiment with different touches, perhaps using a massage lotion to make the movements more pleasant.

Some people find that knowledge obtained during self-exploration exercises may later be shared with a partner. Explorations of one's own body may provide the motivation to apply the same process to exploring and examining the body of a partner. Exchanging information can be immensely valuable in increasing both comfort with and knowledge about each other. A later section, "Sensate Focus," elaborates on mutual exploration.

Self-Stimulation

Self-stimulation is an effective way for a person, male or female, to learn about and experience sexual response. It is a time that can be enjoyed for itself, and the knowledge acquired can be shared with a partner. Many people have some negative feelings about masturbation that intrude on sensations of pleasure. Changing these negative attitudes and increasing self-knowledge may take some time, but the rewards can be worth the effort.

There are many variations of self-stimulation, and you can experiment to find what is most enjoyable. Some people think of masturbation as making love to themselves. They treat themselves as they would a special lover, with soft lights, music, clean sheets, fragrant oils, and lots of time to develop arousal slowly and tenderly. It may be helpful to include several erogenous zones. Concentrate your stroking on areas that feel particularly pleasurable. While lubricating materials like body lotion, oil, or saliva will often improve sensations, women should be careful to avoid using any non-water-soluble lubrications (such as vaseline) in the vagina.

If you choose to experiment with these self-stimulation exercises, it is important to remember that the major purpose of the experience is to become more aware of your body's sensations. You may find it helpful to experiment with several positions. Some people find that lying on their back is best; others prefer to stand or sit. To enhance the sensual experience, many people use sexual fantasy. Further information on self-stimulation has been provided in Chapter 9, and there is more discussion later in this chapter in the section titled "Becoming Orgasmic: Strategies for Women." This discussion is written specifically for women for whom self-stimulation may be particularly helpful in overcoming orgasmic difficulties. However, it may have applicability for men, too. In the next few paragraphs, we will look at ways of sharing exploration and problem-solving with a partner.

SHARING WITH A PARTNER

A variety of sexual activities shared with a partner may enhance one's sexual potential. The activities suggested here include both communication and touching exercises that may improve the overall quality of a couple's sexual sharing. In later sections we will discuss methods for dealing with specific sexual difficulties of either sex. Many of these suggestions are equally applicable to either heterosexually or homosexually oriented couples. Some specific approaches for homosexual individuals, similar to those developed for heterosexual couples, are outlined in Masters and Johnson's recent publication, *Homosexuality in Perspective* (1979).

The suggestions we offer may be most helpful to couples who feel trust and warmth for each other. Difficulties with interpersonal conflict or lack of caring can interfere with the potential benefits of the various exercises we will outline, and counseling may be needed to help resolve such relationship problems.

Communicating Feelings and Problems

Before discussing specific ways of dealing with sexual difficulties, we want to stress again the importance of communication. Many people find it difficult to talk about the sexual area of their relationships, but failure to communicate needs and expectations can hinder the resolution of sexual problems and may even contribute to some difficulties.

One of the primary benefits of sex therapy, whether it is learning to have orgasms with partners, how to overcome rapid ejaculation, or almost any other shared problem, is that couples participating together in the treatment process often develop more effective communication skills. The following account, from one of our students, reflects this potential benefit:

When you first discussed the "squeeze technique" [discussed later in this chapter] in class, I was excited to try it out with my partner. However, I didn't know how to talk about it. It wasn't like he had never mentioned his problem before. He would say he was sorry he was so fast, and that maybe it would get better with time. Finally, I asked him to come to class with me the day you showed the film demonstrating the technique. Man, did we do a lot of talking after it was over. He was anxious to give it a try, and we felt that with your lectures and the movie, we could do it on our own. At first we made some mistakes, like not doing enough sensate focus and him waiting too long to tell me to put the squeeze on. In fact, it was only when we were really talking openly that things began to work well. He showed me how he liked to be stimulated, things he had never told me before. During sensate focus we shared a lot of feelings. He became much more aware of my needs and what I needed to be satisfied. We really started getting into a lot of variety in our lovemaking, whereas before it had usually consisted of just kissing and intercourse. By the way, the squeeze technique did work in slowing him down, but I think the biggest benefit has been breaking down the communication barriers. Now the talking is almost as fun as the doing and it sure makes sex a whole lot better! (Authors' files)

Communication itself may not solve a sexual difficulty. It is, however, a very important element, for it is helpful not only in working out a specific problem but also in establishing and maintaining mutual understanding that can make a relationship stronger.

Sensate Focus

One of the most useful couple-oriented activities for mutually enhancing sexual enjoyment is the *experience of sensate focus*. Masters and Johnson labeled this technique and use it as a basic step in the treatment of many sexual problems. It can be extremely helpful in reducing anxiety from goal orientation and increasing communication, pleasure, and closeness. It is by no means a technique only appropriate for sex therapy but is rather an option for all couples. The following guidelines may be modified to fit your personal needs.

The setting you choose for experiencing sensate focus is important. Find a quiet place, free of ringing telephones and noisy doorbells—a special place just for the two of you. Set the mood in a way that makes each of you comfortable—perhaps some soothing music, candles, a crackling fire in the fireplace.

The sensate focus experience requires that one partner be the "giver" and the other the "receiver." For the first session, decide who will be the giver and who will be the receiver. If it is difficult to arrive at a mutual decision, simply flip a coin. After both partners remove all their clothes, the one who is the receiver stretches out in a comfortable position and allows the giver to gently caress, touch, and explore his or her entire body, as shown in Figure 17.1. Explore everywhere, remaining attuned to your partner's response to your touch. Avoid concentrating on specific goals such as producing sexual arousal or orgasm. In the first few sessions, Masters and Johnson

FIGURE 17.1 SENSATE FOCUS

The process of sensate focus, whereby partners sensually explore each other's body, can contribute to the mutual enhancement of a couple's sexual enjoyment.

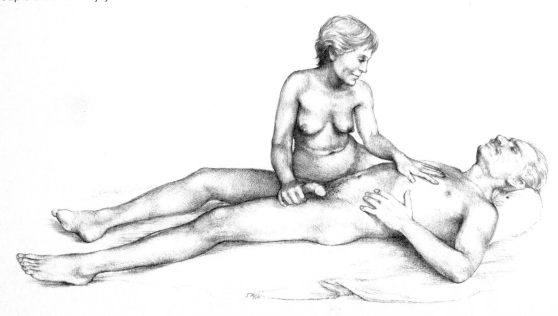

have their patients touch all over the body, excluding the genitals. After the couple experiences comfort and pleasure with this step, nondemand touching of the genitals is included in the total body sensate focus.

Allow yourself to experience the pleasure of both giving and receiving. Both verbal and nonverbal reactions may be helpful in indicating your preferences for location and intensity of touching. Be sure to let your partner know if you find something unpleasant or distracting and ask for things you enjoy.

Continue the caressing for as long as it feels good to both of you. Rather than reversing your roles during the same session, it is often preferable to wait until next time to change roles. We make this suggestion because many people have difficulty completely surrendering to the sensual pleasuring by another when they feel the necessity to "keep track of how many minutes I owe them when my turn is over."

Sensate focus is an excellent way to learn to respond erotically with all areas of the body. It is also a good vehicle for learning the exquisitely sensitive areas on the bodies of partners. We strongly recommend it, not only as a way to begin sexual intimacies, but also as an ongoing practice to enhance sexual sharing and maintain total body sensuality.

Active-Receptive Communication Exercise

A technique related to sensate focus is *active-receptive communication*. This exercise can help couples learn to communicate about sensations more effectively. It can be beneficial to practice communicating about touching each other by first experimenting with a nongenital area. Decide on a part of your body that is comfortable for both of you—the hand, the foot, or the back of the neck, for instance. This is the area you will focus upon, following these steps:

1. Touch and explore your partner in ways that are pleasurable to your hand. Notice the different textures and colorations. Experiment using your lips, tongue, face, hair, and other parts of your body to give caresses.
2. Continue touching as the receiving partner gives continual verbal feedback regarding how the touching feels and what kinds of stroking she or he desires.
3. The receiving individual, when desiring a specific kind of caress, communicates this by guiding the partner's hand with his or her own hand.
4. Trade active and receptive roles and repeat the preceding three steps.

When both partners are comfortable with these steps, repeat the process, substituting genital touching, oral sex, or both, to help establish effective communication in these areas.

An excellent position for genital caresses is to rest your head on your partner's thigh while you visually, manually, or orally explore his or her genitals. Another common position is for the giver to sit upright on a bed, back against the cushioned headboard or pillows. The receiver then sits between the giver's legs with the receiver's back resting against his or her partner's chest, as shown in Figure 17.3.

Self-Stimulation with a Partner Present

It can be particularly valuable for couples to let each other know what kind of touching they find arousing. Masturbating in the presence of a partner may be a way to share this kind of information (Figure 17.2). A woman describes how she accomplished this:

> When I wanted to share with my partner what I had learned about myself through masturbation, I felt super uptight about how to do it. Finally, we decided that to begin with, I would be in the bedroom and he would be in the living room, knowing I was masturbating. Then he would sit on the bed, not looking at me. The next step was for him to hold and kiss me while I was touching myself. Then I could be comfortable showing him how I touch myself. (Authors' files)

Couples who feel comfortable incorporating self-stimulation into their sexual relationship open many options for themselves. When one of them feels sexual and the other

FIGURE 17.2 SELF-STIMULATION WITH PARTNER PRESENT

Masturbating in the presence of a partner can be an effective way for an individual to indicate what kind of touching she or he finds arousing.

does not, that person can masturbate with the other present, perhaps touching, perhaps kissing. This may sometimes lead to more shared sexual activity:

Occasionally, when I don't feel like having sex my wife will coax me into taking a shower with her while she masturbates with the shower head massager. Sometimes it's just nice to hold her and feel her respond. Other times, watching her getting turned on gets me going and we end up making love in the shower. (Authors' files)

The experiences suggested in the preceding pages may all be helpful in increasing sexual satisfaction, whether an individual or couple have a specific difficulty or whether the goal is to find out more about themselves. Beyond these general exercises, though, there may be particular sexual difficulties that can be highly troublesome. Specific exercises or techniques can sometimes aid in reducing or overcoming these problems. A number of difficulties were described in Chapter 16, and in the remainder of this chapter, we will look at some strategies that have been used to deal with them. For purposes of clarity and easy reference, these difficulties are organized according to whether they are primarily female or male sexual problems. As in the discussions of sexual difficulties in the previous chapter, however, we should stress that these discussions are not only applicable to one gender. Men can gain some understanding of both themselves and female partners from reading the section on specific female difficulties; and women can gain similarly from reading the discussions about difficulties and techniques for men.

SPECIFIC SUGGESTIONS FOR WOMEN

The following paragraphs suggest procedures that may be helpful to women in learning to increase sexual arousal and to reach orgasm by themselves or with a partner and also in dealing with vaginismus.

Becoming Orgasmic: Strategies for Women

Learning effective self-stimulation is often recommended for women who have never experienced orgasm. One advantage to self-stimulation is that a woman without a partner can learn to become orgasmic. For a woman with a sexual partner, becoming orgasmic first by masturbation may help to develop a sense of sexual autonomy that can increase the likelihood of satisfaction with a partner.

Therapy programs are based on progressive self-awareness activities that a woman does at home between therapy sessions. The step-by-step activities are often presented by a therapist in a small group of women who want to learn to experience orgasm. Women in the group also provide each other with support and encouragement. These same steps are also used in individual sex counseling. Both individual and group counseling for anorgasmic women can provide information, permission-giving, and individualized problem-solving.

Another source of guidance for learning to experience orgasms comes from books such as *For Yourself: The Fulfillment of Female Sexuality* by Lonnie Barbach (1975) or *Becoming Orgasmic: A Sexual Growth Program* by Julia Heiman and Leslie and Joseph LoPiccolo (1976). The following is a brief outline of the steps in the self-discovery group therapy program adapted from Barbach's book:

1. *Time commitment.* Set aside one hour every day to do the "homeplay" exercise.
2. *Mirror exercise.* Using a full-length mirror, look at your nude body from all angles. Examine uncritically the shapes, colorations, and textures of the different areas.
3. *Body exploration.* Using your hands, and body lotion or powder if desired, explore your entire body, from your face to your toes. Take lots of time and focus on the feelings in your fingertips and your body. Notice differences in sensation. Compare having your eyes open and closed.
4. *Vulva self-exam.* Locate and explore the different structures of the vulva. Learn and practice Kegel exercises (outlined in Chapter 4).
5. *Self-stimulation.* Find and use a lotion or oil which contains no alcohol and is water soluble. Use this on your vulva to enhance the touch sensations. For the first several sessions, experiment and discover genital touches which are pleasurable, but do not attempt to reach orgasm. It's very important to remove the goal orientation of orgasm at this point. If you feel yourself becoming very aroused, reduce the stimulation. Then begin again, allowing yourself to become slightly more aroused than previously. Focus on the pleasurable sensations. Allow yourself to have erotic fantasies if you so desire. Experiment with Kegel squeezes during stimulation.
6. *Orgasm.* Once you are becoming aroused from self-stimulation and believe you want to proceed to orgasm, continue the touching that is most arousing. If interfering thoughts or feelings arise, allow yourself to be aware of them and then refocus on the sensations. If you experience difficulty "letting go," it may be helpful to try acting out an orgasm—exaggerate the movements and sounds you associate with orgasm.
7. *Use of a vibrator.* Vibrators are a potentially pleasurable option for self-stimulation. They are sometimes used to help an anorgasmic woman experience sexual climax for the first time. A vibrator is often less tiring to use and supplies more intense stimulation than the fingers. For women who have not experienced orgasm after a couple of weeks of daily self-stimulation exercises, using a vibrator is sometimes recommended. The more intense stimulation may help her have her first orgasm so she knows that she can experience this response. After she has a couple of orgasms with the vibrator, it would be helpful to stop using it and return to manual stimulation so she learns to respond in this manner, too. This is important because it is easier for her partner to replicate a woman's own touch than the stimulation of a vibrator. Changing back to manual stimulation will facilitate learning to have orgasms with a partner.

If following these exercises does not result in orgasm and this concerns you, that does not necessarily mean that something is "wrong." It may be that you could benefit by reading more. The books listed earlier should be helpful, and your sexuality course teacher may have other suggestions. Counselors are also available, as mentioned earlier, to answer questions and provide more personal assistance. Sharing discoveries with a partner may be another area to explore.

Experiencing Orgasm with a Partner

As we saw in Chapter 16, origins of difficulties in reaching orgasm may be highly complex, involving conditioning and experiences of which a person may not even be consciously aware. This is one reason why any step-by-step guidelines for learning to reach orgasm should be thought of as aids, not solutions. The steps that follow are intended for couples. They are based on techniques developed in a therapy context.

After the couple is comfortable with the sensate focus exercises described earlier, they proceed to genital exploration. The exercise is called a *sexological exam.* Each partner takes turns visually exploring the other's genitals, locating all the parts discussed in Chapters 4 and 5. After looking thoroughly, they experiment with touch, noticing and sharing what different areas feel like (Barbach, 1975).

The next step is for the woman to stimulate herself in her partner's presence. The woman can use self-stimulation methods that she has learned are effective and share her arousal or orgasm with her partner. Her partner can be holding and kissing her or lying beside her, as was shown in Figure 17.2. This step is often a difficult one, and some women begin by asking their partners to be in another room while they are masturbating. Slowly, as the woman determines she is ready for the next step, her partner can be progressively closer and more involved (Barbach, 1975).

Nondemanding manual-genital pleasuring is now begun by the partner. The couple can do this in any position that suits them. Masters and Johnson (1970) recommend the position illustrated in Figure 17.3. The partner leans slightly back, propped with pillows. The woman sits between her companion's legs with her back supported by her partner's chest. The woman places her hand over the partner's hand on her genitals to guide the stimulation. A lotion or oil can be used to increase sensation. Her partner is to make no assumptions about how to touch, but rather to be guided by the woman's words and hand. The purpose of initial sessions is for the partner to discover what is arousing to the woman rather than to produce orgasm. If the woman thinks she is ready to experience orgasm, she indicates to her partner to continue the stimulation until climax is achieved. Orgasm will probably not occur until after several sessions.

There are several specific techniques that couples can use to increase a woman's arousal and the possibility of orgasm during intercourse. The first has to do with initiating intercourse. Rather than beginning intercourse after a certain number of minutes of "foreplay" or when there is sufficient lubrication, a woman's own feeling of what might be called "readiness" can be the signal. Not all women may experience this feeling of readiness, but for those who do, beginning intercourse at this time may enhance the resultant erotic sensations.

FIGURE 17.3 BACK-TO-CHEST POSITION FOR GENITAL SENSATE FOCUS

A woman who wants increased stimulation during coitus may benefit from direct manual stimulation of her clitoris (see Chapter 9, Figures 9.6 and 9.8). This often results in greater arousal and sometimes in orgasm. The female-on-top intercourse position is commonly used in this situation. After both partners are aroused—the man with an erection and the woman with adequate lubrication—and feel ready for intercourse, she sits astride and guides his penis into her vagina. She remains motionless for several moments, allowing both of them to be aware of sensations. Then she begins slow, exploring pelvic movements with the intention of discovering what is pleasurable to her. Her partner is to be receptive to her movements rather than actively initiating his own (Masters and Johnson, 1970). *The Hite Report* emphasizes the importance of female-initiated movements:

Orgasms during intercourse in this study usually seemed to result from a conscious attempt by the woman to center some kind of clitoral area contact for herself during intercourse, usually involving contact with the man's pubic area. This clitoral stimulation during intercourse can be thought of then as basically stimulating yourself while intercourse is in progress. Of course, the other person must cooperate. This is essentially the way men get stimulation during intercourse. They rub their penises against our vaginal walls so that the same area they stimulate during masturbation is being stimulated during intercourse. In other words, you have to get the stimulation centered where it feels good. (Hite, 1976, p. 276)

Additionally, a woman can experiment with positions and pelvic thrusts that create more intense internal sensations.

The next step is for the woman to stimulate her clitoris manually during intercourse. She may also use a vibrator, as is shown in Figure 17.4. Some men report the vibrations transmitted to their penis as pleasurable. Then she teaches her partner to touch her clitoris (Barbach, 1975). One way for him to be able to touch her clitoris is to turn his hand slightly and use his thumb. The side-to-side coital position also works well for either of them to touch her clitoris. The woman may also find it helpful to experiment with Kegel exercises during penetration.

After several sessions of the woman's controlling pelvic movements and incorporating manual stimulation, the man initiates nondemanding thrusting. Experimen-

FIGURE 17.4 THE USE OF AN ELECTRIC VIBRATOR FOR
CLITORAL STIMULATION DURING COITUS

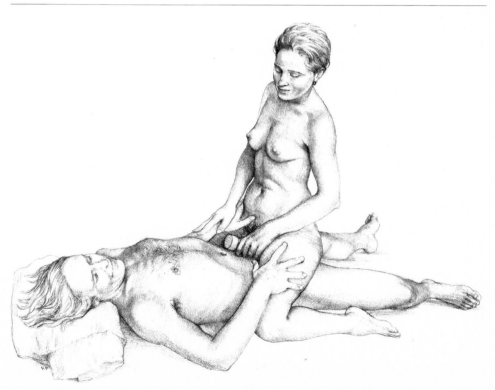

tation with other coital positions can be included. Some couples may wish to experiment with reaching orgasm without direct clitoral stimulation. Kaplan (1974) suggests the use of the *bridge maneuver*. In this, manual stimulation during intercourse is employed until the woman is very close to orgasm. Then manual stimulation is stopped and she actively moves her pelvis to provide sufficient stimulation to induce orgasm. In using maneuvers like the "bridge," we caution against deciding arbitrarily that this technique might be "better" than techniques that involve continuing manual stimulation to orgasm. As Kaplan comments:

> We reassure her and her husband that their reliance on clitoral stimulation to achieve orgasm is a normal and authentic response. . . . We emphasize that it is possible for partners . . . [who use these techniques] . . . to have a gloriously rich and fulfilling sex life, providing neither feels that this is an inferior mode of sexual expression. We try in this way to undo the myths surrounding "vaginal" orgasm and the unrealistic ideal of invariable simultaneous orgasms and universal female orgasm on intercourse.
> (pp. 398–99)

The techniques just described are useful in exploring ways of relating sexually, and they may allow a woman to experience orgasm in some cases. A number of books are available for couples who want more information than we have had space to present here; some of these are listed in the "Suggested Readings" at the end of this chapter.

Dealing with Vaginismus

Treatment for vaginismus usually begins during a pelvic exam, with the therapist or a consulting physician demonstrating the vaginal spasm reaction to the couple. The woman is then sometimes given relaxation and self-awareness exercises to do in the privacy of her own home. These include a soothing bath, general body exploration, and manual external genital pleasuring. The next steps pertain specifically to resolving the vaginismus. She puts some lubricant, such as K-Y Jelly, at the vaginal opening and practices inserting a fingertip gently into her vagina. This may take several sessions. Once she can do this comfortably, she inserts her entire finger into the vaginal canal. After relaxing with her finger inside, she is to consciously contract and relax the vaginal muscles as with Kegel exercises. The next step is for her to insert two, then three, fingers and continue to practice vaginal muscle contractions and relaxation. Dilators, cylindrical shapes of graduated sizes, which the woman inserts into her vagina, are also sometimes used to accustom the vaginal muscles to stretching. Once she can comfortably insert one size, she allows it to remain in her vagina for several hours. Concurrent with these "homeplay" exercises she will meet with her therapist to discuss her reactions.

After she has completed the preceding steps her partner joins her in "homeplay" assignments. He visually examines her vulva and proceeds to insert his fingers or dilators following the same steps she did. Open communication between the couple is essential during these steps. After the man can insert three fingers with no vaginal muscular spasm, the couple continues to the next step, vaginal-penile penetration.

The penis and vaginal opening are well lubricated. The woman slowly guides her partner's penis into her vagina. Once the penis is inside the couple remain motionless while she experiences vaginal containment of the penis. After a few moments, he withdraws his penis. This will be repeated and as they continue to be comfortable with penetration, pelvic movements and pleasure focusing will be incorporated. Masters and Johnson (1970) report 100% success in alleviating vaginismus using this method. However, more current research indicates that vaginismus can be difficult to treat successfully, especially in relationships in which couples have never had penile-vaginal intercourse (LoPiccolo, 1982).

SPECIFIC SUGGESTIONS FOR MEN

In the following paragraphs we outline methods for dealing with the common difficulties of rapid ejaculation and erectile inhibition. We also discuss a way of treating the less common condition of ejaculatory inhibition. As in the preceding discussion of women's sexual difficulties, we caution that the origins of such problems are complex and that solutions are frequently not simple. Again, we refer readers who are interested in pursuing this topic to "Suggested Readings" and also to the discussion about therapy assistance at the end of this chapter.

Lasting Longer

Although rapid ejaculation is a common dissatisfaction, the probability for positive change is quite good. Most professional sex therapists use a multiphased program that focuses on the stop-start or squeeze techniques. These successful approaches to learning ejaculatory control are quite easy to implement, even, in some cases, without professional guidance. There are also simpler strategies for helping to delay ejaculation, and we will discuss these first. Women readers and men for whom rapid ejaculation is not a problem may find the following discussion valuable simply because they would sometimes like sexual interactions to last longer.

Ejaculate More Frequently   Men with rapid ejaculation problems sometimes find that they can delay ejaculation when they are having more frequent orgasms. If partner sex is not a viable option, frequent masturbation to orgasm can be helpful.

Change Positions   Excessive muscle tension is detrimental to a man who ejaculates rapidly. All things being equal, increased myotonia is typically associated with a rapid sexual response cycle. Aside from certain exotic acrobatic positions, the male-on-top position is about the worst way to have intercourse for a man who wants to delay ejaculation. This is particularly true if he subscribes to Alex Comfort's (1972) definition of a gentleman: "A gentleman is defined as one who takes his weight on his hands" (p. 135). The muscle tension from supporting his own weight as he thrusts results in a more rapid ejaculation.

Many men gain a desirable amount of control by lying on their backs (see Figure 9.6 for variations of female-on-top positions). An important point to note is that this position by itself is not sufficient; another essential aspect is relaxation. One couple reported to us a lack of success in applying this suggestion. In fact, the male partner's orgasm was occurring more rapidly than before. Closer questioning revealed that he was maintaining his old custom of energetic pelvic movements. Thus, he was moving not only his own weight but that of his partner as well, increasing muscle tension to even higher levels than before. Encouraged to relax totally during coitus, he found that he was able to prolong intercourse. Both partners were then able to fully enjoy what had once been a fleeting and anxiety-ridden experience.

Immediate results do not always follow this position modification. Sometimes a man will experience a degree of increased arousal, stemming from the novelty of this position, that will temporarily counteract its tendency to delay ejaculation. Also, his partner may be more responsive, and he may be further excited by the increased opportunity to observe her reactions. However, after some experience with this change in position, he often experiences the advantages of increased relaxation.

"Come Again!" In view of our earlier discussion of the male refractory period, it is clear that sexual activity that follows initial male orgasm will not typically be characterized by rapid ejaculation. However, few men or their partners consider or explore the potential for slowed responsiveness after first climax. This is largely due to the belief that male orgasm is the end point of sexual interaction. Many men might be pleased with the results of exploring the potential for continued interaction.

Talk with Each Other Communicating during coitus may help the couple prolong the experience. It is often essential to slow down or completely cease movements if climax is to be delayed. A partner may find it difficult to anticipate the precise moment to reduce or stop stimulation unless she or he is clearly informed by the other.

Some men find that intercourse can be maintained for very long periods of time if they allow sexual tension to rise and fall between plateau and excitement phase levels of arousal. Not uncommonly, men report an added sense of control that comes with repeated episodes of going to the brink of orgasmic release, reducing stimulation to allow tensions to subside somewhat, and then moving once again to the edge. Often, time and practice facilitate this modulated form of activity, particularly if the partners continue to communicate.

Consider Alternatives In minimizing performance anxiety about rapid ejaculation (and most of the other problems discussed here), it is often useful to think of intercourse as just one of the several options for sexual sharing. Many people have discovered that reaching orgasm during intercourse is not necessary to pleasure, particularly if other successful methods of orgasm-producing stimulation are used. Occasionally, a man will find that manual stimulation, oral-genital contact, using a vibrator, and so forth will reduce his performance anxiety enough to considerably improve his staying power. It can be comforting to know that there are many options for obtaining and giving sexual pleasure. It is also important to realize that an activity may be very enjoyable even when it does not produce orgasm.

Have a "Small Orgasm"   According to Masters and Johnson and many other researchers, when a man reaches the point of "ejaculatory inevitability" (synonymous with the emission stage of orgasm, described in Chapter 6), nothing can be done to avert a complete ejaculation. However, there is more recent evidence that some men have the ability to shut down the second stage of ejaculation, right at its beginning, to experience what amounts to a minor or "small orgasm." This typically takes the form of one or two muscle contractions and a small amount of seminal fluid emission. Such an experience is often later marked by the continued ability to keep a complete erection and increased ejaculatory control. A full ejaculation almost always occurs following the initial small orgasm(s) but often after a significantly protracted period of coital activity.

We have surveyed several hundred of our male students about the occurrence of small orgasms. Ten to 15 percent have consistently reported this phenomenon in their sex lives; some practice it with a high degree of regularity. Of this group, many have remarked on the "staying power" advantages of having small orgasms. Some students have experimented with this response after first learning about it in class. In the following account one male student relates his experience:

Probably the most fascinating and informative piece of classroom information I learned and was able to put into practice was the fact that an orgasm and an ejaculation can be two different functions. This is interesting because I had always associated an orgasm with expulsion of semen, and could hardly comprehend a male continuing sexual intercourse after ejaculation. (Authors' files)

I first experimented in this area with masturbation. At the point of climax, I would relax the muscles in my penis and slightly apply pressure as if trying to urinate. The feeling was good, and some semen was released. I was able to do this a total of three times before reaching a complete orgasm. The amount of semen released each time was less than my usual ejaculation; however, the total amount expelled was greater than ever before. (Authors' files)

My wife and I are very much alike in degree of sexual excitement. However, there are times—as was mentioned in class—when one of us needs to prolong the excitement level in order to reach an orgasm together. There was such an occasion, just awhile back, where I reached the plateau level much faster than my wife. I then applied the same technique experimented with in masturbation. I was able to ejaculate twice before reaching a full orgasm. This tended to increase my wife's excitement, which increased my arousal, shortly allowing us to reach an orgasm together. Wow, it worked! (Authors' files)

The reports we have received are only tentative evidence, and experimental investigation is needed to find out more about small male orgasms and their incidence. However, enough men have spoken convincingly of the benefits of small orgasm to convince us that it does deserve further evaluation. At present, our best suggestion is for personal exploration and experimentation, either with a partner or during masturbation.

The Stop-Start and Squeeze Techniques   The method most commonly associated with treatment for rapid ejaculation is the *squeeze technique* popularized by Masters and Johnson (1970). Their approach is a modification of a technique developed earlier by James Semans (1956). Semans, a urologist, hypothesized that rapid ejaculation stems from a man's lack of awareness of the neuromuscular sensations that precede orgasm and ejaculation. The man who ejaculates rapidly, for whatever reasons, has not noticed this sensory feedback, yet such awareness is essential to bringing any reflex function under control.

Working from this assumption, Semans developed a stop-start technique. This technique is learned in several training sessions, and is designed to prolong the sensations prior to orgasm, thereby affording the man a chance to become acquainted with, and ultimately to control, his ejaculatory reflex. The partner is instructed to stimulate the man's penis, either manually or orally, to the point of impending orgasm. At this time, stroking is stopped until the preejaculatory sensations subside.

The strategy advocated by Masters and Johnson follows essentially the pattern developed by Semans, with the added component of squeezing the penis. When the man is on the brink of orgasm, he signals his partner to cease stimulation and to squeeze. Figure 17.5 illustrates the proper application of this technique. As indicated, the thumb is placed on the frenum and two fingers are positioned on the other side of the penis, one above and one below the corona. Strong pressure must then be applied for a few seconds until the man loses the urge to ejaculate. (At the same time, a portion of his erection is typically lost.) Sometimes, two hands are required to apply sufficient pressure. This squeezing will not cause pain or injury, and occasionally, his partner needs to be assured of this. A man with rapid ejaculation can place his fingers directly over his partner's fingers, demonstrating how hard to squeeze to produce the desired results. After applying the squeeze, his partner should refrain from further stimulation for a period of 15–30 seconds. While a variety of positions can be used during these training sessions, most commonly couples will use an approach approximating that shown in the figure.

Masters and Johnson have introduced another type of squeeze technique, called the *basilar squeeze*. After the man has practiced with the regular squeeze technique and has developed some ejaculatory control, either the man or woman can apply firm pressure on the top and bottom of the base of the penis. This has the advantage of not requiring the man to remove his penis from the vagina during intercourse to apply the squeeze.

It is generally suggested that training sessions such as those just described last around 15–30 minutes and occur as often as once a day, for several days or weeks. During each session the couple repeats the stimulation and squeeze or stop-start procedure several times and then allows ejaculation to occur on the last cycle. At the same time, the couple should reach an agreement about sexual stimulation and orgasm for the man's partner. If this is desired, they can engage in noncoital activity.

A man undergoing this procedure will usually experience immediately observable benefits. As his ejaculatory control improves appreciably, the couple progresses

FIGURE 17.5 THE SQUEEZE TECHNIQUE FOR
TREATMENT OF RAPID EJACULATION

543

(*Top*) The position couples assume during initial training session
with this method, (*lower left*) the proper gripping of the penis for
applying the squeeze technique, and (*lower right*) the basilar
squeeze.

to coital interaction employing the woman-astride position shown in Figure 17.6. This position is especially well-suited for this stage because a slight shift of the woman's pelvis permits the man's penis to be withdrawn so the squeeze can be applied. The couple can also stop moving if they are using the stop-start technique. This technique is continued as the man experiences progressive improvement. In most cases the man is able to learn to prevent a too-hasty orgasm (Masters and Johnson report a 98% success rate).

A major advantage of Seman's stop-start technique and "squeeze" variations is the almost inevitable improvement of communication that results when two people treat rapid orgasm. As Masters and Johnson note, "Aside from the obvious control improvement, the greatest return from use of the squeeze technique is improved communication both at verbal and non-verbal levels for the marital unit" (1970, p. 105).

Recently it has been demonstrated that a man can benefit from using the squeeze technique on himself during solo sessions of masturbation. However, to gain the full returns of improved communication, we encourage couples to share in this experience whenever practical.

We have considered several approaches to overcoming the problem of premature ejaculation. Although couple-oriented approaches such as the stop-start and the squeeze technique have the advantages of leading to better communication and cooperation, any of the other suggested avenues of change may be enough to reduce or resolve this difficulty, and combinations of techniques are often even more effective. [However, do not combine the squeeze technique and having a "small orgasm" because there is some chance of rupturing the seminal vesicle (LoPiccolo, 1982).] For example, it is unlikely that a man will experience a hasty climax during intercourse when he is relaxing in the male supine position, and at the same time, recovering from the refractory effects of an earlier orgasm shared with his partner. There is a wide array of possible combinations. Experiment a little to find what works best for you. Most important, trust that change can occur. Once you begin to experience some improvements, one powerful benefit will most likely become apparent, namely a marked lowering of performance anxiety. The reduction of this pressure undoubtedly accounts, at least in part, for continued long-term gains you can expect to maintain.

Dealing with Erectile Difficulties

With the exception of organically caused erection difficulties, anxiety is the major stumbling block to erectile response. Therefore, all behaviorally focused approaches to this problem concentrate on reducing or eliminating anxiety. A major goal is to create an atmosphere in which the man is able to achieve some success with obtaining an erection, thus restoring his confidence and diminishing performance fear.

Initially, a couple should spend their intimate moments engaged in non-demanding caresses. The sensate focus experiences discussed earlier are ideally suited for this purpose. Often it is helpful not to touch the genitals during these first encounters. The emphasis is placed on sensual pleasure as each person lightly touches, strokes, and explores his or her partner's body. It is also important that both members of the pair understand that these exercises in pleasuring are not designed to produce an erect penis. Neither person should enter into the experience expecting this. If an erection should occur, fine; if it goes away, do not worry. The main point is that the time spent touching is not goal oriented. For this reason, it is often helpful to place a mutually agreed-upon specific restriction on coitus and ejaculation. The following account shows how one man reacted to the regimen imposed by his therapist:

When I was told that intercourse was off-limits, at least for the time being, I couldn't believe how relieved I felt. After years of trying to make my body get up for a performance, suddenly the doctor's advice eliminated this pressure. It was like being given permission to feel again. If I couldn't get hard, so what? After all, I was told not to use it even if it happened. Looking back, I think those first few times touching and getting touched by my wife were the first really worry-free pleasurable times I had experienced in years. Soon I was getting erections all over the place, and the problem was resisting the urge to jump the gun on the therapy timetable. (Authors' files)

An urge to take shortcuts on the therapy timetable can be a potential problem. Such impulsiveness may be counterproductive. Avoiding intercourse and ejaculation does not necessarily mean that a man's partner may not have an orgasm. If a couple wants to, they can agree in advance for the partner to have an orgasm at the close of a session by whatever mode of stimulation seems comfortable to both (self-stimulation or being touched by partner, oral stimulation, and so on). One key restriction is that such activity is noncoital and does not result in ejaculation by the man who has the erectile difficulty.

The elimination of pressure to perform helps to lessen the anxiety felt by the erection-inhibited man. A man often begins to have erections during these times of intimate pleasuring. This can be a very positive experience for him and his partner, demonstrating that erections will occur spontaneously in an atmosphere of mutual sharing.

When anxiety is reduced and the couple has progressed in their sensate focus exercises to a point where both feel comfortable with the newly discovered pleasures of body exploration, it is time to move to the next phase. Note that while the man who has experienced arousal difficulties will probably have begun to have spontaneous erections by this time, their occurrence is not essential to deciding to move forward. The critical condition is that both partners feel relaxed and positive about their new-found, mutually experienced sensuality.

In the next phase, the couple directs their attention toward whatever kinds of genital stimulation are particularly arousing to the man. This may consist of manual or oral pleasuring, or both. The intercourse ban is still in effect. If the man achieves a complete erection, his partner should stop whatever actions have aroused him.

Sometimes people are perplexed at this suggestion, thinking that the logical next step would be to progress to penetration. However, in view of the past history of the vast majority of men troubled by erectile inhibition, it is critical that his erection be allowed to subside at this point. The purpose of this is to alter the man's belief that once an erection is lost, it will not return, no matter how much he and his partner work to make it happen again. A concern like this is common among men who have erectile difficulties, and it may be based on a collection of real experiences ranging from frantic efforts to use nighttime erections before they are lost to the anxiety-producing occurrence of watching spontaneous erections subside before penetration can be accomplished.

It is important that someone with these concerns be shown that they can be overcome. This can usually be best accomplished through positive experiences such as a repeated pattern of arousal, subsiding of erection, and arousal once again. When his partner stops providing optimal stimulation, the man allows his erection to subside. This may take several minutes of nonstimulation if the level of arousal is very high. This time can be spent holding each other close or exchanging nongenital caresses. When his erection has completely gone down, the man's partner again resumes the genital pleasuring that produced the original reaction. Once he experiences that erections can be lost and regained, the fear that he has "had it" if he loses the first one is diminished.

Occasionally, a man will experience a recurrence of erection-inhibiting fears during these exercises. In such cases, it is helpful to remind him to relax and focus his attention on pleasuring his partner through sensate focus. It may sometimes be necessary to move back a step to emphasize nondemand pleasuring if he continues to have difficulty responding to the stimulate-stop-restimulate phase of treatment.

The final phase of treatment, for heterosexual couples who desire intercourse, involves penetration and coitus. A good procedure for accomplishing this is to begin with sensate focus, with the man on his back and his partner astride. The couple can then move to genital stimulation; then, when he has an erection, she lowers herself onto his penis, maintaining stimulation by gentle movements of her pelvis. If his penis remains erect, vaginal stimulation should be continued until he reaches orgasm. Permission to be "selfish" is quite helpful at this point (Kaplan, 1974). By this, we mean the man should be instructed to concentrate exclusively on his own erotic pleasures. If worries such as "Is she going to come?" or "Am I doing it well?" intrude on his own sensual feelings, he should shift his attention back to his own sensations. Sometimes this concern for self is easier to put into practice if both have agreed that her orgasm will be a matter of mutual consideration after he has experienced his.

Occasionally, a man will lose his erection after penetration. If this happens, it is good procedure for his partner to again provide the kind of oral or tactile stimulation that originally produced his erection. If his response continues to be blocked, it is wise to stop genital contact, returning once again to the original nondemand pleasuring of sensate focus rather than forcing efforts to "make it happen." Erection loss after penetration is not uncommon, and couples should be encouraged not to be overly anxious if it should happen.

A few successful coital encounters will generally alleviate erectile inhibition. Should the problem recur, the couple is now experienced in techniques they can use to avoid establishing a pattern of difficulty.

Some men who have impaired erectile functioning as the result of a medical problem make a very satisfactory sexual adjustment to the absence of erection by emphasizing and enjoying other ways of sexual sharing. In cases where illness or injury have left a man permanently unable to have erections, the option for a surgically implanted penile prosthesis is also available. Since the surgery is expensive and involves some risks, it is wise to carefully evaluate this option. There are two basic types of penile implants. One consists of a pair of semirigid rods placed inside the cavernous bodies of the penis. A potential disadvantage to this method is that the penis is always semierect. The second type of penile prosthesis is an inflatable device that enables the penis to be either flaccid or erect (Figure 17.7). Two inflatable cylinders are implanted into the cavernous bodies of the penile shaft. They are connected to a fluid-filled reservoir located near the bladder and to a pump in the scrotal sac. When a man wants an erection, he squeezes the pump several times, and the fluid fills the collapsed cylinders and produces an erection. When an erection is no longer desired, a release valve causes the fluid to go back into the reservoir. Neither of these devices can restore sensation or the ability to ejaculate if they have been lost due to medical problems. They do, however, provide an alternative for men who want to mechanically restore their ability to have erections.

Treatment in Short-Term Relationships Recently, we have encountered several male students who have sought us out for advice on how to best deal with

FIGURE 17.7 A PENILE PROSTHESIS

This inflatable device enables the penis to be either flaccid or erect.

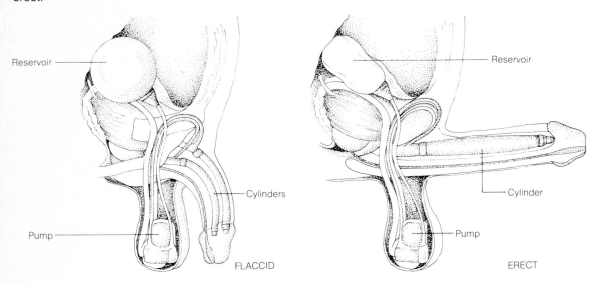

Reservoir

Reservoir

Cylinders

Cylinder

Pump

Pump

FLACCID

ERECT

erectile difficulties that have just surfaced in their lives. Often they are not inclined toward involving their partner(s)—perhaps they have no primary companions—in a time-consuming therapy regimen. Furthermore, it is often unnecessary to implement such an elaborate program in the case of a short-lived problem. Rather, what is called for is a modified procedure, also designed to reduce performance anxiety. Consider the following account:

A young man sought our advice regarding an abortive attempt to have intercourse for the first time with a new romantic interest. It seems that their attempt at sexual intimacy had been preceded by heavy drinking, which no doubt contributed to his inability to obtain an erection. The reason for perceived failure was primarily organic, but its impact on his psyche was of a psychological and potentially lasting variety. He was quite upset by the experience, stating adamantly that he had "never had any trouble before." It seemed unnecessary and inappropriate to involve his partner in a protracted period of therapy. Rather, we simply suggested that next time they were intimate, they concentrate their efforts on mutual sensual pleasuring, not being concerned with intercourse as an endpoint goal. The results were gratifying for each in that it both reduced the pressure and opened new options for erotic pleasure. (Authors' files)

Sometimes people, both men and women, may find it very difficult to suggest to a partner that nondemand stimulation is what they need to help overcome performance anxiety. In this regard, we would like to share a strategy that we have found to be of particular value for many individuals. This approach to sensual sharing has broad applicability, both to people troubled by anxiety-induced difficulties and to others who seek to enhance their sexual experiences. At an early point in a developing intimate relationship, we suggest that you begin sexual sharing with a period of mutual exploration, a time when each may acquire knowledge about the other's body, feelings, sensitivities, and needs. Make an agreement to avoid genital sex during the initial stages. This can reduce anxiety and give you a chance to experience mutual discovery without the pressure of a goal orientation.

For a man or woman who has had difficulties in previous sexual encounters, the opportunity to feel and respond spontaneously, with no need to perform, can be a valuable experience. In addition to reducing performance anxieties, this approach may provide a wealth of knowledge about each other's needs and desires, information that may then be used to enhance sexual sharing.

Reducing Ejaculatory Inhibition

As with erectile difficulties, a behavioral "reconditioning" approach is generally used in the treatment of ejaculatory inhibition. In addition, psychotherapy aimed at reducing conflicts in the relationship may be helpful when dislike or anger toward a partner contributes to a man's difficulty with ejaculatory inhibition. The reconditioning plan is outlined in the following paragraphs. The program is suitable for either a heterosexual or homosexual couple. However, for the purposes of descriptive simplicity, we will assume a male-female pair.

Therapy usually begins with a few days of sensate focus, during which time the man should not attempt to have an ejaculation, either intravaginally or by some other form of stimulation. If his partner desires orgasm, this may be accomplished in whatever fashion is comfortable to both, excluding coitus. It is desirable for a man to maintain this consideration for his partner's needs throughout the reconditioning program.

When they have become comfortable with the nondemand pleasuring of sensate focus, the couple may move on to the next phase of treatment. Now the man should experience ejaculation by whatever method is most likely to be successful. Ideally, this will involve his partner so that he may begin to associate his orgasmic pleasure with her. Frequently, the man begins by masturbating himself after first being stimulated to a highly aroused state by his partner. If he is uncomfortable masturbating in her presence, he can leave the room after being aroused by her touch and immediately stimulate himself to orgasm. Perhaps after some experience with this activity, he will feel comfortable remaining in her presence while he masturbates, preferably with her participation through kissing, fondling, or holding him. The essential idea is for him to begin connecting his partner's presence and activity with his own pleasure. Many couples may find that they can move successfully from sensate focus to the man receiving stimulation from his partner without the intervening step of his solo masturbation.

Once both partners feel comfortable with the man's self-stimulation in the woman's presence, the couple may move on to the next phase, where she attempts to bring him to orgasm with manual or oral stimulation. Communication is especially important at this time. The man can greatly heighten his pleasure and arousal by demonstrating or verbalizing what feels best to him. It may take several days or longer before his partner's stimulation produces an ejaculation. There is no need to rush or feel panicked if it does not happen immediately. Most therapists agree that once he can reach orgasm by her touch, an important step has been accomplished.

When he is ejaculating consistently in response to her stimulation, the couple may move on to the final phase of treatment where ejaculation takes place during penetration. The female partner assumes the woman-astride position, sitting over the man who is lying on his back. She then stimulates him to the point where he signals that he is about to reach orgasm, at which time she inserts his penis and begins active pelvic thrusting. If he starts to ejaculate before insertion is completed, this should not be viewed as a cause for concern. If he does not ejaculate shortly after penetration, she should withdraw his penis and resume manual stimulation. When he is again about to ejaculate, she reinserts his penis and they continue stimulation by pelvic thrusting.

Once he experiences a few intravaginal ejaculations, the mental block that is usually associated with ejaculatory inhibition often disappears. After a few experiences with penetration followed immediately by ejaculation, the man may acquire confidence in his capacity to ejaculate intravaginally. At this point, the couple may wish to concentrate on prolonging coital contact. Typically, he will begin to enter his partner at lower levels of excitement rather than at the moment of impending orgasm. It may be useful to apply some of the techniques for lasting longer discussed earlier. It frequently happens that a stage is reached during which no noticeable improvement occurs, and this can take place at any point in the program. In this case, the couple may need to let some time pass before trying to move on to the next stage.

Ejaculatory inhibition may involve complex factors. Nevertheless, based on limited clinical data, it appears that the probability of overcoming the problem in a therapy program is good. Masters and Johnson (1970) report success with 10 of the 17 men they treated for this difficulty. Generally, the prognosis is better when the condition occurs independently of severe relationship problems.

TREATMENT FOR INHIBITED SEXUAL DESIRE

Many aspects of treatment for inhibited sexual desire are similar to specific suggestions for resolving other sexual problems. These include encouraging erotic responses through self-stimulation and arousing fantasies; reducing anxiety with appropriate information and sensate focus exercises; and enhancing sexual experiences by improving communication, increasing skill in initiation and refusal of sexual activity, and expanding one's repertoire of sexual activities (LoPiccolo, 1980a).

ISD appears to be more difficult to treat than other sexual problems, and is more likely to require intensive therapy than problems like rapid ejaculation, primary anorgasmia, or vaginismus (Kaplan, 1979). The goal for treatment of ISD is to modify the person's pattern of inhibiting his or her erotic impulses. To achieve this, the therapist helps the client to understand the underlying motivation to suppress sexual feelings and the reasons "why" he or she refuses sexual intimacy. Kaplan combines specific suggestions for activities with insight therapy to help the person understand and resolve unconscious conflicts about sexual pleasure and intimacy.

After exploring the information and suggestions in this text and other readings, you may continue to experience considerable sexual dissatisfaction. Perhaps you may find it difficult to progress beyond a particular stage in an exercise program. At this point you may decide to seek professional help. A skilled therapist can offer useful information, emotional support, a perspective other than your own, and specific problem-solving techniques, all of which may help you make the desired changes in your sexual life.

Many people are apprehensive about going to see a sex therapist, and it can be helpful to have some idea about what to expect. Each therapist works differently, but most follow certain steps. At the first interview the therapist will help the person or couple to clarify the problem and their feelings about it, and to understand what their goals are for therapy. The therapist will usually ask questions about when the difficulty first began, how it has developed over time, what the person thinks has caused it, and what he or she has already tried to resolve the problem. The therapist will likely gather some information about medical history and current physical functioning and then make referrals, if necessary, for further physical screenings. Over the next few sessions the therapist may gather more extensive sexual, personal, and relationship histories. Some therapists use written questionnaires to help gather information and clarify problems.

Once the therapist and the individual or couple more fully realize the nature of the difficulty, the therapist helps the client understand and overcome obstacles to meeting their therapy goals as the sessions continue. The therapist will often give "homework" assignments such as self-stimulation or sensate focus exercises for the client(s) to do between therapy sessions. Successes and difficulties with the assignments are then discussed at subsequent meetings. Therapy is terminated when the clients' goals are reached. It is often helpful for clients to leave with a plan for continuing and maintaining progress. The therapist and clients may also plan one or more follow-up sessions.

Selecting a Therapist

Depending on your situation, you may wish to see a therapist alone or with your partner. Many women who want to learn to experience orgasm may not have an available partner or may decide they prefer to attain orgasm initially by self-stimulation; the same may be the case for men with premature ejaculation or erection problems. Masters and Johnson believe that a couple's sexual functioning, including difficulties one or the other may experience, is based on the interaction between the two people. Therefore, their counseling is done with both partners. Masters and Johnson have also promoted the use of male and female cotherapists to work with heterosexual couples.

Another option in some areas is small group therapy. Small groups in sex therapy were first extensively used with women who had not yet experienced orgasm.

These women's groups combine in-group sharing and support with self-discovery exercises (Barbach, 1975). This model is also being used for groups of men (Zilbergeld, 1975) and couples (Baker and Nagata, 1978; McGovern et al., 1976) experiencing sexual difficulties. One advantage of group therapy is that it is usually less expensive than individual therapy. Also, group members often gain knowledge and support from sharing with each other.

Once a person has determined she or he wants help from a sex therapist, how is a therapist selected? To locate a therapist you might ask your sexuality course instructor or health-care practitioner for referrals. If you are concerned about having a nonsexist focus to your therapy, you can call your local National Organization for Women (NOW) chapter. They may have a list of therapists from whom to choose. Homosexual individuals or couples may find it helpful to contact a gay rights organization for names of therapists who are supportive of their clients' sexual orientations. Your doctor or friends may know therapists whom they might recommend, and your county or state psychological association can also provide names of licensed clinical psychologists in your area. County medical societies have lists of names of psychiatrists. Also, the American Association of Sex Educators, Counselors and Therapists (AASECT) can send you the names of therapists in your area who have applied and qualified for AASECT certification.*

After consulting some of the above sources you will have several choices. There are many factors to consider in making your selection. A basic criterion is training. Professionals from a variety of backgrounds do sex therapy. The title *sex therapist* does not assure competence: there are few regulations on use of that title. At this time, there are few advanced degree programs in sex therapy. Rather, a professional who has specialized in this area is likely to have credentials as a psychiatrist, psychologist, social worker, or educational or pastoral counselor. To do sex therapy, he or she should also have participated in sex therapy training, supervision, and workshops. It is highly appropriate for you to inquire about the specific training and certification of a prospective therapist.

To help determine if a specific therapist will meet your needs, you may wish to discuss the following points at your first meeting:

1. What do you want from therapy? You and your therapist should reach an agreement on your and his or her goals. This agreement is sometimes referred to as the therapy contract.
2. What is the therapist's approach? You can ask about the general process (what the therapist will do) in the therapy sessions and what kind of participation is expected of you.
3. How do you feel about talking with a therapist? Therapy is not intended to be a light social interaction. It can be difficult. At times it may be quite uncomfortable for a client to discuss personal sexual concerns. However, for therapy to be useful, you will want to have the sense that the therapist is open and willing to understand you.

*The address is AASECT, 5010 Wisconsin Avenue N.W., Suite 304, Washington, D.C., 20016.

After this initial interview you can decide to continue with this therapist or ask for a referral more appropriate to your needs. If you become dissatisfied once you begin therapy, discuss your concerns with your therapist. Decide jointly, if possible, whether to continue or to seek another therapist. It is usually best to continue for several sessions before making a decision to change. Occasionally, clients expect magic cures rather than the hard and rewarding work therapy often demands.

Fees and Ethics

Another consideration may be the cost of therapy. Fees vary considerably. Psychiatrists are usually on the upper end of the fee scale, psychologists are in the middle, and social workers and counselors are usually on the lower end. A higher fee does not necessarily indicate better sex therapy skills. Some mental health agencies and private practitioners offer sliding fee schedules based on the client's income.

Finally, it is considered highly unethical for professional therapists to engage in sexual relationships with clients. If at any time your therapist makes verbal or physical sexual advances towards you, you have every right to leave immediately and terminate therapy. It would be helpful to others who may be victims of this misuse of professional power if you report this incident to local professional organizations.

In conclusion, sex therapy can be a useful tool for individuals and couples who want to resolve their sexual difficulties. The process of sex therapy may also have additional benefits. The individuals and couples who have successfully met their goals may experience increased self-confidence and emotional satisfaction (Clement and Pfäfflin, 1980), and they may improve the effectiveness of their communication and be more assertive and emotionally expressive with each other (Tullman et al., 1981). The combined efforts of the therapist and client are an important element in this process, which can replace doubt and anxiety with the joy of satisfying sexual sharing.

SUMMARY

THE PLISSIT MODEL OF SEX THERAPY

1. The PLISSIT model outlines four progressive levels of sex therapy: permission, limited information, specific suggestions, and intensive therapy.

SELF-KNOWLEDGE

2. It is helpful to begin with ourselves as we attempt to actualize our sexual potentials. Self-knowledge may include procedures for improving self-awareness and for self-pleasuring activities.

3. Self-stimulation is an effective way for an individual to learn about and experience sexual response. It is a time that can be enjoyed for itself and the knowledge acquired can be shared with a partner.

SHARING WITH A PARTNER

4. A variety of sexual activities, shared with a partner, may enhance sexual potential. Included in this category are an assortment of touching and communication exercises.

5. The experience of sensate focus, nondemand pleasuring shared by sexual partners, is an excellent vehicle for mutually enhancing sexual potentials.

6. Masturbating in each other's presence may be an excellent way for a couple to indicate to each other what kind of touching they find arousing.

SPECIFIC SUGGESTIONS FOR WOMEN

7. Therapy programs for anorgasmic women are based on progressive self-awareness activities.

8. Women who wish to become orgasmic while sharing with a partner may benefit from programs that commence with sensate focus, mutual genital exploration, self-stimulation, and nondemand genital pleasuring by the partner.

9. A couple may increase the probability of female orgasm during penetration by incorporating knowledge acquired during sensate focus and nondemand pleasuring, and by combining manual stimulation with penetration.

10. Treatment for vaginismus generally involves promoting increased self-awareness and relaxation. Insertion of a lubricated finger (first one's own and later the partner's) into the vagina is an important next step in overcoming this condition. Penile insertion is the final phase of treatment for vaginismus.

SPECIFIC SUGGESTIONS FOR MEN

11. A variety of approaches may help a man learn to delay his ejaculation. Potentially helpful suggestions include ejaculating more frequently, using a more relaxed intercourse position, having a second orgasm, openly communicating a need to modulate movements, including noncoital activity in sexual sharing, and experimenting with small orgasms.

12. If a couple has the time and inclination to work together in resolving rapid ejaculation difficulties, application of the stop-start or squeeze methods is usually effective.

13. A symptom-focused behavioral approach has proven quite successful in treating psychologically based erectile inhibition. This treatment method has several phases: sensate focus, followed by genital stimulation, then penetration.

14. Surgically implanted penile prostheses are options for men who have a permanent, physiologically caused inability to experience erections.

15. The use of nondemand pleasuring can be an effective preventive intervention in the early development of erectile difficulty.

16. A behavioral approach for the treatment of ejaculatory inhibition combines sensate focus with self- and partner manual stimulation to ultimately lead to intravaginal ejaculation.

TREATMENT FOR INHIBITED SEXUAL DESIRE

17. Problems with inhibited sexual desire often require more intensive therapy to help a person understand and change their suppression and avoidance of sexual feelings.

GUIDELINES FOR SEEKING PROFESSIONAL ASSISTANCE

18. Professional counseling is often helpful and sometimes necessary in overcoming sexual difficulties.

19. A skilled therapist can offer useful information, emotional support, a perspective other than your own, and specific problem-solving techniques.

20. A lack of regulations governing sex therapy suggests that we should be careful in selecting a therapist or cotherapists. Referrals may be given by sex educators, physicians, or a variety of organizations including AASECT or women's groups.

SUGGESTED READINGS

Castleman, Michael. *Sexual Solutions*. New York: Simon & Schuster, 1980. An excellent book that encourages readers to clarify their personal conditions for positive sexual experiences.

Kaplan, Helen. *The Illustrated Manual of Sex Therapy*. New York: Quadrangle/New York Times, 1975. A readable and beautifully illustrated book with clearly explained steps in the behavioral treatment of sexual difficulties.

LoPiccolo, Joseph, and LoPiccolo, Leslie (Eds.). *Handbook of Sex Therapy*. New York: Plenum, 1978. An edited text that synthesizes research and writing in the field of sex therapy. It is somewhat technical but highly appropriate reading for the student seriously interested in the field of sex therapy.

McCarthy, Barry; Ryan, Mary; and Johnson, Fred. *Sexual Awareness: A Practical Approach*. San Francisco: Boyd & Fraser, 1975. A straightforward and sensitive guide to improving self-awareness and pleasure in sexuality. The book offers suggestions for enhancement programs for men, women, and couples.

Rosenberg, Jack. *Total Orgasm*. New York: Random House, 1973. Based on body-work therapies, this book suggests breathing, movement, and meditation exercises to increase sexual awareness and pleasure.

18

Sexually Transmitted Diseases

TWO COMMON VAGINAL INFECTIONS
  Trichomoniasis
  Moniliasis
GONORRHEA
SYPHILIS
NONGONOCOCCAL URETHRITIS
HERPES
PUBIC LICE
GENITAL WARTS
PREVENTION OF SEXUALLY TRANSMITTED DISEASES
  Some Steps for Prevention
SUMMARY
SUGGESTED READINGS

*I*n this chapter we will discuss a variety of diseases that may be transmitted through sexual interaction. These are commonly called *STDs* or *sexually transmitted diseases*. Some of these conditions may be spread nonsexually as well as through sexual contact (for example, pubic lice, herpes, and genital warts). The term *venereal disease (VD)* is sometimes used interchangeably with STD. However, the VD label is traditionally applied only to those conditions whose mode of transmission is almost always sexual contact (for example, gonorrhea and syphilis). Thus, the title of this chapter, Sexually Transmitted Diseases, is a much broader topic that encompasses the more limited category of VD.

Gonorrhea and herpes are major health problems in the United States. Other STDs, such as trichomoniasis, pubic lice, and yeast infections, are even more prevalent than gonorrhea. It is quite possible that you will experience at least one of the STDs described in this chapter. The probability of this occurring is greatest if you are (or come in close contact with) a sexually active, nonmonogamous individual.

Our purpose in including a chapter on STDs is not to scare readers into celibacy or monogamy. Rather, we would like to present a realistic picture of what a sexually transmitted disease is, how it can be recognized, what should be done to treat it, and what preventive measures can be taken. Furthermore, we trust that increased knowledge about STDs will lead to thoughtful consideration of other people who might be involved. There are good reasons for letting them know if they might be affected and for taking proper preventive action and treatment. These are our motives for including a chapter on this topic in this book—particularly in view of the facts that many STDs are on the increase, that relatively little prevention is currently practiced, and that most of these diseases can be successfully treated.

It is not entirely clear why the incidence of STDs is so high. Undoubtedly, a number of factors are operating in what many writers and health authorities have labeled an epidemic. Increasing sexual activity among young people, particularly women (see Chapter 13), has commonly been advanced as a prime reason for the accelerating rate of STDs. A related contributory effect of "sexual liberation" has been an increasing tendency to have multiple sexual partners, particularly during one's youth when the incidence of STDs is the highest. It is also believed that increased use of birth control pills and the IUD have contributed to the rising rates by reducing use of two contraceptive methods, vaginal spermicides and the condom, both known to offer some protection against sexually transmitted diseases.

It is possible, too, that women who use the pill may actually become more susceptible to certain STDs. This is still a highly controversial theory among specialists in this area of medicine. It is based on the fact that an excellent environment for STD organisms exists in a part of the cervix where its outer cover meets with the inner lining. This area becomes more exposed during pregnancy or after about six months of oral contraceptive use (Wear and Holmes, 1976).

The spread of STDs is facilitated by the unfortunate fact that many of these diseases do not produce obvious symptoms. In some cases, particularly among women, there may be no outward signs at all. Under these circumstances, people may unknowingly infect others. In addition, feelings of guilt and embarrassment that often accompany having an STD may prevent people from seeking adequate treatment or informing their sexual partners.

It is possible that the effect of these factors could be counterbalanced through general public understanding of STDs and their prevention. Unfortunately, this has not happened. We hope this widespread ignorance will eventually be overcome by the development of more meaningful sex education at all levels of society.

The following sections focus on the most common sexually transmitted diseases. These are outlined in Table 18.1. If you desire more information, we recommend contacting your county health service or VD clinic or calling the VD National Hotline.* These services will answer questions, send free literature, and, most important, give you the name and telephone number of a local physician or public clinic that will treat STDs free or at minimal cost.

TWO COMMON VAGINAL INFECTIONS

There are several kinds of vaginal infections that may be transmitted through sexual interaction. Because they are also frequently contracted through nonsexual means, they are not generally referred to as venereal diseases. *Leukorrhea* or *vaginitis* are general terms applied to a variety of vaginal infections characterized by a whitish discharge. The secretion may also be yellow or green in color because of the presence of pus cells, and it often has a disagreeable odor. Additional symptoms of vaginitis may include irritation and itching of the genital tissue, burning during urination, and pain around the vaginal opening during intercourse.

Vaginal infections are far more common than some of the more serious STDs like gonorrhea and syphilis. Practically every woman experiences one or more of these infections during her life. Under typical circumstances, many of the organisms that cause vaginal infections are relatively harmless. In fact, some routinely live in the vagina, and they cause no trouble unless something alters the normal vaginal environment and allows them to overgrow. The vagina normally houses bacteria (*Lactobacilli*) that help to maintain a healthy vaginal environment. The pH balance of the vagina is usually sufficiently acidic to ward off most infections. However, certain conditions may alter the pH toward the alkaline side, and this may leave a woman vulnerable. Some factors that may increase the likelihood of vaginal infection include antibiotic therapy, use of contraceptive pills, menstruation, pregnancy, wearing nylon underwear, douching, and lowered resistance from stress or lack of sleep. The vast majority of vaginal infections are either trichomoniasis or moniliasis.

Trichomoniasis

Trichomoniasis is caused by a one-celled parasite called *Trichomonas vaginalis*.

Incidence and Transmission   In females, trichomoniasis is far more common than any other STD. It afflicts roughly 25% of all women. However, not all infected

*The VD National Hotline can be dialed toll-free 8:00 A.M. to 8:00 P.M. weekdays and 10:00 A.M. to 6:00 P.M. weekends. The number is 1-800-227-8922 (in California, 1-800-982-5883).

TABLE 18.1 COMMON SEXUALLY TRANSMITTED DISEASES (STDs): MODE OF TRANSMISSION, SYMPTOMS, AND TREATMENT

STD	Transmission	Symptoms	Treatment
Trichomoniasis	*Trichomonas vaginalis* organism is passed through genital sexual contact; or less frequently by towels, toilet seats, or bathtubs used by an infected person.	White or yellow vaginal discharge that has an unpleasant odor; vulva is sore and irritated.	Metronidazole (Flagyl), a prescription drug.
Moniliasis (yeast infection)	The *Candida albicans* fungus may accelerate growth when the chemical balance of the vagina is disturbed; it may also be transmitted through sexual interaction.	White, "cheesey" discharge; irritation of vaginal and vulvar tissue.	Vaginal suppositories of Mycostatin or candicidin.
Gonorrhea ("clap")	*Neisseria gonorrhoeae* ("gonococcus") bacteria is spread through genital, oral-genital, or genital-anal contact.	Most common symptoms in men are a cloudy discharge from the penis and burning sensations during urination. If untreated, complications may include inflammation of scrotal skin and swelling at the base of testicle. In women, some green or yellowish discharge is produced. At a later stage, pelvic inflammatory disease may develop.	Penicillin, tetracycline, or erythromycin.
Syphilis	*Treponema pallidum* ("spirochete") is transmitted from open lesions during genital, oral-genital, or genital-anal contact.	*Primary stage:* A painless chancre appears at the site where spirochete entered the body. *Secondary stage:* The chancre disappears and a generalized skin rash develops. *Latent stage:* There may be no observable symptoms. *Tertiary stage:* Heart failure, blindness, mental disturbance, and many other symptoms. Death may result.	Penicillin, tetracycline, or erythromycin.
Nongonococcal urethritis (NGU)	Primary causes are believed to be *Chlamydia trachomatis* and T-strain *Mycoplasma* most commonly transmitted in coitus. Some NGU may result from allergic reactions or from *Trichomonas* infection.	Inflammation of the urethral tube. A man has a discharge from the penis and irritation during urination. A woman may have a mild discharge of pus from the vagina, but often shows no symptoms.	Tetracycline or erythromycin.

Continued on next page

TABLE 18.1 CONTINUED

STD	Transmission	Symptoms	Treatment
Herpes	Genital herpes appears to be transmitted primarily by vaginal, oral-genital, or anal sexual intercourse. Oral herpes is transmitted primarily by kissing.	One or more small red, painful bumps (papules) appear in the region of the genitals (genital herpes) or mouth (oral herpes). The papules develop into painful blisters that eventually rupture to form wet, open sores.	A variety of treatments may reduce symptoms, but no known cure exists.
Pubic lice ("crabs")	*Phthirus pubis,* or pubic lice, are spread easily through body contact or through shared clothing or bedding.	Persistent itching. Lice are visible and may often be located in pubic hair or other body hair.	Preparations such as A-200 pyrinate or Kwell (gamma benzene).
Genital warts (venereal warts)	Primarily spread through genital, anal, or oral-genital interaction.	Warts are hard and yellow-gray on dry skin areas; soft, pinkish-red, and cauliflower-like on moist areas.	Surface applications of podophyllin; large warts may require surgical removal.

individuals have noticeable symptoms. Men may carry the infection, too, but it is quite difficult to spot this condition because they generally show no observable symptoms. Nevertheless, some authorities believe that most male sex partners of infected women carry the trichomonas organism in their urethra or under the foreskin if they are uncircumcised.

The trichomonas organism is hardy and can survive outside the body for several hours on a moist object or in water. Thus, it is possible for a woman to become infected if her genitals come in close contact with a towel, washcloth, toilet seat, or other object used by an infected person. It is also believed that the organism may enter a woman's vagina if she uses a swimming pool or bathtub that has been used by an infected individual. However, the main mode of transmission appears to be through genital sexual contact.

Symptoms and Complications The most common symptom of trichomoniasis infection in women is an abundant, frothy white or yellow vaginal discharge that has an unpleasant odor. The discharge frequently irritates the tissues of the vagina and vulva, causing them to become inflamed, itchy, and sore. The infection is usually limited to the vagina and sometimes the cervix, but occasionally the organism may invade the urethra, bladder, or Bartholin's glands. Some health specialists believe that long term trichomonal infection may damage the cells of the cervix and increase susceptibility to cervical cancer. However, prompt, effective treatment prevents permanent cervical damage.

Infected males rarely have any observable symptoms. Occasionally, there may be a slight, whitish discharge from the penis accompanied by some sensations of tickling, itching, or burning in the urethral tract.

Treatment   An effective treatment for this condition is administration of the prescription drug metronidazole, marketed under the trade name Flagyl. To avoid passing the disease back and forth, it is important that the male partner(s) of the infected woman also take the treatment even if they show no symptoms of the disease. The drug generally produces a cure within 10–14 days. Users of this medication should not consume alcohol during the course of therapy, because the combination of the drug and alcohol can produce undesirable side effects. One other important caution should be noted in the use of metronidazole. There is some concern at the present time that the drug may be linked to cancer. A woman may wish to discuss this with her physician before agreeing to use it.

Moniliasis

Moniliasis, also commonly referred to as monilia or a yeast infection, is caused by a yeastlike fungus called *Candida albicans*.

Incidence and Transmission   The microscopic Candida organism is normally present in the vagina of many women; it also inhabits the mouth and large intestine of large numbers of men and women. A disease state results only when certain conditions allow the yeast to overgrow other microorganisms in the vagina. This accelerated growth may result from pregnancy, use of birth control pills, or diabetes—conditions that increase the amount of sugar stored in vaginal cells (*Candida albicans* thrives in the presence of sugar). If a nonpregnant woman has repeated yeast infections, it may be advisable for her to be tested for diabetes or other blood sugar disorders. Another factor is the use of oral antibiotics that reduce the number of *Lactobacilli*, mentioned earlier as important for a healthy vaginal environment. This permits Candida to multiply rapidly. Monilia often accompanies other infectious organisms, particularly Trichomonas. It is the second most common vaginal infection in women, surpassed in frequency only by trichomoniasis.

If the yeast organism is not already present in the woman's vagina, it may be transmitted to this area in a variety of ways. It may be conveyed from the anus on the surface of a menstrual pad, or transmitted through sexual interaction, since the organism may be harbored under the foreskin of an uncircumcised man. It may also be passed from a partner's mouth to a woman's vagina during oral sex.

Symptoms   Yeast infections do not generally produce the profuse, unpleasant smelling vaginal discharges typical of trichomoniasis. Instead, a woman may notice that she has a white, clumpy discharge that looks something like cottage cheese. In addition, monilia is often associated with intense itching and soreness of the vaginal and vulva tissues, which typically become red and dry. A woman who has a yeast infection may find coitus quite painful, and irritation from intercourse may worsen the infection.

Treatment   The best treatment for yeast infections consists of vaginal suppositories or cream, usually nystatin (Mycostatin) or candicidin. Since Candida is a hardy organism, treatment should be continued for the prescribed length of time (usually two to four weeks) even though symptoms may disappear in two days. In cases of very resistant infections, oral nystatin tablets may be used to reduce the amount of Candida in the large intestine and to help prevent the woman from reinfecting herself from her own anus.

GONORRHEA

Gonorrhea, known in street language as "clap," is a venereal disease caused by a bacterium, *Neisseria gonorrhoeae* (also called "gonococcus").

Incidence and Transmission Gonorrhea is a very common communicable disease. Approximately one million cases of gonorrhea are reported annually in the United States, and these may represent only a quarter to a third of the actual cases that occur each year (U.S. DHEW, 1980). Roughly 20,000 new cases of gonorrhea are reported each week (Amstey, 1981). There is a very high rate of occurrence among younger people: more than one-half of reported infections in this country involve people under 25 years of age. Evidence suggests that women have slightly greater than a 50% chance of developing gonorrhea after a single exposure to an infected partner. In contrast, a man who has intercourse once with an infected woman has a lower risk, probably around 20% to 25%, of contracting the disease (Rein, 1977). The risks for both sexes increase with repeated exposures.

Survival of the gonococcus microorganism is facilitated by the warm mucous membranes found in the tissues of the genitals, anus, and throat. Its mode of transmission is by sexual contact—penile-vaginal, oral-genital, or genital-anal. It has generally been assumed that gonococci do not survive when removed from the body's mucous membranes and that therefore one cannot contract this disease from toilet seats, drinking cups, towels, or other objects used by an infected person. However, research has shown that gonococci may survive for up to 24 hours on a moist towel (Elmros and Larson, 1972). Another study (Gilbaugh and Fuchs, 1979) found that gonococci contained in the urethral discharge from male patients with diagnosed gonorrhea remained viable on a toilet seat and toilet paper for two to three hours. However, these researchers caution: "The ability of the gonococcus to survive for several hours in dried purulent discharge on toilet seats or toilet paper suggests a possible source for nonsexual acquisition of gonorrhea. Our data in no way prove that such transmission can occur . . ." (p. 93). It is noteworthy that these investigators were unable to find any gonococci in random samplings from toilet seats in 72 public restrooms.

Symptoms Early symptoms of gonorrhea infection are more likely to be evident in men. Roughly 80%–90% of infected males have noticeable initial signs; as many as 80% of infected women will not detect the disease until it has progressed considerably. This marked discrepancy in early signs of the disease makes it imperative for men to inform their sexual partners once they are diagnosed as having gonorrhea. In view of the fact that some men are also asymptomatic, it is equally important for infected women to tell their partners they have gonorrhea. (Box 18.1

offers some suggestions that may be helpful when telling a partner about an STD infection.) Besides ethical and moral considerations, there are good legal reasons for informing a partner of gonorrhea infection. In one case, a Wyoming jury awarded $1.3 million in damages to a woman who suffered long-term complications from being infected by a man who knew he had gonorrhea at the time of their sexual involvement but failed to inform her of his condition.

Early symptoms in the male In men, early symptoms typically appear within three to five days after sexual contact with an infected person. However, symptoms may show up as early as one day or as late as two weeks after contact. The two most common signs of infection are a bad-smelling, cloudy discharge from the penis (particularly evident when the penis is "milked" from base to head) and burning sensations during urination. About 30%–40% of infected men also have swollen and tender lymph glands in the groin. These early symptoms often clear up on their own without treatment. However, this is no guarantee that the disease has been eradicated by the body's antibody system. The bacteria may still be present and a man may infect a partner.

Complications in the male If the infection goes without treatment for two to three weeks, it may spread up the genitourinary tract. Here, it may involve the prostate, bladder, kidneys, and testicles. Most men who continue to harbor the gonococcus have only periodic flareups of the minor symptoms of discharge and burning during urination. In a small number of men, however, the bacteria cause abscesses to form in the prostate. These may result in fever, painful bowel movement, difficulty in urinating, and general discomfort. In approximately one out of five men who remain untreated for longer than a month, the bacteria move down the vas deferens to infect the epididymis on the back of one or both testicles. Generally only one side is infected initially, usually the left. The symptoms of *epididymitis* may include a sensation of heaviness in the affected testicle, inflammation of the scrotal skin, and the formation of a small area of hard, painful swelling at the bottom of the testicle.

A common early symptom of gonorrhea in men is a cloudy discharge from the penis.

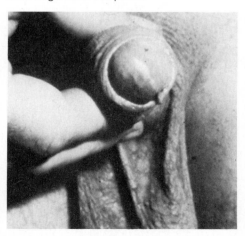

BOX 18.1 TELLING A PARTNER

Most of us would find it difficult to discuss with our lover(s) the possibility that we may have transmitted a disease to him or her during sexual sharing. Due to the stigma often associated with STDs, it can be bad enough admitting to having one of these diseases. The need to tell others (maybe even several others) that they may have "caught" something from you may seem to be a formidable task. You might fear that such a revelation will jeopardize a valued relationship, or worry that you will be considered "dirty." In relationships presumed to be monogamous, a person might fear that telling his or her partner about an STD will threaten mutual trust. "However, lovers who attempt to conceal a sex-related illness risk a good deal more in the long run than those who have the courage to discuss the situation right away" (Castleman, 1980, p. 230).

Not disclosing the existence of an STD risks the health of one's partner(s). Many people may not have symptoms and thus may not become aware that they have contracted a disease until they discover it for themselves, perhaps only after they have developed serious complications. Furthermore, if a lover remains untreated, she or he may reinfect you even after you have been cured by medical treatment. Unlike some diseases, like measles and chicken pox, STDs do not provide immunity against future infections. You can get one, give it to your lover, be cured, and then get it back again if he or she remains untreated (a process some health authorities call "ping-pong VD").

The following suggestions may provide some guidelines for telling a partner about your STD. Remember, these are only suggestions that have worked for some people. They may need to be modified to fit your particular circumstances. This is a sensitive issue that requires thoughtful consideration and planning.

1. Be honest. There is nothing to be gained by downplaying the potential risks associated with STDs. If you tell a partner, "I have this little drip, but it probably means nothing," you may regret it. Stick with the facts and be sure your partner understands the importance of obtaining a medical evaluation.
2. Even if you suspect that your partner may have been the source of your infection, there is little to be gained by blaming him or her. Instead, you may wish to simply acknowledge that you have the disease and are concerned that your partner gets proper medical attention.
3. Your attitude may have considerable impact upon how your partner receives the news. If you display high levels of anxiety, guilt, fear, or disgust, your partner may reflect these feelings in her or his reponse. Try to simply present the facts in as clear and calm a fashion as you can manage.
4. Be sensitive to your partner's feelings. Be prepared for reactions of anger or resentment. These are understandable

Continued on next page

initial responses. Being supportive and demonstrating a willingness to listen without becoming defensive may be the best tactics for diffusing negative responses.

5. Engaging in sexual intimacies after you become aware of your condition and before you obtain medical assurances that you are no longer contagious and/or inform your partner is clearly inappropriate.

6. Medical examinations and treatments for STDs, when necessary, can be a financial burden. Offering to pay for some or all of these expenses may help

to maintain (or re-establish) good will in your relationship.

7. In the case of a disease like herpes, where recurrences are unpredictable and the possibility of infecting a new partner is an ongoing concern, it is probably a good idea to tell him or her about your herpes before sexual intimacies take place. You may wish to preface your first sexual interaction by saying "There is something we should talk over first." Be sure to emphasize that herpes is usually preventable when proper precautions are taken.

Even after successful treatment, gonococcal epididymitis leaves scar tissue, which can block the flow of sperm from the affected testicle. Sterility does not usually result, since this advanced complication of gonorrhea in men is usually restricted to only one testicle. However, if treatment is still not carried out at this point, the infection may spread to the other testicle, rendering the man permanently sterile.

Early symptoms in the female   As mentioned earlier, women are often unaware of the early signs of gonorrheal infection. The primary site of infection, the cervix, may become inflamed without producing any observable symptoms. A green or yellowish discharge usually results, but since this is rarely heavy, it commonly remains undetected. A woman who is very aware of her vaginal secretions (perhaps from using the mucus method of birth control), is more likely to note the infection during these early stages. Sometimes the discharge may be irritating to the vulva tissues. However, when a woman seeks medical attention for an irritating discharge, her physician may fail to consider gonorrhea since many other infectious organisms produce this symptom. Also, for reasons that are not understood, as many as 50% of women who have gonorrhea also have trichomoniasis, and this condition may mask the presence of gonorrhea. Consequently, it is essential for any woman who thinks she may have gonorrhea to make certain that she is tested for gonorrhea when she is examined. (A Pap smear is not a test for gonorrhea.)

Complications in the female   It is not uncommon for the Bartholin's glands to be invaded by the gonococcus organism. When this happens there are usually no symptoms. The anus may also become infected through the "bridge" provided by vaginal discharge or menstrual blood.

Far more serious complications result from spread of the disease within the internal reproductive organs and pelvic cavity. In at least one-half of women who remain untreated for two or more months, the bacteria spread from the vagina and cervix up through the uterus and into the fallopian tubes. The infection may move very rapidly during menstruation. The gonococcus organisms infect the inner walls of the tubes, forming pus that may eventually leak out into the lower abdominal cavity and onto the ovaries. These tissues, in turn, may also become swollen and inflamed. At this point the woman is suffering from what is known as *pelvic inflammatory disease* (PID), the symptoms of which often include disrupted menstrual periods, pain in the lower abdomen, high temperature, nausea, vomiting, and headache. Even when effective treatment is introduced at this point, scar tissue in the fallopian tubes leaves about 20%–30% of women sterile. A woman who has had PID should be cautioned about the use of the IUD as a method of birth control. An IUD does not prevent fertilization of an egg (see Chapter 11 for an explanation of how the IUD prevents pregnancy); thus, the much smaller sperm cell may negotiate a partially blocked area and fertilize an ovum that subsequently becomes lodged in the scarred tube. The result is a tubal pregnancy, a dangerous health hazard to the woman.

Another serious complication that may result from PID is the development of tough bands of scar tissue adhesions that may link several pelvic cavity structures (tubes, ovaries, uterus, and so forth) to each other, to the abdominal walls, or to both. These adhesions can cause severe pain during coitus or when a woman is standing or walking.

Other complications in both sexes   In a tiny percentage of both women and men, gonorrhea bacteria enter the bloodstream and produce chills, fever, loss of appetite, a skin rash on the extremities, and arthritic pain in the joints. If arthritic symptoms develop, quick treatment is essential to avoid permanent joint damage. In very rare cases, the gonococcus organism may invade the heart, liver, spinal cord, and brain.

An infant may develop a gonococcal eye infection after passing through the birth canal of an infected woman. The use of silver nitrate or penicillin eye drops immediately after birth averts this potential complication. There are a few rare cases recorded where adults have transmitted the bacteria to their eyes by touching this region immediately after handling their genitals. That is one reason why it is important to wash with soap and water immediately after self-examination.

Oral contact with infected genitals may result in transmission of the gonococcal bacteria to the throat, causing pharyngeal gonorrhea. The primary symptom of this condition is a sore throat. Rectal gonorrhea may be caused by anal intercourse or, in a woman, by transmission of the bacteria from the vagina to the anal opening in menstrual bleeding or vaginal discharge. This form of gonorrhea is characterized by itching and rectal discharge.

The incidence of rectal gonorrhea among homosexual men who engage in anal intercourse is sharply on the rise (Lebedeff and Hochman, 1980). In view of the growing acceptance of both oral sex and anal intercourse within our society, it is likely that both pharyngeal and rectal gonorrhea are increasing among heterosexual individuals as well. Since infections of the throat or anus often do not produce observable symptoms, it is very important to examine laboratory cultures taken from the throats or anuses of people who have engaged in oral-genital or anal intercourse with those suspected of having gonorrhea. Health practitioners will often overlook these important tests unless a person requests the throat and/or anal cultures. Treatment for these two conditions is the same as that for genital gonorrhea.

Treatment   Since gonorrhea is often confused with other ailments, it is important to make the correct diagnosis before treatment. This is accomplished by culturing material taken from the male urethra or female cervix (a painless process). After a positive diagnosis, penicillin is generally the treatment of choice. For people allergic to this medication, tetracycline or erythromycin may be used. About 90% of infected individuals respond quickly to treatment. However, the remaining 10% are more resistant and may require more extensive or different treatment. A reduction in symptoms does not necessarily imply total cure, and it is essential that a follow-up negative culture be obtained before a person may conclude that she or he is free of the infection.

In recent years, a new strain of penicillin-resistant gonorrhea has emerged in the United States. This strain has been traced to Southeast Asia. It is theorized that it developed as a result of the common use of low doses of black-market penicillin. These low doses killed the less viable gonococcus organisms, but they allowed the more hardy ones to survive and develop some tolerance to the medication. This produced gonococcus bacteria with even greater resistance to penicillin. The emergence of penicillin-resistant gonorrhea may also be related to an increased use of antibiotics in general, a process that tends to weed out susceptible gonococci, leaving the naturally more resistant ones still alive. Regardless of causes, the increased resistance of gonococci to penicillin has resulted in a necessary increase in the curative dose from 150,000 units of penicillin in the 1940s to several million units at the present time (Hubbard, 1977). In cases where an infection does not respond to penicillin other medication must be used. The drug spectinomycin has been generally successful in combating this new development (Berg and Harrison, 1981).

SYPHILIS

Syphilis is a venereal disease that is caused by a thin, corkscrewlike organism called *Treponema pallidum* (also commonly called a "spirochete").

Incidence and Transmission   Syphilis is far less common than gonorrhea. However, statistics released by the National Centers for Disease Control revealed that the number of reported cases of syphilis increased by 33% during the three-year period from 1977 to 1980 (20,399 in 1977 versus 27,204 in 1980). Many health authorities estimate that the real number of syphilis cases may be three times these figures, and it has been estimated that as many as half a million people in the United States have untreated syphilis (Chiappa and Forish, 1976). Whatever its frequency, syphilis should not be taken lightly. Unlike most STDs, syphilitic infection may result in death.

Like the gonococcus organism, *Treponema pallidum* requires a warm and moist environment for survival. It is transmitted almost exclusively from open lesions of infected individuals to the mucous membranes or skin abrasions of sexual partners through penile-vaginal, oral-genital, or genital-anal contacts. Syphilitic organisms may also be transmitted from an infected pregnant woman to her unborn child through the placental blood system. The resulting congenital syphilis can cause death or extreme damage to infected newborns. If the disease is successfully treated before the fourth month of pregnancy, the fetus will not be affected. Therefore, pregnant women should be tested for syphilis sometime during their first three months of pregnancy.

Symptoms and Complications If untreated, the disease may progress through four phases of development. These are known as the primary, secondary, latent, and tertiary stages. A brief description of each follows.

Primary syphilis In its initial or primary phase, syphilis is generally manifested in the form of a painless sore called a *chancre* (pronounced "shanker"), which appears at the site where the spirochete organism enters the body (see Figure 18.1). In women who have coitus with infected men, this sore most commonly appears on the inner vaginal walls or cervix. It may also appear on the external genitals, particularly the labia. In men, the chancre most often occurs on the glans of the penis. It may also

FIGURE 18.1 SYPHILITIC CHANCRES

Chancres as they appear on the penis and on the labia. Chancres develop in the first or primary stage of syphilis.

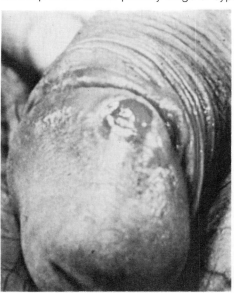
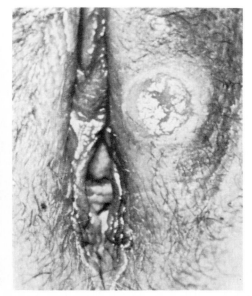

show up on the penile shaft or on the scrotum. People who have had oral sex with infected individuals may develop a sore on their lips or tongue. Anal intercourse may result in chancres appearing in or around the anus. The following is an excellent description of the chancre sore:

When the chancre first develops, it is a dull red bump about the size of a pea. The surface of the bump soon breaks down and the chancre becomes a rounded, dull red, open sore which may be covered by a yellow or grey crusty scab. The chancre is painless and does not bleed easily. In about 50% of cases, the chancre is surrounded by a thin pink border. The edges of the chancre are often raised and hard, like the edges of a button. The hardness may spread to the base of the chancre and eventually to the surrounding tissue, making the whole area feel hard and rubbery. (Cherniak and Feingold, 1973, p. 30)

In view of the painless nature of the chancre, it often goes undiscovered when it occurs on internal structures like the rectum, vagina, or cervix. Even when it is noticed, some people do not seek treatment. Unfortunately (from the long term perspective), the chancre generally heals without treatment in one to five weeks after its initial appearance. For the next few weeks the person typically has no symptoms but may infect an unsuspecting partner. After about six weeks have gone by (perhaps as little as two weeks or as long as six months), the disease progresses to the secondary stage.

Secondary syphilis   This phase is characterized by the appearance of a skin rash on the body that may range from barely noticeable to severe, with raised bumps that have a rubbery hard consistency. While the rash may look terrible, it typically does not hurt or itch. If the earlier appearance of a chancre was not sufficient to cause a person to seek treatment, the occurrence of the skin rash, if at all noticeable, generally prompts a visit to a physician. Even if treatment is not provided, the rash eventually subsides within a few weeks, sometimes longer. Rather than being eliminated, however, the disease enters the potentially more dangerous latent phase.

Latent syphilis   This stage can last for several years, and during this time there may be no observable symptoms of the disease. Nevertheless, the infecting organisms may continue to multiply, preparing for the final, most horrendous stage of syphilitic infection. After one year of the latent stage has elapsed, the infected individual is no longer contagious to sexual partners (Cherniak and Feingold, 1973). However, a pregnant woman with syphilis in any stage can pass the infection to her unborn fetus.

Tertiary syphilis   Research has revealed that one-third to one-half of all people who fail to obtain treatment after entering the latent phase of syphilis are affected by the tertiary stage later in life (Wear and Holmes, 1976). The final manifestations of syphilis can be horrible, often resulting in death. They occur anywhere from three to 40 years after initial infection and may include such conditions as heart failure, blindness, ruptured blood vessels, paralysis, skin ulcers, liver damage, and severe mental disturbance. Depending on the extent of the damage, treatment even at this late stage may be beneficial.

Treatment   The treatment for syphilis is highly effective and virtually the same as that employed in cases of gonorrhea. It consists of the use of antibiotics such as penicillin. All individuals who have been treated for this disease should have several blood tests (the method of diagnosis) after the completion of treatment to make certain that they are completely free of the *Treponema pallidum* organism.

NONGONOCOCCAL URETHRITIS

Any inflammation of the urethra tube that is not caused by gonorrhea is called *nongonococcal urethritis* or *NGU*. Until 1974 it was not known what organisms were the cause of this very common condition. Prior to this time it was also common to call it nonspecific urethritis, or NSU. Now it is believed that two separate microscopic organisms, *Chlamydia trachomatis* and *T-strain Mycoplasma*, are the primary causes of NGU (Wear and Holmes, 1976). Occasionally, NGU may result from invasion by other infectious agents (such as trichomonas, fungi, or bacteria), allergic reactions to vaginal secretions or irritation by soaps, vaginal contraceptives, and deodorant sprays.

Incidence and Transmission NGU is quite common among men, often surpassing the frequency of gonorrhea in the record of some VD clinics. In the United States, it is not required that NGU be reported to health authorities. However, there is mounting evidence that it is increasing at a faster rate than gonorrhea and may be twice as common (Felman and Nikitas, 1981). While it generally produces urinary tract symptoms only in men, there is evidence suggesting that women harbor the chlamydia or T-strain mycoplasma organisms.

The most common forms of NGU, caused by the earlier described infectious organisms, are no doubt transmitted by coitus. The fact that it rarely occurs in men who are not involved in sexual interaction supports this contention.

Symptoms and Complications Men who contract NGU often manifest symptoms similar to those of gonorrheal infection, including discharge from the penis and mild burning during urination. Often the discharge is less pronounced than that which occurs with gonorrhea; it may be evident only in the morning before urinating.

Women infected with chlamydia or T-strain mycoplasma are generally unaware of the disease until they are informed that NGU has been diagnosed in a male partner. They frequently show no symptoms, although there may be some itching, burning on urination, and a mild discharge of pus from the vagina. (Cultures may reveal the presence of the causative organism.) An infected woman may have the infection for a long period of time, during which she may pass it to sexual partners. Chlamydia present in the cervix of a pregnant woman may contaminate the eyes of her infant at birth and produce a chronic infection that can result in mild scarring of the cornea of the eyes.

The symptoms of NGU generally disappear after two to three months without treatment. However, the disease may still be present and, if left untreated in women, may result in cervical inflammation or pelvic inflammatory disease and may spread in some cases to the prostate and/or epididymis of an infected man (Holmes and Stamm, 1981). In rare cases NGU produces a form of arthritis.

Treatment   Many physicians assume that any penile discharge is caused by gonorrhea, and thus they may fail to diagnose NGU. Some even begin treatment for gonorrhea before confirming its existence with laboratory tests. In view of the fact that the common treatment for gonorrhea, penicillin, is not effective against NGU, it is important that an infected person make certain there has been a laboratory diagnosis before receiving treatment. A few days of tetracycline therapy usually clears up the condition. Erythromycin is used on individuals who are allergic to tetracycline.

HERPES

Herpes is caused by a virus called *Herpes simplex*. A virus is a parasite that invades, reproduces, and lives within a cell, thereby disrupting normal cellular activities. There are five different herpes viruses that infect humans, the most common being type 1 (HSV-1) and type 2 (HSV-2). Type 1 is generally confined to nongenital areas and is typically manifested as fever blisters or cold sores in the mouth or on the lips (oral herpes). Type 2 generally causes sores below the waist, on and around the genital areas (genital herpes). Occasionally, type 1 affects the genital area and, conversely, type 2 may produce a cold sore or fever blister in the mouth area.

The most common method of diagnosing herpes is direct observation by a physician. In most cases the clinical symptoms accompanying a herpes outbreak, together with a thorough patient history, will yield an accurate diagnosis. There are also a number of laboratory tests designed to detect herpes virus infections and one or more of these may be used in cases where the diagnosis is in question. The most accurate of these tests involves culturing a small sample taken from the base of an active lesion (Loveless, 1982). If the virus grows in the culture medium, a definitive diagnosis of HSV can be made.

Incidence and Transmission   Recent evidence suggests that perhaps as many as 20 million Americans may have genital herpes in an active or latent form (Dailey, 1981; Rapp, 1982). Statistics released by the National Centers for Disease Control reveal a ninefold increase in the number of cases of genital herpes between 1966 and 1979. There may be as many as 600,000 new cases and three to four million recurrences of genital herpes each year (Holmes, 1982). In addition to herpes infections of the genitals, countless millions of people have oral herpes.

Genital herpes appears to be transmitted primarily by penile-vaginal, oral-genital, or genital-anal sexual contact. Oral herpes may be transmitted by kissing, sharing towels, drinking out of the same cup, and so on. A person who has oral sex performed on her or him by a partner who has a cold sore or fever blister in the mouth region may develop genital herpes of either the type 1 or type 2 variety.

When any blisters or sores of herpes are present, it is extremely important that a person avoid bringing them into contact with someone else's body through touching, sexual interaction, or kissing. The value of a condom in preventing transmission of genital herpes is not certain since the viral particles are so small that they may pass through the pores of a condom (Vines, 1982). Toilet articles, towels, eating and drinking utensils, and so on should not be shared during the time of herpes eruptions.

Individuals may also spread the virus from one part of their body to another by touching a sore and then scratching or rubbing somewhere else, a process referred to as *autoinoculation*. It is very important for people with herpes to wash their hands thoroughly with soap and water after a sore is touched. It is better to avoid touching the sores if possible.

Symptoms and complications The symptoms associated with HSV-1 and HSV-2 infections are quite similar. The primary or initial episodes generally occur two to 12 days after exposure to the virus. Genital herpes symptoms consist of one or more small, red, painful bumps, called *papules*, that usually appear in the genital region. In women, the areas most commonly infected are the labia. The inner vaginal walls and cervix may also be affected. In men, the infected site is typically the glans or shaft of the penis. Homosexual men and heterosexual women who have engaged in anal intercourse may develop eruptions in and around the anus.

Soon after their initial appearance, the papules rapidly develop into tiny painful blisters filled with a clear fluid containing highly infectious virus particles (see Figure 18.2). The body then attacks the virus with white blood cells, causing the blisters to become filled with pus. Soon the blisters rupture to form wet, painful, open sores surrounded by a red ring (health practitioners refer to this as the period of "viral shedding"). A person is highly contagious during this time. About 10 days after the first appearance of the papule, the open sore forms a crust and begins to heal, a process that may take as long as 10 more days. There may be other symptoms accompanying genital herpes, including swollen lymph nodes in the groin, fever, muscle aches, and headaches. In addition, urination may be accompanied by a burning sensation and women may experience increased vaginal discharge.

Oral herpes is characterized by the formation of papules on the lips, and sometimes on the inside of the mouth and on the tongue and throat. (HSV-1 only

FIGURE 18.2 GENITAL HERPES BLISTERS

Genital herpes blisters as they occur on the penis and on the labia.

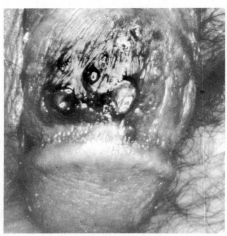
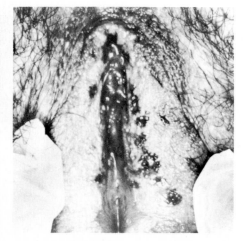

infrequently occurs within the mouth and it should not be confused with canker sores.) These blisters tend to crust over and heal within 10 to 16 days. Other symptoms of oral herpes include fever, general muscle aches, swollen lymph nodes in the neck, flulike symptoms, increased salivation, and possible bleeding in the mouth.

After complete healing, one cannot assume he or she will not experience a recurrence of the infection. Unfortunately, the herpes virus does not typically go away. Instead, it retreats up the nerve fibers leading from the infected site, ultimately finding a resting place in either the nerve cells that lie adjacent to the lower spinal column, in the case of genital herpes, or, in oral herpes, the virus becomes lodged in nerve cells lying in the cheek. The virus may remain dormant in these cells, without causing any apparent damage, perhaps for the individual's lifetime. However, in many cases there will be periodic flareups as the virus retraces its path back down the nerve fibers leading to the genitals or lips.

Many people never experience a recurrence of herpes following the initial or primary infection. Research suggests that approximately 40% of people who have undergone a primary episode of oral herpes experience at least one recurrence. The comparable figures for genital herpes are 30% to 70% (Gunn and Stenzel-Poore, 1981). Individuals who experience recurrences may do so frequently or only occasionally. Studies have shown that the more extensive the primary attack, the greater the chance of recurrence (Holmes, 1982). The symptoms associated with recurrent attacks tend to be milder than primary episodes and the disease tends to run its course more quickly, averaging 7 to 10 days (Gunn and Stenzel-Poore, 1981; Holmes, 1982).

A variety of factors may trigger reactivation of the herpes virus, including emotional stress, acid food, sunburn, cold, poor nutrition, being overtired or "run down," and trauma to the skin region affected. One person noted:

For several years I have been having a herpes outbreak on my lips. It usually happens just once a year and coincides with the start of fishing season when I sit in a boat too long without protection from the sun. Now that I am aware of the pattern, I plan to take proper precautions in the future. (Authors' files)

Recurrences may also be more frequent in cases where the genitals are kept tightly enclosed and warm, such as by panty hose, nylon underwear, or tight jeans (Gunn and Stenzel-Poore, 1981). There is wide individual variation in triggering factors and it is often difficult to associate a specific event with the onset of a recurrent herpes infection.

The majority of people prone to recurrent herpes outbreaks, perhaps as many as 75%, experience some type of *prodromal* symptoms that give advance warning of an impending eruption (Grossman, 1981). These indications include itching, burning, throbbing or "pins and needles" tingling at the sites commonly infected by herpes blisters, and sometimes pain in the legs, thighs, groin, or buttocks. Many health authorities believe that a person may be infectious from this stage through the appearance of the lesions and up to the time they have completely healed. Consequently, to avoid transmitting the disease, a person should avoid direct contact from the time he or she first experiences prodromal symptoms until the sores have completely healed. Even during an outbreak, it is possible to continue intimacies with a partner as long as infected skin does not come in contact with healthy skin. During this time individuals may wish to experiment with other kinds of sensual pleasuring such as sensate focus (see Chapter 17), hugging, and orally or manually stimulating a partner.

Some people may not experience a relapse of genital herpes until several years after the initial infection. Therefore, if you have been in what you believe is a sexually exclusive relationship and your partner shows symptoms or transmits the virus to you, it does not necessarily mean that he or she contracted the disease from someone else during the course of your relationship.

During their initial episode of genital herpes infection, most women have blisters on the cervix as well as the labia. The cervical sores may continue to produce infectious viral material for as long as 10 days after the labia sores have completely healed. Consequently, it is wise to take the additional precaution of avoiding coitus for a 10-day period after any external sores heal. Recurrent episodes of genital herpes in women do not typically involve the cervix.

While the sores are painful and bothersome, it is very unlikely that men will experience any major physical complications of herpes. Women, however, may be faced with two very serious, although quite uncommon, complications: cancer of the cervix and infection of the newborn. There is strong evidence that the risk of developing cervical cancer is higher among women who have had genital herpes (Rapp, 1982; Wear and Holmes, 1976). Fortunately, the great majority of women infected with herpes will never develop cancer of the cervix. Nevertheless, it is advisable for all women, particularly those who have had genital herpes, to obtain an annual cervical Pap smear for the rest of their lives. Some authorities recommend that women with genital herpes should have this test every six months (Gunn and Stenzel-Poore, 1981).

A newborn may be infected with genital herpes while passing through the birth canal. The greatest risk of transmitting the disease to the infant occurs when the mother's herpes eruption coincides with the time of delivery. In such cases, cesarean section is often performed to minimize risk to the child (about one-half of newborns infected with genital herpes will either be severely damaged or die). If the woman does not have open sores at the time of delivery, the probability of the baby's contracting the disease is extremely low. In fact, there is very little chance of infecting newborns with herpes if the attending obstetrician is aware of the disease in his or her patient and tests for herpes outbreaks during the course of pregnancy. Pregnant women may have herpes present in their cervical areas even when they are without symptoms. Therefore, it is very important that they be laboratory monitored during the late stages of their pregnancies (Nahmias, 1982).

There is one additional serious physical complication of herpes that both sexes should be aware of. Occasionally, a person will transfer the virus to an eye after touching a virus-shedding sore. This may lead to a severe eye infection known as ocular herpes or *herpes keratitis* (usually caused by HSV-1). Ocular herpes is the number one cause of cornea transplants in the United States (Fraunfelder, 1982). This complication may be best prevented by not touching the herpes sores. If contact cannot be avoided, thoroughly wash the hands with hot water and soap immediately after touching the lesions. There are effective treatments for this condition, but they must be started quickly to avoid eye damage.

Many people who have recurrent herpes outbreaks are troubled with mild to severe psychological distress. Some health authorities believe that emotional pain is the biggest problem associated with herpes. One recent survey of 3148 individuals with recurrent herpes revealed that 84% attributed periodic episodes of depression to herpes, 70% experienced a definite sense of isolation, 53% said they avoided potentially intimate situations, and 25% indicated that at one time or another they had experienced self-destructive feelings (American Social Health Association, 1981). In view of the physical discomfort associated with the disease, the unpredictability of recurrent outbreaks, and the lack of an effective cure (see next section), it is no small wonder that people who have herpes undergo considerable stress. We believe that becoming better informed about herpes may help to alleviate some of these emotional difficulties. Certainly, herpes is not the dread disease that some people believe it to be. In fact, countless numbers of individuals have learned to cope quite effectively with it.

When I first discovered I had herpes several years ago my first reaction was "Oh no, my sex life is destroyed!" I was really depressed and angry with the person who gave me the disease. However, with time I learned I could live with it and I even began to gain some control over it. Now, on those infrequent occasions when I have an outbreak, I know what to do to hurry up the healing process. Most of the time things are just the same as before I got it, and my sex life is only occasionally disrupted. (Authors' files)

Treatment   At the time of this writing there is no medical treatment proven to be effective in curing either oral or genital herpes. However, there is mounting optimism among medical researchers who are pursuing an effective treatment on many fronts. More information about herpes was acquired in the first two years of the 1980s than in all previous years of research (Rapp, 1982).

Current treatment strategies are designed to reduce discomfort and to speed healing during an outbreak of herpes. There are a number of ways to obtain relief from the discomfort associated with herpes. The following list of suggestions, adopted in part from the *Herpes Handbook* (Gunn and Stenzel-Poore, 1981) and a lecture by health practitioner Carol Winter (1982) may be helpful. The effectiveness of these suggestions varies from person to person, and we encourage people to experiment with the various options available to find an approach to symptom relief that best meets their needs.

1. Keeping herpes blisters clean and dry will lessen the possibility of secondary infections, significantly shorten the period of viral shedding, and reduce total time to lesion healing (Grossman, 1981). Washing the area with warm water and soap is adequate for cleaning. After bathing, dry the area thoroughly by patting it gently with a soft cotton towel or by blowing it with a hair dryer set

on cool. Since moisture that occurs naturally in the genital area may slow the healing process, it can be helpful to sprinkle the dried area liberally with cornstarch or baby powder. It is desirable to wear loose clothing that does not trap the moisture (cotton underwear absorbs moisture, but nylon traps it).

2. A number of health practitioners recommend a soothing soak in a warm bath to which a drying agent such as Epsom salts or Burow's solution has been added. This can help to relieve local pain and discomfort of lesions while increasing circulation in the infected area. However, there is some evidence that after prolonged soaking the normal skin adjacent to infected areas may become more susceptible to invasion by the herpes virus. Consequently, it is probably wise to limit the frequency and duration of these soaks.

3. Two aspirin every three to four hours may help to reduce the pain and itching. Ice packs applied directly to the lesions (avoid wetting with melt water) may also provide temporary relief from these symptoms. Keeping the area liberally powdered may also alleviate itching.

4. Some people have an intense burning sensation when they urinate if the urine comes into contact with herpes lesions. This discomfort may be reduced by pouring water over the genitals while you void or by urinating in a bathtub filled with water. It may help to dilute the acid in the urine by drinking lots of fluids (avoid liquids that make the urine more acidic, like cranberry juice).

5. Since stress has been implicated as a triggering event in recurrent herpes, it is a good idea to try to reduce this negative influence. There are a variety of approaches to stress reduction, including learning relaxation techniques, practicing yoga or meditation, and obtaining counseling about ways to better cope with daily pressures.

6. An individual prone to repeated relapses of herpes may obtain some benefit from keeping records of life events occurring immediately before an eruption (this may be done either after the fact or as part of an ongoing journal). You may be able to recognize certain common precipitating events, like fatigue, acid food, or sunlight, that may be avoided in the future.

7. A number of drugs, potentially helpful in combating herpes, have been investigated in recent years. The most encouraging development in this area is the recent FDA approval of acyclovir (sold under the trade name Zovirax Ointment 5%). Initial studies with this drug suggest that it shortens the duration of episodes of herpes eruptions and reduces symptom severity (Holmes, 1982). Apparently, acyclovir will not save cells already infected but will reduce invasion of adjacent healthy cells (Rapp, 1982). The major benefits of acyclovir seem to be on initial rather than recurrent herpes outbreaks. We must emphasize that acyclovir, while representing a significant breakthrough in the treatment of herpes, is not a cure at the present time. However, injectable acyclovir is being investigated with the hope that it may act to prevent recurrent herpes infections (Treichel, 1982). Interferon, a natural antiviral compound produced by our bodies, may also prove helpful

in the treatment of herpes. Some preliminary investigations indicate that interferon may reduce the frequency of recurrent episodes. Unfortunately, the availability of interferon for experimentation is extremely limited.

PUBIC LICE

Pubic lice, more commonly called "crabs," belong to a group of parasitic insects called biting lice. They are known technically as *Phthirus pubis*. Although very tiny, adult lice are visible to the eye. They are yellowish-gray in appearance, and under magnification they resemble a crab, as Figure 18.3 shows. A pubic louse generally grips a pubic hair with its claws and sticks its head into the skin, where it feeds on tiny blood vessels.

Incidence and Transmission   Pubic lice are quite common and are seen frequently in public health clinics and by private physicians. They are frequently transmitted during sexual contact when the pubic areas of two individuals are brought together. Crabs may live for as long as one day away from the body, particularly if their stomachs are full of blood. They may drop off onto underclothes, bedsheets, sleeping bags, and so forth. Eggs deposited by the female louse on clothing or bedsheets may survive for several days. Thus, it is possible to get lice by sleeping in someone else's bed or by wearing his or her clothes. Furthermore, a successfully treated person may be reinfected by being exposed to her or his own unwashed sheets or underclothes. Pubic lice do not necessarily limit themselves to the genital areas. They may be transmitted, usually by fingers, to the armpits or scalp.

Symptoms   Most people begin to suspect something is amiss when they start itching. Suspicions become stronger when scratching brings no relief. However, a few people seem to have great tolerance for the bite of a louse, experiencing very little if any discomfort. Self-diagnosis is possible by simply locating a louse on a pubic hair.

FIGURE 18.3 A PUBIC LOUSE, OR "CRAB"

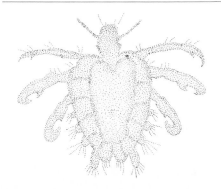

Treatment   Self-treatment is possible by obtaining an over-the-counter preparation known as A-200 pyrinate. Another commonly employed treatment is Kwell (gamma benzene), available by prescription (often a phone call to your physician will be sufficient). Be sure to follow the accompanying instructions carefully. It is advisable to apply the solution to all areas where there are concentrations of body hair—the genitals, armpits, scalp, and even eyebrows. This should be followed by a reapplication seven days later (eggs take seven days to hatch). Be sure to wash all clothes and sheets that were used prior to treatment.

GENITAL WARTS

Warts that appear on the genitals, sometimes called venereal warts, are caused by a virus similar to that which produces warts on other parts of the body.

Incidence and Transmission   Genital warts are perhaps the least common of the STDs discussed in this chapter, but they are being seen today with increasing frequency. It is believed that they are primarily transmitted by vaginal, anal, or oral-genital sexual interaction. However, warts have been known to appear on people who are not sexually active or whose only sexual partner shows no sign of the condition.

Symptoms   The average incubation period for genital warts is about three months after contact with an infected person. In women, they most commonly appear on the bottom part of the vaginal opening. They may also occur on the perineum, the vaginal lips, the inner walls of the vagina, and the cervix. In men, they commonly occur on the glans, foreskin, or shaft of the penis. In moist areas (such as the vaginal opening and under the foreskin) they are pink or red and soft with a cauliflower-like appearance. On dry skin areas, they are generally hard and yellow-gray.

Treatment   Unless they are quite large, genital warts are treated, under medical supervision, with a surface application of podophyllin, a dark resinlike material. The podophyllin must be washed off with soap and water six hours after application to avoid a possible toxic reaction. One treatment may be sufficient to cause the warts to dry up and fall off. Occasionally, a second or sometimes extended period of treatment is necessary. Cauterization by electric needle, freezing with liquid nitrogen, or surgical removal is sometimes necessary with very large or persistent warts.

PREVENTION OF SEXUALLY TRANSMITTED DISEASES

Many approaches to curtailing the spread of sexually transmitted diseases have been advocated. These range from attempting to prohibit sexual activity among young people to providing easy public access to information about the symptoms of STDs,

Health departments often provide screening and treatment for sexually transmitted diseases.

along with free medical treatment. Consistent with the latter focus is an effort by most public health agencies to trace and treat any sexual partners with whom an infected person had contact. While public health codes require physicians to report all cases of venereal disease, in practice it seems that the majority of such instances go unreported. With nonsexually transmitted diseases like influenzas, chicken pox, or measles, this method of reporting and tracing potentially infected individuals has proved extremely successful in curtailing widespread epidemics. However, STDs present unique problems. Beyond embarrassment, there may be fear of the reactions of infected partners. In many states, nonmarital sex is against the law, creating the added problem of implicating a partner in crime. Fortunately these laws are rarely enforced, and most public clinics are willing to treat patients even if they refuse to reveal the names of sexual partners.

Unfortunately, the approaches mentioned here have not been successful in curbing the rapid spread of sexually transmitted diseases. For this reason, it becomes doubly important to stress a variety of specific preventive measures that may be taken by an individual or couple. Clearly, abstinence is one virtually sure-fire method to avoid an STD infection. However, this alternative is not especially popular. There is a variation on the theme of abstinence worth noting. Perhaps you are married or living with someone in a generally monogamous relationship but have a brief sexual encounter with a casual acquaintance. Out of concern for yourself and your primary partner, it would be wise to avoid sexual relations with him or her for at least seven to eight days after your contact with the third party to allow symptoms of an STD to develop. Gonorrhea and herpes, two extremely common STDs, will generally show up during this period. Unfortunately, other diseases like syphilis, NGU, and genital warts may take several weeks to surface, and for most people this long a period of abstinence is not a practical alternative.

Being monogamous yourself and having a disease-free partner who is also monogamous is another way to prevent contracting a sexually transmitted disease. Yet sometimes it is difficult to be certain your partner is monogamous, even if you are. In addition, neither abstinence nor monogamy is an acceptable alternative to many people. It is to those of you who fit into these categories that the following suggestions are primarily directed.

Prostitutes and certain medical practitioners have known for a long time that a collection of specific procedures, some of which are quite simple to put into effect, can help to reduce a person's chances of getting an STD. Unfortunately, preventive measures (other than abstinence) have not been stressed publicly with the same enthusiasm that has been directed toward dispensing information on the symptoms and treatment of STDs. The lack of emphasis on practical preventive techniques often reflects an underlying societal consciousness that views STDs as "little helpers" in scaring off young people who might otherwise experiment with sex. For example, in California before 1971 it was a criminal offense for an individual to provide another with a VD preventive. Furthermore, some people feel quite uncomfortable with promoting prevention because of the implied assumption that nonmarital intercourse is condoned. However, the reality of contemporary sexual behavior indicates a need for some practical preventive procedures.

Some Steps for Prevention

We will outline several methods of prevention—steps that can be taken before, during, or shortly after sexual contact to reduce the likelihood of contracting an STD. Many of these methods are effective against the transmission of a variety of diseases. Several are applicable to oral-genital and anal-genital contacts in addition to genital-genital interaction. None are 100% effective, but each acts to significantly reduce the chances of infection. Furthermore—and this cannot be overemphasized—the use of preventive measures may help to curtail the booming spread of STDs. Since most infected people have sexual contact with one or more partners before they realize they have a disease and seek treatment, improved prevention rather than better treatment seems to hold the key to reducing these unpleasant accompaniments to sexual expression. The following quote elaborates on this point of view:

A clinician who diagnoses and cures a symptomatic gonorrhea infection accomplishes very little toward curbing the disease; for on the average each patient has already infected one additional person prior to diagnosis and cure. The prevention of one infection, in contrast, also prevents all of the subsequent cases which would otherwise stem from that case through the years ahead. It is not unrealistic to estimate that the prevention of one gonorrhea infection today will also on the average prevent several hundred additional gonorrhea infections during the next two decades. (Brecher, 1975, pp. 325–326).

Some of the suggestions included in the following discussion are discussed in detail in an excellent article written by Edward Brecher titled "Prevention of the Sexually Transmitted Diseases" (*Journal of Sex Research*, 1975, 11, pp. 318–328). Those of you interested in more detailed information on this topic might wish to refer to his article.

Inspection of Your Partner's Genitals   Examining your partner's genitals, prior to coital or oral contact, may reveal the symptoms of an STD. Herpes blisters, vaginal and urethral discharges, chancres and rashes associated with syphilis, genital warts, and pubic lice may be easily seen. In most cases, symptoms will be more evident in a man. If he is uncircumcised, be sure to retract the foreskin. The presence of a discharge, unpleasant odor, sores, blisters, rash, warts, or anything else out of the ordinary should be viewed with some concern. "Milking" the penis is a particularly effective way to detect a suspicious discharge. This technique, sometimes called the "short-arm inspection," involves grasping the penis firmly and pulling the loose skin up and down the shaft several times, applying pressure on the base-to-head stroke. Next, part the urinary opening to see if any cloudy discharge is present.

People may frequently find it difficult to conduct such an inspection before sexual sharing. Occasionally, just the request "let me undress you" will provide some opportunity to examine your partner's genitals. Perhaps some sensate focus pleasuring, discussed in Chapter 17, will provide the opportunity for more detailed visual exploration. Some people suggest a shower before sex with an eye toward examining their partner. While this may be quite helpful for noting visible sores, blisters, and so forth, the soap and water may also remove the visual and olfactory cues associated with a discharge.

If you note signs of infection, you may justifiably and wisely elect not to have sexual relations. Your intended partner may or may not be aware of his or her symptoms. Therefore, it is important that you explain your concerns. Some people may decide to continue their sexual interaction, using some of the methods of protection described in the following sections. Others might choose a form of sexual sharing that avoids either coitus or oral-genital contact like manual stimulation or solo masturbation while being held by the other person.

Washing the Genitals Before or After Sexual Contact   There is some difference in opinion about the effectiveness of soap and water washing of the genitals before sexual interaction. One problem is that the organisms infecting a man, even when removed from the external penis, often are harbored within the urethra and thus may be forced to the outside during sexual arousal or ejaculation. However, there can be little doubt that washing has some benefits (Buchan, 1973). This technique is generally more effective when applied to the man, although washing the vulva can also be helpful.

Some people may find it difficult to suggest that their partner allow them to wash their genitals before having sex. However, this may be accomplished unobtrusively by including the washing of the penis and vulva in the sex play that occurs in the shower or bathtub. Others may quite frankly announce that they are cleansing their partner's genitals for their mutual protection. Some individuals suggest that a woman douche before coitus as a preventive measure. However, frequent douching may be harmful to a woman, and its effectiveness in preventing transmission of an STD is likely to be quite limited.

After sexual contact, thorough washing of the genitals and surrounding area with soap and water is highly recommended as a preventive procedure when transmission of an infection is a possibility. We are not suggesting that this procedure should always follow sexual sharing. In fact, many lovers with long term relationships would find it unnecessary and possibly even offensive, implying that a person is somehow unclean after sex.

Promptness is very important in post-sex washing, probably as important as thoroughness. Some people might object to jumping out of bed to wash, as it may break the relaxed mood. For those uncomfortable with letting their partner know they are taking this precaution, perhaps simply announcing you need to go to the bathroom (a not uncommon need after sex) will be enough. Sometimes, the suggestion of a post-sex shower will be happily received.

Women and men can also wash their genitals while sitting over the washbowl. First fill it with warm soapy water, then turn your back to it and boost yourself up to straddle it. In this position it is relatively easy to thoroughly wash your exposed genitals with a soapy washcloth. In France, where both men and women use the *bidet* (a low-built basin with hot and cold running water, easy to squat over) after intercourse, there is a remarkably low gonorrhea rate (Brecher, 1975).

Urination after coitus may have some limited benefits, particularly to men. Many infectious organisms do not survive in the acid environment created by urine. Urinating may also flush out disease-causing organisms.

It has been suggested that women douche after intercourse with a partner who may have an STD. This procedure may be somewhat effective in preventing disease, particularly when a medicated douche preparation is used (Singh et al., 1972). However, as with douching before coitus, the preventive value of this procedure should be carefully weighed against its potentially damaging effects.

Vaginal Prophylaxis During Coitus Most women and men, when they consider the range of available birth control options, are not aware that the foams, creams, and jellies currently on the market offer some protection against a variety of sexually transmitted diseases, including gonorrhea, syphilis, and trichomoniasis (Bolch and Warren, 1973; Singh et al., 1972). This is an important additional benefit of vaginal contraceptive products.

The Condom as a Prophylactic Device   It has been known for decades that condoms effectively prevent transmission of some STDs. Unfortunately, this benefit has not been as actively promoted in the United States as it has been in other countries, most notably Sweden. The condom seems to be one of the great under-rated aids to sexual interaction. Used in combination with vaginal spermicides, it is effective as a preventer of both undesired conception and transmission of many diseases. It is most valuable in the prevention of gonorrhea, trichomoniasis, moniliasis, syphilis, and NGU. It is less effective against warts and herpes and has no value in combating pubic lice. Condoms are particularly practical in sexual encounters where the couple has not thoroughly evaluated a method of birth control appropriate for their respective life styles and where the lack of a monogamous affiliation increases the possibility of contracting a sexually transmitted disease.

Post-Contact Medication   Occasionally, a person may engage in sexual relations where the possibility of contracting an STD seems quite high. Perhaps certain symptoms were detected during or after the sexual sharing. What can be done? Observing a period of abstinence while waiting for symptoms to appear seems a good practice to follow. In addition, it has long been known that taking tetracycline after high-risk exposure dramatically reduces the possibility of developing a variety of STDs (Wear and Holmes, 1976). A word of caution is in order here, however. Routine prophylactic treatment with any antibiotic you might have around the house is not advisable. It is much better to consult with your private physician or local VD clinic.

Routine Medical Evaluations   Many authorities recommend that sexually active individuals should routinely visit their physician or local VD clinic for periodic check-ups, even when no symptoms of disease are evident. In view of the number of people, both women and men, who are symptomless carriers of STDs, this seems like very good advice. How often these examinations should be conducted is a matter of opinion. Our advice to people in this category is that they should preferably have check-ups every three months, certainly no less than twice a year.

SUMMARY

1. In the United States there is an increasing incidence of diseases that are transmitted sexually (STDs). However, public understanding of STDs, particularly preventive measures, has not shown a comparable increase.

TRICHOMONIASIS

2. Trichomoniasis is the most common STD in women. Male partners of infected women are thought to carry the Trichomonas organism in their urethra or prostate. Its primary mode of transmission is through sexual contact.

3. The primary symptom of trichomoniasis in women is an abundant, unpleasant-smelling vaginal discharge often accompanied by inflamed, itchy, and painful genital tissues. Men are rarely symptomatic.

4. Infected women and their male sexual partners may be successfully treated with the drug Flagyl.

MONILIASIS

5. Moniliasis is a yeast infection that affects many women. Pregnancy, diabetes, using birth control pills, and treatment with oral antibiotics are conditions often associated with monilia infection.

6. Symptoms of yeast infections include a white, clumpy discharge and intense itching of the vaginal and vulvar tissues.

7. Yeast infections respond quite well to treatment with antibiotic vaginal suppositories.

GONORRHEA

8. Gonorrhea, a very common communicable disease in the United States, is a bacterial infection transmitted by sexual contact.

9. Early symptoms of gonorrhea infection are more likely to be manifested by men, who will probably have a discharge from the penis and burning during urination. The early sign in women, if detectable, is a mild vaginal discharge that may be irritating to vulvar tissues.

10. Complications of gonorrhea infection in men include prostate, bladder, and kidney involvement, and, infrequently, gonococcal epididymitis that may lead to sterility. In women, gonorrhea may lead to pelvic inflammatory disease, sterility, and abdominal adhesions.

11. Most cases of gonorrhea respond well to penicillin treatment. In cases of allergic or resistant reactions to penicillin, alternative drugs are available.

SYPHILIS

12. Syphilis is far less common, but potentially more damaging, than gonorrhea. It is almost always transmitted by sexual contact.

13. If untreated, syphilis may progress through four phases: primary, characterized by the appearance of chancre sores; secondary, distinguished by the occurrence of a generalized skin rash; latent, a several-year period of no overt symptoms; and tertiary, during which the disease may produce cardiovascular disease, blindness, paralysis, skin ulcers, liver damage, and severe mental pathology.

14. Syphilis may be treated by penicillin at any stage of its development.

NONGONOCOCCAL URETHRITIS

15. Nongonococcal urethritis (NGU) is a very common infection of the urethral passage typically seen in men. It is primarily caused by two infectious organisms transmitted during coitus.

16. Symptoms, most apparent in men, include penile discharge and mild burning during urination. Women may have a minor vaginal discharge and are thought to harbor the infecting organisms.

17. Penicillin is not effective against NGU, making definitive diagnosis a must. A few days of tetracycline therapy usually clears up the condition.

HERPES

18. There are five different herpes viruses, the most common being type 1, which produces cold sores, and type 2, which infects the genital area. Occasionally, type 1 is found below the waist and type 2 in the mouth area. Type 2 is transmitted almost exclusively by sexual contact; type 1 may be passed by kissing, or by using toilet articles or utensils of an infected person.

19. The presence of painful sores is the primary symptom of herpes. A person is highly contagious during a herpes eruption. Genital herpes may predispose a woman to cervical cancer and infect her newborn child, producing severe damage or death of the infant.

20. There is no known cure for herpes. Treatment is symptomatic, aimed at reducing pain and speeding the healing process.

PUBIC LICE

21. Pubic lice ("crabs") are tiny biting insects that feed on small blood vessels in the pubic region. They may be transmitted through sexual contact or by using sheets or clothing contaminated by an infested individual.

22. The primary symptom is severe itching that is not relieved by scratching; sometimes pubic lice can be seen.

23. A variety of prescription and nonprescription medications effectively kill pubic lice.

GENITAL WARTS

24. Genital warts are primarily, but not exclusively, transmitted by sexual contact. They are successfully treated by surface application of podophyllin.

PREVENTION OF STDs

25. The combined efforts to curtail the spread of STDs, including increasing the public's knowledge about them, offering free medical care, and requiring physicians to report all cases of VD, have not been successful.

26. To curb the rising tide, more emphasis needs to be placed on prophylactic (preventive) measures.

27. Other than abstinence and monogamy, both unacceptable to many sexually active people, there are a variety of potentially valuable preventive steps that may be taken by a concerned individual or couple.

28. These include inspection of your partner's genitals, disinfection of the genitals prior to or after sexual contact, vaginal prophylaxis during coitus, use of a condom, routine medical evaluations, and, in certain cases of high-risk exposure, the use of post-coital medication.

SUGGESTED READINGS

Corsaro, Maria, and Korzeniowsky, Carole. *STD: A Commonsense Guide*. New York: St. Martin's, 1980. An excellent, concise, clearly written book that provides important information about a variety of STDs in language easily understood by a lay person.

Gunn, Terri, and Stenzel-Poore, Mary. *The Herpes Handbook*. Portland, Oregon: Venereal Disease Action Council. A comprehensive guide to the physical and emotional aspects of genital and oral herpes. $2.00 per copy which includes mailing in an unmarked envelope. Make checks payable to V.D.A.C. To order, write: HERPES HANDBOOK, OHSU–L220A, Portland, Oregon 97201.

Montreal Health Press. *VD Handbook*. Montreal: MHP, 1977. A comprehensive, well-written discussion of the many varieties of sexually transmitted diseases. Available for 50 cents from VD Handbook, P.O. Box 1000, Station G, Montreal, Quebec H2W 2NI, Canada.

Wear, Jennifer, and Holmes, King. *How to Have Intercourse Without Getting Screwed*. Seattle: Madrona, 1976. Contains up-to-date information on sexually transmitted diseases (also contraception and abortion) written in a candid, easy-to-read style. An excellent source book for individuals who wish to make responsible and informed decisions in sexual matters.

Resources

The Herpes Resource Center (formerly HELP), 260 Sheridan Avenue, Palo Alto, California 94306; (415) 328–7710. For an annual membership fee of $12, this excellent service provides a quarterly journal complete with up-to-date information about herpes, access to local chapters (support groups), and a private telephone information, counseling, and referral service.

PART SIX

Social Issues

19

Atypical Sexual Behavior

EXHIBITIONISM
OBSCENE PHONE CALLS
VOYEURISM
SADOMASOCHISM
FETISHISM
TRANSVESTISM
SUMMARY
SUGGESTED READINGS

*I*n this chapter we will focus on a number of sexual behaviors that have been variously labeled as deviant, perverted, aberrant, or abnormal. More recently, the terms variant and *paraphilia* (meaning "beyond love") have been used to describe these somewhat uncommon manifestations of sexual expression. These labels are less emotionally laden and judgmental, and therefore preferable to the others. However, in our experiences dealing with and discussing variant sexual behaviors, only one common characteristic seems to stand out. Simply stated, each behavior, in its fully developed form, is not typically expressed by most people in our society. Therefore, we have elected to use the label *atypical* to describe these behaviors.

There are many degrees of atypical behavior. Like many other sexual expressions discussed in this book, the behaviors singled out in this chapter represent extreme points on a continuum. Atypical sexual behaviors exist in many gradations, ranging from mild, infrequently expressed tendencies to full-blown, regularly manifested behaviors. Despite the term atypical, many of us may recognize some degree of such behaviors or feelings within ourselves—perhaps manifested at some point in our lives, perhaps mostly repressed, or perhaps emerging in very private fantasies.

A second point has to do with the state of our knowledge about these behaviors. In most of the discussions that follow, readers will probably note that the person who shows the atypical behavior is usually male. For some of the activities discussed in this chapter, this is an accurate impression. In other instances, however, the tendency to assume that males are predominantly involved may be influenced by the somewhat biased nature of differential reporting and prosecution. Female exhibitionism, for example, is far less likely to be reported than is a similar kind of behavior in a male.

A third consideration is the impact of these behaviors both upon the person who exhibits them and upon others to whom they may be directed. People who manifest unusual sexual behaviors often depend upon these acts for sexual satisfaction. The behavior is an end in itself. It is also likely that their unconventional behavior will alienate others. Consequently, these people often find it very difficult to establish satisfying relationships with partners. Instead, their sexual expression may assume a solitary, driven, even compulsive quality. Research also suggests that such acts may have harmful effects upon others (Altrocchi, 1980). People who are unwilling recipients of variant sexual expressions, such as peeping or exposing, may be psychologically traumatized. They may feel that they have been violated, that they are vulnerable to physical abuse, and may develop fears that such unpleasant episodes will recur. This is one reason why many of these behaviors are illegal. Many people who encounter such acts are not adversely affected. Because of this, and the fact that these behaviors do not generally involve physical or sexual contact with another, many authorities view them as minor sex offenses (sometimes called "nuisance" offenses). However, recent evidence suggests that some people progress from nuisance offenses to more serious forms of sexual abuse, a finding that may lead to a reconsideration of their classification as minor offenses. We will examine this issue in more detail later in this chapter and in the next.

Finally, please note that the terms we use in this chapter refer to behaviors, not to people. While it may be convenient to label people as transvestites, voyeurs, fetishists, and the like, such labeling is inappropriate and potentially oppressive. For example, even when a person's primary mode of sexual expression is genital exposure, it would be misleading to label him or her an exhibitionist. This would be comparable to labeling someone who has a tendency to squint their eyes an eye squinter. "Hi, Jack, I would like you to meet Tom—he is an eye squinter." Sounds ludicrous, doesn't it? Is it any more sensible to label people by how they express their sexuality? Many of the individuals you will read about in the following pages live productive lives, exhibiting no overtly detectable behaviors that result in their being labeled abnormal or undesirable by the general public. It is much more appropriate to speak of voyeuristic or masochistic behavior rather than calling people voyeurs or masochists.

Six forms of behavior will be outlined in the following pages; they are among the most frequently expressed atypical behaviors in our society. We will briefly discuss each behavior, looking at how it is expressed, some of the common characteristics of those exhibiting it, and the various factors thought to contribute to its development. More severe forms of sexual victimization, such as rape, incest, and child abuse, will be discussed in the next chapter. Many forms of variant sexual expression are not included in this text. Those interested in finding more information will have no difficulty locating ample material among the many books and articles written about this topic.

EXHIBITIONISM

Exhibitionism, often called "indecent exposure," refers to behavior where an individual (usually a male) exposes his genitals to an involuntary observer (usually an adult woman or female child). Sexual gratification is typically obtained by masturbating shortly thereafter using mental images of the "victim's" reaction to increase arousal. Some people may have orgasm triggered by the very act of exposure, and a few may masturbate while exhibiting themselves. Exposure may occur in a variety of locations, most of which allow for easy escape. Subways, relatively deserted streets, parks, and cars with a door left open are common places for exhibitionism to occur. However, sometimes a private dwelling may be the scene of an exposure, as revealed in the following account.

One evening I was shocked to open the door of my apartment to a naked man. I looked long enough to see that he was underdressed for the occasion, and then slammed the door in his face. He didn't come back. I'm sure my look of total horror was what he was after. But it is difficult to keep your composure when you open your door to a naked man. (Authors' files)

Certainly, many of us have exhibitionistic tendencies—we may go to nude beaches, parade before admiring lovers, or wear provocative clothes or scanty swimwear. However, such behavior is considered appropriate by a society that in many ways exploits and celebrates the erotically portrayed human body. The fact that legally defined exhibitionistic behavior involves generally unwilling observers sets it apart from the more acceptable variations of exhibitionism just described.

Exhibitionism accounts for more arrests for sexual offenses than any other single form of behavior (Allen, 1969; Freese, 1972). Our knowledge of who shows this behavior is based almost exclusively on studies of the arrested offender, a fact that may make the sample unrepresentative. This sampling problem is common to many other forms of atypical behavior that come under the criminal code.

From the available data, however limited, it would appear that most people who exhibit themselves are adult males in their 20s or 30s, and over one-half are or have been married. They are often very shy, nonassertive people who feel inadequate and insecure. They may function quite efficiently in their daily lives and be commonly characterized by others as "nice, but kind of shy." Sexual relationships with others are likely to have been quite unsatisfactory. Many were reared in atmospheres characterized by puritanical and oppressive attitudes toward sexuality.

There are a number of hypotheses about the factors that influence the development of exhibitionistic behavior. Many of the individuals manifesting such behavior may have such powerful feelings of personal inadequacy that they are afraid to reach out to another person out of fear of rejection. Their exhibitionism may thus be a limited attempt to somehow involve others, however fleetingly, in their sexual expression. Limiting contact to briefly opening a raincoat before dashing off minimizes the possibility of overt rejection.

Some men who expose themselves may be looking for affirmation of their masculinity. Others, feeling isolated and unappreciated, may simply be seeking attention they desperately crave. A few may feel anger and hostility toward people, particularly women, who have failed to notice them or who, they believe, have caused them emotional pain. In these circumstances exposure may be a form of reprisal designed to shock or frighten the people they see as the source of their discomfort.

Occasionally, exhibitionism may be associated with more extreme psychopathology. It is not uncommon to observe such activity in emotionally disturbed, intellectually handicapped, or mentally disoriented individuals. The behavior can sometimes represent a generalized limited awareness of what society defines as appropriate actions, or a breakdown in personal ethical controls, or both.

In contrast to the public image of an exhibitionist as one who lurks about in the shadows, ready to grab hapless victims and drag them off to ravish them, the majority of men who fall into this category are probably unlikely to physically assault or rape anyone (Tollison and Adams, 1979). Yet the word "victim" is not entirely inappropriate, in that observers of such exhibitionistic episodes may be emotionally traumatized by the experience. Some may feel that they are in danger of being raped or otherwise harmed. A few, particularly young children, may develop negative feelings about the genital anatomy from such an experience.

Investigators have noted that some people who expose themselves, probably a small minority, may actually physically assault their victims. Furthermore, it also seems probable that some men progress from exposing themselves to more serious offenses such as rape and child-molesting. In a one-of-a-kind study, Gene Abel (1981), a Columbia University researcher, conducted an in-depth investigation of the motives and behavior of 207 men who were admitted perpetrators of a variety of sexual offenses, including child-molesting and rape. This research is unique in that all participants were men outside of the legal system who voluntarily sought treatment for

A calm response to an act of exhibitionism is not likely to reinforce such behavior.

Spencer— © Punch (Rothco)

"You don't often see a real silk lining, these days . . ."

the sexual offenses they committed after being guaranteed confidentiality. Abel found that 49% of the rapists in his sample had histories of other types of variant sexual behavior, generally preceding the onset of rape behavior. The most common of these were child molestation, exhibitionism, voyeurism, incest, and sadism. These findings do not imply that people who engage in activities like exhibitionism and voyeurism will inevitably develop into rapists. However, it seems clear that some people may progress beyond these relatively minor acts to far more severe patterns of sexual aggression.

While perhaps all of us would like protection against being sexually used without our consent, it seems unnecessarily harsh and punitive to imprison people manifesting exhibitionistic behavior, particularly the first-time offender. In recent years, at least in some locales, there has been some movement toward therapy as an alternative to incarceration. Often therapy is directed toward fostering feelings of personal worth and adequacy, together with supporting the development of more acceptable modes of sexual expression. In addition, various behavioral therapy methods are sometimes used to help the offender gain control over his urge to expose (Rooth and Marks, 1974).

A final note about exhibitionism seems in order. It has to do with ways of responding to such episodes. Most people who express this behavior want to elicit reactions of shock, disgust, fear, or terror. Although it may be difficult not to react in this fashion, a better response would be to calmly ignore it and casually go about your business. In this way you will avoid reinforcing such self-defeating behavior. Of course, it is also important to report such acts to the proper authorities as soon as possible.

OBSCENE PHONE CALLS

The characteristics of people who make obscene phone calls seem to be similar to those who engage in exhibitionism. As one extensive study has indicated (Nadler, 1968), they are typically male, and they often suffer from pervasive feelings of inadequacy and insecurity. Obscene phone calls are frequently the only way they can find to have sexual exchanges. However, when relating to the other sex, these people frequently show greater anxiety and hostility than do individuals inclined toward exhibitionism. This is revealed in the following account:

One night I received a phone call from a man who sounded quite normal until he started his barrage of filth. Just as I was about to slam the phone down, he announced, "Don't hang up. I know where you live (address followed) and that you have two little girls. If you don't want to find them all mangled up, you will hear what I have to say. Furthermore, I expect you to be available for calls every night at this time." It was a nightmare. He called night after night. Sometimes he made me listen while he masturbated. Finally, I couldn't take it any longer and I contacted the police. They were unable to catch him, but they sure scared him off in short order, thank heaven. I was about to go crazy. (Authors' files)

Fortunately, a caller rarely follows up his verbal assault with a physical attack on his victim.

Information about how to deal with obscene phone calls is made available by most local phone company offices. Because they are commonly beseiged by such queries, you may need to be persistent in your request. A few tips are worth knowing; they may even make it unnecessary to seek outside help.

First, quite often the caller has picked your name at random from a phone book, or perhaps knows you from some other source and is just trying you out to see what kind of reaction he can get. Your initial response is critical in determining his subsequent actions. He wants you to be horrified, shocked, or disgusted, so the best response is usually not to react overtly. Slamming the phone down may reveal your emotional state and provide reinforcement to the caller. Simply set it down gently and go about your business. If the phone rings again immediately, ignore it. Chances are he will seek out other, more responsive "victims."

Other tactics may also be helpful. One, used successfully by a former student, is to feign deafness. "What is that you said? You must speak up. I'm hard of hearing, you know!" Setting down the phone with the explanation that you are going to another extension (that you never arrive at) may be another practical solution.

If you are persistently bothered by repeated calls, you may need to take additional steps. There are several possible ways of dealing with the situation. Your telephone company may cooperate in changing your number to an unlisted one at no charge. Another option is to try to trace the call, with local police cooperation (phone-call tracing has become exceedingly efficient in recent years). Some people report success with tapping a ring or some other metallic object against the phone mouthpiece to simulate connecting a recording device. Others cover the mouthpiece partially, announcing "He is on the line again, officer." By all means, do not heed the commonly given advice to blow in the mouthpiece with a police whistle (which may be quite painful and even harmful to the ear) unless you are willing to receive the same treatment from your caller.

VOYEURISM

Voyeurism refers to deriving sexual pleasure from looking at the naked bodies or sexual activities of others, usually strangers, without their consent. A degree of voyeurism is socially acceptable (witness the popularity of R- and X-rated movies and magazines like *Playboy* and *Playgirl*), and it is sometimes difficult to determine when voyeuristic behavior becomes a problem. To qualify as atypical sexual behavior, voyeurism must be preferred to sexual relations with another, and/or it must be indulged in with some risk. People who engage in this behavior are often most sexually aroused when the risk of discovery is high, and this may explain why most are not attracted to places like nudist camps and nude beaches where looking is acceptable (Tollison and Adams, 1979).

The common term "Peeping Tom" correctly implies that this behavior is typically, although not exclusively, expressed by males. Voyeurism includes peering in bedroom windows, stationing oneself by the entrance to the woman's bathroom, and boring holes in the walls of public dressing rooms. Some men have elaborate routes that they travel several nights a week, being occasionally rewarded by a glimpse of bare anatomy or, rarely, by a scene of sexual interaction. The following account reveals one such pattern of repetitive, ritualized voyeuristic behavior.

During my teenage years I never expressed any sexual needs to another person—not that I had any real opportunities. You could count the dates I had all through high school on one hand. But I did have my secret nightlife. Almost every evening, after Mom and Dad were asleep, I would slip out my bedroom window and make the rounds. Sometimes I would only do a "short-circuit," covering just the local neighborhood. Other times I would branch out, traveling for miles over a familiar route. Sometimes days would go by and I wouldn't see anything. Other nights I would get real lucky. There was a high school girl who lived down the street who persisted in undressing in front of her bedroom window. I guess she thought her backyard was secluded enough for such activities. I wonder what she would have thought if she had seen me masturbating in the darkness below? I would fantasize that she would invite me in to share her bed. Actually, if she had made such an offer, I would probably have run the other way. Finally, I tired of such activity. But for a while, it was the major part of my sex life. (Authors' files)

Most people inclined toward voyeurism tend to have some of the same characteristics as people who expose themselves (Gebhard et al., 1965). They often have poorly developed sociosexual skills, with strong feelings of inferiority and inadequacy, particularly as directed toward potential sexual partners. They tend to be very young men, usually in their early 20s. They rarely "peep" at someone they know, preferring strangers instead. Voyeurism is not typically associated with other antisocial behavior. Most individuals who engage in such activity are content to merely look, preferring to keep space between themselves and their "victims." However, in some instances people who engage in voyeurism may go on to more serious offenses such as burglary, arson, assault, and even rape (Abel, 1981; Gebhard et al., 1965; MacNamara and Sagarin, 1977).

It is difficult to isolate specific influences that trigger voyeuristic behavior, particularly since so many of us demonstrate these tendencies in somewhat more controlled fashion. The adolescent or young adult male who displays this behavior is often an individual who feels great curiosity about sexual activity (as many of us do) but, at the same time, feels very inadequate or insecure. Peeping becomes a vicarious fulfillment because he may be unable to consummate sexual relationships with others without experiencing a great deal of anxiety. Some people may also have their voyeuristic behavior reinforced by feelings of power and superiority over those they secretly observe.

SADOMASOCHISM

We have chosen to discuss sadism and masochism under the common category of *sadomasochistic* behavior (also known as SM) because they are mirror images of the same phenomenon, the association of sexual expression with pain. Furthermore, the dynamics of both behaviors are similar and overlapping. Technically, sadomasochism may be defined as obtaining sexual arousal through receiving or giving physical and/or mental pain (Gebhard et al., 1965).

Labeling behavior as sadistic or masochistic is complicated by the fact that many people enjoy some form of aggressive interaction during sexual sharing (such as "love bites") for which the label SM seems inappropriate. Kinsey (1953) found that 10% of the males and 3% of the females in his sample responded erotically to stories with SM themes. Furthermore, over 25% of both sexes reported erotic response to receiving love bites during sexual interaction. More recently, Hunt's survey (1974) found that 10% of males and 8% of females in his sample (under age 35) reported obtaining sexual pleasure from SM activities during interaction with a partner. Although sado-masochistic practices have the potential for being physically dangerous, most people who indulge in these behaviors generally stay within mutually agreed-upon limits, often confining their activities to mild or even symbolic SM acts with a trusted partner.

Individuals with sadistic tendencies are less common than their masochistic counterparts (Gebhard et al., 1965). This imbalance may reflect a general social script—certainly it is more virtuous to be punished than to be the perpetrator of either physical or mental aggression toward another. It is relatively easy to find someone who is willing to inflict pain, particularly for a price. On the other hand, it is often difficult to find someone who is willing to suffer pain at the hands of another, even for a price. We occasionally read of sadistic assaults against unwilling victims. The classic sex murder is often of this nature. In these instances, orgasmic release may be produced by the homicidal violence itself.

Studies of sexual behavior in other species reveal that many nonhuman animals engage in what might be labeled combative or pain-inflicting behavior before coitus. Many observers theorize that such activity has definite neurophysiological value in that it heightens many of the biological accompaniments of sexual arousal, including blood pressure, muscle tension, and hyperventilation (Gebhard et al., 1965). It may be that a number of people engage in this behavior because, for a variety of reasons (such as guilt, anxiety, or apathy), they need additional nonsexual stimuli to achieve sufficient arousal.

Some people may be attracted to SM behavior simply because it represents a marked departure from more conventional sexual practices. Other people who indulge in SM acts may have acquired strong negative feelings toward sex, often believing it is sinful and immoral. For such persons, masochistic behavior provides a guilt-relieving mechanism: either they get their pleasure simultaneously with punishment, or they first endure the punishment to entitle them to ultimate pleasures. Similarly, people who indulge in sadism may be punishing partners for engaging in anything so evil. Furthermore, people who have strong feelings of personal or sexual inadequacy may resort to sadistic acts of dominance over their partners to temporarily alleviate these feelings of inferiority.

FETISHISM

Fetishism refers to sexual behavior in which an individual becomes sexually aroused by focusing on an inanimate object or a part of the human body. As has been the case with the behaviors we have considered so far, it is often difficult to draw the line between normal activities that may have fetishistic overtones and those that are genuinely atypical. Many people are erotically aroused by the sight of undergarments and certain specific body parts like legs, buttocks, thighs, and breasts. Many men, and some women, may use articles of clothing and other paraphernalia as an accompaniment to masturbation or sexual activity with a partner. It is only when a person becomes focused on these objects or body parts to the exclusion of everything else that the term fetishism is truly applicable. In some instances, a person may be unable to experience sexual arousal and orgasm in the absence of the fetish object. In other situations, where the attachment is not so strong, sexual response may occur in the absence of the object, but often with diminished intensity. For some people, fetish objects serve as substitutes for human contact and are dispensed with if a partner becomes available. Some common fetish objects include women's lingerie, shoes (particularly high-heeled), boots (often affiliated with SM themes of domination), hair, stockings (especially black mesh hose), and a variety of leather, silk, and rubber goods.

How does fetishism develop? Perhaps the most common way is through incorporating the object or body part, often through fantasy, in a masturbation sequence where the reinforcement of orgasm strengthens the fetishistic association. This is a kind of classical conditioning in which some object or body part becomes associated with sexual arousal. This pattern of conditioning was demonstrated some years ago by Rachman (1966), who created a mild fetish among male subjects under laboratory conditions by repeatedly pairing a photograph of women's boots with erotic slides of nude females. The subjects soon began to show sexual response to the boots alone. This reaction also generalized to other types of women's shoes.

Only rarely does fetishism develop into an offense that might harm someone. Occasionally, an individual may commit burglary to supply an object fetish:

Some years ago we had a bra stealer loose in the neighborhood. You couldn't hang your brassiere outside on the clothesline without fear of losing it. He also took panties, but bras seemed to be his major thing. I talked to other women in the neighborhood who were having the same problem. This guy must have had a roomful. I never heard anything about him being caught. He must have decided to move on because the thefts stopped all of a sudden. (Authors' files)

Burglary is the most frequent serious offense to be associated with a fetishist inclination. Uncommonly, a person may do something bizarre, such as cut hair from an unwilling person. In extremely rare cases, a man may murder and mutilate his victim, preserving certain body parts for fantasy-masturbation activities.

TRANSVESTISM

The term *transvestism* is applied to behaviors whereby an individual obtains sexual excitement from putting on the clothes of the other sex. In defining transvestism, it is important to emphasize the differences between people who cross-dress to experience sexual arousal, female impersonators (who cross-dress to entertain), male homosexuals who occasionally "go in drag" (cross-dress), and transsexuals who, as we discussed in Chapter 2, cross-dress to obtain a partial sense of physical and emotional completeness rather than for sexual titillation.

A range of behaviors fall under the category of transvestism. Some people prefer to don the entire garb of the other sex. This is often a solitary activity, occurring privately in their homes. Occasionally, a person may go out on the town while so attired, but this is unusual. Generally, the cross-dressing is a momentary activity, producing sexual excitement that often culminates in gratification through masturbation or sex with a partner. In many cases of transvestism, a person becomes aroused by wearing only one garment, perhaps a pair of panties or a brassiere. There is a strong element of fetishism in this behavior that has led many writers to link the two conditions. A distinguishing feature of transvestism is that the article is actually worn instead of just being viewed or fondled.

It would appear that in the majority of instances, it is men who are attracted to transvestism. It is true, though, that our data are somewhat limited, and the opportunities for cross-dressing without detection are obviously much greater for women. Nevertheless, the clinical literature is largely devoid of accounts of women who derive sexual arousal from such behavior. Male cross-dressing occurs primarily among married men with predominantly heterosexual orientations (Benjamin, 1967; Stoller, 1971; Wise and Meyer, 1980). Not uncommonly, men with inclinations toward transvestism work out arrangements with their partners so that cross-dressing may occur at home. The initial reaction of the partners may not be particularly negative. Nevertheless, resentment or disgust may sometimes develop, as revealed in the following account:

The first time my husband asked if he could wear my panties I thought he was joking. When he put them on I could see that he wasn't kidding around. Actually, we had a real good session that night and I guess this kind of blunted my concern. After a while it just started really bugging me. It seems like we can never just make love without his first putting on my underthings. Now I'm sick and tired of it. The whole thing seems real weird. (Authors' files)

As with fetishism and some other atypical behaviors, the development of transvestism often reveals a pattern of conditioning. Reinforcement, in the form of arousal and orgasm, may accompany cross-dressing activities at an early point in the development of sexual interest. This is portrayed in the following anecdote:

When I was a kid, about 11 or 12, I was fascinated and excited by magazine pictures of women modeling undergarments. Masturbating while looking at these pictures was great. Later, I began to incorporate my mother's underthings in my little masturbation rituals, at first just touching them with my free hand, and later putting them on and parading before the mirror while I did my hand-job. Now, as an adult, I have numerous sexual encounters with women that are quite satisfying without the dress-up part. But, I still occasionally do the dress-up when I'm alone, and I still find it quite exciting. (Authors' files)

Occasionally, transvestism is a behavior of the heterosexual male who is striving to explore the feminine side of his personality, an often difficult effort in a society that extols the "Marlboro Man" image. In essence, such men create two separate worlds, the dominant one being their masculine image exhibited on the job and in most relationships, and the private world of dress-up at home where they can express their gentle, sensuous self, which they may perceive as being more feminine.

Most people who engage in transvestism are not inclined to seek professional help. Even when therapy is undertaken, it is unlikely that the behavior will be appreciably altered (Wise and Meyer, 1980).

SUMMARY

1. Atypical sexual behavior refers to a variety of sexual activities that are statistically uncommon in the general population.

2. Such behaviors exist in many gradations, ranging from mild, infrequently expressed tendencies to full-blown, regularly manifested behaviors.

EXHIBITIONISM

3. Exhibitionism refers to behavior where an individual, almost always a male, exposes his genitals to an involuntary observer.

4. People who exhibit themselves are usually young, adult males who have strong feelings of inadequacy and insecurity. Sexual relationships with others, either past or present, are likely to be unsatisfactory.

5. Gratification is usually obtained when the "victim" responds with shock, disgust, or fear. Physical assault is not generally associated with such behavior.

OBSCENE PHONE CALLS

6. The characteristics of individuals who make obscene phone calls are similar to those who engage in exhibitionism.

7. While there may be an element of vicious verbal hostility in obscene phone calls, the caller rarely follows up his verbal assault with a physical attack on his victim.

VOYEURISM

8. Voyeurism refers to obtaining sexual pleasure from looking at the exposed bodies or sexual activities of others, usually strangers.

9. People inclined toward voyeurism, typically males, are often sociosexually underdeveloped, with strong feelings of inferiority and inadequacy.

SADOMASOCHISM

10. Sadomasochism may be defined as obtaining sexual arousal through receiving or giving physical and/or mental pain.

11. Individuals who engage in such behavior may be seeking additional nonsexual stimuli to achieve sufficient arousal. They may also be acting out of deeply rooted beliefs that sexual activity is sinful and immoral.

FETISHISM

12. Fetishism is a form of atypical sexual behavior wherein an individual obtains arousal by focusing on an inanimate object or a part of the human body.

13. Fetishism often is a product of conditioning, where the fetish object becomes associated with sexual arousal through the reinforcement of masturbation-produced orgasm.

TRANSVESTISM

14. Transvestism involves obtaining sexual excitement by cross-dressing. It is usually a solitary activity, expressed by a heterosexual male in the privacy of his own home.

15. As with fetishism, transvestism often evolves through an early pattern of conditioning where reinforcement, in the form of arousal and orgasm, accompanies the cross-dressing activities.

SUGGESTED READINGS

Gebhard, Paul H.; Pomeroy, Wardell B.; Gagnon, John H.; and Christenson, Cornelia V. *Sex Offenders: An Analysis of Types.* New York: Harper & Row, 1965 (also available in paperback from Bantam Books, 1967). A thorough analysis of many types of atypical sexual behaviors which come under the criminal code. Contains excellent information about a variety of psychosocial factors implicated in the development of these behaviors.

Stoller, Robert. "Sexual Deviations." In F. Beach (Ed.), *Human Sexuality in Four Perspectives.* Baltimore: Johns Hopkins Press, 1977 (also available in paperback from same publisher, 1978). Provides a review of several common atypical sexual behaviors with accompanying case examples.

20

Sexual Victimization

PEDOPHILIA
INCEST
SEXUAL HARASSMENT ON THE JOB
    Varieties of Sexual Harassment
    Effects of Sexual Harassment on Victims
    How to Deal with Sexual Harassment
RAPE
    Contemporary Issues
    False Beliefs about Rape
    Rape Victims
    A Partner's Response to Rape
    Men Who Rape
    Treatment of Rapists
    Rape of Males
SUMMARY
SUGGESTED READINGS

A person becomes a sexual victim when he or she is deprived of free choice and forced to comply with sexual acts under duress. Certainly, there are many varieties of victimization—for example, the teenager who threatens to break up with his girlfriend if she "doesn't put out" or the adult who feels compelled to perform a personally repugnant sexual act because his or her partner has threatened to "find it somewhere else." In this chapter we will focus on four particularly abusive and expoitive forms of sexual victimization: pedophilia (child molestation), incest, sexual harassment, and rape. All of these behaviors involve strong elements of coercion, sometimes even violence, in which the perpetrator typically uses his or her power over a victim.

PEDOPHILIA

Child molestation, or *pedophilia* (derived from the Greek "lover of children"), refers to sexual contact between an adult and a child. The definition of pedophilia depends to some extent on how one defines a child and an adult. For example, if an adult male has sexual intercourse with a 15-year-old female, is he guilty of pedophilia, statutory rape, or simply bad judgment? The issue may be further complicated when his partner willingly participates and may, in fact, have been the initiator. Each state has its own legal codes that specify at what age interaction between an adult and a young person is considered *child molestation* (usually under age 12), *statutory rape* (generally 12 to 17), and a consenting sexual act (often 18 or older, but in some states may even be 21). The legal code may appear quite ludicrous at times, particularly in cases involving teenage sex where one partner is technically an adult and the other a minor, even when only one or two years separate their ages.

It is difficult to obtain accurate estimates on the frequency of pedophilia in our society. Relatively few people are actually imprisoned for this offense (and these few are likely to be ostracized and abused by an inmate population that takes a dim view of child molesters). Acts of child molestation are unlikely to be reported, for several reasons. First, a child may not recognize that what has transpired is improper behavior. He or she may be unable to distinguish between expressions of affection and illicit sexual contact. The fact that the offender is often a friend may further confuse the child. A second reason for low reporting stems from the fact that even when a child does inform his or her parents of improper sexual advances, the parents may not believe the child or may be reluctant to expose the child to the stress of legal proceedings. This reluctance to prosecute may be strengthened when the offender is a "friend" or acquaintance of the family.

Child molestation is considered by many to be one of the most heinous of crimes. Many states have meted out life sentences for this crime, and in a few, the death penalty may be applied. Who is the "horrible person" who commits sexual offenses against children? Most investigations reveal a male, perhaps a teenager, but often middle-aged or older, who is shy, conservative, and frequently very moralistic or religious. The majority of these individuals are a family friend, neighbor, or acquaintance of the victim. They often have poor social and sexual relations with other adults, and they may feel inadequate and inferior. Alcoholism, severe marital problems, sexual difficulties, and poor emotional adjustment are additional problems frequently exhibited by child molesters (Kolodny et al., 1979; Rada, 1976). Not uncommonly, these offenders have been sexually victimized themselves during their childhood (Groth, 1979). Occasionally, pedophilia involves homosexual adult-child contacts, but the vast majority of such acts are heterosexual in nature, between an adult male and a female child (Rush, 1980).

In an effort to explain this behavior, many writers have suggested that relating to children represents a way of coping with powerful feelings of inadequacy that are likely to emerge in social/sexual relationships with adults. Many people who seek sexual contacts with children do not relate well to other adults, particularly sexually. A child, as a nonadult, is less threatening. Thus, sexual behavior directed at a child may be an attempt to establish a relationship seemingly unavailable in the adult world, and an individual who lacks the appropriate interpersonal skills to relate effectively with adults may be drawn to a child because he feels more comfortable.

Most adults who relate sexually to a child do not inflict physical harm (McCaghy, 1971). The sexual interaction usually consists of touching and fondling of the child's genital organs (often without removing undergarments). Sometimes the child touches the offender's genitals. Vaginal intercourse or anal penetration is not very common. However, the potential for violent abuse is present, and evidence suggests that some child molesters may progress to more violent sexual offenses, such as rape (Abel, 1981).

While a child may be emotionally traumatized by a sexual encounter with an adult, the effects are generally believed to be transitory. Frequently, the major damage in such cases seems to come from parental reactions to revelations or discovery of such activity. The child, when reporting to the parent, may merely be relaying a sense of discomfort over something he or she does not fully understand. It is when the parents understandably react with extreme agitation that the child is most likely to develop detrimental emotional reactions. The young person may have a sense of being implicated in what now appears, in light of parental reaction, to be something terrible. She or he may come to feel extremely guilty over having participated in such an event. Children may also feel guilty about such experiences even without parental displays of distress, because they sense the guilt of the person who molests them.

It is important that parents respond appropriately to instances of pedophilia involving their children. Such acts should not be ignored! While parents can try to remain calm in the face of their child's revelation, they should take great precautions to see that the child is not alone with the offending party again. In many instances children are repeatedly molested by the same person, and may come to feel a sense of obligation and guilt. It is essential to see that the child is protected from further experiences of this kind.

INCEST

Incestuous behavior is sexual interaction between relatives. Specifically, this includes sexual contact between siblings, or between children and their parents, grandparents, uncles, or aunts. All of these behaviors are illegal in every state. (Sexual contact between first cousins is a gray area, and not all state legal codes contain laws against these unions.) Although its definitions may vary slightly from place to place, incest is one of the few sexual behaviors that is prohibited in virtually every known society.

Despite universal prohibitions against incest, the behavior occurs—although it is difficult to estimate how frequently. Concealment by families and the powerful social taboos against such activity dramatically reduce the chances that incestuous behavior will come to public attention. Recent public attention to the problem of sexual abuse in the home has led some writers to conclude that incest occurs with a much higher frequency than was previously imagined (Weber, 1977). Some writers have estimated that incest, in its various forms, may affect as many as 5% of the population and 10% of American families (Justice and Justice, 1979). Morton Hunt's 1974 study revealed even higher figures—15% of the 2026 subjects in his sample group reported sexual contacts with relatives.

A number of researchers have indicated that female victims of incest outnumber male victims by about 10 to one. However, in a recent survey of 952 college students, 7.7% of the women in the sample and 4.8% of the men reported being sexually molested as children, usually by relatives such as parents, grandparents, aunts, and uncles (*Sexuality Today*, 1981). This study suggests that the incidence of male victims may be much greater than previously believed. This survey also showed that most male victims had been molested by females.

Incest occurs at all socioeconomic levels (Meiselman, 1978). It appears to occur with greater frequency in families disrupted by a variety of problems including severe marital conflict, spouse abuse, alcoholism, unemployment, and emotional illness.

While it is commonly assumed that father-daughter incest is the most prevalent, studies have shown that brother-sister and first-cousin contacts are far more common (Coleman, 1972; Hunt, 1974). Cases of prosecution for incest almost invariably involve father-daughter sex, a fact that has no doubt led to the confusion over which type of incestuous pattern occurs most frequently.

Sexual relations between brothers and sisters are seldom discovered, and when they are, they do not typically elicit the extreme adverse reactions that father-daughter sexual contact often does. Furthermore, it is not uncommon for participating siblings to look favorably upon their shared experiences, particularly if no coercion is involved (Justice and Justice, 1979). In one survey of 796 college students, 15% of the women and 10% of the men reported some type of sexual experience involving a sibling. Reactions to the experiences were equally divided among those who considered them positive and those who considered them negative (Finkelhor, 1980).

Sex between a parent and child is often a different matter. At the time of this writing little is known about mother-son sex. Perhaps the recent evidence that victimization of boys by adult female relatives is more common than previously thought will stimulate more investigations of this pattern of incest. Much more is currently known about father-daughter sex since this is the type of incest that most frequently leads to intervention by child-protection agencies and the legal system.

The incestuous involvement of a father with his daughter typically begins before the female child understands its significance. Often it starts as a kind of playful activity involving wrestling, tickling, kissing, and touching. Over time the father may gradually include touching of the genitals and breasts, perhaps followed by oral and/or manual stimulation of the genitals and intercourse. In most cases the father does not need to use physical force due to his position of authority or the pair's emotional closeness. He may pressure his daughter into such activity by reassuring her that he is "teaching" her something important, by offering rewards, or by exploiting her need for love. Later, when she discovers that the behavior is not appropriate, or finds her father's demands to be unpleasant or excessive, it may be difficult for her to escape from a well-established pattern of sexual activity. Occasionally, a daughter may value the relationship for the special recognition or privileges it brings to her. The incestuous involvement most frequently comes to public attention when she gets angry with her father, often for nonsexual reasons, and "tells on him." Sometimes a mother may discover, much to her horror, what has been transpiring between her husband and daughter. However, just as often, she may be aware of such behavior but remain quiet for various reasons including shame, fear of reprisals, concern about having her family disrupted if her husband is jailed, or because such activity allows her to avoid her husband's sexual demands.

The man who is prosecuted for having an incestuous relationship with his child is often economically disadvantaged, a heavy drinker, unemployed, devoutly religious, and very conservative (Gebhard et al., 1965; Meiselman, 1978). His behavior may result from general tendencies toward pedophilia, severe feelings of inadequacy in adult sexual relations, rejection by a hostile spouse, or as an accompaniment to alcoholism or other psychological disturbances. Not uncommonly, he is a product of a family where patterns of incest were modeled for him by parents, other siblings, or both (Delson and Clark, 1981).

Once detected, a father who engages in sexual relations with his child may be prosecuted under state criminal codes. Sometimes an entire family may be disrupted, with the father imprisoned, the mother faced with economic difficulties, and perhaps the victim and other siblings being placed in foster homes. Separation or divorce may result. These potential consequences of revealing an incestuous relationship place tremendous pressure on the child. For these and other reasons she may be extremely reluctant to tell anyone else in her family, let alone public authorities. Many professionals are hard-pressed to decide which is more traumatic to the victim: the incestuous experience itself or the consequences of its revelation.

There is increasing evidence that father-daughter incest can be a severely traumatizing and emotionally damaging experience with long-term consequences for the child. Many of these victims have difficulty forming intimate adult relationships, particularly with men (Janeway, 1981; Summit and Kryso, 1978). When relationships with men are established, they are frequently devoid of emotional and sexual fulfillment (Meiselman, 1978). Sexual molestation by fathers (or other adults) is not uncommon in the histories of women who seek treatment for sexual difficulties (McQuire and Wagner, 1978). Other difficulties commonly found in these victims include low self-esteem, guilt, shame, a sense of alienation from others, revulsion at being touched, and a predisposition to becoming repeatedly victimized in a variety of ways.

We conclude our discussion of incest with one woman's account of her incestuous victimization:

I was subjected to sexual pressures and advances by my father throughout adolescence, although it seems to have started much earlier with a disarming and subtle conditioning and progression. My feeling of having been betrayed and made unclean and unworthy by these experiences was almost overwhelming. I was so shocked by what was happening that I could find no words to express it. I wanted desperately to be rescued and protected. But I was sure that no one would believe me. I was right. In a desperate moment I confided in one of my brothers. He rejected with disbelief and anger what I said, and told me never to mention it again . . .

It was not easy, at the age of 11, to try alone to cope with my father's sexual advances. He was a very authoritarian father, but he had always been abundantly affectionate and protective. I hardly knew how to resist. He always made sure that no one was at home when he approached me. I had absolutely no frame of reference by which to judge this experience. I clung desperately to an instinctive conviction that this was not normal, although my father tried to convince me that it was. It was a long, exhausting struggle—mine was an adolescence without joy. I grew sullen and solitary and felt I bore a peculiar mark of shame. I feared that people would shrink away from me if they knew what I had experienced, but at the same time and for years afterward I wanted someone to talk to.

I am almost 40 now, and I'm happily married. But sometimes when I look at little girls, I wonder how many of them are trapped in incestuous situations and don't know how to ask for help. (Name withheld, *Ms.*, September 1977, p. 89)

SEXUAL HARASSMENT ON THE JOB

Working Women United Institute, a New York-based research and resource center founded in 1975 to deal exclusively with sexual harassment on the job, offers a brief and succinct definition of this behavior: "Sexual harassment is any unwanted attention of a sexual nature from someone from the workplace that creates discomfort and/or interferes with the job" (Bartlett, 1982, p. 22).

Many working people are subjected to sexual coercion on the job. This form of sexual victimization, while perhaps not as shocking as child molestation, incest, or rape, is nevertheless a major concern that is receiving increasing attention. Some people may consider sexual harassment to be an unimportant or trivial issue. However, victims present a different picture as the following account reveals:

A woman in her late forties was hired as an executive secretary to the head of a small business in California. Her duties included a heavy correspondence load, keeping the social schedule of her boss and his wife, paying all his personal and household bills, and also arranging dates with, buying gifts for, and making motel reservations for the many young women whom he recruited for one-night stands. She was then summoned in the morning to hear about his sexual exploits, and to rehearse with him the details of an overnight business trip he had concocted as an excuse for his wife.

When she objected to such nonbusiness duties, she was told that she was lucky, at her age, to hear about sex at all. When he began to accompany his morning rehearsals with pats on her buttocks and requests for blow jobs, she objected more strongly, but still she felt guilty about having gone along with his lies up to then. He told her she was a "dirty old woman," and she felt ashamed, as if she might somehow have invited his advances. After a number of incidents in which he unzipped his pants in front of her, she finally quit the job she badly needed. Though she had done the secretarial work with great efficiency (and he had hired two women to replace her), he gave her poor work references, and wouldn't support her claim for unemployment insurance. (Lindsey, 1977, p. 47)

How common are such experiences? A number of studies have shown that sexual harassment is extremely widespread. A recent survey of more than 17,000 federal employees found that 42% of the women and 15% of the men surveyed had been sexually harassed (Bartlett, 1982). (Working men are not as likely as women to be victims of sexual coercion. However, men are occasionally sexually harassed by

Sexual harassment creates anxiety and tension in the workplace.

their female, or male, bosses.) In 1976, *Redbook* magazine printed a questionnaire on sexual harassment that was returned by 9000 women. Approximately 88% of these women said they had personally been subjected to sexual harassment at work (Safran, 1976). The *Redbook* respondents were certainly not a probability sample of the general population. However, the high incidence revealed by the survey suggests that sexual harassment is a very common problem for working women.

How do people at the top of the corporate ladder view this problem? A 1981 survey of almost 2000 business executives revealed an apparent difference in how women and men in high level positions assess sexual harassment on the job. Two-thirds of the men indicated they felt that the extent of the problem "is greatly exaggerated" while only one-third of the women respondents agreed with this statement (Safran, 1981).

In the last few years there have been a number of court decisions that have interpreted Title VII of the 1964 Civil Rights Act, which prohibits discrimination in employment on the basis of sex, as also prohibiting unwelcome sexual advances or requests for sexual favors. In 1980 the Equal Employment Opportunity Commission issued guidelines derived from the Civil Rights Act that impose liability on companies for sexual harassment by supervisors unless the company takes immediate and appropriate action. These guidelines emphasize that both verbal and physical harassment are illegal. Furthermore, they also provide legal recourse for other employees if a coworker uses sex to obtain job advancement. Thus, if employee A has sex with a boss and gets promoted, employee B, who is equally qualified for the higher level position, may file suit against the employer, claiming sexual discrimination.

There is evidence that employers are becoming increasingly sensitive to the issue of sexual harassment, perhaps motivated in part by a number of court decisions that have awarded large payments to victims. More and more large companies (including CBS, General Electric, General Motors, IBM, and General Telephone) are establishing programs for supervisors that clarify what harassment is and when a company can be liable for such coercive actions by its supervisors, coworkers, and even customers.

Varieties of Sexual Harassment

Sexual harassment on the job can appear in many forms. Perhaps the most common situation involves a boss or supervisor who requires sexual services from an employee as a condition for keeping a job or for promotion. This is a particularly insidious form of harassment, because when an employee is fired for noncompliance, the supervisor may invent a reason for the termination that can be damaging to the victim's future employment prospects. Employees are well aware of this possibility and thus may feel great pressure to go along with their employer's demands. Retaliation may also occur in other, less dramatic ways that are nevertheless quite damaging. A person may be denied promotion, be demoted to a lesser job, receive a reduction in pay, have vacation requests denied, and so forth.

Sometimes job seekers find that sexual availability is a condition for being hired. A prospective employer may even require a "sample" before putting a new person on the payroll.

What if a worker is subjected to obscenities or made the constant target of sexual jokes? Is this sexual harassment? We certainly believe so, and apparently the courts share this view. In one case a woman engineer—whose coworkers made her job intolerable by such abusive behaviors as loudly speculating about whether she was a virgin and passing around an obscene cartoon about her—complained to her supervisor and was then promptly fired. After several years of trying to obtain legal redress, she was compensated on all counts. The coworkers were found guilty of sexual harassment, and each had to pay her $1,500. The company was required to reinstate her in a higher position and pay all back wages.

Sometimes workers are coerced into providing sexual services to customers or clients of the firm they work for. This is also clearly a form of sexual harassment, for which a company can be liable.

Effects of Sexual Harassment on Victims

The financial ramifications of not complying with sexual coercion on the job may be devastating, especially for people in lower level positions such as clerical and blue-collar workers. Many victims, particularly if they are supporting families, cannot afford to be unemployed. Many find it exceedingly difficult to look for other jobs while maintaining their present employment. If they are fired for refusing to be victimized, they may be unable to obtain employment compensation (unfortunately, harassment is sometimes seen as insufficient reason for quitting a job), and when they do, compensation will probably provide only half of their former salaries. Thus, a person who quits or is fired as a result of sexual harassment faces the prospect of severe financial difficulties.

The victim of sexual harassment may also suffer a variety of emotional and physical effects. In one survey of sexually harassed women, 78% reported experiencing some negative effects, including feeling angry, humiliated, ashamed, embarrassed, and cheap (McKinnon, 1979). Many of these women also felt guilty, as though they had done something to encourage the harassment; some felt that they alone had been singled out for such abuse, an often mistaken notion that can result in a sense of alienation from coworkers. The sense of degradation and helplessness reported by many victims of sexual harassment is similar to that experienced by many rape victims (Safran, 1976).

These feelings of isolation, helplessness, and guilt, together with the very real threat of financial disaster, may cause a victim to acquiesce to the exploitive sexual demands encountered on the job. Very few comply because they feel "flattered" by the sexual attention they receive (McKinnon, 1979; Safran, 1976).

Finally, many victims of sexual harassment report a variety of psychosomatic symptoms that stem directly from the pressures associated with their victimization. These include headaches, stomach ailments, back and neck pain, and a variety of other stress-related ailments.

In the next section we will discuss how a victim of sexual harassment may reduce its potential negative impact by taking appropriate action.

How to Deal with Sexual Harassment

If you face sexual harassment at work, a number of options are available to you. The suggestions listed below, some of which are adapted from an excellent article by Karen Lindsey (1977), provide guidelines for dealing with this exploitive abuse.

1. If the harassment includes actual or attempted rape or assault, you can file criminal charges against the perpetrator.
2. If the coercion has stopped short of rape or assault, you may wish to confront the person who is harassing you. State in clear terms that what he or she is doing is clearly sexual harassment, that you will not tolerate it, and that if it continues you will file charges through appropriate channels.
3. If the offender does not stop the harassment after direct confrontation, it may be helpful to discuss your situation with your supervisor and/or the supervisor of the offender.
4. If neither the harasser nor the appropriate supervisors respond appropriately to your concern, you may want to gather support from your coworkers (you may not be the only victim in your company). Discussing the offense with other sympathetic men and women in your place of work may produce sufficient pressure to terminate the harassment. Be sure of your facts, since such actions could result in a slander lawsuit.
5. Sometimes you can get results by using unorthodox tactics, such as an anonymous posting of the offender's name or picture along with the message, "Warning: This person is a sexual harasser."
6. If your attempt to deal with this problem within your company does not work, or if you are fired, demoted, or refused promotion because of your efforts to end harassment, you may file an official complaint with your city or state Human Rights Commission or Fair Employment Practices Agency (the names may vary locally). You may also ask that the local office of the federally funded Equal Employment Opportunity Commission investigate the situation.
7. Finally, you may wish to pursue legal action to resolve your problem with sexual harassment. Lawsuits may be filed in federal courts under the Civil Rights Act. They may also be filed under city or state laws prohibiting employment discrimination. One lawsuit can be filed in a number of jurisdictions. A person who has been a victim of such harassment is most likely to receive a favorable court judgment if she or he has first tried to resolve the problem within the company before taking the issue to court.

RAPE

Rape, commonly thought of as sexual relations forced by a man upon an unconsenting woman, has occurred throughout history.

The legal definition of rape varies from state to state. Varying degrees of rape are also defined, depending on the particular sexual act or the age of the victim. Most laws define rape as sexual intercourse that occurs under actual or threatened forceable compulsion that overcomes earnest resistance of the victim. There is one notable exception. According to the legal code in most states, a wife cannot press charges of rape against her husband regardless of the force he uses and her resistance to intercourse. Only a few states have recently changed this antiquated law, which assumes a married woman is the unconditional sexual property of her husband.

Statutory rape is intercourse with a person who is legally defined to be under the age of consent. The age of consent varies in different states but is generally 18 years of age. Statutory rape is considered to have occurred regardless of the apparent willingness of the underage partner. Even if the young person lies about his or her age, the older person can be prosecuted for this activity.

Many contemporary attitudes, issues, and laws regarding rape stem from the historical status of women. Until very recently, rape has been institutionalized by law as a violation of the male right of possession of female virginity and exclusive marital sexual access. For example, in ancient Babylonian law, women were considered to be their father's possessions until sold to their husband for a bride price. The amount of payment for the bride was contingent upon her virginity. Therefore, rape of an unmarried woman was considered as theft of the father's market price for his daughter. In England at the close of the thirteenth century, punishment that had previously been reserved only for forcible rape of virgins was extended to include the rape of married women by men other than their husband. The law still maintained that a husband could not legally rape his own wife since she was his possession and sexual relations were his right (Brownmiller, 1975). Today married women in some states are winning the right to prosecute their husbands for rape. At the time of this writing, a husband can be prosecuted for rape, whether married or separated, in 10 states (California, Connecticut, Florida, Iowa, Massachusetts, Minnesota, Nebraska, New Hampshire, New Jersey, and Oregon). However, 13 other states have taken an opposite position by denying both wives and cohabitating women the right to file a rape complaint against their partners.

Both rape and the threat of rape have served to control female sexuality and behavior for centuries. Throughout history, if a woman was to expect even a modicum of protection or recourse against rape, her sexual behavior had to remain within narrowly defined limits; that is, she must have been a virgin or a monogamous wife. The "protection" of women from rape has often been a way of preserving exclusive male sexual rights to chaste women. In the following discussions, we will examine the effects of these historical attitudes on contemporary rape issues.

Contemporary Issues

Significant changes in rape laws and services to rape victims have occurred in the past several years. Legal reform is taking place in the areas of redefinition of the crime and revision of the rules of evidence during rape trials. A few important changes have been made in some states. One is the provision that the threat of force is sufficient coercion—that is, that personal injury does not have to occur for an act to be considered rape. Second, the victim's prior sexual conduct is not permitted as evidence in the trial. Third is the inclusion of the accused man's past sexual offenses. A fourth reform recognizes the victim's right not to have her name printed in the newspaper.

An important impetus for legal reforms has come from the women's movement, which has also challenged societal assumptions about rape. When women organized in the early 1970s to deal with rape issues, they asserted first that the problem of rape stems from the way in which society deals with it. The women's movement involvement began with consciousness-raising groups and conferences. Grass-roots community outreach programs, rape crisis centers, and hotlines were established to provide education, counseling, and procedural information for rape victims and the community. Groups of women began to patrol high-rape areas of cities. Legislative task forces were implemented to change laws. Programs were established in conjunction with police forces, hospitals, and legal systems to provide victim advocate and support services to women who reported being raped (Brownmiller, 1975). In some cities, men have also formed groups to support the women's movement efforts and to examine male attitudes that perpetuate rape.

Recently victims of rape have begun to fight back in civil court. Several have successfully sued their assailants. Property owners and institutions may also be found liable in such procedures. In one landmark case in California a woman who had been raped in her own apartment won the right in appeals court to bring charges against her landlord for negligence in failing to provide adequate safety measures. Colleges and universities have also had legal judgments rendered against them for failure to provide adequate protection for women students who were raped on campus. These de-

Boston women protest night assaults with a mass march.

velopments in rape litigation may prompt insurance companies to demand stricter enforcement of security measures before providing coverage for property owners and institutions.

False Beliefs about Rape

As attitudes have begun to change and research has correspondingly improved, many past beliefs about the crime, the person who rapes, and the victim have been shown to be inaccurate. There is, however, much that remains unknown.

The main reason for our incomplete knowledge has to do with problems of data collecting. We do not have information about the victims of unreported rapes—and rape is the most underreported crime in the United States. It is estimated that as many as eight unreported rapes occur for each one that is reported (Amir, 1971). Many women have been hesitant to report rape because of the social stigma associated with being a rape victim or fear about the potentially humiliating procedures of pretrial and court proceedings. A reflection of this is that cities that offer rape victim advocate programs often find a gradual increase in reported rapes. The support services provided by the programs make it easier for women to go to the authorities. The number of rapes is quite large. There were approximately 56,000 reported rapes in 1975 and by 1979 this figure had risen to 76,000, a 36% increase (Federal Bureau of Investigation, 1975 and 1979). If estimates of unreported rapes are correct, the actual figure in 1979 may have been well over 600,000.

Besides the problem of underreporting, research is complicated by the fact that most available data on men who rape include only those who have been convicted. The characteristics of men in unreported cases and those who were guilty but not convicted have not been widely studied. Inequities in our judicial system also affect the kind of information that is available to researchers. Individuals from low-income groups do not have the social status and financial resources that often help middle- and upper-income people avoid conviction. Conviction rates for rape are also higher in interracial cases. Black men who rape white women are likely to receive heavier sentences than those who rape black women or white men who rape either black or white women (Brownmiller, 1975).

Along with our lack of data, another basis for false beliefs lies in folklore and in assumptions people tend to make. We will discuss a few of these assumptions in the following pages.

False Belief: "Rape Is a Crime of Uncontrollable Sex Drive." Men convicted of rape often excuse their actions based on sexual need (Bromberg and Coyle, 1974). The argument is a weak one, for several reasons. First, relief of sexual tension is readily available through masturbation. Second, statistics reveal that most men who rape are involved in ongoing sexual relationships at the time of the crime or have access to a consenting partner (Amir, 1971; Groth, 1979; Groth and Burgess, 1977). More than 40% are married (MacDonald, 1971). Since sexual release can so easily be obtained in ways other than those that require force, it becomes clear that coercion is a part of the motivation for most of the men who rape. The violation and control of another person provides a sense of power and an opportunity to express hostile and aggressive impulses. Rape is typically an act of violence. The rapist's weapon is his penis.

False Belief: "You Can't Thread a Moving Needle." The belief that women can always successfully ("if they *really* want to") resist a rape attempt is false, for several important reasons. First, men are usually physically larger than women. They have been encouraged to develop their physical strength and agility throughout their lives. Boys' rough-and-tumble play and athletics encourage them to be physically forceful and confident. On the other hand, stereotypical female gender role conditioning trains a woman to be passive—the recipient rather than the initiator of action. Smaller stature is a physical reality, but the way women feel about and use their bodies is learned. Muscles may be admired on men, but they are typically considered unattractive on women. Soft skin and physical weakness are "feminine." Furthermore, a woman's clothing and shoes typically inhibit her efforts to fight or to run. Yet these are only exterior symbols of the passivity, compliance, and submission that "good girls" are encouraged to incorporate in their behavior. (Paradoxically, "good girls" are also supposed to defend their "honor" in spite of being taught to be passive!) These elements of gender role conditioning limit the options a woman believes she has in resisting a rape attack. It simply may not be in her repertoire of behavior to be offensive, aggressive, or to resort to socially unacceptable behaviors to defend herself against the person attacking her.

Second, the man who rapes chooses the time and place. He has the element of surprise on his side. Furthermore, the fear and intimidation a woman usually experiences when attacked works to the assailant's advantage. The use of weapons, threats, or physical force further encourages a woman's compliance. One study revealed that the use of some type of weapon is reported in 50% of the police reports. Furthermore, strong-arm force was present in 75% of the cases (National Institute of Law Enforcement and Criminal Justice, 1978). It has been estimated that many rapes are perpetrated by two or more attackers (Steen and Price, 1977). Increased physical violence is more likely to occur in situations with multiple rapists (Rada, 1977); the intimidation the victim feels is likely to be greater as well.

To state that a woman who wishes to avoid rape can do so is to misunderstand the realities of this crime:

Rape can be the most terrifying event in a woman's life. The sexual act or acts performed are often intended to humiliate and degrade her: bottles, gun barrels and sticks may be thrust into her vagina or anus. She may be compelled to swallow urine or perform fellatio with such force that she thinks she might strangle or suffocate; her breasts may be bitten or burned with cigarettes. In many instances, her hope is to save her life—not her chastity. Her terror may be so overwhelming that she urinates, defecates or vomits. If she escapes without serious outward signs of injury, she may suffer vaginal tears or infections, contact venereal disease, or become impregnated. For months or years afterward, she may distrust others, change residences frequently and sleep poorly. Her friends and family may blame or reject her. (National Institute of Law Enforcement and Criminal Justice, 1978, p. 15)

As the preceding report illustrates, women who are attacked often believe their only choices are to be killed, seriously injured, or raped. Courses on rape prevention sometimes advise women to be passive when attacked, on the assumption that resistance or fighting might increase the potential for violence. Yet such compliance often results in difficulties for a rape victim if she prosecutes. Without clear signs of resistance on her part, chances of a conviction are often reduced. Statistically, rape murders are rare. Serious physical injury occurs in a small minority of cases. However, statistics do not reflect the actual or implied threat of a rape situation.

False Belief: Many Women "Cry Rape."   Historically, women may have chosen to "cry rape" because they were severely condemned when they overstepped the boundaries of virgin or wife. Today false accusations rarely occur, and they are even less frequently carried as far as prosecution. Given the difficulties that exist in reporting and prosecuting a rape, few women or men could successfully proceed with an unfounded rape case.

False Belief: "All Women Want To Be Raped."   Novels and films perpetuate the notion that women want to be raped. Typically, fictionalized rape scenes begin with a woman resisting her attacker, only to melt into passionate acceptance. In the rare cases where male-to-male rape is shown, the violation and humiliation of rape is more likely to be truthfully portrayed.

The fact that some women do have rape fantasies is sometimes used to support the idea that women want to be sexually assaulted. However, there are several factors that clearly discredit this belief. First of all, in a fantasy a person still retains ultimate control. It is important here to understand the distinction between an erotic fantasy and a conscious desire to lose one's free will to someone whose intent is to inflict harm. A basic element in an actual rape is the terrifying powerlessness of the victim. A fantasy carries no threat of physical harm or death; a rape does. Furthermore, many women have internalized ambivalent "good girl versus bad girl" messages about expressing their sexuality. Fantasizing about intense seduction can be a way for a woman to feel accepting of her sexual feelings without having to assume active responsibility for them.

An extremely negative consequence of the belief that women want to be raped is that many rape victims may believe that the rape was basically their fault. Even when they may have simply been in the wrong place at the wrong time, a pervasive sense of personal guilt may remain. Unfortunately, when a victim continues to feel self-blame following a rape, the man who raped her is still indirectly maintaining some control over her life. Rape self-help groups or personal counseling may help a woman resolve these feelings.

False Belief: "It Could Never Happen to Me."   Many women may think that because they are too young, too old, too fat, married, "not that kind of girl," exceedingly cautious, or possess any variety of unique characteristics, they will not be raped. This belief may promote a false sense of security. It also tends, once again, to place blame for the rape on some characteristic or behavior of the victim herself. The truth is that any female is a potential victim.

Rapists show a high degree of arbitrariness in selecting their victims. Victim precipitation (behaviors which contribute to the occurrence of a crime) has been analyzed for a variety of crimes, and a Federal Commission on Crimes of Violence study indicates that only 4% of rapes result from precipitant behavior of the victim. In fact, rape victims were responsible for less precipitant behavior than were victims of homicide, assault, or robbery (Brownmiller, 1975).

Even women who are never raped live daily with the threat of a sexual attack. The possibility of rape makes it more difficult for women to lead independent lives. Even one's home is not a refuge. Although studies vary somewhat, approximately one-third of all rapes occur in the woman's home, usually following illegal entry. The offender's car and home are the next most likely places. The location of the rape is not always the same as where the initial contact between the victim and offender occurs. Although rape can happen to virtually any woman, there are some things that can be done to reduce (but not eliminate) the chance of its occurrence. Some suggestions for prevention, and for coping with the situation if it cannot be prevented, appear in Box 20.1.

Rape Victims

Given the characteristics of rape—the physical violation of the victim, the psychological trauma experienced from such an event, and our societal attitudes about rape—it is understandable that many rape victims suffer long-lasting emotional effects. The emotional repercussions women experience following rape or attempted rape have been labeled *rape trauma syndrome* (Burgess and Homstrom, 1974a, 1974b.).

There are usually two phases of rape trauma. The first, known as the *acute phase*, begins immediately following the rape and may continue for hours, days, and often several weeks. During the first few hours after the attack a woman will tend to react in an expressive or controlled manner. In the expressive reaction, she will likely be crying and obviously upset. In the controlled reaction, a woman will appear subdued and matter-of-fact. She may, however, experience the expressive reaction at a later time.

The feelings many victims report during this phase cover a wide range, often including shame, anger, fear, and self-blame. Other feelings are physical: symptoms such as nausea, sleeplessness, nervousness, and headaches are commonly associated with the emotional stress. Some physical symptoms may be due to the assault itself and not to the emotional trauma. Injuries such as bruises, abrasions, and vaginal or rectal tears require a period of healing.

Fear and nervousness often continue during the second, *long-term reorganization phase*. The woman may fear retaliation by the rapist. Women often change their place of residence during this time. Rape can cause sexual difficulties for the woman; she may have fearful or negative feelings about sexual relations in general, particularly about intercourse.

Women who report a rape to the police and who prosecute the offender will be involved in legal proceedings that will include a recounting of the assault. In the past,

Supportive counseling can help ease the trauma suffered by a rape victim.

the judicial system has been insensitive and sometimes psychologically brutal to rape victims. In recent years there has been considerable improvement as the police and court system attempt to be more sensitive and supportive. A few cities have instituted *Rape Victim Advocate Programs*. These provide a counselor to work with the woman, beginning with the initial report and continuing throughout the prosecution process.

Many women neither report the rape to the police nor tell anyone else. Women who choose this course have the same psychological reactions to their experience as women who report the rape, but do not have the opportunity to express and resolve their feelings. Sometimes the trauma of the rape surfaces later when a woman seeks help for a problem apparently unrelated to the attack.

In summary, rape is usually a very traumatic experience. The passage of time combined with support from others can help alleviate its effects. Hopefully, the many women who are victims of this crime will seek help (counseling can be useful) in resolving a trauma that can interfere with their lives.

A Partner's Response to Rape

The rape of his partner may be a difficult experience for a man. In a sense, he also is victimized by the assault. He may feel a range of emotions including rage, disgust, and helplessness. He may be confused and unsure about how he should react to his lover's victimization. This lack of direction may prove costly because his reactions can

BOX 20.1 DEALING WITH RAPE

While rape is a society-wide problem, it is the rape victim who experiences the direct, personal violation. The suggestions offered below may reduce a woman's chances of being raped. *However, these suggestions are no guarantee of avoiding rape.* Even a woman who leads an extremely cautious and restricted life is a potential victim.

Reducing the Risk of Rape

Rape prevention consists primarily of making it as difficult as possible for a rapist to make you his victim. Many of the following suggestions are common-sense measures against other crimes as well as rape.

1. Install and use secure locks on doors and windows, changing door locks after losing keys or moving into a new residence.
2. Do not open your door to strangers.
3. Lock your car when it is parked, and drive with locked car doors.
4. Avoid dark and deserted areas, and be

Many women take self-defense training to protect themselves.

aware of the surroundings where you are walking. This may help if you need an opportunity to escape.

5. Have house or car keys in hand before coming to the door, and check the back seat before getting into your car.

Many cities have crime-prevention bureaus that will provide further suggestions and home safety inspections.

What to Do in a Threatening Situation

When a woman is approached by a man or men who may intend to rape her, she will have to decide what to do. *Each situation, assailant, and victim is unique: There are no absolute rules.*

1. Run away if you can.
2. Resist if you cannot run. Make it difficult for the rapist. Many men, upon locating a potential victim, test her to see if she is easily intimidated. FBI statistics from 1973 indicate that one-fourth of reported rape offenses were attempted but not completed. Resistance by the woman is responsible for many of the thwarted attempts (Brownmiller, 1975). Active and vociferous resistance— shouting, being "rude," causing a scene, running away, fighting back— may deter the attack.
3. Ordinary rules of behavior do not apply. Vomiting, screaming, acting "crazy," or being passive—whatever a woman is willing to try—can be appropriate responses to a rape situation.
4. Talking can be a way to stall and give the woman a chance to think about what her next best move might be.
5. Self-defense classes are a resource for learning techniques of physical

resistance that can injure or distract the attacker(s) long enough for a woman to escape.

6. Remain alert for an opportunity to escape. In some situations, it may be initially impossible to fight or elude an attacker. However, a woman may later have a chance to deter the attack and escape—for example, if the rapist becomes distracted or a passerby comes on the scene.

What to Do If You Have Been Raped

If a woman has been raped, she will have to decide whether to report the attack to the police.

1. It is advisable to report a rape, even an unsuccessful rape attempt. The information a woman provides may prevent another woman from being raped. Ninety-eight percent of women who reported being raped recommended that other victims report to protect other women (Forcible Rape: Final Project Report, 1978).
2. When she reports a rape, any information the woman can remember about the attack will be helpful—the assaulter's physical characteristics, voice, clothes, car, even an unusual smell.
3. She should call the police as soon as possible; she should not bathe or change her clothes. Semen, hair, material under her fingernails or on her apparel—all may be useful in identifying the person who raped her.
4. Finally, it is important to remember that many women will mistakenly blame themselves for the rape. However, the victim has not committed a crime—the man who raped her has.

have a profound impact upon both his lover's recovery and the future of their relationship. In the following paragraphs we will offer some suggestions for how a man may participate meaningfully in his partner's recovery. These recommendations are adapted from *Sexual Solutions*, an excellent book by Michael Castleman (1980). Our comments are directed to the male partners of female victims. However, the following suggestions are applicable to homosexual individuals whose same-sex partners have been violated.

The last thing a rape victim needs is to have her judgment questioned (Why did you park on a dark side street?). Equally counterproductive is the response of the partner who gets sidetracked by focusing his attention on his own imagined short-comings ("I should have been along to protect you"). The woman has just finished dealing with one violent man (or men), and being confronted with a similar emotional state in her partner (motivated by his desire for revenge against the assailant) is probably not in her best interests.

What she does need is to be listened to. A person comforting a rape victim might understandably try to divert her attention from the terrible event. However, professionals who work with victims of sexual assault have found that many of these people need to talk repeatedly about the assault to come to terms with it. A partner may encourage his lover to discuss the rape in any way that she is able.

A rape victim may recover more quickly when she is able to decide for herself how to deal with the assault. A man may be inclined to ease his partner's burden by taking charge and deciding what should be done in the aftermath of a rape. However, "She should make every decision in response to the assault. She was the person attacked. The important thing is for her to regain a sense of control over her life after being stripped of that control by her attacker(s)" (Castleman, 1980, p. 177). Her partner may suggest alternatives and act as a sounding board while she weighs her options. Nevertheless, all the decisions should ultimately be made by the woman unless she is unable to do so.

In the days, weeks, and even months following the rape a partner can continue to provide empathy, support, and reassurance to a rape victim. He can encourage her to resume a normal life and support her at those moments that she feels particularly vulnerable, fearful, or angry. He can be there to listen, even if it means hearing the same things over and over again. In the event that her assailant is prosecuted, she may be in particular need of support and understanding throughout the often arduous legal proceedings.

Rape victims may need more than their lover or families can provide. Some may require short- or long-term therapy to help ease the trauma of rape and reconstruct their lives. Partners may recognize these needs and encourage their lovers to seek professional help. Similarly, partners of sexually assaulted women may also experience severe conflicts and deep feelings of rage and guilt that they need help coping with. These men may find that a close friend, family member, or professional therapist will listen as they voice their pain and anger. "Men who take care of their own emotional needs tend to provide better support to their lovers" (Castleman, 1980, p. 181).

Resuming sexual activity after a rape may present problems for both the victim and her partner. Rape may precipitate sexual difficulties for the woman; she may not want to be sexually intimate for quite a while. However, some women may desire relations very soon after the attack, perhaps for assurance that their lovers still care for them and do not consider them "tainted." Some women may prefer not to have intercourse for awhile but instead just want to be close and affectionate. Deciding when and how to engage in intimate sharing is best left up to the woman. Her partner's support in this matter is very important. Even when sexual sharing resumes, it may be some time before she is able to relax and again respond the way she did before the attack. A patient, understanding, sensitive partner can help her reach the point where she is again able to experience satisfying sexual sharing.

Men Who Rape

Our awareness of the characteristics of men who rape is based largely on studies of individuals convicted of this crime. We cannot say with certainty that men who rape without being prosecuted or convicted demonstrate traits similar to convicted rapists. Since only 5% of reported rapes result in apprehension of a suspect and less than 3% result in a conviction, a large number of men who rape remain unstudied (National Institute of Law Enforcement and Criminal Justice, 1978). Keeping these limitations in mind, we will outline some of the characteristics of rapists as revealed by research.

Men convicted of rape usually are from a low socioeconomic background (Amir, 1971). Most are young, under 30 years of age (Federal Bureau of Investigation, 1973, 1975, 1979). Their range of physical attractiveness is not distinguishable from any random group of men. Many have a history of prior sexual offenses, such as exhibitionism, voyeurism, or child molestation (Abel, 1981). Rapists are frequently socially inept, have difficulty establishing meaningful interpersonal relationships, have low self-esteem, and feel inadequate (Groth and Burgess, 1977; Pepitone-Rockwell, 1980). Many were subjected to sexual abuse during childhood (Delin, 1978). Rapists are often heavily drinking or drunk when they assault their victims (Rada, 1975). In contrast to men in a matched control group, those convicted of rape appear more likely to express anger by violent aggression (Rada, 1977).

These characteristics may give some clues as to why men rape. Rape is not typically a random, spontaneous, irrational act. Men who rape do so for definite reasons. Many researchers and mental health practitioners believe that it is important to systematically investigate the factors that lead up to a sexual attack. Just what are the motivational and behavioral patterns that precede the act of rape?

Some authorities suggest that a rapist often presents a picture of a man overwhelmed by an increasing sense of failure. His psychological makeup and socioeconomic background ill equip him to cope with economic and social stresses in his life. He may feel powerless, hopeless, and unable to effectively deal with escalating stress. Rape often represents a breaking point for such a man. His violent act may be a way of expressing his rage and frustration against society in general and women in particular. It is an attempt by him to take back some of the power absent from his life. This interpretation is consistent with the current belief that rape is usually an expression of anger and power and not sexual desire (Brownmiller, 1975; Groth et al., 1977; Tollison and Adams, 1979). In fact, one study revealed that many rapists have impaired sexual functioning (such as erectile difficulties and ejaculatory inhibition) during rape attempts (Groth and Burgess, 1977). This does not mean that rape is without sexual meaning or motivation in all cases. There is evidence that some men who rape have eroticized violence. Two separate studies compared the erectile responses of matched groups of rapists and nonrapists to taped descriptions of rape and of mutually consenting sexual activity (Abel et al., 1977; Barbaree et al., 1979). Both experiments found that rapists obtained erections while listening to violent scenes of rape while their nonrapist counterparts did not. Descriptions of consenting sexual activity produced similar levels of arousal in both groups of men.

Efforts to understand the motivational and behavioral factors leading to rape have been consistently hindered by rapists' reluctance to reveal their thoughts or activities for fear they might be used against them in criminal prosecutions. This problem was overcome by Gene Abel (1981), a Columbia University researcher. He developed an elaborate system of confidentiality that allowed over 200 New York sex offenders to seek treatment and to participate in his research without identification and/or prosecution by the criminal justice system. His research is further distinguished by the use of a variety of physiological tools to measure rapists' sexual arousal patterns when exposed to a range of violent and nonviolent sexual themes. Such procedures provide a more reliable method for confirming the accuracy of self-reports and for revealing patterns that might ordinarily be concealed.

Abel found that some of the rapists in his sample had extensive histories of rape and violence fantasies long before becoming rapists. Such a man might have begun masturbating frequently to such fantasies as early as his mid-teens. As he continues this pattern, his deviant urges to rape become progressively stronger. Ultimately his attempts to resist acting on his compulsions fail and he becomes a rapist in fact, not just in fantasy. Earlier we suggested that the violence of rape in some men is eroticized. These observations by Abel suggest at least one possible mechanism whereby this effect is accomplished.

Approximately half of the rapists in Abel's sample had histories of other types of sexual offenses, most notably child molestation, exhibitionism, voyeurism, incest, and sadism. This suggests that the behavior of at least some rapists may escalate through a series of progressively more violent sexual offenses.

Abel also found that rapists are frequently motivated by displaced anger toward women. For example, a man who is unable to express his anger directly to his wife or girlfriend may inappropriately and violently direct that anger at another woman by raping her. The relationship between anger and rape was recently demonstrated in an experimental laboratory study. Marshall (1981) measured sexual arousal to rape stimuli before and after his subjects were confronted by a hostile, angry woman (actually a research colleague who pretended anger toward the subjects). The results indicated that many of his male subjects, following their confrontation with an angry woman, experienced significant increases in their sexual arousal to descriptions of rape.

Finally, Abel reported that some rapists have distorted perceptions of their interactions with rape victims both before and during the assault. They may believe that women want to be coerced into sexual activity, even to the extent of being physically abused. These distorted beliefs may help the rapist justify his reprehensible behavior; his acts are not rape but rather "normal" courtship behavior. Such a man might meet a woman in a bar, take her for a drive, park, and attempt intercourse which he would force if she resisted. Even if he has to "slap her around" to convince her to have sex, he believes he is only acting in accordance with what he perceives to be her wishes and expectations. Afterwards, he may have little or no guilt about his behavior since, in his own mind, it was not rape. Apparently, many people believe that roughing up women is acceptable, that many women get "turned on" by such activity, and that it is impossible to rape a healthy woman against her will (Burt, 1980; Malamuth et al., 1980). Thus, a rapist may find both the impetus for and support of his behavior within the fabric of society.

Treatment of Rapists

Statistics show that most rapists are repeat offenders, and imprisonment does not typically stop them from raping again. These grim facts have prompted the development of specialized treatment programs for convicted rapists in a handful of states (Connecticut, Florida, Minnesota, Oregon, Washington). One approach in these programs is the use of conditioning procedures designed to create aversion to deviant arousal. For example, a man who is sexually aroused when exposed to slides and narrative tapes of violent sexual interaction might be subjected to a putrid odor through a tube in his nose at the precise moment a penile strain gauge registers erectile response. Repeated sessions of this aversion conditioning frequently reduce inappropriate arousal patterns. At the same time the offender's deviant sexual arousal is being reduced, therapists strive to establish or increase his arousal to slides and tapes depicting caring, mutually consensual sexual sharing.

Treatment programs also attempt to teach offenders more appropriate ways to deal with their anger. In the cases of men whose rape behavior is motivated by deeply rooted hatred for people, particularly women, long-term psychotherapy may be required. Sometimes combining reconditioning trials with in-depth psychotherapy is the best approach.

As stated earlier, rapists are sometimes socially inept individuals who have difficulty establishing and maintaining relationships. When these traits are present, treatment may involve teaching the rapist useful social skills and how to develop warm and loving relationships with people. This can be an extremely difficult task in view of the marked amount of emotional deprivation and abuse that distinguishes the backgrounds of many rapists.

The distorted beliefs that often support rape behavior must also be eliminated in effective treatment programs. The rapist needs to learn that actual rape is not like his distorted perception of a woman becoming sexually aroused after being roughed up a bit. He must be taught to view rape as it actually is—a dehumanizing, terrifying experience for a woman who, after being forced against her will, may suffer long-lasting psychological damage.

Rape of Males

Health professionals who work with rape victims know that men are raped. Statistics on the frequency of male victimization are extremely difficult to obtain. Men are probably less likely than women to report that they have been raped. However, there is evidence "that men may be at the same point women were ten years ago on the subject of rape—more assertive, willing to talk and beginning to realize that the victim is not the criminal" (*Sexuality Today*, 1982, p. 1).

Only rarely do men report being sexually assaulted by women (Groth, 1979; Sarrel, 1980). Most of the perpetrators are heterosexual men who often commit their crime with one or more cohorts. As in rape of women, violence and power, not sex, are the driving forces behind the assault. Taking a man sexually may represent for some the ultimate way of degrading and humiliating another. The possibility of being raped is a very serious issue among male homosexuals since they are often the victims of such attacks.

Rape of inmates in penal institutions is a serious problem. Men who do the raping typically consider themselves to be heterosexual. When released, they usually resume sexual relations with women. The men who are rape victims often experience brutal gang assaults, or they may become the sexual partner of one particular dominant inmate for protection from others (Braen, 1980; Brownmiller, 1975).

SUMMARY

PEDOPHILIA

1. Pedophilia refers to sexual contact between an adult and a child. State legal codes vary as to what age interaction between an adult and a young person is considered child molestation.

2. Most individuals who engage in pedophilia are middle-aged or older males who are shy, conservative, and often very moralistic or religious. They frequently have poor social and sexual relations with other adults and may feel inadequate and inferior.

3. Most adults who relate sexually to children do not inflict physical damage. Quite often extreme parental reaction creates more psychological trauma in the child than the act itself.

INCEST

4. Incestuous behavior is sexual interaction between relatives. Brother-sister and first-cousin contacts are the most prevalent forms of this activity.

5. Most incestuous activity that is legally prosecuted is father-daughter sexual contact. The fathers in such cases are often economically disadvantaged, heavy drinkers, unemployed, religious, and very conservative.

6. Father-daughter incest can be an emotionally damaging experience for the child victim, with long-term negative consequences such as low self-esteem and difficulty establishing satisfying sexual and emotional relationships as an adult.

SEXUAL HARASSMENT ON THE JOB

7. Sexual harassment is any unwanted attention of a sexual nature from someone on the job that creates discomfort and/or interferes with the job.

8. Title VII of the 1964 Civil Rights Act prohibits sexual harassment in all its forms. A company can be liable for such coercive actions by its supervisors, coworkers, and customers.

9. Victims of sexual harassment may experience a variety of negative financial, emotional, and physical effects.

RAPE

10. Rape is a crime of violence. It is highly underreported.

11. Significant changes in rape laws regarding legal definition and prosecution proceedings are occurring.

12. The many false beliefs about rape tend to hold the victim responsible for the crime and excuse the attacker.

13. There are some rape prevention tactics that may help reduce the chances of a woman being raped.

14. Rape victims often suffer severe emotional difficulties that are manifested in the two phases of the rape trauma syndrome.

15. A rape victim's recovery from her ordeal may be facilitated by a partner who listens and provides support and encouragement.

16. Men who are convicted of rape are frequently poor, young, socially inept individuals who feel inadequate. Many have a prior history of sexual offenses.

17. Rape is usually an expression of anger and power.

18. Rapists frequently reveal extensive histories of rape and violence fantasies. They also may exhibit displaced anger toward women and distorted perceptions of their rape behavior.

19. There are a few specialized treatment programs for convicted rapists that attempt to reduce deviant arousal patterns, modify distorted belief systems, and teach rapists more appropriate ways of relating to people.

20. Rape of men is a serious problem, particularly in penal institutions. Most of the perpetrators of male rape are heterosexual men.

SUGGESTED READINGS

Brady, Katherine. *Father's Days*. New York: Dell, 1979. A courageous and powerful true story of a woman's sexual victimization by her father.

Brownmiller, Susan. *Against Our Will: Men, Women, and Rape*. New York: Simon & Schuster, 1975. An extremely well-documented, powerful, and illuminating examination of the myths and realities of rape.

Groth, A. Nicholas. *Men Who Rape*. New York: Plenum, 1979. Written by the director of a sex offender program in Connecticut, this book provides important insights into the character and motivation patterns of rapists.

Justice, Blair, and Justice, Rita. *The Broken Taboo: Sex in the Family*. New York: Human Sciences Press, 1979. An important, thought-provoking examination of incest with particular attention to its often devastating consequences.

MacKinnon, Catherine. *Sexual Harassment of Working Women*. New Haven, Conn.: Yale University Press, 1979. An excellent, comprehensive discussion of the nature, extent, and impact of sexual harassment.

Rush, Florence. *The Best Kept Secret: Sexual Abuse of Children*. New York: Atlantic, 1981. A superb, painfully illuminating discussion of the sexual abuse of children. The author details the historical, political, social, and even religious factors that have sanctioned and perpetuated child/adult sex through the ages.

Resources

Rape crisis centers are often listed in the white pages of the phone books of many cities.

21

Sex and the Law

ADULT CONSENSUAL SEXUAL BEHAVIORS
  Nonmarital Intercourse
  Specific Sexual Behaviors
  Homosexual Behaviors
PORNOGRAPHY
  Three Legal Issues
  Effects of Pornography
PROSTITUTION
  Female Prostitutes
  Male Prostitutes
  Economics and Profit from Prostitution
  Issues of Legal Status
SEX LAW REFORM
SUMMARY
SUGGESTED READINGS

*E*very society has certain norms for sexual behavior.* Some of these sexual norms are codified in law. This chapter presents a discussion of some of the laws that relate to sexuality in the United States and some of the social issues that focus on these laws.

Laws generally attempt to regulate the behavior of members of society to protect individuals and property and to insure continuation of the society itself. Sex laws endeavor to serve these and other purposes, as indicated by the many areas of sexuality that are under legal jurisdiction. Some laws pertaining to sexuality attempt to protect the public from acts that have been identified as offensive, for instance, exhibitionism, solicitation, sexual harassment, and voyeurism. Child molestation legislation tries to control exploitation of children. Rape laws are concerned with forcible and coercive sexual relations. Other laws pertaining to consensual acts between adults aspire to define and to prevent "immorality." Laws about procreation determine which contraception, abortion, and conception practices are legal. For example, right-to-life legislation would give the fetus constitutional rights and might make IUD use and abortion due to congenital defects of the fetus illegal. Laws regarding commercialized sex regulate prostitution and pornography. Considering the broad gamut of laws pertaining to sexuality, it may not be too surprising that Kinsey (1948) estimated that 95% of the males in his sample had experienced sex acts defined as illegal.

Many of the legal issues of sexuality do not apply equally in all parts of the country. Some sex laws are federal, covering all the states, while other sex laws are determined by the individual states and vary from one state to another. Penalties for breaking sex laws also differ greatly. Additionally, many of the laws are in a state of flux; for example, the legal status of abortion and the availability of contraceptives to adolescents without parental consent are currently being challenged.

ADULT CONSENSUAL SEXUAL BEHAVIORS

Consensual sexual behavior between adults consists of activities in which the individuals agree to participate. Such acts may be designated as illegal on the grounds of "immorality." Three classifications—nonmarital intercourse, specific sexual behaviors, and homosexual behaviors—will be discussed in the following sections.

Nonmarital Intercourse

Contemporary laws in our society reflect the Judeo-Christian ethic that sexual intercourse is only appropriate within the institution of marriage. These laws reflect long-standing societal concerns for the stability of the family and for property rights. Laws against nonmarital intercourse attempt to insure that those to whom property is

*See the discussion in Chapter 22 on cross-cultural sexuality for a look at the range of sexual norms in different societies.

passed are legitimately heirs of the father. Consequently, married women often have been more harshly prosecuted than married men for engaging in extramarital intercourse.

There are two legal categories for nonmarital sexual intercourse. *Fornication* is intercourse between unmarried adults, and *adultery* is intercourse by a married person with someone other than his or her spouse. In states where fornication and adultery are both crimes, fornication is usually the lesser crime. Laws against *cohabitation* (unmarried people living together) also exist in some states. Laws about nonmarital sex as well as other sexual activities have tended to become less severe through the years. For example, in early American times, adultery was punishable by death (Taylor, 1970).

People are rarely prosecuted for nonmarital intercourse. However, the illegality of sex between unmarried persons can have adverse effects. The law sometimes provides justification in court to discriminate in employment or to demonstrate the "bad character" of a rape victim or a parent seeking custody. Adultery is also often not prosecuted, although adultery was used as grounds for thousands of divorces before divorce by mutual consent became widely available. Although criminal prosecution for cohabitation is unlikely, other difficult legal matters may arise. Property and inheritance rights and responsibility for debts may be difficult to establish after the death of or separation from an unmarried partner (MacNamara and Sagarin, 1977).

Specific Sexual Behaviors

Many of the laws concerning the sexual behavior of consenting adults in private are derived from the Judeo-Christian ethic that viewed procreation as the only justification for sexual intercourse. Therefore, any act that did not provide the possibility of conception was "sinful." In Europe during medieval times, the Catholic church placed very severe restrictions on marital sexual behaviors. Intercourse was legal only in one position, and it was illegal on Sundays, Wednesdays, and Fridays, and during the days before Easter and Christmas. Church confessors were required to inquire specifically about these and other behaviors of their parishioners (Taylor, 1970).

"Immorality" has been codified into laws that define many nonprocreative behaviors as criminal, and many of these laws are still in effect. Although definitions are often vague and vary from state to state, oral-genital intercourse and anal intercourse are categorized as *sodomy* and are classified as felonies in many states. Often the penalties for these "crimes" (described in many statutes as "crimes against nature") are very severe. There is great variability from state to state in the penalties for sodomy. Some states have repealed their sodomy laws completely. In other states where sodomy laws exist, it is important to note that they usually pertain to all adults—married, nonmarried, heterosexual, and homosexual.

Miscegenation refers to a sexual relationship, marital or nonmarital, between persons of different races. Prior to the mid-1960s when antimiscegenation laws were declared unconstitutional in the United States, laws in most southern and several other states forbade sexual relations between white and nonwhite, especially white and black, persons. These laws were enforced selectively; white males were rarely prosecuted for having interracial relationships. Although miscegenation is no longer illegal in the United States, interracial couples often face considerable social pressure (MacNamara and Sagarin, 1977).

Homosexual Behaviors

The laws against homosexual behaviors stem from biblical injunctions against same-sex contact. Laws against homosexual behaviors have been exceedingly punitive. People with a homosexual orientation have been tortured and put to death throughout Western history. In the American colonies, homosexual people were condemned to death by drowning and burning. In the late 1770s, Thomas Jefferson was among the political leaders who suggested lessening the punishment from death to castration for men who committed homosexual acts (Katz, 1976).

Today, official views and actions on homosexuality reflect changed attitudes. The British Wolfenden Report of 1957 advocated removal of criminal sanctions against homosexual behavior. This report was based on a 10-year study by the Committee on Homosexual Offenses and Prostitution. The report maintains that there is no evidence that homosexual behavior contributes to "societal decay"; that personal revulsion by those who believe homosexual behavior to be unnatural or sinful is not a valid reason to override personal privacy or to make an act criminal; that the removal of criminal sanctions against homosexual behaviors in private between consenting adults will not result in an increase in homosexuality; and that private morality is not the law's business. The report recommended that homosexual behavior in private between consenting adults should not be a criminal offense.

As we have seen, sodomy laws are still in the legal codes in many states in our own country. Although they apply to heterosexual as well as homosexual behavior, these statutes are invoked more often against homosexual people. Most arrests for sodomy between same-sex (usually male) partners take place when the act occurs in a public place such as a restroom, theater, or park. In these cases, sexual conduct in public may be the issue rather than (or as well as) homosexuality.

The majority of homosexual arrests are made not for sodomy but for solicitation or for loitering in public places. Most homosexual solicitation is based on subtle gestures and comments that are not highly offensive to public decency—certainly no more so than catcalls, whistles, and comments directed at women by heterosexual men. However, the judicial system in some cities has occasionally used controversial practices to make arrests for homosexual solicitation. Policemen dress in plain clothes and attempt to entice homosexual men to make sexual propositions. If the proposition or "solicitation" occurs, another policeman standing nearby arrests the homosexual man. The police regard this practice as enticement. Others call it entrapment, in other words, inducing people to commit illegal acts. Entrapment is illegal and enticement is legal. The controversy over the definition of this procedure continues in the legal system. (The same practices and issues pertain to prosecution of prostitutes.)

The great majority of homosexual people are never arrested for either solicitation or sodomy because the behaviors occur in private. However, living under the threat of prosecution for being sexual with another consenting adult is an uncomfortable position, especially given the negative attitudes toward homosexuality in our

BOX 21.1 STATES WITH CONSENTING ADULT LAWS AS OF 1982

Alaska	Maine	Oregon
California	Massachusetts	Pennsylvania
Colorado	Nebraska	South Dakota
Connecticut	New Hampshire	Texas
Delaware	New Jersey	Vermont
Hawaii	New Mexico	Washington
Illinois	New York	West Virginia
Indiana	North Dakota	Wyoming
Iowa	Ohio	Source: National Gay Task Force

society. As we saw in Chapter 10, one of the goals of the gay rights movement is to repeal sodomy laws and establish *consensual adult statutes* that decriminalize and legalize sexual activity between consenting adults in private (Box 21.1).

In addition to laws that exist to regulate adult consensual sexual activities, there is a large body of laws in effect that regulate pornography.

PORNOGRAPHY

Pictorial and written representations of sexuality are not a modern invention. Cave drawings depicted sexual activity. Ancient Greek and Roman societies used sexual themes to decorate housewares and public architecture. The ancient Eastern Indian love manual *Kama Sutra*, dating from about 400 A.D., summarized philosophies of sexuality and spirituality in its description of specific sexual techniques. Graphic representations of coitus in Japanese *schunga* paintings and woodcuts from the 1600s and 1700s were regarded as art masterpieces.

A clearcut contemporary definition of pornography is difficult to establish. The United States judicial system has not been able to establish a consistent definition, and individual opinions vary greatly in what is considered to be pornography. Generally speaking, pornography is written, visual, or spoken material, depicting or describing sexual conduct or genital exposure, that is arousing to the viewer. This definition is broad, however. Within it, the continuum could range from suggestive advertisements commonly seen in the media to the explicit portrayal of sexual interaction and sexually oriented violence. The legal controversies about pornography center on what is to be legally defined as "obscene," a term that implies a personal or societal interpretation of what is considered offensive. For purposes of this section, *pornography* will be used

Erotic scenes on a Greek vase.

A Japanese schunga painting.

as a collective term for visual and written materials sold for the purposes of sexual arousal.

Three Legal Issues

The legal processes relating to pornography have centered on three issues: the evaluation of what is obscene, regulations concerning dissemination of sexually explicit materials, and the constitutional right of free speech, as provided by the First Amendment of the United States Constitution.

Attempts at a Legal Definition   Pornography itself is not illegal, but materials considered to be obscene are. This leads us to the dilemma faced by the courts in determining what constitutes obscenity. Early American courts considered material to be obscene if it depraved and corrupted the user. The courts then faced the problem of establishing that a person had been depraved by the materials. The first major challenge to this legal definition of obscenity occurred in the Roth v. United States case (354 US 476), decided by the Supreme Court in 1957. This and subsequent decisions have established three criteria to evaluate obscenity. First, the dominant theme of the work as a whole must appeal to prurient interest in sex. Second, it must be patently offensive to contemporary community standards. Third, it must be without serious literary, artistic, political, or scientific value (Miller v. California 413 US 15, 1973).

The subjectivity of these criteria is reflected in Supreme Court Justice Potter Stewart's comment that pornography is difficult to intelligently define, "But I know it when I see it" (Jacobelis v. Ohio, 379 US 197, 1965), as well as in local differences in interpretation. Community standards of obscenity can vary dramatically. In some areas, particularly in large cities, all manner of explicit sexual films are openly advertised and shown. In other areas, particularly in small communities, magazines like *Playboy* have been banned. Courts, communities, and pornographic entrepreneurs still struggle with the legal determination of obscenity.

Regulating Pornography Dissemination   There have been several legal approaches to the regulation of obscene materials. In 1969, the United States Supreme Court ruled that private possession in the home is not a crime, nor is it subject to government regulation (Stanley v. Georgia, 394 US 557, 1969). However, dissemination of pornography is closely regulated. Federal laws prohibit broadcasting, mailing, importation, and interstate transport of obscene materials.

Most of these pornography dissemination statutes stem from the Comstock Act of 1873 (mentioned in Chapter 11), which made it a felony to deposit any materials of "indecent character" in the U.S. mail. During the first eight years of his involvement in the New York Society for the Suppression of Vice, some of self-appointed censor Anthony Comstock's activities included destroying 27,584 pounds of books; confiscating 1,376,939 "obscene" songs, poems, pamphlets, and catalogs; and recording 976,125 names and addresses of people on mailing lists for pornography (Kilpatrick,

Scully—© Punch (Rothco)

*"Obviously been too long in the making. What was obscene enough
when you started isn't obscene enough now."*

1960). Federal mailing laws have also been invoked in contemporary times in the prosecution of purveyors of obscene materials.

There are other ways of regulating dissemination of pornography. Many cities limit the areas where adult bookstores and movie houses can be located. Containment of bookstores and movie houses by zoning and land-use regulations attempts to protect nonusers of pornography from being visually assaulted by offensive material on the basis of the right to freedom from involuntary exposure to pornography. Because of zoning ordinances, high concentrations of pornographic establishments have arisen in some cities. The "Combat Zone" in Boston and North Beach in San Francisco are examples of such areas.

634

Areas such as North Beach in San Francisco have high
concentrations of "adult" entertainment establishments.

Freedom of Speech   The 1957 Supreme Court decision declared that the First
Amendment guarantee of freedom of speech and of the press did not apply cat-
egorically to obscene materials. Vigorous debate of this position has been presented
by civil libertarians as well as by some of the justices on the Supreme Court. They
maintain that any censorship is unconstitutional, and they support the unrestricted
availability of pornography to adults.

Effects of Pornography

Questions about the effects of pornography have been debated extensively in recent
years from different philosophical perspectives, and a considerable body of research is
emerging. Some of the key questions being raised have to do with whether pornography has a significant effect on behavior, what those effects are, and value
judgments about the messages pornography may transmit about human relationships.

In the late 1960s President Johnson appointed a Commission on Obscenity and
Pornography to study the effects of sexually explicit materials. The commission
studied events following the legalization of pornography in Denmark, analyzed
findings of various self-report and survey research studies in the United States, and
offered recommendations. The commission found that after pornography was legalized in Denmark in the late 1960s there was an initial increase in the number of Danish
people who purchased pornographic materials. After a few years, however, sales to

BOX 21.2 BOOKS BANNED IN SCHOOLS

School boards and their appointed book review committees can legally ban books from classroom use or from the library. Many books have been recently banned from various schools. John Steinbeck's *Grapes of Wrath* was banned from classroom use in Kanawha, Iowa, because a parent complained that the work was "profane, vulgar, and obscene"; and his book, *Of Mice and Men*, was removed from a high school library in Oil City, Pennsylvania, on the basis that it refers to prostitution and contains "vulgarity and profanity." A high school library in Milton, New Hampshire, removed Alexander Solzhenitsyn's work, *One Day in the Life of Ivan Denisovich* because it contained "language you wouldn't allow to be used in the home." The school board of Issaquah, Washington, removed *The Catcher in the Rye* by J. D. Salinger from classroom use,

claiming that it represents an "overall Communist plot" and contains numerous profanities. The Middleville, Michigan, school board banned the same book after several parents complained that it "violates the word of God." Pressure from parents caused a school board to ban *Flowers for Algernon* (on which the movie *Charly* was based) because parents believed that a scene in the book would stir students' "natural impulses." The school board of Miller, Missouri, banned Huxley's *Brave New World* because many parts of the book "make that kind of sex look like fun." Finally, *The American Heritage Dictionary* was removed from a high school because, among other things, a "bed" was defined as a "place for lovemaking." The school board in Anchorage, Alaska, also removed this dictionary because it contained too many "dirty words" (Doyle, 1982).

Danes decreased, and foreign tourists purchased most of the pornography. The commission noted that legalization and increased availability of pornography did not result in an increase in reported sex offenses, although a cause-and-effect relationship is difficult to establish. (For example, there may have been increased tolerance and reduced prosecution of lesser offenses such as exhibitionism.) Also, the commission's analysis of current research found that imprisoned sex offenders had not had more exposure to pornography than had other prison inmates or nonprison populations. In its summary of research on the effects of sexually explicit materials, the commission concluded that no significant, long-lasting changes in behavior were evident in college student volunteer research subjects after being exposed to pornography. On the basis of this information the commission's 1970 report recommended repealing all laws prohibiting access to pornography for adults. However, the U.S. Senate and President Nixon rejected the commission's recommendations.

Controversy and concern about the effects of pornography has continued. One criticism of pornography is that it contributes to unrealistic expectations of male sexual

636   behavior. Pornography often stresses performance and conquest rather than pleasure. It perpetuates the myth that a "real man" is always ready for sex and that sex can be obtained without regard for the other person or the complex nature of the man himself (Zilbergeld, 1978).

Another concern is with pornography that portrays violence toward or degradation of women. Gloria Steinem, editor of Ms. magazine, objects to the woman-hating, often violent portrayal of sexuality found in much pornography. Her definition of pornography is:

> . . . any depiction of sex in which there is clear force, or an unequal power that spells coercion. It may be very blatant, with weapons of torture or bondage, wounds and bruises . . . It may be much more subtle: a physical attitude of conqueror and victim . . . In either case there is no sense of equal choice or equal power. (November 1978, p. 54)

Steinem is concerned that pornography encourages people to eroticize aggressive and dehumanizing attitudes about women. Some feminists believe that pornography that depicts male power and violence toward women promotes a climate in which sexual hostility is encouraged and which contributes to actual violence against women.

Recent research supports the legitimacy of these concerns and questions the commission's findings. A variety of studies indicates that certain types of erotic materials can increase a person's acceptance of actual aggressive behaviors. Research with college men found that sexually explicit films with violence elicit more subsequent aggression toward women than films with consensual sex scenes or scenes without sex or aggression (Donnerstein and Berkowitz, 1981). The researchers express concern that pornography with aggression might stimulate aggressively disposed men to assault women. Another study found that exposure to films in the popular media portraying violent sexuality increased male (but not female) subjects' acceptance of interpersonal violence against women (Malamuth and Check, 1981). These concerns are particularly significant in view of the fact that the prevalence of aggression in pornography has increased in the last few years (Malamuth and Spinner, 1980).

Some research on aggressive pornography and sexual offenders suggests the possibility that certain types of pornography may encourage sexually assaultive behavior. One study found that convicted rapists, as contrasted to other sex offenders, are likely to find the combination of sex and violence in pornography to be particularly stimulating (Goldstein and Kant, 1973); others report that many men who rape have erections while listening to descriptions of violent rape, while most nonrapists do not (Abel et al., 1977; Barbaree et al., 1979).

The conflicting data on the effects of pornography leave many questions unanswered. Some of the differences between the commission's findings and more recent research may be due to the use of physiological measurements of arousal instead of only the use of self-report. Also, sexually violent and coercive materials were not generally employed in the commission's studies. It seems reasonable to conclude, however, that for some people pornography, especially portrayals of rape and violence, may play a part in inducing aggressive behavior.

Definitions of and perspectives on pornography, as well as pornography itself, have changed with time. However, the issues involved, such as freedom of speech, the role of law, effects on human relationships, and considerations of personal and public morality, remain controversial. Another controversial topic related to sex and the law is prostitution, which will be discussed in the next section.

PROSTITUTION

Prostitution is usually understood to be the exchange of sexual services for money. It usually involves a woman selling sexual services to a man, although transactions between two males are also common. Payment for a man's services to a woman are less usual. Prostitution is generally characterized by sexual contacts with multiple partners with whom the contract for the exchange of sexual services for money is explicit. Prostitution is illegal in every state of the United States, except Nevada.

Prostitution has existed throughout history. However, the significance and meaning of prostitution have varied in different times and societies. In ancient Greece the practice was tolerated. During some periods of Greek history, prostitutes were valued for their intellectual, social, and sexual companionship. Prostitution was part of revered religious rituals in other ancient societies. Sexual relations between prostitutes and men often took place within temples and were seen as sacred acts; in some cultures the man in this transaction was considered to be a representative of the diety. In medieval Europe, prostitution was tolerated, and the public baths provided a flourishing opportunity for contacts between customers and prostitutes. And in England during the Victorian era, prostitution was viewed as a scandalous but necessary sexual and social outlet for men, as it was a lesser evil for men to have sexual relations with a prostitute than with another man's wife or daughter (Taylor, 1970).

Prostitutes exist because there is a demand for their services (Cohen, 1980). Customers of prostitutes are usually white, middle-aged, middle class, and married (James et al., 1975), and they patronize prostitutes for various reasons. Sex with a prostitute can provide sexual contact or release without any future commitment or may offer an opportunity to engage in sexual techniques that a partner will not permit.

Prostitutes may be delinquent school dropouts and runaways or well-educated adults. No single theory can explain the motivation for being a prostitute. A combination of psychological, social, environmental, and economic factors is involved. However, studies report a high incidence of childhood sexual abuse in the history of female prostitutes (James and Meyerding, 1977; Satterfield and Listiak, 1982). Many are prostitutes on a part-time basis and otherwise pursue conventional school, work, or social life styles. People who work as prostitutes on a temporary, part-time basis and have other occupational skills can more easily leave prostitution. Many of these men and women have not identified themselves as prostitutes or as "professionals" (Davis, 1978). The full-time prostitute, who is alienated from traditional values, has identified him- or herself as part of the subculture (being arrested facilitates this identification); this person may have little education, no other marketable skills, and usually finds it very difficult to become successfully independent of prostitution.

BOX 21.3 SEXUAL EXPLOITATION OF CHILDREN IN PROSTITUTION AND PORNOGRAPHY

Experts estimate that there may be as many as 2.4 million teenage prostitutes in the United States (United States General Accounting Office, 1982). Teenagers often become prostitutes as a means of survival after they have run away from home. There are extreme instances, such as a seven-year-old boy selling his sexual services for 25¢ to buy food. Many of these young prostitutes have been abused or neglected at home, did not perform well in school, and have poor self-images. They are often seeking adult attention and affection, and they believe at first that prostitution is a life of glamour and adventure.

Pornographers are able to find children—usually between the ages of eight and 16—to willingly participate in making pornographic photographs, video tapes, or movies in exchange for friendship, interest, money, or as a result of threats. Some children, particularly the very young, may not know their photographs are used as pornography. Commercially produced child pornography has declined due to the Protection of Children Against Sexual Exploitation Act of 1977, stricter enforcement, and media attention; but homemade, underground child pornography is still produced (Baker, 1980).

Children involved in prostitution and pornography often suffer emotional distress and have a poor life adjustment. Many develop a concept of themselves as objects to be sold. They frequently have problems with employment because of the stigma of their past and their dissatisfaction with the lower pay of a regular job. They may have difficulty establishing meaningful relationships and are likely to become involved in crime.

Female Prostitutes

There are various types of female prostitutes who service male customers. The variations may relate to a number of characteristics, including public visibility of the woman, the amount of money she charges, and her social class. We will look at a few different categories, defined roughly in terms of the method a woman uses to contact customers. These include streetwalkers, women in brothels or massage parlors, and call girls.

Streetwalkers can be seen on the streets of most large cities. They solicit customers on the street or in bars. They are often from lower socioeconomic backgrounds, and they charge less than other types of prostitutes for their services. Because of their visibility, streetwalkers are easily subject to arrest. Most streetwalkers repeat the cycle of arrest, short jail sentences, and release many times throughout their careers. Even in the few cities where laws inflict penalties on the customer as well as

the prostitute, the male customers of streetwalkers and other prostitutes are rarely arrested.

A *brothel* is a house in which a group of prostitutes work. Brothels were common in earlier American history and remain so in some other countries. They are legal in some areas of Nevada today. Brothels range from expensive establishments to run-down, seedy places. They are usually managed by a "madam" who acts as a hostess and business manager for the house. Prostitutes who work in brothels are somewhat more protected from arrest because they are less visible to the police.

Massage parlors are often seen as a modern "quick service" version of brothels. Some massage parlors offer legitimate massages, nothing more. However, many also provide some sexual services. Intercourse is illegal and may or may not occur as part of the "massage." Manual stimulation (a "local" or "hand finishing") or oral stimulation to orgasm is often arranged for a fee once the customer is in the massage room.

The customer also can often dictate in what state of dress or undress he would like his masseuse to be. One study stated that most of the customers were white-collar businessmen over the age of 35 (Velarde and Warlick, 1973). Zoning or business license laws are sometimes used to attempt to control the location or existence of massage parlors.

Call girls generally earn more than other prostitutes. They often come from middle-class backgrounds. Call girls frequently offer social companionship as well as sexual services to their customers. Their customer contacts are usually made by personal referral, and they often have several regular customers. Their public visibility is minimal, and their risk of arrest is much less than that of the streetwalker. Call girls charge more for their services and provide themselves with attractive wardrobes and apartments—all part of their business expenses. They are also more likely than other types of prostitutes to be given goods such as clothing or living accommodations by regular customers. A case study of call girls is described in Box 3.1 (p. 65).

Male Prostitutes

Men who provide sexual services for women in exchange for money and gifts are called *gigolos*. The role of a gigolo is most similar to that of a call girl because he usually acts as a social companion as well as sexual partner to his customers. Customers are usually wealthy middle-aged women seeking the attentions of attractive young men. There is often a pretense on the gigolo's part of romantic interest in the woman. The exchange of money for services is less explicit than in most interactions between female prostitutes and male customers. It is unknown how common this type of male prostitution is, but it is probably far less common than female prostitution.

Male prostitutes who exchange their sexual services for money with homosexual customers are probably as numerous as female prostitutes but have not been studied as extensively. As with female prostitutes, male prostitutes who cater to homosexual men can be classified into different groups. *Hustlers* make contact with customers on the streets, in gay bars or steam baths, or in public parks or toilets. *Call boys* work similarly to call girls. They have regular customers and are often social companions as well as sexual partners. Call boys find their customers by newspaper advertising or through someone who refers the customer to them. *Kept boys* are partially or fully supported by an older male. *Peer-delinquent prostitutes* often work in small groups and use homosexual prostitution as a vehicle for assault and robbery. Most peer-delinquent prostitutes are between 14 and 17 years old. Their usual modus operandi is for one or more of them to solicit a customer who is willing to pay to perform fellatio on them. The peer-delinquent prostitutes then rob and physically assault the customer. Peer-delinquent prostitutes often define their contacts with customers as a demonstration of their masculinity and heterosexuality to their peers. However, beneath this facade, many have strong homosexual feelings (Allen, 1980).

Some male prostitutes consider themselves to be heterosexual, and they have concurrent female sexual partners and usually return to a heterosexual life style after a brief career in prostitution. Like the peer-delinquent prostitutes, they often restrict the nature of the sexual activities that occur so that the prostitute assumes the more "masculine" role, for example, allowing the customer to perform fellatio on him but not reciprocating (Reiss, 1964).

Economics and Profit from Prostitution

For many men and women who sell sexual services, prostitution is a way of earning a living; most view their work as an economic opportunity. Recognizing the connection between prostitution and economic disadvantage, the 1959 United Nations Commission study of prostitution concluded that creating other economic opportunities for women is important for the prevention of prostitution.

While women and men usually become prostitutes to earn money, the practice provides business for many parties besides the prostitutes. In fact, it may not be as lucrative for the prostitute as it is for the other people involved, either directly or indirectly. Pimps, the criminal justice system, referral agents, and hotel operators all benefit financially from prostitution (Sheehy, 1973). Pimps are men who "protect" the prostitutes (usually streetwalkers) and live off their earnings. (Women are more likely to have pimps than are men.) The illegality of prostitution contributes to the prostitutes' need for a pimp. Pimps bail the women in their "stables" out of jail when they are arrested. They may offer companionship, a place to live, clothing, food, and in some cases, drugs. They often assume a highly controlling, authoritarian relationship with their prostitutes while being financially supported by the women's earnings. Pimps may keep as much as 95% of the streetwalkers' earnings, which they often invest in ostentatious clothing and cars that represent the pimp's status and the prostitute's earning power (Young, 1970).

Because prostitution is illegal, police officers, attorneys, judges, bail bondsmen, and jailers spend part of their work time attempting to control, litigate, or process prostitutes through the judicial bureaucracy. In this way, prostitution provides some of the business for the criminal justice system. (Some people argue that the time and money spent in actions against prostitution impedes the judicial system's effectiveness in working with more serious crimes.) On the other side, organized crime is also often involved in prostitution and profits from it (Sheehy, 1973).

Referral agents also make money from prostitution. Cabdrivers, hotel desk clerks, and bartenders get cash tips from customers as well as from prostitutes for helping establish the contact. Prostitutes who work out of their apartments may have to give doormen, hotel proprietors, and elevator operators an ongoing supply of tips, high rental fees, or sexual services (or any combination thereof) so that they will not report them to the authorities.

Issues of Legal Status

Questions on the legal status of prostitution have been debated for some time in the United States. There are several arguments for maintaining its status as a criminal offense. One view is that, if prostitution were not a punishable offense, many women would take it up, and it would be more difficult to enforce any restrictions on prostitution activities. (This same argument is sometimes offered regarding legal sanctions against homosexual behavior.) Another argument is that it is the responsibility of government to regulate public morals, and that the absence of laws against prostitution signifies governmental tolerance of commercialized vice (United Nations Study on Traffic in Persons and Prostitution, 1959).

There are also arguments against the criminal status of prostitution. Some of these center on the difficulty of effective prosecution. Prostitution flourishes despite criminal sanctions against it, as it has throughout history in most societies where it has been prohibited. Other arguments are concerned with the possible negative results of outlawing prostitution. For instance, its criminal status may encourage connections with organized crime, contribute to the use of police entrapment, and hamper the rehabilitation of prostitutes (who may find it difficult to find other kinds of work once they have a criminal record). There are also arguments that center on discrimination in applying penalties. Customers and prostitutes are equally responsible in the vast majority of cases, but it is the prostitute, and not the customer, who is arrested and prosecuted. Many people who argue for the legalization of prostitution have a different view of the role of government from that held by people who favor its proscription. They maintain that the appropriate role of penal codes is to protect minors and to maintain public order but not to penalize prostitution because it is seen as immoral (United Nations Study on Traffic in Persons and Prostitution, 1959).

There are at least two main alternatives to the criminal status of prostitution. One is its *legalization*; the other is *decriminalization*. An important distinction exists. If legalized, prostitution could be regulated, licensed, and taxed by the government. In some European cities, prostitutes are registered and required to follow certain procedures, such as periodic VD checks, to maintain their licenses. If it were decriminalized, the criminal penalties for prostitution would be removed. Prostitutes would be neither licensed nor regulated. However, decriminalization does not condone prostitution. Laws concerning solicitation and laws against involvement of minors would remain, even if prostitution were legalized or decriminalized.

Some writers favor decriminalization and oppose legalization. The primary objection to legalization is that prostitutes would still be "owned," but now by the government and its regulations and licensing rather than by pimps and their rules. Some people see decriminalization as a better option to allow women more control over the use of their own bodies (Millett, 1976).

The rationale for legalization or decriminalization is based on several factors. Prostitution is usually considered a victimless crime, an act that does not harm the people engaged in it. (However, prostitution may not be victimless in all senses, since as we have seen, the prostitute is often the victim of abuse from customers and pimps and of discriminatory laws and social stigma.) There is a legislative trend to give victimless crimes (including nonsexual laws on such acts as gambling, alcohol use, and drug use) regulatory rather than criminal status. In changing these laws, it is hoped that the criminal justice system can expend more efforts on protection from crimes that harm people or property (Morris, 1973). Also, if prostitution were legal, its association with organized crime might be weakened. Victimization of prostitutes by pimps, customers, the judicial system, and others who profit at their expense would perhaps be reduced.

Some prostitutes have begun to organize for political change and mutual support. The prostitutes' union, COYOTE (Cast Out Your Old Tired Ethics), acts as a collective voice for the issues and concerns of prostitutes' point of view. It is unknown what impact this organization will have on laws pertaining to prostitution.

SEX LAW REFORM

There are several important issues to be considered in the question of sex law reform. These include the right to sexual privacy, victimless crimes, and equality in the laws. None of these issues has a simple answer, due partly to the conflicting values within our pluralistic society.

The right of personal sexual privacy is violated by many of the existing sex laws. Statutes regulating private, consensual sexual behavior between adults are an example. Some legislative action has been taken along these lines. In Griswold v. Connecticut in 1965, the United States Supreme Court ruled that the State of Connecticut could not prohibit the use of contraceptives by married people (381 US 479). They based their decision on the right to privacy of married couples. This decision set a precedent to challenge remaining laws that regulate marital sexual relations. In 1972, the Supreme Court ruled against a statute that prohibited distribution of contraceptives to unmarried people (Eisenstadt v. Baird, 405 US 438, 1972). One of the objections to a law requiring parental notification of a minor receiving prescription contraceptives from a federally funded program is the invasion of doctor-patient privacy (ACLU, 1982).

The right to privacy in consensual adult sexual behavior is increasing as more states repeal their sodomy laws. In 1962, Illinois became the first state to remove criminal offense status from adult consensual behavior. By 1982, 26 states had consenting adult laws (see Box 21.1). The American Law Institute's Model Penal Code recommends removing criminal sanctions from all private adult consensual sexual behavior except prostitution (1962).

Victimless crimes are another focus for law reform. Prostitution is most commonly thought of in this perspective, but consensual adult sexual behaviors, also victimless, are still legally defined as criminal in many states. Pornography might also be considered in this category. The argument for decriminalization of victimless crimes is twofold. The first point is based on the principle that if an act does not harm anyone, it should not be considered as a crime. The second is based on the expense to the already overextended judicial system in prosecuting acts that are not harming anyone. There is also the argument that time and money spent with victimless crimes would be much better used to attack crimes that do endanger others.

The arbitrariness and inequality of many sex laws are of further concern. For example, although prostitutes and their customers commit the act together, usually only the woman is arrested. Homosexuals are more likely to be brought to trial for sodomy than are heterosexual people. The dramatic variations in laws and penalties from state to state are another form of inequality. These inequalities are contradictory to our constitutional right of "justice for all," and changes in sex laws are, in part, an attempt to achieve increased legal equality.

SUMMARY

1. The laws about sexuality cover many different areas including reproduction, exhibitionism, child molestation, rape, voyeurism, pornography, prostitution, and consensual adult behaviors.

2. Kinsey (1948) estimated that 95% of the males in his sample had broken some sex law.

ADULT CONSENSUAL SEXUAL BEHAVIORS

3. Fornication laws cover intercourse between unmarried adults, and adultery laws pertain to intercourse by a married person with someone other than one's spouse. Miscegenation refers to a sexual relationship between persons of different races.

4. Sodomy laws prohibit oral-genital intercourse and anal intercourse. In some states these activities are legally defined as felonies.

5. Sodomy laws and solicitation statutes are used in arrests of homosexual people.

6. The Wolfenden Report from Great Britain recommends the removal of private homosexual behavior between consenting adults as a criminal offense.

PORNOGRAPHY

7. A clear definition of pornography and obscenity has yet to be established by the judicial system. The criteria established by the Supreme Court in attempting to decide what is obscene decree that the dominant theme of the work as a whole must appeal to prurient interest, be offensive to contemporary community standards, and be without serious literary, artistic, political, or scientific value.

8. Legal regulation of pornography occurs through mailing laws and zoning of pornography outlets.

9. The increased availability and legalization of pornography in Denmark was not followed by an increase in reported sex offenses.

10. There is conflicting data on the effects of pornography. The 1970 Commission on Obscenity and Pornography reported that pornography does not have significant, long-lasting effects, but more recent research suggests that sexually explicit materials, especially with violence toward women, increase aggressive behaviors.

PROSTITUTION

11. Streetwalkers, women in brothels or massage parlors, and call girls are broad categories of prostitutes.

12. Male prostitutes who service women are called gigolos and male prostitutes who service men are called hustlers, call boys, kept boys, or peer-delinquent prostitutes.

13. Women or men who turn to prostitution do so, in part, for economic opportunity. However, pimps, the criminal justice system, organized crime, referral agents, and hotel operators also profit from prostitution.

14. Alternatives to the criminal status of prostitution include legalization and decriminalization.

SEX LAW REFORM

15. Questions concerning the right to personal privacy, victimless crimes, and equality of the law are important in considering sex law reform.

Faust, Beatrice. *Women, Sex and Pornography*. New York: Macmillan, 1980. An interesting book on controversial issues.

Great Britain Committee on Homosexual Offenses and Prostitution. *The Wolfenden Report*. New York: Stein and Day, 1963. A thorough and thoughtful investigation into sex laws pertaining to homosexuality and prostitution with concluding recommendations for sex law reform.

Millett, Kate. *The Prostitution Papers*. New York: Ballantine, 1976. A critical exploration into the social meaning of the role of prostitutes in our society which presents an argument opposed to legalization and in favor of decriminalization.

Schultz, Leroy (Ed.). *The Sexual Victimology of Youth*. Springfield, Ill.: Charles C. Thomas, 1980. A variety of papers on various aspects of sexual victimization and young people, including incest, sexual abuse, and pornography.

22

Cross-Cultural Variations in Sexual Expression

SOCIETY AND CULTURE: DEFINITIONS AND OBSERVATIONS
DATA SOURCES: METHODS AND LIMITATIONS
COMPARATIVE ANALYSIS OF SOME SELECTED SEXUAL BEHAVIORS
    Sexuality During Childhood
    Coitus Before Marriage
    Marital Coitus
    Extramarital Coitus
    Female Orgasm
    Noncoital Sex Play
    Sexuality and Aging
    Homosexuality
SUMMARY
SUGGESTED READINGS

*I*n the preceding chapters we have focused almost exclusively on the sexual attitudes and behaviors of people in our own North American society. Many of us have a tendency to view these standards and practices as the only "natural" or appropriate ones. This is understandable, for very few people have experiences with sexuality outside their own culture. In this last chapter we will examine human sexuality across a spectrum of diverse cultures. Sexual expression in other societies is an interesting topic in its own right. However, our reasons for concluding our text with a discussion of cross-cultural patterns go beyond interest. We are convinced that even a brief look at the variations that exist in sexual behavior in other societies will provide us with new perspectives and improved understanding of our own society's sexual standards and values.

It is also conceivable that certain practices often believed to be deviant or inappropriate within our society (for example, homosexuality, extramarital sex, and sex play between children) will be viewed with more understanding when we realize that they are both common and acceptable in many other societies. Furthermore, the study of sexuality across the ethnographic spectrum gives us valuable information about the powerful role that culture plays in shaping our individual sexualities. Finally, a legitimate goal of sex research is to understand the universal features as well as the diversities in human sexual behavior. What better way is there to accomplish this than through a search for patterns of behavior that are shared across cultural boundaries?

SOCIETY AND CULTURE: DEFINITIONS AND OBSERVATIONS

The terms *society* and *culture* appear with great frequency throughout the remainder of this chapter. How we use these terms is clarified in the following quotations from a noted sex researcher, Frank Beach:

A *society* is an enduring, cooperating, self-reproducing group of individuals with organized patterns of interrelationships.

Culture refers to a society's shared patterns of belief, thought, speech and action. A culture is a body of customary beliefs, social forms and material traits characterizing a society or a subdivision thereof. Cultures are the tools with which societies achieve their function. (1978, pp. 7–8)

The meaning of a given act (sexual or otherwise) can be fully understood only by looking at the cultural context within which it occurs. For example, in North American society, sexual overtones are often attributed to two men hugging each other. In contrast, men in Iran (and in many other societies) may heartily embrace each other without any assumption of a sexual component in their behavior.

There is such cultural diversity among the peoples of the world that the very definition of what is sexually arousing may vary greatly. For example, exposed female breasts may trigger sexual interest in the males of one society (certainly most Western ones) while inducing little or no erotic interest in males of a different land. Further-

A woman warrior in New Guinea. In many societies bare female breasts are not generally viewed as erotic stimuli.

more, cultural mandates on the acceptability of sexual activity show enormous variation across cultures. In some societies, such as the Mangaians of Polynesia, sex is highly valued and almost all manifestations of it are considered beautiful and natural. In contrast, other societies, such as the Manus of New Guinea, view any sexual act as undesirable and shameful.

One can take almost any specific sexual behavior and find wide differences in the ways in which it is practiced or viewed in different societies. For example, masturbation by children may be overtly condemned in one society, covertly supported in another, openly encouraged in still another, and even occasionally initiated by parental example, as we will see later in this chapter.

The diversity of sexual expression throughout the world may tend to mask a fundamental generalization that can be applied without exception to all social orders. This is the fact that within the cultural mores of all societies, there are rules regulating the conduct of sexual behavior. While the exact regulations vary from one society to the next, no social order has seen fit to allow sexuality to remain totally unregulated. Thus, the sexual inclinations of human males and females are never allowed free reign within the context of any formally organized social group.

DATA SOURCES:
METHODS AND LIMITATIONS

Most of our data about sexual expression in other societies has been derived from the fieldwork of *ethnographers,* anthropologists who specialize in studying the cultures of different societies. Fieldwork consists of careful observation (the researcher may live with the population for several months or years) and in-depth interviews and discussions. It is a method of study that can produce detailed information about the beliefs and behaviors of a small representative group. Unfortunately, fieldwork has rarely focused on sexual mores and behaviors. Descriptive ethnographies are more often characterized by extended discussions of religion, economics, technology, and social organization.

The scarcity of data about sexual expression is probably due in part to a certain cultural bias on the part of many researchers. Most ethnographers come from Western societies, where there has typically been a reluctance to pursue investigations into private matters. Our limited information also reflects the attitudes of the people being studied. Even when field investigators are comfortable with inquiring about sexual activity, their respondents may not share the same degree of comfort with the subject matter. Most people, whether they live on the plains of Tanzania or on an island in Polynesia, are hesitant to talk openly about their sex lives.

When people do talk about sex, their accounts may present another limitation. To an even greater extent than in our own society, investigations of other societies rely on reported rather than observed sexual behavior, and we must assume that these reports are subject to the same kinds of errors that are outlined in Chapter 3. Most people around the world are probably concerned, to one degree or another, with such things as fear of disclosure and a desire to present themselves or their group in a favorable light.

There are also some limitations to cross-cultural studies that pertain to the biases of the ethnographers. We might expect some of these investigators to have limited objectivity and a tendency to make certain assumptions about other societies on the basis of their own culturally determined attitudes. Most ethnographers are from European or American cultures that have traditionally legitimized sexual expression only within permanent, monogamous marital unions. Consequently, it seems reasonable to suspect that at least some researchers have been inclined to make biased assessments of nonmarital sexual activity. For example, instances of childhood (or premarital, or extramarital) sexual experience may sometimes be overlooked or misinterpreted. Ethnographers are not immune to certain other biases that are by no means culture-bound. For instance, some investigators have reported the frequent use of dildos as aids to female masturbation—accounts that may reflect a widespread masculine assumption that a penis substitute is necessary for female masturbation.

This brief outline of some of the limitations of cross-cultural sex data may give you some perspective on the discussions that follow. We do not mean to imply that such information is totally untrustworthy and irrelevant. Quite to the contrary, some of the available ethnographic descriptions contain valuable data about the richness and diversity of human sexual expression.

While we will draw upon many publications in the discussions that follow, two sources are particularly noteworthy. One is the monumental work by anthropologist Clellan Ford and psychologist Frank Beach, who surveyed many aspects of human sexuality in 190 societies throughout the world. In their classic book, *Patterns of Sexual Behavior* (1951), they also include an excellent comparative analysis of sexual behaviors in nonhuman species. Despite the fact that it was published more than three decades ago, the work of Ford and Beach still remains one of our best sources on cultural variations in human sexual expression.

A more recent source is an excellent reader, edited by Donald Marshall and Robert Suggs, titled *Human Sexual Behavior: Variations in the Ethnographic Spectrum* (1971). It contains detailed essays pertaining to sexual expression in several diverse cultures.

COMPARATIVE ANALYSIS OF SOME SELECTED SEXUAL BEHAVIORS

The remainder of this chapter is devoted to discussions of cultural diversity in sexual attitudes and behaviors. Our treatment here is admittedly brief, due to limitations of space. Limitations of available data also impose restrictions. Certain areas of sexuality have been explored more fully than others. Almost every ethnographic report includes information about marital coitus, for example, whereas virtually none discuss the role of communication in a people's sexual lives. Therefore, our selection of topics reflects information at hand.

We will look mainly at non-Western societies in an attempt to give the reader an appreciation of the tremendous diversity in human sexuality. (The sexual mores of other Western societies are often markedly similar to our own.) While these social groups have been studied at some time during this century (some within the last decade), many have undoubtedly undergone considerable cultural change since the time they were observed. For example, sexual behavior on the island of Mangaia (the southernmost island in the Cook chain in central Polynesia) has been widely discussed since anthropologist Donald Marshall (1971) published the findings of his field research in the 1950s. Many writers consider Mangaia to be one of the most sexually permissive societies in the world. One of the authors of this text, Bob Crooks, visited this island in 1982. His stay was much too brief to allow him to investigate in-depth the cultural changes that have occurred in this society in the roughly 25 years since Marshall's original work. Nevertheless, he noted some important changes and these will be discussed in subsequent sections of this chapter. Keeping in mind the possibility of changes in other societies as well, we will describe the behavior and mores of these social groups in the present tense.

Sexuality During Childhood

As reported in Chapter 13, children are capable of experiencing sexual arousal and even orgasm. However, the expression of such activity shows enormous variation from society to society. In certain social orders, particularly those in the South Pacific and in some areas of Africa, the incidence of extensive prepubertal sexual activity approaches 100% of the population. In more restrictive societies (certainly the United States fits into this category) the frequency of such expression is significantly reduced. Specific activities range from masturbation to partner activity that includes both homosexual contact and heterosexual coitus. We will look briefly at a few examples that give some indication of the variety of attitudes and activities.

Many of the island societies of the South Pacific are very permissive about youthful sexual activity. Children of both sexes may engage in solo masturbation, group masturbation, and sex play with others, including manual manipulation, oral-genital contacts, and coitus. Children may receive extensive verbal instructions about sexual matters. In some areas, they may be allowed to observe adult sexual activity.

Among the Mangaians it is perfectly acceptable for young boys and girls to engage in masturbation as long as they do it in private.* Marshall reported that the sexes are generally segregated from three years of age to nearly adolescence. Crooks noted that this segregation seems to be less pronounced in more recent years. However, it still exists to some degree and acts to curtail heterosexual sex play during this time. However, Mangaian children acquire a great deal of information about sexuality during their early years, as evidenced by their use of detailed vocabulary for describing sexual anatomy and function (for example, they learn several different terms for the clitoris). In the 1950s Marshall noted that it was quite common for an entire Mangaian family of five to 15 members to sleep in one room. Since a good deal of sexual activity occurred at night in this room, Mangaian children had innumerable opportunities to see and hear sexual sharing. In recent years many Mangaians have moved into larger homes with multiple sleeping areas, a change that may reduce the exposure of young people to their parents' nighttime sexual activity.

Like the Mangaians, the children of the Marquesas Islands in French Polynesia develop remarkable sophistication about sex early in life. They also sleep with their parents and siblings in one room, with ample opportunity to observe sexual activity. When a baby boy is fretful, Marquesan parents may masturbate the child, a practice

---

*When they reach adolescence, however, the practice is viewed more negatively. At that time, coitus becomes the dominant form of sexual expression, and persistent masturbation is considered inappropriate and juvenile. This same stigma is attached to postpubertal masturbation in some other societies, including East Bay (described later) and the Bala of Africa.

Families on the South Pacific island of Bali bathe together.

that also occurs among the Bolivian Siriono nomads. Marquesan boys begin masturbating around the age of two or three and may engage in same-sex group activities of this nature by the age of five or six. Boys may also engage in casual homosexual contacts during their youth.

Marquesan girls are also involved in self-stimulation and homosexual contacts from an early age. In addition, girls are given daily treatments of ointments, concocted from herbs, applied to the genitals. This procedure, believed to improve the quality of their adult sex lives, begins at the age of a few weeks and continues to age 12 (Suggs, 1962).

Early childhood masturbation is common in other areas besides the South Pacific. Among the African Bala, a society of villagers who engage in agricultural work and fishing, children of both sexes are given free reign to engage in self-stimulation from a very early age. As in the Marquesas, Bala boys commonly engage in group masturbation.

Within the cultures of some of these permissive societies, there are beliefs that provide a rationale for prepubertal sexual activity. For example, the Chewa, advanced agriculturalists of Central Africa, believe that sexual activity in children is essential to insure adult fertility. The Lepcha farmers of the southeastern Himalayas maintain that girls must be sexually active if they are to undergo normal growth as they develop into adulthood.

Not all Pacific island societies are as permissive toward childhood sexuality as the Mangaians or the Marquesans. On the Melanesian island known as East Bay (a pseudonym that ethnographer William Davenport used to maintain anonymity of the island's inhabitants), boys and girls are segregated as soon as they can walk and are not allowed to converse with or touch one another in public throughout their childhood years. Masturbation is considered normal among boys and thus tolerated; little information exists about female masturbation. In contrast to their restrictions on overt sexual behavior among prepubertal boys and girls, the adults of East Bay do provide children with frank information about sex. In addition, as boys enter adolescence they have the legitimized sexual outlet of homosexual contact with other same-age males or with older men, as will be discussed later in this chapter (Davenport, 1965).

In some areas, restrictions on childhood sexual activity seem to reflect adult views toward sexuality. Among the Manus of New Guinea, for example, all sexual activity on the part of both adults and children is viewed very negatively. Consequently, children experience little in the way of either overt sexual activity or sexual instruction. The children in another New Guinea society, the Dani, also engage in very little childhood sexual activity but for entirely different reasons than the Manus. The Dani people show a remarkable indifference to sex during all phases of the life cycle. Their indifference does not result from formal cultural proscriptions. Instead, they just seem not to be interested. Ethnographer Karl Heider (1976), who studied these healthy, vigorous people extensively in the 1960s, concluded that their sexual indifference is related to their low level of emotional expressiveness.

A few non-Western societies have strong prohibitions against self-stimulation similar to those of North American societies. For example, the African Ashanti forbid their children to masturbate. Little boys growing up in the Kwoma society of New Guinea live in fear of being caught with an erection. Under such circumstances they may have their penises struck with a stick. Some Kwoma boys become so concerned about this possibility that they learn to urinate without touching their penises.

Perhaps the most extreme example of repression of childhood sexuality (indeed, of all aspects of sexual expression) is provided by a rural society of Irish folk who live on a small island off the coast of Ireland, referred to in the literature as Inis Beag (a pseudonym used by ethnographer John Messenger, who studied this society between 1958 and 1966). A strong Christian tradition of sexual repressions dominates this community of farmers and fishers. Nudity is viewed with abhorrence by these people, and only infants are allowed to be completely naked.

Only infants have their entire bodies sponged once a week, on Saturday night; children, adolescents, and adults, on the same night, wash only their faces, necks, lower arms, hands, lower legs, and feet. Several times my wife and I created intense embarrassment by entering a room in which a man had just finished his weekly ablutions and was barefooted; once when this occurred, the man hurriedly pulled on his stockings and said with obvious relief, "Sure, it's good to get your clothes on again." Clothing always is changed in private, sometimes within the secrecy of the bedcovers, and it is usual for the islanders to sleep in their underclothes. (Messenger, 1971, p. 18)

654   Consistent with their taboos on exposure of the body, sex is never discussed in Inis Beag homes when children are present. Apparently, the attitude in this culture is that "after marriage, nature takes its course" (p. 15). The sexes are separated from early childhood. In fact, they may have no close contact with the opposite sex (other than parent and siblings) until marriage, which generally does not occur until men reach their middle 30s and women their mid-20s. The absence of sexual jokes in this culture further attests to its extreme sexual repression. In fact, inhabitants of Inis Beag are so anxiety-ridden about sexual matters that "[e]ven the nudity of household pets can arouse anxiety, particularly when they are sexually aroused during time of heat. In some homes, dogs are whipped for licking their genitals and soon learn to indulge in this practice outdoors" (p. 18).

Coitus Before Marriage

As with childhood sexual activity, an enormous diversity exists in both attitudes toward and expression of premarital coital activity. Some societies, more restrictive than our own, apply strong punishments to those individuals caught indulging in such behavior. At the other extreme, some societies encourage coital expression in unmarried young people.

Most societies we know of are somewhere between these two extremes. The majority of those included in the Ford and Beach survey combine formal cultural prohibitions against premarital coitus with informal acceptance of such behavior—so long as it is not flaunted in public. In other words, the behavior is publicly prohibited but privately tolerated.

With very few exceptions, premarital coitus is considered more acceptable among males than females; apparently, the double standard is widespread in the human family. However, it has been estimated that as many as 70% of non-Western societies either openly approve of or privately accept coital activity among unmarried females (Murdock, 1949). As with the other behaviors discussed in this chapter, a broad range of cultural mores exists.

The Romonum (inhabitants of Romonum Island in the Truk group of the South Pacific) are representative of some of the more permissive societies in this regard. They consider premarital coital activity to be both natural and desirable for both sexes once early adolescence is achieved. Curiously, the Romonum are not permissive about sex play among prepubertal children. Adolescent boys are often introduced to coitus by older women. The practice of children being initiated into coitus by older adults is also common among the Lepcha of the Himalayas. However, in this society it is typically the female who, by age 11 or 12, may be engaging in intercourse with adult males.

First coital experiences occur at an even younger age in the Trobriand society of the Southwest Pacific islands (located off the coast of New Guinea). Here, girls as young as six and boys of 10 or 11 years have their first coital experiences with other children, under adult tutelage.

The Marquesans also openly encourage coitus before marriage (Suggs, 1962). In this society, the circumcision of adolescent boys is considered to be a formal stamp

In many societies circumcision marks the transition from child to man and may provide a formal stamp of approval for engaging in coitus.

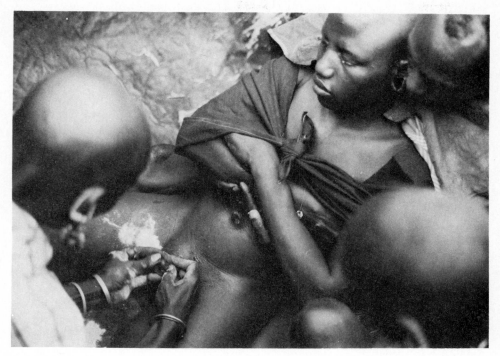

of approval for first experience with coitus, which usually occurs with an older woman who provides appropriate instruction. Girls generally have their initial coital encounters with older males. Throughout adolescence, it is considered normal for girls and boys to have frequent sexual relations. This is generally accomplished through the practice known as night-crawling, where boys enter their chosen lover's house at night and have sexual relations while other family members are sleeping nearby.

The practice of night-crawling also occurs on the island of Mangaia. Here young men, after being formally initiated into the ranks of manhood by a *superincision* ceremony (where the upper flap of foreskin is cut), actively pursue lovers during the nighttime. This phenomenon of entering a young woman's residence and engaging her in coitus with several family members sleeping in the same room is described in the following excerpt:

The basis of the adventurousness of *motoro* (night-crawling) is the fact that the entire Mangaian family sleeps in one room. The adventurous youth will have made a reconnaissance beforehand or will have gotten a report on the condition of the door and window openings from his age mates, including whether the door hinges squeak (if there is a door, which frequently there is not), how soundly the family sleeps, and the state of the father's cigarette lighting lamp (which remains lighted, with the wick turned low all night, near the parents).

A youth bent on courting must first slip out of his own home and then avoid village policemen who are out searching for violators of the nine o'clock curfew. He must then get to the girl's house before other suitors. His effort may be made at sometime between ten o'clock in the evening and midnight; if successful, he may remain until three o'clock in the morning. (Marshall, 1971, p. 129)

Many people might find it hard to believe that such behavior can occur in a room full of people. However, Marshall's informants made it clear that many parents accept this practice because they "fully realize that the custom of night-crawling is the means for their daughter to win her husband" (p. 130).

It appears that night-crawling has lost some of its appeal in the years since Marshall studied Mangaian society. Several of Crooks's adult informants in 1982 stated that it is now an uncommon practice. Some flatly denied it occurs. However, numerous youthful informants confirmed its continued existence, although in significantly altered form. It seems that parents have become less accepting of such behavior. Young men no longer enjoy the benefits of "parents who sleep soundly" while they conduct their nighttime trysts with the daughter. An adolescent male caught in his lover's bedroom, after crawling through her window, stands a good chance of being soundly beaten. His female partner may also be beaten by her angry parents. Apparently some Mangaian adolescents also disapprove of night-crawling. One young 17-year-old woman adamantly stated to Crooks, "I'm a good girl—I'm not one of those."

What happens in permissive societies such as the Mangaians and the Marquesans when an "illegitimate" birth occurs? Davenport provides a general answer: "Societies that permit or encourage premarital sex freedom are organized so that all children born outside marriage are fully provided for and in no way suffer social disabilities or stigma" (1978, p. 146).

Predictably, the few societies that do deny full social status to children born to an unmarried parent typically try to keep all coitus confined to marriage. In reality, the incidence of conception among unmarrieds in permissive societies is somewhat lower than one might expect. This finding is related to the fact that the probability of conception, while varying from individual to individual, is generally lower during the years immediately following menarche (a phenomenon that is known as *adolescent sterility*). The relatively high incidence of pregnancy among unmarried American women is partly related to the marked prolongation of adolescence in our society and the resulting higher age of marriage.

The Mangaians, Trobrianders, and other highly permissive societies are a minority. Most of the societies surveyed by Ford and Beach are characterized by tacit acceptance rather than overt approval of coitus before marriage. For example, the Huichal farmers in Mexico, the Alorese farmers of Indonesia, and the African Bala all have formal codes that censure premarital coitus (although these rules are rarely enforced so long as participating couples do not flaunt their behavior). Our own society is somewhat more restrictive, and a few societies are even more restrictive than ours. For example, such behavior is virtually unknown among the Irish folk who live on Inis Beag. In East Bay, all premarital intercourse is strongly condemned. Male "offenders" in this society are dealt with more harshly than their female partners, in a kind of reverse double standard not known in other societies.

Marital Coitus

Marital coitus is the most common form of adult sexual activity in virtually all societies we know of. There is widespread variation in both the types of coital positions used and the frequency of sexual contact. Most of the ethnographic data focus on frequency of coitus, often to the exclusion of other relevant factors.

While data are limited, there is evidence that each society tends to favor a particular coital position. Whether it is man-on-top, woman-on-top, side-by-side, or some other variation is greatly influenced by the relative social status of the sexes in the society. In social groups such as the Trobrianders, where women are valued, the female-on-top position is often quite common. In societies where women are assigned low social status (for example, Inis Beag), the male-on-top position seems to be preferred (Beigel, 1953). It is interesting to note that improved social status of American women has been paralleled by an increase in the use of coital positions other than the man-on-top (Hunt, 1974; see Chapter 9 for further details).

It has been estimated that most married couples around the world engage in coitus between two and five times per week (Gebhard, 1971). However, in some societies the frequency may range as high as 10 times a night or as low as once or twice a month. Married couples on Mangaia, while somewhat less active than during their premarital days, maintain a coital frequency far greater than that of most Western couples. With marriage, coital emphasis tends to shift from the number of times a man can bring his partner to orgasm during a single session to whether he can copulate with her every night in the week (Marshall, 1971).

Somewhat higher frequency rates are reported among the Australian Aranda, a hunting and food-gathering group who report as many as three to five coital contacts per night. Even higher rates (up to 10 times per night) are reported by the Chagga farmers of Tanzania. Lest the reader believe this figure to be beyond the realm of human potential, note the following quote pertaining to another group of people, the Lepcha of the southeastern Himalayas:

In their youth and young manhood (the period Lepchas call *fleng*) Lepcha men would appear to be remarkably potent; trustworthy people said that when they were first married they would copulate with their wives five or six, and even eight or nine times in the course of the night, though they would be tired the next day. I have no comparable information from women but such statements were often made in mixed company without women present making any comment or in any way expressing incredulity. (Gorer, 1938, p. 329)

In view of the unusual nature of this data, it may be helpful to recall our earlier caution about self-reports. Sometimes individuals in our own culture exaggerate accounts of their sexual activity. The reports of very high rates of coital contact among such societies as the Aranda, Chagga, and Lepcha may be inflated somewhat by these same tendencies to exaggerate. In fact, some people may feel particularly inclined to impress an outsider with accounts of great capacity for sexual performance. (Conversely, reports of low activity levels, as discussed below, may reflect cultural ideals of moderation or restraint.) It is reasonable to maintain a certain degree of critical objectivity when interpreting data obtained from self-reports.

At the other extreme of coital activity, there are societies that report an exceedingly low rate of marital coitus. Couples in the Dani culture of New Guinea seem rarely to have sexual interactions, as evidenced by a very low birth rate. Newlyweds wait for an average of two years for their first coital experiences, and both men and women abstain from intercourse for a period of four to six years after the birth of a child. Relatively low coital frequencies of once per week are reported by married couples within another New Guinea society, the Kerakis. The reported frequency among the Lesu of the South Pacific is approximately twice per week, a figure similar to that of our own society.

Extramarital Coitus

Most societies have more restrictive codes about extramarital sex than they have concerning premarital coitus. Nevertheless, many societies enforce fewer restrictions on extramarital activity than does our own society. Some societies even have formal rules allowing such behavior under special circumstances—during celebrations, as part of the marriage ceremony, or as a form of sexual hospitality. With very few exceptions, men around the world are allowed greater access to extramarital coitus than are women. However, it appears that as many as 60% of non-Western societies studied allow some form of extramarital coitus for wives (Gebhard, 1971). A few examples will illustrate the diversity of this activity in other societies.

The aborigines of western Australia's Arnhem land openly accept extramarital sexual relationships. Both wives and husbands enjoy the same privilege of outside sex, with their nonmarital partners assigned the status of tribal husbands or wives. Such relationships are legally sanctioned within this society, whose members welcome the variety in experience and the break in monotony offered by extramarital involvements. Many also report increased appreciation of and attachment to the spouse as a result of such experiences (Berndt and Berndt, 1951).

The Polynesian Marquesans, while not open advocates of extramarital affairs, nevertheless exhibit covert acceptance of such activity. A Marquesan wife often takes lovers from ranks of young boys and her husband's friends or relatives. Conversely, her husband may have relations with young unmarried girls or with his sisters-in-law. Marquesan culture openly endorses the practices of partner swapping and *sexual hospitality*, where unaccompanied visitors are offered sexual access to the host of the other sex. Sexual hospitality is also practiced by some Eskimo groups where a married female host has intercourse with a male visitor.

Among the Turu of central Tanzania (cultivators and raisers of livestock), marriage is seen primarily as a cooperative, economic, and social bond. Affection between husband and wife is generally thought to be out of place: most people believe that the marital relationship is endangered by the instability of love and affection. While they do not openly endorse it, the Turu have evolved a system of romantic love, called *Mbuya,* that allows them to seek affection outside the home without threatening the stability of the primary marriage relationship and operation of the household.

While rules against the practice of adultery exist in the formal mores of Turu society, there is widespread informal acceptance of the custom of Mbuya. These outside relationships are actively pursued by both husband and wife. Affairs between lovers are generally confined to exchanges of sex and gifts. Not uncommonly, relationships may develop between a husband and his wife's lover (for example, they may help each other with cultivating). Likewise, a wife and her husband's lover may cooperate in tasks like grinding grain and making beer together. Even with such acceptance, lovers are careful not to flaunt their illicit relationships.

In a few societies, such as the Mota of the Pacific Banks Islands, a young, unmarried man may be sexually initiated by an older, married female with the acceptance of her husband. Conversely, among the Banaro of New Guinea it is required that the first coital experiences of the new bride be with her husband's father's "ritual brother" (a nonbiological relationship dictated by cultural custom). Furthermore, all ritual brothers in this society have access to each others' wives.

Many societies are significantly less permissive about extramarital sex than those just discussed. The African Bala, for example, consider the practice to be a serious offense, although it is begrudgingly acknowledged that such behavior will probably occur if a married couple is separated for a long period of time. A double standard exists, so that female but not male adultery may be considered legitimate grounds for divorce. A different inequality between the sexes exists in East Bay, where the penalties for adulterous affairs are much more severe for males than females.

Female Orgasm

With no recorded exceptions, males from virtually every society typically experience orgasm as part of sexual expression. In contrast, the frequency of female orgasm is quite variable, and it seems strongly influenced by the cultural norms of a society. In fact, some writers have suggested that orgasmic response among women is largely culturally determined. According to Margaret Mead, "There seems therefore to be a reasonable basis for assuming that the human female's capacity for orgasm is to be viewed much more as a potentiality that may or may not be developed by a given culture" (1949, p. 217).

There has been a general tendency in Western societies to consider female sexual gratification unimportant. While this is changing, particularly in the United States, there are still significant numbers of Western women who seldom experience orgasm, particularly in repressive cultures. In Inis Beag, where women are ascribed the status of second-class citizens, female orgasm is virtually unknown.

In marked contrast, most island societies of the South Pacific, which collectively tend to value female sexual pleasure, record the routine occurrence of female orgasm during sexual activity. An example is provided by Mangaian culture, where "the Mangaian male lover aims to have his partner achieve orgasm two or three times to his once" (Marshall, 1971, p. 122).

BOX 22.1 FEMALE GENITAL MUTILATION

Some form of female genital mutilation has been practiced at one time in almost all parts of the world (including the United States, from 1890 through the late 1930s). Today it continues in many parts of Africa, the Middle East, and Asia. Women in these parts of the world undergo several types of genital mutilation. The simplest procedure, *circumcision,* consists of cutting off the clitoral hood. Another common practice is the removal of the clitoris itself, called *clitoridectomy.* In the most extreme practice, *genital infibulation,* the clitoris is entirely removed and the labia are cut off, with both sides scraped raw and stitched up (sometimes with thorns) so they grow together, leaving only a small opening for urine and menstrual flow to pass through. Serious gynecological and obstetrical complications often arise from genital infibulation. Fetal death sometimes occurs due to difficult delivery because of extensive vaginal scarring. It is estimated that 30 million women and girls now living have undergone one of these kinds of "surgeries" (Brisset, 1979).

Clitoridectomy is more common than infibulation. It is done by various techniques. In Syria, the clitoris of a newborn girl is rubbed with pepper until nothing remains (Ohm, 1980). Other groups burn the clitoris. A girl of the Nandi people of Africa undergoes ritual clitoridectomy at puberty. After ceremonial dances the group of young women to be initiated go to a special house. Older women rub the young women's clitorises with stinging nettles, which eventually makes the clitoris numb and swollen. The women sing loudly to muffle any cries from the initiates, who try not to shame themselves and their families by showing fear or pain. Early the next day the tribe gathers to watch a woman cut off each girl's clitoris with a curved knife. Following the clitoridectomies, the young women are isolated and taught about housekeeping and proper marital conduct (Mbiti, 1969).

There are various rationales for performing these genital mutilations on females. Often such mutilations are rites of passage from childhood to adulthood. Some social groups mistakenly believe that such a procedure is necessary for hygiene. Others believe that contact with the clitoris is dangerous to the man or, conversely, in the case of infibulation, that the smaller vaginal opening provides greater pleasure to the male during intercourse. These "surgeries" are often thought to "protect" women from sexual over-excitement and to insure virginity before marriage and fidelity after marriage.

A woman who has not undergone a culturally prescribed genital mutilation will often be considered immature or ill-mannered. For example, to call a woman in Sudan *ghalfa,* meaning uncircumcised, would be a grave insult. Young girls are often considered unmarriageable if they do not have the culture-appropriate excision.

In addition to numerous medical problems that arise from these procedures, African and Arab physicians and health workers report widespread sexual problems

Continued on next page

BOX 22.1 CONTINUED

among women who have had clitoridectomies and infibulations. One physician reported that 80% of infibulated women he had examined over the years indicated never having experienced any sexual pleasure. Another physician made a similar report on women who have had clitoridectomies. A Middle Eastern gynecologist asked 300 men who practiced polygamy and had more than one wife whether they preferred women with or without sexual excisions. The great majority of these men—266—reported that they preferred women who had not had "surgeries" because such women enjoyed sex more (Ohm, 1980).

In recent years there has been such an outcry over these practices, particularly from women in Western nations, that the United Nations agreed to suspend its policy of nonintervention in the cultural practices of individual nations. In 1980, the World Health Organization (WHO) and the United Nations Children's Fund (UNICEF) jointly adopted a plan to encourage leaders of nations where such practices occur to use their influence to bring them to an end. Unfortunately, the strength of the cultural tradition for female genital mutilation in many societies will be difficult to overcome.

Noncoital Sex Play

In some societies, noncoital sexual interaction is virtually nonexistent; in others, a broad repertoire of sexual techniques may be used. Touching, oral stimulation, manual stimulation, and mutual masturbation are not commonly employed as substitutes for coitus among heterosexual lovers in most societies. While these activities may be used extensively, this happens most frequently as part of sexual encounters that also include coitus. Orgasm resulting from noncoital sex play is probably much higher in the United States than in most less industrialized societies (Gebhard, 1971).

Kissing on the mouth, universal in Western societies, may be rare or absent in many other parts of the world. Male fondling of the female body, particularly hand on breast, is apparently an activity common to all cultures. Male oral stimulation of the female breast is somewhat less common. Manual stimulation of a partner's genitals is commonly practiced by both males and females in the majority of researched societies (Gebhard, 1971).

Oral sex, both cunnilingus and fellatio, is quite common among island societies of the South Pacific, in industrialized nations of Asia, and in much of the Western world. In Africa, the practice is more prevalent in northern regions. In societies that accept the practice of cunnilingus, fellatio is also almost always present. However, the reverse is not necessarily the case.

Sexuality and Aging

We have only limited cross-cultural data about sexual expression among older men and women. However, there is some evidence to suggest that frequency of activity is related to the status assigned older members of the community. It seems that cultures that value older people tend to be characterized by more frequent sexual expression among aging individuals.

For example, the mountain people of Abkhasia, a Russian state in the Caucasus region, enjoy tremendous longevity, both in total life expectancy and in sexual activity. Sex among married couples is considered a primary pleasure in life, to be pursued for as long as possible. Most Abkhasian couples remain quite active beyond the age of 70 and some even after the age of 100. Aging individuals are ascribed valued social status. They are expected to continue making productive contributions to the family and community—there is no retirement in this society. Moderation is the key cultural ethic: older folks "continue to do what they have always done, but in gradually diminishing amounts" (Beach, 1978, p. 118).

The African Bala also seem to maintain a high degree of sexual vigor in the older years. Ethnographer Alan Merriam (1971) reported asking a small sample of men how many times they had experienced intercourse in the preceding 24 hours. The data, collected each morning for a period of 10 days, revealed that the average frequency for several men over the age of 45 (the oldest was 66) was about 1.5 times each 24-hour period. Again, some caution in interpreting this finding seems necessary. It is possible that being asked daily to report the frequency of coital encounters may have induced Merriam's respondents to temporarily increase their activity levels.

Homosexuality

As with other sexual behaviors, attitudes toward homosexual activity vary greatly. In some societies, such behavior is condemned more vigorously than in our own society. Other societies take a considerably more permissive view, and a few openly approve of same-sex relations. Ford and Beach (1951) found that approximately two-thirds of the 190 societies in their sample accept homosexual activity.

Certain general facts emerge from cross-cultural comparisons of homosexual behavior. First, male homosexuality is more common than lesbianism in most societies. Second, the percentage of males in a given society who participate in homosexual activity sometime during their lives varies from nearly 100%, as in East Bay, to virtually none, as in Mangaia. Third, it appears that the lowest proportions of individuals who are exclusively or nearly exclusively homosexual exist in non-industrialized societies such as those of Africa and the South Pacific. Finally, in all societies for which we have data, homosexual activity has never been shown to be the predominant form of adult sexual behavior.

Some societies encourage their members to engage in homosexual activities. For example, men in the African Siwan society lend their sons to one another for sexual purposes. Virtually all Siwan males engage in homosexual activity, and they discuss these relationships as openly as their heterosexual involvements. Male homosexuality is also an institutionalized aspect of East Bay culture (Davenport, 1965). It is considered normal and acceptable for adolescents to privately engage in mutual masturbation or anal intercourse, and homosexual contacts between adolescent and adult men are also viewed as legitimate forms of sexual expression. As among the Siwan, such contacts may be facilitated by the boy's father, who often chooses the older man for his son.

It appears that East Bay culture's legitimization of homosexual male relations bears some relationship to its strong condemnation of heterosexual coitus outside of marriage. Homosexual contact is viewed largely as a normal, temporary substitute for heterosexual coitus or, in the case of older males without female partners, as an acceptable alternative mode of sexual expression. Despite the fact that virtually all men in East Bay pass through a period of homosexual activity, Davenport was unable to locate any cases of exclusive homosexuality among adult men. East Bay women have no institutionalized homosexual phase and are expected to confine all sexual activity to marriage.

SUMMARY

SOCIETY AND CULTURE: DEFINITIONS AND OBSERVATIONS

1. An awareness of cultural diversity in human sexual expression can provide new perspectives and improved understanding of our own society's sexual standards and values.

2. The meaning of a given sexual act can be fully understood only by looking at the cultural context within which it occurs.

3. All societies have rules regulating the conduct of sexual behavior.

DATA SOURCES: METHODS AND LIMITATIONS

4. Ethnographic data on other societies are often lacking in information about sexual expression. This is due in part to the reluctance of both investigators and respondents to talk openly about private matters.

5. The available data consist primarily of verbal reports rather than observed behavior.

6. The reliability of these reported accounts of sexual behavior in other societies may be somewhat compromised by investigator bias and the tendency of respondents to provide inaccurate information.

COMPARATIVE ANALYSIS OF SOME SELECTED SEXUAL BEHAVIORS

7. The expression of sexuality during the childhood years may vary from societies where it is virtually nonexistent to other social groups where prepubertal children actively participate in coital activity with adult approval.

8. Most societies publicly condemn but privately tolerate discreet coital activity among unmarrieds. A few encourage, or even initiate, such activity in young people. Most societies consider such behavior to be more acceptable among males than females.

9. Marital coitus is the most common form of adult sexual activity in all societies for which data exist. While most married couples engage in coitus two to five times per week, the frequency may range from once a month in one society to as high as 10 times a night in another. Coital position preference in a given society often reflects the social status of the sexes.

10. Most societies are less permissive about extramarital than premarital sex. Some have formal rules allowing such behavior under special circumstances. With very few exceptions, the men of the world are allowed greater access than women to extramarital coitus.

11. The occurrence of female orgasm, in contrast to male orgasm, is quite variable and seems strongly influenced by the cultural norms of a given society. In cultures that repress women, female orgasm tends to be quite rare. In contrast, societies that value female pleasure record the routine occurrence of female orgasm.

12. Noncoital sex play, such as touching, oral sex, and manual stimulation, is more commonly employed as an accompaniment to coitus rather than as a substitute for it.

13. The frequency of sexual activity among older people may be related to the status assigned older members of a community. Cultures that value older people tend to be characterized by more frequent sexual expression among aging individuals.

14. Societal attitudes toward homosexuality vary from vigorous condemnation to outright approval. The frequency of male homosexual behavior, which varies from society to society, is almost always greater than lesbian activity. Homosexuality has never been shown to be the predominant form of adult sexual behavior in any society.

SUGGESTED READINGS

Berndt, Ronald, and Berndt, Catherine. *Sexual Behavior in Western Arnhem Land*. New York: Viking Fund Publications in Anthropology, 1951. A detailed analysis of sexual attitudes and practices of the Australian aborigines.

Davenport, William. "Sex in cross-cultural perspective." In F. Beach (Ed.), *Human Sexuality in Four Perspectives*. Baltimore: Johns Hopkins Press, 1977. (Also available in paperback from same publisher, 1978.) An eminent anthropologist provides an up-to-date comparison of human sexuality in different societies around the world.

Ford, Clellan, and Beach, Frank. *Patterns of Sexual Behavior*. New York: Harper & Row, 1951. A wealth of information about variations in sexual attitudes and behaviors in 190 human societies. Authors Ford and Beach also provide comparative data on sexual expression in other species.

Marshall, Donald, and Suggs, Robert (Eds.). *Human Sexual Behavior: Variations in the Ethnographic Spectrum*. Englewood Cliffs, N.J.: Prentice-Hall, 1971. A superb collection of eight articles that detail the sexual attitudes, behaviors, and mores of societies around the world.

Mead, Margaret. *Male and Female: A Study of Sexes in the Changing World*. New York: Morrow, 1949. Contains a remarkable composite of facts, insights, and speculations pertaining to the impact of various societies on the expression of human sexual behaviors and relationships.

Suggs, Robert. *Marquesan Sexual Behavior*. New York: Harcourt, Brace, and World, 1966. An excellent source for more detailed information about sexual expression in this fascinating Polynesian society.

Glossary

Abortion The spontaneous or medically induced removal of the contents of the uterus during pregnancy.

Abstinence Not engaging in sexual interaction or intercourse.

Adolescence The period of life between the onset of puberty and the cessation of major body growth changes.

Adultery Coitus experienced by a married person with someone other than his or her spouse.

Afterbirth The placenta and amniotic sac following its expulsion through the vagina after childbirth.

Amenorrhea The absence of menstruation.

Amniocentesis A procedure in which amniotic fluid is removed from the uterus and tested to determine if certain fetal birth defects exist.

Amniotic fluid The fluid inside the uterus surrounding the fetus during pregnancy.

Amniotic sac A sac of tissue inside the uterus that encloses the fetus.

Ampulla Upper portions of the vas deferens that undergo muscle contractions during the emission phase of ejaculation.

Anaphrodisiac A substance that allegedly inhibits sexual desire and behavior.

Androgen A class of hormones that promotes the development of male genitals and secondary sex characteristics and influences sexual motivation in both sexes. It is produced by the adrenal glands in males and females and by the testes in males.

Androgyny A blending of typical male and female behaviors in one individual.

Anorexia nervosa An eating disorder that often results in extreme weight loss and cessation of menstruation.

Anorgasmia The absence of orgasm in women.

Antiandrogens A group of drugs that blocks the action of testicular and adrenal androgens.

Aphrodisiac A substance that allegedly arouses sexual desire and increases capacity for sexual activity.

Areola The darkened circular area surrounding the nipple of the breast.

Artificial insemination Introducing semen into the vagina or uterus by means other than coitus to induce conception.

Autoinoculation A process whereby individuals may spread the herpes virus from one part of their body to another by touching a sore and then scratching or rubbing somewhere else.

Autosomes Twenty-two matched sets of chromosomes that do not significantly influence sex differentiation.

Bartholin's glands Two small glands slightly inside the vaginal opening which secrete a few drops of fluid during sexual arousal.

Basal body temperature birth control A method of fertility control based on temperature changes before and after ovulation.

Bisexual A person who feels sexual attraction to or has sexual contact with both sexes.

Brothel A house in which a group of prostitutes works.

Calendar method A method of birth control based on abstinence from intercourse during calendar estimation of fertile days.

Candida albicans A fungus or yeast ordinarily found in the vagina. When excessive amounts of it develop, vaginal irritation results.

Castration Surgical removal of the testes or ovaries.

Cavernous bodies The structures in the shaft of the penis and clitoris that engorge with blood during sexual arousal.

Celibacy The choice not to engage in genital sexual behavior.

Cervical cap A plastic or rubber cover for the cervix that provides a contraceptive barrier to sperm.

Cervix The small end of the uterus which is located at the back of the vagina.

Cesarean section A childbirth procedure whereby the infant is removed through an incision in the abdomen and uterus.

Chancre A raised, red, painless sore that is symptomatic of the primary phase of syphilis.

Chastity Abstention from sexual interaction.

Cilia Tiny hairlike structures that line the inside of various body structures including the fallopian tubes and vas deferens.

Circumcision Surgical removal of the foreskin of the penis.

Clitoral hood The skin that covers the clitoris.

Clitoris A highly sensitive structure of the female external genitals, the only purpose of which is sexual pleasure.

Cohabitation A couple living together and having a sexual relationship without being married.

Coitus A technical term for heterosexual penile-vaginal intercourse.

Colostrom A thin fluid secreted by the breasts during late pregnancy and the first few days following delivery.

Combination pill Contraceptive pills that contain both estrogen and progestin.

Complete celibacy The choice to engage neither in masturbation nor in interpersonal sexual contact.

Condom See *prophylactic*.

Consensual adult statutes Laws that maintain that private, consensual sexual behavior between adults is not illegal.

Contraception Techniques, drugs, or devices to prevent conception.

Corona The rim of the penile glans.

Corpora cavernosa See *cavernous bodies*.

Corpus luteum A yellowish body that forms on the ovary at the site of the ruptured Graafian follicle and secretes progesterone.

Corpus spongiosum See *spongy body*.

Cowper's glands Two pea-sized glands located in the male alongside the base of the urethra that secrete an alkaline fluid during sexual arousal.

Cremasteric muscle A muscle located in the spermatic cord that elevates the testicles when voluntarily or involuntarily contracted.

Cremasteric reflex Contractions of the cremasteric muscle induced by stroking the inner thigh.

Crura The innermost tips of the cavernous bodies that connect to the pubic bones.

Cryptorchidism A condition in which the testicles fail to descend from the abdominal cavity to the scrotal sac.

Culpotomy Female sterilization procedure when the incision to locate the tubes is made at the back of the vagina.

Culture A society's shared patterns of belief, thought, speech, and behavior.

Cunnilingus Oral stimulation of the vulva.

Cystitis An inflammation of the urethra or bladder, characterized by discomfort during urination.

Decriminalization Removing criminal penalties for activities previously defined as criminal.

Diaphragm A birth control method consisting of a latex dome on a flexible spring rim which is inserted into the vagina with contraceptive cream or jelly.

Differentiation The fetal development of characteristic male and female external and internal sex organs.

Dildo A penis-shaped device used for vaginal or anal insertion.

Douching To rinse out the vagina with plain water or a variety of solutions. Usually unnecessary for hygiene, and too-frequent douching can result in vaginal irritation.

Ductus deferens See *vas deferens*.

Dysmenorrhea Pain or discomfort before or during menstruation.

Dyspareunia Pain or discomfort during intercourse.

Ectopic pregnancy A fertilized ovum that implants in a location other than the uterus, usually in the fallopian tubes.

Effaced cervix Flattening and thinning of the cervix that occurs before and during childbirth.

Ejaculation The process whereby semen is expelled out of the body through the penis.

Ejaculatory ducts Two short ducts located within the prostate gland.

Ejaculatory inhibition A sexual difficulty whereby the male does not ejaculate inside the vagina.

Emission phase The first stage of male orgasm in which the seminal fluid is gathered in the urethral bulb.

Endocrine system A system of ductless glands that produces hormones and secretes them directly into the bloodstream.

Endometriosis A condition in which uterine tissue grows on various parts of the abdominal cavity.

Endometrium The tissue that lines the inside of the uterine walls.

Epididymis The structure along the back of each testicle wherein sperm maturation occurs.

Episiotomy An incision in the perineum that is sometimes made during childbirth.

Erectile inhibition A sexual difficulty whereby a man's penis does not become erect in response to sexual stimulation.

Erection The process of the penis or clitoris engorging with blood and increasing in size.

Erogenous zones Areas of the body that are particularly responsive to sexual stimulation.

Estrogen A class of hormones that produces female secondary sex characteristics and affects the menstrual cycle. Also found in lesser amounts in males.

Estrogen replacement therapy (ERT) The use of supplemental estrogen during and after menopause.

Ethnographers Anthropologists who specialize in studying the cultures of different societies.

Excitement phase Masters and Johnson's term for the first phase of the sexual response cycle in which engorgement of sexual organs and an increase in muscle tension, heart rate, and blood pressure occur.

Exhibitionism The act of exposing one's genitals to an unwilling observer.

Expulsion phase The second stage of male orgasm during which the semen is expelled out of the penis by muscular contractions.

Extramarital relationships Consensual or nonconsensual sexual relationships with people other than one's marital partner.

Faking orgasms A sexual difficulty whereby a person secretly pretends to experience orgasm during sexual interaction.

Fallopian tubes Two tubes that extend from each side of the uterus wherein the egg and sperm travel.

Fellatio Oral stimulation of the penis.

Fetishism Obtaining sexual excitement primarily or exclusively from an inanimate object or a particular part of the body.

Fimbriae Fringelike ends of the fallopian tubes into which the released ovum enters.

First-stage labor The initial stage of childbirth in which regular contractions begin and the cervix dilates.

Follicle-stimulating hormone (FSH) A pituitary hormone. Secreted by a female during the secretory phase of the menstrual cycle, it stimulates the development of ovarian follicles. In males, it stimulates sperm production.

Forceps Instruments shaped like salad tongs that are sometimes used during childbirth to assist the passage of the infant out of the birth canal.

Foreplay Usually defined as the kissing, touching, or oral-genital contact preceding coitus.

Foreskin A covering of skin over the penile or clitoral glans.

Fornication A pejorative (also legal) term sometimes used to label coitus between two unmarried persons.

Frenulum See *frenum.*

Frenum A highly sensitive, thin fold of skin that connects the foreskin with the underside of the penile glans.

Fundus The upper, rounded portion of the uterus.

Gender identity How one psychologically perceives self as either male or female.

Gender nonconformity A lack of conformity to stereotypic masculine and feminine behaviors.

Gender role A collection of attitudes and behaviors that are considered normal and appropriate in a specific culture for people of a particular sex.

General sexual dysfunction A sexual difficulty labeled by Helen Singer Kaplan whereby a woman does not experience vaginal lubrication during sexual interaction.

Genes The basic units of heredity.

Genitals The sexual organs of males and females.

Genital tubercle The area on a fetus that develops into the male and female external genitals. It is undifferentiated prior to six weeks of age.

Gigolos Men who provide social companionship and sexual services to women for financial gain.

Glans The head of the penis or clitoris; richly endowed with nerve endings.

Gonadotropins Pituitary hormones that stimulate activity in the gonads (testes and ovaries).

Gonads The male and female sex glands—ovaries and testes.

Gonorrhea A sexually transmitted disease that initially causes inflammation of mucous membranes.

Graafian follicle A small swelling on the ovary from which a mature ovum is discharged.

Grafenberg spot Glands and ducts located in the anterior wall of the vagina below the urethra. Some women may experience sexual pleasure, arousal, orgasm, and an ejaculation of fluids from stimulation of the Grafenberg spot.

Group marriage Several adults living together wherein each member of the group maintains what are considered marital relationships with more than one other person.

Gynecology The medical practice specializing in women's health and diseases of the reproductive and sexual organs.

Hermaphroditism A condition in which biological characteristics of both sexes are present.

Herpes A disease, characterized by blisters on the skin in the regions of the genitals or mouth, which is caused by a virus and is easily transmitted by sexual contact.

Heterosexual A person whose primary social, emotional, and sexual orientation is toward members of the other sex.

Homophobia Irrational fears of homosexuality, the fear of the possibility of homosexuality in oneself, or self-loathing toward one's own homosexuality.

Homosexual person A person whose primary erotic, psychological, emotional, and social orientation is toward members of the same sex.

Homosocial Relating socially primarily with members of the same sex.

Hormones Chemical substances produced by endocrine glands that affect the functioning of other organs.

Human chorionic gonadotropin (HCG) A hormone that is detectable in the urine of a pregnant woman about a month after conception.

Hustlers Male prostitutes who sexually service other males.

H-Y antigen A substance present on the surface of cells in all normal male tissue that triggers the transformation of the embryonic gonads into testes.

Hymen Tissue that partially covers the vaginal opening.

Hypogonadism Impaired hormone production in the testes that results in androgen deprivation.

Hypothalamus A portion of the brain that regulates several body processes.

Hysterectomy The surgical removal of the uterus.

Imperforate hymen A hymen that completely seals the vaginal opening.

Impotence See *erectile inhibition.*

Incest Sexual interaction between close relatives other than husband and wife.

Inferior vena cava A major source of blood supply to and from the uterus.

Inguinal canal The canal through which the testes travel during fetal development from inside the abdomen to the scrotum.

Inhibited sexual desire (ISD) A lack of interest in sexual fantasy and activity.

Inhibition of vaginal lubrication A sexual difficulty that refers to a lack of lubrication during sexual interaction.

Interstitial cells Cells located between the seminiferous tubules that are the major source of androgen in males.

Intrauterine device (IUD) A small plastic device of varying shape that is inserted into the uterus for contraception.

Introitus The opening to the vagina.

Intromission Insertion of the penis into the vagina.

Kegel exercises A series of exercises that strengthen the muscles underlying the external female or male genitals.

Klinefelter's syndrome A rare condition characterized by the presence of two X chromosomes and one Y (XXY).

Labia majora The outer lips of the vulva.

Labia minora The inner lips of the vulva on both sides of the vaginal opening.

Lactobacilli Bacteria that help maintain a healthy vagina.

Laparoscope The instrument used to locate the tubes during one type of female sterilization procedure.

Laparoscopy A common procedure for female sterilization.

Legalization Making legal previously defined illegal activities and regulating, licensing, or taxing the activities.

Lesbian A woman whose primary social, emotional, and sexual attraction is toward members of the same sex.

Leukorrhea A general term applied to a variety of vaginal infections characterized by an excessive discharge.

Leydig's cells See *interstitial cells*.

Libido A term commonly used to denote sexual motivation.

Limbic system A subcortical brain system composed of several interrelated structures that influences the sexual behavior of humans and other animals.

Lochia A reddish uterine discharge that occurs following childbirth.

Luteinizing hormone (LH) The hormone secreted by the pituitary gland that stimulates ovulation in the female. In males, it is called ISCH and it stimulates production of androgens by the testes.

Masturbation Stimulation of one's own genitals to create sexual pleasure.

Menarche The initial onset of menstrual periods in a young woman.

Menopause Cessation of menstruation due to the aging process or surgical removal of the ovaries.

Menstrual synchrony The development of congruent menstrual cycle timing that sometimes occurs among women who live in close proximity.

Menstruation The sloughing off of the built-up uterine lining that takes place if conception has not occurred.

Midwife A woman who has had training as a birth attendant.

Miscarriage The spontaneous premature termination of a pregnancy. Also known as a spontaneous abortion.

Miscegenation Sexual relationships between persons of different races.

Mittelschmerz A sensation of pain or aching in the abdomen that sometimes occurs during ovulation.

Moniliasis A fungus organism that causes inflammation of the vaginal walls when it is present in an excessive amount.

Mons veneris A triangular mound over the pubic bone above the vulva.

Mores Established customs and beliefs in a given culture.

Mucosa Moist tissue of mucous membrane that lines certain body areas such as the penile urethra, vagina, and mouth.

Mucus method A birth control method that is based on the cyclical changes of the cervical mucus.

Müllerian ducts A pair of ducts in the embryo that develop into female reproductive organs.

Multiparous A woman who has given birth one or more times.

Multiple orgasms Experiencing more than one orgasm within a short time period.

Myotonia Muscle tension.

Neisseria gonorrhoeae The name of the bacteria that cause a gonorrhea infection.

Nocturnal emission Involuntary ejaculation during sleep, also known as a "wet dream."

Nocturnal penile tumescence (NPT) test An erection-monitoring procedure done during sleep in a specially equipped lab.

Nongonococcal urethritis An inflammation of the male urethral tube caused by other than gonorrhea organisms.

Nulliparous   A woman who has never given birth.

Oophorectomy   Surgical removal of the ovaries.

Open marriage   A marriage in which spouses develop, with the other's permission, intimate relationships with other people as well as the marital partner.

Oral-genital stimulation   Mouth to genital contact to create sexual pleasure.

Orchidectomy   The surgical procedure for removing the testes.

Orgasm   A series of muscular contractions of the pelvic floor muscles occurring at the peak of sexual arousal.

Orgasm phase   A term coined by Masters and Johnson to describe the third phase of the sexual response cycle in which rhythmic muscular contractions of the pelvic floor occur.

Os   The opening in the cervix that leads to the interior of the uterus.

Ovaries   Two female sex glands that produce ova and sex hormones.

Ovulation   The release of a mature ovum from the Graafian follicle of the ovary.

Ovum   The female reproductive cell.

Pap smear   A screening test for cervical cancer.

Paramenstrual   The time period several days prior to and during menstruation.

Paraphrasing   A listener summarizing the speaker's message in his or her own words.

Partial celibacy   Choosing not to engage in interpersonal sexual contact but continuing to engage in masturbation.

Passing   Appearing to be heterosexual and avoiding presenting oneself as homosexual.

Pederasty   A practice in ancient Greece and Sparta in which an older man would take a young man as a lover and student.

Pedophilia   Sexual contact between an adult and a child.

Peer-delinquent prostitutes   Male prostitutes who usually work in groups and use prostitution as a means to assault and rob their customers.

Pelvic inflammatory disease (PID)   An infection in the uterus and pelvic cavity.

Penis   A male sexual organ consisting of the internal root and external shaft and glans.

Perineum   The area between the vagina and anus of the female and the scrotum and anus of the male.

Petting   Physical contact including kissing, touching, and manual or oral genital stimulation but excluding coitus.

Peyronies disease   Abnormal fibrous tissue and calcius deposits in the penis.

Pheromones   Certain odors produced by the body that relate to reproductive functions.

Phimosis   A condition characterized by an extremely tight penile foreskin.

Pimp   A prostitute's business manager.

Pituitary gland   A gland located in the brain that secretes hormones that influence the activity of other endocrine glands.

Placenta   A disc-shaped organ attached to the uterine wall and connected to the fetus by the umbilical cord. Nutrients, oxygen, and waste products pass between mother and fetus through its cell walls.

Placenta previa   A birth complication where the placenta is between the cervical opening and the infant.

Plateau phase   Masters and Johnson's term for the second phase of the sexual response cycle in which muscle tension, heart rate, blood pressure, and vasocongestion increase.

Pornography   Visual and written materials of a sexual nature that are sold for purposes of sexual arousal.

Postpartum period   The first several weeks following childbirth.

Premarital sex   A term commonly used to categorize coitus that occurs before marriage.

Premature ejaculation   See *rapid ejaculation.*

Premenstrual tension syndrome   Symptoms of physical discomfort and emotional irritability that occur two to 12 days prior to menstruation.

Prepared childbirth   An education process about birth that can involve information, exercises, breathing, and working with a labor coach.

Prepuce   See *foreskin.*

Preputial glands   Small lubricating glands located in the foreskin of the penis.

Priapism Prolonged and uncomfortable penile erection.

Primary erectile inhibition A sexual difficulty of a man who has never experienced an erection with a partner.

Primary erogenous zones Areas of the body that contain dense concentrations of nerve endings.

Primary orgasmic dysfunction Helen Singer Kaplan's label for a woman who has never experienced orgasm.

Probability sample A type of limited research sample in which every individual in the total population about which one wishes to draw inferences has an equal chance (probability) of being included.

Prodromal symptoms Symptoms that give advance warning of an impending herpes eruption.

Progesterone The hormone produced by the corpus luteum of the ovary that causes the uterine lining to thicken.

Progestin-only pill A contraceptive pill that contains a small dose of progestin and no estrogen.

Proliferative phase The phase of the menstrual cycle in which the ovarian follicles mature.

Pronatalism Attitudes and policies that encourage parenthood for all couples.

Prophylactic A latex or membrane sheath that fits over the penis and is used for protection against unwanted pregnancy and sexually transmitted diseases. Also used in a general sense as anything that aids in disease prevention.

Prostaglandins Hormones that are used to induce uterine contractions and fetal explusion for second trimester abortions.

Prostatectomy Surgical removal of the prostate.

Prostate gland A gland located at the base of the bladder that produces the greatest portion of the volume of seminal fluid released during ejaculation.

Prostatitis Inflammation of the prostate.

Prostitution The exchange of sexual services for money.

Puberty The stage of life between childhood and adulthood during which the reproductive organs mature.

Pubic lice Lice that primarily infest the pubic hair and are transmitted by sexual contact.

Pubococcygeal (PC) muscle A muscle surrounding the vaginal opening.

Rape Sexual intercourse that occurs without consent under actual or threatened force.

Rape trauma syndrome The emotional difficulties women experience after they have been raped.

Rapid ejaculation A sexual difficulty of a man who ejaculates so rapidly as to impair his own or his partner's pleasure.

Recanalization The spontaneous rejoining of the vas deferens following sterilization.

Refractory period The period of time following orgasm in the male during which another orgasm cannot be experienced.

Relationship contract A mutually agreed upon set of rules, plans, and philosophies related to an interpersonal relationship.

Resolution phase The fourth phase of the sexual response cycle as outlined by Masters and Johnson in which the sexual systems return to their nonexcited state.

Retrograde ejaculation Process by which semen is expelled into the bladder instead of out of the penis.

Rugae The folds of tissue in the vagina.

Sadomasochism (SM) The act of obtaining sexual arousal through receiving (masochism) or giving (sadism) physical or psychological pain.

Scrotum The pouch of skin of the external male genitals that encloses the testicles.

Secondary erectile inhibition A sexual difficulty of a man who has experienced and maintained erections in past sexual interactions but is presently having difficulty with this response.

Secondary erogenous zones Areas of the body that have become erotically sensitive through learning and experience.

Secondary sex characteristics The physical characteristics other than genitals that indicate sexual maturity, such as body hair, breasts, and deepened voice.

Second-stage labor The middle stage of labor in which the infant descends through the vaginal canal.

Secretory phase   The phase of the menstrual cycle in which the corpus luteum develops and secretes progesterone.

Semen   A viscous fluid ejaculated through the penis that contains sperm and fluids from the prostate, seminal vesicles, and Cowper's glands.

Seminal fluid   See *semen*.

Seminal vesicles   Two small glands adjacent to the terminals of the vas deferens that secrete an alkaline fluid conducive to sperm motility.

Seminiferous tubules   Thin, coiled structures in the testes in which sperm are produced.

Sensate focus   A process of touching and communication used to enhance sexual pleasure and to reduce performance pressure.

Sex chromosomes   A single set of chromosomes that influences biological sex determination.

Sexual aversion   Extreme and irrational fear of sexual activity.

Sexual harassment   Unwanted attention of a sexual nature from someone at the workplace.

Sexually transmitted diseases   Diseases that are transmitted by sexual contact.

Sexual orientation   The gender to which a person is attracted.

Smegma   A cheesy substance of glandular secretions and skin cells that sometimes accumulates under the foreskin of the penis or hood of the clitoris.

Socialization   The process whereby our society conveys to the individual behavioral expectations for his or her gender.

Society   An enduring, cooperative group of people with organized patterns of interrelationships.

Sodomy   An ill-defined legal category for noncoital genital contacts such as oral-genital and anal intercourse.

Speculum   An instrument with two blades used to open the vaginal walls during a gynecological exam.

Sperm   The male reproductive cell.

Spermatic cord   A cord attached to the testicle that contains the vas deferens, blood vessels, nerves, and cremasteric muscle fibers.

Spermatogenesis   Sperm production.

Spermicide   Chemical substances used in contraceptives that kill sperm.

Spongy body   A chamber that forms a bulb at the base of the penis, extends up into the penile shaft and forms the penile glans.

Spontaneous abortion   Commonly called a *miscarriage*, the fetus is expelled from the uterus early in pregnancy before it can survive on its own outside the uterus.

Squeeze technique   A treatment technique for rapid ejaculation consisting of squeezing the penis at the base of the glans or at the base of the shaft.

Statutory rape   Intercourse with a person under the legal age of consent.

Stereotype   A generalized notion of what a person is like that is based only on that person's sex, race, religion, ethnic background, or a similar criterion.

Swinging   The exchange of marital partners for sexual interaction.

Syphilis   A sexually transmitted disease caused by an organism called *Treponema pallidum* or spirochete.

Target organs   Organs and cells that are influenced by certain specific hormones.

Testicle   Male gonad inside the scrotum that produces sperm and sex hormones.

Testosterone   A major male hormone produced by the testes.

Third-stage labor   The last stage of childbirth in which the placenta separates from the uterine wall and comes out of the vagina.

Toxemia   A dangerous condition during pregnancy in which high blood pressure occurs.

Toxic shock syndrome   A disease that may cause a person to go into shock, occurring most commonly in menstruating women.

Transsexual   A person whose psychological gender identity is opposite to his or her biological sex.

Transvestism   Deriving sexual arousal from wearing clothing of the opposite sex.

Trichomoniasis   A form of vaginitis caused by a one-celled protozoan called *Trichomonas vaginalis*.

Trimesters   Three-month segments dividing the nine months of pregnancy.

Trophoblast cells   Cells of the placenta that secrete human chorionic gonadotropin (HCG).

Tubal ligation Female sterilization by cutting the fallopian tubes.

Turner's syndrome A rare condition characterized by the presence of only one unmatched X chromosome (XC).

Tyson's glands Small glands under the corona of the penis on either side of the frenum.

Urethra The tube through which urine passes from the bladder to outside the body.

Urethral bulb The portion of the urethra in the male between the urethral sphincters.

Urethral sphincters Two muscles, one located at the base of the bladder in both sexes and another located below the prostate in the male.

Urology The medical specialty dealing with reproductive health and genital diseases of the male and urinary tract diseases in both sexes.

Uterus A pear-shaped organ inside the female pelvis within which the fetus develops.

Vagina A stretchable canal in the female that opens at the vulva and extends about four inches into the pelvis.

Vaginismus A sexual difficulty that describes a woman who experiences involuntary spasmodic contractions of the muscles of the outer third of the vagina.

Vaginitis Inflammation of the vaginal walls caused by a variety of vaginal infections.

Vas deferens Two sperm-carrying tubes that begin at the testes and end at the urethra.

Vasectomy Male sterilization procedure that involves removing a section from each vas deferens.

Vasocongestion The engorgement of blood vessels in particular body parts in response to sexual arousal.

Vasovasectomy Surgical reconstruction of the vas deferens after vasectomy.

Venereal disease Contagious diseases whose mode of transmission is almost always sexual contact.

Vernix caseosa A waxy, protective substance on the fetus's skin.

Vestibular bulbs Two bulbs, one on each side of the vaginal opening, that engorge with blood during sexual arousal.

Vestibule The area of the vulva inside of the labia minora.

Virgin A person who has not experienced coitus.

Voyeurism The act of obtaining sexual gratification by observing undressed or sexually interacting people without their consent.

Vulva The external genitals of the female, including the mons veneris, labia majora, labia minora, clitoris, and urinary and vaginal openings.

Withdrawal A method of birth control in which the male withdraws the penis prior to ejaculation.

Wolffian ducts The internal duct system of the embryo that develops into male reproductive structures.

Zygote The single cell resulting from the united sperm and egg cells.

Bibliography

Abel, G. The evaluation and treatment of sexual offenders and their victims. Paper presented at St. Vincent Hospital and Medical Center, Portland, Ore., October 15, 1981.

————, Barlow, D., Blanchard, E., and Guild, D. The components of rapists' sexual arousal. *Archives of General Psychiatry*, 1977, 34, 895–903.

Abou-David, K. Epidemiology of carcinoma of the cervix uteri in Lebanese Christians and Moslems. *Cancer*, 1967, 20, 1706–1714.

ACLU of Oregon Newsletter, March/April 1982, 20.

Adams, J. *Understanding Adolescence*. Boston: Allyn and Bacon, 1973.

Adams, M., Oakley, G., and Marks, J. Maternal age and births in the 1980s. *Journal of the American Medical Association*, 1980, 247, 493–494.

Addiego, F., Belzer, E., Comolli, J., Moger, W., Perry, J., and Whipple, B. Female ejaculation: A case study. *Journal of Sex Research*, 1981, 17, 13–21.

Alan Guttmacher Institute. *11 Million Teenagers: What Can Be Done About the Epidemic of Adolescent Pregnancies in the United States*. New York: Planned Parenthood Federation of America, 1976.

Allen, C. *A Textbook of Psychosexual Disorders*. London: Oxford University Press, 1969.

Allen, D. Young male prostitutes: A psychosocial study. *Archives of Sexual Behavior*, 1980, 9, 399–426.

Allon, N., and Fishel, D. Singles bars. In N. Allon (Ed.), *Urban Life Styles*. Dubuque, Ia.: W. C. Brown, 1979.

Altrocchi, J. *Abnormal Behavior*. New York: Harcourt Brace Jovanovich, 1980.

American Law Institute. *Model Penal Code: Proposed Official Draft*. Philadelphia: American Law Institute, 1962.

American Medical Association Council on Pharmacy and Chemistry. "Germicidal" soaps. *Journal of the American Medical Association*, 1944, 124, 1195–1201.

American Social Health Association. Help membership HSV survey. *The Helper*, 1981, 3, 1–5.

Amir, M. *Patterns in Forcible Rape*. Chicago: University of Chicago Press, 1971.

Amstey, M. Asymptomatic gonorrhea in pregnancy. *Medical Aspects of Human Sexuality*, 1981, 15, 52–60.

Annon, J. *The Behavioral Treatment of Sexual Problems*, Vol. 1. Honolulu: Enabling Systems, 1974.

Anthony, E., Green, R., and Kolodny, R. *Childhood Sexuality*. Boston: Little, Brown, 1982.

Antunes, C., Stolley, P., Rosenshein, N., Davies, J., Tonascia, J., Brown, C., Burnett, L., Rutledge, A., Pokempner, M., and Garcia, R. Endometrial cancer and estrogen use. *New England Journal of Medicine*, 1979, 300, 9–13.

Aquinas, T. *Summa Theologica* II, III, ed. T. Gilbey. New York: Doubleday, 1975.

Armentrout, J., and Burger, G. Children's reports of parental child-rearing behavior at five grade levels. *Developmental Psychology*, 1972, 7, 44–48.

Arms, S. *Immaculate Deception*. Boston: Houghton Mifflin, 1975.

Arthur, C. Customized cervical cap: Evolution of an ancient idea. *Journal of Nurse-Midwifery*, 1980, 34, 25–33.

Athanasiou, R., Shaver, P., and Tavris, C. Sex. *Psychology Today*, July 1970, 39–52.

Atkin, C. Changing male and female roles. In M. Schwarz (Ed.), *TV and Teens: Experts Look at the Issues*. Reading, Mass.: Addison-Wesley, 1982.

Baker, C. Preying on playgrounds: The sexploitation of children in pornography and prostitution. In L. Schultz (Ed.), *The Sexual Victimology of Youth*. Springfield, Ill.: Charles C. Thomas, 1980.

Baker, H. Transsexualism—problems in treatment. *American Journal of Psychiatry*, 1969, 125, 118–124.

Baker, L., and Nagata, F. A group approach to the treatment of heterosexual couples with sexual dissatisfactions. *Journal of Sex Education and Therapy*, 1978, 4, 15–18.

Baldwick, R. *Dinner at Magny's*. London: Harmondsworth Press, 1973.

Bandura, A., and Walters, R. *Social Learning and Personality Development*. New York: Holt, Rinehart, and Winston, 1963.

Barbach, L. *For Yourself: The Fulfillment of Female Sexuality*. Garden City, N. Y.: Doubleday, 1975.

Barbaree, H., Marshall, W., and Lanthier, R. Deviant sexual arousal in rapists. *Behavior Research and Therapy*, 1979, 17, 215–22.

Barfield, R., Wilson, C., and McDonald, P. Sexual behavior: Extreme reduction of postejaculatory refractory period by midbrain lesions in male rats. *Science*, 1975, 189, 147–149.

Barlow, D., Silverstein, C., and Bieber, I. New frontiers in human sexuality. *Contemporary Psychology*, 1980, 25, 355–359.

Bartell, G. Group sex among the mid-Americans. *Journal of Sex Research*, 1970, 6, 113–130.

Bartlett, K. Sexual harassment may be issue of '80s. *The Oregonian*, Feb. 28, 1982, A22.

Bauman, K. Volunteer bias in a study of sexual knowledge, attitudes, and behavior. *Journal of Marriage and the Family*, 1973, 35, 27–31.

Beach, F. (Ed.). *Human Sexuality in Four Perspectives*. Baltimore: Johns Hopkins Press, 1978.

Becker, J., Skinner, L., Abel, G., and Treacy, E. Incidence and types of sexual dysfunctions in rape and incest victims. *Journal of Sex and Marital Therapy*, 1982, 8, 65–74.

Behavior Today. Leboyer babies—a first follow-up from France. November 29, 1976, 3.

Beigel, H. The meaning of coital postures. *International Journal of Sexology*, 1953, 4, 136–143.

Bell, A., and Weinberg, M. *Homosexualities: A Study of Diversity Among Men and Women*. New York: Simon and Schuster, 1978.

———, Weinberg, M., and Hammersmith, S. *Sexual Preference: Its Development in Men and Women*. Bloomington: Indiana University Press, 1981.

Belzer, E. Orgasmic expulsions of women: A review and heuristic inquiry. *Journal of Sex Research*, 1981, 17, 1–12.

Bem, S. The measurement of psychological androgyny. *Journal of Consulting and Clinical Psychology*, 1974, 42, 155–162.

———. Sex role adaptability: One consequence of psychological androgyny. *Journal of Personality and Social Psychology*, 1975, 31, 634–643.

———, and Lenney, E. Sex typing and the avoidance of cross-sex behavior. *Journal of Personality and Social Psychology*, 1976, 33, 48–54.

———, Martyna, W., and Watson, C. Sex-typing and androgyny: Further explorations of the expressive domain. *Journal of Personality and Social Psychology*, 1976, 34, 1016–1023.

Benjamin, H. Transvestism and transsexualism in the male and female. *Journal of Sex Research*, 3, 1967, 107–127.

Benson, R. *Handbook of Obstetrics and Gynecology*. 4th rev. ed. Los Altos, Calif.: Lange Medical Publications, 1971.

———. *Handbook of Obstetrics and Gynecology*. 5th rev. ed. Los Altos, Calif.: Lange Medical Publications, 1974.

Berg, S., and Harrison, W. Spectinomycin as primary treatment of gonorrhea in areas of high prevalence of penicillinase-producing *N. gonorrhoeae*. *Sexually Transmitted Diseases*, 1981, 8, 38–39.

Bermant, G., and Davidson, J. *Biological Bases of Sexual Behavior*. New York: Harper & Row, 1974.

Berndt, R., and Berndt, C. *Sexual Behavior in Western Amhem Land*. New York: Viking Fund Publications in Anthropology, 1951.

Bernstein, R. The Y chromosome and primary sexual differentiation. *Journal of the American Medical Association*, 1981, 245, 1953–1956.

Berscheid, E., and Walster, E. Physical attractiveness. In L. Berkowitz (Ed.), *Advances in Experimental Social Psychology*, Vol. 7. New York: Academic Press, 1974.

Bevson, J. Lovemaking with myself. *Changing Men*, January 1975, 1.

Bidgood, F. Sexuality and the handicapped. *Siecus Report*, 1974, 2, 2.

Bieber, I., Dain, H., Dince, P., Drellich, M., Grand, H., Gundlach, R., Kremer, M., Rifkin, A., Wilbur, C., and Bieber, T. *Homosexuality*. New York: Vintage Books, 1962.

Bierce, A. *The Devil's Dictionary*. New York: World, 1943.

Billings, E., Billings, J., and Catarinch, M. *Atlas of the Ovulation Method*. Collegeville, Minn.: Liturgical Press, 1974.

Bloch, D. Sex education practices of mothers. *Journal of Sex Education and Therapy*, 1978, 4, 7–12.

Block, J. Issues, problems, and pitfalls in assessing sex differences. *Merrill-Palmer Quarterly*, 1976, 22, 283–308.

Block, N., and Tessler, A. Transsexualism and surgical procedures. *Medical Aspects of Human Sexuality*, 1973, 7, 158–161.

Bolch, J. Academy questions routine circumcision. *The Oregonian*, Oct. 20, 1981, Section C, p. 4.

Bolch, O., and Warren, J. In vitro effects of Emko on *Neisseria gonorrhoeae* and *Trichomonas vaginalis*. *American Journal of Obstetrics and Gynecology*, 1973, 115, 1145–1148.

Bongaarts, J. Infertility after age 30: A false alarm. *Family Planning Perspectives*, 1982, 14, 75–78.

Bonica, J. *Principles and Practice of Obstetric Analgesia and Anesthesia*, Vols. 1 and 2. Philadelphia: F. A. Davis, 1972.

Boston Collaborative Drug Surveillance Program. Oral contraceptives and venous thromboembolic disease, surgically confirmed gallbladder disease and breast tumors. *Lancet*, 1973, 1, 1399–1404.

———. Surgically confirmed gallbladder disease, venous thromboembolism and breast tumors in relation to postmenopausal estrogen therapy. *New England Journal of Medicine*, 1974, 290, 15.

Boston Women's Health Book Collective. *Our Bodies, Ourselves*. New York: Simon and Schuster, 1976.

Boswell, J. *Christianity, Social Tolerance, and Homosexuality*. Chicago and London: University of Chicago Press, 1980.

Braen, G. Examination of the accused: The heterosexual and homosexual rapist. In C. Warner (Ed.), *Rape and Sexual Assault*. Germantown, Md.: Aspens Systems Corp., 1980.

Brazelton, T. Effects of prenatal drugs on the behavior of the neonate. *American Journal of Psychiatry*, 1973, 126, 1261–1266.

Brecher, E. *The Sex Researchers*. New York: New American Library, 1971.

———. Prevention of the sexually transmitted diseases. *Journal of Sex Research*, 1975, 11, 318–328.

Bremer, J. *Asexualization*. New York: Macmillan, 1959.

Brenner, W. Evaluation of contemporary female sterilization methods. *Journal of Reproductive Medicine*, 1981, 26, 439–453.

Briddell, D., and Wilson, G. Effects of alcohol and expectancy set on male sexual arousal. *Journal of Abnormal Psychology*, 1976, 85, 225–234.

Brisset, C. Female mutilation: Cautious forum on damaging practices. *The Guardian*, March 18, 1979, 12–15.

Broderick, C. Sexual behavior among preadolescents. *Journal of Social Issues*, 1966, 22, 6–21.

———. Heterosexual interests of suburban youth. *Medical Aspects of Human Sexuality*, 1971, 5, 83–100.

Bromberg, W. and Coyle, E. Rape: A compulsion to destroy. *Medical Insight*, 1974, 22, 21–25.

Brooks, J., Ruble, D., and Clark, A. College women's attitudes and expectations concerning menstrual-related changes. *Psychosomatic Medicine*, 1977, 39, 289–298.

Broverman, I. Sex-role stereotypes: A current appraisal. *Journal of Social Issues*, 1972, 28, 59–78.

Brownmiller, S. *Against Our Will: Men, Women, and Rape*. New York: Simon and Schuster, 1975.

Buchan, W. *Domestic Medicine: A Treatise on the Prevention and Cure of Diseases*. Boston: Printed by Joseph Bumstead for James White and Ebenezer Larkin, 1973.

Burdoff, P. *No More Menstrual Cramps and Other Good News*. New York: G.P. Putnam's Sons, 1980.

Burgess, A., and Holmstrom, L. Rape trauma syndrome. *American Journal of Psychiatry*, 1974(a), 131, 981–986.

———. *Rape: Victims of Crisis*. Bowie, Md.: Robert J. Brady, 1974(b).

———, and Holmstrom, L. Rape: Sexual description and recovery. *American Journal of Orthopsychiatry*, 1979, 49, 648–657.

Burt, M. Cultural myths and supports for rape. *Journal of Personality and Social Psychology*, 1980, 38, 217–230.

Buscaglia, L. *Love*. Greenwich, Conn.: Fawcett Books, 1972.

Byrne, D. A pregnant pause in the sexual revolution. *Psychology Today*, July 1977, 67–68.

———, Ervin, C., and Lamberth, J. Continuity between the experimental study of attraction and "real life" computer dating. *Journal of Personality and Social Psychology*, 1970, 16, 157–165.

Cadwallader, M. Marriage as a wretched institution. In Jack and Joann DeLora (Eds.), *Intimate Lifestyles: Marriage and Its Alternatives*. Pacific Palisades, Calif.: Goodyear, 1975.

Caggiula, A. Analysis of the copulation-reward properties of posterior hypothalamic stimulation in male rats. *Journal of Comparative and Physiological Psychology*, 1970, 70, 399–412.

———, and Hoebel, B. Copulation—reward site in the posterior hypothalamus. *Science*, 1966, 153, 1284–1285.

Calderone, M. The sex information and education council of the U.S. *Journal of Marriage and Family*, 1965, 27, 533–534.

Calhoun, L., Selby, J., and King, E. The influence of pregnancy on sexuality: A review of current evidence. *Journal of Sex Research*, 1981, 17, 139–151.

California State Department of Education. Guidelines for evaluation of instructional materials with respect to social content. *Curriculum Frameworks and Instructional Materials Unit*, March 1979.

Campbell, A. The American way of mating, marriage Si, children only maybe. *Psychology Today*, May 1975, 37–43.

Campbell, M. Anomalies of the genital tract. In M. Campbell and J. Harrison (Eds.), *Urology*, Vol. 2. Philadelphia: W. B. Saunders, 1970.

Cannon, K., and Long, R. Premarital sexual behavior in the sixties. *Journal of Marriage and Family*, 1971, 33, 36–39.

Caplan, B. In the Foreword of Brodyaga, L., Gates, M., Singer, S., Tucker, M., and White, R. *Rape and Its Victims: A Report for Citizens Health Facilities and Criminal Justice Agents*. Washington, D.C.: U.S. Department of Justice, November 1975.

Cappiello, J., and Grainger-Harrison, M. The rebirth of the cervical cap. *Journal of Nurse-Midwifery*, 1981, 26, 13–18.

Carswell, R. Historical Analysis of Religion and Sex. *Journal of School Health*, 1969, 39, 673–683.

Carter, A., Cohen, E., and Shorr, E. The use of androgens in women. *Vitamins and Hormones*, 1947, 5, 317–391.

Castleman, M. *Sexual Solutions*. New York: Simon and Schuster, 1980(a).

———. Sperm crisis. *Medical Self-Care*, Spring 1980(b), 26–27.

———. Men, lovemaking and cramps. *Medical Self-Care*, Spring 1981, 21.

Cautley, R., Beebe, G., and Dickinson, R. Rubber sheaths as venereal disease prophylactics. *American Journal of the Medical Sciences*, 1938, 195, 155–163.

Centers for Disease Control. Increased risk of hepatocellular adenoma in women with long-term use of oral contraception. *Morbidity and Mortality Weekly Report*, 1977, 26, 293.

———. Annual summary 1980: Reported morbidity and mortality in the United States. *Morbidity and Mortality Weekly Report*, 1981, 29, 54.

Chase, H., and Ducat, C. *Constitutional Interpretation*. St. Paul, Minn.: West, 1979.

Cherniak, D., and Feingold, A. *VD Handbook*. Montreal: Montreal Press, 1973.

Chiappa, J., and Forish, J. *The VD Book*. New York: Holt, Rinehart, and Winston, 1976.

Childs, A. Acute symbiotic psychosis in a post-operative transsexual. *Archives of Sexual Behavior*, 1977, 6, 37–44.

Chvapil, M., and Droegemueller, V. Collagen sponge in gynecologic use. *Obstetrics and Gynecology Annual*, 1981, 10, 363–73.

Clanton, G. and Smith, L. *Jealousy*. Englewood Cliffs, N.J.: Prentice-Hall, 1977.

Clappison, V. Anorexia nervosa and related eating disorders. Unpublished manuscript, January 30, 1981.

Clark, D. *Loving Someone Gay*. Millbrae, Calif.: Celestial Arts, 1977.

————. *Living Gay*. Millbrae, Calif.: Celestial Arts, 1979.

Clarke, J. The unmarried marrieds: The meaning of the relationship. In J. Eshleman and J. Clarke (Eds.), *Intimacy, Commitment, and Marriage*. Boston: Allyn and Bacon, 1978.

Clement, U., and Pfäfflin, F. Changes in personality scores among couples subsequent to sex therapy. *Archives of Sexual Behavior*, 1980, 9, 235–244.

Clifford, R. Development of masturbation in college women. *Archives of Sexual Behavior*, 1978, 7, 559–573.

Cochran, W., Mostetler, F., and Tukey, J. *Statistical Problems of the Kinsey Report on Sexual Behavior in the Human Male*. Washington, D.C.: The American Statistical Association, 1954.

Cohen, B. *Deviant Street Networks*. Lexington, Mass.: Lexington Books, 1980.

Coleman, E., and Edwards, B. *Brief Encounters*. New York: Anchor Books, 1980.

Coleman, J. *Abnormal Psychology and Modern Life*. Glenview, Ill.: Scott, Foresman, 1972.

Comfort, A. *Sex in Society*. London: Duckworth, 1963.

————. *The Joy of Sex*. New York: Crown, 1972.

Commission on Obscenity and Pornography. *The Report of the Commission on Obscenity and Pornography*. New York: Bantam, 1970.

Commission on Population Growth and the American Future. *Population and the American Future*. Washington, D.C.: U.S. Government Printing Office, 1972.

Condoms. *Consumer Reports*, 1979, 44, 583–589.

Constantine, L., and Constantine, J. *Group Marriage*. New York: Collier Books, 1973.

Cooke, C., and Dworkin, S. *The Ms. Guide to a Woman's Health*. New York: Anchor Books, 1979.

Csikzentmihalyi, M. Love and the dynamics of personal growth. In K. Pope (Ed.), *On Love and Loving*. San Francisco: Jossey-Bass, 1980.

Cummings, E. *e. e. cummings: a selection of poems*. New York: Harcourt, Brace, and World, 1961.

Cvetkovich, G., Grote, B., Lieberman, J., and Miller, W. Sex role development and teenage fertility-related behavior. *Adolescence*, 1978, 13, 231–236.

Dailey, D. The pregnant male. *Journal of Sex Education and Therapy*, 1978, 4, 43–44.

Dailey, J. Controlling herpes with food. *Sexology Today*, February 1981, 33–35.

————. Women and orgasm: Breakthrough discovery. *Sexology Today*, April 1981, 17–20.

Davenport, W. Sexual patterns and their regulation in a society of the Southwest Pacific. In F. Beach (Ed.), *Sex and Behavior*. New York: John Wiley, 1965.

————. Sex in cross-cultural perspective. In F. Beach (Ed.), *Human Sexuality in Four Perspectives*. Baltimore: Johns Hopkins Press, 1978.

David, H. Psychological studies in abortion. In J. Fawcett (Ed.), *Psychological Perspectives on Population*. New York: Basic Books, 1973.

Davis, K. Sex on campus: Is there a revolution? *Medical Aspects of Human Sexuality*, 1971, 5, 128–142.

Davis, N. Prostitution: Identity, career, and legal-economic enterprise. In J. Henslin and E. Sagarin (Eds.), *Studies in the Sociology of Sex*. New York: Schocken Books, 1978.

Debrovner, C., and Shubin-Stein, R. Sexual problems associated with infertility. *Medical Aspects of Human Sexuality*, March 1976, 161–162.

Degler, C. *At Odds, Women and the Family in America from the Revolution to the Present*. Oxford: Oxford University Press, 1980.

Delaney, J., Lupton, M., and Toth, E. *The Curse, A Cultural History of Menstruation*. New York: E.P. Dutton, 1976.

DeLatiner, B. The teenage pregnancy epidemic. *McCall's*, July 1978, 45.

Delgado, J. *Physical Control of the Mind*. New York: Harper & Row, 1969.

Delin, Bart. *The Sex Offender*. Boston: Beacon Press, 1978.

Delson, N., and Clark, M. Group therapy with sexually molested children. *Child Welfare*, 1981, 50, 161–174.

DeMartino, M. How women want men to make love. *Sexology*, October 1970, 4–7.

Dennerstein, L., Wood, C., and Burrows, G. Sexual response following hysterectomy and oophorectomy. *Obstetrics and Gynecology*, 1977, 49, 92–96.

Derogatis, L., Meyer, J., and Gallant, B. Distinctions between male and female invested partners in sexual disorders. *American Journal of Psychiatry*, 1977, 134, 385–390.

Deschin, C. Teenagers and venereal disease: A sociological study of 600 teenagers in NYC social hygiene clinics. *American Journal of Nursing*. 1963, 63, 63–67.

Diamond, M. Human sexual development: Biological foundations for social development. In F. Beach (Ed.), *Human Sexuality in Four Perspectives*. Baltimore: Johns Hopkins Press, 1977.

————. Sexual identity and sex roles. In V. Bullough (Ed.), *The Frontiers of Sex Research*. Buffalo: Prometheus Press, 1979.

————, and Karlen, A. *Sexual Decisions*. Boston: Little, Brown, 1980.

Dickinson, R. *Atlas of Human Sex Anatomy*. Baltimore: Williams and Wilkins, 1949.

Dick-Read, G. *Childbirth Without Fear*. 2d rev. ed. New York: Harper & Row, 1959.

Dion, K., Bersheid, E., and Walster, E. What is beautiful is good. *Journal of Personality and Social Psychology*, 1972, 24, 285–290.

Dodson, B. *Liberating Masturbation*. New York: Betty Dodson, 1974.

Donnerstein, E., and Berkowitz, L. Victim reactions in aggressive erotic films as a factor in violence against women. *Journal of Personality and Social Psychology*, 1981, 41, 710–724.

Dorfman, R., and Shipley, T. *Androgens: Biochemistry, Physiology and Clinical Significance*. New York: John Wiley, 1956.

Dörner, G. *Hormones and Brain Differentiation*. Amsterdam: Elsevier Publishing Co., 1976.

———. Sex-hormone-dependent brain differentiation and reproduction. In J. Money and H. Musaph (Eds.), *Handbook of Sexology*. New York: Elsevier/North-Holland Biomedical Press, 1977.

———, Rohde, W., Stahl, F., Krell, L., and Masius, W. A neuroendocrine predisposition for homosexuality in men. *Archives of Sexual Behavior*, 1975, 4, 1–8.

Doty, R., Ford, M., Preti, G., and Huggins, G. Changes in the intensity and pleasantness of human vaginal odors during the menstrual cycle. *Science*, 1975, 190, 1316–1318.

Dover, K. *Greek Homosexuality*. Cambridge, Mass.: Harvard University Press, 1978.

Downey, L. Intergenerational change in sex behavior: A belated look at Kinsey's males. *Archives of Sexual Behavior*, 1980, 9, 267–317.

Doyle, R. American Library Association Office of Intellectual Freedom. Personal correspondence, 1982.

Dutton, D., and Aron, A. Some evidence for heightened sexual attraction under conditions of high anxiety. *Journal of Personality and Social Psychology*, 1974, 30, 510–517.

Dweck, C. Sex differences in the meaning of negative evaluation in achievement situations: Determinants and consequences. Paper presented at the meeting of the Society for Research in Child Development, Denver, April 1975.

Eastman, N., and Hellman, L. *Williams' Obstetrics*. 12th edition. New York: Appleton-Century-Crofts, 1961.

Eber, M. Gender identity conflicts in male transsexualism. *Bulletin of the Menninger Clinic*, 1980, 1, 31–38.

Edmiston, S. How to write your own marriage contract. *Ms.*, Spring 1972, 66.

Ehrhardt, A. Prenatal androgenization and human psychosexual behavior. In J. Money and H. Musaph (Eds.), *Handbook of Sexology*. New York: Elsevier/North-Holland Biomedical Press, 1977.

Elias, J., and Gebhard, P. Sexuality and sexual learning in childhood. *Phi Delta Kappan*, 1969, 50, 401–405.

Ellis, A. *Sex Without Guilt*. Secaucus, N.J.: Lyle Stuart, 1966.

Ellis, H. *Studies in the Psychology of Sex*. New York: Random House, 1906.

Ellison, C. A critique of the clitoral model of female sexuality. Paper presented to the American Psychological Association, Montreal, September 4, 1980.

Elmros, T., and Larsson, P. Survival of gonococci outside the body. *British Medical Journal*, 1972, 2, 403–404.

Embrey, M. Oxytocins and the uterus. In E. Phillip, J. Barnes, and M. Newton (Eds.), *Scientific Foundations of Obstetrics and Gynecology*. Chicago: William Heinemann, 1977.

Erikson, E. Youth and the life cycle. In D. Hamachek (Ed.), *The Self in Growth, Teaching and Learning*. Englewood Cliffs, N.J.: Prentice-Hall, 1965.

Federal Bureau of Investigation. *Uniform Crime Reports for the United States*. Washington, D.C.: U.S. Department of Justice, 1973, 1975, and 1979.

Fein, G., Johnson, D., Kesson, N., Stork, L., and Wasserman, L. Sex stereotypes and preferences in the toy choices of 20 month old boys and girls. *Developmental Psychology*, 1975, 11, 527–528.

Felman, Y., and Nikitas, J. Nongonococcal urethritis. *Journal of the American Medical Association*, 1981, 245, 381–386.

Finkelhor, D. Sex among siblings: A survey on prevalence, variety, and effects. *Archives of Sexual Behavior*, 1980, 9, 171–194.

Fisher, C., Gross, J., and Zuch, J. Cycle of penile erection synchronous with dreaming (REM) sleep. *Archives of General Psychology*, 1965, 12, 29–45.

Fisher, W., and Byrne, D. Sex differences in response to erotica? Lover versus lust. *Journal of Personality and Social Psychology*, 1978, 36, 117–125.

Fleming, M., Cohen, D., Salt, P., Jones, D., and Jenkins, S. A study of pre- and postsurgical transsexuals: MMPI characteristics. *Archives of Sexual Behavior*, 1981, 10, 161–170.

———, Steinman, C., and Bockneck, G. A reply to Meyer and Reter. *Archives of Sexual Behavior*, 1980, 9, 451–456.

Ford, C., and Beach, F. *Patterns of Sexual Behavior*. New York: Harper & Row, 1951.

Foreman, H., Stade, B., and Schlesselman, S. Intrauterine device usage and fetal loss. *Obstetrics and Gynecology*, 1981, 58, 669–677.

Foster, A. Relationships between age and sexual activity in married men. *Journal of Sex Education and Therapy*, 1979, 5, 21–26.

Frank, D., Dornbush, R., Webster, S., and Kolodny, R. Mastectomy and sexual behavior: A pilot study. *Sexuality and Disability*, 1978, 1, 16–26.

Frank, E., Anderson, C., and Rubinstein, D. Frequency of sexual dysfunction in "normal" couples. *New England Journal of Medicine*, 1978, 299, 111–115.

———, ———, and ———. Marital role strain and sexual satisfaction. *Journal of Consulting and Clinical Psychology*, 1979, 47, 1096–1103.

Fraser, I., Radonic, I., and Clancy, R. Successful pregnancy after occlusion therapy for high-titre sperm antibodies. *Medical Journal of Australia*, 1980, 1, 324–325.

Fraunfelder, F. Ocular herpes. Paper presented at the Herpes Symposium, Oregon Health Sciences University, Portland, April 2, 1982.

Freeman, E., Rickels, K., Huggins, G., Celso-Ramon, G., and Polin, G. Emotional distress patterns among women having first or repeat abortions. *Obstetrics and Gynecology*, 1980, 55, 630–636.

Freese, A. Group therapy with exhibitionists and voyeurs. *Social Work*, March 1972, 44–52.

Freud, S. 1905. Three essays on the theory of sexuality. In *Standard Edition*, Vol. VII. London: Hogarth Press, 1953.

Friedman, R., Hurt, S., Arnoff, M., and Clarkin, J. Behavior and the menstrual cycle. *Signs*, 1980, 5, 719–738.

Frisch, R., and McArthur, J. Menstrual cycles: Fatness as a determinant of minimum weight for height necessary for their maintenance or onset. *Science*, 1974, 185, 949–951.

———, Wyshak, G., and Vincent, L. Delayed menarche and amenorrhea in ballet dancers. *New England Journal of Medicine*, 1980, 303, 17–19.

Fromm, E. *The Ability to Love.* New York: Farrar, Straus and Giroux, 1965.

Fuchs, E. *The Second Season: Life, Love and Sex for Women in the Middle Years.* Garden City, N.Y.: Anchor Books, 1978.

Gadpaille, W. *The Cycles of Sex.* New York: Scribner's, 1975.

Gagnon, J. *Human Sexualities.* Glenview, Ill.: Scott, Foresman, 1977.

Gaitwell, N., Loriaux, D., and Chase, T. Plasma testosterone in homosexual and heterosexual women. *American Journal of Psychiatry*, 1977, 134, 117–119.

Gardner, L., and Neu, R. Evidence linking an extra Y chromosome to sociopathic behavior. *Archives of General Psychiatry*, 1972, 26, 220–222.

Gebhard, P. Factors in marital orgasm. *Journal of Social Issues*, 1966, 22, 88–95.

———. Postmarital coitus among widows and divorcees. In P. Bohannan (Ed.), *Divorce and After.* New York: Doubleday, 1970.

———. Human sexual behavior: A summary statement. In D. Marshall and R. Suggs (Eds.), *Human Sexual Behavior: Variations in the Ethnographic Spectrum.* Englewood Cliffs, N.J.: Prentice-Hall, 1971.

———, Gagnon, J., Pomeroy, W., and Christenson, C. *Sex Offenders: An Analysis of Types.* New York: Harper & Row, 1965.

Gibb, G., and Millard, R. Research on repeated abortion: State of the field. *Psychological Reports*, 1981, 48, 415–424.

Gilbaugh, J., and Fuchs, P. The gonococcus and the toilet seat. *New England Journal of Medicine*, 1979, 301, 91–93.

Gilmartin, B. Swinging: Who gets involved and how? In R. Libby and R. Whitehurst (Eds.), *Marriage and Alternatives:*

Exploring Intimate Relationships. Glenview, Ill.: Scott, Foresman, 1977.

Ginsberg, G., Frosch, W., and Shapiro, T. The new impotence. *Archives of General Psychiatry*, 1972, 26, 218–220.

Glick, P. A demographer looks at American families. *Journal of Marriage and the Family*, 1975, 37, 15–26.

———, and Norton, A. Frequency, duration, and probability of marriage and divorce. *Journal of Marriage and the Family*, 1971, 33, 307–313.

———, and ———. *1979 Update: Marrying, Divorcing, and Living Together in the U.S. Today.* Washington, D.C.: Population Reference Bureau, 1979.

———, and Spanier, G. Married and unmarried cohabitation in the United States. *Journal of Marriage and the Family*, 1980, 42, 19–30.

Gochros, H. Counseling gay husbands. *Journal of Sex Education and Therapy*, 1978, 4, 6–10.

Goepp, R. Personal communication, April 1982.

Goethals, G. Love, marriage, and mutual growth. In K. Pope (Ed.), *On Love and Loving.* San Francisco: Jossey-Bass, 1980.

Golbus, M., Loughman, W., Epstein, C., Halbasch, G., Stephens, J., and Hall, B. Prenatal genetic diagnosis in 3000 amniocenteses. *New England Journal of Medicine*, 1979, 300, 157–163.

Goldberg, M., Edmonds, L., and Oakley, G. Reducing birth defect risk in advanced maternal age. *Journal of the American Medical Association*, 1979, 242, 2292–2294.

Goldberg, P. Are women prejudiced against women? *Transaction*, April 1968, 28–30.

Goldstein, M., and Kant, H. *Pornography and Sexual Deviance.* Berkeley: University of California Press, 1973.

Gordon, S. *The Sexual Adolescent.* North Scituate, Mass.: Duxbury Press, 1973.

Gorer, G. *Himalayan Village.* London: Michael Joseph Ltd., 1938.

Gottman, J., Notarius, C., Gonso, J., and Markman, H. *A Couple's Guide to Communication.* Champaign, Ill.: Research Press, 1976.

Goy, R. Experimental control of psychosexuality. *Philosophical Transactions of the Royal Society of London Biological*, 1970, 259, 149–162.

Grafenberg, E. The role of urethra in female orgasm. *International Journal of Sexology*, 1950, 3, 145–148.

Granberg, D., and Granberg, B. Abortion attitudes, 1965–1980: Trends and determinants. *Family Planning Perspectives*, 1980, 12, 250–261.

Great Britain Committee on Homosexual Offenses and Prostitution. *The Wolfenden Report* (American edition). New York: Stein and Day, 1963.

Green, R. *Sexual Identity Conflict in Children and Adults.* New York: Basic Books, 1974.

————. Sexual identity of 37 children raised by homosexual or transsexual parents. *American Journal of Psychiatry*, 1978, 135, 692–697.

Greenbank, R. Are medical students learning psychiatry? *Pennsylvania Medical Journal*, 1961, 64, 989–992.

Greene, B., Lee, R., and Lustig, N. Conscious and unconscious factors in marital infidelity. *Medical Aspects of Human Sexuality*, 1974, 8, 87–105.

Greenwald, H. *The Call Girl*. New York: Ballantine Books, 1958.

————. *The Elegant Prostitute: A Social and Psychoanalytic Study*. New York: Walken, 1970.

Griffiths, P., Merry, J., Browning, M., Eisinger, A., Huntsman, R., Lord, E., Polani, P., Tanner, J., and Whitehouse, R. Homosexual women: An endocrine and psychological study. *Journal of Endocrinology*, 1974, 63, 549–556.

Griffitt, W. Environmental effects on interpersonal behavior: ambient effective temperature and attraction. *Journal of Personality and Social Psychology*, 1970, 15, 240–244.

Grossman, J. Herpes: Dry lesions may shorten periods of viral shedding. *Sexually Transmitted Diseases Bulletin*, 1981, 1, 4.

Groth, A. *Men Who Rape*. New York: Plenum Press, 1979(a).

————. Sexual trauma in the life histories of rapists and child molesters. *Victimology: An International Journal*, 1979(b), 4, 10–16.

————, and Burgess, A. Rape: A sexual deviation. *American Journal of Orthopsychiatry*, 1977, 47, 400–406.

————, ————, and Holmstrom, L. Rape: Power, anger and sexuality. *American Journal of Psychiatry*, 1977, 134, 1239–1243.

Gunn, T., and Stenzel-Poore, M. *The Herpes Handbook*. Portland, Ore.: Venereal Disease Action Council, 1981.

Gurel, L. National Gay Task Force. Personal communication, March 1982.

Hamburg, M. Observations concerning family planning education in China. *Siecus Report*, 1981, 10, 23–25.

Hamilton, E. *Sex, with Love*. Boston: Beacon Press, 1978.

Hamilton, J. Demonstrable ability of penile erection in castrate men with markedly low titers of urinary androgen. *Proceedings of the Society of Experimental Biology and Medicine*, 1943, 54, 309.

Hampson, J. L., and Hampson, J. G. The ontogenesis of sexual behavior in man. In W. Young (Ed.), *Sex and Internal Secretions*. Baltimore: Williams and Wilkins, 1961.

Hanckel, F., and Cunningham, J. *A Way of Love, A Way of Life*. New York: Lothrop, Lee & Shepard, 1979.

Hand, J. Surgery of the penis and urethra. In M. Campbell and J. Harrison (Eds.), *Urology*, Vol. 3. Philadelphia: W. B. Saunders, 1970.

Hare-Mustin, R., and Broderick, P. The myth of motherhood: A study of attitudes toward motherhood. *Psychology of Women Quarterly*, 1979, 4, 114–28.

Harlap, S., Shiono, P., and Ramcharan, S. Spontaneous foetal losses in women using different contraceptives around the time of conception. *International Journal of Epidemiology*, 1980, 9, 49–56.

Harlow, H., and Harlow, M. The effects of rearing conditions on behavior. *Bulletin of the Menninger Clinic*, 1962, 26, 13–24.

Hartman, W., and Fithian, M. *Treatment of Sexual Dysfunction*. New York: Jason Aronson, 1974.

Haseltine, F., and Ohno, S. Mechanisms of gonadal differentiation. *Science*, 1981, 21, 1272–1278.

Hass, A. *Teenage Sexuality*. New York: Macmillan, 1979.

Hatch, J. Psychophysiological aspects of sexual dysfunction. *Archives of Sexual Behavior*, 1981, 10, 49–63.

Hatcher, R., Stewart, G., Stewart, F., Guest, F., Schwartz, D., and Jones, S. *Contraceptive Technology 1980–1981*. 10th rev. ed. New York: Irvington Publishers, 1980.

————, ————, ————, ————, Stratton, P., and Wright, A. *Contraceptive Technology 1978–1979*. 9th rev. ed. New York: Irvington Publishers, 1978.

Health, R. Pleasure and brain activity in man. *Journal of Nervous and Mental Disease*, 1972, 154, 3–18.

Heider, K. Dani sexuality: A low energy system. *Man*, 1976, 11, 188–201.

Heim, N. Sexual behavior of castrated sex offenders. *Archives of Sexual Behavior*, 1981, 10, 11–19.

Heiman, J. The physiology of erotica: Women's sexual arousal. *Psychology Today*, April 1975, 90–94.

————. Female sexual response patterns. *Archives of General Psychiatry*, 1980, 37, 1311–16.

————, LoPiccolo, L., and LoPiccolo, J. *Becoming Orgasmic: A Sexual Growth Program for Women*. Englewood Cliffs, N.J.: Prentice-Hall, 1976.

Heimer, L., and Larsson, K. Drastic changes in the mating behavior of male rats following lesions in the junction of diencephalon and mesencephalon. *Experientia*, 1964, 20, 460–461.

Heinrichs, W., and Adamson, G. A practical approach to the patient with dysmenorrhea. *Journal of Reproductive Medicine*, 1980, 25, 236–242.

Helsinga, K., Schellen, A., and Verkuyl, A. *Not Made of Stone: The Sexual Problems of Handicapped People*. Springfield, Ill.: Charles C. Thomas, 1974.

Henderson, S. Reversal of female sterilization: Comparison of microsurgical and gross surgical techniques for tubal anastomosis. *American Journal of Obstetrics and Gynecology*. 1981, 139, 73–9.

Hess, E. Attitude and pupil size. *Scientific American*, April 1965, 46–54.

Heston, L., and Shields, J. Homosexuality in twins. *Archives of General Psychiatry*, 1968, 18, 149–160.

Hite, S. *The Hite Report: A Nationwide Study of Female Sexuality*. New York: Dell Books, 1976.

————. *The Hite Report on Male Sexuality*. New York: Alfred A. Knopf, 1981.

Hitt, J., Hendericks, S., Ginsberg, S., and Lewis, J. Disruption of male but not female sexual behavior in rats by medial forebrain bundle lesions. *Journal of Comparative and Physiological Psychology*, 1970, 73, 377–384.

Hoffman, M., and Saltzstein, H. Parent discipline and the child's moral development. *Journal of Personality and Social Psychology*, 1967, 5, 45–57.

Holmes, K. Natural history of herpes: Current trends in treatment. Paper presented at the Herpes Symposium, Oregon Health Sciences University, Portland, April 2, 1982.

————, and Stamm, W. Chlamydial genital infections: A growing problem. *Hospital Practice*, October 1979, 105–117.

Hook, E. Rates of chromosome abnormalities at different maternal ages. *Obstetrics and Gynecology*, 1981, 282–284.

Hooker, E. The adjustment of the male overt homosexual. *Journal of Projective Techniques*, 1957, 21, 18–31.

Hoover, R., Gray, L., and Cole, P. Menopausal estrogens and breast cancer. *New England Journal of Medicine*, 1976, 295, 401–405.

Hotchkiss, R. How will an operation on the prostate affect a man's sex life? *Sexual Behavior*, August 1971, 14.

Hoult, T., Henze, L., and Hudson, J. *Courtship and Marriage in America*. Boston: Little, Brown, 1978.

Howe, B., Kaplan, R., and English, C. Repeat abortions: Blaming the victims. *American Journal of Public Health*, 1979, 69, 1242–46.

Howley, C. The older primipara: Implications for nurses. *JOGN Nursing*, 1981, 10, 182–185.

Hubbard, C. *Family Planning Education*. St. Louis: C.V. Mosby, 1977.

Hulka, B., Chambless, L., Kaufman, D., Fowler, W., and Greenberg, B. Protection against endometrial carcinoma by combination-product oral contraceptives. *Journal of the American Medical Association*, 1982, 247, 475–477.

Hunt, M. *Sexual Behavior in the 1970s*. Chicago: Playboy Press, 1974.

————, and Hunt, B. *The Divorce Experience*. New York: Signet, 1977.

Hutt, C. *Male and Female*. New York: Penguin, 1973.

Jacobs, P., Brenton, M., Melville, M., Brittain, R., and McClemont, W. Aggressive behavior, mental subnormality, and the XYY male. *Nature*, 1965, 208, 1351–1353.

Jacoby, S. 49 million singles can't all be right. *New York Times Magazine*, February 17, 1974, 37–43.

Jacques, J., and Chason, K. Cohabitation: Its impact on marital success. *Family Coordinator*, 1979, 28, 35–39.

James, J., and Meyerding, J. Early sexual experience as a factor in prostitution. *Archives of Sexual Behavior*, 1978, 7, 31–42.

————, Withers, J., Haft, M., Theiss, S., and Own, M. *The Politics of Prostitution*. Seattle: Social Research Associates, 1975.

Janeway, J. Incest: A rational look at the oldest taboo. *Ms.*, November 1981, 61 ff.

Jay, K. Coming out as process. In G. Vida (Ed.), *Our Right to Love*. Englewood Cliffs, N.J.: Prentice-Hall, 1978.

Jick, H., Alexander, W., Rothman, K., Hunter, J., Holmes, L., Watkins, R., D'Ewart, D., Danford, A., and Madsen, S. Vaginal spermicides and congenital disorders. *Journal of the American Medical Association*, 1981, 245, 1329–1332.

————, Walker, A., and Rothman, K. The epidemic of endometrial cancer: A commentary. *American Journal of Public Health*, 1980, 70, 264–267.

Johnson, W. Key factors in the sex education of the mentally retarded. Keynote address of Planned Parenthood Conference, Seattle, December 2, 1971.

Justice, B., and Justice, R. *The Broken Taboo: Sex in the Family*. New York: Human Sciences Press, 1979.

Kallman, F. Comparative twin study on the genetic aspects of male homosexuality. *Journal of Nervous and Mental Disease*, 1952(a), 115, 283–298.

————. Twin and sibship study of overt male homosexuality. *American Journal of Human Genetics*, 1952(b), 4, 136–146.

Kaplan, H. *The New Sex Therapy: Active Treatment of Sexual Dysfunction*. New York: Brunner/Mazel, 1974.

————. Hypoactive sexual desire. *Journal of Sex and Marital Therapy*, 1977, 3, 3–9.

————. *Disorders of Sexual Desire*. New York: Brunner/Mazel, 1979.

Karacan, I. Clinical value of nocturnal erection in the prognosis and diagnosis of impotence. *Medical Aspects of Human Sexuality*, 1970, 4, 27–34.

Karp, L. The arguable propriety of preconceptual sex determination. *American Journal of Medical Genetics*, 1980, 6, 185–187.

Katchadourian, H. *The Biology of Adolescence*. San Francisco: W. H. Freeman, 1977.

Katz, J. *Gay American History*. New York: Avon, 1976.

Kegel, A. Sexual function of the pubococcygeus muscle. *Western Journal of Surgery*, 1952, 60, 521–524.

Kephart, W. Some correlates of romantic love. *Journal of Marriage and the Family*, 1967, 29, 470–474.

Kilpatrick, J. *The Smut Peddlers*. Garden City, N.Y.: Doubleday, 1960.

Kimmel, D. Adult development and aging: A gay perspective. *Journal of Social Issues*, 1978, 34, 113–130.

King, F. Roll me over, lay me down. In D. Stillman and A. Beatts (Eds.), *Titters*. New York: Collier Books, 1976.

Kinsey, A., Pomeroy, W., and Martin, C. *Sexual Behavior in the Human Male*. Philadelphia: W. B. Saunders, 1948.

————, ————, ————, and Gebhard, P. *Sexual Behavior in the Human Female*. Philadelphia: W. B. Saunders, 1953.

Kirkendall, L. The case against circumcision. *Sexology Today*, May 1981, 56–59.

Klaich, D. *Woman Plus Woman: Attitudes Towards Lesbianism*. New York: Simon and Schuster, 1974.

Klaus, M., and Kennel, J. *Journal of Maternal Infant Bonding*. St. Louis: C. V. Mosby, 1976.

Koch, J., and Koch, L. The urgent drive to make good marriages better. *Psychology Today*, September 1976, 33.

Kohlberg, L. A cognitive-developmental analysis of children's sex-role concepts and attitudes. In E. Maccoby (Ed.), *The Development of Sex Differences*. Stanford, Calif.: Stanford University Press, 1966.

Kolodny, R. Adolescent sexuality. Paper presented at the Michigan Personnel and Guidance Association annual convention, Detroit, November 1980.

————, Masters, W., and Johnson, V. *Textbook of Sexual Medicine*. Boston: Little, Brown, 1979.

Kols, A., Rinehart, W., Piatrow, P., Doucette, L., and Quillan, W. Oral contraceptives in the 1980s. *Population Reports*, Series A(6), May-June 1982.

Kosnik, A., Carroll, W., Cunningham, A., Modras, R., and Schulte, J. *Human Sexuality: New Directions in American Catholic Thought*. New York: Paulist Press, 1977.

Krantzler, M. *Creative Divorce*. New York: New American Library, 1975.

Kreuz, L., Rose, R., and Jennings, J. Suppression of plasma testosterone levels and psychological stress. *Archives of General Psychiatry*, 1972, 26, 479–482.

Kron, R., Stein, M., and Goddard, K. Newborn sucking behavior affected by obstetrical sedation. *Pediatrics*, 1966, 37, 1012–1016.

Kujansuu, E., Kivinen, S., and Tuimala, R. Pregnancy and delivery at the age of forty and over. *International Journal of Gynecological Obstetrics*, 1981, 19, 341–345.

Kupperman, H., and Studdiford, W. Endocrine therapy in gynecologic disorders. *Postgraduate Medicine*, 1953, 14, 410–425.

Kutchinsky, B. The effect of easy availability of pornography on the incidence of sex crimes: The Danish experience. *Journal of Social Issues*, 1973, 29, 163–182.

La Barre, M. *The Double Jeopardy. The Triple Crisis, Illegitimacy Today*. New York: National Council on Illegitimacy, 1969.

Lader, L. *Abortion*. Indianapolis: Bobbs-Merrill, 1966.

Lamaze, F. *Painless Childbirth*. Chicago: Henry Regnery, 1956.

Lane, M., Arley, R., and Sobrero, A. Successful use of the diaphragm and jelly in a young population: Report of a clinical study. *Family Planning Perspectives*, 1976, 8, 81–86.

Langone, J. A new view of impotence. *Discover*, May 1981, 74–76.

Lapides, J. The key to urinary infections. *The Female Patient*, 1980, 5, 11–14.

Larned, D. Caesarean births: Why they are up 100 percent. *Ms.*, October 1978, 24–30.

Lasswell, M., and Lasswell, T. In T. Hoult, L. Henze, and J. Hudson (Eds.). *Courtship and Marriage in America*. Boston: Little, Brown, 1978.

Lavin, J., Stephens, R., Miodovnik, M., and Barden, T. Vaginal delivery in patients with a prior cesarean section. *Obstetrics and Gynecology*, 1982, 59, 135–148.

Laws, J., and Schwartz, P. *Sexual Scripts: The Social Construction of Female Sexuality*. Hinsdale, Ill.: Dryden Press, 1977.

Lebedeff, D., and Hochman, E. Rectal gonorrhea in men: Diagnosis and treatment. *Annals of Internal Medicine*, 1980, 92, 463–466.

Leboyer, F. *Birth Without Violence*. New York: Alfred A. Knopf, 1975.

Lederer, W., and Jackson, D. False assumption 3: That love is necessary for a satisfactory marriage. In F. Morrison and V. Borosage (Eds.), *Human Sexuality: Contemporary Perspectives*. 2d rev. ed. Palo Alto, Calif.: Mayfield, 1977.

Levin, A., Schoenbaum, S., Monson, R., Stubblefield, P., and Ryan, K. Association of induced abortion with subsequent pregnancy loss. *Journal of the American Medical Association*, 1980, 243, 2495–2499.

Levin, R., and Levin, A. Sexual pleasure: The surprising preferences of 100,000 women. *Redbook*, September 1975, 38.

————, and ————. The *Redbook* report on premarital and extramarital sex. *Redbook*, October 1975, 51.

Levine, M. Sex education in the public elementary and high school curriculum. In D. Taylor (Ed.) *Human Sexual Development*. Philadelphia: Davis, 1970.

Levinson, D. *The Seasons of a Man's Life*. New York: Alfred A. Knopf, 1978.

Lewis, A., and Hoghughi, M. An evaluation of depression as a side effect of oral contraceptives. *British Journal of Psychiatry*, 1969, 115, 697–701.

Lewis, M. Parents and children: Sex-role development. *School Review*, 1972(a), 80, 229–240.

————. State as an infant-environment interaction: An analysis of mother-infant interaction as a function of sex. *Merrill-Palmer Quarterly*, 1972(b), 18, 95–121.

Lewis, R. The swinger. In F. Robinson and N. Lehrman (Eds.), *Sex American Style*. Chicago: Playboy Press, 1971.

————. Parents and peers: Socialization agents in the coital behavior of young adults. *Journal of Sex Research*, 1973, 9, 156–162.

Libby, R. Creative singlehood as a sexual life-style: Beyond marriage as a rite of passage. In R. Libby and R. Whitehurst (Eds.), *Marriage and Alternatives: Exploring Intimate Relationships*. Glenview, Ill.: Scott, Foresman, 1977.

Linde, R., Doelle, G., Alexander, N., Kirchner, F., Vale, W., Rivier, J., and Rabin, D. Reversible inhibition of testicular steroidogenesis and spermatogenesis by a potent gonadotropin-releasing hormone agonist in men. *New England Journal of Medicine*, 1981, 305, 663–667.

Lindsey, K. Sexual harassment on the job. *Ms.*, November 1977, 47 ff.

Lisk, R. Increased sexual behavior in the male rat following lesions in the mammillary region. *Journal of Experimental Zoology*, 1966, 161, 129–136.

Lloyd, C. The influence of hormones on human sexual behavior. In E. Astwood and C. Cassidy (Eds.), *Clinical Endocrinology*, Vol. 2. New York: Grune and Stratton, 1968.

Lobsenz, N. Sex and the senior citizen. *The New York Times Magazine*, January 20, 1974, 87–91.

LoPiccolo, J. Low sexual desire. In S. Leiblum and L. Pervin (Eds.), *Principles and Practice of Sex Therapy*. New York: Guilford Press, 1980(a).

———. The human sexual dilemma: New clinical approaches and perspectives. Paper presented in seminar in Portland, Ore., October 22, 1980(b).

———. Personal communication, July 1982.

———, and Heiman, J. The role of cultural values in the prevention and treatment of sexual problems. In C. Qualls, J. Wincze, and D. Barlow (Eds.), *The Prevention of Sexual Disorders*. New York: Plenum, 1978.

Loraine, J., Adamopoulos, D., Kirkham, K., Ismail, A., and Dove, G. Patterns of hormone excretion in male and female homosexuals. *Nature*, 1971, 234, 552–554.

Lothstein, L. Psychotherapy with patients with gender dysphoria syndromes. *Bulletin of the Menninger Clinic*, 1977, 41, 563–582.

———. The psychological management and treatment of hospitalized transsexuals. *Journal of Nervous and Mental Disorders*, 1978, 166, 255–262.

———. The aging gender dysphoria (transsexual) patient. *Archives of Sexual Behavior*, 1979, 8, 431–444.

———. The postsurgical transsexual: Empirical and theoretical considerations. *Archives of Sexual Behavior*, 1980, 9, 547–563.

Loveless, M. Clinical and laboratory diagnosis of herpes. Paper presented at the Herpes Symposium, Oregon Health Sciences University, Portland, April 2, 1982.

Luker, K. *Taking Chances: Abortion and the Decision Not to Contracept*. Berkeley: University of California Press, 1975.

Luloff, P. Adolescents: Sexuality active but unhappy. *Sexuality Today*, June 26, 1978.

Lumby, M. Homophobia: The quest for a valid scale. *Journal of Homosexuality*, 1976, 2, 39–47.

Lunde, D., and Hamburg, D. Techniques for assessing the effects of sex hormones on affect, arousal and aggression in humans. *Recent Progress in Hormone Research*, 1972, 28, 627–663.

MacDonald, A., and Games, R. Some characteristics of those who hold positive and negative attitudes towards homosexuals. *Journal of Homosexuality*, 1974, 1, 9–27.

MacDonald, J. *Rape: Offenders and Their Victims*. Springfield, Ill.: Charles C. Thomas, 1971.

Macklin, E. Unmarried heterosexual cohabitation on the university campus. In J. Wiseman (Ed.), *The Social Psychology of Sex*. New York: Harper & Row, 1976.

———. Review of research on nonmarital cohabitation in the United States. In B. Murstein (Ed.), *Exploring Intimate Life Styles*. New York: Springer, 1978.

———. Nontraditional family forms: A decade of research. *Journal of Marriage and the Family*, 1980, 4, 11–24.

MacLean, P. New findings relevant to the evolution of psychosexual functions of the brain. In J. Money (Ed.), *Sex Research: New Developments*. New York: Holt, Rinehart, and Winston, 1965.

MacNamara, D., and Sagarin, E. *Sex, Crime, and the Law*. New York: Free Press, 1977.

Maddux, H. *Menstruation*. New Canaan, Conn.: Tobey, 1975.

Madore, C., Hawes, W., Many, F., and Hexter, A. A study on the effects of induced abortion on subsequent pregnancy outcome. *American Journal of Obstetrics and Gynecology*, 1981, 139, 516–521.

Malamuth, N., and Check, J. The effects of mass media exposure on acceptance of violence against women: A field experiment. *Journal of Research in Personality*, 1981, 15, 436–446.

———, Haber, S., and Feshback, S. Testing hypotheses regarding rape: Exposure to sexual violence, sex differences, and the "normality" of rapists. *Journal of Research in Personality*, 1980, 14, 121–137.

———, and Spinner, B. A longitudinal content analysis of sexual violence in the best-selling erotica magazines. *Journal of Sex Research*, 1980, 16, 226–237.

Malatesta, V., Pollack, R., Wilbanks, W., and Adams, H. Alcohol effects on the orgasmic-ejaculatory response in human males. *Journal of Sex Research*, 1979, 15, 101–107.

Marmor, J. (Ed.). *Homosexual Behavior*. New York: Basic Books, 1980.

Marshall, D. Sexual behavior on Mangaia. In D. Marshall and R. Suggs (Eds.), *Human Sexual Behavior: Variations in the Ethnographic Spectrum*. Englewood Cliffs, N.J.: Prentice-Hall, 1971.

Marshall, W. *Human Growth and Its Disorders*. New York: Academic Press, 1977.

———. The evaluation of sexual aggressives. Paper presented at the Third Annual Conference on the Evaluation and Treatment of Sexual Aggressives, San Luis Obispo, Calif., 1981.

Martin, C. Factors affecting sexual functioning in 60–79-year-old married males. *Archives of Sexual Behavior*, 1981, 10, 399–420.

Martin, D. Microsurgical reversal of vasectomy. *American Journal of Surgery*, 1981, 142, 48–50.

Martin, D., and Lyon, P. *Lesbian-Woman*. New York: Bantam, 1972.

Martinson, F. Childhood sexuality. In B. Wolman and J. Money (Eds.), *Handbook of Human Sexuality*. Englewood Cliffs, N.J.: Prentice-Hall, 1980.

Maslow, A., and Mintz, N. Effects of esthetic surroundings: I. Initial effects of three esthetic conditions upon perceiving "energy" and "well-being" in faces. *Journal of Psychology*, 1956, 41, 247–254.

————, and Sakoda, J. Volunteer-error in the Kinsey study. *Journal of Abnormal and Social Psychology*, 1952, 47, 259–267.

Masters, W. Update on sexual physiology. Paper presented at the Masters and Johnson Institute's postgraduate workshop on human sexual function and dysfunction, St. Louis, October 20, 1980.

————, and Johnson, V. Orgasm, anatomy of the female. In A. Ellis, and A. Abarbonel (Eds.), *Encyclopedia of Sexual Behavior*, Vol. 2. New York: Hawthorn Books, 1961.

————, and ————. *Human Sexual Response*. Boston: Little, Brown, 1966.

————, and ————. *Human Sexual Inadequacy*. Boston: Little, Brown, 1970.

————, and ————. *The Pleasure Bond*. New York: Bantam, 1976.

————, and ————. *Homosexuality in Perspective*. Boston: Little, Brown, 1979.

Maugh, T. Male "pill" blocks sperm enzyme. *Science*, 1981, 212, 314.

May, R. *Love and Will*. New York: W. W. Norton, 1969.

Mayleas, D. The impact of tiny feet on love. *Self*, August 1980, 105–110.

Mbiti, J. *African Religions and Philosophy*. New York: Praeger Publishers, 1969.

McArthur, L., and Resko, B. The portrayal of men and women in American television commercials. *Journal of Social Psychology*, 1975, 97, 209–220.

McCaghy, C. Child molesting. *Sexual Behavior*, August 1971, 16–24.

McCary, J. *Sexual Myths and Fallacies*. New York: Schocken, 1973.

McClintock, M. Menstrual synchrony and suppression. *Nature*, 1971, 229, 244–245.

McConnel, J. *Understanding Human Behavior*. New York: Holt, Rinehart, and Winston, 1977.

McGovern, K. Personal communication, June 28, 1982.

————, Kirkpatric, D., and LoPiccolo, J. A behavioral group treatment program for sexually dysfunctional couples. *Journal of Marriage and Family Counseling*. October 1976, 2, 397–404.

McGuire, L., and Wagner, N. Sexual dysfunction in women who were molested as children: One response pattern and suggestions for treatment. *Journal of Sex and Marital Therapy*, 1978, 4, 11–15.

McKinnon, K. *The Sexual Harassment of Working Women*. New Haven: Yale University Press, 1979.

McNeil, E., and Rubin, Z. *The Psychology of Being Human*. San Francisco: Canfield Press, 1977.

Mead, M. *Male and Female: A Study of Sexes in the Changing World*. New York: William Morrow, 1949.

————. *Sex and Temperament in Three Primitive Societies*. New York: William Morrow, 1963.

Meiselman, K. *Incest*. San Francisco: Jossey-Bass, 1978.

Mendelson, J. Marijuana and sex. *Medical Aspects of Human Sexuality*, 1976, 10, 23–24.

Menning, B. Counseling infertile couples. *Contemporary OB/GYN*, 1979, 13, 101–108.

Merriam, A. Aspects of sexual behavior among the Bala. In D. Marshall and R. Suggs (Eds.), *Human Sexual Behavior: Variations in the Ethnographic Spectrum*. Englewood Cliffs, N.J.: Prentice-Hall, 1971.

Messenger, J. Sex and repression in an Irish folk community. In D. Marshall and R. Suggs (Eds.), *Human Sexual Behavior: Variations in the Ethnographic Spectrum*. Englewood Cliffs, N.J.: Prentice-Hall, 1971.

Meyer-Bahlburg, H. Sex hormones and male homosexuality in comparative perspective. *Archives of Sexual Behavior*, 1977, 6, 297–325.

Meyer, J., and Reter, D. Sex reassignment follow-up. *Archives of General Psychiatry*, 1979, 36, 1010–1015.

Michael, R., Bonsall, R., and Warner, P. Human vaginal secretions; volatile fatty acid content. *Science*, 1974, 186, 1217–1219.

Millett, K. *The Prostitution Papers*. New York: Ballantine, 1976.

Milligan, D. Homosexuality: Sexual needs and social problems. In R. Bailey and M. Brake (Eds.), *Radical Social Work*. New York: Pantheon, 1975.

Milton, C., Pierce, C., and Lyons, M. *Little Sisters and the Law*. Washington, D.C.: American Bar Association Female Offender Resource Center, 1977.

Minton, J., Foecking, D., Webster, D., and Matthews, R. Caffeine, cyclic nucleotides, and breast disease. *Surgery*, 1979, 86, 105–109.

Mittwoch, U. *Genetics of Sex Differentiation*. New York: Academic Press, 1973.

Money, J. Components of eroticism in man: The hormones in relation to sexual morphology and sexual desire. *Journal of Nervous and Mental Disease*, 1961, 132, 239–248.

————. Psychosexual differentiation. In J. Money (Ed.), *Sex Research, New Developments*. New York: Holt, Rinehart, and Winston, 1965.

————. The strange case of the pregnant hermaphrodite. *Sexology*, August 1966, 7–9.

————. Cytogenetic and other aspects of transvestism and transsexualism. *Journal of Sex Research*, 1967, 3, 141–143.

————. *Sex Errors of the Body: Dilemmas, Education, Counselling*. Baltimore: Johns Hopkins Press, 1968.

————. Clitoral size and erotic sensation. *Medical Aspects of Human Sexuality*, 1970, 4, 95.

————. Ablatio penis: Normal male infant sex—reassigned as a girl. *Archives of Sexual Behavior*, 1975, 4, 65–72.

————. *Love and Love Sickness*. Baltimore: Johns Hopkins Press, 1980.

————. Genetic and chromosomal aspects of homosexual etiology. In J. Marmor (Ed.), *Homosexual Behavior*. New York: Basic Books, 1980.

————, and Ehrhardt, A. Prenatal hormonal exposure: Possible effects on behavior in man. In R. Michael (Ed.), *Endocrinology and Human Behavior*. London: Oxford University Press, 1968.

————. *Man Woman/Boy Girl*. Baltimore: Johns Hopkins Press, 1972.

————, ————, and Masica, D. Fetal feminization induced by androgen insensitivity in the testicular feminizing syndrome: Effect on marriage and maternalism. *Johns Hopkins Medical Journal*, 1968, 123, 105–114.

————, Hampson, J., and Hampson, J. An examination of some basic sexual concepts: The evidence of human hermaphroditism. *Bulletin of Johns Hopkins Hospital*, 1955, 97, 301–319.

————, and Primrose, C. Sexual dimorphism and dissociation in the psychology of male transsexuals. *Journal of Nervous and Mental Disorders*, 1968, 147, 472–486.

————, and Yankowitz, R. The sympathetic-inhibiting effects of the drug Ismelin on human male eroticism, with a note on Mellaril. *Journal of Sex Research*, 1967, 3, 69–82.

Montagu, A., and Matson, F. *The Human Connection*. New York: McGraw-Hill, 1979.

Mooney, T., Cole, T., and Chilgren, R. *Sexual Options for Paraplegics and Quadraplegics*. Boston: Little, Brown, 1975.

Morgan, A. Psychotherapy for transsexual candidates screened out of surgery. *Archives of Sexual Behavior*, 1978, 7, 273–283.

Morgan, E. The Puritans and sex. In M. Gordon (Ed.), *The American Family in Social-Historical Perspective*. New York: St. Martin's Press, 1978.

Morin, J. *Anal Pleasure and Health*. Burlingame, Calif.: Down There Press, 1981.

Morris, J. *Conundrum*. New York: Harcourt Brace Jovanovich, 1974.

Morris, N. The law is a busybody. *The New York Times Magazine*, April 18, 1973, 58–64.

Moseley, D., Fellingstad, D., Harley, H., and Heckel, R. Psychological factors that predict reaction to abortion. *Journal of Clinical Psychology*, 1981, 37, 276–279.

Mosher, B., and Whelan, E. Postmenopausal estrogen therapy: A review. *Obstetrical and Gynecological Survey*, 1981, 36, 467–475.

Moss, H. Sex, age and state as determinants of mother-infant interaction. *Merrill-Palmer Quarterly*, 1967, 13, 19–36.

Munjack, D., and Oziel, L. *Sexual Medicine and Counseling in Office Practice*. Boston: Little, Brown, 1980.

Murdock, G. *Social Structure*. New York: Macmillan, 1949.

Murphy, N., and Fain, T. Psychobiological factors in sex and gender identity. Paper presented to the AASECT conference in Portland, Ore., October 19, 1978.

Murray, M. Sexual problems in nursing mothers. *Medical Aspects of Human Sexuality*, October 1976, 75–76.

Murstein, B. *Love, Sex and Marriage Through the Ages*. New York: Springer, 1974.

————. Swinging or comarital sex. In B. Murstein (Ed.), *Exploring Intimate Life Styles*. New York: Springer, 1978.

Nadler, R. Approach to psychodynamics of obscene telephone calls. *New York Journal of Medicine*, 1968, 68, 521–526.

Naeye, R. Coitus and associated amniotic-fluid infections. *New England Journal of Medicine*, 1979, 301, 1198–1200.

Nahmias, A. Herpes, pregnancy and the neonate. Paper presented at the Herpes Symposium, Oregon Health Sciences University, Portland, April 2, 1982.

National Institute of Law Enforcement and Criminal Justice. *Forcible Rape Final Project Report*. Washington, D.C.: U.S. Government Printing Office, March 1978.

Nelson, J. Selecting the optimum oral contraceptive. *Journal of Reproductive Medicine*, 1973, 11, 135–141.

Neuberger, J., Nunnerely, H., Davis, M., Portman, B., Laws, J., and Williams, R. Oral-contraceptive-associated liver tumors: Occurrence of malignancy and difficulties in diagnosis. *Lancet*, 1980, 1, 273–276.

Newcomb, M., and Bentler, P. Assessment of personality and demographic aspects of cohabitation and marital success. *Journal of Personality Development*, 1980, 4, 11–24.

Nieshclag, E., Wickings, E., and Breuer, H. Chemical methods for male fertility control. *Contraception*, 1981, 23, 1–10.

Norman, J., and Harris, M. *The Private Life of the American Teenager*. New York: Rawson Wade, 1981.

Novak, E., Jones, G., and Jones, H. *Novak's Textbook of Gynecology*. 8th ed. Baltimore: Williams and Wilkins, 1970.

Nowak, J., Rodunda, R., and Young, N. *Handbook on Constitutional Law 1978*. St. Paul, Minn.: West, 1978.

Ohm, W. Female circumcision. *Sexology Today*, June 1980, 21–25.

Olds, J. Pleasure centers in the brain. *Scientific American*, 1956, 193, 105–116.

O'Neill, N., and O'Neill, G. *Open Marriage*. New York: M. Evans, 1972.

Onlofsky, J. Sex-role orientation, identity formation, and self-esteem in college men and women. *Sex Roles*, 1977, 3, 561–576.

Orlando. [pseud.] Bisexuality: A choice not an echo. *Ms.*, October 1978, 60.

Ory, H., Rosenfield, A., and Landman, L. The pill at 20: An assessment. *Family Planning Perspectives*, 1980, 12, 278–283.

Page, J. *The Other Awkward Age*. Berkeley, Calif.: Ten Speed Press, 1977.

Palson, C., and Palson, R. Swinging in wedlock. *Society*, 1972, 9, 43–48.

Pauly, I. The current status of the change of sex operation. *Journal of Nervous and Mental Disorders*, 1968, 147, 460–471.

Paxter, J., O'Hare, D., Nelson, F., and Svigir, M. Two years' experience in New York City with the liberalized abortion law—progress and problems. *American Journal of Public Health*, 1973, 63, 524–535.

Penfield, J. Contraception and female sterilization. *New York State Journal of Medicine*, 1981, 81, 255–258.

Pepitone-Rockwell, F. Counseling women to be less vulnerable to rape. *Medical Aspects of Human Sexology*, January 1980, 145–146.

Peplau, L. What homosexuals want in relationships. *Psychology Today*, March 1981, 28–38.

———, Rubin, Z., and Hill, C. Sexual intimacy in dating relationships. *Journal of Social Issues*. 1977, 33, 86–109.

Perry, J., and Whipple, B. Pelvic muscle strength of female ejaculators: Evidence in support of a new theory of orgasm. *Journal of Sex Research*, 1981, 17, 22–39.

Pfeiffer, E. Sex and aging. In L. Gross (Ed.), *Sexual Issues in Marriage*. New York: Spectrum, 1975.

Pfuhl, E. The unwed father: A "non-deviant" rule breaker. *Sociological Quarterly*, 1978, 19, 113–128.

Pheterson, G., Kiesler, S., and Goldberg, P. Evaluation of the performance of women as a function of their sex, achievement, and personal history. *Journal of Personality and Social Psychology*, 1971, 19, 114–118.

Phoenix, C., Goy, R., Gerall, A., and Young, W. Organizing action of prenatally administered testosterone propionate on the tissues mediating mating behavior in the female guinea pig. *Endocrinology*, 1959, 65, 369–382.

Pietropinto, A., and Simenauer, J. *Husbands and Wives*. New York: Times Books, 1979.

Pomeroy, S. *Goddesses, Whores, Wives, and Slaves: Women in Classical Antiquity*. New York: Schocken Books, 1975.

Pomeroy, W. Why we tolerate lesbians. *Sexology*, May 1965, 652–654.

Portland Town Council. *See* The Portland Town Council.

Powdermaker, H. *Life in Lesu*. New York: W. W. Norton, 1933.

Preston, S. Estimating the proportion of American marriages that end in divorce. *Sociological Methods and Research*, 1975, 3, 435–460.

Proctor, F., Wagner, N., and Butler, J. The differentiation of male and female orgasm: An experimental study. In N. Wagner (Ed.), *Perspectives on Human Sexuality*. New York: Behavioral Publications, 1974.

Puzo, M. *The Godfather*. Greenwich, Conn.: Fawcett, 1969.

Raboch, J., Mellon, J., and Starka, L. Klinefelter's syndrome: Sexual development and activity. *Archives of Sexual Behavior*, 1979, 8, 333–340.

Rachman, S. Sexual fetishism: an experimental analogue. *Psychological Record*, 1966, 16, 293–296.

Rada, R. Alcoholism and forcible rape. *American Journal of Psychiatry*, 1975, 132, 444–446.

———. Alcoholism and the child molester. *Annals of the New York Academy of Sciences*, 1976, 273, 492–496.

———. Commonly asked questions about the rapist. *Medical Aspects of Human Sexuality*. 1977, 11, 47–56.

Randell, J. Pre-operative and post-operative status of male and female transsexuals. In R. Green and J. Money (Eds.), *Transsexualism and Sex Reassignment*. Baltimore: Johns Hopkins Press, 1969.

Rapp, F. Structure and function of the virus: Latency of herpes simplex virus. Paper presented at the Herpes Symposium, Oregon Health Sciences University, Portland, April 2, 1982.

Rebeta-Burditt, J. *The Cracker Factory*. New York: Bantam, 1978.

Rein, M. Epidemiology of gonococcal infections. In R. Roberts (Ed.), *The Gonococcus*. New York: John Wiley, 1977.

Reinisch, J., and Karow, W. Prenatal exposure to synthetic progestins and estrogens: Effects on human development. *Archives of Sexual Behavior*, 1977, 6, 257–288.

Reiss, A. The social integration of queers and peers. In H. Becker (Ed.), *The Other Side*. New York: Free Press, 1964.

Research Forecasts, Inc. *The Tampax Report: A Summary of Survey Results on a Study of Attitudes toward Menstruation*. New York: Tampax Incorporated, 1981.

Reuben, D. *Everything You Always Wanted to know about Sex*. New York: Bantam, 1969.

Rhodes, R. Sex and sin in Sheboygan. *Playboy*, August 1972, 186–190.

Rich, A. *Of Woman Born*. New York: W. W. Norton, 1976.

Riedman, S. Change of life. *Sexology*, July 1961, 808–813.

Ritter, T. The people's home medical book. In R. Barnum (Ed.), *The People's Home Library*. Cleveland: R. C. Barnum, 1919.

Ritz, S. Growing through menopause. *Medical Self-Care*, Winter 1981, 15–18.

———. How to deal with menstrual cramps. *Medical Self-Care*, Spring 1981, 17–22.

Robbins, M., and Jensen, G. Multiple orgasm in males. *Journal of Sex Research*, 1978, 14, 21–26.

Roberts, E., Kline, D., and Gagnon, J. *Family Life and Sexual Learning.* Cambridge, Mass.: Project on Human Sexual Development, 1978.

Robinson, D., and Rock, J. Intrascrotal hyperthermia induced by scrotal insulation: Effect on spermatogenesis. *Obstetrics and Gynecology*, 1967, 29, 217–223.

Robinson, P. What liberated males do. *Psychology Today*, July 1981, 81–84.

Roby, P. Politics and criminal law: Revision of the New York State penal law on prostitution. *Social Problems*, 1969, 17, 18–109.

Rogers, C. *Client-Centered Therapy: Its Current Practice, Implications, and Theory.* Boston: Houghton Mifflin, 1951.

Rooth, F., and Marks, I. Persistent exhibitionism: Short-term response to aversion, self-regulation, and relaxation treatment. *Archives of Sexual Behavior*, 1974, 3, 227–248.

Rosenkrantz, P., Vogel, S., Bee, H., Broverman, I., and Broverman, D. Sex-role stereotypes and self concepts in college students. *Journal of Consulting and Clinical Psychology*, 1968, 32, 287–295.

Rosenman, M. *Loving Styles.* Englewood Cliffs, N.J.: Prentice-Hall, 1979.

Roy, R., and Roy, D. Is monogamy outdated? In E. Morrison and V. Borosage (Eds.), *Human Sexuality: Contemporary Perspectives.* Palo Alto, Calif.: National Press Books, 1973.

Rubin, E., Lieber, C., Altman, K., Gordon, G., and Southren, A. Prolonged ethanal consumption increases testosterone metabolism in the liver. *Science*, 1976, 191, 563–564.

Rubin, I. *Sexual Life After Sixty.* New York: Basic Books, 1965.

Rubin, J., Provenzano, F., and Luria, Z. The eye of the beholder: Parents' views on sex of newborns. *American Journal of Orthopsychiatry*, 1974, 44, 512–519.

Rubin, L. *Worlds of Pain: Life in the Working Class Family.* New York: Basic Books, 1976.

Rubin, Z. Measurement of romantic love. *Journal of Personality and Social Psychology*, 1970, 16, 265–273.

———. *Liking and Loving.* New York: Holt, Rinehart, and Winston, 1973.

Ruble, D., and Brooks-Gunn, J. Menstrual myths. *Medical Aspects of Human Sexuality*, June 1979, 110–127.

Rush, F. *The Best Kept Secret: Sexual Abuse of Children.* Englewood Cliffs, N.J.: Prentice-Hall, 1980.

Russell, M. Sterilization. In A. Ellis and A. Abarbanel (Eds.), *The Encyclopedia of Sexual Behavior*, Vol. 2. New York: Hawthorn, 1961.

Saario, T., Jacklin, C., and Tittle, C. Sex role stereotyping in public schools. *Harvard Educational Review*, 1973, 43, 386–416.

Safran, C. What men do to women on the job: A shocking look at sexual harassment. *Redbook*, November 1976, 148 ff.

———. Sexual harassment: The view from the top. *Redbook*, March 1981, 47–51.

Saghir, M., and Robins, E. *Male and Female Homosexuality: A Comprehensive Investigation.* Baltimore: Williams and Wilkins, 1973.

Saldana, L., Schulman, H., and Reuss, L. Management of pregnancy after cesarean section. *American Journal of Obstetrics and Gynecology*, 1979, 135, 555–560.

Salmon, U., and Geist, S. Effect of androgens upon libido in women. *Journal of Clinical Endocrinology and Metabolism*, 1943, 3, 235–238.

Salsberg, S. Is group marriage viable? *Journal of Sex Research*, 1973, 9, 325–333.

Sarlin, M., and Altshuler, D. Group psychotherapy with deaf adolescents in a school setting. *International Journal of Group Psychotherapy*, 1968, 18, 337–344.

Sarrel, P. Male rape. Paper presented at the Annual Meeting of the International Academy of Sex Research, Phoenix, Ariz., November 1980.

Satterfield, S., and Listiak, A. Juvenile prostitution: A sequel to incest. Paper presented at the 135th meeting of the American Psychiatric Association, Toronto, May 15–21, 1982.

Sawyer, C. Reproductive behavior. In J. Field (Ed.), *Handbook of Physiology. Section I: Neurophysiology.* Washington, D.C.: The American Physiological Society, 1960.

Scanlon, J. Obstetric anesthesia as a neonatal risk factor in normal labor and delivery. *Clinics in Perinatology*, 1974, 1, 465–482.

Schmidt, G., and Sigusch, V. Sex differences in responses to psychosexual stimulation by films and slides. *Journal of Sex Research*, 1970, 6, 268–283.

Schneebaum, T. Notes and observations on Mascho Amarataire and Huachipairi. In C. A. Tripp, *The Homosexual Matrix.* New York: McGraw-Hill, 1975.

Schon, M., and Sutherland, A. The role of hormones in human behavior. III. Changes in female sexuality after hypophysectomy. *Journal of Clinical Endocrinology and Metabolism*, 1960, 20, 833–841.

Schwartz, P., and Blumstein, P. Bisexuality: Some sociological observations. Paper presented at the Chicago Conference on Bisexual Behavior, October 6, 1973.

Seaman, B., and Seaman, G. *Women and the Crisis in Sex Hormones.* New York: Bantam, 1978.

See, P. The more, the merrier? In J. R. Delora and J. S. Delora (Eds.), *Intimate Life Styles.* 2d rev. ed. Pacific Palisades, Calif.: Goodyear, 1975.

Semans, J. Premature ejaculation, a new approach. *Southern Medical Journal*, 1956, 49, 353–358.

Sevely, J., and Bennett, J. Concerning female ejaculation and the female prostate. *Journal of Sex Research*, 1978, 14, 1–20.

Sexuality Today. More men report rape, but it's still just the tip of the iceberg. April 5, 1982, 5.

————. Negative vs. positive coercion key to adult sexual problems in molested girls. July 13, 1981, 4.

Shanegold, M. Sports and menstrual function. *The Physician and Sportsmedicine.* 1980(a), 8, 66–70.

————. Pregnancy. In C. Haycock (Ed.), *Sports Medicine for the Athletic Female.* Oradell, N.J.: Medical Economics, 1980(b).

Shaul, S., Bogle, J., Hale-Harbaugh, J., and Norman, Ann. *Toward Intimacy: Family Planning and Sexuality Concerns of Physically Disabled Women.* New York: Human Sciences Press, 1978.

Sheehan, K., Casper, R., and Yen, S. Luteal phase defects induced by an agonist of luteinizing hormone-releasing factor: A model for fertility control. *Science,* 1982, 215, 170–172.

Sheehy, G. *Hustling.* New York: Delacorte, 1973.

Sherfey, M. *The Nature and Evolution of Female Sexuality.* New York: Random House, 1972.

Shettles, L. Predetermining children's sex. *Medical Aspects of Human Sexuality,* June 1982, 172.

Shostak, A. Abortion as fatherhood lost: Problems and reforms. *Family Coordinator,* 1979, 28, 569–574.

Siiter, R., and Unger, R. Sex-typing versus sex-role stereotyping: It all depends on your reference group. Paper presented at the meeting of the Eastern Psychological Association, Washington, D.C., April 1978.

Singh, B., Cutler, J., and Utidijian, H. Studies on the development of a vaginal preparation providing both prophylaxis against venereal disease and other genital infections and contraception. *British Journal of Venereal Diseases,* 1972, 48, 57–64.

Slater, P. Sexual adequacy in America. *Intellectual Digest,* November 1973, 17–20.

Slone, D., Shapiro, S., Kaufman, D., Rosenberg, L., Miettinen, O., and Stolley, P. Risk of myocardial infarction in relation to current and discontinued use of oral contraceptives. *New England Journal of Medicine,* 1981, 305, 420–424.

Smith, J., and Smith, L. Co-marital sex and the sexual freedom movement. *Journal of Sex Research,* 1970, 6, 131–142.

Smith, K. The homophobic scale. In G. Weinberg, *Society and the Healthy Homosexual.* New York: Anchor, 1973.

Smith, M., and Paulson, D. The physiologic consequences of vas ligation. *Urological Survey,* 1980, 30, 31–34.

Sokolov, J., Harris, R., and Hecker, M. Isolation of substances from human vaginal secretions previously shown to be sex attractant pheromones in higher primates. *Archives of Sexual Behavior,* 1976, 5, 269–274.

Solomon, R. The love lost in cliches. *Psychology Today,* October 1981, 83–94.

Sommer, B. The effect of menstruation on cognitive and perceptual motor behavior: A review. *Psychosomatic Medicine,* 1973, 35, 515–34.

Sontag, S. The double standard of aging. *Saturday Review,* September 23, 1972, 29–38.

Sorenson, R. *Adolescent Sexuality in Contemporary America.* New York: World, 1973.

Spence, J., Helmreich, R., and Stapp, J. Ratings of self and peers on sex role attributes and their relation to self-esteem and conceptions of masculinity and femininity. *Journal of Personality and Social Psychology,* 1975, 32, 29–39.

Speroff, L., Blass, R., and Kase, N. *Clinical Gynecologic Endocrinology and Infertility.* Baltimore: Williams and Wilkins, 1978.

Spezzano, C., and Waterman, J. The first day of life. *Psychology Today,* December 1977, 11, 110.

Starr, B., and Weiner, M. *The Starr-Weiner Report on Sex and Sexuality in the Mature Years.* New York: Stein and Day, 1981.

Steege, J. Female factors which contribute to premature ejaculation. *Medical Aspects of Human Sexuality,* 1981, 15, 73–74.

Steen, E., and Price, J. *Human Sex and Sexuality.* New York: John Wiley, 1977.

Stein, P. *Single.* Englewood Cliffs, N.J.: Prentice-Hall, 1976.

Steinem, G. Erotica and pornography—a clear and present difference. *Ms.,* November 1978, 53.

Stephan, W., Berscheid, E., and Walster, E. Sexual arousal and heterosexual perception. *Journal of Personality and Social Psychology,* 1971, 20, 93–101.

Stevens, M. Lesbian mothers in transition. In G. Vida (Ed.), *Our Right to Love.* Englewood Cliffs, N.J.: Prentice-Hall, 1978.

Stimson, A., Wase, J., and Stimson, J. Sexuality and self-esteem among the aged. *Research on Aging,* 1981, 3, 228–239.

Stolkowski, J., and Choukroun, J. Preconception selection of sex in man. *Israel Journal of Medical Sciences,* 1981, 17, 1061–1067.

Stoller, R. The term "transvestism." *Archives of General Psychiatry,* 1971, 24, 230–237.

Straw, T. Visual impairment. In D. Bullard and S. Knight (Eds.), *Sexuality and Physical Disability.* St. Louis: C.V. Mosby, 1981.

Street, R. *Modern Sex Techniques.* New York: Archer House, 1959.

Subak-Sharpe, G. Is your sex life going up in smoke? *Today's Health,* August 1974, 37–41.

Suggs, R. *The Hidden Worlds of Polynesia.* New York: Harcourt, Brace, and World, 1962.

Sullivan, W. Boys and girls are now maturing earlier. *The New York Times,* January 24, 1971.

Summit, R., and Kryso, J. Sexual abuse of children: A clinical spectrum. *American Journal of Orthopsychiatry*, 1978, 48, 237–251.

Tanner, M., Pierce, B., and Hale, D. Toxic shock syndrome. *Western Journal of Medicine*, 1981, 134, 477–484.

Tatum, H., and Connell-Tatum, E. Barrier contraception: A comprehensive overview. *Fertility and Sterility*, 1981, 36, 1–12.

Tavris, C. Masculinity. *Psychology Today*, January 1977, 34.

———, and Sadd, S. *The Redbook Report on Female Sexuality*. New York: Delacorte Press, 1977.

Taylor, J. In R. Haber and C. Eden (Eds.), *Holy Living*. Rev. ed. New York: Adler, 1971.

Taylor, M., and Lockwood, W. Toxic-shock syndrome. *Journal of the Mississippi State Medical Association*, 1981, 22, 194–198.

Taylor, R. *Sex in History*. New York: Harper & Row, 1970.

Tessler, A., and Krahn, H. Varicocele and testicular temperature. *Fertility and Sterility*, 1966, 17, 201–203.

The Portland Town Council. *A Legislative Guide to Gay Rights*. Portland, Ore.: The Portland Town Council, 1976.

Thoman, E., Liderman, P., and Olsen, J. Neonate-mother interaction during breast feeding. *Developmental Psychology*, 1972, 6, 110–118.

Tollison, C., and Adams, H. *Sexual Disorders: Treatment, Theory, Research*. New York: Gardner Press, 1979.

Tordjman, G., Thierrée, R., and Michel, J. Advances in the vascular pathology of male erectile dysfunction. *Archives of Sexual Behavior*, 1980, 9, 391–398.

Tourney, G. Hormones and homosexuality. In J. Marmor (Ed.), *Homosexual Behavior*. New York: Basic Books, 1980.

Trause, M., Kennell, J., and Klaus, M. Parental attachment behavior. In J. Money and H. Musaph (Eds.), *Handbook of Sexology*. New York: Elsevier/North-Holland, 1977.

Treichel, J. Drug against surface herpes approved. *Science News*, 1982, 121, 247.

Tripp, C. *The Homosexual Matrix*. New York: McGraw-Hill, 1975.

Trussell, J., and Westoff, C. Contraceptive practice and trends in coital frequency. *Family Planning Perspectives*, 1980, 12, 246–249.

Tullman, G., Gilner, F., Kolodny, R., Dornbush, R., and Tullman, G. The pre- and post-therapy measurement of communication skills of couples undergoing sex therapy at the Masters and Johnson Institute. *Archives of Sexual Behavior*, 1981, 10, 95–99.

Unger, R. *Female and Male*. New York: Harper & Row, 1979.

United Nations Commission. Study on Traffic in Persons and Prostitution. ST/SOA/5D/8, 1959.

United States Bureau of the Census. *Statistical Abstract of the United States: 1978*. 99th edition. Washington, D.C.: U.S. Department of Commerce, 1978.

United States Department of Health, Education, and Welfare. Public Health Service and Centers for Disease Control STD Fact Sheet, Edition 35. Atlanta, Ga., 1980.

United States General Accounting Office. *Sexual Exploitation of Children—A Problem of Unknown Magnitude*. Gaithersburg, Md.: U.S. General Accounting Office, 1982.

Van Dis, H., and Larsson, K. Induction of sexual arousal in the castrated male rat by intracranial stimulation. *Physiological Behavior*, 1971, 6, 85–86.

Van Putten, T., and Fawzy, J. Sex conversion surgery in a man with severe gender dysphoria. *Archives of General Psychiatry*, 1976, 33, 751–753.

Vaughn, E., and Fisher, A. Male sexual behavior induced by intracranial electrical stimulation. *Science*, 1962, 137, 758–760.

Veevers, J. Voluntarily childless wives: An exploratory study. *Sociology and Social Research*, 1973, 57, 356–366.

Velarde, A., and Warlick, M. Massage parlors: the sensuality business. *Society*, 1973, 11, 63–74.

Vessey, M., Peto, R., Johnson, B., and Wiggins, P. A long-term follow-up study on women using different methods of contraception: An interim report. *Journal of Biosocial Science*, 1976, 8, 373–427.

Vines, N. Psychological aspects of recurrent genital herpes. Paper presented at the Herpes Symposium, Oregon Health Sciences University, Portland, April 2, 1982.

Vinick, B. Remarriage in old age. *The Family Coordinator*, 1978, 27, 359–363.

Wagner, G., Bro-Rasmussen, F., Willis, E., and Nielsen, M. New theory on the mechanism of erection involving hitherto undescribed vessels. *Lancet*, February 20, 1982, 416–418.

Wagner, N., and Sivarajan, E. Sexual activity and the cardiac patient. In R. Green (Ed.), *Human Sexuality: A Health Practitioner's Text*. Baltimore: Williams and Wilkins, 1979.

Walfish, S., and Myerson, M. Sex role identity and attitudes toward sexuality. *Archives of Sexual Behavior*, 1980, 9, 199–203.

Walinder, J., and Thuwe, I. *A social-psychiatric follow-up study of 24 sex reassigned transsexuals*. Copenhagen: Scandinavian University Books, 1974.

Wallerstein, E. *Circumcision*. New York: Springer, 1980.

Walster, E., and Walster, G. *A New Look at Love*. Reading, Mass.: Addison-Wesley, 1978.

Waxenberg, S., Drellich, M., and Sutherland, A. Changes in female sexuality after adrenalectomy. *Journal of Clinical Endocrinology*, 1959, 19, 193–202.

Wear, J., and Holmes, K. *How to Have Intercourse Without Getting Screwed*. Seattle: Madrona, 1976.

Webb, J., Millan, D., and Stolz, C. Gynecological survey of American female athletes competing at the Montreal Olympic Games. *Journal of Sports Medicine and Physical Fitness*, 1979, 19, 405–412.

Weber, E. Sexual abuse begins at home. *Ms.*, April 1977, 64–67.

Weidiger, P. *Menstruation and Menopause*. New York: Alfred A. Knopf, 1976.

Weinberg, G. *Society and the Healthy Homosexual*. New York: Anchor, 1973.

Westoff, C., and Jones, E. The secularization of U.S. Catholic birth control practices. *Family Planning Perspectives*, 1977, 9, 203–207.

Whitam, F. The prehomosexual male child in three societies: The United States, Guatemala, Brazil. *Archives of Sexual Behavior*, 1980, 9, 87–99.

Wiest, W. Semantic differential profiles of orgasm and other experiences among men and women. *Sex Roles*, 1977, 3, 399–403.

Williams, P., and Smith, M. Interview in "The First Question." London: British Broadcasting System Science and Features Department film, 1979.

Wilson, G., and Lawson, D. Effects of alcohol on sexual arousal in women. *Journal of Abnormal Psychology*, 1976, 85, 489–497.

Winter, C. Comfort measures. Paper presented at the Herpes Symposium, Oregon Health Sciences University, Portland, April 2, 1982.

Wise, T., and Meyer, J. Transvestism: Previous findings and new areas for inquiry. *Journal of Sex and Marital Therapy*, 1980, 6, 116–128.

Wolfe, L. The sexual profile of that Cosmopolitan girl. *Cosmopolitan*, September 1980, 254–265.

Wolfenden Report. See Great Britain Committee on Homosexual Offenses and Prostitution.

Women on Words and Images. *Dick and Jane as Victims*. Princeton, N.J., 1972.

————. *Channeling Children: Sex Stereotyping on Prime Time TV*. Princeton, N.J., 1975.

Wood, G., and Ruddock, E. *Vitalogy*. Chicago: Vitalogy Association, 1918.

Woods, N. *Human Sexuality in Health and Illness*. St. Louis: C.V. Mosby, 1975.

World Health Organization Scientific Group Review. *Steroid Contraception and the Risk of Neoplasm*. Geneva, Switzerland: Technical Report Series No. 619, 1978.

Wright, M., and McCary, J. Positive effects of sex education on emotional patterns of behavior. *Journal of Sex Research*, 1969, 5, 162–169.

Yllo, K. Nonmarital cohabitation: Beyond the college campus. *Alternative Lifestyles*, 1978, 1, 37–55.

Young, W. Prostitution. In J. Douglas (Ed.), *Observations of Deviance*. New York: Random House, 1970.

Zabin, L., and Clark, S. Why they delay: A study of teenage family planning clinic patients. *Family Planning Perspectives*, 1981, 13, 205–217.

Zellman, G., and Goodchilds, J. Becoming sexual in adolescence. In E. Allgeier and N. McCormick (Eds.), *Gender Roles and Sexual Behavior*. Palo Alto, Calif.: Mayfield, 1982.

Zelnick, M., and Kantner, J. Sexual and contraceptive experiences of young unmarried women in the United States, 1976 and 1971. *Family Planning Perspectives*, 1977, 9, 55–71.

————, and ————. Sexual activity, contraceptive use, and pregnancy among metropolitan-area teenagers: 1971–1979. *Family Planning Perspectives*, 1980, 12, 230–237.

Zilbergeld, B. Group treatment of sexual dysfunction in men without partners. *Journal of Sex and Marital Therapy*, 1975, 1, 204–214.

————. *Male Sexuality: A Guide to Sexual Fulfillment*. Boston: Little, Brown, 1978.

————, and Evans, M. The inadequacy of Masters and Johnson. *Psychology Today*, August 1980, 29–43.

Zussman, L., Zussman, S., Sunley, R., and Bjornson, E. Sexual response after hysterectomy-oophorectomy: Recent studies and reconsideration of psychogenesis. *American Journal of Obstetrics and Gynecology*, 1981, 140, 725–729.

Credits

PHOTOS

4: Owen Franken/Stock, Boston, Inc.
9: © René Burri/Magnum Photos, Inc.
14 (left): Courtesy San Francisco Public Library
14 (right): The Bettmann Archive, Inc.
15 (left): The Bettmann Archive, Inc.
15 (right): © Paramount Pictures Corporation
24: Courtesy T. T. Puck, *The Mammalian Cell as Microorganism*, Oakland, Calif.: Holden-Day, Inc., 1972.
31: J. Money and A. Ehrhardt, *Man and Woman, Boy and Girl,* Baltimore: Johns Hopkins University Press, 1972.
40 (left): Derek Bayes, *Life Magazine,* © 1960 Time Inc.
40 (right): © Henry Grossman
44 (left): © Leonard Freed/Magnum Photos, Inc.
44 (right): © Bill Owens/Jeroboam, Inc.
53: © Robert Azzi 1980/Woodfin Camp & Associates
54: Judy Lutticken
69: Wallace Kirkland, *Life Magazine,* © 1948 Time Inc.
73: United Press International
88: William Thompson
90: (b) © Baron Wolman; (c), (d) Courtesy of Deryck Calderwood and Mark Schoen
108: © Baron Wolman
130: William Thompson
144 (left): Editorial Photocolor Archives, Inc.
144 (right): Burk Uzzle/© 1968 Magnum Photos, Inc.
145: Photos courtesy of Deryck Calderwood and Mark Schoen
159: John Brook, Boston
195: Culver Pictures, Inc.
197: © Joan Liftin/Archive Pictures, Inc.
198: © Robert Burroughs/Jeroboam, Inc.
205: Anestis Diakopoulos/Stock, Boston, Inc.
212: Peter Southwick/Stock, Boston, Inc.
217: © Mary Ellen Mark/Archive Pictures, Inc.
241: © Charles Harbutt/Archive Pictures, Inc.
247: © Robert Foothorap/Jeroboam, Inc.
264: © Robert Vernon Wilson/Natur'l Photography
266: "The Garden of Delights" by Hieronymus Bosch (detail)/Mas
276: Reproduced by permission of G. P. Putnam's Sons and Weidenfeld and Nicholson Ltd., from *Erotic Art of the East,* Philip Rawson ed., p. 43 copyright © 1969 by Philip Rawson
283: © Mark Tuschman
306: Photo courtesy of Frank Hermann and Margaret Berman
308: Carole Latimer/Camera Press/Photo Trends
309: © Rose Skytta/Jeroboam, Inc.
317: Peter Southwick/Stock, Boston, Inc.

326: The Sophia Smith Collection (Women's History Archive), Smith College, Northampton, MA 01063
339: William Thompson; IUDs courtesy of Planned Parenthood Association of San Mateo County
343: William Thompson; contraceptives courtesy of Planned Parenthood Association of San Mateo County
347: William Thompson; cervical caps courtesy of Woman's Health Center, San Francisco General Hospital
349 (right): William Thompson
351: Courtesy of Pharmacists Planning Service, Inc., P.O. Box 1336, Sausalito, CA 94965
353: William Thompson
361: Jean-Pierre Laffont/Sygma
384: E. W. Byrd, Jr. and D. Epel
385: Carnegie Institution of Washington, Dept. of Embryology, Davis Division
390: John Brook, Boston
393: Alta Bates Hospital, for use of facilities and staff assistance
398: Irene Barki/Woodfin Camp & Associates
399: © Michael Alexander 1982
405: John Brook, Boston
412: © Richard Kalvar/Magnum Photos, Inc.
413: Phelps-Rapho
414: © Fredrick Bodin/Stock, Boston, Inc.
415: © Josef Koudelka/Magnum Photos, Inc.
423: Paul S. Conklin
432: © Bill Aron/Jeroboam, Inc.
457: © Elizabeth Hamlin/Stock, Boston, Inc.
466: © Laurence Cameron/Jeroboam, Inc.
470: © Charles Harbutt/Archive Pictures, Inc.
475 (left): Patricia Hollander Gross/Stock, Boston, Inc.
475 (right): © James Motlow/Jeroboam, Inc.
485: George Bellerose/Stock, Boston, Inc.
487: Anestis Diakopoulos/Stock, Boston, Inc.
495: © Judy S. Gelles/Stock, Boston, Inc.
501: © Bettye Lane
563, 568, and 572: Centers for Disease Control, Venereal Disease Control Division, Public Health Service, Department of Health and Human Services
607: Judy Lutticken
612: Ellis Herwig/Stock, Boston, Inc.
617: © Bettye Lane
631 (top): Photographie Giraudon
631 (bottom): Sipa Press/Editorial Photocolor Archives
639: Charles Gatewood/Stock, Boston, Inc.
648: The Bettmann Archive, Inc.
652: Ken Heyman
655: George Rodger/Magnum Photos, Inc.

EXCERPTS, ETC.

Masters and Johnson excerpts on pp. 99, 141, 148–149, 169, 181, 394, and 484 and Figures 6.3 and 6.4 on pp. 170–171 from *Human Sexual Response* by William H. Masters and Virginia E. Johnson. Little, Brown and Company, 1966.

Breast self-examination information on p. 109 from American Cancer Society.

Sarton poem on p. 112 from *Collected Poems 1930–1973* by M. Sarton, copyright © 1974 by W. W. Norton & Company, Inc., New York, N.Y.

Excerpt on p. 162 reproduced by Special Permission of PLAYBOY Magazine; copyright © 1978 by Playboy.

Figure 6.2 on p. 168 from *Disorders of Sexual Desire* by H. Kaplan, Brunner/Mazel, New York, 1979.

Hite excerpts on pp. 181, 271, 308, 514, and 536–537 reprinted with permission of Macmillan Publishing Co., Inc., from *The Hite Report* by Shere Hite. Copyright © 1976 by Shere Hite.

Addiego et al. excerpt on p. 182 from "Female Ejaculation: A Case Study" by F. Addiego, E. Belzer, J. Cornolli, W. Moger, J. Perry, and B. Whipple, *Journal of Sex Research,* 1981, 17, 13–21. Reprinted by permission of the Society for the Scientific Study of Sex, publisher of *The Journal of Sex Research.*

Rebeta-Burditt excerpt on p. 219 from *The Cracker Box* by Joyce Rebeta-Burditt. Copyright © 1977 by Joyce Rebeta-Burditt. Macmillan Publishing Company, Inc.

Bevson excerpt on p. 259 from "Lovemaking with Myself" by J. Bevson, *Changing Men,* January, 1975, 1.

Bidgood excerpt on p. 285 from "Sexuality and the Handicapped" by F. Bidgood, *Siecus Report,* 1974, 2, 2.

Smith excerpt on p. 296 from George Weinberg, *Society and the Healthy Homosexual,* St. Martin's Press, Inc., New York. Copyright © 1973 by George Weinberg.

Bell et al. excerpts on pp. 297, 298, 299, 301, and 302 from *Sexual Preference: Its Development in Men and Women* by Allan Bell et al., Bloomington: Indiana University Press, 1981.

Hatcher et al. tables on pp. 331, 337, and 341 from Robert A. Hatcher et al., *Contraceptive Technology, 1980–1981,* 10th rev. ed. © 1980 by Irvington Publishers, Inc., New York. Reprinted with permission from Irvington Publishers, Inc., New York.

"Dear Abby" on p. 313 copyright © 1981 Universal Press Syndicate.

Letter on p. 315 by Don Dufford. Used by permission.

Rich excerpt on p. 389 from *Of Woman Born, Motherhood as Experience and Institution* by Adrienne Rich. Copyright © 1976 by W. W. Norton & Company, Inc., New York, N.Y.

Dailey excerpt on p. 393 from "The Pregnant Male" by D. Dailey, *Journal of Sex Education and Therapy,* 1978, 4, 43–44. Used with permission of *Journal of Sex Education and Therapy.*

Spezzano and Waterman excerpt on p. 404 from "The First Day of Life," by C. Spezzano and J. Waterman, *Psychology Today,* December 1977, 11, 110. Reprinted from *Psychology Today* magazine. Copyright © 1977 Ziff-Davis Publishing Company.

Kinsey et al. excerpt on p. 410 and adapted Figure 10.1 on p. 292 from *Sexual Response in the Human Male* by Alfred C. Kinsey, Wardell B. Pomeroy, and Clyde E. Martin. The Kinsey Institute for Sex Research, Bloomington, Indiana, 1948.

Kinsey et al. excerpts on pp. 69, 410–411, and 413 from *Sexual Response in the Human Female* by Alfred C. Kinsey, Wardell B. Pomeroy, and Clyde E. Martin. The Kinsey Institute for Sex Research, Bloomington, Indiana, 1953.

Sontag excerpt on pp. 476–477 from "The Double Standard of Aging" by Susan Sontag, *Saturday Review,* September 23, 1972, 29–38.

Lobsenz excerpt on p. 477 from "Sex and the Senior Citizen" by N. Lobsenz, *The New York Times Magazine,* January 20, 1974, 87–91. Copyright © 1974 by The New York Times Company. Reprinted by permission.

Vinick excerpt on p. 487 from "Remarriage in Old Age" by B. Vinick, *The Family Coordinator,* 1978, 27, 359–363. Copyright 1978 by the National Council on Family Relations. Reprinted by permission.

Slater excerpt on p. 499 from "Sexual Adequacy in America" by P. Slater, *Intellectual Digest,* November 1973, 17–20.

Brecher excerpt on pp. 580–581 from "Prevention of the Sexually Transmitted Diseases" by E. Brecher, *Journal of Sex Research,* 1975, 11, 318–328. Reprinted by permission of the Society for the Scientific Study of Sex, publisher of *The Journal of Sex Research.*

Excerpt on p. 606 from *Ms.,* September 1977, p. 89. Copyright © 1977 Ms. Foundation for Education and Comm., Inc.

Lindsey excerpt on pp. 606–607 from "Sexual Harassment on the Job" by Karen Lindsey, *Ms.,* November 1977, pp. 47 ff. Copyright © 1977 Ms. Foundation for Education and Comm., Inc.

Index

Abortion
induced, 359–364
medical procedures for, 360–361
repeat, 364
right-to-life vs. prochoice, 360
spontaneous, 382–383
Abstinence, contraceptive, 358
Active-receptive communication exercise, 531
Acyclovir, for genital herpes, 576
Adolescence
contraceptive use and, 426–428
double standard in, 419–420
homosexuality and, 428–429
masturbation and, 421
ongoing sexual relationships and, 422–423
parents and, 437–439
petting and, 422
physical changes in, 417–419
pregnancy and, 426
sexual intercourse and, 424–426
virginity and, 420–421
Adolescent sterility, 656
Adrenalectomy, sexual behavior and, 155
Adultery, 628
Afterbirth, 396
Aging
double standard of, 475–477
sexuality and, 474–487
cross-culturally, 662
Alcohol
pregnancy and, 387
sexuality and, 67, 163–165
Amenorrhea, 122
Amniocentesis, 388
Amniotic fluid, 388
Amphetamines, sexual behavior and, 164, 165
Amyl nitrate, sexual behavior and, 164, 165–166
Analingus, 275
Anal intercourse, homosexual, 310
Anal stimulation, 275
Anaphrodisiacs, 166–167
Anatomical sex, 20
Anatomy, sexual; see Female sexual anatomy; Male sexual anatomy
Androgens, 27
fetal, 27–33
homosexuality and, 301–302
libido and, 155
male sexual behavior and, 153–155
sexual arousal and, 166
Androgyny, 33–34, 52–55, 443–445

Anemia, intrauterine device and, 340
Anorgasmia, 511–515
Antiandrogens, 154
Antibiotics, for cystitis, 93
Antigay rights, 316–318
Antihypertensive drugs, sexual functioning and, 167
Anxiety
erectile inhibition and, 511
rapid ejaculation and, 516–517
sexual difficulties and, 500
Aphrodisiacs, 163–166
Aphrodite, 143, 163
Aquinas, St. Thomas, 11
Areola, 107, 108
Arousal, sexual; see Sexual arousal
Arthritis, sexual functioning and, 504
Artificial embryonation, 380
Artificial insemination, 380
Authentic love, 210
Autoinoculation, 572
Autosomes, 23

Bacterial infections, vaginal, 101
painful coitus and, 505
Barbach, Lonnie, 534
Barbiturates
sexual behavior and, 164, 166
sexual response and, 505
Bartholin's glands, 95
Basal body temperature, ovulation and, 355
Basilar squeeze, 542–544
Beach, Frank, 647, 650
Bell, Alan, 80–81, 295, 297, 298, 301, 305–307, 312
Bem, Sandra, 54–55
Bieber, Irving, 299
Billings, E. L., 355
Biopsy, 104
Birth control, shared responsibility and, 327–329, 336–337, 338, 345, 347, 350, 354, 356, 359, 362; see also Contraceptive methods
Birthing clinics, 398–399
Bisexuality, 293
Blindness, sexuality and, 287
Blood clots, oral contraceptive usage and, 334
Body image, disability and, 283–284
Brain, 156–158
limbic system of, 156, 157
Breast cancer, 110–111
estrogen replacement therapy and, 480
Breast feeding, 404–406

Breast lumps, 110–111
Breasts, 106–108
external and internal structures of, 107
sexual response cycle and, 177
Breast self-examination, 108–110
Brecher, Edward, 581
Bridge maneuver, 538
Brothels, 639
Bulbourethral glands, 133
Burglary, fetishism and, 597

Calderone, Mary, 430
Calendar method of birth control, 355
Call boys, 640
Call girls, 65, 640
Cancer
breast, 110–111, 480
cervical, 104, 146–147
genital herpes and, 574
circumcision and, 146–147
endometrial, 479
penile, 146
prostate, 132–133
castration and, 154
estrogens for, sexual response and, 505
testicular, 129–130
Candicidin, for moniliasis, 561
Candida albicans, 560–561
Cantharides, 164, 165
Case studies, in sex research, 63–64, 65
Castration, 153–154
prostate cancer and, 154
"Casual sex," 206–207
Cavernous bodies, 134
Celibacy, 253–254
Cerebral palsy, sexuality and, 286–287
Cervical cancer, 104, 146–147
genital herpes and, 574
Cervical caps, 346–347
Cervix, 103–104
Cesarean section, 401–402
Chancre, syphilitic, 568–569
Childbirth, 394–402
birthplace alternatives and, 398–400
episiotomy and, 401
medical intervention in, 400–402
postpartum period of, 402–406
practices of, 396–397
sexual interaction after, 406
stages of, 395–396
Childhood
homosexuality and, 416
independency issues in, 437–438
lack of sexual communication in the family and, 224

Childhood (*continued*)
masturbation in, 430–431
negative learning about sexuality and, 429–430
nudity and, 435–437
positive models in, 431–435
sexual behavior in, 411–416
Child molestation, 602–603
homosexuality and, 318
Child-rearing, androgynous, 443–445
Chlamydia trachomatis, 570
Chromosomes
abnormalities in, 24–26, 388
sexual differentiation and, 23–24, 32–33
Cigarette smoking
pregnancy and, 387
sexual motivation and, 167
Circumcision, 134, 146–149
Clitoral hood, 91
Clitoridectomy, 180, 660–661
Clitoris, 91–92, 179–181
Cocaine, sexual behavior and, 164, 165
Cohabitation, 451–454
Coital anorgasmia, 513
Coital positions, 275–281
man above, face-to-face, 277–278
rear-entry, 281
side, face-to-face, 280
woman above, face-to-face, 278–279
Coitus
adolescent, 424–426
extramarital, cross-culturally, 658–659
introitus after, 94
marital, cross-culturally, 7, 8, 657–658
nonmarital, laws against, 627–628
painful
in men, 506
in women, 505–506
premarital, cross-culturally, 7, 8, 654–657
use of a vibrator for clitoral stimulation and, 537
vaginal prophylaxis and, 582
woman astride position, 544
Coitus interruptus, 357
Collagen sponge, 370
Colostrum, 391
Colposcopy, 104
Combination pill, 330
side effects of, 334
Comfort, Alex, 188, 539
Communication, sexual; *see* Sexual communication
Companionate love, 210–211
Conception
alternative methods of, 380–381
enhancing possibility of, 379–380
process of, 104–105
Condoms
contraceptive, 350–354

prophylactic, 583
Consensual extramarital relationships, 463–466
Consensual sexual behavior, adult, 627–630
Contraceptive methods
abstinence from coitus, 358
adolescent use of, 426–428
basal body temperature, 355
cervical caps, 346–347
comparison of, 329–330
condoms, 350–354
diaphragm, 342–346
douching, 357–358
effectiveness of, 330, 331
induced abortion, 359–364
intrauterine devices, 337–342
mucus method, 354–355
new directions in, 368–370
oral, 330–337
ovulation method, 354–355
postcoital, 358–359
rhythm method, 355
sterilization, 364–367
vaginal spermicides, 348–350
withdrawal, 357
Contracts, relationship, 460–461
Copper 7, 338, 339, 358
Copper T, 338, 339
Corona, 134, 136
Corpus luteum, 114
Courtly love, 13, 14
Cowper's glands, 133
Crabs, 577–578
Cremasteric reflex, 129
Criticism, in sexual communication, 239–245
Crura
clitoral, 91
penile, 134
Cryosurgery, 104
Cryptorchidism, 127–128
Culpotomy, 365
Culture, definition of, 647
Cunnilingus, 274
cross-culturally, 661
Cystitis, 92–93
prevention of, 93
Cysts, breast, 110

Dalkon Shield, 341
Davenport, William, 653, 656
Deafness, sexuality and, 287
Dehumanization, pornography and, 636
Delgado, José, 158
Depression, sexual difficulties and, 500
DES; *see* Diethylstilbestrol
Developmental disabilities, sexuality and, 287–288
Diabetes, sexual functioning and, 504
Diaphragm, 342–346

advantages of, 345
disadvantages of, 345–346
insertion of, 342–344
Dick-Read method of childbirth, 397
Diethylstilbestrol (DES), 358, 386
Dilation and evacuation (D and E), 361
Dildoes, 308
Dionysus, 143
Direct observation, in sex research, 64
Divorce, 467–470
Dodson, Betty, 87, 255–256
L-dopa, sexual behavior and, 164, 166
Double standard, 495–498
adolescent, 419–420
of aging, 475–477
Douching, 101
contraceptive, 357–358
Down's syndrome, 388
Dreams, erotic fantasy and, 265–270
Drug addiction, pregnancy and, 386
Dysmenorrhea, 121–122
Dyspareunia, 505–506

Ectopic pregnancy, 105, 341
Ehrhardt, Anke, 32, 36
Ejaculation, 139–142
emission phase of, 139
expulsion phase of, 140
lasting longer, 539–545
partial, 518
rapid, 515–517
retrograde, 141–142
Ejaculatory duct, 131–132
Ejaculatory inhibition, 378, 517–519
reducing, 548–550
Ellis, Albert, 202
Ellis, Havelock, 16, 167
Embryo transfer, 380–381
Emotional difficulties, sexual difficulties and, 500
Empathy, 223
Endocrine system, 27, 153
Endometrial cancer, estrogen replacement therapy and, 479
Endometriosis, 506
Endometrium, 104
Entrapment, homosexual, 316, 629
Epididymis, 129, 131
Epididymitis, 563
Episiotomy, 401
childbirth and, 94
Erectile inhibition, 510–511
case study in, 512
dealing with, 545–549
Erection, 138–139
Erogenous zones, 158–160
Erotic fantasies, 156
dreams and, 265–270
rape, 615
sharing, 268–269
ERT; *see* Estrogen replacement therapy

Erythromycin, for nongonococcal
    urethritis, 571
Estradiol, 27, 106
Estrogen, 27, 106
    female sexual behavior and, 155
    in oral contraceptives, 330, 358
    for prostate cancer, sexual response
        and, 505
Estrogen replacement therapy (ERT), for
    menopause, 479–480
Ethnography, 649–650
Excitement, 171–173
    in the older female, 480
    in the older male, 483
Exhibitionism, 590–593
Experimental research, in sex research,
    64–66, 67
Extramarital relationships, 461–466

Facial expression, 246
Fallopian tubes, 104–105
Fantasy; see Erotic fantasies
Feedback, in sexual communication,
    229–231
Fellatio, 274
    cross-culturally, 661
    homosexual, 310
Female external genitalia, during the
    sexual response cycle, 172, 174
Female genitalia, manual stimulation of,
    272
Female infertility, 377–378
Female orgasm, 179–183
    clitoris and, 92
    cross-culturally, 659
    rapid, 517
    vaginal vs. clitoral myth, 179–181
Females, genetic determination of, 24
Female sexual anatomy; see also Vulva
    external, 89–94
    internal, 97–106
        cervix, 103–104
        cross section of, 97
        fallopian tubes, 104–105
        ovaries, 105–106
        uterus, 104
        vagina, 97–103
Female sexual behavior
    gonadal hormones and, 155
    homosexual, 304–305, 307–309
Female sexual functioning, 99–100,
    111–122
    tubal ligation and, 365–366
Female sterilization, 365–366
Fertilization, 104–105
Fetal development, 383–385
Fetal viability, abortion and, 359
Fetishism, 596–597
Fibroadenomas, breast, 110
Fimbriae, 104
Flagyl; see Metronidazole

Follicle-stimulating hormone (FSH),
    menstrual cycle and, 114
Forceps, childbirth, 401
Ford, Clellan, 650
Foreplay, 5
Foreskin, 134
    circumcision of, 146–149
Fornication, 628
Freedom of speech, pornography and,
    634
Frenum, 135, 136
Freud, Sigmund, 16, 299
Friendship, without sex, 204–205
Frigidity; see Anorgasmia
FSH; see Follicle-stimulating hormone
Fundus, 104

Gay community, 314
Gay rights, 314–319
Gebhard, Paul, 66
Gender, 20–21
Gender identity, 21
    as a biological process, 23–33
    interactional model of, 35–36
    social learning factors and, 33–35
Gender nonconformity, 301–302
Gender roles, 21–22
    androgyny and, 52–55
    historical roots of, 12–16
    impact of, on sexuality, 47–52
    socialization of, 43–47
    stereotypes based on, 41–43
Genes, 24
Genetic sex, 20
Genital examinations; see
        Self-examinations, genital
Genital herpes, 571–577
Genitalia
    before- and after-sexual contact
        disinfection of, 581–582
    before-sexual contact inspection of,
        581
    external, prenatal differentiation of,
        28–29
    female
        during the sexual response cycle,
            172, 174
        manual stimulation of, 272
        mutilation of, 660–661
    following sex-change surgery, 38, 39
    internal, prenatal differentiation of,
        27–28
    male
        during sexual response cycle, 176
        manual stimulation of, 134–136,
            272
    negative feelings toward, 101
Genital infibulation, 660–661
Genital tubercle, 28
Genital tuberculosis, castration and, 153
Genital warts, 578

Gigolos, 640
Glans
    clitoral, 91–92
    penile, 134
Gonadal sex, 26–27
Gonadotropin-releasing factors, 114
Gonadotropins, 114
    function of, in puberty, 417
Gonads
    development of, 26
    hormones produced by, 27, 153–155
Gonococcus, neonatal eye infection and,
    566
Gonorrhea, 562–567
    painful coitus and, 506
Gossypol, 368–369, 370
Graafian follicle, 115
Grafenberg, Ernest, 181
Grafenberg spot, 100, 181–183
Gray Panthers, 477
Greenwald, Harold, 65
Group marriage, 465–466
Guilt, 202
    masturbation and, 258

Handicapped individuals, sexuality and,
    281–288
HCG; see Human chorionic
    gonadotropin
Hearing, sexual arousal and, 162
Heart attacks, sexual problems following,
    504
Heath, Robert, 157–158
Heider, Karl, 8, 653
Heiman, Julia, 534
Hermaphroditism, 26–27, 30–31
Herpes keratitis, 574
Herpes simplex, 571–577
Hite, Shere, 77–78, 181, 271, 513–514
Home birth, 399–400
Homophobia, 295–297
Homosexuality, 74–75, 80–81, 290–319
    adolescent, 428–429
    biological theories of, 300–303
    "causes" of, 297–303
    childhood, 416
    "coming out," 310–314
    cross-culturally, 293–294, 662–663
    the law and, 314–319, 629–630
    life styles in, 303–314
    pathological model of, 63–64
    psychosocial theories of, 298–300
    relationships and, 304–307
    sexual expression and, 307–310
    societal attitudes and, 293–297
Homosexual solicitation, 629
Homosocial, 419
Hormone replacement therapy, 155
Hormones, 27; see also specific hormone
    sex differentiation and, 27–33
    sexual motivation and, 152–155

Hormone therapy, for transsexuals, 38
Hospital birth, 400
Hot flashes, 479
Human chorionic gonadotropin (HCG),
    pregnancy detection and, 382
Hunt, Morton, 75–76, 292, 458, 459,
    469–470
Hustlers, male, 640
H-Y antigen, 26
Hymen, 93–94
Hypertension, oral contraceptives and,
    335
Hypogonadism, 153
Hypothalamic releasing factors, 114
Hypothalamus, 33
    puberty and, 417
Hysterectomy, 104, 106
Hysterosalpingogram, 377

Impotence; see Erectile inhibition
Incest, 603–606
Indecent exposure, 590–593
Induced abortion, 359–364
Infatuation, 208
Infertility, 377–379
    female, 377–379
    male, 378
        scrotal temperature and, 128
Infibulation, genital, 660–661
Inhibited sexual desire (ISD), 507–508
    treatment for, 550
Intercourse, penile-vaginal; see Coitus
Interferon, for genital herpes, 576
Interpersonal distance, 246
Interviews, in sex research, 59–61
Intimacy, 196
    development of, 211–214
    parental, as a positive childhood
        model, 431–435
Intrauterine devices (IUDs), 337–342
    advantages of, 340
    disadvantages of, 340–342
    morning-after insertion of, 358–359
Introitus, 93–94
    after intercourse, 94
IUDs; see Intrauterine devices

Jealousy, love and, 197–199

Kallman, F. J., 300
Kantner, John, 79–80, 425
Kaplan, Helen Singer, 167–168, 478,
    494, 507–508, 513, 538
Kegel, Arnold, 95
Kegel exercises, 95–96, 136–137
Kinsey, Alfred, 16, 61, 142, 156, 160,
    187, 291–292, 308, 410–413,
    424–426, 461–463, 484
Kinsey group, 66–72
Klinefelter's syndrome, 25

Labia
    genital herpes and, 572
    syphilitic chancre and, 568
Labia majora, 91
Labia minora, 91
Labor, stages of, 395–396
Lactation, 405–406
Lamaze, Bernard, 397
Lamaze method of childbirth, 397
Laparoscopy, 365
    diagnostic, 377–378
LeBoyer, Frederick, 397
LeBoyer method of childbirth, 397
LeBoyer's warm water bath, 397
Lesbianism, 12–13; see also
        Homosexuality
Leukorrhea, 558
Leydig's cells, 130
LFR agonist, 370
LH; see Luteinizing hormone
LHRH agonist, 368
Libido
    androgens and, 155
    menopause and, 478
Lice, pubic, 577–578
Limbic system, 156, 157
Lippies loop, 339
Listening, in sexual communication,
        229–231
Lobotomy, as a treatment for
        homosexuality, 295
Lochia, 406
LoPiccolo, Joseph, 534
LoPiccolo, Leslie, 534
Love, 195–202
    definition of, 195–196
    jealousy and, 197–199
    measurement of, 196–197
    sex and, 201–202
    types of, 208–211
LSD, sexual behavior and, 164, 166
Lumpectomy, 110
Luteinizing hormone (LH), menstrual
        cycle and, 114
Luther, Martin, 11

McGovern, Kevin, 552
Madonna stereotype, 13
Male birth control pill, 368–369
Male genitalia, manual stimulation of,
        134–136, 272; see also Male
        sexual anatomy
Male infertility, 378
Maleness, desirability of, 42
Male refractory period, 185, 186
Males, genetic determination of, 24
Male sexual anatomy, 126–137
    Cowper's glands, 133
    during ejaculation, 139–142
    penis, 134–137
    prostate gland, 132–133

scrotum, 126–127
    seminal vesicles, 132
    sexual response cycle and, 176
    testes, 127–131
    vas deferens, 127, 131–132
Male sexual behavior; see also specific
        behavior
    gonadal hormones and, 153–155
    homosexual, 304–305, 309–310
Male sexual functioning, 137–149
    circumcision and, 146–149
    ejaculation, 139–142
    erection, 138–139
    penis size and, 142–146
    vasectomy and, 366–367
Male sterilization, 366–367
Marijuana, sexual behavior and, 164,
        165
Marriage, 454–460
    divorce and, 467–470
    extramarital relationships and,
        461–466
    group, 465–466
    open, 463–464
    widowhood and, 470
Marshall, Donald, 6–7, 650, 655–656
Martin, Clyde, 66
Massage parlors, 639–640
Mastectomy, 110–111
Masters and Johnson, 16, 64, 72–75,
        99, 118, 140–141, 145,
        148–149, 168–171, 173, 181,
        187, 189, 270, 300, 394, 460,
        480–484, 496, 515, 518–519,
        542
Masturbation, 254–265; see also
        Self-exploration; Self-stimulation
    adolescent, 421
        parental reactions to, 430–431
    childhood, 416
    cross-culturally, 8, 651–653
    female, 92, 263
    historical perspectives on, 254–256
    through life cycle, 258–261
    male, 262–263
    purposes of, 256–258
    techniques of, 261–265
Maternal age, 388–389
May, Rollo, 199, 202, 210
Mead, Margaret, 34, 659
Medicaid, abortion and, 360
Meiosis, 23
Menarche, 113, 417–418
Menopause, 478–479
    estrogen for sexual interest and, 505
Menstrual cycle, birth control and,
        354–357
Menstrual synchrony, 114
Menstruation, 111–122
    adolescent, 113–114
    changes during, 115

Menstruation (*continued*)
  menstrual phase of, 117–118
  mood and performance during, 119–120
  orgasm and, 118
  physiology of, 113–115
  problems in, 121–122
  proliferative phase of, 115–116
  secretory phase of, 117
  sexual activity and, 118, 120
Mental retardation, sexuality and, 287–288
Messenger, John, 653–654
Metronidazole, for trichomoniasis, 560
Midwifery, 396, 399
Miscarriage, 382–383
  intrauterine devices and, 341
Miscegenation, 628–629
Mittelschmerz, 116
Money, John, 25, 32, 35, 36
Moniliasis, 561–562
Mons veneris, 89–91
Morris, Jan, 40
Mucus method of birth control, 354–355
Müllerian ducts, 28
Multiple orgasm, 186–189
Multiple sclerosis, sexual functioning and, 504
Mumps, adult male and, 378
Mutative relationship, 210
Mutual empathy, 223
Mycostatin; *see* Nystatin
Myotonia, 170–171

Narcotics
  pregnancy and, 386
  sexual response and, 505
Needle aspiration, 110
Neisseria gonorrhoeae, 561
Neonate, gonococcal eye infection in, 566
NGU; *see* Nongonococcal urethritis
Nicotine, sexual functioning and, 167
Night-crawling, 655–656
Nipple
  female, 107, 108
  sexual response and, 177
Nocturnal emissions, 142
Nocturnal penile tumescence (NPT) test, 505
Noncoital sex play, cross-culturally, 661
Nonconsensual extramarital sex, 461–463
Nongonococcal urethritis (NGU), 570–571
Nonresponse, in sex research studies, 60–61
Nonverbal sexual communication, 245–248
Nudity, 435–437, 653

Nursing homes, sexuality and aging in, 477–478
Nystatin, for moniliasis, 56l

Obscene phone calls, 593–594
Obscenity, definition of, 632; *see also* Pornography
Olds, James, 156
O'Neill, George, 463–464
O'Neill, Nena, 463–464
Oophorectomy, 106
Open marriage, 463–464
Oral contraceptives, 330–337
  advantages of, 333
  disadvantages of, 334–336
Oral-genital stimulation, 273–275
  "69," 273
Orchidectomy, 153
Orgasm, 178–183
  difficulties in, 511–520
    anorgasmia, 511–515
    ejaculatory inhibition, 517–519
    faking, 519–520
    rapid ejaculation, 515–517
    rapid orgasm in women, 517
  female, 179–183
    clitoris and, 179–181
    cross-culturally, 659
    rapid, 517
  menstruation and, 118
  multiple, 186–189
  in the older female, 481
  in the older male, 483
  sexual therapy and, 535–538
Orgasmic, becoming, for women, 533–535
Ovarian follicle development, 116
Ovaries, 105–106
  hormones produced by, 27
  surgical removal of, 106
Ovulation, 106, 116
  basal body temperature and, 355
  implantation and, 384
Ovulation method of birth control, 354–355
Ovum, 23
Ovum transfer, 380

Pap smear, 103–104
Paraphilia, 589
Paraphrasing, in sexual communication, 231
Paraplegics, sexuality and, 285–286
Parent-child contact, after childbirth, 402–404
Parenthood, optional, 374–376
Parents
  adolescents and, 437–439
  as shapers of gender roles, 43–45
Partial ejaculation, 518
Passionate love, 208–209

Pederasty, 6
Pedophilia, 602–603
"Peeping Tom," 594
Peer-delinquent prostitutes, 640
Peer group, and gender role socialization, 45
Pelvic exam pregnancy detection, 382
Pelvic inflammatory disease (PID), 566
  intrauterine devices and, 341
Penicillin
  for gonorrhea, 567
  for syphilis, 570
Penile cancer, 146
Penile prosthesis, 547, 548
Penile strain gauge, 68
Penile-vaginal intercourse; *see* Coitus
Penis, 134–137
  ejaculation from, 139–142
  erection of, 138–139
  exercises for, 136–137
  genital herpes and, 572
  health care of, 137
  interior structure of, 135
  syphilitic chancre and, 568
  tactile stimulation of, 134–136
Penis size, self-esteem and, 142–146
Perineum, 94
Petting, adolescent, 422
Peyronies disease, 506
Pheromones, 161
Phimosis, 148
Physical attractiveness, 200
PID; *see* Pelvic inflammatory disease
Pimps, 641
Placenta, 386
  attachment to uterine wall, 387
Placenta previa, 400
Plateau, 173–178
  in the older female, 480–481
  in the older male, 483
Playfulness, 214
PLISSIT model, of sex therapy, 525–526
Podophyllin, for genital warts, 578
Polyandry, 455
Polygamy, 455
Pomeroy, Wardell, 66
Pornography, 630–637
  effects of, 634–637
  freedom of speech and, 634
  legal definition of, 632
  regulating dissemination of, 632–633
Postpartum blues, 402
Postpartum period, 402–406
  breast feeding during, 404–406
  parent-child contact during, 402–404
  sexual interaction during, 406
Potassium nitrate, 167
Pregnancy, 383–394
  adolescent, 426
  amniocentesis and, 388
  detection of, 382

Pregnancy (*continued*)
ectopic, 105, 341
fears about, sexual dissatisfaction and, 502–503
fetal development in, 383–385
man's experience of, 391–393
prenatal care during, 385–388
sexual interaction during, 393–394
woman's experience of, 389–391
Premarital sex
cross-culturally, 654–657
incidence of, 424–426
Premature ejaculation; *see* Ejaculation, rapid
Premenstrual tension syndrome, 121
Prenatal care, 385–388
Prepared childbirth, 397
Prepuce
female, 91
male, 134
Preputial glands, 146
Priapus, 143, 144
Primary anorgasmia, 513
Primary ejaculatory inhibition, 518
Primary erectile inhibition, 510
Probability sample, 60
Progestasert T, 338, 339, 340
Progestational compounds, 27
Progesterone, 27, 106
menstrual cycle and, 114
time-release, as female contraceptive, 369
Progestin, 30
in oral contraceptives, 330, 333, 358
Pronatalism, 374
Prostaglandin induction, in terminating second-trimester pregnancies, 361–362
Prostate cancer, 132–133
castration and, 154
hormones for, sexual response and, 482
Prostatectomy, 482
Prostate gland, 132–133, 482
Prostatitis, 132, 482
Prostitutes
female, 65, 638–640
male, 640–641
Prostitution, 637–643
economics of, 641
legal status of, 641–643
Psychedelic drugs, sexual behavior and, 164, 166
Psychosexual development, 429–439
Psychotherapy, transsexualism and, 38
Puberty, 417
Pubic lice, 577–578
Pubococcygeal muscles, in masturbation, 263

Quadraplegics, sexuality and, 285–286
Questionnaires, in sex research, 59–61

Rape, 610–624
false accusations of, 615
false beliefs about, 613–616
homosexual, 623–624
partner's response to, 617–621
reducing the risk of, 618–619
sexual difficulties and, 500–501
statutory, 611
underreporting of, 617
victims of, 616–617
Rape trauma syndrome, 616
Recanalization, 366
Redbook report, 76, 459, 608
Refractory period, 185, 186
in the older male, 484
Rejection, management of, 207–208
Relationships
contracts in, 460–461
extramarital, 461–466
homosexual, 304–307
maintaining satisfaction in, 214–220
phases of, 211–214
sex and, 202–208
Reproduction, Judeo-Christian view of, 10–12
Resolution, 183–185
in the older female, 481
in the older male, 484
Response, 213
Retrograde ejaculation, 141–142
Rhythm method of birth control, 355
Right-to-life, 360
Rogers, Carl, 231
Rubin, Lillian, 459–460
Rubin, Zick, 196–197

Sadomasochism, 595–596
Saline injection abortion method, 362
Saltpeter, 167
Sanger, Margaret, 325
Schools, and gender role socialization, 45–46
Scrotum, 126–127
Seaman, Barbara, 336
Seaman, Gideon, 336
Secondary anorgasmia, 513
Secondary ejaculatory inhibition, 518
Secondary erectile inhibition, 510–511
Secondary sex characteristics
development of, 417–419
female, 106–108
sex hormones and, 27
Self-awareness, sexual satisfaction and, 526–528
Self-concept, sexual difficulties and, 500
Self-disclosure, in sexual communication, 234–235
Self-esteem, penis size and, 142–146
Self-examinations, genital
female, 87–89
male, 129–130

Self-exploration, 261–262; *see also* Masturbation; Self-stimulation
Self-knowledge, and sexual satisfaction, 526–528
Self-love, 211
Self-stimulation, 528; *see also* Masturbation
with partner present, 532–533
Semans, James, 542
Semen, 133–134
Seminal fluid, 132
Seminal vesicles, 132
Seminiferous tubules, 130
Sensate focus, 160, 530–531
back-to-chest position for, 536
Services to Ongoing Mature Aging, 477
Sex; *see also* Coitus
"casual," 206–207
concept of, 20–21
love and, 201–202
relationships and, 202–208
Sex-change surgery, 38–40
genitals after, 39
Sex characteristics, secondary
development of, 417–419
female, 106–108
sex hormones and, 27
Sex determination, preconceptual, 381
Sex education, 439–443
Sex hormones
differentiation of sex structures and, 27–33
secondary sex characteristics and, 27
Sex language, street vs. clinical, 225
Sex law reform, 643
Sex murder, 596
Sex offenders, pornography and, 635–636
Sex organs
homologous, 30
prenatal development of, 27–33
Sex play
childhood, 415–416
cross-culturally, 661
Sex-for-reproduction, 10–12
Sex research; *see also* Masters and Johnson
Bell and Weinberg, 80–81
evaluation of, 81
Hite Report, 77–78
Hunt report, 75–76
Kinsey group and, 66–72
methods of, 59–66
Redbook report, 76, 77–78
Sorenson, 78–79
summary of, 70–71
technology and, 68
Zelnick and Kantner, 79–80
Sex-role reversal, 296–297
Sex structures, internal, prenatal differentiation of, 27–33

Sex talk; see Sexual communication
Sexual activity, menstruation and, 118
Sexual adjustment and disability,
    281–288
  blindness and, 287
  body image and, 283–284
  cerebral palsy and, 286–287
  deafness and, 287
  developmental disabilities and,
    287–288
  spinal cord injury and, 285–286
  stereotypes about, 282
Sexual arousal
  alcohol and, 67
  difficulties in, 509–511
  female, 99–100
    clitoris and, 92
  hearing and, 162
  role of hormones in, 152–155
  smell and, 160–161
  taste and, 161–162
  touch and, 158–160
  vaginal lubrication and, 99–100
  vision and, 160
Sexual aversion, 509
Sexual behavior, 253–288
  adolescent, 419–429
  adult consensual, 627–630
  anaphrodisiacs and, 166–167
  aphrodisiacs and, 163–165
  celibacy, 253–254
  cross-culturally, 6–10, 650–663
  cultural legacy in, 5–6
  female
    gonadal hormones and, 155
    homosexual, 304–305, 307–309
  in infancy and childhood, 411–416
  male
    gonadal hormones and, 153–155
    homosexual, 304–305, 309–310
  marriage and, 454–460
  masturbation, 254–265, 421
  psychosocial factors in, 3–4
Sexual communication, 223–249
  criticism in, 239–245
  difficulties in, 224–227
  during coitus, 540
  getting started, 227–229
  impasses in, 248–249
  listening and feedback in, 229–231
  making requests in, 236–239
  nonverbal, 245–248
  sexual difficulties and, 502
  sexual dissatisfaction and, 529
  your partner's needs and, 232–236
Sexual desire
  difficulties with, 506–509
  treatment of difficulties, 550
Sexual difficulties
  arousal difficulties, 509–511
  desire phase difficulties, 506–509

double standard and, 495–498
goal orientation and, 498–499
interpersonal factors in, 501–503
narrow definition of sexuality and, 498
negative childhood learning and,
    494–495
organic factors in, 504–506
orgasm difficulties, 511–520
origins of, 493–506
personal factors in, 499–501
vaginismus, 520–521
Sexual functioning, aging and, 484–487;
    see also Female sexual
    functioning; Male sexual
    functioning
Sexual harassment, 606–610
Sexual intercourse; see Coitus
Sexuality
  adolescent, 419–429
  aging and, 474–487
    cross-culturally, 662
  androgynous, 443–445
  childhood, 410–416
    cross-culturally, 651–654
  impact of gender roles on, 47–52
  infertility and, 378–379
Sexual liberation, adolescent, 420–421
Sexually transmitted diseases (STDs),
    557–583; see also specific type
  common, 559
  prevention of, 578–583
  telling a partner about, 564–565
  vaginal infections, 558–561
Sexual motivation
  anaphrodisiacs and, 166–167
  aphrodisiacs and, 163–166
  hormones and, 152–155
Sexual needs, discovering your partner's,
    232–236
Sexual orientation, sexual difficulties and,
    503
Sexual orientation continuum, 291–293
Sexual response cycle
  breast changes during, 177
  excitement in, 171–173
  female
    patterns of, 170
    variability of, 185
  female external genitalia during, 172,
    174
  Kaplan's three-stage model of,
    167–168
  male, 171
  male sexual anatomy during, 176
  in the older female, 480–481
  in the older male, 482–484
  orgasm in, 178–183
  phases of, 168–185
  plateau in, 173–178
  resolution, 183–185
  sexual differences in, 185–189

vaginal and uterine changes during,
    175
Sexual satisfaction
  active-receptive communication
    exercise and, 531
  communication and, 529
  for men, 539–550
  orgasm with a partner and, 535–538
  partner and, 528–533
  self-awareness and, 526–528
  self-knowledge and, 526–528
  self-stimulation with a partner present
    and, 532–533
  sensate focus and, 530–531
  for women, 533–539
Sexual therapy, 551–553
  orgasm and, 535–538
  PLISSIT model of, 525–526
Sexual variety, 218–220
Shaft
  clitoral, 91
  penile, 134
Shettles, Landrum, 381
Silver nitrate, 566
Single living, 449–450
Situational anorgasmia, 513
Slater, Philip, 499
Sleepcrawling, 7
Smegma, 91, 146
Smell, sexual arousal and, 160–161
Socialization, 43
Society, definition of, 647
Sodomy, law and, 629
Sorenson, Robert, 78–79, 425
Spanish fly, 164–165
Spectinomycin, for gonorrhea, 567
Speculum, in vaginal examinations, 103
Sperm, 23
Spermatogenesis, 130
Spermicides, vaginal, 348–350
Spinal-cord injury, sexuality and,
    285–286
Spongy body, 134
Spontaneous abortion, 382–383
Squeeze technique, 542–545
Statutory rape, 611
Stereotypes, gender-based, 41–43,
    46–47; see also Gender roles
Sterility, adolescent, 656
Sterilization, 364–367
  female, 365–366
  male, 131, 366–367
Steroids, 27
Streetwalkers, 638–639
Suction curettage, 360–361
Suggs, Robert, 650
Sulfa, for cystitis, 93
Superincision, 7
"Supermale syndrome," 25–26
Surrogate mothers, 381
Surveys, in sex research, 59–63

Survey sample, 60
Swinging, 464–465
Syphilis, 567–570

Taste, sexual arousal and, 161–162
Television, and gender role stereotypes, 46–47
Testes, 127–131
  hormones produced by, 27
  self-examination of, 127, 129
Testicular cancer, 129–130
Testicular feminizing syndrome, 32
Testosterone, 27
  as a contraceptive, 368
Tetracycline
  for nongonococcal urethritis, 571
  pregnancy and, 386
Thalidomide, 386
Touching
  nonverbal communication through, 247–248
  sexual arousal and, 158–160
  shared, 270–272
Toxemia, pregnancy and, 400
Toxic shock syndrome (TSS), 122–123
Tranquilizers, sexual motivation and, 167
Transsexualism 36–40; see also
      Sex-change surgery
Transvestism, 36, 597–599
Treponema pallidum, 567–568
Trichomonas vaginalis, 558
Trichomoniasis, 101, 558–560
  painful coitus and, 505
Trophoblast cells, 382
T-strain Mycoplasma, 570
Tubal ligation, 365–366
Turner's syndrome, 25

Tyson's glands, 146

Urethra, female, 92
Urethral bulb, ejaculation and, 139
Urethral opening, female, 92–93
Urethral sphincters, ejaculation and, 139
Urethritis, nongonococcal, 570–571
Urology, 137
Uterine wall, placenta attached to, 387
Uterus, 104
  positions of, 104, 105
  sexual response cycle and, 175
  surgical removal of, 106

Vaccine, antisperm, 369
Vagina, 97–103
  chemical balance of, 100–101
  insensitivity of, 92
  sexual response cycle and, 175
Vaginal health care, 102–103
Vaginal infections, 101–102, 558–561
Vaginal lubrication, 99–100
  inadequate, painful coitus and, 505
  inhibition of, 100, 509–510
Vaginal photoplethysmograph, 68
"Vaginal ring," 369
Vaginismus, 520–521
  relieving, 538–539
Vaginitis, 101
  prevention of, 101–102
Validating, 249
Van de Velde, Theodore, 16
Varting, 98
Vas deferens, 127, 131–132
Vasectomy, 131, 366–367
Vasocongestion, 170
  vaginal lubrication and, 99

Vasovasectomy, 367
Venereal disease; see Sexually
      transmitted diseases
Vernix caseosa, 383
Vestibular bulbs, 94–95
Vestibule, 92
Viability, fetal, abortion and, 359
Vibrators, 263–265
  usage during coitus, 537
Victimless crimes, 643
Victorian sex roles, 14–15
Virginity, adolescence and, 420–421
Vision, sexual arousal and, 160
Voyeurism, 594–595
Vulva, 89–94
  structures and variations of, 90
  underlying muscles of, 95–96
  underlying structures of, 94–95

Warts, genital, 578
Weinberg, Martin, 80–81, 295, 297, 299, 305–307, 311, 312–314
Wet dreams, 142, 269
Widowhood, 470
Witch hunting, 13, 14
Wolffian ducts, 28

X chromosomes, 23–25
XYY male, 25–26

Y chromosomes, 23–26
Yeast infections, 101, 560–561
  painful coitus and, 505

Zelnick, Melvin, 79–80, 425–426
Zilbergeld, Bernie, 74, 126, 136–137
Zygote, 104

Gloria C. Luten